CURRENT LEGAL PROBLEMS 2005

Volume 58

CURRENT LEGAL PROBLEMS 2005

VOLUME 58

Edited by
JANE HOLDER
and
COLM O'CINNEIDE

OXFORD
UNIVERSITY PRESS

OXFORD
UNIVERSITY PRESS

Great Clarendon Street, Oxford OX2 6DP

Oxford University Press is a department of the University of Oxford.
It furthers the University's objective of excellence in research, scholarship,
and education by publishing worldwide in

Oxford New York

Auckland Cape Town Dar es Salaam Hong Kong Karachi
Kuala Lumpur Madrid Melbourne Mexico City Nairobi
New Delhi Shanghai Taipei Toronto

With offices in

Argentina Austria Brazil Chile Czech Republic France Greece
Guatemala Hungary Italy Japan Poland Portugal Singapore
South Korea Switzerland Thailand Turkey Ukraine Vietnam

Oxford is a registered trade mark of Oxford University Press
in the UK and in certain other countries

Published in the United States
by Oxford University Press Inc., New York

© Oxford University Press, 2006

The moral rights of the authors have been asserted

Crown copyright material is reproduced under Class Licence
Number C01P0000148 with the permission of OPSI
and the Queen's Printer for Scotland

Database right Oxford University Press (maker)

First published 2006

British Library Cataloguing in Publication Data
Data available

Library of Congress Cataloging in Publication Data
Data available

Typeset by Newgen Imaging Systems (P) Ltd., Chennai, India
Printed in Great Britain
on acid-free paper by
Biddles Ltd., King's Lynn

ISBN 0–19–928539–X   978–0–19–928539–6

1 3 5 7 9 10 8 6 4 2

Editors' Preface

As in previous years, this volume reflects the varied nature (and high standard) of the legal academy. Notwithstanding the diversity of subject matter and methodology, and the application of different social and legal theories (feminist theory and systems theory amongst them) a consistent theme of this volume is the dynamics of legal change, particularly that instigated by the human rights agenda. A good example of this theme is provided by Daniel Farber in his account of the judicial response to avowedly anti-terrorist measures in the United States. He shows how, unfortunately, recent events have provided opportunities for evaluating not just adherence (or otherwise) to human rights principles (and the rule of law) in a United States facing the so-called 'war against terrorism', but also the ease by which constitutional checks on abuses of human rights may be dismantled, creating a 'law-free' zone. However, Farber explains how the judicial response to this has been to reject the Government's position, leading him to conclude that the rule of law has proved unexpectedly tenacious. In the next two papers, dealing with the strikingly similar threat to human rights in the United Kingdom in this context, Conor Gearty applauds and explains the human rights victory, and the legal structure of rights that lies behind the *Belmarsh* decision, and Ralph Wilde examines the extra-territorial reach of the Human Rights Act 1998. The common thread between these papers is the role of the judiciary in the determination of certain fundamental rights. This is also the key issue of Edwin Cameron's paper on the Sharpeville Six judgment (originally the Bentham Club's Presidential address in 2004) in which his highlighting of the treatment of these and several other defendants at a time of 'national trauma' leads to the regretful conclusion that miscarriages of justice occur across a whole range of jurisdictions, and that in certain circumstances they cannot be prevented by judicial interpretations of the rule of law.

Returning to the knock-on effects of the Human Rights Act, Jonathan Rogers colourfully highlights the clashes that occur between domestic criminal law and human rights, focusing on the exercise of prosecutorial discretion. In doing so he makes clear that the impact of the Act extends beyond the attribution of rights to the determination of legal practice. That rights relating to personality may be influenced and complicated by human right norms is just one of the subjects of Robin Morse's extensive comment on freedom of the press and private international law.

The trammeling, indeed disregarding, of rights is vividly described by Jo Bridgeman in her work on failures in the healthcare system—in this case the taking of organs from children after their death without parental consent—and the corresponding failure of law. Bridgeman explains such failures from a feminist perspective and by invoking systems theory, amounting to an important critique of aspects of the law of tort and negligence.

The dramatic transformation of legal practice—amounting to a 'velvet revolution'—is the subject of Linda Mulcahy's research into the aftermath of the Woolf reforms in which she views, also from a feminist perspective, 'cultures of adversarialism' and the marginalization of certain voices in the civil justice arena. Somewhat controversially she asks whether the shift towards cultures of cooperation can ever be fully achieved whilst masculine ideology and methodology dominate legal practice and education. Law's response to social movements is similarly charted by Alison Diduck in her evaluation of 'shifting familiarity' in law. By this Diduck explains that a whole range of relationships are now legally recognised as familial—that those with whom we are familiar have become our family. She attributes this shift in part to law's new(ish) culture of equality and non-discrimination. Importantly, the changes described by Diduck may be more tangential and less deliberate than those engendered by the Woolf reforms, but they are no less influenced by policy, particularly ideas of shared responsibility and the withdrawal of the state in relationships of care. This leads Diduck to conclude that instead of being primarily concerned with the legal boundaries which demarcate what is meant by 'family', this example of radical legal change is more about how individual rights and responsibilities accrue from different relationships and how law distributes these.

Jo Shaw's main concern is equality as a central and evolving legal concept in the European Union, particularly as it has been absorbed into the mainstream of policy making. This process of 'mainstreaming' is viewed by Shaw both as a theoretical approach and as a political strategy. Additionally she explores the relationship between notions of gender equality and diversity, reaching important conclusions about the 'constitutional promise' as well as the symbolic importance of provisions in EU law which are intended to achieve gender equality.

A theoretical approach to the connection between legal change—'decent burials for dead concepts!'—and legal reasoning is advanced by James Penner in a major critique of Dworkin's analogy between scientific inquiry and legal reasoning. Penner's concuding plea is for a broader 'intellectual' history of the way the law operates. In contrast, Vivienne

Brown's concern is with rights and duties and the way in which they make up legal relations. Bravely, she offers a fascinating reformulation of Hohfeld's scheme of rights.

The state of the art of several key legal disciplines forms the second half of this volume, with many of the papers advancing areas ripe for reform. For example John Armour addresses a fundamental question 'Who should make corporate law?', arguing that regulatory competition between Member States' company laws is likely to be a better way to stimulate the development of appropriate legal rules than is the EU legislative process. In addressing this issue he offers an expansive perspective on company law, and the inevitable impacts of EU law in this area. Reinhard Zimmermann surveys the impact of the incorporation of consumer contract law, often as a result of EC legislation, within the time-honoured and venerable structure of the German Civil Code. He characterises the impact of this process of incorporation as having 'effectively converted the BGB into a permanent building site'. However, he then concludes with the graphic observation that 'a building site humming with the cheery voices of craftsmen and artisans may be a more appropriate metaphor for a modern code of private law than a museum in which only the hushed voices of the occasional tourist group can be heard': this encapsulates neatly the energy that law reform can engender even in the most venerable of institutions.

Michael Spence also analyses the continuous development of legal doctrine in the field of trade mark law, and how various 'topoi', or commitments to particular ideas about specific legal concepts, shape and influence this development. He sees trade mark law as wandering between the *topos* of 'property' and the *topos* of 'speech', and argues compellingly for the greater normative value of the latter approach. He also situates these questions of legal doctrine within a wider economic and cultural context, as does Mark Freedland in his magisterial analysis of the unfolding evolution of the law of the personal employment contract, and of the 'functional deficiencies' that exist in our employment laws. Catherine Redgwell, also grapples with the question of how the evolution of legal norms can keep pace with the pace of biotechnological advances, and how international standards can be framed to address the new environmental challenges thrown up by these scientific developments (this was her inaugural lecture). Taken together, a central theme of how legal systems respond to new and dynamic scientific, social, economic and cultural shifts is visible in every paper in this volume, which can be perhaps described as the overarching current problem for all those who engage with the law.

Finally, we would like to express our thanks to all those who chaired this year's lectures—Lord Woolf of Barnes, Mr Justice Collins, Mr David Zilkha, Mavis MacLean, Dame Brenda Hale, Professor Ian Dennis, Lord Justice Sedley, Lord Justice Neuberger, Lord Justice Jacob, Lord Rodger of Earlsferry, Lord Hoffmann, Lord Justice Auld, Professor Malcolm Grant and Lord Justice Steyn.

Jane Holder and Colm O'Cinneide
UCL
2005

Contents

Unlawful Combatants: Military Detention, Terrorism, and the Rule of Law

Daniel A Farber[1]

Introduction

The unprecedented attacks of 11 September 2001 have prompted far-reaching responses by the United States. After 9/11, Congress passed a resolution—the Authorization for Use of Military Force Resolution (AUMF)—authorizing the President to 'use all necessary and appropriate force' against any 'nations, organizations, or persons' that he determines 'planned, authorized, committed, or aided' in the attacks. Pursuant to this and other legal authority, the United States commenced military actions in Afghanistan and a host of other actions against al Qaeda and its supporters around the world. Of particular importance for present purposes, the Bush Administration claimed that the U.S. military was authorized to detain suspected al Qaeda supporters as unlawful combatants, indefinitely and without legal recourse.[2] I should note that the Administration has taken this position regarding all active supporters of al Qaeda regardless of whether those individuals are directly involved in terrorist acts.

U.S. treatment of 'unlawful combatants' raises critical questions of international law, U.S. constitutional law, statutory interpretation, and legal theory. Among these questions are whether the procedures prescribed in the Geneva Conventions apply in determining the status of suspected al Qaeda supporters captured on battlefields; whether some or all Taliban members might qualify as prisoners of war; the definition of torture under international and domestic law; the statutory restrictions on the use of military commissions; and the existence of legal limits on

[1] I would like to thank David Caron and Dianne Farber for helpful comments.
[2] An overview of the Administration's actions and of the initial judicial response (prior to the Supreme Court's rulings) can be found in R Iraola, 'Enemy Combatants, The Courts, and the Constitution' (2003) 56 Okl L Rev, 565.

the terms of detention.[3] All of these issues relate to the correct application of legal rules to anti-terrorist activities.

But a more fundamental question was raised by the Government's actions, and in particular its claim that military detention was not subject to legal constraints. That more fundamental question was not, 'which legal rules apply?'. Instead, it was, 'does law apply here *at all*?'. Overall, as one seasoned observer explains, '[t]he view of the Bush Administration has been consistent: that the location at which a non-citizen is held, the battlefield conditions under which he was seized, the absence of uniform, or a threat to willingly cause civilian deaths will preclude any significant form of judicial review for almost anyone whom the administration suspects of involvement with terrorists'.[4] In a series of memoranda and presidential decisions, the Bush Administration attempted to clear a law-free zone for the actions against al Qaeda. Given the shocking and unprecedented nature of 9/11, perhaps this effort was understandable. But as we will see, this effort has been notably unsuccessful.

The upshot was a victory for the rule of law. This evocative phrase has served as a rallying cry for centuries, though it lacks any clear-cut defini-tion. Rather, the rule of law involves a cluster of concepts.[5] Of these concepts, two are most relevant for current purposes. The first is the supremacy of legal authority, so that officials as well as citizens are gov-erned by laws. The second is the availability of impartial legal forums to enforce the law, replacing the 'rule of men' with the 'rule of law'. These two concepts come together in the idea of due process, for without

[3] For discussion of these and other issues, see B Ackerman, 'The Emergency Constitution' (2004) 112 Yale LJ, 1029; A Barak, 'The Role of a Supreme Court in a Democracy, and the Fight Against Terrorism' (2003) 58 U Miami L Rev, 125; N Feldman, 'Choices of Law, Choices of War' (2002) 25 Harv JL & Pub Pol'y, 457; H Hongju Koh, 'The Spirit of the Laws' (2002) 43 Harv Int'l LJ, 23; D Luban, 'The War on Terrorism and the End of Human Rights' (Summer 2002) 22 Phil & Pub Pol'y Q, 9. My concern here is with the legality rather than the wisdom of these measures, but doubts have also been raised on that score. Professor Heymann, for example, argues that; 'the military order deprives the United States of its historic claim of moral leadership among the world's nations in matters of fairness to individuals charged with crime, leaving us in the company of dictators like President Robert Mugabe of Zimbabwe. It makes even more difficult future efforts at military coalition-building and will deny us the benefits of legal cooperation with our closest allies in the forms of extradition and mutual assistance. Finally, it will leave lasting doubt about the honesty of convictions in the wake of secret trials with secret evidence'. P B Heymann, 'Terrorism, Freedom and Security: Winning Without War' (Boston: MIT Press 2003), 95.

[4] Ibid, 96. Professor Heymann adds: 'Though our danger is far less than the danger that Israel faces, our willingness to abandon the most fundamental judicial protections of personal security has been far greater'.

[5] For analysis of the various threads of the rule of law ideal, see R H Fallon Jr., 'The Rule of Law' as a Concept in Constitutional Discourse' (1997) 97 Colum L Rev, 1.

the right to notice and a hearing before an impartial decisionmaker, the rule of law means little in practice. These basic aspects of the rule of law were put at issue by the Bush Administration's detention policy.

It is a familiar view—and not without empirical support—that law goes silent in the face of battle; or, as it is sometimes said, war may function as a black hole into which constitutional rights vanish.[6] The view that law falls out of the picture during dire emergencies has a respectable intellectual pedigree (and not just from apologists for dictatorship).[7] In the immediate aftermath of 9/11, it seemed likely that the 'War Against Terrorism' might become a case in point. The fact that it has not is a tribute to the stubborn efforts of certain civilian and military lawyers, the resistance of the courts, and the influence of domestic and international opinion.

I will begin by discussing in detail the position taken by the Bush Administration in the aftermath of 9/11. I will then consider in turn the judicial response on two crucial points: the availability of a judicial forum to raise legal challenges to detention, and the mandate for due process in the handling of individual cases.

The Effort to Create a Law-Free Zone

On 13 November 2001, President Bush issued a 'military order' regarding the detention of terrorists.[8] The order invokes his powers as 'President and as Commander in Chief of the Armed Forces', specifically including two statutory provisions dealing with military commissions discussed below. Section 1 of the order makes seven findings, of which the most important are (a) and (e). Finding (a) states that '[i]nternational terrorists, including members of al Qaida, have carried out attacks ... on a scale that has created a state of armed conflict ...'. Finding (e) states that, '[t]o protect the United States and its citizens, and for the effective conduct of military operations and prevention of terrorist attacks, it is necessary for individuals subject to this order under section 2 to be detained, and, when tried, to be tried for violations of the laws of war and other applicable laws by military tribunals'.

---

[6] Heymann, 'Terrorism, Freedom and Security', (n 3 above) 161 (attributing this phrase to Kathleen Sullivan).

[7] For a thorough discussion of this and related questions, see O' Gross, 'Chaos and Rules: Should Responses to Violent Crises Always be Constitutional' (2003) 112 Yale LJ, 1011.

[8] The order is most readily accessible on the White House website, *www.whitehouse. gov/news/releases/2001/*.

Section 2 defines who is subject to this order, or more precisely, authorizes the President to do so in the future. The President need merely make a written finding that there is 'reason to believe' that a person was a member of al Qaeda, has engaged in acts of international terrorism against the United States, or has harboured such individuals. The President must also find that 'it is in the interest of the United States that such individual be subject to this order'. Essentially, then, the targets of the order consist of everyone who has assisted al Qaeda or engaged in terrorism against the United States—or more precisely, those who are suspected of doing so by the President. Individuals covered by this order do not include U.S. citizens.

Section 3 provides for detention of these individuals, who are to be 'treated humanely' and 'afforded adequate food, drinking water, shelter, clothing, and medical treatment'. Section 4 then provides that '[a]ny individual subject to this order shall, when tried, be tried by military commission for any and all offenses triable by military commission that such individual is alleged to have committed and may be punished in accordance with the penalties provided under applicable law, including life imprisonment or death'. Subsection (c) sketches the procedures for such trials, which are to provide a 'full and fair trial'. The order does call for the participation of 'attorneys for the individual subject to this order', but with relaxed procedural rules: suspension of all rules of evidence except relevance, conviction and sentencing by two-thirds of the members of the commission, and wide power to prevent unauthorized disclosure of information. Thus, the order falls far short of providing the sorts of procedural protections available in the United States in criminal cases or even in military courts martial.

Finally, section 7 of the order provides that individuals 'shall not be privileged to seek any remedy or maintain any proceeding, directly or indirectly, or to have any such remedy or proceeding sought on the individual's behalf, in (i) any court of the United States, or any State thereof, (ii) any court of any foreign nation, or (iii) any international tribunal'.

Three months later, this order was supplemented by a classified order from the President (not fully declassified until June 2004). In this memorandum, President Bush rejected the application of the Geneva Convention to supporters of al Qaeda, whether captured during the Afghanistan conflict or elsewhere. Although international law is not my focus in this paper, a brief consideration of the memo is helpful to round out the picture. In the first paragraph of the memo, the President concludes that 'the war against terrorism ushers in a new paradigm, one in which groups with broad, international reach commit horrific acts against innocent civilians, sometimes with the support of states'. 'Our Nation recognizes', the memo continues, 'that this new paradigm—ushered in not by us, but by terrorists—requires new thinking in the law of war, but thinking that should nevertheless be consistent with the principles of Geneva'.

The second paragraph of the memo considers the application of the Geneva Conventions to al Qaeda and the Taliban. As to al Qaeda, the memo concludes:

I accept the legal conclusion of the Department of Justice and determine that none of the provisions of Geneva apply to our conflict with al Qaeda in Afghanistan or elsewhere throughout the world because, among other reasons, al Qaeda is not a High Contracting Party to Geneva.

The President rejected the sweeping argument that because Afghanistan is a failed state, the Geneva Conventions did not apply to the conflict as a whole. He did not, however, provide Taliban supporters with POW status. (The State Department had argued that individual Taliban supporters might receive such status.)[9] The President went on to conclude that common Article 3 of Geneva (a provision included in all of the Geneva conventions) did not apply to either al Qaeda or Taliban detainees 'because, among other reasons, the relevant conflicts are international in scope and common Article 3 applies only to "armed conflict not of an international character".' In addition, the memo finds that 'Taliban detainees are unlawful combatants and, therefore, do not qualify as prisoners of war under Article 4 of Geneva'. Nevertheless, 'as a matter of policy', the memo directs the armed forces to 'continue to treat detainees humanely and, to the extent appropriate and consistent with military necessity, in a manner consistent with the principles of Geneva'.

This memo was based in part on the now-famous advice of Alberto Gonzales.[10] Gonzales argued that 'the war against terrorism is a new kind of war' and continued:

The nature of the new war places a premium on other factors, such as the ability to quickly obtain information from captured terrorists and their sponsors in order to avoid further atrocities against American civilians, and the need to try terrorists for war crimes such as wantonly killing civilians. In my judgment, this

---

[9] Memorandum from C L Powell to Counsel to the President, 'Draft Decision Memorandum for the President on the Applicability of the Geneva Convention to the Conflict in Afghanistan', 26 January 2002.

[10] Memorandum for the President, from A R Gonzales, 'Decision re Application of the Geneva Convention on Prisoners of War to the Conflict with al Qaeda and the Taliban', 25 January 2002.

new paradigm renders obsolete Geneva's strict limitations on question of enemy prisoners and renders quaint some of its provisions requiring that captured enemy be afforded such things as commissary privileges, scrip (i.e., advances of monthly pay), athletic uniforms, and scientific instruments.

Gonzales argued, however, that the U.S. would continue to be constrained by several factors: '(i) its commitment to treat the detainees humanely and, to the extent appropriate and consistent with military necessity, in a manner consistent with the principles of GPW, (ii) its applicable treaty obligations, (iii) minimum standards of treatment universally recognised by the nations of the world, and (iv) applicable military regulations regarding the treatment of detainees'. As is also well-known, the Gonzales memo was sharply contested by the legal adviser to the State Department, William H. Taft IV, who argued that the Geneva Convention should apply to Taliban detainees in Afghanistan.[11] But the President ultimately sided with Gonzales except to the extent that he was willing to classify Taliban members as unlawful combatants under Geneva rather than as being entirely outside the purview of the Geneva Conventions.

Besides eliminating the substantive provisions of Geneva as applied to al Qaeda, the President's decision also had the effect of eliminating various hearing requirements mandated by the conventions.[12] Under Article 82 of Geneva III, prisoners of war may be tried only by a 'military court' unless the detaining power's laws explicitly permit the use of a civilian court, and any procedure must 'offer the essential guarantees of independence and impartiality as generally recognized'. Moreover, under Article 106, the prisoner must have the same right of appeal as a member of the detaining power's own armed forces. These provisions might arguably apply at least to some Taliban soldiers. Also pursuant to Article 6, '[s]hould any doubt arise as to whether persons, havng committed a belligerent act and having fallen into the hands of the enemy', constitute POWs, 'such persons shall enjoy the protection of the Present Convention until such time as their status has been determined by a competent tribunal'. Article 6 might apply to Taliban and perhaps to some of their al Qaeda supporters in Afghanistan. Common Article 3 imposes other requirements in an 'armed conflict not of an international character occurring in the territory of one of the High Contracting Parties'. In such conflicts, punishment is not allowed 'without previous judgment

[11] Memorandum to Counsel to the President, 'Comments on Your Paper on the Geneva Convention', 2 February 2002.

[12] A detailed critique of the President's position and its legal rationale can be found in D Jinks and D Sloss, 'Is the President Bound by the Geneva Conventions?' (2004) 90 Cornell L Rev 97.

pronounced by a regularly constituted court, affording all the judicial guarantees which are recognized as indispensable by civilized parties'. Thus, where they apply, the Geneva Conventions not only provide substantive protection but require significant procedural safeguards beyond those promised in the President's detention order.

Failure to comply with Geneva could potentially be more than an international embarrassment if the Conventions apply. Under a federal statute, the War Crimes Act of 1997,[13] war crimes committed by U.S. nationals or members of the armed forces are subject to life imprisonment (or to the death penalty if the victim dies). A war crime is defined to include, *inter alia*, 'any conduct ... defined as a grave breach' in the Geneva Conventions and any violation of Common Article 3. Geneva III, article 130, lists 'wilfully depriving a prisoner of war of the rights of fair and regular trial prescribed in this Convention' as a grave breach. Thus, failure to follow proper procedures before imposing punishment on detainees could potentially be a serious federal offence, even a capital one. The President sought to avoid these potential consequences, and with them the need to provide procedural protection, by ruling the Geneva Conventions completely inapplicable to al Qaeda and its supporters, and by classifying Taliban as unlawful combatants.

I have referred to these presidential actions as attempting to create a law-free zone; and yet, even on their own terms, they do not quite succeed in doing so. True, they attempt to block conventional legal constraints such as the ordinary requirements of criminal procedure and the normal international rules governing detainees. The presidential order also attempts to shut off any access to the judicial system. But still these actions brush up against the law.

First, of course, is the fact that the President apparently solicited advice from lawyers—his own White House counsel and the Office of Legal Counsel in the Department of Justice (OLC). (Others, such as military and State Department lawyers were excluded from the process as much as possible.) Admittedly, given the functions of these offices and their political character, he was unlikely to receive unpalatable advice. But the fact remains that he did seek to establish the legality of his actions, rather than merely announcing that the dire crisis required him to act 'above the law'.

Second, the President's detention order invoked at least the form of law. 'Trials' of detainees were to take place, based on 'charges' and with a fair 'hearing'. Military lawyers were to serve as prosecutors and defence counsel. Involving military lawyers in the process was to prove a fateful

---

[13] 18 USC 2441.

step. An old saying has it that 'military justice is to justice as military music is to music'. Whatever historical truth that saying may have had, today's military lawyers are committed to procedural fairness. As discussed later, the result of their involvement was a much more elaborate set of procedures, still falling a bit short of the usual requirements of the Uniform Code of Military Justice, but far more balanced than the summary proceedings suggested by the curt language of the President's order.

Nevertheless, the main thrust of the detention order was to sweep away domestic legal restraints. Access to the courts was purportedly eliminated, as were civilian criminal trials and their accompanying restrictions. The application of the War Crimes Act was allegedly avoided by the President's later directive on the Geneva Conventions. America is a notoriously litigation-prone and law-bound society. What made the Administration's chief lawyers think they could escape the clutches of the legal system?

The main answer to that question lies in two World War II-era decisions by the Supreme Court, *Johnson v Eisentrager*[14] and *Ex parte Quirin*.[15] These cases require close examination.

Quirin upheld a military tribunal's jurisdiction over a group of German soldiers (one an American citizen). The group had been taken by German submarine to the U.S. coast, where they landed, buried their uniforms, and headed inland to conduct a campaign of sabotage. Because they were not in uniform, the German soldiers were classified as spies rather than prisoners of war and were subject to the death penalty. In attacking the jurisdiction of the military tribunal, their lawyers relied on a famous case, *Ex parte Milligan*,[16] which had roundly condemned the use of military tribunals against civilians during the Civil War. *Milligan* held that military tribunals could not be used so long as the civil courts remained open and functioning. But the Court distinguished *Milligan* on the ground that Milligan had been a longtime resident of a loyal state and a civilian rather than an enemy belligerent. Despite the seemingly absolute language of the Sixth Amendment to the Constitution, requiring jury trials in all criminal cases, the Court found an implicit exception based on historical context—particularly the application of martial law during the American Revolution.

Quirin was decided under highly unusual circumstances at the onset of World War II. Some scholars questioned whether it remained good law. Nevertheless, on its own terms, it seems to authorize the use of military tribunals to try violations of the law of war by enemy belligerents, even if

---

[14] 339 US 763 (1950).   [15] 317 US 1 (1941).   [16] 71 US 2 (1866)

those belligerents are also U.S. citizens. To apply this ruling, all that seemed necessary was to classify al Qaeda supporters as enemy belligerents, which seemed natural enough once the struggle against them was categorized as a 'war against terrorism'. This would make them subject to military trial for violations of the laws of war. There remained some conceptual (and practical) puzzles, in terms of defining what kind of affiliation with terrorists would render a person an enemy belligerent and in terms of specifying the application of the laws of war in this context. But *Quirin* provided a firm foundation for the constitutionality of military tribunals.

This left, however, the problem of how to keep the U.S. courts from reviewing the cases. In *Quirin* itself, the trials took place within the United States. But a later case, also arising from World War II, suggested a method for avoiding the jurisdiction of the federal courts.

The defendants in *Johnson v Eisentrager*[17] were associated with the German armed forces in China. After the German surrender, they continued to furnish intelligence to the Japanese. They were tried by U.S. military authorities in China for violating the laws of war by continuing to engage in hostilities after the surrender. The issue before the Supreme Court was whether the federal courts had jurisdiction to entertain a *habeas* petition on their behalf. The Court began its analysis by remarking that it knew of 'no instance where a court, in this or any other country where the writ is known, has issued it on behalf of an alien enemy who, at no relevant time and in no stage of his captivity, has been within its territorial jurisdiction'.[18] The Court then discussed the tenuous legal rights of enemy aliens before turning to the jurisdictional issue. The lower court had held that the defendants had a constitutional entitlement to seek *habeas*. The Supreme Court found this untenable. For one thing, military commanders would be required even during active hostilities to ship *habeas* petitioners to the U.S. to appear before the court.

One might expect this to be the end of the opinion, but the Court then went on somewhat puzzlingly to deal with the merits of the defendants' claims that their trial by military commission was unconstitutional. The explanation seems to lie in the structure of the lower court's opinion. The lower court had reasoned that *habeas* is a 'subsidiary procedural right that follows from possession of substantive constitutional rights'.[19] The Supreme Court concluded, on the contrary, that the Bill of Rights did not have extra-territorial application in the context of military occupation. Finally, the Court considered the facial validity of the charges against the

---

[17] n 14 above.   [18] Ibid, 768.   [19] Ibid, 781.

defendants and concluded that the military commission had jurisdiction
over them. Concluding that 'we find no basis for invoking federal judicial
power in any district', the Court held that the petition was properly
dismissed.[20]

The OLC encapsulated the opinion as follows: 'In the critical passage
that most nearly summarizes the Court's holding, the *Eisentrager* Court
based its conclusion on the fact that the prisoners were seized, tried, and
held in territory that was outside the sovereignty of the United States
and outside the territorial jurisdiction of any court of the United States'.
In my view, that was a fair reading of the holding of the *Eisentrager*
Court, though it does require viewing the final portions of the opinion
as *dicta* of the worst kind—not only unnecessary to the holding
but issued despite an acknowledged lack of jurisdiction. Thus, on
OLC's reading of *Eisentrager*, *habeas* jurisdiction is strictly limited by
geography.

The problem was to find the appropriate place of confinement, safely
within U.S. control but hopefully not part of the United States for
purposes of *habeas* jurisdiction. The choice was the U.S. military base at
Guantánamo Bay, Cuba (GBC). The United States holds Guantánamo
under a perpetual lease that gives it complete control of the base but
purports to reserve 'ultimate sovereignty' in Cuba. In relying on
Eisentrager to preclude *habeas* jurisdiction, the President must have
known that he was taking a risk. OLC did 'conclude that the great weight
of legal authority indicates that a federal district court could not properly
exercise habeas jurisdiction over an alien detained at GBC'.[21] But even
OLC communicated less than its usual certainty about the correctness
of the President's position because of the ambiguous legal status of
Guantánamo. The OLC memo concludes:

A detainee could make a non-frivolous argument that jurisdiction does exist over
aliens detained at GBC, and we have found no decisions that clearly foreclose the
existence of habeas there .... While we believe that the correct answer is that
federal courts lack jurisdiction over habeas petitions filed by alien detainees held
outside the sovereign territory of the United States, there remains some litigation
risk that a district court might reach the opposite result.

In short, OLC's message to the President about *habeas* was, 'don't blame
us if this doesn't work'. What happened, however, turned out to be a more
serious loss for the government than OLC had feared.

[20] 339 US 763 (1950), 790.
[21] Memorandum for W J Haynes, II from P F Phibin and J C Yoo, 'Possible Habeas
Jurisdiction over Aliens Held in Guantanamo Bay, Cuba', 28 December 2001.

Restoring Access to Courts

The initial *habeas* litigation was promising to the government. In *Coalition of Clergy v Bush*,[22] a group of lawyers, journalists, and clergy sought *habeas* on behalf of all of the Guantanamo detainees. The district court found that the petitioners lacked standing and also that the court lacked *habeas* jurisdiction under *Eisentrager*. The court of appeals for the Ninth Circuit agreed that the petitioners lacked sufficient connection with the detainees to file as 'next friend' on their behalf. In a signal of possible future difficulties, however, the appellate court vacated the portion of the district court ruling regarding *habeas* jurisdiction. The D.C. Circuit, on the other hand, fully accepted the government's reading of *Eisentrager*.[23] So far, so good, from the government's perspective. But then two clouds appeared on the horizon. The first cloud issued from the Ninth Circuit. After the Ninth Circuit's first opinion, the brother of one of the detainees refiled on behalf of his brother. The Ninth Circuit concluded that the United State exercise of complete territorial jurisdiction over Guantanamo was sufficient to allow *habeas* under *Eisentrager*, regardless of whether Cuba formally retained 'sovereignty' over the base.[24] The second, more ominous cloud, came from the Supreme Court, which agreed to review the contrary holding of the D.C. Circuit in a case filed on behalf of another detainee.

When it came, the Supreme Court's decision in *Rasul v Bush*[25] was a more severe loss for the Government than might have been expected. Not only did the Court find *habeas* jurisdiction, but it did so on unexpectedly broad grounds. Correspondingly, the Court read *Eisentrager* very narrowly. It portrayed *Eisentrager* as considering only whether *habeas* was available as a matter of constitutional right. This constitutional analysis, in turn, was necessitated only because of an earlier ruling that statutory jurisdiction did not extend to persons held outside any federal judicial district. But that statutory ruling was overruled in a later case, eliminating the statutory gap that confronted the Court in *Eisentrager*. The Court also rejected the argument that *habeas* jurisdiction should not extend to Guantanamo under the presumption against extra-territorial application of statutes: Guantanamo was sufficiently subject to U.S. control to qualify as U.S. territory.

[22] 310 F3d 1153 (9th Cir 2002).
[23] *Al Odah v United States*, 321 F3d 1134 (DC Cir 2003), cert. granted. 540 U.S. 1003 (2003).   [24] *Gherebi v Bush*, 374 F3d 727 (9th Cir 2004).
[25] 124 S Ct 2686 (2004).

To cap the government's defeat, the Supreme Court also held that
'nothing in *Eisentrager* or in any of our other cases categorically excludes
aliens detained in military custody outside the United States from the
"privilege of litigation" in U.S. courts'.[26] The Court continued with
a reminder that the Alien Torts Claim Act 1789 gives aliens alone
the 'privilege of suing for an actional "tort . . . committed in violation of the
law of nations or a treaty of the United States" '.[27] Thus, the Court concluded, '[t]he fact that petitioners in these cases are being held in military
custody is immaterial to the question of the District Court's jurisdiction
over their nonhabeas claims'.[28] So, by invoking the general jurisdiction of
the district courts, detainees could avoid whatever territorial limits
remained on *habeas* after *Rasul*.

To complete the government's misery, the Court also made clear its
view of the legal sufficiency of the complaint. A footnote to the opinion
reads:

Petitioners' allegations—that, although they have engaged neither in combat
nor in acts of terrorism against the United States, they have been held in
Executive detention for more than two years in territory subject to the long-
term, exclusive jurisdiction and control of the United States, without access to
counsel and without being charged with any wrongdoing—unquestionably
describe "custody in violation of the Constitution or laws or treaties of the
United States".[29]

Three justices dissented, joining an opinion by Justice Scalia. A certain
amount of hyberbole is common in American dissenting opinions, and so
Justice Scalia's reading of the majority opinion may be taken with a grain
of salt. Nevertheless, the dissent was an indication of the seriousness of
the government's loss. In Justice Scalia's characteriszation, the decision
'boldly extends the scope of the habeas statute to the four corners of the
earth'.[30] He complained that, '[f]rom this point forward, federal courts
will entertain petitions from these prisoners, and others like them around
the world, challenging actions and events far away, and forcing the courts
to oversee one aspect of the Executive's conduct of a foreign war'.[31] Justice
Scalia's dissent closes with the following observation: 'For this Court to
create such a monstrous scheme in time of war, and in frustration of our
military commanders' reliance upon clearly stated prior law, is judicial
adventurism of the worst sort'.[32]

Although it is too soon to be sure, the early indication is that the lower
courts will give *Rasul* a broad reading, fulfilling Justice Scalia's fear that

[26] 124 S Ct 2698.   [27] Ibid, at 2699.   [28] Ibid.   [29] Ibid, 2698 n 15.
[30] 124 S Ct 2706.   [31] Ibid, 2707.   [32] Ibid, 2711.

habeas jurisdiction might extent to the ends of the earth. Last December, a federal district court extended *habeas* jurisdiction well beyond Guantánamo and indeed beyond anything even arguably describable as U.S. territory.[33] Petitioners alleged—and provided some supporting evidence—that Omar Abu Ali is a U.S. citizen who was arrested over a year ago in Saudi Arabia at the request of the U.S. government. As Judge Bates said, 'Abu Ali was not captured on a battlefield or in a zone of hostilities—rather, he was arrested in a university classroom while taking an exam'.[34] FBI agents watched his interrogation by Saudi police as well as conducting their own interrogations, and government officials were allegedly aware that he had been tortured.[35] Allegedly, 'Saudi officials have described the detention privately as a United States matter, have acknowledged publicly that the United States has been involved throughout his detention, and have told United States officials that they would release Abu Ali at the request of the United States'.[36] On this basis, Judge Bates held that discovery was warranted to determine the truth of the accusations, this discovery to be 'expeditious but cautious, consistent with the substantial and delicate interests of foreign relations potentially involved'.[37]

As Judge Bates observed, the petitioners had already offered 'considerable' evidence, which the government had made almost no effort to rebut.[38] I wish that I could say with complete confidence that discovery will result in evidence conclusively rebutting the petitioner's charges about his treatment. Because discovery involves intrusion into relations with a foreign power, it is possible that higher courts will intervene to prevent inquiry into the extent to which the Saudis are merely acting on behalf of the U.S. In any event, Judge Bates' ruling makes clear the potential sweep of the *habeas* statute after *Rasul*; the likelihood that a court would assert *habeas* jurisdiction over a person who is in the formal custody of a foreign power would have seemed remote even a year ago.

Rasul grants *habeas* jurisdiction to the courts, but the question remains whether the lower courts will use that jurisdiction to oversee the legality of the detentions at Guantánamo. To my mind, it seems clear that the Supreme Court intended such review and that the *habeas* statute requires it. But at least one district judge has ruled to the contrary, just recently, and it remains to be seen how this story will play out.

---

[33] Memorandum Opinion of Dec. 16, 2004, in *Ali v Ashcroft*, 350 F Supp 2d 28 (DDC 2004).   [34] Ibid, at 30.

[35] Ibid, at 31–32, 36.   [36] Ibid, at 33.   [37] Ibid, at 69.

[38] Ibid, at 67.

Re-establishing Due Process

Rasul made it clear, at the very least, that the courts are open to accused unlawful combatants and that they cannot constitutionally be held if they are not in fact within that category. But this leaves a bit of a puzzle about how to determine the facts. The district court could conduct a *de novo* hearing and make its own independent determination of status. But this would essentially amount to a trial on war crime charges, which seems to obviate the whole point of military detention and trial. On the other hand, the right to *habeas* would be meaningless if the government could answer the petition with a simple averment of unlawful combatant status. The Supreme Court wrestled with this problem in *Hamdi v Rumsfeld*,[39] along with the broader question of the government's right to detain citizens as enemy combatants.

Hamdi, an American citizen, was captured in Afghanistan and after some intermediate stops was detained at a naval brig in Charleston, SC. No charges were filed against Hamdi, but the Government claimed the right to detain him incommunicado indefinitely as an 'unlawful combatant'. His father filed a *habeas* petition on his behalf. His father asserted that Hamdi went to Afghanistan to do 'relief work' less than two months before 11 September and could not have received military training. In response to the petition, the Government filed a declaration from Michael Mobbs, a Defense Department official. The Mobbs declaration alleges various details regarding Hamdi's trip to Afghanistan, his affiliation there with a Taliban unit during a time when the Taliban was battling U.S. allies, and his subsequent surrender of an assault rifle.[40]

There was no majority opinion, though there was a strong consensus against the Government's position. Four Justices, led by Justice O'Connor, held that Hamdi was entitled to some form of due process hearing. Four other Justices, in two different opinions, would have held his detention squarely unlawful. Two of those Justices joined portions of O'Connor's opinion in order to provide a majority for some disposition of the case. The remaining member of the Court, Justice Thomas, agreed with the Government's view that the Mobbs declaration (which the lower court had characterized as conclusory hearsay) provided a sufficient basis for Hamdi's indefinite detention. Justice O'Connor's opinion seems to

---

[39]   124 S Ct, 2686 (2004).

[40]   For background on the case, and review of the somewhat complex proceedings in the lower courts, see C I Lugosi, 'The Rule of Law or Rule by Law: The Detention of Yaser Hamdi' (2003) 30 Am J Crim L, 225.

represent the pivotal position on the Court and is likely to be regarded as controlling in future cases. But before turning to a detailed consideration of her views, some general observations about the ruling are in order.

Hamdi obviously presented a very serious and difficult constitutional issue. On the one hand, the potential for abuse in allowing arbitrary detentions is plain. On the other hand, the threat of terrorism is a new one; we do not know its exact parameters or those of the response; and other democratic nations such as Britain and Israel have found it necessary to make some sacrifices of civil liberties to combat terrorist campaigns. Of the various opinions, Justice O'Connor's made the most serious effort to reconcile the two interests. She found authorization for the detention in the Congressional resolution, ducking any need to consider inherent presidential authority. But she was only willing to endorse the detention power in cases like Hamdi's, involving enemy action in a war zone, leaving other cases to the future but implying that the category of enemy combatants was narrow. For reasons I have discussed elsewhere, I believe that this is a correct reading of the precedents and of U.S. constitutional history.[41]

Justice Souter's opinion also seemed willing to allow such detention as a narrow exception. Justice Souter recognized, I think properly, that the President may have some emergency detention powers even apart from statute. He observed, also appropriately, that the long-term detention of Hamdi and others could hardly be considered an emergency action. Moreover, he strongly suggested that the Government's action could not be lawful unless it accorded with the Geneva Convention rather than being 'outside the customary usages of war'.[42] Justice Souter emphasized that in deciding the case, 'we are heirs to a tradition given voice 800 years ago by Magna Carta, which, on the barons' insistence, confined executive power by the "law of the land" '.[43]

The positions of the other Justices can be quickly summarized. Justice Thomas, as we read his opinion, came close to giving the President a blank cheque to engage in detention during wartime, though perhaps not to impose criminal punishments through military tribunals. Justices Scalia and Stevens took an equally forthright but opposing view. They denied the existence of any right to treat American citizens who 'fight for the other side' as prisoners of war. In their view, after it detains citizens, the government must either bring criminal charges promptly or release them. Scalia and Stevens recognized only one source of flexibility, the power of Congress to suspend the writ of *habeas corpus*. Not only is this

---

[41] D A Farber, *Lincoln's Constitution* (Chicago: University of Chicago Press, 2003).
[42] 124 S Ct, 2658–2659.   [43] Ibid, 2659.

a draconian remedy, but if invoked it might be far more destructive of civil liberties than a judicially defined solution.

Justice O'Connor's statement acknowledged a power of detention but also began to stake out limits: for example, detention cannot be solely for the purposes of interrogation and cannot extend beyond the armed conflict at question. Justice O'Connor was thus faced with the difficult question of how to determine whether Hamdi fell within what she called the 'narrow category' of unlawful combatants. She attempted to provide a fair process for determining the facts, allowing the Government to begin the process by filing factual affidavits but then allowing Hamdi the chance to provide evidence in rebuttal.

Justice O'Connor's opinion was not necessarily ideal or the only reasonable approach. She might have done more to limit more clearly the permissible category of unlawful combatants and to make it clear that any inherent presidential power was very narrow. ('Take the keys and lock him up' is fine in nursery rhymes but no way to run a democratic society.) Her suggested procedures may or may not turn out to be as workable and fair as she suggested. Nevertheless, her opinion is admirable for its princi-pled stand against arbitrary arrests and for its effort to find a solution that also respected our constitutional history and the need for some flexibility in protecting national security.

Hamdi is also notable as evidence that—contrary to some cynical views of the American judiciary—ideology is not everything, even in the hardest constitutional cases. The critical vote for Justice O'Connor's position was Justice Breyer, commonly considered a member of the liberal block. Chief Justice Rehnquist, a strong conservative voice, also allied himself with O'Connor's centrist views. In the meantime, the two most conserv-ative members of the Court (Thomas and Scalia) came to diametrically opposite conclusions, and Scalia was joined by Justice Stevens, the most liberal member of the Court.

Hamdi leaves open some important questions. Justice O'Connor's opinion was cautious in its treatment of the detention issue. She remarked that there was 'some debate about the proper scope' of the term enemy combatant, and that the 'Government has never provided any court with the full criteria that it uses in classifying individuals as such'.[44] Consequently, she limited herself to individuals like Hamdi, who was allegedly ' "part of or supporting forces hostile to the United States or coalition partners" in Afghanistan and who "engaged in an armed conflict against the United States" there'.[45] Justice O'Connor did not address the

---

[44] 124 S Ct, 2639.   [45] Ibid.

position of individuals whose activities were not part of conventional warfare. She did hold, however, that the 'permissible boundaries of the category [of enemy combatants] will be defined by the lower courts as subsequent cases are presented to them'.[46]

A second question relates to form and length of detention. In justifying detention, Justice O'Connor repeatedly referred to the preventive, non-punitive purposes for detaining 'prisoners of war'.[47] Citing the Geneva and Hague Conventions, O'Connor said that it is 'a clearly established principle of the law of war that detention may last no longer than active hostilities'.[48] She added, 'Certainly, we agree that indefinite detention for the purpose of interrogation is not authorized'.[49] Moreover, She hinted that indefinite preventive detention might undermine the argument for the validity of detention:

[W]e understand Congress' grant of authority for the use of "necessary and appropriate force" to include the authority to detain for the duration of the relevant conflict, and our understanding is based on longstanding law-of-war principles. If the practical circumstances of a given conflict are entirely unlike those of the conflicts that informed the development of the law of war, that understanding may unravel.[50]

But on the facts presented, Justice O'Connor saw no need to confront that problem so long as 'United States troops are still involved in active combat in Afghanistan'.[51]

The remaining question was the form of hearing. Justice O'Connor held that a *habeas* court could accept a government affidavit 'so long as it also permits the alleged combatant to present his own factual case to rebut the Government's [*habeas*] return'.[52] Justice O'Connor also commented on the possibility of a hearing outside the court: 'There remains the possibility that the standards we have articulated could be met by an appropriately authorized and properly constituted military tribunal. Indeed, it is notable that military regulations already provide for such process in related instances, dictating that tribunals be made available to determine the status of enemy detainees who assert prisoner-of-war status under the Geneva Convention'.[53] Importantly, the Court also remarked that Hamdi 'unquestionably has the right to access to counsel in connection with the proceedings on remand'.[54]

The most important aspect of *Hamdi* may not rest in its specific holding but rather on the willingness of eight members of the Court to subject the

---

[46] Ibid, 2642.   [47] Ibid, 2640–41.   [48] Ibid, 2641.   [49] Ibid.
[50] Ibid, 2642.   [51] Ibid.   [52] Ibid, 2652.   [53] Ibid, 2651.
[54] Ibid, 2652.

Government's action to legal constraint. *Hamdi* was a resounding defeat for the Government's effort to evade the rule of law through creation of a law-free zone. Justice O'Connor's opinion made clear in no uncertain terms that the rule of law continues to apply:

> Striking the proper constitutional balance here is of great importance to the Nation during this period of ongoing combat. But it is equally vital that our calculus not give short shrift to the values that this country holds dear or to the privilege that is American citizenship. It is during our most challenging and uncertain moments that our Nation's commitment to due process is most severely tested; and it is in those times that we must preserve our commitment at home to the principles for which we fight abroad.[55]

Unfinished Business

Recall that in its memo on *habeas*, the OLC conceded that a court might conclude, contrary to its analysis, that *habeas* did extend to Guantánamo. The memo also discussed the possible consequences of such a judicial ruling. Because I can hardly improve on it as a description of the issues opened up by the *Rasul* decision, it is worth quoting the relevant paragraph in full:

> You have also asked us about the potential legal exposure if a detainee successfully convinces a federal district court to exercise habeas jurisdiction. There is little doubt that such a result could interfere with the operation of the system that has been developed to address the detainment and trial of enemy aliens. First, a habeas petition would allow a detainee to challenge the legality of his status and treatment under international treaties, such as the Geneva Conventions and the International Covenant on Civil and Political Rights. Thus, a court could review, in part, the question whether and what international law norms may or may not apply to the conduct of the war in Afghanistan, both by the United States and its enemies. Second, a detainee could challenge the use of military commissions and the validity of any charges ... Third, although the Supreme Court in *Ex Parte Quirin*, 317 U.S. 1 (1942) foreclosed habeas review of the procedures used by military commissions, a petition could argue that subsequent developments in the law of habeas corpus require the federal courts to review the constitutionality of military commission procedures today. Fourth, a petition might even be able to question the constitutional authority of the President to use force in Afghanistan ....

As an aside, I would say that this paragraph seemingly suggests some degree of discomfort with the proposed course of action, since it forecasts

---

[55] 124 S Ct, 2648.

very serious consequences for the President's policies if the litigation risk were to materialize. As of course it did.

Even before *Rashid*, the Administration had been pressured to improve the trial procedures before military commissions. The American Bar Association called for procedures guided by the principles of law available in courts martial and in conformity with Article 14 of the International Covenant on Civil and Political Rights.[56] Within the Defense Department, military lawyers also pressed for greater procedural protections. On 21 March 2002, the department issued Miliary Commission Order No. 1. Section 5 of the order provides procedural restrictions, including: (a) a requirement of proof beyond a reasonable doubt, (b) access by the defence to exculpatory evidence held by the prosecution, (c) a right to remain silent, (d) the right to present witnesses and cross-examine opposing witnesses, and (e) a presumptive right of the defendant to be present at all proceedings. Another order provided a detailed description of what offence could be charged under the law of war.[57]

Pursuant to these orders, charges have been filed against several individuals. A review of the complaints, which is available on the Defense Department's website, shows that the primary charge is conspiracy. For example, an Australian named David Hicks is charged as follows:

19. [The defendant] in Afghanistan, from on or about January 1, 2001 to on or about December 2001, willfully and knowingly joined an enterprise of persons who shared a common criminal purpose and conspired and agreed with Nuammad Atef (a/k/a Abus Hafs al Masri), Saif al Adel, Usama bin Laden, and other members and associates of the al Qaeda organizations, known and unknown, to commit the following offenses triable by military commission: attacking civilians; attacking civilian objects; murder by an unprivileged belligerent; destruction of property by an unprivileged belligerent; and terrorism.

The Hicks complaint is also of interest because of the nature of the overt acts charged in pursuit of the conspiracy. His primary affiliation was apparently not with al Qaeda itself but with a Pakistani terrorist association called Lashkar e Tayyiba (LET). Most of the allegations concern Hicks's involvement in al Qaeda training courses. Hicks then allegedly joined al Qaeda fighters at Kandahar airport, where he guarded a tank, and then after a week joined others who were in engaged in combat against Coalition forces. The other two charges are attempted murder (for firing on coalition forces 'while he did not enjoy combat immunity')

---

[56] American Bar Association Task Force on Terrorism and the Law, Report and Recommendations on Military Commissions 16 (4 January 2002).

[57] Department of Defense, Military Commission Instruction No. 2 (30 April 2003).

and aiding the enemy. Thus, the charges amount to general collaboration with al Qaeda combined with involvement in combat in Afganistan.

The charges against other defendants are similar. Salim Ahmed Hamdan was a driver and bodyguard for bin Laden who was charged with conspiracy. So was another defendant who served as a driver, bodyguard, and delivery person. Alia al Balul did media work for bin Laden, including recruiting videos and a video glorifying the attack on the USS *Cole*. Ibrahim al Qosi's primary duties were as a financial officer, though he also served as a bodyguard and driver. Interestingly enough, one of the charges against him is that he fought alongside Chechnyan rebels against the Russians.

The defence has filed a motion to dismiss the conspiracy charges on the ground that the law of war does not include any general offense of conspiracy. A full discussion of this point would go well beyond the scope of this paper. The Government's conspiracy charges seem worrisome on two grounds. First, conspiracy laws give great latitude to the prosecution, even in the presence of all of the safeguards of the federal criminal law system. In a system where procedural protections are weaker, the imbalance between prosecution and defence is even stronger. Second, the boundaries of conspiracy law are capacious, to say the least, and under U.S. law every participant in the conspiracy is fully responsible for the acts committed by any one of them in furtherance of the conspiracy. This is an exceptionally wide net of liability, and one that the United States ought to think twice about before embracing as a principle of international law.

In any event, these charges must be a disappointment to those who hoped military tribunals would be used to punish those who planned and executed specific terrorist attacks such as 9/11. Nor has the prosecution focused solely on those who committed specific belligerent acts in violation of the laws of war. Rather, the theory is that all active al Qaeda supporters are outlaws under the laws of war.

I wonder how thoroughly the Government has thought through the broader implications of its conspiracy theory. The U.S. has a variety of nonmilitary individuals engaged in security and covert operations in Iraq and elsewhere. At least some of these activities might be considered belligerent actions by individuals outside the uniformed military, and therefore under the U.S. theory chargeable as violations of the law of war. Some covert actions may also be conducted in ways that are not in accordance with the laws of war. Under the theories espoused by the U.S. in the Guantánamo cases, one might begin to worry about the potential scope of liability for those who are tangentially connected with these operations. Moreover, the U.S. has sometimes supported military and paramilitary operations by insurgents or their opponents, and to the extent the U.S. has advance knowledge of violations of international law, the conspiracy theory might operate to enlarge the scope of state liability under international law. In any event, given the Bush Administration's general attitude towards international law, it seems a bit ironic that the prosecutors are pressing a theory that may expand the reach of the laws of war very substantially.

How the conspiracy issue will eventually be resolved is unknown. What does seem clear is that the federal courts will ultimately have to determine whether the charges constitute offenses triable by military commission. Given that *habeas* jurisdiction exists under *Rasul*, the government must show that the defendants are not being punished in violation of the laws or treaties of the United States. Even in *Eisentrager*, over fifty years ago, the Court found it necessary to assure itself of the legal validity of the charges.

In the meantime, another of OLC's concerns is also being realised. The federal courts are indeed involving themselves in review of the procedures used by the tribunals and their validity under the Geneva Convention. In *Hamdan v Rumsfeld*,[58] Judge Robertson invalidated the current plan for trials before military commissions. Applying the Third Geneva Convention, he held that the defendant could be tried only by court-martial, with the full protections provided by the Uniform Code of Military Justice, unless a competent tribunal first determined that he was not entitled to POW status. The current system of military commissions was inadequate because it permitted the introduction of evidence outside the presence of the accused for security reasons. Judge Robertson abstained from deciding another claim: whether the use of military commissions would violate Common Article 3.

Judge Robertson rejected the Government's argument that the defendant 'was captured, not in the course of a conflict between the United States and Afghanistan, but in the course of a 'separate' conflict with al Qaeda'.[59] He concluded that the effort to separate the two conflicts 'finds no support in the structure of the Conventions themselves, which are triggered by the place of the conflict, and not by what particular faction a fighter is associated with'.[60] It is notable that in support of this position

---

[58] 344 F Supp 2d 152 (DDC 2004).　　　[59] Ibid, 160.

[60] Ibid, 161. While this article was in press. Judge Robertson's decision was reversed by an appellate panel, which held *inter alia* that the Geneva Conventions are not judicially enforceable and that al Qaeda is not covered by the Convention in any event. See *Hamdan v Rumsfeld*, 415 F 3d 33 (D C Cir 2005). A petition for review in the Supreme Court was filed on August 8, 2005.

he relied on an *amicus* brief filed by a group of highly distinguished retired military lawyers, and on the State Department memo taking issue with Gonzales on the question. Under Army regulations, the defendant's assertion of POW status was enough to place that status 'in doubt' and therefore to entitle him to treatment as a POW until a competent tribunal determined otherwise.

The court also rejected the Government's argument that Common Article 3 was inapplicable because it applied only to civil wars, relying on the contrary language of the International Court of Justice. Finally, Judge Robertson held that the Geneva Conventions were judicially enforceable because the treaties were self-executing and therefore part of the 'Supreme Law of the Land' under the Constitution. Consequently, he ordered that no trial could go forward until the procedural flaws were cured and that the defendant had to be released from special detention into the general population at Guantánamo. In other words, everything OLC feared might happen if Guantánamo were subject to *habeas* jurisdiction seemed to be coming to pass.

Nevertheless, the Administration remains unrepentant. Two months after Judge Robertson's ruling, Gonzales reiterated his support for his original position, precluding POW treatment for al Qaeda fighters in Afghanistan. Specifically, he said:

I think the decision not to apply Geneva in our conflict with Al Qaeda was absolutely the right decision for a variety of reasons ... First of all, it really would be a dishonor to the Geneva Convention. It would honor and reward bad conduct. It would actually make it more difficult, in my judgment, for our troops to win in our conflict against Al Qaeda. It would limit our ability to solicit information from detainees. It would require us to keep detainees housed together where they could share information, where they could coordinate their story, they could plan attacks against guards. It would mean that they would enjoy combat immunity from prosecutions for certain war crimes. And so for a variety of reasons, it makes absolutely no sense.[61]

Mr. Gonzales also maintained that it was appropriate to consider revisions to the Geneva Convention given the new type of enemy involved.

In the meantime, there is the question of what to do about detainees who will not be subject to trial, including 'hundreds of people now in

---

[61] E Lichtblau, 'Gonzales Speaks Against Torture During Hearing', *New York Times*, 7 January 2005. The headline is a little misleading. What Gonzales said was: 'And of course we want to, of course, meet basic standards of conduct with respect to treatment of Al Qaeda, but information is very, very important. And if there are ways we can get that information, especially, for example, through inducements, it seems to me that there is a responsibility of this government to exercise those means'.

military and CIA custody whom the government does not have enough evidence to charge in courts'.[62] One proposal is to build prisons in their homelands, where they would be detained by their national governments. In the meantime, the Defense Department plans to ask Congress to fund a 200-person prison to hold these lifetime prisoners in more comfortable settings. The U.S. apparently also uses as an interrogation technique the threat of transferring prisoners to countries that practice torture.[63] Now that the federal courts have asserted jurisdiction, one can only wonder about their reaction to such plans. The federal courts will also have to consider recent news reports, based on declassified documents, of widespread abuse of prisoners at Guantánamo. For instance, one FBI agent 'reported seeing detainees chained hand and foot in fetal positions, in barren cells with no chair, food, or water'.[64]

There are new judicial rulings on an almost weekly basis, and it remains to be seen how the litigation will ultimately be resolved. (For example, very recently, another federal judge ruled that detainees at Guantánamo have no cognizable constitutional rights, in what appears to me to be a flat refusal to follow the Supreme Court's dictates in footnote 15 of the *Rasul* decision).[65] Moreover, the Government may be able to avoid judicial interference by keeping its activities secret, though the press has proved surprisingly successful in uncovering illicit activities. Finally, as events at Abu Ghraib show, the rules purportedly in place to protect detainees may not be applied as a matter of practice. So there is much ground for concern.

The Administration was clearly successful in at least one regard: it changed the frame of the debate by challenging what had previously been unchallenged legal fundamentals. It is disturbing that at this late date we are forced to struggle to obtain the protection of the very 'law of the land' that the barons thought they had got at Runnymede. Yet this has also had

[62] D Priest, 'U.S. Prepares Long-Term Plan for Jailing of Terror Suspects', *San Francisco Chronicle*, 2 January 2005.

[63] In general, as Professor Heymann explains: 'The administration has shown unexplained and untraditional preferences for coercive interrogation over electronic and other surveillance as a way of learning about the plans and associates of someone suspected of terrorism. It has authorized coercion short of torture for non-citizens outside the United States in forms Israel has found illegal. It has sent foreign suspects to states that practice torture'. Heymann, *Terrorism, Freedom and Security*, (n 3 above), 109.

[64] M Isikoff, 'Unanswered Questions', *Newsweek*, 17 January 2005, 36.

[65] Memorandum and Order in *Kahlif v Bush* (D.D.C. No. 1:04–1142, 19 January 2005) (Leon J.) So far as I can tell, Judge Leon regarded the footnote as *dictum*, though he does not quite say so. In any event, it is unusual for a trial judge to deflect such clear and obviously relevant language from a Supreme Court opinion in connected litigation. The following week, another judge in the same district ruled to the contrary.

its benefits. Many of those fundamentals were universally understood but nowhere articulated definitively. They are now laid down in Supreme Court opinions, to which the Administration is now forced to pay at least lip service.

The Administration has, however reluctantly, conceded that it is not above the law. In his confirmation hearing, Gonzales referred specifically to the *Hamdi* decision: 'We in the executive branch, of course, understand that there are limits upon presidential power; very, very mindful of Justice O'Connor's statement in the *Hamdi* decision that "a state of war is not a blank check for the president of the United States" with respect to the rights of American citizens'.[66]

The question remains whether, in some extreme situations, the executive should be empowered to act without regard for normal legal constraints. Whatever may be said about that question as a theoretical matter, at the very least the executive would have to make a convincing case that the dire nature of the emergency required an extralegal response. The Government's failure to make such a case is evidenced by the sceptical responses of so many federal judges, many of them in general political sympathy with the Administration. Indeed, it is notable that Chief Justice Rehnquist himself, a stalwart conservative and often a strong supporter of presidential authority, rejected the Government's position in *Hamdi*.

When I was a law student, the dean of my law school was fond of repeating the adage that 'the law is a seamless web'. The events discussed here suggest that we might want to amend that phrase. Law is not only a seamless web but a sticky one, difficult to shake loose. Stickiness is not absolute, and under sufficiently extreme circumstances perhaps the web can be brushed away. But centuries of legal evolution have left behind a dense network of adhesive threads, and escaping their entanglement is no easy task. In short, the rule of law has proved unexpectedly tenacious. For that we must be grateful.

---

[66] Memorandum and Order in *Kahlif v Bush* (D.D.C. No. 1:04–1142, 19 January 2005) (Leon J.).

Human Rights in an Age of Counter-Terrorism: Injurious, Irrelevant or Indispensable?

Conor Gearty

Introduction

It might seem churlish to have insisted on the question mark in the title to this paper, when civil libertarians, human rights activists and liberals everywhere were still basking in the glory of what has been widely applauded as the finest 'human rights' judgment ever handed down by a British court: the decision of the nine judge panel in (for want of better shorthand) the *Belmarsh* internment case, decided on 16 December 2004[1]. The title may seem even odder on account of the fact that this chapter is indeed about the inter-relationship of UK anti-terrorism law and the UK Human Rights Act 1998. It does not address large issues of international relations or of global politics, in which arenas it can indeed be credibly argued that human rights ideology has underpinned horrible violence and neo-colonial aggression.[2] Nor is the remit comparative: there will be little in what follows about how badly other countries have behaved: Guantánamo in particular has been well-served in this year's series of *Current Legal Problems* papers[3] as has the extra-jurisdictional reach of the European Convention on Human Rights,[4] and neither shall

---

[1] *A (FC) and others (FC) v Secretary of State for the Home Department; X (FC) and Another (FC) v Secretary of State for the Home Department* [2004] UKHL 56. The case was decided one day after the then Secretary of State for the Home Department and chief patron of the impugned legislation, David Blunkett, had departed from office as a result of developments on an unrelated matter.

[2] C A Gearty, 'Is the Idea of Human Rights Now Doing More Harm than Good?', available from *http://www.lse.ac.uk/Depts/human-rights/index_documents.htm*. See also S Khan, 'War on Terrorism' in *New Civilisation*, Autumn 2004, 26–31.

[3] DA Farber, 'Unlawful Combatants: Military Detention, Terrorism, and the Rule of Law', [2005] *Current Legal Problems*, ch 1 above (27 January 2005).

[4] R Wilde, 'The Extraterritorial Application of the Human Rights Act' [2005] *Current Legal Problems*, ch 3 below (24 February 2005).

be dealt with here. The focus is determinedly provincial, albeit with European elements at the edge of our field of vision.

If we are concerned in the main with UK law in general, and the House of Lords decision in particular, how can it even be suggested that the human rights model, exemplified in the *Belmarsh* case, does anything other than reflect the indispensability of human rights in an age of counter-terrorism? Certainly both with that decision and with the conduct of the debate on the terrorism proposals that followed it in the Spring of 2005, we can now dispel the notion that 'human rights' are *irrelevant*. But injurious? It is clear that the *Belmarsh* ruling deserves to be applauded by civil libertarians and that it warrants the plaudits that it has received. The purpose of this paper is to explain the case in conventional case-note style but also to explore how it came about, how a deeply critical perspective on the detention powers in the Anti-terrorism, Crime and Security Act 2001, one that was thought extremist, eccentric—downright radical in fact—in the autumn of that year (when the Bill was enacted, in the immediate aftermath of the attacks of 11 September), should have become so obvious, so full of common sense, that it could within three years have been capable of securing the support of eight of nine members of the appellate committee of the House of Lords, the United Kingdom's *de facto* Supreme Court. In conducting this inquiry, particular attention will be paid to the role of the new language of human rights (new because fully in place in UK law only since 2 October 2000[5]) in producing this outcome, a role that, as we shall see, was not insubstantial.[6]

If the first inquiry is into this human-rights-friendly question of how its language seems to have come to triumph, the second is into how this human rights victory, and the legal structure of rights that lies behind it, might nevertheless be 'injurious' to the war on terrorism, either internationally or domestically, or both. This is where we come to the Prevention of Terrorism Act 2005, a piece of legislation that would not have been enacted when it was had it not been for the *Belmarsh* decision. How the judgment could conceivably be 'injurious' in this way hinges on where we see the idea of respect for human rights fitting within the campaign against terrorism: the more central we see human rights, the more likely we are to regard the ruling as a coherent part of our societal engagement with terrorism; on the other hand, the more tangential or peripheral or

---

[5] The Human Rights Act 1998 (Commencement No. 2) Order 2000, SI 2000/1851.

[6] C A Gearty, '11 September 2001, Counter-terrorism, and the Human Rights Act' (2005) 32 Journal of Legal Studies 18. Cf K D Ewing, 'The Futility of the Human Rights Act' [2004] PL 829. An excellent study is B Dickson, 'Law versus Terrorism: Can Law Win?' [2005] *European Human Rights Law Review*, 11.

downright hostile we view human rights as being in the 'war against terror', the more likely we are to regard the case as unhelpful at best, downright destructive at worst, pedantic legalism in action, something to be evaded, got round, rather than admired and implemented in spirit as well as in bare, minimalist deeds. The mirror image of these positions also holds: the less we are captured by the idea of the war on terrorism the more we are likely to admire the ruling; the greater our anxiety about terror the less we are likely to applaud it. These various alternatives will be examined in more detail later. With the bombings in London in July 2005 and the likelihood at the time of writing of yet further legislation on terrorism, the nature of the inter-relationship between counter-terrorism law and human rights is likely to continue to be at the forefront of public debate for some time to come. This paper concentrates on the 2005 Act but it may well be that many of the points made here about the nature of human rights reasoning when put under the strain of perceived counter-terrorism necessity will also apply to legislation that, at the time of writing, has not yet taken specific shape.

The *Belmarsh* Decision in Legal Context

The details of the ruling are well-known.[7] Nine men went before the appellate committee, challenging an earlier Court of Appeal decision[8] which had upheld their detention without trial under Part 4 of the Anti-terrorism, Crime and Security Act 2001. The men, with eight others,[9] had each been certified under section 21 of that Part as persons reasonably believed by the Home Secretary to be terrorists whose presence in the United Kingdom constituted a 'risk to national security.'[10] As such they would in the normal course of events have expected to have been detained and deported from the country. However under well-established human rights law, the authorities may not remove a person to another jurisdiction

---

[7] For a very good review of the judgment which places it in context in a way that is also being attempted here, see C Walker, 'Prisoners of "War All the Time" ' [2005] *European Human Rights Law Review* 50.

[8] *A and Others v Secretary of State for the Home Department* [2002] EWCA Civ 1502, [2004] QB 335.

[9] At the time of the Home Secretary's statement to the House of Commons on 26 January 2005, one had had his certificate cancelled by SIAC, one had had his certificate discharged by the Home Secretary, two had left for other countries, three had been transferred to Broadmoor, and another had been granted bail: see HC Debs, 26 January 2005, cols 305–324. Shortly before new legislation had been enacted to supersede the part 4 detention power, the remaining foreign suspects had all been ordered to be released on bail: *Guardian*, 12 March 2005.   [10] s 21(1).

in a situation where that person 'faces the prospect of torture or inhuman treatment'.[11] So it was accepted that while persons certified under section 21 could leave the country voluntarily, or be sent to a safe third country if there was one that would receive them, none of these men could be removed against their will to any place in which they were likely to come to this sort of serious harm. It followed from this that neither could they simply be held indefinitely on the pretence that the detention was pending removal, given that such a removal was for all practical purposes well nigh impossible: Article 5 of the European Convention on Human Rights, dealing with the right to liberty, has an exception for detention 'with a view to deportation' but it has been widely understood, not least by the European Court of Human Rights,[12] not to extend to this kind of *de facto* permanent detention.

Given that, on his estimation, the Secretary of State had on his hands a number of suspected international terrorists, the obvious next thing to have done, given this impossibility of removal, might well have been thought to have been to charge them. It was not as though UK law, at the end of 2001, was lacking in possible offences that such people might be thought capable of having committed. The advantage of deploying the criminal code in this way would have been that it would also have reached suspected UK terrorists.[13] Nor were such laws few and far between. Far from it: a plethora of crimes were on offer on the anti-terrorism menu. The first rank of these obviously included murder, criminal damage and various offences against the person, together with their inchoate equivalents, attempting, inciting or merely conspiring with others to do any of these things. There was also a large second tier of crimes. A depressing legacy of the thirty-year IRA campaign of violence in the United Kingdom has been the building-up of an arsenal of anti-terrorism laws, some sensible, some opportunist, some redundant almost from their inception, some (in every sense) reactionary, and these had been rendered a permanent feature of UK law, in an expanded form, in the Terrorism Act 2000, a measure which had received the Royal Assent some fourteen months before the 11 September attacks.[14]

[11] Lord Bingham of Cornhill, n 1 above, para. 9 referring to the effect of *Chahal v United Kingdom* (1996) 23 EHRR 413. See further *R (Ullah) v Special Adjudicator*; *Thi Lien Do v Secretary of State for the Home Department* [2004] UKHL 26, [2004] 3 All ER 785.

[12] *Chahal*, n 11 above, para. 113.

[13] Lord Bingham of Cornhill remarked in his speech in the *Belmarsh* case: 'A person who commits a serious crime under the criminal law of this country may of course, whether a national or non-national, be charged, tried and, if convicted, imprisoned': n 1 above, para. 9.

[14] C Walker, *Blackstone's Guide to the Anti-terrorism Legislation* (Oxford University Press, 2002).

That legislation embraced a very wide definition of terrorism[15] which was then used to underpin a series of specifically terrorist offences. No fewer than 23 of the 64 sections in the first six parts of this Act (covering the substance of terrorism law in the United Kingdom as a whole) deal directly with criminal offences. Nor are these crimes all obscure or parasitic on rarely deployed administrative powers. Any kind of instruction or training in firearms or explosives is a crime, as is inviting someone to take part in such training—and this includes even training which is to take place outside the UK.[16] Collecting information 'of a kind likely to be useful to a person committing or preparing an act of terrorism' or merely possessing this kind of information is a crime.[17] A person 'commits an offence if he directs, at any level, the activities of an organisation which is concerned in the commission of acts of terrorism', with the punishment here being up to life imprisonment.[18] Then there is the bizarre double thought-crime to be found in section 57: 'A person commits an offence if he possesses an article in circumstances which give rise to a reasonable suspicion that his possession is for a purpose connected with the commission, preparation or instigation of an act of terrorism'. A special offence of inciting terrorism overseas allows the authorities to proceed against people here, and punish them as though that which they had incited (murder, offences against the person, criminal damage) had actually occurred, despite the incitement being specifically to commit acts of such terrorism abroad, with it being 'immaterial whether or not the person incited is in the United Kingdom at the time of the incitement'.[19]

It is right to stress that these offences were on the statute book and available for use[20] at the time that the decision was made to introduce the detention provisions that were later to form Part 4 of the Anti-terrorism, Crime and Security Act. They had frequently been very controversial when first mooted. An unprecedented expansion of conspiracy law, to include offences contemplated outside the United Kingdom, for example, had been smuggled into UK law off the back of the parliamentary reaction to the Omagh tragedy in the summer of 1998, with which of course it had no logical connection whatsoever.[21] This had been just an exceptionally egregious example of a normal mode of acting in this field.

---

[15] Terrorism Act 2000 s 1 covers more than acts of politically motivated violence against the person and/or property: see text at n 99 below. [16] Ibid, s 54.

[17] Ibid, s 58. [18] Ibid, s 56.

[19] Ibid, especially sub-s 4 from which the quoted extract is derived.

[20] As they had been from 19 February 2001: Terrorism Act 2000 (Commencement No. 3) Order 2001 SI 2001/421.

[21] Criminal Justice (Terrorism and Conspiracy) Act 1998, s 5, adding a new section, s 1A, to the Criminal Law Act 1977.

Apart from 1998, the same thing had occurred in 1939,[22] 1974[23] and 1996.[24] Laws such as these were often displayed (not least by the Government[25]) as the widest and most effective of such laws in the democratic world. What none of those who opposed them (both when first introduced and when later consolidated in the 2000 Act) could possibly have imagined was that even these swingeing prosecutorial powers would themselves be so useless, so incapable of deployment against the menace of suspected international terrorists, that they would make the detention without trial of foreign nationals an alleged necessity—while being apparently *at exactly the same time* sufficient to cope with *exactly the same kind* of dangerous people who happened to hold British passports. It was as though the Terrorism Act 2000 had contained a saving clause at the end, rendering its provisions, and the criminal law generally, inapplicable to irremovable foreign persons inclined to lawlessness for political reasons.

It will be necessary later to come back to why these various laws were thought to be unusable, and we shall do so in considering the options open to the authorities in the aftermath of the appellate committee's ruling. This was what was later to be exposed as the logical flaw in the detention scheme that the Government came up with in Autumn 2001, after it had ruled out both expulsion despite human rights law and prosecution under the mainstream criminal law. This also proved to be the chink in the armour of derogation through which an entire coach and horses of human rights principle, driven by our senior judges, was later able to drive, destroying practically all of the Government's defences from the inside. Building on this inherently dubious national/non-national distinction, the scheme that was eventually adopted and set out in the Act was largely parasitic upon pre-existing immigration law, providing for the detention of persons who were suspected international terrorists only insofar as they were subject to that law. The 2001 Act borrowed certain features from earlier internment models, such as those deployed in Britain during the First and Second World Wars,[26] and in Northern

---

[22] Prevention of Violence (Temporary Provisions) Act 1939.

[23] Prevention of Terrorism (Temporary Provisions) Act 1974.

[24] Prevention of Terrorism (Additional Powers) Act 1996.

[25] 'In addition to the provisions in the general criminal law, the United Kingdom has some of the most developed and sophisticated anti-terrorism legislation in the world': Home Office, *Counter-terrorism Powers: Reconciling Security and Liberty in an Open Society. A Discussion Paper* (Cm 6147, February 2004), para. 17.

[26] K D Ewing and C A Gearty, *The Struggle for Civil Liberties. Political Freedom and the Rule of Law in Britain* (Oxford University Press 2000), chs 2 and 8. The leading study is A W B Simpson, *In the Highest Degree Odious. Detention without Trial in Wartime Britain* (Clarendon Press: Oxford, 1992).

Ireland in the early 1970s.[27] Efforts were definitely made to ameliorate the draconian dimensions that might be thought inherent in any system of executive detention: following once more an immigration precedent, an appellate system of a moderately decent sort was put in place,[28] special legal functionaries were appointed to put the suspects' case (albeit without being instructed by or being responsible directly to them)[29], a kind of bail was allowed,[30] and various other half reminders of decency were thrown into the repressive pot,[31] like confetti at a funeral.

But despite these ameliorations, the 'problem' of human rights law had also to be addressed. The Human Rights Act, fully in effect for little over a year when the post 11 September legislative crisis reached its boiling point, demanded that ministers make a declaration of compatibility or incompatibility in respect of all legislative proposals they brought to Parliament.[32] This was a legal duty, not susceptible to avoidance via a few weasel words about security and the need for action. The detention that was being planned was in all probability in breach of Article 5's right to liberty. There is a provision in the European Convention on Human Rights which allows the flouting of certain rights in narrowly defined circumstances.[33] This had been used in the past,[34] and was indirectly available via section 14 of the Human Rights Act itself. In the autumn of 2001, the Government decided to press this rights-destruct button. It took the form of the Human Rights Act 1998 (Designated Derogation) Order 2001.[35] This order referred, as the relevant override clause in the European Convention on Human Rights[36] required it to do, to the existence of a public emergency in the United Kingdom threatening the life of the nation. It asserted:

There exists a terrorist threat to the United Kingdom from persons suspected of involvement in international terrorism. In particular, there are foreign nationals present in the United Kingdom who are suspected of being concerned in the commission, preparation or instigation of acts of international terrorism, of being members of organisations or groups which are so concerned or of having links with members of such organisations or groups, and who are a threat to the national security of the United Kingdom.[37]

[27] J Bowyer Bell, *The Irish Troubles. A Generation of Violence 1967–1992* (Gill and Macmillan: Dublin, 1993), especially ch 7.

[28] Special Immigration Appeals Commission Act 1997, as amended by the Anti-terrorism, Crime and Security Act 2001, part 4, especially s 35.

[29] Ibid, especially s 27.   [30] Ibid, s 24.   [31] Ibid, ss 25, 26 and 28.

[32] Human Rights Act 1998 s 19.   [33] Art 15.

[34] Eg *Brannigan and McBride v United Kingdom* (1993) 17 EHRR 539.

[35] Human Rights Act 1998 (Designated Derogation) Order 2001, SI 2001/3644. Designated under s 14 of the Act. Lord Scott of Foscote had his doubts about the procedure: see n 1 above paras. 150–160.   [36] Art 15.

[37] The wording is at Lord Bingham of Cornhill, n 1 above para. 11. Note that a derogation from art 9 of the International Covenant on Civil and Political Rights 1966 was also effected.

Interestingly in view of the explicit acknowledgement of the national/
non-national distinction, the derogation was restricted to Article 5 of
the Convention, and did not extend to the guarantee against non-
discrimination in the enjoyment of Convention rights which is set out in
Article 14 of the same Convention, a provision that is also incorporated
into UK law via the Human Rights Act. Perhaps this was just an oversight; perhaps the legal advisers thought they could get the scheme within
Article 14.[38]

As the inevitable legal challenges got under way following the deployment of this detention power (immediately and in a blaze of publicity
directly after the Royal Assent[39]), no court has been prepared to challenge
the assertion that an emergency existed or continues to do so, with eight
of the nine lords agreeing with the Special Immigration Appeals
Commission (SIAC) and the Court of Appeal on this point. The exception was Lord Hoffmann in the Lords who, in a passage of great intensity
which has already been widely quoted in the media, directly challenged
the assumption that al Qaeda could conceivably threaten the nation, 'a
social organism, living in its territory (in this case, the United Kingdom)
under its own form of government and subject to a system of laws which
expresses its own political and moral values'.[40] Osama binLaden and his
cohorts were no Spanish Armada or Nazi regime; '[t]here may be some
nations too fragile or fissiparous to withstand a serious act of violence. But
that is not the case in the United Kingdom.'[41] Nor was it true of the
Spanish whose 'legendary pride' would not allow even the 'hideous crime'
of the Madrid bombings to destroy their system of government.[42] There
was 'no doubt that we shall survive Al-Qaeda'.[43] And then the dramatic
conclusion to his lordship's speech:

> The real threat to the life of the nation, in the sense of a people living in
> accordance with its traditional laws and political values, comes not from terror-
> ism but from laws such as these. That is the true measure of what terrorism
> may achieve. It is for Parliament to decide whether to give the terrorists such
> a victory.[44]

This argument nearly won over Lord Bingham; it was 'not without
misgivings (fortified by reading the opinion of my noble and learned
friend Lord Hoffmann)' that his lordship came to the conclusion that he

---

[38] The prohibition on discrimination in art 14 is not so broad as the wording would
appear to indicate, allowing for discrimination where this can be objectively justified: see
Belgian Linguistics Case (No 2) (1968) 1 EHRR 252, especially para. 10 at 284.
[39] (2002) 12 *Statewatch*, no 1, 11.   [40] n 1 above, para. 91.
[41] Ibid, para. 95.   [42] Ibid, para. 96.   [43] Ibid, para. 96.
[44] Ibid, para. 97.

should 'resolve this issue against the appellants'.[45] The European Court of Human Rights had taken a fairly expansive view of what could constitute a threat to the life of the nation[46] and in any event this kind of judgment was essentially political. His lordship did not

> accept the full breadth of the Attorney General's argument on what is generally called the deference owed by the courts to the political authorities. It is perhaps preferable to approach this question as one of demarcation of functions or what *Liberty* in its written case called 'relative institutional competence'. The more purely political (in a broad or narrow sense) a question is, the more appropriate it will be for political resolution and the less likely it is to be an appropriate matter for judicial decision. The smaller, therefore, will be the potential role of the court. It is the function of political and not judicial bodies to resolve political questions. Conversely, the greater the legal content of any issue, the greater the potential role of the court, because under our constitution and subject to the sovereign power of parliament it is the function of the courts and not of political bodies to resolve legal questions.[47]

It is suggested that this is a passage of immense significance. Hopefully as it seeps into the consciousness of advocates, especially treasury counsel in their various forms, there will be less reliance in court on shapeless invocations of judicial deference or on question-begging assertions of the existence of something called the 'discretionary area of judgment'. Lord Bingham has served an important reminder that it all depends on function: judges do what they are good at unless Parliament has specifically taken the subject from them; judges do not swim into the deep end of policy where they are manifestly out of their depth.[48] Was Lord Bingham right to say with the majority that the issue of whether or not there is an emergency lay 'very much at the political end of the spectrum'?[49] The answer—despite the power of Lord Hoffmann's intervention—must surely be yes. It is not for judges to engage in assessment of future risks, and in a democracy those who are accountable to the electorate must be the people with the responsibility to assess the nature of the threat to a people's way of life. If the assessment is fabricated or otherwise untenable, or if the political leaders making the assessment are not to be trusted, then that is a matter for political not legal resolution. Lord Hoffmann's comments are very useful additions to an important discussion, but it is not one that judges wearing their judicial hats are entitled to have.

---

[45] n1 above, para. 26. These misgivings were shared by Lord Scott of Foscote at para. 154 and Lord Rodger of Earlsferry at para. 165. See also Lord Hope of Craighead at para. 116.

[46] Especially in *Lawless v Ireland (No 3)* (1961) 1 EHRR 15.

[47] n 1 above, para. 29.

[48] C A Gearty, *Principles of Human Rights Adjudication* (Oxford University Press, 2004), especially ch 6. [49] n 1 above, para. 29.

The same is not the case when it comes to an assessment of what may be done to protect the life of the nation. Article 15 requires that any measures taken by a Member State in derogation of its obligations under the Convention should not go beyond what is 'strictly required by the exigencies of the situation'. Now here is something that lawyers can confidently get their hands on, testing the proportionality of responses to actions and threats of actions is something with which judges are institutionally entirely familiar: it crops up across the whole spectrum of the law, and especially frequently in public law. The appellants relied on the well-known test in *de Freitas v Permanent Secretary of Ministry of Agriculture, Fisheries, Lands and Housing*.[50] In determining whether a limitation is arbitrary or excessive, the court must ask itself:

[w]hether: (i) the legislative objective is sufficiently important to justify limiting a fundamental right; (ii) the measures designed to meet the legislative objective are rationally connected to it; and (iii) the means used to impair the right or freedom are no more than is necessary to accomplish the objective.[51]

As far as the first of these was concerned, the majority were in no doubt that a fundamental right was engaged, for solid Convention but also impeccable common law reasons; as Lord Hoffmann put it, '[f]reedom from arbitrary arrest and detention is a quintessentially British liberty, enjoyed by the inhabitants of this country when most of the population of Europe could be thrown into prison at the whim of their rulers'.[52] To Lord Hope of Craighead, it was 'impossible ever to overstate the importance of the right to liberty in a democracy'.[53] The Attorney General's effort to extend the requirement of judicial quiescence into this area was unsuccessful. As Lord Bingham put it, while 'any decision made by a representative democratic body must of course command respect, the degree of respect will be conditioned by the nature of the decision'[54], and while for this reason the Attorney was 'fully entitled to insist on the proper limits of judicial authority' he was 'wrong to stigmatise judicial decision-making as in some way undemocratic.'[55]

Freed by these robust preliminaries to engage in a meaningful way with the inquiry into rational connection and necessity, there could only be

---

[50] [1999] 1 AC 69, given a fresh lease of life in *R (Daly) v Secretary of State for the Home Department* [2001] UKHL 26, [2001] 2 AC 532.   [51] [1999] 1 AC 69 at 80.

[52] n 1 above, para. 87. See Lord Bingham of Cornhill at para. 36; Lord Nicholls of Birkenhead at para. 74; and Baroness Hale of Richmond at para. 222.

[53] Ibid, Lord Hope of Craighead, para. 100.

[54] Ibid, Lord Bingham of Cornhill, para. 39.

[55] Ibid, para. 42; see further Lord Nicholls of Birkenhead at paras. 79–83; Lord Hope of Craighead at paras. 107 and 116; and Lord Rodger of Earlsferry at para. 177.

one outcome. There were flaws in the scheme even without taking into account the central problem of the national/non-national divide. The measures permitted suspected international terrorists to leave the country if they could, '[b]ut allowing [such a person] to leave our shores and depart to another country, perhaps a country as close as France, there to pursue his criminal designs, is hard to reconcile with a belief in his capacity to inflict serious injury to the people and interests of this country.'[56] The provisions were potentially capable of being extended beyond alQaeda, and it was only as a result of an executive concession that they would not be: this was no way to arrange matters in relation to such a fundamental liberty.[57] The powers were very wide: '[s]omeone who has never committed any offence and has no intention of doing anything wrong may be reasonably suspected of being a supporter on the basis of some heated remarks overheard in a pub.'[58] Perhaps somewhat carried away by the implications of the power rather than the way it had hitherto been deployed, Lord Scott of Foscote commented,

Indefinite imprisonment in consequence of a denunciation on grounds that are not disclosed and made by a person whose identity cannot be disclosed is the stuff of nightmares, associated whether accurately or inaccurately with France before and during the Revolution, with Soviet Russia in the Stalinist era and now associated, as a result of section 23 of the 2001 Act, with the United Kingdom.[59]

Above all, though, there was the problem of the laws not extending to British nationals. If other means were acceptable for this kind of 'homegrown' suspected terrorist (whom no-one denied existed), then why were these measures not also acceptable for the tiny category of international suspects whom it had been judged essential to detain? As Lord Hope remarked, almost in exasperation, if 'the threat is as potent as the Secretary of State suggests, it is absurd to confine the measures intended to deal with it so that they do not apply to British nationals, however strong the suspicion and however grave the damage it is feared they may cause.'[60] Lord Nicholls of Birkenhead thought that the 'principal weakness in the government's case [lay] in the different treatment accorded to

---

[56] Ibid, Lord Bingham of Cornhill, para. 33 summarising the submission of the appellants on this point. See Lord Hope of Craighead at paras. 127 and 133 and Baroness Hale of Richmond at para. 230.

[57] Ibid, Lord Bingham of Cornhill, para. 33: 'It is not ... acceptable that interpretation and application of a statutory provision bearing on the liberty of the subject should be governed by implication, concession and undertaking'.

[58] Ibid, Lord Hoffmann, para. 87.

[59] Ibid, Lord Scott of Foscote, para. 155.

[60] Ibid, Lord Hope of Craighead, para. 133. See also Lord Rodger of Earlsferry at paras. 178, 183, 188–189; and Baroness Hale of Richmond at para. 228.

nationals and non-nationals';[61] the authorities had, he thought, 'vouchsafed no persuasive explanation of why national security calls for a power of indefinite detention in one case but not the other.'[62] To Lord Bingham, it seemed 'reasonable to assume that those suspected international terrorists who are UK nationals are not simply ignored by the authorities.'[63] One had already been granted bail,

on condition (among other things) that he wear an electronic monitoring tag at all times; that he remain at his premises at all times; that he telephone a named security company five times each day at specified times; that he permit the company to install monitoring equipment at his premises; that he limit entry to his premises to his family, his solicitor, his medical attendants and other approved persons; that he make no contact with any other person; that he have on his premises no computer equipment, mobile telephone or other electronic communications device; that he cancel the existing telephone link to his premises; and that he install a dedicated telephone link permitting contact only with the security company. The appellants suggested that conditions of this kind, strictly enforced, would effectively inhibit terrorist activity. It is hard to see why this would not be so.[64]

We will need presently to return shortly to the fairly relaxed attitude Lord Bingham, and indeed the appellants, seem to have had towards such extraordinarily draconian restrictions on freedom as these, and what implications this might have now for the implementation of alternatives to detention. But for the present the point stands as a knock-out blow against detention without trial.

Deprived of his carapace of judicial deference, the Attorney General simply had no answer to their lordships on the meaninglessness of the national/non-national distinction.[65] The ruling's devastating effect was such that it spread from the issue of derogation into the separate and independent ground of appeal based on a breach of the right to non-discrimination in the enjoyment of their right to liberty which the appellants enjoyed under Article 14 of the Convention. This ground (as has been noted earlier) had survived untruncated or otherwise qualified by the derogation order which had tried (unsuccessfully as it turned out) to neutralise the more obviously engaged right to liberty.[66] This had been

---

[61] Baroness Hale of Richmond, para. 76.
[62] Ibid, para. 78. See also Lord Hope of Craighead at para. 129.
[63] Ibid, para. 35.   [64] Ibid, para. 35.
[65] Put perhaps best of all by Baroness Hale of Richmond: 'The conclusion has to be that it is not necessary to lock up the nationals. Other ways must have been found to contain the threat which they present. And if it is not necessary to lock up the nationals it cannot be necessary to lock up the foreigners. It is not strictly required by the exigencies of the situation': ibid, para. 231.
[66] See the argument as set out in the speech of Lord Bingham of Cornhill, ibid, paras. 45–54.

the main battleground in both SIAC and the Court of Appeal,[67] and in the Lords the Attorney General mounted a 'far-reaching submission'[68] that a 'sovereign state may control the entry of aliens into its territory and their expulsion from it' and that it followed from this both that the Convention permitted 'the differential treatment of aliens as compared with nationals' and that international law 'sanction[ed] the differential treatment, including detention, of aliens in times of war or public emergency.'[69] But the majority were having none of these new general rules.[70] An extensive review of the international law position led Lord Bingham to describe the effect of the materials he had considered to be 'inimical' to the submission.[71] To Lord Hope it was simply the case that a 'state is not permitted to discriminate against an unpopular minority for the good of the majority'.[72] Close to the conclusion of her speech, and just three paragraphs from the end of the whole case, Baroness Hale of Richmond summed up why the detention provisions could not stand in a system of democracy which 'values each person equally':[73]

No one has the right to be an international terrorist. But substitute 'black', 'disabled', 'female', 'gay', or any other similar adjective for 'foreign' before 'suspected international terrorist' and ask whether it would be justifiable to take power to lock up the group but not the 'white', 'able-bodied', 'male' or 'straight' suspected international terrorists. The answer is clear.[74]

The Decision in Its Wider Political and Legal Context

The speeches of these eight senior judges amount collectively to what is the finest assertion of civil liberties that has emerged from a British court since at least *Entick v Carrington*.[75] The substance of the principles which the judges develop, the power of the application of those principles to the facts before the court, and—perhaps above all—the strength of the language used by the members of the appellate committee to communicate their findings all mark the case out as pretty well unique in the annals of UK legal history, this or that *dictum* by Lord Denning[76] and Lord Templeman aside.[77] This language point is not an insubstantial one.

---

[67] n 8 above; decision of the Special Immigration Appeals Commission (SIAC), 30 July 2002. [68] Lord Bingham of Cornhill, n 1 above, para. 55.
[69] Ibid.
[70] Ibid, Lord Bingham of Cornhill, paras. 56–63; Lord Nicholls of Birkenhead at para. 84; and Lord Hope of Craighead at paras. 101 and 136–137. [71] Ibid, para. 63.
[72] Ibid, para. 136. [73] Ibid, para. 237. [74] Ibid, para. 238.
[75] (1765) 19 St Tr 1030. [76] *Gouriet v Union of Post Office Workers* [1978] AC 435.
[77] *Re M* [1994] 1 AC 377.

The senior judiciary have travelled a very long way since they not only found against the newspapers in the first *Spycatcher* case but at the same time—maddeningly or magnificently depending on your taste—initially refused to give their reasons because they were off on holiday.[78] Now they all seem to know their Habermas: communication is the only truth, and if we don't say it in a way that is understood it won't have happened. *Dicta* from the case have flowed into the news reportage of the decision,[79] underpinned interrogation of Ministers in Parliament[80] and greatly assisted public opinion in forming a view as to the legitimacy of the ruling.

But what is the 'ruling' precisely? As Lord Scott candidly remarked from a legal point of view, the effect of the decision is 'nil'.[81] It is precisely this 'nilness' that is—paradoxically it might be thought—the main exhibit in explaining the case's unique potency. For the judgment decided nothing at all, or at least nothing tangible in the form of immediate or even delayed releases from Belmarsh.[82] It was genuinely an exercise in communication, an explosion of righteous anger aimed at the other branches of the state and the general public; it was not an order of release to a prison governor. The Human Rights Act, with its insistence that declarations of incompatibility should not have legal effect, ensured that it could not be other than this. It would seem clear that lawyers for the appellants would have had clearly in mind when addressing the appellate committee the fact that the judges could not themselves make the final call on the applicants' detention,[83] and it is something that must have been very much in the judges' minds. Their liberal fingerprints would not be—could not be—the last to be found on these men should they be released; the Home Secretary's and/or Parliament's imprimatur would also have to be impressed. And with such power comes responsibility, and

---

[78] *Attorney General v Guardian Newspaper Ltd* [1987] 3 All ER 316.

[79] Usefully collated in the *Guardian*, 18 December 2004. For a fascinating example see the column by John Gulliver in the *Camden New Journal*, 17 February 2005, 19, where a sentence from Lord Hoffmann's judgment is given particular attention, in bold in a special display.

[80] David Winnick MP, Proceedings of the Select Committee on Home Affairs, 8 February 2005.   [81] n 1 above, para. 144.

[82] But note that as of January 2005, only seven persons were being held in detention solely under the Part 4 power, with there having been one granted conditional bail, one unconditionally released, two transferred to secure hospitals and the remainder having been charged with conventional crimes and transferred to remand status pending Crown Court trial: Lord Carlile of Berriew, Anti-terrorism, Crime and Security Act 2001 Part IV Section 28 Review 2004 (February 2005), para. 31. By the time the new legislation introduced in response to the Lords' judgment had received the royal assent, all those detained under part 4 had been granted bail: *Guardian* 12 March 2005.

[83] A point made in the course of discussion at a meeting of the Human Rights Lawyers' Association at the Law Society, 17 January 2005.

in particular responsibility for anything that might subsequently go wrong. In this field we lawyers, dedicated as our entire profession is to the science of retrospective wisdom, too often take too little account of what is on many decision-makers' minds: the horror of the next atrocity, and the fear that—reasonably or unreasonably—they will find the scapegoat's burden descending firmly on to their shoulders.[84] It was a great thing for the judges to know, even if only at the back of their minds, that they could never be held directly responsible for their ruling even if they were incorrect or (more likely) if things were in fact to go horribly wrong and it was thought as a result that they had been incorrect. Because of the legal unenforceability of declarations of incompatibility, another set of public officials, probably elected officials, would be in the front line. And as all academics know, the flower that is a liberal conscience can much more easily be made to flourish when it is nurtured in a way that avoids all contact with the weeds of real life.

This might explain the House of Lords decision but it does not tell us why the Court of Appeal took such a different line. There is a subsidiary mystery here that needs to be unravelled: a court of appeal headed by that fearless liberal Lord Woolf of Barnes, a judge who had chosen to appear on BBC World's *HardTalk* in the very week the 2001 Act received the Royal Assent in order specifically to express great anxiety about Part 4, nevertheless finding in favour of the authorities when the matter comes before it, on all points. At first glance it looks as though Lord Woolf is the real loser from the Lords decision, his liberalism having been revealed to be as vacuous and as empty as social democrats say liberalism always is. But on reflection the issue would seem to resolve itself more into one of timing. When the Court of Appeal gave judgment in this case, on 25 October 2002,[85] the powers were less than a year old, and 11 September 2001 had been only thirteen months before. The atmosphere was still tense, the expectation of an attack high. The corrosive effect on confidence of the spurious WMD intelligence in Iraq lay in the future. With one exception, no important public body or international organisation had by this point made a case against part 4, the critical comments being still then supplied by old reliables like *Liberty*.[86] The exception was the Council of Europe's Commissioner for Human Rights, Mr Gil Robles,

---

[84] 'No Minister will take the one in 10 million chance of being the person who lets the Queen be assassinated': R Hattersley, *Guardian*, 7 February 2005, 16.

[85] The hearing was on 7–9 October, with judgment given on 25 October 2002.

[86] There were general interventions by the Parliamentary Assembly (Resolution 1271 (24 January 2002)) and the Committee of Ministers (Guidelines on Human Rights and the Fight Against Terrorism (11 July 2002)) of the Council of Ministers: see Lord Bingham of Cornhill, n 1 above, para. 57.

whose interventions throughout this period have been brave, constructive and immensely to the point.[87] But less than two months after Lord Woolf's Court of Appeal decision came the report of the Privy Counsellor Review Committee with its swingeing criticism of the whole underlying rationale of the detention power.[88] This was the key turning point in the public mood, not the first shout that 'the Emperor has no clothes' but the first by a set of persons which had been confidently expected to clothe the naked emperor with a fine new suit to last well into the future. By the time the Lords came to deliver their speeches, there was an array of national and international documentation on which they could draw to support their arguments.[89] There has also been as Lord Hoffmann described it 'the fiasco over Iraqi weapons of mass destruction.'[90] And crucially, in December 2004 there had been no violent attacks: the authorities had to pay the price for what we must assume had been at that point their quiet success in the anti-terrorism arena.

So far we have been concerned with the beneficial dimensions of the *Belmarsh* case when viewed from the human rights perspective. This one case, dramatic though it is, should not however be allowed entirely to obscure the appallingly deferential approach the courts have taken before and since to the exercise by the executive of the swingeing anti-terrorism powers contained in both the 2000 and the 2001 Acts. This is not the place for a comprehensive review of the case law,[91] but mention can be quickly made of such dreary lowlights as upholding police anti-terrorism powers of stop and search that were being in fact deployed against peaceful protestors[92] and the relaxed attitude the courts have taken to the admissibility of torture evidence by executive and judicial authorities—as long as such torture as might be alleged is being done abroad.[93] It is doubtful that the

---

[87] Commissioner for Human Rights, Opinion 1/2002 (28 August 2002): see Lord Bingham of Cornhill, n 1 above, para. 57.

[88] Privy Counsellor Review Committee, *Anti-terrorism, Crime and Security Act 2001 Review: Report* HC 100, 18 December 2003.

[89] Lord Bingham of Cornhill, n 1 above, paras. 57–65; also Lord Hope of Craighead at para. 105. We now know that the Council of Europe's Committee for the Prevention of Torture had also been very critical, but its report had not at the time been made public: 'UK treatment of terror suspects "inhumane" ', *Guardian*, 10 June 2005.

[90] n 1 above, para. 94. See also Lord Scott of Foscote at para. 154: 'judicial memories are no shorter than those of the public and the public have not forgotten the faulty intelligence assessments on the basis of which United Kingdom forces were sent to take part, and are still taking part, in the hostilities in the Gulf.'   [91] Ewing, n 6 above.

[92] *R (Gillen) v Metropolitan Police Commissioner* [2004] EWCA Civ 1067.

[93] *A v Secretary of State for the Home Department (No 2)* [2004] EWCA Civ 1123; cf *R (Al-Skeini and Others) v Secretary of State for Defence* [2004] EWHC 2911 (Admin). Both cases are under appeal, the first to the House of Lords, the second to the Court of Appeal.

Belmarsh detention case is other than a one-off, a particular and exceptional decision which results from a variety of different considerations all coming together at the same time—many of which have been highlighted in the course of this paper—and that it is not the start of a new liberal trend.[94] Depressingly we should remind ourselves that the court in the *Belmarsh* case could not do anything directly; in all the cases where the judges could actually have achieved an outcome directly, they have come down unequivocally on the side of the authorities.

There is also the question of how inclined the courts are for a long fight. After the London bombings in July 2005, the Government made clear its determination not to allow the judges to get in the way of what the authorities saw as the new realities of national security that now governed the situation. As far as the *Belmarsh* judgment itself is concerned, much will depend on the judicial perception of the executive's response to the decision. Certainly it has not been ignored as technically it could have been (at least until an adverse Strasbourg ruling, and perhaps even then). The new Home Secretary admitted in a session before the Home Affairs Select Committee on 8 February that it was 'difficult not to acknowledge some truth in criticism' of the national/non-national distinction.[95] The alternative of deporting suspects in a way which secures their human rights to the satisfaction of the courts remains an option: the Home Secretary has indicated that he is in the process of negotiating with certain key Middle Eastern and North African countries to achieve memoranda of understanding with them in relation to their treatment of potential deportees.[96] Approached with goodwill on both sides, this is a perfectly reasonable outcome to strive towards, and the judicial checks against improper removals are presently fairly well entrenched in our law, and unlikely to be set aside or savagely diluted in the short to medium term.[97]

In early March 2005, the Home Secretary also persuaded Parliament to pass fresh legislation providing for 'a new scheme of control orders

---

[94] Certainly the case has not stimulated any resurgence of judicial commitment to the protection of civil liberties: see *Quinn v Prosecutor Fiscal, Dumbarton* High Court of Justiciary (AC) 16 March 2005; *R (Brehony) v Chief Constable of Greater Manchester Police* [2005] EWHC 640 (Admin); *Austin v Metropolitan Police Commissioner* [2005] EWHC 480 (QB).

[95] House of Commons Select Committee, 8 February 2005, oral evidence of the Home Secretary.   [96] See the ministerial statement at HC Debs, 26 January 2005, col 307.

[97] During the summer of 2005, negotiations to obtain diplomatic assurances to secure the removal of persons from the jurisdiction began in earnest. But for evidence of a lack of good faith here see Human Rights Watch, '*Still at Risk' Diplomatic Assurances No Safeguard against Torture* (April 2005) (*http://www.hrw.org/reports/2005/eca0405/*); and for a worrying indication of the inter-relationship between the executive and judicial branches in this field see *Youssef v Home Office* [2004] EWHC 1884 (QB).

applicable to *all* suspected terrorists irrespective of whether they are British or foreign nationals'.[98] This law reaches not only al Qaeda and suspected 'international terrorists' but all 'terrorists' including 'British home-grown' and Northern Ireland based varieties. It is worth repeating that the definition of 'terrorism' in the 2000 Act is far wider than is popularly assumed, covering politically, religiously or ideologically motivated serious violence to the person and serious damage to property but also similarly motivated conduct creating either 'a serious risk to the health or safety of the public or a section of the public' or which is 'designed seriously to interfere with or seriously to disrupt an electronic system'.[99] It does also need to be acknowledged that there has been a growth in direct action groups which regard lawless action as a route to their (often single issue) political goals and which fall within the outer reaches of this definition; Fathers 4 Justice, people for and against hunting, and (a recent example) the brief flowering of a cell within Manchester allegedly determined by whatever means available to them to keep Manchester United under its then-current ownership.[100] These proposed control orders would appear to be modelled on the ever expanding and apparently popular ASBO jurisdiction which has been rendered largely human rights proof courtesy of the House of Lords.[101] After a large-scale Parliamentary revolt, the Government conceded a greater range of safeguards on the issuing of such orders than it had initially intended,[102] including regular reportage to Parliament[103], independent review[104] and a renewal clause of a modestly tougher form than usual.[105] Quite possibly there is enough here—together with a promise to derogate if house arrest proper is to be introduced[106]—to satisfy the senior judiciary that their criticism has truly been taken on board.[107] The July bombings have made this rather more likely.

But standing back a bit, we need to ponder the kind of society that we are helping to create here: a new class of restricted persons, perhaps

---

[98] Statement to the Commons, 22 February 2005. The measure became the Prevention of Terrorism Act 2005.   [99] Terrorism Act 2000, s 1.

[100] *Guardian*, 9 February 2005.

[101] *R (McCann) v Manchester Crown Court* [2002] UKHL 39, [2003] 1 AC 787. For a powerful critique, see A Ashworth, 'Social Control and "Anti-Social Behaviour": the Subversion of Human Rights?' (2004) 120 LQR 263.

[102] Cf the actual measure with the Home Secretary's statement of 22 February 2005 summarising the effect of what were then merely proposals.

[103] Prevention of Terrorism Act 2005, s 14.

[104] Ibid. Cf ministerial statement, 26 January 2005, col 308; House of Commons Select Committee, 8 February 2005, oral evidence of the Home Secretary; Home Secretary's statement to the Commons of 22 February 2005.

[105] Prevention of Terrorism Act 2005, s 13.   [106] Ibid, s 4.

[107] Certainly the derogation has been removed: The Human Rights Act 1998 (Amendment) Order 2005, SI 1071/2005.

running into hundreds—thousands, who knows?—whose suspected involvement in extra-parliamentary political activity has been judged by their political opponents in government to have created risks of various sorts which warrant these non-criminal controls being imposed on them, possibly of a draconian sort, possibly of indefinite duration—but without the due process that previous generations have regarded as essential to justice where issues of liberty and political freedom have been engaged. The proposed orders will not be criminal; nor (unless there has been a need to derogate) will they be imposed by a court.[108] They will not depend on proof of wrongdoing or even imminent wrongdoing of any sort. The evidence on which they are based will not be exposed to adversarial scrutiny. And yet their effect will be more severe on individuals, perhaps also on their families, dependants and friends, than many criminal sanctions. It is true that the ASBO rulings and the cases already decided under the terrorism legislation point unequivocally in the direction of judicial deference, and that unless there is a repeat, or series of repeats of the spirit of the *Belmarsh* ruling, these orders may well in due course fall to be justified by the British courts as (in Strasbourg terms) both the result of fair procedures (under Article 6) and 'necessary in a democratic society' under Articles 8–11, and therefore in *perfect compliance with* the human rights of the individuals affected by them.[109] Yet it is surely not in keeping with, if not the letter, then the supposed principles behind human rights that so diluted and attenuated a procedure should, in human rights terms, get away scot-free.[110]

At the top end of the control orders scale will be house arrest of the type that we earlier saw Lord Bingham and counsel for the appellants in the *Belmarsh* case accept (in a tactical concession that each may in due course have cause to regret) as a credible alternative to detention. The Act makes clear that such orders would be restricted to a narrow set of situations and that a derogation from the European Convention would be required and would be sought.[111] But as we have already seen, the kinds of condition needed to achieve proper house arrest are draconian indeed, perhaps

---

[108] Prevention of Terrorism Act 2005, s 1. Derogating control orders may exceptionally also be made by the Home Secretary: ibid, s 3(1).

[109] For a well expressed and an informed view from the Bar see T. Owen, 'Clarke's folly', *The Guardian*, 8 March 2005, G2 10–11.

[110] Note the serious concerns of the Joint Committee on Human Rights: *Prevention of Terrorism Bill: Preliminary Report* (Ninth Report of Session 2004–05, HL 61, HC 389). The Council of Europe's Commissioner for Human Rights has been sharply critical of the new powers: Report of the Commissioner for Human Rights on his Visit to the United Kingdom, 4–12 November 2004 (Comm DH (2005) 6, 8 June 2005), paras. 9–25.

[111] Prevention of Terrorism Act 2005, s 4. See further ministerial statement, 26 January 2005, col 308; House of Commons Select Committee, 8 February 2005, oral evidence of the Home Secretary.

sufficiently savage to raise an issue as to compatibility with the non-derogable Article 3 prohibition on the imposition of inhumane and degrading treatment. *The Economist* called the plan 'shocking'[112] when it was first mooted and it was right to do so. There are also all those ancillary problems that attend the implementation of repressive law: how are the restrictions to be policed? Are there any exceptions for illness, family bereavement, or the like? Such problems of authoritarian law enforcement have already arisen in the context of the bail conditions imposed in one case that obtained this kind of release under the old regime.[113] And there is the frightening prospect of an arrest and detention in what the Home Secretary has called 'accommodation owned and managed by the Government'[114] which it seems would need to be described by other than the traditional word for such a place, a prison. This looks very like internment by the back door. The legislation could produce a derogation order after a single atrocity which in turn could then lead to the detention of suspects in government centres. The United Kingdom as a whole is just two legal steps away from *de facto* internment—and neither involves the need for fresh primary legislation. This dismal scenario has been made possible even without the intervention of the new legislation that is, at the time of writing [August 2005], expected to be put before Parliament sometime in Autumn 2005.

Conclusion

The alternative that dare not speak its name is so simple as to be unutterable in polite circles: charge or release. This applies as much to any new legislation that is proposed as it does to control orders and the potential new house arrest powers and indefinite detention under the 2001 Act. We have a very strong prosecutorial team determined to protect the public within the ordinary law and this has led to numerous arrests and charges under the current law—the ordinary law of murder, criminal damage and offences against the person and so on as well as the special terrorism law.[115] The fact

---

[112] See its leading article, 'Taking Britain's Liberties', 5 February 2005, 9. To similar effect is a leading article in the *Financial Times*: 'The Responsibilities of Opposition. The Government's Anti-terrorist measures must be blocked', 18 February 2005, 16.

[113] *G v Secretary of State for the Home Department* [2004] EWCA Civ 265, and the refusal of Mahmoud Abu Rideh and another detainee to accept bail under the old system if it was conditional on house arrest: 'Suspects spurn house arrest', *Guardian*, 1 February 2005, 1. By the time the new measure had received its royal assent, however, all detainees had been granted bail: *Guardian*, 12 March 2005.

[114] Ministerial statement, 22 February 2005.

[115] The Metropolitan Police Commissioner Sir Ian Blair has reportedly observed that there have been 'over 700 arrests under the Terrorism Act 2000, of which more than half

of this action against terrorism should be much more widely celebrated than it is at present; the Home Secretary is surely right about this[116]—the more the public knows about the action that has already been taken, the less pressure there will be for yet more laws.[117] There is no need for further laws to make prosecutions easier, such as the rather ominous 'acts preparatory to terrorism' crime of French origin that has been doing the rounds recently.[118] What would make prosecutions easier would be a relaxation of the absolute prohibition on the use of intercept evidence in court,[119] a reform now supported by a huge range of informed opinion in this country, *Liberty*,[120] the Metropolitan Police Commissioner,[121] the Director of Public Prosecutions,[122] Lord Carlile of Berriew[123] the independent reviewer of Part 4 among them,[124] and opposed only (so far as one can tell) by serving members of the intelligence services—even some of their most distinguished retired colleagues have deserted them.[125] In an otherwise confident series of parliamentary performances on terrorism law, the Home Secretary seems invariably to descend into a kind of gibberish when forced to explain why exactly such material may never ever be used to secure the prosecution of all these dangerous terrorists he goes on about.[126] Not being quite on top of the technological issues seems not exactly an overwhelming argument against, apart from being embarrassing given that practically everywhere else now permits its use in court.

have ended in a judicial disposal of one sort or another', with 119 of those arrested under the Act being charged with terrorist offences and a further 135 with offences under the general criminal law: *Guardian*, 7 February 2005, 4.

[116] House of Commons Select Committee of Home Affairs, 8 February 2005, oral evidence of the Home Secretary.

[117] This may involve lifting current restrictions on the reporting of terrorist trials: see the call to this effect by the Metropolitan Police Commissioner Sir Ian Blair: *Guardian*, 7 February 2005.

[118] Statement of the Home Secretary, House of Commons, 22 February 2005; House of Commons Select Committee on Home Affairs, 8 February 2005. See also Lord Carlile, Anti-terrorism, Crime and Security Act 2001, Part 4, Section 28 Review 2003, para. 123.

[119] Regulation of Investigatory Powers Act 2000, s 17.

[120] *Liberty's* Response to the Government's White Paper, August 2004, 43–44.

[121] Sir Ian Blair: see 'Intelligence agencies and Police at odds over wire-tap evidence', *Guardian*, 8 February 2005, 9. [122] *New Statesman*, 7 February 2005.

[123] n 82 above, para. 39.

[124] See further Lord Lloyd of Berwick, *Inquiry into Legislation Against Terrorism* (Cm 3420, 1996), ch 7, especially para. 7.25; Privy Counsellors' Review, n 88 above, paras. 208–215, Report of the Joint Committee on Human Rights, HC 713 of 2003–2004, July 2004, para. 56; and the Northern Ireland Human Rights Commission, *Countering Terrorism and Protecting Human Rights*, Belfast, September 2004, 13–17.

[125] See the reported comment by Stella Rimington, ex head of MI5, that the refusal to use such evidence was 'ridiculous': 'Intelligence agencies and police at odds over wire-tap evidence', *Guardian*, 8 February 2005, 9.

[126] Secretary of State for the Home Department, ministerial statement, House of Commons, 26 January 2005, col 307.

The issue is an important one because it flushes out who is genuinely committed to making the criminal process work, and who would prefer to operate entirely in the shadows.[127] It is extraordinarily disappointing that the new Home Secretary has decided (for the time being at least) to side with the forces of extra-legality. There are signs, though, that the new terrorism proposals in the autumn will include some movement on this key issue.

We can now conclude this paper by setting out two alternative future histories. In early February 2005, the Prime Minister of the United Kingdom of Great Britain and Northern Ireland publicly apologised to the Guildford Four and the Maguire Seven for their wrongful imprisonment over the Guildford, Woolwich and other bombings in Britain in 1974.[128] Will some future Prime Minister be making similar apologies in future years to the victims of miscarriage in which this very same Prime Minister is now actively conniving? Is it the fate of every political generation to acknowledge only the mistakes of their predecessors while drawing absolutely no lessons at all for themselves? Or—and it is a bleaker guess about the future—will there be no such apologies because the wrongs done now to our system of liberty and freedom will have become so entrenched as to be accepted by our future leaders and communities entirely without any concern or even a sense of loss?[129] This is what John Stuart Mill, that magnificent champion of so much that is good about what our culture has become, had to say about such a possibility, in a passage even more relevant today than when it was first penned:

A good despotism is an altogether false ideal, which practically (except as a means to some temporary purpose) becomes the most senseless and dangerous of chimeras. Evil for evil, a good despotism, in a country at all advanced in civilisation, is more noxious than a bad one; for it is far more relaxing and enervating to the thoughts, feelings, and energies of the people. The despotism of Augustus prepared the Romans for Tiberius. If the whole tone of their character had not first been prostrated by nearly two generations of that mild slavery, they would probably have had spirit enough left to rebel against the more odious one.[130]

---

[127] One of the more revealing arguments against allowing in such evidence is that of some 'senior anti-terrorist officials' that 'it would never reach normal standards of proof. It would be difficult to prove that intercepted information had not been tampered with': *Guardian*, n 125 above. But this is an argument against its use anywhere and not just in court.

[128] 'After 16 years of waiting, an apology at last for the Guildford Four', *Guardian*, 10 February 2005, 3.

[129] 'I have a horrible feeling that we are sinking into a police state': Mr George Churchill-Coleman, former head of Scotland Yard's anti-terrorist squad: *Guardian*, 28 January 2005, 1.

[130] *Representative Government*, first published 1861, cited from J S Mill, *Three Essays* (Oxford University Press, 1975) 185.

The Extraterritorial Application of the Human Rights Act

*Ralph Wilde**

Introduction

A striking feature of some of the commentary on certain post 9/11 extraterritorial activities—notably the US detention of several hundred individuals at its Naval Base in Guantánamo Bay, Cuba—is the suggestion that these activities take place in a 'legal black hole.'[1]

This paper considers the UK position, in particular the applicability of the Human Rights Act 1998 to UK activities abroad. Although much attention has been given to the Bush Administration's resistance to the application of certain US constitutional safeguards to Guantánamo— an argument rejected by the Supreme Court in the *Rasul* case in 2004[2]— perhaps less well known are the somewhat similar arguments made by the UK government in relation to the applicability of the Human Rights Act to its actions in Iraq. These arguments prompt us to examine the broader question addressed here: when does the Human Rights Act apply to the UK outside UK territory?

The General Position in Relevant International Treaties on Civil and Political Rights

Relevant International Treaties

The Human Rights Act is concerned with civil and political rights and also a right to property and a right to education, taking these rights from the

* Reader, UCL Faculty of Laws. The author has acted as a consultant in the capacity of legal adviser to the applicants in the *Quark* case (see below, n 14). The views expressed herein are independent of this work and do not necessarily reflect the views of any of the parties to that case. Warm thanks are due to James Crawford, Colin Warbrick and Rosalyn Higgins for feedback, and to Silvia Borelli and Daniel Geron for research assistance.
[1] R Wilde, 'Legal "Black Hole"? Extraterritorial State Action and International Treaty Law on Civil and Political Rights', 26 (3) Michigan Journal of International Law (2005) 739.
[2] *Rasul v Bush*, 124 S Ct 2686 (2004).

European Convention on Human Rights (ECHR) and certain provisions from its Protocols.[3] In international law, the UK is subject to other treaty obligations in addition to the ECHR and its Protocols that *also* protect these rights, apart from the property right.[4] The International Covenant on Civil and Political Rights (ICCPR) and its Second Optional Protocol (ratified by the UK) cover all the civil and political rights under the Act.[5] Certain civil and political rights are also contained in the Convention on the Rights to the Child (CRC); a prohibition on torture, inhumane and degrading treatment is contained in the Convention against Torture (CAT); the International Covenant on Economic, Social and Cultural Rights (ICESCR) contains a right to education; the 1926 Slavery Convention and the 1956 Supplementary Slavery Convention contain a prohibition on slavery and institutions or practices similar to slavery; and the 1951 Refugee Convention and its 1967 Protocol contain a *non refoulement* obligation that has since been replicated, in a somewhat more expansive fashion, through a constructive interpretation of the ECHR and the ICCPR and is also explicitly provided for in the case of torture in the CAT.[6]

---

[3] Human Rights Act 1998 (hereinafter 'HRA'); European Convention for the Protection of Human Rights and Fundamental Freedoms, Rome, 4 November 1950, ETS, No. 5, ratified by the UK on 8 March 1951 (hereinafter 'ECHR'); Protocol to the Convention for the Protection of Human Rights and Fundamental Freedoms, 20 March 1952, ETS, No. 9, ratified by the UK on 3 November 1952 (hereinafter 'ECHR Protocol No. 1'); Protocol No. 13 to the Convention for the Protection of Human Rights and Fundamental Freedoms concerning the Abolition of the Death Penalty in All Circumstances, 3 May 2002, ETS, No. 187, ratified by the UK on 10 October 2003 (hereinafter 'ECHR Protocol No. 13').

[4] In addition, the UK may well be subject to many of the same obligations as a matter of customary international law, although the precise scope of such coverage is unclear and beyond the scope of this chapter.

[5] International Covenant on Civil and Political Rights, New York, 16 December 1966, 999 UNTS 171, ratified by the UK on 20 May 1976 (hereinafter 'ICCPR'); Second Optional Protocol to the International Covenant on Civil and Political Rights, Aiming at the Abolition of the Death Penalty, New York, 15 December 1989, UN Doc. A/RES/44/128, ratified by the UK on 10 December 1999 (hereinafter 'ICCPR Second Optional Protocol'). As far as the death penalty is concerned, there is a slight difference between the absolute prohibition of the death penalty in all circumstances contained in ECHR Protocol No. 13 and the ICCPR Second Optional Protocol which allows for the possibility of reserving the right to apply the death penalty in times of war 'pursuant to a conviction for a most serious crime of a military nature committed during wartime' (Art 2). However, the UK has not entered any such reservation.

[6] Convention on the Rights of the Child, New York, 20 November 1989, 1577 UNTS 3, ratified by the UK on 16 December 1991 (hereinafter 'CRC'); Convention against Torture and Other Cruel, Inhuman or Degrading Treatment or Punishment, New York, 10 December 1984, 1465 UNTS 85, ratified by the UK on 8 December 1988) (hereinafter 'CAT'); Art 13, International Covenant on Economic, Social and Cultural Rights, New York, 16 December 1966, 993 UNTS 3, ratified by the UK on 25 May 1976 (hereinafter

In what circumstances do these relevant international treaty obligations apply to the UK extra-territorially? Due to space limitations, the following examination will not cover the obligations in the 1951 Refugee Convention and its 1967 Protocol.

The Concept of 'jurisdiction' in International Treaties on Civil and Political Rights

All the obligations under the ICCPR and its Second Protocol, the ECHR and its Protocols and the CRC, and the obligation to take measures to prevent acts of torture under the CAT do not operate in a 'free standing' sense, simply in relation to the acts or omissions of the UK anywhere in the world. Rather, the UK is obliged to respect, protect and fulfil the rights contained in these instruments or, in the case of the CAT, is subject to a particular obligation to take 'effective legislative, administrative, judicial or other measures to prevent acts of torture' within its 'jurisdiction'.[7]

Although the ICESCR does not contain any reference to the *spatial* scope of application (other than Article 14 which conceives the state's obligation in relation to the provision of primary education in terms of 'metropolitan territory or other territories under its jurisdiction')[8], in the recent *Wall Advisory Opinion* on the Israeli-constructed barrier in the Palestinian territories, the International Court of Justice held that the ICESCR applied to Israel in the occupied territories on the grounds that such territories fell within Israel's 'territorial jurisdiction' since Israel was the 'occupying Power,' for the purposes of a separate area of law—the law of belligerent occupation under international humanitarian law.[9] Since the Court gave no definition of this term, but discussed the ICESCR after considering the meaning of 'jurisdiction' in the ICCPR, one can perhaps assume that the Court had the same meaning in mind in relation to both instruments.

'ICESCR'); International Convention with the Object of Securing the Abolition of Slavery and the Slave Trade, Geneva, 26 September 1926, 60 LNTS 253, ratified by the UK on 18 June 1927 (hereinafter '1926 Slavery Convention'); Convention on the Abolition of Slavery, the Slave Trade, and Institutions and Practices Similar to Slavery, Supplementary to the International Convention signed at Geneva on 25 September 1926, Geneva, 7 September 1956, ratified by the UK on 30 April 1957 (hereinafter '1956 Supplementary Slavery Convention'); Convention Relating to the Status of Refugees, Geneva, 28 July 1951, 189 UNTS 137, ratified by the UK on 11 March 1954 (hereinafter 'Refugee Convention'); Protocol relating to the Status of Refugees, New York, 31 January 1967, 606 UNTS 267, ratified by the UK on 4 September 1968.

  [7] ECHR, Art 1; ICCPR, Art 2; CRC, Art 2; CAT, Art 2.   [8] ICESCR, Art 14.

  [9] *Legal Consequences of the Construction of a Wall in the Occupied Palestinian Territory*, ICJ Advisory Opinion of 9 July 2004, available at *www.icj-cij.org/icjwww/decisions.htm* (hereinafter *'Wall Advisory Opinion'*), para. 112.

It is clear that 'jurisdiction' covers the state's own territory; less clear are the precise circumstances in which it subsists extraterritorially. No definition of the term is given in these instruments, and the extraterritorial meaning of it has been discussed in relatively few cases.[10] Nonetheless, as explained in more detail below, from these cases it is possible to discern the broad contours of a definition. Extraterritorial jurisdiction subsists when the state exercises power, control or authority over either territory—what might be termed the *spatial* basis for jurisdiction—or individuals—what might be termed the *personal* basis for jurisdiction.

Colonial Clauses

In addition to this 'jurisdiction' regime of extraterritorial applicability, the ECHR and its Protocols and the 1951 Refugee Convention all contain a 'colonial clause' allowing the UK to make a declaration that the rights contained in the treaty are to apply in 'territories for whose international relations it is responsible', a term referring at the time to colonial and Trust territories, and what are now designated by the UK as 'Overseas Territories' (formerly 'dependent territories'), covering former colonies that remain administered by the UK but do not form part of UK territory.[11] Similarly, the 1926 Slavery Convention contains an 'opt-out' clause which allows states parties to declare that their acceptance of the Convention does not bind some of the territories placed under their jurisdiction,[12]

---

[10] Eg, *Cyprus v Turkey*, European Court of Human Rights, Judgment of 10 May 2001, *Reports 2001-IV* (hereinafter '*Cyprus v Turkey*'); *Loizidou v Turkey (Preliminary Objections)*, European Court of Human Rights, Judgment of 23 March 1995, *Series A*, No. 310 (hereinafter '*Loizidou (Preliminary Objections)*'); *Loizidou v Turkey (Merits)*, European Court of Human Rights, Judgment of 18 December 1996, *Reports 1996-VI* (hereinafter '*Loizidou (Merits)*'); *Banković v. Belgium and 16 Other Contracting States*, European Court of Human Rights, Admissibility Decision, 12 December 2001, *Reports 2001-XII* (hereinafter '*Banković*'); *Öcalan v Turkey*, European Court of Human Rights, Admissibility Decision, 4 December 1999, obtainable from *www.echr.coe.int* (hereinafter '*Öcalan (Admissibility decision)*'); *Öcalan v Turkey (Merits)*, European Court of Human Rights, Judgment of 12 March 2003, obtainable from *www.echr.coe.int* (hereinafter '*Öcalan (Merits)*'); *Öcalan v Turkey*, Application No. 46221/99, European Court of Human Rights [Grand Chamber], Judgment of 12 May 2005, obtainable from *www.echr.coe.int* (hereinafter '*Öcalan (Grand Chamber)*'); *Ilascu and Others v Moldova and Russia*, European Court of Human Rights, Judgment of 4 July 2004, obtainable from *www.echr.coe.int*; *Issa and Others v Turkey (Merits)*, European Court of Human Rights, Judgment of 16 November 2004, available at *www.echr.coe.int* (hereinafter '*Issa*'); *WM v Denmark*, Application No. 17392/90, European Commission of Human Rights, Admissibility Decision of 14 October 1992, reported in (1992) 15 *EHRR CD* 28 (hereinafter '*WM v Denmark*').

[11] ECHR, Art 56 (formerly 63); Refugee Convention, Art 40.

[12] Slavery Convention 1926, Art 9: 'At the time of signature or of ratification or of accession, any High Contracting Party may declare that its acceptance of the present Convention does not bind some or all of the territories placed under its sovereignty,

whilst the 1956 Supplementary Slavery Convention, although providing that '[t]his Convention shall apply to all non self-governing, trust, colonial and other non-metropolitan territories for the international relations of which any State Party is responsible', requires states to specify to which territories the Convention applies.[13]

As explained more fully below, the conventional position is that, regardless of whether the test for the extraterritorial exercise of 'jurisdiction' mentioned above is met (eg through the exercise of effective territorial control), the ECHR and its Protocols do not apply to Overseas Territories unless these instruments have been expressly extended to the Territories in question. The effect of this conventional position is that there are two mutually exclusive regimes determining the extraterritorial applicability of the ECHR and its Protocols: for Overseas Territories, an explicit 'colonial clause' extension is required; for everywhere else, the existence of a factual situation amounting to the exercise of 'jurisdiction' is necessary.

Under the ICCPR and the ICESCR, by contrast, no express extension to Overseas Territories is required; thus if the 'jurisdiction' test is met, these instruments apply. As mentioned, they contain all the rights in the ECHR and its Protocols apart from the right to property.

Existing Position in UK Case Law

The few English cases to date on the extraterritorial applicability of the Human Rights Act have all made a central assumption: the position under the Human Rights Act follows exclusively that under the ECHR and its Protocols.[14] The general reason for this is that the Act was

jurisdiction, protection, suzerainty or tutelage in respect of all or any provisions of the Convention; it may subsequently accede separately on behalf of any one of them or in respect of any provision to which any one of them is not a Party'.

[13] Supplementary Slavery Convention 1956, Art 12(1): 'This Convention shall apply to all non self-governing, trust, colonial and other non-metropolitan territories for the international relations of which any State Party is responsible; the Party concerned shall [...] at the time of signature, ratification or accession declare the non-metropolitan territory or territories to which the Convention shall apply *ipso facto* as a result of such signature, ratification or accession.' The UK has not utilized the faculty to opt-out contained in the 1926 Slavery Convention (see *http://untreaty. un.org/ENGLISH/bible/englishinternetbible/ part1/chapterXVIII/treaty3.asp*), and, when ratifying the 1956 Convention, it specified that the Convention applies to all the UK Overseas Territories (see Foreign and Commonwealth Office, 'Treaties applying to UK Overseas Territories, Human Rights', available at *http://www.fco.gov.uk/Files/KFile/UKOTHumanRightsTreaties.pdf*).

[14] *R. (on the application of Al-Skeini and others) v Secretary of State for Defence* [2004] EWHC Admin 2911, 14 December 2004 (hereinafter '*Al Skeini*'); *R. (Quark Fishing Ltd) v*

intended to 'incorporate' most of the rights in the Convention and its Protocols into English law. Under this view, then, one has to separate out the position under the ECHR and its Protocols from that under the other relevant international human rights treaties above and consider only the ECHR and its Protocols when interpreting the scope of the Act. This has had three principal consequences in terms of the extraterritorial scope of the Act.

In the first place, as explained more fully below, the Divisional Court in the *Al-Skeini* case concerning Iraq defined the extraterritorial meaning of 'jurisdiction' under the ECHR in a narrower fashion than is the position in human rights law generally, disregarding the notion of a broad doctrine of control/power/authority exercised over individuals in favour of a narrower category of actions in embassies, ships, aircraft and detention facilities. Although, as I shall explain below, this is an incorrect reading of the ECHR, it would be even more difficult to sustain if the frame of reference moved beyond that particular treaty.

In the second place, taking the view that the position under the Act follows the position under the ECHR and its Protocols exclusively, rather than the UK's international human rights obligations generally, means that the Act applies extraterritorially in Overseas Territories only if a 'colonial clause' extension has been made; this would not be necessary if the approach taken under the ICCPR and the ICESCR—which do not require express extension—were adopted.

In the third place, following the ECHR and its Protocols in particular, rather than international human rights law generally, brings in the possibility of adopting an idea developed from a *dictum* by the European Court of Human Rights in the *Banković* case concerning the NATO bombing of what was then the Federal Republic of Yugoslavia (FRY, now called Serbia and Montenegro) in 1999: that the Act only applies to the actions of the UK extraterritorially if such actions occur in other contracting states to the Convention—within the Convention's 'legal space.' In the *Al-Skeini* case this notion was affirmed in relation to acts involving the exercise of control over territory but not in a residual category of particular acts conducted on ships, aircraft, embassies and detention facilities. Although as I shall explain below this is an incorrect reading of the *Banković dictum*, it would not even be relevant (other than perhaps in relation to the property right) if the frame of reference went beyond the ECHR and its Protocols and took in the other international human rights treaties.

Secretary of State for Foreign & Commonwealth Affairs [2004] EWCA Civ. 527, 29 April 2004 (herinafter '*Quark*'); *R. (on the application of B) v Secretary of State for Foreign and Commonwealth Affairs* [2004] EWCA Civ 1344, 18 October 2004 (hereinafter '*B*. case').

In this paper I argue that the central assumption of tying the Act to the ECHR and its Protocols exclusively, and the particular conclusions drawn by the Divisional Court in *Al-Skeini* about the extraterritorial applicability of the ECHR and its Protocols, are incorrect.

The correct international law basis for understanding the extraterritorial application of the Act is the UK's international human rights law obligations generally, including, but not limited to, the ECHR and its Protocols. Because of this, there *is* a general doctrine of extraterritorial applicability in circumstances where the UK exercises control/power/authority over individuals; the 'legal space' limitation, whatever its merits (which are, as will be explained, dubious) is *inapplicable* to the Act (other than possibly in relation to the property right) since no such limitation operates with respect to the ICCPR and the ICESCR; and the extraterritorial applicability of the Act to the UK's Overseas Territories in most cases *should not depend* on whether the ECHR and its Protocols have been extended to these territories, but rather, as is the case with other foreign territories under the ECHR and its Protocols, simply whether the 'jurisdiction' test is met.

The Terms of the Human Rights Act

The Act renders what it calls 'Convention rights' part of English law. The content of that class of rights is determined by inclusion in a list drawn from some of the articles from the Convention and its Protocols contained in Schedule 1 of the Act.[15] These articles are concerned exclusively with *rights*—they say nothing about the nature of the *obligation* or *obligations* borne by the UK government in relation to them. As previously discussed, under the Convention an overall obligation is introduced by coupling each of the articles setting out the rights with Article 1, which states that

The High Contracting Parties shall secure to everyone within their jurisdiction the rights and freedoms defined in Section I of this Convention.[16]

In the case of Overseas Territories, as previously mentioned, there is also the provision in Article 56, and equivalent provisions in the ECHR Protocols, providing for rights to be expressly extended in such territories.

The Human Rights Act, however, does not adopt the obligation contained in Article 1, nor does it contain a 'colonial extension clause' as in ECHR Article 56. Instead, it contains its own special set of obligations.

---

[15] HRA, s 1 and Sch 1.   [16] ECHR, Art 1.

In the first place, under Section 3 the courts are obliged, so far as it is possible to do so, to read and give effect to primary and subordinate legislation in a way that is compatible with these rights and if this is not possible, under Sections 4, 5 and 10 provision is made for the courts to make a declaration of incompatibility and for Parliament to take remedial action in such instances.[17] In the second place, Section 6(1) states that, subject to certain exceptions, 'It is unlawful for a public authority to act in a way which is incompatible with a Convention right'[18] and sections 7 to 9 provide for certain remedies to those complaining of a breach of Section 6.[19] As far as the Section 6 obligation, then, there is a different conception of responsibility to that under the Convention: the issue is simply who is carrying out the act, *not also*, as in the Convention, where this act takes place. Clearly the plain meaning of an obligation conceived in this manner is that it applies to *all* acts of a public authority, regardless of whether they take place within or outside UK territory.

But doesn't the fact that the Act was intended to incorporate the rights in the Convention also mean that Parliament intended to incorporate the type of *obligation* operating under that Treaty, even if it did not articulate this expressly?

As far as the long title to the Bill containing the Act is concerned, it is stated that one of the Bill's purposes is '.... to give further effect to rights and freedoms guaranteed under the European Convention on Human Rights.'[20] What are being given *effect* to here are simply the rights—had Parliament intended also to refer to the particular regime of *obligation* under the Convention, the phrase would need to be worded differently, perhaps stating an intention to give further effect to the *guarantee* of rights under the Convention.

The Act does however require the courts to take into account Strasbourg jurisprudence. Since clearly this jurisprudence *is* concerned not only with Convention rights but also the obligation to secure them under Article 1 and/or the relevance of any Article 56 extensions, do we not see here an intention to adopt the regime concerning extraterritorial

---

[17] HRA, ss 3 and 4.

[18] Ibid, s 6(1).   [19] Ibid, ss 7–9.

[20] Ibid, long title. *Bennion on Statutory Interpretation* states that: 'The long title (formerly and more correctly called the title) appears at the beginning of the Act. It is a remnant from the Bill which on royal assent became the Act. Its true function pertains to the Bill rather than the Act. It sets out in general terms the purposes of the Bill, and under the rules of parliamentary procedure (at least in the House of Commons) should cover everything in the Bill..... Although thus being of a procedural nature, the long title is nevertheless regarded by the courts as a guide to legislative intention'. Francis Bennion, *Statutory Interpretation: A Code* (4th ed., 2004) (hereinafter '*Bennion on Statutory Interpretation*') part XV, Sec. 245, p. 620.

applicability set out in the ECHR and its Protocols exclusively? The problem with drawing such a conclusion is that the obligation in the Act is simply to 'take account' of Strasbourg jurisprudence when 'determining a question which has arisen in connection with a Convention right,' and only when this is 'relevant to the proceedings in which that question has arisen'.[21] This clearly falls short of a position whereby the meaning of rights and the scope of state obligations under the Convention and its Protocols is to be adopted by the Act.

Clearly one can disaggregate Strasbourg determinations on the meaning of ECHR and/or ECHR Protocol provisions into those aspects bound up in the particular way obligations are conceived under Article 1, and other aspects relevant more generally to the right concerned. So, for example, one could look to Strasbourg jurisprudence on the *meaning* of inhumane and degrading treatment under ECHR Article 3, without also following the formulation taking Article 3 together with Article 1 and, where relevant, Article 56, that the state is obliged not to perpetrate such treatment only within its jurisdiction and/or when an Article 56 'extension' has been made. Equally, nothing in the obligation to take into account Strasbourg jurisprudence when 'relevant' prevents the English courts from taking into account any other considerations that would also be relevant to statutory interpretation.

The text of the Act, then, suggests that although the rights it contains are based on provisions in the Convention—and for this reason are called Convention rights—Parliament did not necessarily intend the nature of government *obligations* under the Act to follow the jurisdictional limitation adopted under Article 1 of the Convention.

Presumption of Territorial Application

Turning from the plain meaning of the Act to principles of statutory interpretation, one such principle is that in the absence of an intention expressed to the contrary, it is assumed that Parliament intends that legislation shall apply only territorially.[22]

---

[21] HRA, s 2.

[22] *Ex p Blain In re Sawers*, 12 Ch D 522 (1879) at 528 *per* Brett LJ; see also *Cooke v Charles A Vogeler Co* [1901] AC 102. *Bennion on Statutory Interpretation* states: 'Unless the contrary intention appears, Parliament is taken to intend an Act to extend to each territory of the United Kingdom but not to any territory outside the United Kingdom' (section 106 (Presumption of United Kingdom extent)). 'Unless the contrary intention appears, and subject to any privilege, immunity or disability arising under the law of the territory to

However, it is doubtful whether this applies to statutes concerning the state's human rights obligations. One of the main justifications normally given for the presumption that statutes do not apply extraterritorially is that this ensures consistency with the United Kingdom's international obligations, given the presumption that Parliament has legislated in conformity with these obligations.[23] Entirely separate from, and dealing with a different matter when compared with, human rights obligations, international law contains a set of rules concerning what is also called the exercise of 'jurisdiction.' Here, the term has a related but distinct meaning from its use in international human rights law: the scope of application and enforcement of UK criminal law to individuals. Unlike human rights law, where the term is used to denote a particular activity that, if present as a matter of fact, triggers the operation of substantive obligations, under this area of law the rules are concerned with determining when the UK is *permitted* to engage in a particular activity.

Under this separate area of law, the UK is only permitted to exercise this 'jurisdiction' extraterritorially—eg the English criminal law applying to acts taking place outside the UK—in a narrow set of circumstances. The principle behind this is that the UK should not normally be entitled to infringe the sovereignty of other states by applying its law to individuals in those states, which in normal circumstances are to be subject to the exclusive criminal jurisdiction of the host state.

which an enactment extends (that is within which it is law), and to any relevant rule of private international law, an enactment applies to all persons and matters within the territory to which it extends, but not to any other persons and matters.' Ibid, section 128 (General principles as to application).

The principle is stated in the following more expansive way in *Halsbury's Laws of England*: 'There is a presumption that Parliament does not assert or assume jurisdiction which goes beyond the limits established by the common consent of nations, and, provided their language admits. Acts are to be applied so as not to be inconsistent with the comity of nations or with the established principles of international law. Thus general words in an Act may be presumed to be limited so as to have effect within the effective jurisdiction of Parliament only.' *Halsbury's Laws of England* (4th ed., reissue, 1995), Vol. 41-1, 'Statutes', para. 1317.

On the limits deriving from 'comity of nations' and 'international law, see *Le Louis* (1817) 2 Dods 210; *The Annapolis* (1861) Lush 295; *R v Wilson* (1877) 3 QBD 42; *Bloxam v Favre* (1883) 8 PD 101 at 104 (affd (1884) 9 PD 130, CA); *Colquhoun v Brooks* (1889) 14 App Cas 493, HL; *Re AB & Co* [1990] 1 QB 541, CA; *Re Martin, Loustalan v Loustalan* [1990] P 211 at 233, CA; *Philipson-Stow v IRC* [1961] AC 727 at 745, [1960] 3 All ER 814 at 821, HL; *Rothmans of Pall Mall (Overseas) Ltd v Saudi Arabian Airlines Corpn* [1981] QB 368, [1980] 3 All ER 359, CA. By virtue of the sovereignty of Parliament, the presumption mentioned must give way before a clearly expressed intention: *Mortensen v Peters* (1906) 8 F 93 at 103.

[23] *Ex p. Blain*, n 22 above, at 527, *per* James LJ: 'in the absence of express legislative provision, compelling me to say that the Legislature has done that which, in my opinion, would be a violation of international law, I respectfully decline to hold that it has done anything of the kind.'

However, human rights law does not operate in this way: the law in question is not being applied—in the sense of imposing obligations—to *individuals* abroad; rather, it applies to the UK. Clearly the UK applying its law to its own acts in a foreign state is not an infringement on the sovereignty of that state (of course, the fact that the UK is *acting* in the foreign state might be a violation of sovereignty, but that is a separate matter).

In the *Roma Rights* case the House of Lords assumed without explanation that the obligation not to discriminate on racial grounds in the Race Relations Act 1976, applied to UK immigration officials operating in Prague Airport.[24] This adds some weight to the argument that the 'territorial' assumption is inapplicable in the case of human rights obligations.

The UK's Other International Human Rights Obligations—Introduction

A more significant principle of statutory interpretation relates to the UK's international human rights law obligations generally, including, but not limited to, the ECHR and its Protocols. Before considering the relevance of this principle, and applying it to the Act, it is necessary to explain in more detail the framework of international human rights law summarized at the start of this paper.

As mentioned above, for each right under the Act apart from the property right there are at least two separate relevant sources of international treaty obligation. In understanding the nature of the UK's international obligations with respect to these rights, one therefore has to take into account not only the Convention, but also these other sources of treaty obligation. Moreover, insofar as there is a divergence in scope between different sources of obligation in relation to the rights protected under various instruments (eg a particular right having a broader meaning in one instrument than another), one ultimately has to look to the broadest formulation in appreciating the full extent of the UK's obligations.

To what extent do these international obligations apply to UK actions outside its territory? I shall address this question below, beginning with the extraterritorial meaning of 'jurisdiction' in the relevant treaties generally, and then turning to the relevance of 'colonial clauses' in certain human

---

[24] *R v Immigration Officer at Prague Airport and another (Respondents) ex parte European Roma Rights Centre and others (Appellants)* [2004] UKHL 55, 9 December 2004 (hereinafter '*Roma Rights* case'); see the opinion of Lady Hale.

rights treaties and the 'legal space' idea from the *Banković* case mentioned above.

The Extraterritorial Meaning of 'jurisdiction' in Human Rights Treaties

The Relevance of the Public International Law Term 'jurisdiction'

In the *Banković* case the European Court of Human Rights seemed to suggest that the meaning of 'jurisdiction' in the ECHR should reflect the meaning of that term in public international law generally;[25] as mentioned above, in public international law the term refers to rules prescribing the particular circumstances where a state is *legally permitted* to exercise its *legal authority* over a particular situation (eg prosecuting its own nationals for crimes committed abroad). Insofar as the Court intended to make this suggestion, it does not fit with how it and other international human rights bodies have approached the issue in other cases, which is to define extraterritorial jurisdiction as a *factual* test, regardless of whether such a situation is lawful. For example, the Court held that Turkey's presence in Northern Cyprus constituted the exercise of jurisdiction for the purposes of the ECHR because of the degree of control exercised (see below), stressing that such jurisdiction could subsist on this basis regardless of the legality of the exercise of control (Turkey's presence in Northern Cyprus was unlawful).[26] The UN Human Rights Committee recently stated in relation to the ICCPR that the principle of making available the enjoyment of Covenant rights to all individuals regardless of nationality

... applies to those within the power or effective control of the forces of a State Party acting outside its territory, *regardless of the circumstances in which such power or effective control was obtained*, such as forces constituting a national contingent of a State Party assigned to an international peace-keeping or peace-enforcement operation.[27]

---

[25] *Banković*, n 10 above, paras 59–61.

[26] *Loizidou (Preliminary Objections)*, n 10 above, para. 62; *Loizidou (Merits)*, n 10 above, paras. 52–56. See also *Cyprus v Turkey*, n 10 above, para. 77.

[27] UN Human Rights Committee, General Comment No. 31, 'The Nature of the General Legal Obligation on States Parties to the Covenant', Eightieth session (2004), in *Compilation of General Comments and General Recommendations Adopted by Human Rights Treaty Bodies*, UN Doc. HRI\GEN\1\Rev.7 (2004), at 192 (hereinafter 'General Comment 31'), para. 10, emphasis added.

So the UK could be exercising extraterritorial jurisdiction without a valid international legal basis for doing so, and its human rights obligations would not be inapplicable simply by virtue of the illegality.

In its *Wall Advisory Opinion*, the International Court of Justice stated in relation to the ICCPR that,

. . . while the exercise of jurisdiction is primarily territorial, it may sometimes be exercised outside the state territory.[28]

The Court went on to say that:

Considering the object and purpose of the International Covenant on Civil and Political Rights, it would seem natural that, even when such is the case, States parties to the Covenant should be bound by its provisions.[29]

Here, then, the Court is clearly being descriptive about the exercise of jurisdiction, reflecting the fact that states do not normally exercise it *as a matter of fact* outside territory. In the *Banković* case, the European Court of Human Rights made a similar observation, that jurisdiction is 'essentially' *territorial*, with *extraterritorial* jurisdiction subsisting only in 'exceptional' circumstances.[30] However, in this observation the European Court, perhaps influenced by the idea (discussed before) of limiting the meaning of extraterritorial jurisdiction to that which is legally permissible, seemed to be suggesting that somehow the 'exceptional' character of extraterritorial jurisdiction should be understood not only in a purely factual sense; it should also have purchase in defining the boundaries of the meaning of 'jurisdiction' in international human rights law in a limited fashion, and should do so in an autonomous manner from the factual exceptionalism. The autonomous nature of this exceptionalism creates the possibility that even if a state *is* acting 'exceptionally' as a *matter of fact* outside its territory, such a situation might not fall within its 'jurisdiction' for the purposes of human rights law.

The *Banković* case was the first case to adopt this approach, which is not found in earlier ECHR cases, or the jurisprudence of other international human rights treaty bodies, including the UN Human Rights Committee, or the International Court of Justice in the *Wall Advisory Opinion*. It was, however, adopted in the recent *Al-Skeini* case before the High Court.[31] It remains to be seen whether this idea is taken up more generally, but insofar as it is adopted it clearly serves to narrow the range of circumstances in which jurisdiction is understood to subsist extraterritorially as a matter of law.

---

[28] *Wall Advisory Opinion*, n 9 above, para. 109.   [29] Ibid.
[30] *Banković*, n 10 above, para. 67.   [31] *Al-Skeini*, n 14 above, paras. 245 and 269.

The Spatial and Personal Bases for Jurisdiction

In the case law and other authoritative statements on the ICCPR and the ECHR, the term 'jurisdiction' has been understood in the extraterritorial context in terms of the existence of a connection between the state and either the territory in which the relevant acts took place—a *spatial* connection—or the individual affected by them—a *personal* connection.

Although there is less authoritative commentary on the extraterritorial applicability of the CRC and the CAT, the meaning of 'jurisdiction' under these instruments is arguably the same as under the ICCPR, ECHR and their Protocols. On the CRC, the ICJ appeared to assume this in affirming the applicability of this treaty to Israel's presence in the occupied territories in the *Wall Advisory Opinion*.[32] On the CAT, the UN Committee Against Torture (the mechanism set up to monitor compliance with the CAT), in its comments on the UK,[33] assumes that 'jurisdiction' includes the exercise of control over territory—the *spatial* connection.

We shall now consider in detail the meaning of each type of connection—*spatial* and *personal*—that can amount to the exercise of 'jurisdiction'.

Jurisdiction as a Spatial Relationship—Control over Territory

Beginning with the approach that conceives the target of the relationship *spatially*, here the exercise of 'jurisdiction' amounts to asserting control over a particular territorial space, within which the state is obliged to secure individual rights in a generalized sense. Such a generalized approach can be understood as an analogue to the approach taken to the state's obligations in its own territory, and reflects the general principle of state responsibility for extraterritorial activity, as articulated in the *Namibia Advisory Opinion* of the International Court of Justice in 1971, where the Court stated that South Africa was

... accountable for any violations ... of the rights of the people of Namibia. The fact that South Africa no longer has any title to administer the Territory does not

[32] *Wall Advisory Opinion*, n 9 above, para. 113. In paras. 118–111 the Court discusses the potential for the term 'jurisdiction' under the ICCPR to subsist extraterritorially, concluding in the affirmative. After considering the position under the ICESCR, it turns to the CRC, and concludes extraterritorial applicability simply on the basis that obligations in that instrument are conceived in relation to the state's 'jurisdiction.' One can perhaps conclude that this assumption is made in the light of the Court's earlier discussion about the meaning of the same term in the ICCPR, and on the basis that the term has the same meaning in both instruments, since otherwise the Court would have to conduct an enquiry into the meaning of 'jurisdiction' in the CRC similar to that which it conducted in relation to the ICCPR.

[33] Conclusions and recommendations of the Committee Against Torture: United Kingdom, UN Doc. CAT/C/CR/33/3, 25 November 2004, in particular para. 4 (b).

release it from its obligations and responsibilities under international law towards other States in respect of the exercise of its powers in relation to this Territory. Physical control of a territory, and not sovereignty or legitimacy of title, is the basis of State liability for acts affecting other States.[34]

The *spatial* approach to the target involved in the jurisdiction concept of human rights law was articulated in the *Loizidou, Cyprus v Turkey*, and *Banković* cases before the European Convention of Human Rights system, and affirmed by the English High Court in *Al-Skeini*.[35]

The *Loizidou* and *Cyprus v Turkey* cases concerned the question of Turkey's responsibility for certain aspects of the situation in northern Cyprus. In its 1995 judgment on preliminary objections in *Loizidou*, the European Court of Human Rights stated that

... the responsibility of a Contracting Party may ... arise when as a consequence of military action—whether lawful or unlawful—it exercises effective control of an area outside its national territory. The obligation to secure, in such an area, the rights and freedoms set out in the Convention derives from the fact of such control ... [36]

In its judgment on the merits, the Court affirmed the previous statement, and stated that

[I]t is not necessary to determine whether .... Turkey actually exercises detailed control over the policies and actions of the authorities of the 'TRNC'. It is obvious from the large number of troops engaged in active duties in northern Cyprus ... that her army exercises effective overall control over that part of the island. Such control, according to the relevant test and in the circumstances of the case, entails her responsibility for the policies and actions of the 'TRNC' ... Those affected by such policies or actions therefore come within the 'jurisdiction' of Turkey for the purposes of Article 1 of the Convention ... [37]

In general, then, the test is 'effective control' over territory; the existence of this factual situation gives rise to a responsibility to secure the rights within the Convention in the territory concerned.

On the facts in Northern Cyprus, the Court emphasized that Turkey exercised effective control operating 'overall;' in such circumstances, it

---

[34] *Legal Consequences for States of the Continued Presence of South Africa in Namibia (South West Africa) notwithstanding Security Council Resolution 276 (1970)*, Advisory Opinion of 21 June 1971, *ICJ Reports 1971*, p. 16, at para. 118.

[35] *Loizidou (Preliminary Objections); Loizidou (Merits); Cyprus v Turkey; Banković*, n 10 above; *Al-Skeini*, n 14 above, para. 248.

[36] *Loizidou (Preliminary Objections)*, n 10 above, para. 62, cited in *Loizidou (Merits)*, n 10 above, para. 52.

[37] *Loizidou (Merits)*, n 10 above, para. 56 and *Loizidou (Preliminary Objections)*, n 10 above, paras. 63–64.

was unnecessary to identify whether the exercise of control was detailed. So if the UK is in overall control of a territorial unit, everything within that unit falls within its 'jurisdiction,' even if at lesser levels powers are exercised by other actors (eg if particular activities are devolved to other states or local actors). In the *Cyprus v Turkey* judgment, the Court stated that:

> ... [H]aving effective overall control over northern Cyprus... [Turkey's] responsibility cannot be confined to the acts of its own soldiers or officials in northern Cyprus but must also be engaged by virtue of the acts of the local administration which survives by virtue of Turkish military and other support. It follows that, in terms of Article 1 of the Convention, Turkey's 'jurisdiction' must be considered to extend to securing the entire range of substantive rights set out in the Convention and those additional Protocols which she has ratified, and that violations of those rights are imputable to Turkey.[38]

In the *Banković* case, the Court made the following general statement on the issue of effective control:

> ... the case-law of the Court demonstrates that its recognition of the exercise of extra-territorial jurisdiction by a Contracting State is exceptional: it has done so when the respondent State, through the effective control of the relevant territory and its inhabitants abroad, as a consequence of military occupation or through the consent, invitation or acquiescence of the Government of that territory exercises all or some of the public powers normally to be exercised by that Government.[39]

Recalling the backdrop to the Northern Cyprus cases, we see the Court in *Banković* emphasising a further feature of those cases which was not actually emphasized in the Court's consideration of the exercise of jurisdiction in them. For the Court in *Banković*, the issue is control over territory that is not only 'effective' but also involves the exercise of 'some or all of the public powers normally to be exercised' by the local government. Whereas indeed such powers were exercised by Turkey in northern Cyprus, their exercise was not seen by the Court as a prerequisite to the exercise of jurisdiction in the northern Cyprus cases: the only issue was the exercise of 'effective control.' The statement in *Banković* then, should be taken in a somewhat loose sense as a general description of the factual circumstances in which the court had previously found the exercise of jurisdiction ('it has done so'), rather than as either an accurate statement of the *salient* facts in those previous cases, or, indeed, a statement of the key factual elements that must subsist in order for extraterritorial jurisdiction to subsist under the 'effective control' heading. It is notable in this regard

---

[38] *Cyprus v Turkey*, n 10 above, para. 77.   [39] *Banković*, n 10 above, para. 71.

that in its application of the law to the facts of the case, the Court made no statement, either explicit or implicit, touching on the question of whether or not the relevant acts—the bombing—involved the exercise of powers normally to be exercised by the local government.[40]

The test, then, is 'effective control' over territory. What this amounts to in practice is difficult to ascertain, because it has only been considered fully in the case of Northern Cyprus, where there was a clear level of overall control by the Turkish military, and the *Banković* case, where the European Court of Human Rights held that aerial bombardment did not constitute the exercise of control over territory.[41]

As far as the applicability of the ECHR to the UK in Iraq is concerned, HMG disputes that its presence since 2003 involves the necessary level of control to bring parts of that country within UK 'jurisdiction' for the purposes of the ECHR.[42] The High Court in *Al-Skeini* avoided having to determine this question by holding that jurisdiction on the basis of effective control could not subsist in territories outside the legal space of the ECHR (see below).

In the November 2004 decision of the European Court of Human Rights in *Issa*, the Court adopted a 'beyond reasonable doubt' standard of proof when determining whether Turkish troops exercised effective control in an area of northern Iraq in the context of allegations of unlawful killing by the troops,[43] and concluded that this standard was not met, and that the killings did not therefore fall within Turkish jurisdiction for the purposes of the application of its ECHR obligations.[44] Since the facts are often disputed and difficult to verify in the case of extraterritorial state actions, the question of what standard of proof applies is an important one. It remains to be seen whether this strict standard will be applied in future cases as a general test when facts are in dispute; in *Issa* the Court adopted it because the case concerned unlawful killing and such a test had been used previously in non-extraterritorial cases on that particular issue.[45]

---

[40] *Banković*, n 10 above, paras. 75 and 76.   [41] *Banković*, ibid.

[42] See, eg, the letter from the UK Armed Forces minister, Adam Ingram MP, to Adam Price MP on 7 April 2004 (quoted below, text relating to note 60); a similar position seems to have been taken by the UK Foreign Secretary, Jack Straw, who made the following statement in relation to the applicability of the ECHR to the UK in Iraq, invoking by contrast the situation in Turkish-occupied northern Cyprus: '[T]he citizens of Iraq had no rights at all under the ECHR prior to military action by the coalition forces; furthermore, the UK does not exercise the same degree of control over Iraq as existed in relation to the Turkish occupation of northern Cyprus.' Jack Straw, MP, Written Answer, House of Commons, 'European Convention on Human Rights,' 19 May 2004, Hansard Vol. 421, Part No. 89, Column 1083W.   [43] *Issa*, n 10 above, para. 76.

[44] Ibid, para. 81.   [45] Ibid, para. 76.

Jurisdiction as an Individual Relationship—Control over Persons

International human rights treaty monitoring bodies have also understood extraterritorial jurisdiction in terms of some kind of connection operating between the state and an *individual*, rather than whether the area in which the control is exercised is itself under the state's control. This connection has been understood variously as *control* (like the spatial relationship discussed already), *power* or *authority*.

In the *Coard* case seventeen petitioners complained to the Inter-American Commission of Human Rights about their treatment, including detention, by United States' forces in the first days of its invasion of Grenada in 1983.[46] Although the 'jurisdiction' test is not contained in the relevant instrument—the American Declaration of the Rights and Duties of Man—under consideration, the Commission decided to use this term as the basis for considering the scope of the obligations contained within the instrument, stating that

... jurisdiction ... may, under given circumstances, refer to conduct with an extraterritorial locus where the person concerned is present in the territory of one state, but subject to the control of another state—usually through the acts of the latter's agents abroad. In principle, the inquiry turns not on the presumed victim's nationality or presence within a particular geographic area, but on whether, under the specific circumstances, the State observed the rights of a person subject to its authority and control.[47]

This definition of 'jurisdiction' is potentially wide enough to cover the exercise of control over individuals, regardless of whether the area within which such control is exercised is itself under the control of the state. Although of course the UK is not a party to the Charter of the Organization of American States and thus not subject to the obligations contained within the Declaration, this *dictum* is helpful as an authoritative statement on the meaning of a particular obligation of the same kind as that contained within the ECHR and its Protocols and the ICCPR and its Protocols.

The *WM* case before the European Commission of Human Rights concerned the acts and omissions of Danish diplomatic officers committed

---

[46] *Coard et al v United States* (Case No. 10.951), Inter-American Commission on Human Rights, Report No. 109/99, 29 September 1999, in Annual Report of the Inter-American Commission on Human Rights 1999, *OAS Doc.* OEA/Ser.L/V/II.106, Doc. 6 rev, Chapter III, obtainable from *http://www.cidh.oas.org/annualrep/99eng/Merits/UnitedStates10.951.htm*, paras. 1–4.   [47] Ibid, para. 37 (footnotes omitted).

within the Danish Embassy in East Berlin in 1988. In that case the Commission stated that:

... authorised agents of a State, including diplomatic or consular agents, bring other persons or property within the jurisdiction of that State to the extent that they exercise authority over such persons or property. In so far as they affect such persons or property by their acts or omissions, the responsibility of the State is engaged.[48]

The *Öcalan* case concerned Abdullah Öcalan, the leader of the Kurdish Workers Party (the PKK), who was arrested in Kenya, flown by Turkish agents to Turkey and detained before being tried and convicted of activities aimed at bringing about the secession of a part of state territory, and sentenced to death.[49] The Grand Chamber of the Court, confirming the position of the Chamber in this regard, stated that

... the applicant was arrested by members of the Turkish security forces inside an aircraft registered in Turkey in the international zone of Nairobi Airport. It is common ground that directly after being handed over to the Turkish officials by the Kenyan officials, the applicant was under effective Turkish authority and therefore within the 'jurisdiction' of that State for the purposes of Article 1 of the Convention, even though in this instance Turkey exercised its authority outside its territory.[50]

As in the *WM* case, here the Court fails to state explicitly on what basis 'effective Turkish authority' was being exercised; specifically, we are not told whether it concerned the relationship between Turkey and the applicant, or Turkey and the location where Turkey held the applicant. The Court's choice of pertinent facts, however, does perhaps suggest the former. No reference is made as to whether the aircraft or the 'international zone' in which it was located were controlled by Turkey (the fact that the aircraft was registered in Turkey is insufficient for such control to be assumed), and the only description given of the acts of Turkish officials concerns their behaviour towards the applicant (eg physically forcing him back to Turkey) rather than their behaviour in relation to the space in which the applicant was held.

In the *Roma Rights* case concerning UK immigration officials in Prague Airport, Lady Hale, in her comments on discrimination law with which the majority agreed, seemed to assume that the ICCPR applied to the situation at issue.[51] Similarly, Lord Steyn held that in conducting

---

[48] *WM. v Denmark*, n 10 above, 'The Law', para. 1.

[49] *Öcalan (Admissibility Decision)*, n 10 above, Section I within 'The Facts.'

[50] *Öcalan (Grand Chamber)*, n 10 above, para. 91. See also the virtually identical statement of the Chamber in *Öcalan (Merits)*, n 10 above, para. 93.

[51] Lady Hale, *Roma Rights* case, n 24 above, paras. 98–99.

immigration decisions in Prague the UK 'purported to exercise governmental authority' and that because of its discriminatory nature this operation 'placed the United Kingdom in breach' of the ICCPR.[52] These *dicta* do not discuss the jurisdiction test under the ICCPR, nor does Lord Steyn define 'governmental authority' and explain in what way the Prague operations involved the exercise of such authority, but given the nature of the activities—making determinations on immigration status with respect to individuals—one can perhaps construct from these *dicta* a definition of one aspect of the 'jurisdiction' test as the exercise of 'governmental authority' over individuals.

In its General Comment 31 on Article 2 of the ICCPR, the UN Human Rights Committee stated that the jurisdictional test in Article 2.1

... means that a State party must respect and ensure the rights laid down in the Covenant to anyone within the power or effective control of that State Party.[53]

Here, then, we have a clear statement affirming jurisdiction on the basis of a personal target—'anyone'—and relationship between the state and this target described in terms of 'power or effective control.'

Taking these three cases and the General Comment together, we see a suggestion that extraterritorial jurisdiction can subsist when it exercises power (General Comment 31) control/effective control (*Coard*/General Comment 31) or authority (*WM* case, *Öcalan*, and *Roma Rights*) over individuals, quite apart from whether control is being exercised over the territory in which the acts take place.

In the *Al-Skeini* case concerning UK soldiers in Iraq, the High Court rejected the idea of a broad, 'personal' basis for extraterritorial jurisdiction as far as the ECHR is concerned, holding instead that there were two types of extraterritorial jurisdiction according to Strasbourg jurisprudence: the 'effective control of an area' doctrine (ie jurisdiction conceived *spatially*), and a residual, narrow category of activities conducted by state agents in particular circumstances, 'exemplified by embassies, consulates, vessels and aircraft,' and including, on the facts of the particular case, 'a British military prison, operating in Iraq with the consent of the Iraqi sovereign authorities, and containing arrested suspects.'[54]

This finding does not fit with the Strasbourg jurisprudence discussed above. More broadly, it is at odds with the jurisprudence and other authoritative commentary under other legal instruments concerning the identical concept of 'jurisdiction.' These problems make it likely that the

---

[52] Lord Steyn, *Roma Rights* case, n 24 above, para. 45.
[53] General Comment 31, n 27 above, para. 10.
[54] *Al-Skeini*, n 14 above, para. 287.

finding will not survive when the case goes to higher courts. Moreover, on its own terms it only purports to be an interpretation of the position under the ECHR, not the group of international legal instruments considered in this section generally.

'Colonial Clauses'

As mentioned earlier, the ECHR and its Protocols and the Refugee Convention contain a 'colonial clause' allowing the UK to make a declaration that the rights contained in the treaty would apply in what are now called 'Overseas Territories,'[55] and somewhat similar provisions exist in the 1926 Slavery Convention and the 1956 Supplementary Slavery Convention.

Similar extension clauses were not included in later human rights treaties, including the ICCPR, the ICESCR, the CRC and the CAT, which therefore apply to the UK in such territories on the same basis as they apply to the UK in other territories (eg if the 'jurisdiction' test is met under the ICCPR), without the need for an express extension.

As far as the ECHR and its Protocols are concerned, in many cases the UK exercises a degree of control over Overseas Territories to bring them within the ECHR 'jurisdictional' test mentioned earlier, raising the question as to whether the UK's obligations in that treaty in particular would apply on 'jurisdictional' grounds even if a 'colonial clause' declaration has *not* been made. The few cases on this issue have held that for overseas territories, the only way ECHR obligations can apply is through a 'colonial clause' declaration.[56] This position is being challenged by the applicants in the *Quark* case concerning South Georgia.[57]

Absent a successful challenge to the established position, the scope of any 'colonial clause' declarations will be dispositive of whether the UK's ECHR obligations apply to its activities in its Overseas Territories. Although the UK has made a series of declarations under several instruments covering various territories, there are some curious anomalies, notably in the decision to extend the ECHR itself to certain territories, but

---

[55] ECHR, Art 56 (formerly 63); ECHR Protocol No. 1, Art 4; ECHR Protocol No. 13, Art 4; Refugee Convention, Art 40.

[56] *Gillow v United Kingdom*, Application No. 9063/80, European Court of Human Rights, Judgment of 24 November 1986, *Series* A, No. 109, para. 62; *Bui Van Thanh v United Kingdom*, Application No. 16137/90, European Commission of Human Rights, Admissibility Decision, 12 March 1990, 65 *DR* 330, pp. 4–5; see also *Yonghong v Portugal*, Application No. 50887/99, European Court of Human Rights, Admissibility Decision, 25 November 1999, *Reports 1999-IX*, p 3.   [57] *Quark*, n 14 above.

not the first Protocol to the Convention (a separate treaty) which contains the right to property.[58] This is at issue in *Quark*, since the UK has extended the ECHR but not the first Optional Protocol to South Georgia, and the case concerns an alleged breach of the property right in the Protocol.[59]

The conventional position on the 'colonial clause' extension of the ECHR and its Protocols creates the potential for a divergent situation under the ECHR and its Protocols when compared with the ICCPR and the ICESCR because of the different basis on which those treaties apply extraterritorially. Given the overlap in the rights covered as between the ECHR and its Protocols, on the one hand, and the ICCPR and the ICESCR, on the other, a situation may arise where the nature of the UK's actions in an 'Overseas Territory' meet the jurisdictional test, and on the facts impact on the enjoyment of a particular right common to both sets of treaties, but only the obligation in the ICCPR or the ICESCR applies because the UK has not made an express extension of the relevant part of the ECHR or its Protocols. This situation does *not* prevail in the *Quark* case, since the right at issue in the case—the right to property—is contained only in ECHR Protocol No. 1, not also in the ICCPR or the ICESCR.

Is the Extraterritorial Applicability of the ECHR Limited to the 'legal space' of Contracting Parties?

In a letter written in response to a Parliamentary question submitted by Adam Price MP, UK Armed Forces Minister Adam Ingram stated in 2004 that:

[T]he European Convention on Human Rights is intended to apply in a regional context in the legal space of the Contracting States. It was not designed to be applied throughout the world and was not intended to cover the activities of a signatory in a country which is not signatory to the Convention. The ECHR can have no application to the activities of the UK in Iraq because the citizens of Iraq had no rights under the ECHR prior to the military action by the Coalition Forces.[60]

Assuming that Minister Ingram is using the term 'signatory' to refer to a state that has signed *and* ratified the Convention, this passage suggests that a particular action taken by one contracting state in the territory of another state would not be governed by the Convention obligations of the first state, if the second state is not also a party to the Convention.

[58] ECHR Protocol No. 1.   [59] *Quark*, n 14 above.

[60] The Rt Hon Adam Ingram MP, Ministry of Defence, Letter to Adam Price MP, 7 April 2004.

Under this view, although as discussed above the concept of 'jurisdiction' under the ECHR is not limited to a state's own territory, the very applicability of the treaty itself is limited to the overall territory of contracting states. So states acting outside the territorial space of the ECHR are not bound by their obligations in that instrument, even if they are exercising effective control over territory and/or individuals. This is a severe limitation as far as the ECHR is concerned, since most of the world's states, including some of the key sites of extraterritorial action by the UK (eg Iraq), and all the world's least developed states fall outside the 'legal space' of the ECHR.

The *Banković dictum*

The possibility of making such an argument exists because of a *dictum* by the European Court of Human Rights in the *Banković* case concerning the NATO bombing of what was then called the Federal Republic of Yugoslavia (FRY) in 1999. In that case, the Court stated that the ECHR applies

...in an essentially regional context and notably in the legal space (*espace juridique*) of the Contracting States .... The Convention was not designed to be applied throughout the world, even in respect of the conduct of Contracting States.[61]

It is clear that this *dictum* does not support some of the assertions made by the Minister. Although his remark about the 'design' of the Convention echoes the phrase used by the Court, his remark that the Convention was not 'intended' to cover the activities of a contracting party in the territory of a non-contracting party finds no counterpart. The Court states that the Convention operates 'essentially in a regional context'—the word 'context' hardly a clear reference to a territorial area (it could equally refer to a regional grouping of states, irrespective of where they act)—and 'notably in the legal space (*espace juridique*) of the Contracting states'—a clear reference to a territorial area, but not one, because of the word 'notably,' that necessarily means that the Convention applies *only* in this area. Despite the Minister's unequivocal assertion, then, neither of these particular remarks in *Banković* necessarily excludes the application of the Convention to the activities of Contracting States outside the territory of the Council of Europe.

---

[61] *Banković*, n 10 above, para. 80.

But what of the Court's comment that '[T]he Convention was not designed to be applied throughout the world, even in respect of the conduct of Contracting States'? Even if the other remarks in that passage are not helpful either way, does this not suggest a general approach in favour of the Minister's assertion? Such a comment could indeed mean that in all circumstances, the Convention does not apply to the actions of contracting parties outside the legal space of the Council of Europe.

In the first place, it is notable that the Court refers to what the Convention 'was not designed' for. This is necessarily a historical comment; certainly, it is concerned with the original wishes of the framers—though, it must be said, without any supporting evidence—but by itself it says nothing about whether this supposed intent is determinative more than fifty years after the Convention was enacted. The Strasbourg organs have been consistently willing to interpret the Convention as a 'living instrument'[62] creating the possibility that obligations can be understood in a manner not necessarily foreseen by the drafters.

In order to consider whether this supposed original intent is relevant now, it is necessary to clarify how exactly the Court applied it to the facts in *Banković*, the extent to which that application was determinative of the outcome in the case, and more broadly whether the existence of a current limitation along these lines is compatible with other Strasbourg cases.

As for *Banković*, the case concerned the spatial basis for extraterritorial jurisdiction: whether the NATO bombing campaign constituted an exercise of effective control over FRY territory so as to bring it within the 'jurisdiction' of the respondent states. One of the applicants' submissions invoked the earlier *Cyprus v Turkey* case concerning the exercise of control over northern Cyprus—part of Cyprus, a contracting state—by Turkey—another contracting state. In that case, the Court held that it

... must have regard to the special character of the Convention as an instrument of European public order (*ordre public*) for the protection of individual human beings and its mission, as set out in Article 19 of the Convention, 'to ensure the observance of the engagements undertaken by the High Contracting Parties'... Having regard to the applicant Government's continuing inability to exercise their Convention obligations in northern Cyprus, any other finding would result in a regrettable vacuum in the system of human-rights protection in the territory in question by removing from individuals there the benefit of the Convention's

---

[62] *Tyrer v United Kingdom*, Application No. 5856/72, European Court of Human Rights, Judgment of 25 April 1978, *Series A*, No. 26, para 31; *Soering v United Kingdom*, Application No. 14038/88, European Court of Human Rights, Judgment of 7 July 1989, *Series A*, No. 161, para 101; *Loizidou* (*Preliminary Objections*), n 10 above, para. 71. See also D J Harris, J M O'Boyle & C Warbrick, *Law of the European Convention of Human Rights* (Butterworths: 1995), pp. 7–9.

fundamental safeguards and their right to call a High Contracting Party to account for violation of their rights in proceedings before the Court.[63]

As one part of their argument that the NATO bombing constituted the exercise of effective territorial control, the applicants in *Banković* suggested that if the Court concluded in the negative on this point, this would 'leave a regrettable vacuum in the Convention system of human rights protection,' and would therefore raise the same concern highlighted by the Court in *Cyprus v Turkey*. The Court responded by emphasizing that in *Cyprus v Turkey* it was concerned with the specific type of vacuum created where a population reside in a state that is a party to the Convention— and have therefore already been granted rights under it—but the state is unable to secure those rights because the territory is occupied by another Convention state. The Court asserted that this type of vacuum was 'entirely different' to the vacuum being suggested by the applicants in *Banković*,[64] presumably because the FRY was not a Convention state. It then made its 'legal space' remark:

> In short, the Convention is a multi-lateral treaty operating, subject to Article 56 of the Convention, in an essentially regional context and notably in the legal space (*espace juridique*) of the Contracting States. The FRY clearly does not fall within this legal space. The Convention was not designed to be applied throughout the world, even in respect of the conduct of Contracting States. Accordingly, the desirability of avoiding a gap or vacuum in human rights' protection has so far been relied on by the Court in favour of establishing jurisdiction only when the territory in question was one that, but for the specific circumstances, would normally be covered by the Convention.[65]

This consideration of the 'vacuum' submission and invocation of the 'legal space' doctrine came *after* the Court had already reached a conclusion rendering the case inadmissible, having earlier concluded that the nature of the air strikes by NATO states in the then FRY did not render this territory under the jurisdiction of the states concerned as far as the exercise of effective control was concerned.[66] In principle, the nature of the submission was such that it had the potential to affect all other findings, something perhaps reflected in the way the Court designated it as a distinct argument *and* one that operated 'more generally.'[67] However, the fact that the Court only addressed such a general consideration after *already* disposing of the earlier submissions *without* considering it suggests that it did not play a key part of the outcome of the case.

---

[63] *Cyprus v Turkey*, n 10 above, para. 78.   [64] *Banković*, n 10 above, para. 80.
[65] Ibid (footnote omitted).
[66] Ibid, para. 75.   [67] Ibid, para. 79 ('Fifthly and more generally').

Of course, even if the Court's observations here can be considered in some sense *obiter*, they are an indication of the Court's views on the issue, and we must therefore consider what exactly they amount to even if they do not have strict precedential value.

The first point to make is that the Court's consideration of the original 'design' of the Convention, although reading like a general doctrine, is invoked in the specific context of a submission concerned with an underlying reason for applying the Convention extraterritorially—the avoidance of a vacuum in protection. Moreover, its application in the case is only by way of explaining why, *so far*, this particular underlying reason has been relied upon in the case law in favour of establishing jurisdiction only in relation to actions within the Council of Europe. This is not quite the same thing as saying that the 'legal space' idea *prevented* this particular vacuum concern from being capable of establishing jurisdiction in relation to actions outside the Council of Europe. Given the use of the word 'accordingly,' the most one can conclude is that the Court is pointing out that the current circumstances in which the vacuum concern has been invoked are on all fours with an idea of the original intent of the Convention.

The comment is limited to a historical analysis of the Court's case law, and does not by itself rule out the possibility of a different finding in future cases. To be sure, the Court decided not to take such a step in *Banković*, but in failing to do so having simply explained that it hasn't done so in the past, in a manner in accordance with some idea of the original design of the Convention, it is hardly giving a clear indication that it is *prevented* from doing so.

Moreover, the Court is invoking the 'legal space' idea only in relation to the possibility of being able to *rely on one particular underlying reason* for establishing extraterritorial jurisdiction. This is not the same thing as being able to found extraterritorial jurisdiction itself. It reflects the way in which the 'legal space' concern was treated by the Court in *Cyprus v Turkey*. In that case, the Court affirmed its earlier finding in the *Loizidou* case on the same issue—whether Turkey's presence in Northern Cyprus constituted an exercise of jurisdiction for the purposes of the Convention. In *Loizidou*, the Court held that the

> . . . responsibility of a Contracting Party could also arise when as a consequence of military action – whether lawful or unlawful – it exercises effective control of an area outside its national territory. The obligation to secure, in such an area, the rights and freedoms set out in the Convention, derives from the fact of such control whether it be exercised directly, through its armed forces, or through a subordinate local administration . . . [68]

---

[68] *Loizidou (Merits)*, n 10 above, para. 52.

Crucially, nothing in *this* finding of extraterritorial jurisdiction based on effective control hinges on the presence or absence of a vacuum in protection within the Council of Europe; obligation derives simply from the 'fact' of 'control.' In *Cyprus v Turkey*, the Court affirmed this determination[69] and *then* turned to the particular vacuum issue, holding that 'any other finding' would give rise to this vacuum. Here, then, the Court is giving a reason why a finding *it has already made* serves an important policy objective. This is not the same as suggesting that the necessity of realizing such a policy objective *has* to be present before such a finding can be made. In other words, the Court is remarking that in the particular facts of this case, founding jurisdiction on the basis of effective territorial control serves a particular policy objective; it is *not* asserting that this policy need *has* to be an issue before the exercise of jurisdiction can be found.

The *Al-Skeini* Case

However, in December 2004 the English Divisional Court concluded in the *Al-Skeini* case concerning allegations of abuse by UK soldiers in Iraq that it *was* necessary to establish this *particular underlying* reason—avoiding a vacuum in protection within the Council of Europe when one contracting state acts in another—in order for extraterritorial jurisdiction to exist on the basis of effective control over territory.[70] The Divisional Court acknowledged the findings in *Loizidou* and *Cyprus v Turkey*, observing that in the light of these cases

... it might have been possible to say that, because Turkey's same argument had been dealt with in ... *Loizidou* ... without the benefit of the additional reasoning found in ... *Cyprus v. Turkey* ..., therefore one could pick and choose between the two analyses.[71]

The first thing to say about this is that, as mentioned earlier, there are not two 'analyses' here in the sense of two alternative legal tests—the additional factor was discussed in *Cyprus v Turkey* only in terms of a good reason for a decision the Court had already come to; the cases are identical in terms of the actual *test* they adopt for jurisdiction on the basis of effective control, viz. simply the fact of such control.

Be that as it may, for the Divisional Court what is 'critical' was how the additional factor considered in *Cyprus v Turkey* was then treated the later case of *Banković*.[72] This treatment changed everything: although in *Banković* the vacuum consideration was 'raised by the applicants ... in a

---

[69] *Cyprus v Turkey*, n 10 above, para. 76.   [70] *Al-Skeini*, n 14 above, paras. 276–7.
[71] Ibid, para. 276.   [72] Ibid.

form designed to assist themselves'—ie as a good policy reason for finding the exercise of jurisdiction—it was 'turned against them by the [European] Court for its *true import*,'[73] the true import being that actually it was a *requirement* for jurisdiction to subsist. What explanation does the Divisional Court give for this assertion of a 'true import'? It simply invokes the 'legal space' comment from the *Banković* case mentioned earlier.

However, as we have seen, the passage from *Banković* does not actually support this conclusion. The European Court's comments, which did not seem to be determinative of the outcome of the case, concern an idea—the 'legal space'—conceived only in terms of the original 'design' of the Convention, invoked only by way of explaining how a certain line of cases have come about, without clearly stating that it would prevent other cases that did not fit with the idea, and only discussed in relation to one particular good reason for a finding of extraterritorial jurisdiction, not whether extraterritorial jurisdiction itself exists, either generally or on the basis of effective control.

In sum, a careful consideration of the Court's *dictum* in *Banković* leads to the conclusion that the Court did not hold that the European Convention does not apply to Contracting States outside the territory of other Contracting States, either generally or, as the Divisional Court held in *Al-Skeini*, in cases involving effective control over territory.

Other Strasbourg Cases, including *Issa*

This conclusion is reinforced by other Strasbourg jurisprudence. The *WM* case decided before *Banković* found the exercise of jurisdiction by Denmark acting in what was then East Berlin, at that stage outside the legal space of the Convention,[74] and as we have seen in *Loizidou* and *Cyprus v Turkey*, in cases where the exercise of jurisdiction was found by states acting *within* other contracting states, the fact that the action took place within the territory of a contracting state was never invoked by the Court as a prerequisite for the exercise of jurisdiction.

Moreover, cases *since Banković* have also found the exercise of jurisdiction by states acting outside the Council of Europe. A case involving jurisdiction conceived in a personal sense would be *Öcalan*, where a chamber of the Court held that the actions of Turkish agents in relation to the alleged abduction of Abdullah Öcalan in Kenya—not a Convention state—took place within Turkish 'jurisdiction.'[75] This holding was subsequently

---

[73] Ibid, emphasis added.   [74] *WM v Denmark*, n 10 above.
[75] *Öcalan (Merits)*, n 10 above, para. 93.

affirmed by the Grand Chamber when the case came before it.[76] A case affirming the possibility of jurisdiction conceived in a spatial sense operating outside the Council of Europe is that of *Issa*, again against Turkey, this time in relation to its actions in northern Iraq—the very state at issue in *Al-Skeini*. At the merits stage, the Court stated that it

... does not exclude the possibility that, as a consequence of this military action, the respondent State [Turkey] could be considered to have exercised, temporarily, effective overall control of a particular portion of the territory of northern Iraq. Accordingly, if there is a sufficient factual basis for holding that, at the relevant time, the victims were within that specific area, it would follow logically that they were within the jurisdiction of Turkey (and not that of Iraq, which is not a Contracting State and clearly does not fall within the legal space (*espace juridique*) of the Contracting States.[77]

As the Divisional Court stated in *Al-Skeini*, this suggests that the 'effective control of an area doctrine is essentially a territorial doctrine.'[78] Given its conclusion as to the meaning of the *Banković dictum*, for the Divisional Court the finding in *Issa* was at odds with that earlier *dictum*: 'the doctrine that there is any difference between the *espace juridique* of the Convention and any other space anywhere in the world' had been 'entirely sidelined.'[79] The Divisional Court faced a choice, then, between two supposedly different positions. It opted for its view of the *Banković* position by dismissing the *Issa dictum* in three different ways.

How the Court in *Al-Skeini* Dismissed *Issa*

In the first place, the Divisional Court called into question the European Court's motivation for making its comment in *Issa*. In that case, the European Court considered both *spatial* and *personal* bases for jurisdiction, on the latter concluding on the facts that the alleged human rights violations in question were not proved to have been committed by Turkish soldiers.[80] In the light of this finding on the *personal* basis for jurisdiction, the Divisional Court viewed the European Court's decision to consider also the *spatial* basis for jurisdiction as taking it 'out of its way' to an issue 'it could have avoided.'[81] The Divisional Court puzzled that it is 'not plain' why the European Court did this—presumably meaning that there was no obvious purpose for doing so in terms of the reasoning of the

---

[76] *Öcalan (Grand Chamber)*, n 10 above, para. 91 (quoted above, text relating to note 50).
[77] *Issa*, n 10 above, para. 74. See also *Issa and Others v Turkey*, Application No. 31821/96, Admissibility Decision of 30 May 2000, available at *www.echr.coe.int*.
[78] *Al-Skeini*, n 14 above, para. 219.   [79] Ibid.
[80] *Issa*, n 10 above, paras. 76–81.   [81] *Al-Skeini*, n 14 above, para. 205.

judgment—and because of its puzzlement offered its own conjectural reason: the European Court

... was conscious that claims arising out of the 2003 invasion of Iraq might in due course need consideration.[82]

Here, then, we have the suggestion that the European Court is making a statement it did not need to make for the purposes of judging the case before it, and the speculation that this was motivated by a desire to stake out a position on the applicability of the ECHR to Iraq for wider consumption.

The problem with this comment, which of course undermines the significance of the *dictum* as far as the case is concerned, is that it mis-perceives the relationship between the factual tests under the *spatial* and *personal* headings of jurisdiction as far as state responsibility is concerned. The Divisional Court seems to assume that because the factual test for responsibility under the *personal* heading was not met—the violations could not be imputed to Turkish soldiers—responsibility could not be founded under the *spatial* heading. However, the test under the latter heading, unlike that under the former, does not require the particular acts or omissions giving rise to the alleged violation to be those of agents of the state or actors acting on behalf of it: the key thing here is that they take place within territory that is under the overall control of the state. In the *Cyprus v Turkey* case, which concerned *inter alia* complaints in relation to the actions of the local Turkish Cypriot authorities, as opposed to the Turkish troops occupying Northern Cyprus, in finding Turkey responsible for those actions the Court stated that

[I]t is not necessary to determine whether... Turkey actually exercises detailed control over the policies and actions of the authorities of the 'TRNC'. It is obvious from the large number of troops engaged in active duties in northern Cyprus... that her army exercises effective overall control over that part of the island. Such control, according to the relevant test and in the circumstances of the case, entails her responsibility for the policies and actions of the 'TRNC'... Those affected by such policies or actions therefore come within the 'jurisdiction' of Turkey for the purposes of Article 1 of the Convention... Her obligation to secure to the applicant the rights and freedoms set out in the Convention therefore extends to the northern part of Cyprus.[83]

It follows, then, that in *Issa* the Court was *not* able to dispose of the case merely through its finding on the facts in relation to the *personal* heading

---

[82] Ibid.
[83] *Loizidou (Merits)*, n 10 above, para. 56 and *Loizidou (Preliminary Objections)*, n 10 above, paras. 63–64.

of jurisdiction; although the same sets of facts were of course being considered in relation to both headings of jurisdiction, this consideration operated differently as between the two, and a negative finding under one heading would not necessarily rule out a positive finding under the other.

Turning to the Divisional Court's second basis for dismissing the *Issa dictum*, here the focus was on the European Court's finding on the existence of jurisdiction in the *spatial* category. For the Divisional Court, because the European Court held on the facts that Turkey did not exercise the necessary control over the area to meet the jurisdictional test, it followed that the Court's *dictum* that, if this test was met, the Convention would apply (and that the extraterritorial application of the Convention under the *spatial* heading was not therefore limited to Council of Europe territories) was 'on any view *obiter*.'[84]

This is a bizarre finding: the European Court needed to affirm the relevance of the legal test before applying it—it would make no sense to consider whether Turkey exercised effective control over the area of territory in Iraq if a supposed *espace juridique* limitation would in any case bar the applicability of the Convention—moreover, a court not finding a legal test met on the facts does not necessarily render that court's statement on the meaning of that test *obiter*: what is crucial is whether the finding is determinative of the outcome of the case. If it does, then the Court's articulation of the legal principle being applied forms the heart of the case. As we have seen, because the *spatial* and *personal* bases of jurisdiction are separate, and a finding of one can be made without a finding of the other, it follows that *both* findings in this case determined its outcome. In consequence, the Court's statement of the legal principle it applied in considering the *spatial* basis for jurisdiction forms part of the reasoning of the case, and is not *obiter*.

Indeed, it is remarkable that the Divisional Court made this observation, given the questionable juridical significance of the *Banković dictum* in determining the outcome of that case.

However, the Divisional Court offered a third ground for dismissing the *Issa dictum*:

> . . . in our judgment the dicta in *Issa* . . . are inconsistent with *Bankovic* and the development of the Strasbourg jurisprudence in the years immediately before *Bankovic*. In a sense *Issa* seems to us to look back to an earlier period of the jurisprudence, which has subsequently made way for a more limited interpretation of article 1 jurisdiction. It may well be that there is more than one school of thought at Strasbourg; and that there is an understandable concern that modern

---

[84] *Al-Skeini*, n 14 above, para. 202.

events in Iraq should not be put entirely beyond the scope of the Convention: but at present we would see the dominant school as that reflected in the judgment in *Bankovic* and it is to that school that we think we owe a duty.[85]

Thus the Divisional Court drops the notion of precedent in favour of an idea of what it considers to be the 'dominant' approach within Strasbourg jurisprudence as a whole, following this approach even if flatly contradicted by the most recent case on the issue. Setting aside the problematic nature of this line of reasoning, what is certainly worth considering is the fact that *Issa* is only a Chamber decision whereas *Banković* was a judgment of the Grand Chamber.

None of this is ultimately relevant, however, since the issue of resolving a conflict between *Issa* and *Banković* only arises if the Divisional Court was correct in its finding on *Banković*, which it was not. The correct reading of *Banković* leads to the conclusion that there is no 'legal space' restriction; the later finding by the Court in *Issa* is therefore in harmony with this earlier decision, something which the Court itself affirmed in *Issa*.[86] There is no contradiction, and so no choice to be made, let alone a choice made on the questionable grounds adopted by the Divisional Court in *Al-Skeini*.

Conclusion on the Position Under the ECHR

It will be recalled that in *Banković* the European Court of Human Rights said that

The Convention was not designed to be applied throughout the world, even in respect of the conduct of Contracting States

What is clear from post-*Banković* cases like *Öcalan* and *Issa* is that, in tune with the notion that the Convention is a 'living instrument,' this idea of the original design of the Convention—whatever its truth in terms of the intentions of the drafters—has given way to the notion that the Convention *does* apply to the actions of Contracting States outside the territory of other Contracting States and on the basis of control exercised over either individuals or territory.

The English Divisional Court's mistaken reading of *Banković* in relation to jurisdiction founded on the exercise of control over territory in the *Al-Skeini* case creates the strong possibility that its finding will not survive challenges in higher English courts and/or the European Court of Human

---

[85] Ibid, para. 265.

[86] In its invocation of *Banković* in its comments on the legal nature of the 'effective control over territory' test.

Rights. As things currently stand, the 'legal space' notion is of doubtful significance in operating as a limitation on the extraterritorial application of the ECHR, but it is clearly something that the present UK government will attempt to invoke in order to achieve this effect.

Beyond the ECHR

The *espace juridique* idea has only been put forward in the context of the ECHR, and has not been taken up by any other human rights treaty bodies such as the UN Human Rights Committee in its comments on the ICCPR. It might be argued, then, that even if the doctrine has some limiting effect, it is specific to the ECHR and is not of general application to human rights treaties, notably the ICCPR. So even if on 'legal space' grounds the ECHR does not apply to the UK's exercise of jurisdiction in the territory of non-ECHR-contracting states (or does apply to such jurisdiction but only in the narrow circumstances outlined in *Al-Skeini*), the ICCPR is not limited in this way. Alternatively, the doctrine *could* be applied to other human rights treaties, but of course for those 'universal' treaties it would not have much of a limiting effect, since most states in the world fall within their 'legal space.' Significantly, Iraq is a party to the ICCPR.

International Human Rights Treaties—Overview

Given what has been said about the extraterritorial applicability of the ICCPR, CRC and ICESCR, what we can see, then, is that as a matter of these international human rights treaty law obligations, with the exception of the property right, the UK is obliged to secure all the rights that it has made part of English law through the Human Rights Act in any instance where it exercises control over either individuals or territory abroad, regardless of whether, in the case of UK Overseas Territories, an express extension of the relevant parts of the European Convention and its Protocols have been made, and regardless of whether or not the territory concerned is part of the territory of a state party to the ECHR.

Interpreting the Act

In the light of this picture in international treaty law generally, how should we understand the extraterritorial application of the Human Rights Act? One key principle of statutory interpretation is of course the presumption mentioned earlier that, absent an express contrary provision, Parliament intended to legislate in conformity with the UK's international human rights obligations. Does this require that the rights under the Act apply extraterritorially in the same manner as they apply in international law?

It might be argued that compliance doesn't necessarily require this. A narrower framework of application—limited to UK territory, say, or limited according to the mistaken interpretation of the European Convention discussed earlier—would not go as far as international human rights law generally, specifically the regime under the ICCPR, but it wouldn't *violate* this broader framework. The key thing in terms of conformity to that broader framework would be whether the UK actually adhered to it when acting abroad. In other words, the UK is only obliged not to violate rights abroad; it isn't also obliged to enshrine such an obligation as a matter of its own domestic law.

The problem with this approach is that the UK is also obliged, in the words of the ICCPR, 'to take the necessary steps . . . to adopt such laws or other measures as may be necessary to give effect to the rights recognized' in the Covenant.[87] One aspect of this is ensuring a framework for adhering to its obligations in relation to these rights as a matter of internal practice. In other words, being bound to observe these rights as a matter of international law is not enough: the state must also take steps internally to ensure that the international obligation is followed. The most obvious way in which this happens is through the provision of a 'domestic remedy': domestic redress for individuals complaining of rights violations.

But does this have to be an English law remedy when it relates to acts committed abroad? Indeed, it might be more appropriate in terms of accessibility for a remedy process to be operated in the territory itself. However, for many UK extraterritorial actions the UK is granted sweeping privileges and immunities in the legal system of the country in which it operates, thereby preventing such a remedy in that legal system. Equally, the military court martial system that has led to convictions of UK soldiers for abuses in Iraq clearly falls short of a remedy as far as serving the interests of the victims are concerned, even if it does implement the UK's international obligations in terms of sanctioning those committing human rights abuses.

It is in this broader context that the English courts must understand the significance of applying the Human Rights Act extraterritorially—in failing to enable this either partially or fully, they risk further narrowing

---

[87] ICCPR, Art 2(2).

the range of domestic remedies available, thereby contributing to a state of affairs constituting a breach of the UK's obligations in this regard. Adopting the presumption that Parliament did not intend to act inconsistently with the UK's international law obligations in the light of this broader context, then, it is necessary to interpret the Human Rights Act so as to apply extraterritorially in the same way as the equivalent areas of human rights law operate on the international level.

Conclusion

One main impetus for enacting the Human Rights Act was to end the situation where the UK government was subject to a broader set of human rights obligations in the civil and political sphere in international law than was the case under English law. Although the Act rectified this in large measure by taking most of the rights of the Convention and its Protocols and rendering them part of English law, the trend so far in the few cases on this issue is to conceive the extraterritorial applicability of these rights in a manner falling short of the position in international law. So although a particular right exists in both areas of law, its applicability is narrower in one than in the other, running counter to Parliament's intention to create greater harmony between the domestic and international position.

This is a key moment in the development of this area of law. As has been suggested, the flaws in the High Court's decision in the *Al-Skeini* case create the possibility that higher courts will rectify what is currently a mistaken view of the 'legal space' *dictum* in *Banković* and the scope of extraterritorial jurisdiction based on the exercise of control/power/authority over individuals. More fundamentally, what also needs to be revisited is the underlying assumption that an exclusively Convention-based approach should be followed.

Given the precise manner in which the HRA adopted most of the rights, but not the general obligation, of the Convention and its Protocols, the qualified manner in which the Act obliges the courts to look to Strasbourg jurisprudence in construing the Act, and Parliament's general intention to legislate in conformity with the UK's international obligations, the courts need to move beyond an exclusive focus on the Convention and its Protocols to the relevant areas of international human rights law generally in understanding the extraterritorial application of the Act.

When Judges Fail Justice

*Mr Justice Edwin Cameron**

It is a privilege and a pleasure for me to be with you this evening. The presidency of the Bentham Club is a particular honour. Its sole duty is to deliver tonight's lecture. In fulfilling this office I hope you will not deal with me as Hazlitt, that astute and acerbic English Romantic essayist, dealt with Bentham.[1] He denounced him for writing in a 'barbarous philosophical jargon, with all the repetitions, parentheses, formalities, uncouth nomenclature and verbiage of law-Latin'. Hazlitt—who could, as they say, 'get on a roll'—certainly did so in his critique of Bentham, whom he accused of writing 'a language of his own that darkens knowledge'. His final rebuke to Bentham was the most piquant: 'His works', he said, 'have been translated into French—they ought to be translated into English.' I trust that we will not tonight need the services of a translator.

To introduce my theme I want to take you back nearly twenty years, to 3 September 1984. The place is in South Africa—a township 60 km south of Johannesburg. It is called Sharpeville. At the time its name already had ineradicable associations with black resistance to apartheid—and with the brutality of police responses to it. On 21 March 1960, 24 years before, the police gunned down some sixty unarmed protestors—most of them shot in the back as they fled from the scene.

That bloody event intensified political consciousness in the township, which as the decades passed continued to seethe with resistance to apartheid. The day I recount was also bloody. But the blood was not that of protestors—it was blood drawn by them: that of four local councillors, who served in the local authority structures the apartheid government created in the early 1980s to try to legitimate its increasingly precarious rule over the black urban population.

One death that day was particularly bloody, and particularly poignant. It was the murder of Mr Kuzwayo Jacob Dlamini, the deputy mayor of

* Revised version of the Bentham Lecture delivered at University College, London, on 24 March 2004.
[1] *The Spirit of the Age* (1824/5). I am grateful to Tim Trengove-Jones of the School of Languages and Literature at University of the Witwatersrand for the reference and the quotations.

the local authority covering Sharpeville. His council had decided on an increase in service levies. The increase was to come into effect on 1 September 1984. The decision enraged residents. Council members were seen to be doing the bidding of, and benefiting from, their apartheid masters, and on Monday 3 September 1984 the whole area erupted in violent rebellion.

Early in the morning, protestors converged on Dlamini's Sharpeville home, pelting it with stones. Police arrived and tried to persuade him to leave under escort. Poignantly, perhaps bravely, certainly unwisely, Dlamini refused. A short while later he paid a hideous price. The crowd surrounded his house. Armed with a pistol, he shot into them, wounding one. They then shattered his windows and threw petrol bombs inside, causing a conflagration. Dlamini was forced out. Holding his pistol, he tried to escape. But members of the crowd set upon him. One of them dispossessed Dlamini of his firearm. He was then stoned. While insensate from his injuries, he was set alight with petrol. He died a terrible death at the scene, succumbing to head wounds and to petrol burns.

Nine months later, eight Sharpeville residents were put on trial for their lives for the murder of Kuzwayo Jacob Dlamini. The murder was horrible, and the State was determined to secure convictions—and death sentences. Their case became an international *cause célèbre* when the trial judge sentenced six of the accused to death, and when five judges of the Appellate Division of the Supreme Court of South Africa confirmed their convictions and sentences.[2] The international outrage focused on two particular features of the case. The first was the appeal court's rejection of certain of its own previous pronouncements that a murder conviction required proof of a causal connection between the accused's actions and the victim's death. The second was the shocking absence of mercy in the death sentences imposed on all six.

Until the Sharpeville Six judgment, appellate judges in South Africa had adopted conflicting approaches to the question whether, for a conviction of murder, proof was required that a causal connection existed between the accused's actions and the victim's death. The appeal court now ruled that it was enough if someone with murderous intent engages in overt conduct associating himself with the murderous actions of others. No doubt incensed by the harshness of the death sentences, some extravagant comment abroad misinterpreted and misrepresented the effect of the court's decision. It was wrongly suggested that the court had ruled that mere presence at a crime scene might be enough to secure

---

[2] *S v Safatsa and others* 1988 (1) SA 868 (A).

a murder conviction. That has never been the case in South African law: and neither the Sharpeville Six judgment nor any critical commentators within South Africa, including myself, suggested otherwise. The judgment required that an accused must himself have murderous intent, and must moreover engage in overt conduct that associates himself with the murderous actions of the actual perpetrators.[3]

It is on this basis that the Constitutional Court, applying a carefully balanced standard of constitutional fairness, has upheld the doctrine of common purpose insofar as it dispenses with the necessity for causal connection between accused and fatal consequence.[4]

But in the case of at least one of the Sharpeville Six, about the causative effect of whose conduct there was reasonable doubt, the appeal court's refusal to consider the harsh consequences of the doctrine in the sentencing process led to a shocking outcome. Accused 4 was a young woman called Theresa Ramashamola. Her plight was the second focus for the international outcry. The evidence placed her near the events, which after Dlamini's pistol shot had wounded one of the crowd she encouraged by shouting that he should be killed. Later, when another woman sought to intercede for the dying man, Theresa slapped her. For this, her sole contribution to the murderous events, she was sentenced to hang. There was no proof, or indeed any suggestion, that her conduct had incited or instigated or encouraged the deeds of the actual killers.[5]

The verdicts and sentences seemed extraordinarily harsh. In academic writing[6] and in contributions to the popular press I vehemently attacked the courts' findings. I accused the appeal court of 'widening the doctrines of criminal liability in response to evidence of township revolt'. My criticisms were quoted in the London *Times* and elsewhere; they helped, I believe, to bring Lord Scarman and other dignitaries into the debate. This earned me a personal attack from the Chief Justice, who—clearly holding me responsible for the extravagant misinterpretations of the judgment abroad—labelled criticism of the judgment 'shocking and

---

[3] As emphasised in *S v Mgedezi and others* 1989 (1) SA 687 (A) 705–706, *per* Botha JA (Smalberger and MT Steyn JJA concurring), applying a notably more rigorous standard of factual scrutiny than in *Safatsa*: see 1989 *Annual Survey of South African Law*, 598.

[4] *S v Thebus and another* 2003 (6) SA 505 (CC), *per* Moseneke J on behalf of a unanimous Court on this point.

[5] *S v Safatsa and others*, n 2 above, 894F–G (' . . . it must be accepted without doubt, in my opinion, that no such causal connection can be found to have been proved. This is particularly obvious in the case of accused Nos 2 and 4 . . . ')

[6] 'Inferential reasoning and extenuation in the case of the Sharpeville Six' (1988) 2 South African Journal for Criminal Justice 243–260.

disgraceful'. He also lodged a complaint against me with the Bar Council. By a majority of eleven votes to one, it rejected his attempt to have disciplinary action instituted against me.[7]

In helping to fuel international protests against the death sentences, and in later forming part of the appellate team for the Six (led by Sydney Kentridge QC, who returned from London to argue the case), I did not find it necessary to differentiate between their individual cases. But as a trained lawyer, I found the sentence passed on Theresa Ramashamola, and the conviction of another of the accused, particularly 'bizarre and shocking', as I wrote at the time.[8]

The fact that accused 3 was convicted at all was especially distressing and outrageous. The evidence against five of those sentenced to hang came from eyewitnesses who placed each of them directly at the murderous scene. By contrast, in the case of accused 3 there was no eyewitness evidence. The case against Oupa Moses Diniso rested on inference alone. He was sentenced to hang by lawyerly logic—and the logic in question seemed to me to be shocking in its patent inadequacy.

The murder occurred on 3 September. The police arrested the first accused in the case 67 days later, on 9 November 1984. Within an hour accused 1 (in the language prosecutors put to police witnesses to avoid eliciting inadmissible hearsay evidence), 'made a report' to the police. The 'report' concerned the whereabouts of the pistol taken from the deceased during his mortal struggle. In pursuance of what they were told, three policemen set out from their offices with accused 1. He took them to the home of accused 3. On arrival, the police asked accused 3 if he knew about a firearm allegedly in his possession. He immediately answered 'Yes', and offered to hand it to them. He rummaged in his ceiling, and amidst cardboard boxes and suitcases retrieved a pistol, which he handed to the police. The firearm, a 9mm Star pistol, became exhibit 1 at the trial. It was proved to have belonged to, and to have been licensed in the name of, the murder victim.

Accused 3 told the police that he had taken the pistol from a group of children who were involved in the rioting on 3 September 1984

---

[7] The Minister's and the judges' attacks on my part in the campaign to save the Sharpeville Six and other criticisms of apartheid judges are documented by the late Professor Etienne Mureinik, 'Law and Morality in South Africa' (1988) 105 South African Law Journal 457. Prakash Diar, the Six's attorney, wrote a moving testimony: *The Sharpeville Six* (McLelland & Stewart, London and Toronto, 1990). The bitter counterattack by the appeal court judge who wrote the judgment in the Sharpeville Six case is in *S v Mgedezi and others*, n 3 above, 702–703. My co-authors and I riposted in the 1989 *Annual Survey of South African Law* 598. The Six were released from prison in 1991 as part of a deal between the outgoing apartheid government and the African National Congress.

[8] 'Inferential reasoning', n 6 above, 260.

near the home of councillor Dlamini. He denied involvement in the murder.

He later changed this story slightly. In a statement to a magistrate twelve days later, he repeated that he obtained the pistol from some children. But he now said this happened not on the day of Dlamini's murder, but on the day after, Tuesday 4 September. The youths were no longer involved in the rioting, but arguing about the weapon, which, one said, they had found in a scrapyard. In court he denied that he told the police that he obtained it on the day of the insurrection.

Neither accused 1 nor 3 proffered any explanation for why accused 1 was able to direct the police to the location of the deceased's pistol at the home of accused 3. It was on this evidence, and this evidence alone, that accused 3 was sentenced to hang.

South African law has taken over from English law a practical maxim, rather grandly dubbed 'the doctrine of recent possession'. It is really a rule of inference to the effect that someone caught with 'hot goods' sufficiently soon after a crime without an innocent explanation may reliably be inferred to have obtained the goods through participation in the crime itself. The South African courts have adopted the maxim, and it has played a useful role in convicting accused where the only reasonable inference from possession is guilt of the crime the goods themselves evidence.[9]

But the doctrine of recent possession was clearly inapposite here. Accused 3 was arrested 67 days after the murder. His mere possession of the murdered man's property could not connect him with the crime. There had to be something more. But was there anything?

The trial court found extra inferential material in accused 3's own statements and conduct, and in the conduct of accused 1. Accused 1 was identified as one of the active perpetrators of the murder by the deceased's wife, by an independent witness, and by a poignant declaration of the deceased, who in his dying moments rebuked accused 1, Mojalefa Reginald Sefatsa, by his nickname, 'Ja-Ja'.

So the evidence unquestionably placed him there. And because accused 1 took the police to the home of accused 3, where the dead man's pistol was found, the trial court concluded that 'the only inference' was that accused 3 had wrested the weapon from him in his dying moments. Added to this was the fact that accused 3 had changed his story; and, in addition, refused to accept that the pistol produced in court was the one he took from his ceiling. What sealed this apparent logic, in both courts,

---

[9] *S v Skweyiya* 1984 (4) SA 712 (A) (possession of burgled goods fifteen days after break-in, even without any adequate exculpatory explanation, not enough to conclude that possessor participated in burglary itself).

Edwin Cameron

was that he could give no explanation of how accused 1 knew that he had the firearm.[10]

The flaws in this reasoning, nearly twenty years after Mr Dlamini's murder, and nearly seventeen years after the appeal court decision, seem to me as patent now as they did then.

In convicting accused 3, the appeal court abandoned its own established principles. In particular there were two. The first required that the inference of guilt be the only reasonable inference from the proved facts. The second reminded judges that accused persons frequently lie about details for a variety of reasons that may be compatible with their innocence. One such reason may be a misguided recourse to falsehood for fear that the truth will not ensure exculpation.

On the proved facts accused 3 certainly lied, but his untruths were both trivial and readily explicable. The difference between his initial story about the weapon and what he later said seems insubstantial, and the shift from the day of the murder to the day after more than readily explicable on the basis that he wanted to place some distance between his acquiring it and the murder. Even an innocent person might foolishly try to do that.

Why did accused 3 have no explanation for accused 1 bringing the police to his home? Well, why not? Sixty seven days is nine weeks, two full months and seven days; and in a township, as in any area of crowded human habitation, there are many sources of information and repetition. That the two accused knew each other and that accused 1 knew where accused 3 lived was scarcely incriminating. It hardly strains the imagination to think that accused 1 could have heard from the youths—to take at face value accused 3's first explanation—that they had handed the dead man's weapon to accused 3.

There is a further possibility—one so obvious that, even after nearly twenty years, it still seems remarkable that neither court professed to contemplate it. It is that accused 1, having wrested the weapon from the deceased, handed it to accused 3 for safe keeping, and that—for obvious reasons—neither chose when the game was up to disclose this to the police.[11]

---

[10] The appeal court said it could find 'no warrant for disagreeing' with the trial court: 'Having regard to the nature of the lies told by accused 3 in his evidence, and particularly to the explanation he gave to [the police] as to when and where he obtained the pistol, coupled with his professed inability to explain how accused 1 would have known that he had the pistol, I am of the view that the trial court was fully justified in drawing the inference, as being the only reasonable inference, that accused 3 was the person who had dispossessed the deceased of his pistol'.

S v Safatsa, n 2 above, 891–892 *per* Botha JA (Hefer JA, Smalberger JA, Boshoff AJA and MT Steyn AJA concurring).

[11] If this was the 'report' accused 1 made to the police, it would have incriminated accused 3 as an accessory to the murder, which would explain why it was inadmissible.

What makes this plausible is accused 3's ready response when confronted at his door by the police in the company of accused 1. He acknowledged having the pistol, and readily retrieved it and handed it to the police, when it is by no means certain that a search would have uncovered it. This suggests that he had nothing to hide—or at least that at that point he did not realise the mortal peril that inferred conclusions would place him in.

These possibilities are not only reasonable. They are patent. Yet they were ignored by the trial court and glossed over by the appeal court. The short and incontrovertible point is this. The fact that accused 3 was in possession of the incriminating object, and that accused 1 took the police to his home, by themselves prove no more and no less than that accused 1 knew that accused 3 had the murder victim's pistol. No amount of evasive or untruthful conduct by either accused can add to the inferential weight of that evidence. Beyond it lies only doubt, uncertainty and speculation—in this case, mortally dangerous doubt, uncertainty and speculation.

In defiance of the elementary precepts of criminal justice, accused 3 was never given the benefit of that doubt. Instead, he was sentenced to hang. While the Six were on death row in Pretoria Central Prison, I wrote, with what even now seems to me to be a degree of measured understatement, that the conviction of accused 3, and the death sentence passed on Theresa Ramashamola, 'cannot be said to be in accordance with the standards of judicial reason that one is entitled to expect from a judicial system that calls itself civilised'.[12]

To me the verdict seemed an outrageous curvature of the laws of logic and fairness—a miscarriage of justice symptomatic of the extremities apartheid was inflicting on the legal system. It still does. Fortunately, the Sharpeville Six did not die on the gallows. After months of international outcry, the trial judge, on the day before their scheduled execution, had second thoughts. In response to an application to re-open their case, he granted a stay just sixteen hours before they were due to hang. If they had been hanged, a gross miscarriage of justice would surely have occurred. The international outcry saved their lives. It also saved the country from the explosion that was certain to have followed. In addition, I thought, then and now, it spared the South African judiciary the ignominy their execution would have earned it.

What happened? Why did the Sharpeville Six judges overlook or ignore what seemed to be elementary tenets of civilised reasoning? The question is haunting: and it is by no means unique to South Africa.

The judges may have suspected that the 'report' was more incriminating—that accused 1 identified accused 3 as at the scene. But that would have been intolerably speculative.

[12] 'Inferential reasoning', n 6 above, 260.

In the case of Ethel and Julius Rosenberg, who were sentenced to death by electrocution for passing atomic secrets to the Russians, the final plea brought on their behalf before the Supreme Court of the United States involved a principle that one of the Justices in the divided decision that followed described as 'too elemental for citation of authority'.[13] It concerned the benefit of subsequent amelioration. The question before the Court was whether a convict should have the benefit of an ameliorative punishment introduced after the commission of the crime.

The Rosenbergs were convicted of conspiracy to commit espionage. The prosecution was brought under the Espionage Act of 1917. This entrusted the decision on the death penalty to the trial judge. Many thought that the presiding judge, Judge Kaufman, was bent on exacting the extreme penalty from them. In sentencing the couple to death, he considered their crime as 'worse than murder', putting the blame for the Korean War on them:

... with the resultant casualties exceeding 50,000 and who knows but that millions more of innocent people may pay the price of your treason. Indeed, by your betrayal you undoubtedly have altered the course of history to the disadvantage of our country.[14]

That assessment is now recognised as grotesquely exaggerated. Two recent commentators, no apologists for the Rosenbergs or the left-wing activists of the time, state that the punishment 'far exceeded the crimes':

Even most of those who were persuaded that Julius Rosenberg had [spied], believe that his death sentence should never have been issued or carried out. As for Ethel Rosenberg, the material drawn from KGB archives for this book, along with previously available information, suggests that although she knew of her husband's long and productive work for Soviet intelligence, at most she played only a minor supporting role in that work. In a less-pressured legal and political environment, her actions might have led only to a brief jail term, perhaps not even to her arrest.[15]

Even in the perfervid climate of that time it is doubtful that a unanimous jury could have been found to sentence the couple to death; and it is on this point that their last appeal was pinned. The 1946 Atomic Energy Act, which came into effect on 31 July 1946, prescribed that the penalty of death could be imposed for atomic espionage:

only upon recommendation of the jury and only in cases where the offense was committed with intent to injure the United States.

---

[13] *Rosenberg et al v United States* 346 US 273 (1953) 312 (Douglas J, dissenting).
[14] Quoted in part in the dissenting opinion of Justice Douglas at 346 US 312, and available more fully at *www.law.umkc.edu/faculty/projects/ftrials/rosenb/ROS_SENT.HTM*.
[15] A Weinstein and A Vassiliev, *The Haunted Wood: Soviet Espionage in America—the Stalin Era* (1999) 342.

The overt acts alleged in the indictment were committed in 1944 and 1945, before the 1946 Act came into effect; but the conspiracy to commit espionage with which they were charged was from 1944 until 1950. This meant that the crime of which they were convicted, and for which the death penalty was imposed, occurred within the period of the statute providing an ameliorated punishment.

Despite this, the Supreme Court, in a verdict announced at noon on the day of the Rosenbergs' scheduled execution, voted by six to three not to grant a stay in order to hear full argument on the point. The Rosenbergs were executed that night at 23h00. The Court's reasons were filed 27 days later. Chief Justice Vinson, delivering the main opinion, took the technical view that the 1946 Act 'did not repeal or limit the provisions' of the 1917 Act.[16]

Justice Jackson, with whom the other five members of the majority concurred, said that to give the Rosenbergs the benefit of the 1946 penalty provisions would 'open the door to retroactive criminal statutes', which 'would rightly be regarded as a most serious blow to one of the civil liberties protected by our Constitution'. This argument has a particular air of bogus expediency that does not wash well with history. Application of a subsequent ameliorative provision for the benefit of a criminal can hardly invoke the spectre of retro-active enforcement of criminal penalties to the detriment of others.

In a third opinion, Justice Clark, with whom the majority again concurred, held that 'where Congress by more than one statute proscribes a private course of conduct, the Government may choose to invoke either applicable law'.[17] To his judgment he added a sonorous postscript: 'Our liberty is maintained only so long as justice is secure. To permit our judicial processes to be used to obstruct the course of justice destroys our freedom.'[18]

The implication was that 'the course of justice' required the execution of the Rosenbergs, and that a decision against would imperil liberty. These arguments the three dissenters showed up for the tawdry makeweights they were. Justice Black called the Chief Justice's argument that the courts could give effect to either statute 'a strange argument in any case, but . . . still stranger . . . in a case which involves matters of life and death'.[19]

Justice Frankfurter pointed out that the jury could have found only one conspiracy—and that was the conspiracy averred in the indictment, which lasted from 1944 to 1950. The ameliorating statute accordingly

---

[16] n 13 above, 289. [17] Ibid, 294. [18] Ibid, 296. [19] Ibid, 299.

covered it. As for the Court's argument that the government could choose under which statute to prosecute, he said that it needed 'only statement' to be rejected:

Nothing can rest on the prosecutor's caprice in placing on the indictment the label of the 1917 Act or of the 1946 Act. To seek demonstration of such an absurdity, in defiance of our whole conception of impersonality in the criminal law, would be an exercise in self-stultification . . .

These considerations . . . cut across all the talk about repeal by implication and other empty generalities on statutory construction.[20]

The dissent of Justice Douglas—who had issued the stay the majority vacated—was the most emphatic and the most sombre: ' . . .[I]t is too elemental for citation of authority that where two penal statutes may apply—one carrying death, the other imprisonment—the court has no choice but to impose the less harsh sentence.'[21]

Rebecca West described the execution of the Rosenbergs as 'an act as discreditable to our civilization as the crime it punished'.[22] In that act the Supreme Court of the United States participated by its rejection of an elementary principle of criminal justice. Their deaths, at the height of the McCarthyite furore in the United States, raised and continue to raise haunting questions about the utility of legal principle in times of great national anxiety and preoccupation with threat.

This country, the source of so many of the salutary principles of the criminal law applied in Anglophone and common law jurisdictions across the world, itself does not escape the charge that its judges have at crucial times failed justice. The instance I cite concerns a character on any account less engaging than the Rosenbergs or the Sharpeville Six. It is the case of William Joyce, Lord Haw-Haw, who was hanged for treason at Wandsworth Prison on 3 January 1946. Joyce was a fascist and an anti-Semite who when the war broke out left England for Germany, from where between 18 September 1939 and 30 April 1945 he broadcast virulent Nazi propaganda to England. He was captured near the Danish border four weeks after his last broadcast, returned to England and put on trial for treason.

His trial was called 'the most spectacular of all the war-crimes trials that were to take place in England'.[23] Joyce's adherence to the Nazi cause was indisputable and was proved with ease. The difficulty was that he was not a British subject. He was born in Brooklyn, New York, in 1906, of an Irish

---

[20] *Rosenberg et al v United States* 346 US, 306–307.   [21] Ibid, 312.
[22] Quoted in C Franklin, *World-Famous Trials*, 283.
[23] F Selwyn, *The Crime of Lord Haw-Haw* (1987), 191.

father who emigrated to the United States in 1888 and became a naturalised American. Joyce's mother was English, but she also became American, for when she returned to her native town in Lancashire in 1917, she was required to register as an alien. Joyce was therefore a natural-born American citizen. He never acquired British citizenship.

Joyce's family went to Ireland when he was a boy and then came to England in 1921, when he was fifteen. Twelve years later, in 1933, he applied for a British passport. In doing so he described himself as 'a British subject by birth'. This was false. He also claimed that he had been born in Galway, Ireland. This too was false. But his lies secured Joyce a British passport. He renewed it in 1938 and again in 1939, just one week before the war broke out. It was on this passport that he left the country to adhere to the German cause.

The indictment alleged that Joyce committed treason between 18 September 1939 and 2 July 1940 when his passport expired. That Joyce, as an alien, owed the Crown allegiance while he was resident in the realm was undisputed. But no non-subject had ever been tried in England for the crime of treason committed abroad, and indeed there was no reported case of any court in the United Kingdom that had assumed jurisdiction to try an alien for an offence committed abroad.[24] The questions his trial raised were whether a British court could try an alien for a crime committed abroad; and, if it could, whether the fact that Joyce had applied for and obtained a British passport imposed on him a duty of allegiance during its currency even when he was no longer in any British realm.[25]

On these questions, the trial judge, Mr Justice Tucker, instructed the jury that Joyce owed allegiance to the British crown through his possession of the passport renewed in his name in August 1939, and that nothing happened thereafter to put an end to the allegiance he owed.[26] Joyce appealed to the Court of Appeal on the grounds that the trial court had wrongly assumed jurisdiction to try him, and that the judge had wrongly instructed the jury that he owed allegiance to the Crown. The Court of Appeal dismissed his appeal in November.

But the Attorney-General granted a certificate that his case involved a 'point of law of exceptional public importance'. The House of Lords heard Joyce's appeal in December 1945. A week before Christmas they announced their decision. By a majority of four to one they dismissed the appeal. Only Lord Porter dissented.

---

[24] See the argument of Slade QC on behalf of Joyce reported at [1946] AC 360.
[25] See J W Hall (ed), *The Trial of William Joyce* (1946), 15. Hall's introduction to his volume is also in J Mortimer, *Famous Trials* (originally edited by H & JH Hodge) (1984), 346–376.　　　　　[26] Hall (ed), *Joyce*, n 25 above, 215 (summing up).

In reasons furnished four weeks after Joyce was executed, the majority held that a passport, even one falsely obtained by an alien not entitled to it, not only gives rights but imposes duties.[27] The argument on behalf of Joyce that a passport is only a request to a foreign potentate and a command to a British representative to afford the holder assistance, from which no right to protection is derived when the holder is in fact not a British subject,[28] was rejected. The Crown in issuing a passport, the Lords held, assumed 'an onerous burden', which conferred on the holder substantial privileges. By claiming the protection of the Crown, he thereby pledged the continuance of his fidelity.[29]

Lord Porter dissented on the ground that it was for the jury to decide whether the duty of allegiance Joyce owed while in England had continued after he left for Germany. This would depend on whether he retained and used his passport until 18 September 1939, the date of his first broadcast. If he did not, he could not be guilty of treason. There was no evidence that Joyce had kept the passport. Indeed, 'he may have used it only to gain admittance to Germany and may then have discarded it.'[30] A reasonable jury, properly directed, may have considered that Joyce's allegiance had terminated on his departure from England. Pointing in this direction, Lord Porter observed, were the fact that the passport was not found in Joyce's possession 'nor anything further known of it', his statement that he intended becoming naturalised in Germany, and his acceptance of a post from the German state.[31] The judge's ruling was therefore wrong, and the appeal ought to have been upheld.[32]

Even leaving aside the pivotal and questionable decision on the point of law, Lord Porter's stand on the necessity for a jury determination of the continuance of Joyce's allegiance seems quite unanswerable.

The defensive tone of the speech by the Lord Chancellor, Lord Jowitt, seems to reflect this. It contains an attempt at self-justification:

It is not for his Majesty's judges to create new offences or to extend any penal law and particularly the law of high treason, but new conditions may demand a reconsideration of the scope of the principle. It is not an extension of penal law to apply its principle to circumstances unforeseen at the time of its enactment, so long as the case is fairly brought within its language.[33]

---

[27] *Joyce v Director of Public Prosecutions* [1946] AC 347 (HL) 369.
[28] Argument of Slade QC on behalf of Joyce, at [1946] AC 353.
[29] *Joyce v DPP*, n 27 above, 370–371.   [30] Ibid, 380.   [31] Ibid, 381–382.
[32] R West, *The Meaning of Treason* (1949, 1965, Virago edition 1982) surprisingly errs in her assessment of the significance of Lord Porter's dissent, saying that he regarded Tucker J's summing up 'as a misdirection to the jury on a minor technical point' (p. 52).
[33] *Joyce v DPP*, n 27 above, 366.

The question for history is whether the conduct of William Joyce was fairly brought within the criminal law of England. Writing almost immediately after the events, JW Hall was openly sceptical. Existing law, he pointed out, suggested that 'the protection of the bearer is the object of a passport, but not that the right to protection springs from the passport'. This, he said, 'seems to have been a novel doctrine in the present case'.[34] That a non-citizen should be hanged for treason by a novel doctrine itself seems to be an affront to justice.

Hall also observed, drily, that the reasoning underlying the Lords' decision was 'a legitimate subject of legal discussion':

[I]t would be untrue to pretend that it meets with unanimous acceptance among lawyers, many—possibly a majority—of whom thought the appeal would succeed.[35]

He doubted whether Joyce's broadcasts deserved hanging. If fear of a public outcry inhibited a reprieve, he said, 'the first function of a legal system is to substitute the reasoned and dispassionate judgment of the law for the clamour of popular prejudice'. But, he said, there would not have been an outcry:

for very much to my surprise I have found, with a universal reprobation of Joyce's conduct, an almost equally universal feeling, shared by lawyers and laymen, servicemen and civilians, that (with the utmost respect to the eight out of the nine learned judges) the decision was all wrong, and that an unmeritorious case has made bad law. The feeling, and it is, I believe, strong and widespread, is not so much that Joyce, having been convicted, should have been reprieved, but that he should not have been convicted.[36]

The *Manchester Guardian* at the time wished that Joyce had been convicted 'on something more solid than a falsehood'.[37] Writing in 1965, AJP Taylor echoed this. He concluded that Joyce had been 'executed on a trumped-up charge', whose 'tawdry basis' was allegiance through his passport. In substance, Taylor thought, the charge against Joyce was not proved, while 'technically, [he] was hanged for making a false statement when applying for a passport, the usual penalty for which is a small fine.'[38]

Taylor's criticism is overblown. But misgivings have rightly persisted about both Joyce's conviction and his execution, and the suspicion is inescapable that the law was tailored to his case. If he had evaded capture

---

[34] Hall (ed), *Joyce,* n 25 above, 29.   [35] Ibid, 33.   [36] Ibid, 35–36.
[37] Quoted in *The Trial of William Joyce—Notes from the Editors,* 'Introduction by T.G. Barnes', 14 (attributing another source), and in Selwyn, *Lord Haw-Haw,* n 23 above, 212.
[38] *Joyce—Notes,* n 37 above, 13.

for just a year or two, there seems little doubt that he would have escaped the gallows.[39] Even Rebecca West, who was dismissive about others' misgivings about Joyce's verdict, conceded that there was:

some merit behind the public's regret that Joyce had been sentenced to death... We are all afraid lest the treatment of Joyce had been determined by our emotions and not by our intellects: that we had been corrupted by our Nazi enemies to the extent of calling vengeance by the name of justice.[40],

As a response to the moral issues the Second World War created for judges, the decision of the majority of the House of Lords in *Joyce v DPP* ranks as scarcely more creditable than that in *Liversidge v Anderson*,[41] and the dissent of Lord Porter, though less memorably phrased, as courageous, truthful and unanswerable as that of Lord Atkin.

What do these cases tell us about the law? Each involved defendants in peril for their lives during a time of great national trauma:

- *Joyce* in the bleak aftermath of the Second World War, while Britain was enervated from its struggle, with the spectre of what a Nazi victory would have entailed still fresh;
- *Rosenberg* during the great fear of Communist subversion and attack that held the United States in thrall in the early 1950s; and
- the *Sharpeville Six* at the height of white South Africa's final crisis of governance, as the townships exploded and mob rule seemed to threaten.

Each case was decided amidst controversy; and its result was immediately attacked as unjust and incorrect and a misapplication of the law. The flaws in the three decisions were not revealed only by hindsight—and the passing decades have vindicated the dissenters, and with them the contemporary critics.

Each could moreover have been decided according to available legal doctrine. These were not cases where the law seemed to have reached its limit, where conflicting rule or principle abounded, where innovation seemed essential, or the uncertain slopes of legal creativity had to be surmounted. None of the cases involved intrinsically difficult, novel or even particularly interesting questions. Nor were they cases decided

---

[39] Selwyn, *Lord Haw-Haw*, n 23 above, 212. Selwyn also observes percipiently (p. 222): 'In the story of his downfall there are too many voices hinting at a failure of justice to leave one entirely at ease. It is as if the tenacity of his defender and the fairness of his prosecutor counted for less than some communal and unconscious compulsion of the time.'

[40] *The Meaning of Treason*, n 32 above, 52.

[41] [1941] 3 All ER 338, 1942 AC 206 (HL).

wrongly because of the absence of adequate advocacy. Each was strenuously argued and the courts in each were enjoined to accept the available doctrine.

The cases indeed called for the conservative application of existing legal principle. In the first the House of Lords had available to it the existing law of allegiance governing non-resident aliens; in the second, the Supreme Court an elementary principle of justice concerning subsequent extenuation; in the third, the Appellate Division the basic rules of inferential logic. Yet in each the judges, or those in the majority, rejected what was accessible to them.

What the cases also have in common is that, despite the judges' failure to apply existing legal principles, it has never been suggested that the decisions were the product of untoward influence or political subservience or corrupt adherence to improper or ulterior motive. Decisions can of course be corrupt, and judges can be corrupted. This occurs in the absence of honest commitment to legal principle. The judges of Nazi Germany and of Stalin's Soviet Union were corrupt in this way. It has even been suggested that the decision of the majority of the United States Supreme Court in *Bush v Gore*[42] was bent by partisan political allegiance.

But in each of the three cases I have discussed the good faith and conscientiousness of the prevailing judges have never been put in doubt. Wrong they may have been; lacking in rigour and perhaps even in courage; but by their own lights not alien to an honest effort to apply the law.

Lords Macmillan and Wright, who found against Joyce, are rated highly amongst the last century's law lords. Most of the justices who held against the Rosenbergs went on, a year later, to decide *Brown v Board of Education*,[43] often cited as a moral high point of judicial determination. In South Africa, the transition to democracy unexpectedly made me the colleague, in my first years in the Supreme Court of Appeal, of two of the members of the Sharpeville Six bench, with both of whom I sat frequently in appeals. One is a man of compassionate religious conviction whose long appellate career has justly earned him stature. The other, even in retirement, has such a commanding intellect and judicial presence that President Mbeki appointed him last year to head a highly charged inquiry into whether the National Director of Public Prosecutions had been an apartheid spy. His conduct of the investigation gained him national renown and respect.

The fact that these cases were decided by judges not overtly or demonstrably swayed by political expedient makes them in some sense more

---

[42] 531 US 98 (2000); see A Dershowitz, *Supreme Injustice: How the High Court Hijacked Election 2000* (Oxford University Press, 2001).   [43] 347 US 483 (1954).

troubling. Corruption for political expedient or financial gain is a fraud upon the law. Its effects, while devastating, are plain. While not always easy to apply, the remedy is not complicated. It has nothing to do with legal principle or its application.

But if otherwise conscientious judges fail justice when accused are in peril of their lives, as did the House of Lords, the Supreme Court and the Appellate Division, then it raises questions about the utility of law and of legal process at just those times when they are most needed.

Why then did the judges fail justice? What the cases seem to have in common is that currently available legal doctrine, if applied, dictated an outcome that seemed unpalatable or even unmerited—in the case of Joyce, his escaping a conviction of treason on what seemed very close to a technicality; in the case of the Rosenbergs, evasion of the electric chair on a lately proffered, formalistic argument of statutory applicability; in the case of the Sharpeville accused, their walking free when suspicion reasonably suggested their involvement in the murder.

In each case it seems that the judges must have flinched from the outcome. It is in this sense that the cases were the converse of those contemplated by the adage 'hard cases make bad law'. That adage forbids the deflection of legal principle for compassionate reasons in order to accommodate cases that appeal to the judge's sympathy.

Our cases illustrate the opposite—the deflection of legal principle because the outcome repelled the judges' sympathies. The conventional adage warns against the pursuit of seemingly benign consequences because of damage to legal values. Our cases show the converse—the damage caused to legal values by deflection of principle in order to avoid seemingly malign consequences.

Apart from the fact that in two of the cases the consequences were quite fatal for their subjects, the damage the decisions caused to belief in the law and its consistent application was enormous.

The reason is obvious. The test of law cannot be its application where consensus exists about a palatable outcome. The true test is when its application yields consequences that are most unpalatable. Our cases warn us that in times of crisis the law, even when its application seems clear, and even when it is administered by honest and well-meaning judges, might offer no safe refuge for those in peril. They suggest that the fabric of legal principle and legal reasoning is often fragile, and its values all too precarious.

They also offer more heartening instruction, however, for the best purpose in looking back is to see better ahead; and in looking back it is a grave error to patronise the failings of the past, by thinking that the mistakes we discern in them are too obvious for us to make ourselves.

To think so is to miss the point, for history's challenges are cyclical, and its moral confrontation never-ending.

For lawyers and judges, this means that cases like *Liversidge v Anderson*, *Joyce v DPP*, *Rosenberg v US* and the Sharpeville Six will recur; and the guise in which they will recur will not be the Nazi menace of the 1930s and 1940s, or the Communist subversion of the 1940s and 1950s, or the threat of mob violence white South Africans created for themselves in the 1980s. They will find new forms in which to challenge our commitment to legal principle and the rule of law.

They already have. For the threat to modern civilisation posed by religious extremists (who come in many forms) offers particularly challenges to the law and its values. The challenge to us as lawyers is not to degrade the principles and the values we hold civilised by failing justice, but to apply them also when we find the result of their application least acceptable.

In the 27th FA Mann lecture last year,[44] Lord Steyn pointed eloquently to one imminent challenge: the invocation of the courts' jurisdiction over those detained at Guantánamo Bay by the United States government because they are suspected of involvement in the al Qaeda terrorist network.[45] There will be others. As these challenges present themselves to us, as judges, academics and practitioners, our fidelity to law will be tested by our willingness to accept what may seem to be unpalatable outcomes.

There was certainly suspicion that Oupa Moses Diniso was at that terrible scene when Mr Dlamini was murdered in Sharpeville in 1984. But it was never proved. And William Joyce was certainly a Nazi adherent who spattered vile propaganda over England when it was at its most vulnerable. But in doing so he did not commit treason. And the Rosenbergs, it seems increasingly clear, did pass atomic secrets to the Russians. But by established principles of civilised justice they did not deserve to die.

Judges failed justice in each of their cases. Their failure teaches us important lessons not only about the fragility of the craft we profess, but about our own fallibility in applying it. But these cases, or their equivalents, will be back. As they already are. They are back in as unattractive, threatening and unpalatable guises as when their first manifestations were decided. The difference is that we have the opportunity to learn from our predecessors' failures. The accretion of wisdom from failed experience is one—and only one—of the marvels of legal reasoning and the proud history of the values that it invokes.

---

[44] Lord Steyn, 'Guantánamo Bay: The Legal Black Hole', 27th FA Mann Lecture, 25 November 2003.

[45] Which the United States Supreme Court has happily resolved in favour of the courts' jurisdiction in *Rasul v Bush* 124 S.Ct. 2686 (2004) (US).

Prosecutors, Courts and Conduct of the Accused Which Engages a Qualified Human Right

Jonathan Rogers[*]

In this paper, I wish to examine some of the problems which arise when a person is accused of criminal conduct which engages a qualified right under the European Convention Human Rights (ECHR), and where he claims that his prosecution or punishment violates that right. This is a broad topic, and so I should immediately draw attention to two important limitations which are contained within my opening sentence. First, the concentration upon the 'qualified' rights means that I will only be discussing the compatibility of criminal proceedings with Articles 8, 9, 10, and 11 of the ECHR.[1] Second, I will not be discussing exactly when conduct of the accused *does* 'engage' one of these rights: rather, I shall sidestep the issue of engagement by discussing only cases where human rights lawyers would readily agree that the circumstances of the conduct as the defendant alleges them to be were clearly such that one of these rights *is* engaged.[2] One familiar example of the sort of case which I have in mind is the liability of a sado-masochist under section 20 of the Offences Against the Person Act 1861, for injuring a consenting partner:[3] he may claim that criminal proceedings violate his right of privacy under

---

[*] I am grateful to those of my colleagues at UCL who challenged some of my ideas in this paper after I delivered my lecture, and especially to the (anonymous) referees who also suggested how I might better present them. I remain fully responsible for the contents, errors and all.

[1] Sometimes there may be a violation of one of these Articles only if read together with the right against discrimination in Art 14. But, as is well known, a state cannot violate Art 14 in isolation, and so a violation is still only possible if the conduct of the accused engaged one of the rights in Arts 8–11.

[2] See instead A Ashworth and B Emmerson, *Human Rights and Criminal Justice* (Sweet & Maxwell, 2001) ch 8 which deals with the scope of these Articles and cites the case law concerning prosecutions for conduct which arguably engages those rights.

[3] He would be liable for any injuries in domestic law notwithstanding the consent of his partner if he intended to cause harm for the sake of its enjoyment: *R v Brown* [1993] 2 All ER 75 (HL).

Article 8(1) ECHR. Another example is the prosecution of a political activist for insulting or alarming another, under section 5 of the Public Order Act 1986:[4] he will claim that proceedings violate his right to freedom of expression under Article 10(1) ECHR. My reason for limiting this Paper to the qualified rights is that they expressly allow state interference in the enjoyment of a right in order to promote or protect certain state interests, and my purpose in this Paper is to discuss how the justifications for state interference should apply to the process of prosecution and to the infliction of punishment.

Justifying State Punishment

It will be as well to say a few introductory words about the qualified Convention rights and about the importance of theories of crime reduction before I outline my arguments in this Paper. I should say something at once about the justifications which are open to the state for criminalising and punishing conduct which engages a qualified Convention right. In each of Articles 8–11, there is a second paragraph which justifies state interference. Article 10(2) of the ECHR is typical, and it justifies state interference with free speech where it is:

prescribed by law[5] and . . . necessary[6] in a democratic society in the interests of national security, territorial integrity or public safety, for the prevention of disorder or crime, for the protection of health or morals, for the protection of the reputation or rights of others, for preventing the disclosure of information received in confidence, or for maintaining the authority and impartiality of the judiciary.

It follows that, if an activity might engage the right under Article 10, then the state which proposes to punish for it must act with the aim of pursuing any of those state interests. If there is no such conceivable aim, then the prosecution will necessarily be incompatible with the Convention right.

---

[4] For a recent overview of the scope of this offence, see A Geddis, 'Free Speech Martyrs or Unreasonable Threats to Social Peace?—"Insulting" Expression and section 5 of the Public Order Act 1986' [2004] PL 853.

[5] This requirement will be satisfied provided that the legislature has enacted a criminal offence with sufficient precision to allow well-informed citizens to predict what behaviour may be prohibited by it. I shall say no more about that, not least because in the context of punishment, any interference *not* prescribed by law ought to found a separate violation under Art 7 of the ECHR.

[6] The courts in Strasbourg read this to mean '*absolutely* necessary', and even more importantly, they also read in the words 'and proportionate' afterwards. See *Handyside v United Kingdom* (1979–1980) 1 EHRR 737 at paras. 48–49, *The Sunday Times v United Kingdom* (1979) 2 EHRR 245 at 277–278.

Thus a prosecution for treason[7] would be incompatible with Article 10 of the ECHR if the accused person had done no more than to advocate the peaceful abolition of the monarchy, since that conduct would engage the right under Article 10(1) and punishment of it could not conceivably be necessary to preserve any of the state interests which are listed under Article 10(2).[8] So, if that were the natural meaning of the words which define the offence, then the courts would have to (re)interpret the legislation, 'so far as it is possible to do so' in order to find an interpretation which would avoid the conviction of the accused. In such cases then, defence lawyers, so far unable to challenge gross examples of over-criminalisation by the legislature, may now argue that punishment of the accused would violate a Convention right.

But we should not get too excited by this. Unless the prosecutor over-looks the Convention right altogether, he is unlikely to prosecute where there is not even arguably a relevant state interest to be protected. Moreover, these state 'interests', as we can see, are very broadly described. Far more typical are those examples with which we started, where one can see that a prosecution *might* be connected with the promotion of a state interest. For example, the punishment of the consensual sado-masochist might be needed in order to 'protect health or morals' (or perhaps 'the rights of others', if there is some doubt over the consent of the victim). Similarly, one might argue that the prosecution of the protester is necessary and proportionate to protect 'the rights of others' if there is evidence that others were alarmed or offended by the conduct of the accused.[9] So the questions which will concern us in this article will be how it can be said to be necessary and proportionate to seek the punishment of anyone in order to protect or promote any of the relevant state interests (ie the protection of health and morals, or the rights of others, etc)? To say that one can safeguard health *by punishment of one who has done something to risk another's health* clearly presupposes much about what punishment can achieve, and inevitably this area of law engages much of the literature about purposes of punishment in the criminal law.

---

[7] Contrary to s 3 of the Treason Act 1848, which includes acts which 'imagine . . . to depose our Most Gracious Lady the Queen . . . from the style, honour, or royal name of the imperial crown of the United Kingdom'.

[8] *R v Attorney-General, ex parte Rusbridger* [2003] UKHL 38 (HL).

[9] But we should note right away that punishment of conduct which engages a right cannot be justified on the basis that it would be necessary to 'prevent crime', *if that were to refer to the same crime for which the defendant is being punished*, for that would be circular. The state interest in 'preventing crime' is allowed in the ECHR because it may instead justify *other* state interferences, eg in detecting criminal activity which itself does not engage any human right. See, eg, *Khan v United Kingdom* (2000) 8 BHRC 310.

That being so, it is astonishing how little attention has been given to this point in academic journals, and even in the case law. Only the European Court of Human Rights has referred in terms to an aim of punishment which can explain it as needed to secure a state interest, namely general deterrence,[10] whilst our domestic courts seem to have managed to avoid explicit reference to *any* purpose of punishment. But there can be little doubting that some theory of crime reduction, and probably general deterrence more often than not, is uppermost in their minds. For example, the House of Lords recently decided that it would not infringe a juror's right of free expression to punish him for contempt of court when he disclosed jury deliberations to the family of the defendant, since jurors were warned about the offence of contempt and moreover the juror 'would know that he could draw his worries to the attention of the trial judge before the jury returned their verdict'.[11] If all the warnings given by the judge and by court officials are to be ineffective (as they were in that case) and if 'maintaining the authority and impartiality of the judiciary' is an important state interest (which it is held to be), then it is reasonable to conclude that it is necessary and proportionate to punish the recalcitrant juror in order to convey the seriousness of the offence to future jurors, and by so doing, *to deter them* from the temptation of unauthorised disclosures.

One might object to that. The purpose of punishment here might simply be the communication of the values which underpin the offence of contempt of court, and it may be neither here nor there whether punishment would have a deterrent effect. Indeed, the objection might continue, theories of general deterrence (and to some extent other measures of crime reduction too) are not only prone to cause injustice but there is very little empirical support for the intuitive notion that punishment to reinforce the messages of the substantive law does affect behaviour.[12] But to say that a state must justify its decision to punish by reference to crime reduction is not at all to decry the alternative theories of denunciation, retribution or communication, and so on. Surely we *do* sometimes punish for one or more of these reasons alone. Rather, it is to say that to seek to communicate the value of the criminal law may suffice as a general theory of punishment, but not where the conduct of the accused engaged a qualified Convention right. The right (eg to privacy)

---

[10] *Laskey, Jaggard and Brown v United Kingdom* (1997) 24 EHRR 39 at para. 44. I shall discuss this case further below: see the text relating to n 40 below.

[11] *Attorney-General v Stotcher* [2005] UKHL 36 (HL) at para. 29.

[12] P Robinson and J Darley 'Does Criminal Law Deter? A Behavioural Science Investigation' (2004) 24 OJLS 173

should only be trumped by a compelling utilitarian value, and the mere communication of a competing value (eg the state interest in the health of its citizens) will not suffice, at least not unless the benefits of communication (ie about the risks which certain conduct poses to health) might, at least arguably, include the possibility of a reduction in the type of activity which is being punished.[13]

In fact, the best authority for the privileged role of crime reduction in determining substantive criminal law as it is affected by human rights is to be found in the doctrine of positive obligations, under which compliance with a Convention right requires the state to criminalise certain conduct and to prosecute offenders[14] in order to safeguard as best it can the rights of victims. Thus, states have been found to be in violation of the Convention where sexual[15] or physical abuse of children[16] is harder to prosecute successfully than it has any good reason to be. Here, the test for deciding whether the state needs to take extra measures to punish the offender rather than, say, make a remedy in tort available to the victim, is whether the extra deterrent effect of the criminal law is needed to prevent the repetition of such conduct.[17] Admittedly, it need not follow from the privileged role of deterrence in the doctrine of positive obligations that there is an equally privileged role for deterrence when the state wishes to interfere with a Convention right of the accused. When the state is already prepared to seek punishment, so the argument goes, it might be allowed to choose from a number of purposes of punishment. The answer to this, however, is not to allow communication as a purpose of punishment when the conduct of the accused engages a right, but rather to allow the state a generous measure of appreciation in deciding whether punishment is likely to have a worthwhile effect in crime reduction. The question in each case should be whether a state might, or might not, legitimately insist that it is necessary and proportionate for it to seek to punish conduct for the purposes of reducing the harm to the state interest which is associated with that activity, notwithstanding that empirical evidence

---

[13] Art 18 ECHR ensures that the pursuance of a legitimate state interest must be *the* motivating force behind state interference ('The restrictions permitted under this Convention to the said rights and freedoms shall not be applied for any purpose other than those for which they have been prescribed').

[14] The United Kingdom was required six years ago, in *A v United Kingdom* (1999) 27 EHRR 611, to do more than it had been doing (essentially by reforming the criminal law) to offer effective deterrence to parents who beat their children. See generally J Rogers, 'Applying the Doctrine of Positive Obligations in the European Convention on Human Rights to Domestic Substantive Criminal Law in Domestic Proceedings' [2003] Crim LR 690.

[15] *X and Y v Netherlands* (1985) 8 EHRR 235, *MC v Bulgaria* Application No 39272/98.　　　　　　　　　　　　　　　[16] *A v United Kingdom*, n 14 above.

[17] J Rogers, 'Applying the Doctrine', n 14 above, 693–694.

of the efficacy of that punishment may be lacking. This means that, in comparison with the doctrine of positive obligations, much more needs to be said about deference to Parliament (or about the margin of appreciation,[18] if one is discussing the review by the European Court of Human Rights in Strasbourg) when one discusses the justification of punishment raised by the state itself for its use of punishment in the protection of one of its own interests.

I am now in a position to outline my arguments in this paper. In the first part, I shall discuss the situation where the prosecution must persuade the judge that, on the facts of the case, it can be said to be necessary and proportionate to punish the accused in order to protect a state interest. We shall discuss in particular how the mysteries of specific and general deterrence might be debated in the courtroom, and will conclude the part with some observations about the respective responsibilities of the prosecutor and the judge. In the second part, I shall discuss the relatively rare occasions where it is clearly the legislative view that it is necessary to punish *all* instances of a certain activity in order to protect a state interest, and that no distinctions need to be made depending upon the facts of the case. I shall argue that additional duties fall upon the prosecutor when exercising prosecutorial discretion in such cases. Having suggested this distinction between offences where the compatibility of prosecution and punishment with the relevant Convention right should depend upon the facts of the case, and those offences where it does not, in the third part I shall criticise the judiciary for having blurred this distinction thus far, mostly because they have been too quick to defer to the generalised judgments of Parliament.

Offences Where Justifying Punishment Depends on the Circumstances of the Alleged Offence

How, then, should one decide whether (say) punishing a sado-masochist is necessary and proportionate for the protection of health? The simplest view would be that one should take a generic view of such matters: since punishing at least some sado-masochists might be effective in protecting health, it should be possible to punish *all* sado-masochists for that purpose, and to trust that prosecutorial discretion would weed out cases

---

[18] For analysis of the argument that the margin of appreciation is a doctrine of international law which need not be applied in domestic law, see H Fenwick, 'The Right to Protest, the Human Rights Act and the Margin of Appreciation' (1999) 62 MLR 491 at 500–505.

where very little danger to any of the health of the participants was evident, or that such cases could at the least attract lesser sentences. This generic view would certainly be the simplest solution as far as determining the criminal liability of the accused is concerned, since it would effectively preserve the status quo. But it overlooks the fact that a state might interfere with a Convention right simply by its decision to criminalise an activity,[19] even if its public prosecutors never intend to initiate proceedings. Provided that those whose activities are criminalised would not 'sleep soundly at night' through fear of prosecution there is a violation by the state.[20] So to criminalise an activity simply because that would cover a few instances where punishment might be necessary would likely be disproportionate to the aim of crime reduction. Yet there might be a pressing need to provide for punishment of those very few cases. So, the solution should be to criminalise the activity but for it to be understood that in those cases where punishment is unnecessary or disproportionate, the defendant should have more than a hopeful expectation of non-prosecution—rather he should be able to deny liability in court, so that he can sleep as soundly at night as does anyone else who has not committed a crime. If he argues successfully that there is no need to punish his particular commission of the offence in order to protect any state interest, then the court would have to find an imaginative way to interpret the legislation (so far as it is possible to do so[21]) so as to procure his acquittal, or to find further developments to the common law[22] to the same effect.

This is the preferred solution. That the accused can, at least usually,[23] require from the court a fact-sensitive assessment of the necessity to punish him (when his conduct engaged a human right) can be gleaned from the case of *Handyside v United Kingdom*, where the applicant, charged under the Obscene Publications Act 1959, argued that there was no need to punish him because his publication did not risk the corruption of morals. Though the European Court found that the state was entitled to view his particular publication differently (and thus his punishment

---

[19] *Norris v Ireland* (1989) 13 EHRR 186

[20] But consider the facts of *Rusbridger*, n 8 above, where their Lordships had no doubt that the Editor of *The Guardian* slept soundly at night without fear of being prosecuted for treason. Since his complaint about the law was said to be purely hypothetical, their Lordships declined to declare as unlawful the decision of the Attorney-General not to categorically rule out prosecution for treason.   [21] Human Rights Act 1998 s 3(1).

[22] Ibid, s 6(1) provides that courts must not act (or fail to act) incompatibly with a Convention right, though they must apply of course incompatible legislation which cannot be read down under s 3(1): see s 6(2).

[23] We will discuss the exceptions to this in 'Offences where justifying punishment does *not* depend upon the circumstances, of the alleged offence', below.

did not violate his right to freedom of expression), nonetheless it agreed that its review

covers not only the basic legislation but also the decision applying it, even one given by an independent court.[24]

But exactly what features about the alleged conduct of the accused might affect the need to punish him? It is submitted that, since punishment must be necessary to forward a particular aim of crime reduction, we must first identify a particular purpose of punishment which meets that aim. There may be a difference between the necessity to punish for specific deterrence and a need to punish for general deterrence, for example, as we shall soon see.[25] If a necessity to punish can be established, then in assessing the proportionality of punishment, we should consider primarily the extent to which the accused risked harm to the state interest in the circumstances of his case. As a guiding rule, the greater the harm risked by the accused, the more likely that it might be proportionate to punish him in the hope of reducing the activity in the future. But if no harm, or virtually no harm, was risked then punishment will always be disproportionate.[26] But there are very many possible factors which might affect either the necessity to punish or the proportionality of any punishment. In the rest of this Part, I shall consider further the relevance of some factors which may be relevant to what I deem to be the two most troublesome methods of crime reduction,[27] namely specific deterrence and then general deterrence.

Punishing for Specific Deterrence

Where the aim is specific deterrence, the ECHR requirement of 'necessity' must refer to the probability that nothing less than punishment is likely to prevent the defendant from continuing his activities. The court which tries the accused must therefore be offered at least some evidence that lesser measures have been tried to discourage the defendant from his activities, or that such measures would be so unlikely to succeed that the state should immediately try the most drastic measure of all (punishment). Perhaps the most straightforward example of the state justifying punishment in order to specifically deter an individual is the seminal case *Handyside v United Kingdom*.[28] The accused had published

---

[24] n 6 above at para. 49.   [25] See below, text relating to no 46 below.
[26] This is subject again to the exceptions which we shall discuss in 'Offences where justifying punishment does *not* depend upon the circumstances, of the alleged offence', below.
[27] If the offence is extremely serious, then the aim of punishment might instead be incapacitation.   [28] n 6 above.

what he called 'The Little Red Schoolbook'. In the early 1970s, apparently, it was not so obviously a book giving frank and explicit advice on sexual matters, but some of the material was informative and since that was the object of the book, Article 10(1) was engaged. But the state authorities took the view that the book could corrupt young people and on separate occasions confiscated a total of some 1,208 copies under the Obscene Publications Act 1959. This was but a fraction of the print of run of 20,000 copies however, and Handyside was undeterred. Believing that the book was not obscene, he tried to defy the authorities by storing most of his copies elsewhere, and he continued to distribute them for sale. Then he was successfully prosecuted for the possession of the books which had been confiscated. In Strasbourg, the European Court of Human Rights accepted that, applying a margin of appreciation, it could be said that the book did risk the corruption of morals,[29] and its finding of no violation by the United Kingdom seems to accept that punishment was necessary for specific deterrence. Only after being punished did Handyside agree to revise those parts of the book which were thought capable of corrupting young minds, and so his punishment could be said to have been 'absolutely necessary' to meeting the state's purpose.

We should note that great emphasis is placed on Handyside's initial refusal to hand over all of his books; it was said to be a matter which helped to justify his prosecution and punishment.[30] The impression from *Handyside* is that, if specific deterrence is the aim, then lesser alternatives (such as the confiscation in this case, or perhaps an arrest and caution in other cases) must first have been exhausted. But it is not necessary to show that punishment will *necessarily* have the desired effects either; it should simply suffice that it ought now to be tried. Generally speaking, deterrence may be tried where those whom one seeks to deter are *capable of* understanding the link between their actions and future punishment (and that will apply where almost anyone of sound mind does a premeditated act); one should not make allowances for their *unwillingness* to be deterred.[31] We should also notice that, on the facts of the case, it could be said that Handyside risked the corruption of youth to such an extent that some punishment was proportionate. He

---

[29] For example, no mention was made in the book of the criminal law which applied to some of the activities discussed. Today one is likely to object that such a book could hardly possibly corrupt morals at all; in which case, of course, it would be unnecessary to punish, or indeed to take any other state action in relation to it, for the protection of morals. See Ashworth and Emmerson, *Human Rights and Criminal Justice*, n 2 above, 232.

[30] n 6 above, at para. 58. [31] J Rogers, 'Applying the Doctrine', n 14 above, 702.

designed the cover of his Schoolbook to make it look like a standard school textbook, and he made it further likely that corruptible youngsters would buy the book in all innocence by issuing it at a very low price. There were no obvious precautionary steps, such as a warning of the contents on the cover of the book.[32] It should also be noted, if one remains unconvinced about the proportionality of punishing such conduct (perhaps because one is generally unconvinced about punishment for the sake of protecting morals), that it is always possible for the court to pass a low penalty so as to make the total degree of state interference proportionate to the level of harm risked by the defendant. But a sentence should not be *raised* on account of the aim to specifically deter: the invocation of specific deterrence serves so as to justify (some) punishment in the first place and should not affect the sentencing level, which should not be higher than it needs to be to reflect the seriousness of the offence.[33]

It is possible, however, to imagine cases where the risk to the state interest is so low that the state should prefer to tolerate the prospect that the defendant might repeat his or her conduct. That will depend upon the state interest in question as well as the degree of risk to it posed by the conduct of the accused. This is perhaps the best way to analyse the issues raised by the decision of the High Court in *Percy v DPP*.[34] That is to say, that proportionality of punishment was the issue in this case; certainly the necessity to punish alone might easily have been established, given the repetitive nature of the appellant's vociferous public protests against government policy.[35] Mrs Percy was charged under section 5 of the Public Order Act 1986 for insulting American soldiers outside an American army base in the United Kingdom while protesting against the Star Wars project of President George W Bush. She had been convicted by the magistrates who thought that her conduct fell under s 5 as normally interpreted and

---

[32] It is worth noting that Art 10(2) specifically says that the privilege of free speech carries with it 'duties and responsibilities' and the European Court in *Handyside* referred to this in upholding the action of the United Kingdom, n 6 above at para. 49, as though to suggest that the words had some material significance and were not merely part of a sermon by the drafters of the ECHR.

[33] See generally Criminal Justice Act 2003 ss 148(2) and 153(2).

[34] [2001] EWHC Admin 11125.

[35] This was not discussed by the High Court, but see a separate case *Percy v DPP* [1995] 1 WLR 1382, and *http://news.bbc.co.uk/1/hi/england/humber/4555131.stm*, where it is reported that a judge refused to impose an ASBO on Mrs Percy (after her conviction for obstructing a constable in the execution of his duty, in a separate incident from that considered in the text) because this was thought to be a disproportionate curtailment upon free speech.

that, by reference to Article 10(2) punishment could be said to be necessary to protect 'the rights of others'. But the High Court held that the magistrates needed to decide whether punishment *of her* was proportionate to meet that end, and more attention needed to be given to the exact level of risk of giving offence to the soldiers which she created. As the Divisional Court put it, some insults which would distress some people would be 'water off a duck's back' to another.[36] The rights of people not to feel insulted by the non-threatening expression of sincerely held views in public is not such a pressing state interest that some risk to it might not be tolerated if punishment (on top of the harms already caused by the decision to prosecute) is the only measure which might prevent it.[37] Much of *Percy v DPP* can be strongly approved, especially the *dictum* that the prosecution needs to satisfy the court of the necessity to punish the accused.[38] It needs only to be added that in this case it was easy to give effect to Mrs Percy's Convention right, since (applying s 3(1) of the Human Rights Act 1998) it would have been open to the magistrates to decide that her conduct was 'reasonable' within the meaning of section 5(3)c of the Public Order Act.[39]

Punishing for General Deterrence

Where the prosecutor seeks *general* deterrence through punishment, then the possible effects of punishment upon the defendant are no longer decisive. The necessity to punish will instead be established by showing that nothing less than punishment of one person for an action which threatens a state interest will suffice in order that *others* might moderate

[36] n 34 above, at para. 28.

[37] It is easy to distinguish Percy's case from the later decision in *DPP v Hammond* [2004] EWHC 69 (Admin). Hammond carried signs with the banner 'Stop Lesbianism' and preached loudly to passers by in the street. *His* punishment too was necessary to stop him from provoking disorder in the future (since, when he was warned that he was provoking a breach of the peace, he replied that he knew of this, and nonetheless intended to continue); but it was arguably proportionate as well, insofar as the risk it carried of causing disorder was greater than that of Percy's conduct violating the rights of others (and the disorder was itself potentially more serious).

[38] However, Mrs Percy's conviction for obstruction of the highway was not challenged, though presumably it might have been, and on much the same grounds. Consequently, we do not know whether the High Court was prepared to let her conduct go unpunished altogether.

[39] n 34 above, at para. 26. Admittedly, to say that the *defendant's* conduct was 'reasonable' is a strained way of expressing the real reason for the acquittal, which is that it is *not* reasonable for the *state* to punish her. But, since the statute is silent on what constitutes 'reasonable' conduct, one might argue that Parliament intended the courts to be able to develop a whole range of new defences as might be required.

their actions accordingly. In this respect, the question mirrors the approach to punishing for specific deterrence: the question for the court is not whether punishment of one *will* succeed in deterring others, but rather whether lesser action by the state has at least been tried to that same effect (unless it would be so clearly doomed to failure that it does not need to be tried). In this context, the court will consider the alternative ways in which the norms of the criminal law might be conveyed to the public in such a way as might alter its behaviour, such as by an educative campaign. In *Laskey v United Kingdom* it was expressly stated that the purpose of punishing those involved in risky sado-masochistic practices was general deterrence (of conduct which poses a risk to the state interest in health).[40] No further explanation was offered as to whether punishment could be said to be necessary to meet that objective, but it is hard indeed to see here how any alternative, such as an educative campaign, could realistically have been effective in deterring or reducing this particular activity.[41] One can certainly see how the European Court of Human Rights felt able to distinguish this case from the facts of *R v Wilson*[42], where a husband tattooed the buttocks of his wife with a hot iron at her instigation. One might imagine that so few people would be so inclined to do anything as dangerous as this[43] that is not necessary to seek to deter others from doing it, or that, if it is, the very small number of those who would be deterred would render any punishment to be disproportionate towards the aim of protecting health.

The analysis of proportionality of punishment also mirrors that which should apply to specific deterrence, with just the important difference that in the case of general deterrence one is considering the likely effects of punishment of the accused upon the behaviour of *others*. Thus again, we should look at the level of harm to the state interest which was *risked* by the accused, and at the level of that risk, rather than at the harm which actually occurred. The harm which *was* caused should be regarded simply as (rebuttable) evidence that the risks of that harm had been of a substantial nature; but conversely it may be possible to justify punishment where it appears to be a matter of good fortune that more serious harm was not in fact caused. Thus the complaint of *Laskey* that the members of the group did not cause any serious injury to themselves would probably not

---

[40] n10 above.

[41] The European Court of Human Rights noted at this point the view of Lord Jauncey in the House of Lords that there was 'no suggestion that they and their associates are the only practitioners of homosexual sado-masochism in England and Wales': see ibid, para 49.

[42] [1996] 3 WLR 125 (CA).

[43] Save perhaps for masochistic pleasure; but (unlike *R v Brown*) there was no element of that in the facts of *R v Wilson*.

have been decisive even if it had been accepted. In the view of the European Court of Human Rights:

... the State authorities were entitled to have regard not only to the actual seriousness of the harm caused—which as noted above was considered to be significant—but also ... to the potential for harm inherent in the acts in question. In this respect it is recalled that the activities were considered by Lord Templeman to be 'unpredictably dangerous'.[44]

It should be added that since the state wishes to communicate the punishment of the accused to a wider audience, it must take into account the risk of over-deterrence, ie that its message might be misunderstood or would have an undesired chilling effect upon activities which would in fact be lawful. A proper understanding of this should help us to understand why prosecutions under s5 of the Public Order Act 1986 should rarely succeed where a right under Article 10 is engaged, even if the manner of the protest posed some threat to the 'rights of others'. The right to protest may be much undermined by any prosecution under s5 of the Public Order Act 1986, and it may not be understood that a particular person is being punished *because of the risk to a state interest*. It might be thought that she is being punished instead for her views.[45] In recognising this, we might give effect to the notion that freedom of speech is particularly to be protected.[46] So we can see that it may be disproportionate to punish a protester for *specific deterrence* if the curtailment of her right to protest would be particularly burdensome for her, and also disproportionate to punish her for *general deterrence* of insulting behaviour because the message to the public which the state wishes to rely upon may be misinterpreted.

One might conclude from this last point that often it will not matter whether the state seeks specific or general deterrence as a way of reducing the conduct of the accused in order to protect the relevant state interest. Success in one might indicate success in the other, and similarly failure to persuade the court of the need to deter specifically might presage a similar failure in relation to general deterrence. But this need not always be the case. Where it is very clear that the defendant is not disposed towards reoffending (or perhaps is unlikely to have another opportunity to do so, as in *Attorney-General v Stotcher*, the case of the juror who revealed

---

[44] n 40 above, at para. 46.

[45] I assume here that this would alarm the public more than the thought that a person might be punished for imparting confidential information, even though that too may engage Art 10. cf *Attorney-General v Stotcher*, n 11 above.

[46] See, eg *Handyside*, n 6 above, at para. 48, *Lingens v Austria* (1986) 8 EHRR 407 at paras. 41–42.

the jury's confidential deliberations)[47] then punishment will have to be justified in terms of general deterrence. Conversely, where few other people would be inclined to imitate the defendant's conduct, then punishment for general deterrence may be both unnecessary and disproportionate and the court should concentrate instead upon the need to use punishment to specifically deter the defendant. This brings us to conclude this part with some observations of the role of the court when the prosecutor seeks punishment of conduct which engaged a Convention right but which also posed some degree of risk to a state interest.

The Responsibilities of the Judge and the Prosecutor

So far, I have assumed that the debate about whether it is necessary and proportionate to punish the defendant will take place in the courtroom. This, it is submitted, is right but the point deserves some attention. Let us start with the responsibilities of the judge, or magistrate as the case may be.

Provided that the court is satisfied that the conduct of the accused engaged a Convention right (which should be a matter of law) then much should depend upon whether the prosecutor seeks specific or general deterrence. In practice, one might tend to assume that it is the latter, and if indeed the prosecutor seeks only to persuade the court that punishment would be justified for specific deterrence, then he perhaps ought to bear an evidential (and legal) burden that there is a risk of repetition of the defendant's conduct. This might be satisfied by the contents of a pre-sentence report, or by the defendant's previous convictions or cautions. The accused person may himself wish to give evidence that he is unlikely to reoffend, if he has already decided to admit the facts upon which the charge is based and to challenge the prosecution solely on human rights grounds. The law of evidence as it relates to risks of future behaviour is likely to develop independently in the near future because of its pivotal importance in deciding whether to impose an anti-social behaviour order,[48] and the same principles ought to apply in this human rights context.

However, most questions which will need to be resolved on the issue of state justification of punishment will be evaluative in nature, and much

---

[47] n 11 above.

[48] The court must be satisfied that 'an order is necessary to protect relevant persons from further anti-social acts by [the defendant]': Crime and Disorder Act 1998 s 1(1)b. See P Ramsay 'What is Anti-Social Behaviour?' [2004] Crim LR 908 at 915. Generally a pattern of previous offending seems to suffice to establish the necessity, but see *R v Lee (Kirkby)* [2005] WL 1382369 (CA) at para. 7.: 'There must be a demonstrable necessity for such an order . . . The need must be considered against the background of the facts of each individual case'.

will depend upon the quality of argument on both sides as well as the willingness of the court to entertain the human rights arguments. On this point, we might observe the warning in *Percy v DPP* that it was insufficient for the magistrate to 'merely state'[49] that interference with the Convention right of the accused was proportionate: rather, he needed to give fuller reasons, not least so that the reviewing court could be sure that he had not misdirected himself about the relevant factors. Unfortunately the tendency of both magistrates and judges to declare only their conclusions upon the proportionality of punishment has nonetheless continued, and I shall suggest the deeper reasons for this in 'Judicial Attitudes and deference to parliament', below. We should also add here that the decision on state justification should not be left to a jury.[50] It may be that a jury might have a role to play in determining whether the level of risk (say, to the health of a consenting partner in a sado-masochist encounter) was of a high or low level, but only isolated questions of fact such as this should be left to the jury, and only where their verdict should follow from their conclusion. In such a case, the judge will already have balanced the need to deter and the proportionality of punishment (or not), depending upon whether the level of risk was high (or not). So, although he might leave the jury to convict or to acquit depending upon its own assessment of the level of risk, the balancing tests required by the Convention right will have been undertaken by the judge and he would only leave the question of the level of risk to the jury if the case depended upon it and if the point was in dispute between the parties.[51]

The responsibility of the prosecutor which most needs discussion in this context relates to the exercise of prosecutorial discretion. The first stage of the test which is prescribed by section 5.1 of the Code for Crown Prosecutors[52] is, as is well known, the 'evidential test'. The application of this test (which requires that the prosecutor should consider it more likely than not that he will prove guilt in court[53]) clearly includes an assessment of success in defeating a human rights based argument which might be raised by the defendant, and he should discontinue the case where he is sure that the magistrates or judge will reinterpret the legislation or

[49] n 34 above, para. 33.
[50] *R v Taylor (Paul)* [2002] 1 Cr App R 37 (CA) at para. 31.
[51] Of course, the jury would always have the final say in any contested Crown Court trial: *R v Wang* [2005] UKHL 9 (HL). It could not be stopped from returning a perverse acquittal by adopting its own viewpoint on the applicability of the Convention right, but a judge might properly warn it to take its instructions on the issues which need to be resolved from himself only.
[52] References to the Code in this article are to the fifth edition (2004), accessible via *www.cps.gov.uk*   [53] Section 5.3 of the Code.

develop the common law in order to acquit the defendant in order to give effect to his Convention right. This, then, serves as one safeguard that prosecutions will not be lightly brought where the conduct of the accused engaged a Convention right, but it is a safeguard which applies equally to all alleged offences. The question is whether the defendant should have a greater right to seek judicial review of a decision to prosecute him if the prosecution is likely to fail, on the basis that the engagement of his right should give him greater protection against a carelessly brought prosecution?

There is, in fact, some *obiter* indication from the House of Lords that to bring a doomed prosecution is an 'unlawful act' within the meaning of section 6(1) of the Human Rights Act.[54] Such an act would of course be unlawful as soon as it is done: it would not make a difference if the prosecution were later to be voluntarily discontinued.[55] But it should be pointed out that their Lordships had in mind the hypothetical prosecution for advocating republicanism, where the Convention right under Article 10(1) would be clearly engaged and where, equally clearly, the state could not be said to be pursuing any of the aims under Article 10(2). It is submitted that their *dicta* should be restricted to such a case as this, where the prosecutor shows complete disregard for the Convention right, and is simply automatically applying the criminal law as it is found in the statute. To stop such a prosecution as this would be consistent with our existing law, which allows judicial review of a decision to prosecute where the decision is prompted by 'dishonesty, *mala fides* or where there is some exceptional circumstance'[56]. This is because a decision to prosecute for an offence where it should be obvious that the conduct of the accused engaged a Convention right and that a court would find any punishment to be unjustified would constitute an 'exceptional circumstance'. The advantage of seeking relief through the High Court in this way would be that if the defendant were to succeed in showing that the decision to prosecute was an 'unlawful act', then the court will have a discretion as to whether to award damages, as it feels appropriate, applying the criteria to determine 'just satisfaction' under s 8(3) of the Human Rights

---

[54] *Rusbridger*, n 8 above at para. 40, *per* Lord Scott.

[55] See, for example, *B v United Kingdom* 53760/00, *The Times*, 18 February 2004. Prosecutors will now advise police when making decisions to charge suspects, and so care will have to be taken at an early stage. However, it will be possible for the suspect to be released on bail while the prosecutor awaits further evidence, or, as in this sort of case, while he considers the human rights implications of charging the suspect. See details of the 'statutory charging scheme' in Part Four and Schedule Two of the Criminal Justice Act 2003, and see section 6 of the Code for Crown Prosecutors on the 'Threshold Test' which applies where it is too early to make a decision about charging but where it is inappropriate to release the suspect on bail.

[56] *R v DPP, ex parte Kebilene and Others* [2000] 2 AC 326 (HL).

Act 1998,[57] in addition to quashing the decision to prosecute. Perhaps a relevant factor here would be whether the defendant had disclosed at the earliest possible stage in the proceedings that he intended to rely upon a Convention right.

But it should not be possible to seek judicial review before the trial in a case such as *Percy*, where it is a matter of argument whether any punishment might be proportionate for the purpose of deterring the accused from further conduct which poses a risk to a right of another. This is because the reason which generally limits judicial review of decisions to prosecute applies as much, or perhaps even more, to cases such as this. That reason is that satellite litigation delays, and adds to the cost of, the anticipated criminal proceedings, to a greater extent than can be justified by the likelihood that the court will be able to pronounce in advance upon the prospects that the prosecution will succeed.[58] Only when the evidence is heard in a criminal trial will the judge and jury have the fullest picture of the extent to which the conduct of the accused risked a relevant state interest, and (if the issue is one of necessity to punish to specifically deter) the court might need an opportunity to hear from the defendant before making its decision.[59] Even if the facts are agreed between the parties, it is desirable that the application of human rights law to the facts, unless already clearly covered by existing authority, be decided upon by the courts. It is more appropriate that the courts should decide unclear points of human rights law than that the prosecutors should resolve them against themselves behind closed doors,[60] and a prosecutor who proceeds in good faith[61] should not be liable to have his decision reviewed on account of his optimism that he might persuade the court of the necessity to punish the accused. In such a case the accused must wait to make his defence at his trial.

Where exceptionally judicial review is available of a decision to prosecute (which has been taken in good faith), it should only be where the

---

[57] Much legal expenditure and strain might be endured pending trial, and a financial remedy might be appropriate where the prosecutor has neglected to consider the purpose of his prosecution and then casually drops the case when it reaches court.

[58] *Kebilene*, n 56 above, 369–370.

[59] The defendant will not of course be compelled to testify, but, especially if specific deterrence is an issue and where the prosecution has satisfied its evidential burden, then one imagines that a court will be inclined to find against a silent defendant in many cases, even without reference to Criminal Justice and Public Order Act 1994 s 35.

[60] See the opinion of Lord Hobhouse in *R (on the application of Mrs Dianne Pretty) v DPP and Secretary of State for the Home Department* [2001] UKHL 61 (HL) at para. 121. We shall return to this important case in the second part of this paper below.

[61] As already mentioned, decisions to prosecute are already reviewable where there is evidence of bad faith from the prosecutor: *Kebilene*, n 56 above.

evidential test can clearly be argued not to be met. There should be no corresponding avenue of review where the accused means only to argue that the prosecution does not serve the public interest. Certainly, any attempt to review the decision or, to similar effect, to try to invoke the abuse of process jurisdiction at the beginning of the trial, on the basis that the judge might disapprove of the decision to bring proceedings should be rejected.[62] This should not cause undue hardship, because (unlike other offences where no Convention right is engaged) the prosecutor will already have given thought to whether he can persuade the court that it is necessary to punish the accused for a particular reason as part of his application of the evidential test. So there is little prospect of a trivial prosecution which serves no particular purpose being brought on account of this restriction.

Moreover, the more suitable ways of ensuring that both the evidential and public interest tests are met surely lie within the internal workings of the Crown Prosecution Service itself. The Law Commission has suggested that there should be a requirement to seek the leave of the Director of Public Prosecutions to bring a prosecution for an offence where it is particularly likely that a Convention right might be engaged *and* where particular harm might be caused by the institution of a prosecution.[63] There is much merit to this proposal, which would not only act as a control over private prosecutions but would also (if all of the Law Commission's recommendations were to be implemented) lead to decisions being taken at a higher level within the CPS than is currently the case.[64] Ideally, the CPS would draw up its own internal policy guidelines for prosecutions in the cases which typically raise human rights issues; and where it is unusual for an offence to raise a human rights issue

---

[62] There is some authority for this: see *R v Taylor*, n 50 above, at paras. 20, 31.

[63] The importance of this second criterion should not be overlooked. It is on account of this that the Law Commission does not propose a consent provision for offences under s 5(1) of the Public Order Act 1986; for notwithstanding the likelihood that in many cases the freedom of expression will be engaged, the Law Commission thinks it reasonable that the defendant should wait to try to resist liability in court. However, it suggests that a consent provision may be required in relation to s 1 of the Child Abduction Act 1984 where often great harm and disruption to the defendant's family life may be caused by the mere institution of the prosecution process. See Law Commission *Consents to Prosecutions* (1998) *www.lawcom.gov.uk/docs/lc255.pdf* at paras. 6.21–6.39.

[64] Importantly, it also recommends that it should not be possible, as it currently is on account of the Prosecution of Offences Act 1985, s 1(7) for that permission to be granted on behalf of the DPP by any Crown Prosecutor. Rather, the Law Commission recommends that the power should be delegable only to the Head of Central Casework: ibid at para. 7.35. There is certainly good reason to believe that Crown Prosecutors do not attach any particular importance to cases where, formally, they have to give consent on behalf of the DPP when deciding to proceed: see *R v Jackson* [1997] Crim LR 293.

(such as the charge of inflicting grievous bodily harm where the harm occurred consensually in a sado-masochistic encounter) the case should be routinely referred to a senior prosecutor when the defendant has indicated his intention to rely upon a Convention right in his defence.[65]

Offences Where Justifying Punishment Does *not* Depend on the Circumstances of the Alleged Offence

We will now turn to the exceptional cases where, although a right was engaged by the conduct of the accused, the state might legitimately aim to punish him in order to pursue a recognised state interest *regardless of the possible absence of any risk to the state interest on the facts of the case.* This would be an exception to the *Handyside* principle that a court must review the application of legislation to a case, and not just the basic legislation itself, which principle we have discussed in the first part of this paper;[66] but I will argue here that Parliament might legitimately decide upon such punishment, on what might be termed the 'slippery slope' principle of criminalisation. We shall turn right away to this principle.

The 'Slippery Slope' Principle of Criminalisation

This wide principle of criminalisation seems to be accepted implicitly both in Strasbourg and domestically. It applies where the legislature decides that if conduct which (on its facts) does not threaten a state interest thereby goes unpunished, then it is *inevitable* that other citizens (even if acting in good faith) will think that the conduct is, or has become, legal in a wider range of cases which may transcend the individual case. They may consequently perform conduct which *does* threaten a state interest. That leap will occur, in the view of the legislature, because those other citizens will be unable to appreciate the extent to which they themselves might be risking the relevant state interest. In other words, it may be thought that they will be unable to make a correct assessment of the risk of harm to the state interest on so many occasions that it is necessary to stop them from acting at all. Further, if the state interest is a particularly

---

[65] The accused must disclose the 'general nature' of his defence before the trial: see the Criminal Procedure and Investigations Act 1996 s 5 (6)a, and ss 6A–6B of the Act as inserted by Part Five of the Criminal Justice Act 2003. In many cases, it will be appropriate for him to seek a human rights ruling on assumed facts at a preparatory hearing (which may then be appealed before the trial begins): Criminal Procedure and Investigation Act 1996 s 29.   [66] See text relating to n 28 above.

pressing one, it may be also be *proportionate* to punish even the defendant whose conduct did not pose any risk, as though he were somehow lucky that he did not put at risk the state interest. I do not mean to be original when I call this the 'slippery slope' principle of criminalisation.[67] We are entitled to feel sceptical of this principle, but nonetheless it enjoys some philosophical background. A slippery slope argument may properly be made *either* where there may be 'horrible results' at the end of the slope, perhaps because persons will have no logical reference point at which to halt the slide down the slope, perhaps because it is only the psychological impact of the blanket nature of the prohibition which is already saving us from these results; *or* where the removal of the blanket ban will lead to 'arbitrary results' because loose concepts will need to be employed in order to distinguish different cases.

There have already been two high profile cases where the House of Lords has effectively held that criminalisation on the basis of the slippery slope principle may be compatible with a Convention right of the accused. The first of these is Mrs Pretty's tragic request that the Director of Public Prosecutions should undertake not to prosecute her husband for any act of assisted suicide which he might later commit, on the basis that the right under Article 8 was engaged[68] and that there should be no need to punish to deter assisted suicide where (as in this case) the principal's wish to die was uncoerced, fully informed and committed.[69] On the facts of the case, so the argument went, there would be no need to punish in order to 'protect the rights of others' (the only conceivable state interest in Article 8(2)) because there would have been no risk to any rights of his wife. But both the House of Lords and subsequently the European Court of Human Rights[70] thought that the state was entitled to reason (and had so reasoned in passing section 2 of the Suicide Act 1961) that if

---

[67] I am grateful to my colleague Michael Freeman for referring me to the valuable essay by B Williams 'Which Slopes are Slippery?' in *Moral Dilemmas in Modern Medicine*, M Lockwood (ed), (Oxford University Press, 1985) 126–137 where the distinction drawn in the text was first made.

[68] It might be noted that the European Commission of Human Rights had doubted whether the rights *of the abettor* of suicide are engaged by Art 8: *R v United Kingdom* (1983) 33 DR 270, but both the House of Lords and the European Court of Human Rights were prepared to consider the issue of justification in this case since the prohibition of assisted suicide (in the view of the European Court) also engaged Mrs Pretty's rights under Art 8.

[69] Such notions as 'lack of coercion' and 'commitment' are the 'loose concepts' which would necessarily be employed if the law of assisted suicide were to be liberalised. Thus, arguably, the slippery slope might lead to 'arbitrary' as well as to 'horrible' results, though the latter results (ie the possible pressure put on the elderly and infirm to end their lives) were sufficient to decide the case against the Prettys.

[70] *Pretty v United Kingdom* (2002) 35 EHRR 1.

someone in Mr Pretty's position were to go unpunished, then other persons would think it legal to assist their terminally ill loved ones—but with the best will in the world, there may be that extra degree of pressure upon the partner or other loved one which the abettors themselves would be unable to perceive.[71] Lord Bingham invoked Dr Johnson in saying that 'Laws are not made for particular cases but for men in general'[72] and, in the context of assisted suicide, his Lordship noted that:

It is not hard to imagine that an elderly person, in the absence of pressure, might opt for a premature end to life if that were available, not from a desire to die or a willingness to stop living, but from a desire to stop being a burden to others.[73]

It was also thought that the possibility of punishing of Mr Pretty was proportionate to ward off this possibility. However the European Court reached this conclusion on the basis that both sentencing and prosecutorial discretion was available in cases of this sort.[74] We shall return to the importance of prosecutorial discretion very shortly.

The second case where the 'slippery slope principle' has been recognised is *R v Shayler*,[75] where a former MI5 officer passed secret information to a newspaper and was charged under sections 1 and 4 of the Official Secrets Act 1989. He relied upon his right to freedom of expression but it was held that it was necessary to punish the unauthorised revelation of *any* secret by a former agent for the 'protection of national security'. Their Lordships noted that the nature of the blanket ban meant that one might be punished for revealing the most innocuous[76] of secrets—but it was accepted that what may seem innocuous to one agent may be the 'missing piece of a jigsaw' to a foreign agent and that an individual agent could not always know the difference.[77] Since the agent could always seek authorisation to

---

[71] The point is well discussed by D Lamb, *Down the Slippery Slope: Arguing in Applied Ethics* (London: Croon Helm, 1988), 68–71. The author points out that 'even if the problem of ascertaining the influence of narcotics or severe pain could be resolved there still remains the fact that the scope of voluntary decisions is necessarily undetermined' and adds that most individuals are accustomed only to making decisions which, to some greater or lesser extent, are reversible.   [72] *Ex parte Pretty*, n 60 above at para. 29.

[73] Ibid at para. 20. See too the opinion of Lord Steyn at para. 62.

[74] Although the Court did accept the view of the House of Lords that the Director of Public Prosecutions had no liberty to grant a proleptic immunity from prosecution, ibid at paras. 39, 65 and so its remarks are intended to refer only to prosecutorial discretion which is exercised *after* the offence has allegedly been committed.   [75] [2002] UKHL 11.

[76] Whether a secret is 'innocuous' seems to require us to reason with another 'loose concept', and so arguably this slippery slope argument also combines the fear of both 'arbitrary' and 'horrible' results.

[77] Even their Lordships, who thought that the Official Secrets Act 1989 was very broad, accepted this argument. See the opinions of Lord Hope at paras. 84–85, and Lord Hutton at paras. 100–101.

disclose material which is covered by the Official Secrets Act 1989, and since a refusal to authorise a revelation of information could be judicially reviewed under the principles of proportionality,[78] it could only tend towards danger to national security to allow any agent to be his own judge of the safety of revealing unauthorised material. Again it was noted that prosecutorial discretion had to be exercised, in this case by the Attorney-General, and this was thought to be a further safeguard against a prosecution being brought over a trivial matter where the agent's assessment of the safety of the material clearly would be correct, even if he had not sought clearance for it.[79] Nonetheless, the agent would be liable if a prosecution were to be brought: he would not be able to point in court to the negligible risk to national security so as to resist criminal liability. So we now turn to look at the exercise of prosecutorial discretion in such cases as *Pretty* and *Shayler*.

The Role of the Prosecutor in 'Slippery Slope' Cases

In *Pretty*, the European Court of Human Rights said that it was proportionate for the state to allow for punishment in all cases of assisted suicide because there was a 'system of enforcement . . . which allows due regard to be given in each case to the public interest in bringing the prosecution'.[80] The Court said nothing more about what was required in such a system, however. The first observation to be made is that if prosecutorial discretion is to be exercised favourably to the defendant, then it must be on the basis of the 'public interest' test, because, assuming that there is admissible evidence of the act of assisted suicide, or of unauthorised disclosure of state secrets, etc, then there is nothing further to consider which relates to the legal proof of the guilt of the accused. Slippery slope cases differ here from the cases considered in the first part of this paper, where the engagement of the human right directly affects the 'evidential test'.

How, then, might prosecutors decide not to proceed with 'slippery slope' cases on 'public interest' grounds? The answer is not obvious. To make a general decision not to continue with less serious cases (presumably those where there is little or no apparent risk to the state interest) would seem to be inconsistent with the principle that a prosecutor should take the law as he finds it to be, a principle which was confirmed in the *Pretty* litigation itself.[81] Further, in a relatively trivial case the court itself

---

[78] *R (on the application of Daly) v Secretary of State for the Home Department* [2001] UKHL 26.   [79] *Shayler*, at para. 35 n 75 above, (Lord Bingham)
[80] n 70 above at para. 74.
[81] n 60 above at paras. 65, 121, *Kebeline*, n 56 above, at paras. 340, 394.

could usually render the punishment proportionate to the aim of the state in exercising its sentencing discretion.[82] But moreover, to rewrite the law of assisted suicide by devising categories of lesser seriousness would seem to be inconsistent with the operation of the slippery slope principle itself (which is to discourage by punishment *all* such activity, even the seemingly innocuous, precisely *because* it is by deciding that any proscribed activity is harmless that greater harms are thought to become inevitable). The problem is essentially this: the logic of the slippery slope principle tends to discourage distinctions based on the perceived seriousness of an offence, at least in so far as those distinctions relate to the perceived danger to the state interest. *All* punishment is 'necessary' and *some* punishment will always be 'proportionate', and any policies of prosecution which sought to undermine this legislative framework would surely be *ultra vires*.[83]

But prosecutors can still devise policies relating to assisted suicide *without* purporting to rewrite the law or doing anything else which undermines the slippery slope principle. They might identify cases of assisted suicide where it is likely to be disproportionate to prosecute on account of factors which have nothing to do with the perceived seriousness of the offence, such as where the defendant himself is ill or depressed *at the time of the decision to prosecute*. There is no reason why policies should not be devised which advise against prosecution on grounds which relate to the effects on the defendant of being *prosecuted*, because such factors do not purport to undercut the seriousness of what the defendant has done.[84]

Perhaps the best way in which to apply the requirement in *Pretty* that there should be a 'system' of enforcement at the stage of prosecutorial

---

[82] Indeed the sentence should be reviewable on the stringent proportionality grounds which are said to apply generally to all decisions which interfere with a Convention right: *Daly*, n 78 above.

[83] Richard Tur has argued that the Director of Public Prosecutions should be obliged to have, and to promulgate, a policy for cases of assisted suicide; but then Tur regards the DPP as having a proper role in perfecting the *legal* definition of assisted suicide. See R Tur, 'Legislative Technique and Human Rights: The Sad Case of Assisted Suicide' [2003] Crim LR 3 at 9–10. Tur writes that 'it is unsatisfactory to say to such citizens that they assist suicide at their own risk of prosecution and conviction however morally compelling their particular circumstances', but he does not acknowledge that it is precisely the inherently risky nature of assisting suicide (that is, a risk that the rights of others will inadvertently be abused) which explains why the state maintains a 'slippery slope' justification of punishment.

[84] At the same time, the prosecutor would not have to weigh this factor if the 'offence is serious': s 5.10(g) of the fifth Code for Crown Prosecutors (2004). Note that there is a difference between saying that the perceived seriousness of the case should determine the decision to prosecute (which would be wrong in the case of a slippery slope offence) and saying that an approximate assessment of its seriousness might be made in order to determine the weight to be given to *other* factors.

discretion would be to require the prosecutor to involve the defendant in his decision making process and to offer a reason for a decision to proceed.[85] This will at least reassure the defendant that irrelevant factors have not been considered, or that relevant factors have not been ignored (or, if this is not so, then the process will enable him better to seek judicial review).[86] The defendant who thus suffered from depression at the time of his act should be given an opportunity to persuade the prosecutor of his version of the facts (even if that would not amount to a denial of guilt in law) and to argue why he should not be prosecuted. The prosecutor must make an assessment as fairly as he can. He must give the accused a fair chance to convince him of his own version of the facts, and should also have regard to any independent evidence which might support the account of the defendant. Further, the Crown Prosecution Service should keep a record of all previous cases where it was arguable that a Convention right was engaged and where a decision was made whether or not to proceed. These previous decisions should be referred to when making future decisions in order that decisions are made consistently in accordance with stated policy (unless the policies have subsequently changed).

A requirement to consider previous decisions and to give reasons to the accused should enable the latter to seek review of a decision to prosecute where there is indeed no evidence that he did risk a state interest. But this begs the question whether judicial review should be an available remedy for a casual exercise of the public interest test? This would appear to be new law, but it is submitted that in the formula of *Kebilene*, it can be said to be an 'exceptional circumstance'.[87] It is indeed highly exceptional that the compatibility of punishment with a human right of the defendant should at least partially depend upon 'a system of enforcement' run by prosecutors. Where so much responsibility is delegated to prosecutors, it is proper that their reasoning (and the consistency of their reasoning) should be reviewable.

If it is right to say that judicial review should be available because the defendant has a right that the decision to prosecute him should be carried out carefully, after due consultation, then judicial review should be sought *before* the trial begins, although there seems to be no reason why the

---

[85] There have been regular calls for prosecutors to give reasons for their decisions to defendants as well as to victims: see eg A Ashworth, 'The 'Public Interest' Element in Prosecutions' [1987] Crim LR 595 at 605–6. But the practice has regrettably never taken root and the fifth Code for Crown Prosecutors (2004) is as silent upon the subject as its predecessors.

[86] Although this will depend upon the extent to which the prosecutor can be expected to disclose any policies which might exist about prosecuting the offence in question. See generally C Hilson 'Judicial Review, Policies and the Fettering of Discretion' [2002] PL 11.   [87] n 56 above.

defendant should not wait until the appropriate moment in the criminal justice process to plead abuse of process on the same grounds.[88] The judge's duty to review the exercise of discretion by the prosecutor might be triggered by the defendant raising evidence that his conduct did engage a Convention right and that the prosecutor was made aware of that evidence. The challenge should be successful where the prosecutor could not explain his decision by reference to the Code for Crown Prosecutors (or in relation to other more detailed policy guidance which might exist) in the light of arguments raised by the defendant and of past practice. I suggest, however, that a *Wednesbury* level of review would be appropriate, so that only the most extreme of cases (such as where the surviving defendant is not expected to live much longer) might be stopped on the basis that the decision to prosecute was irrational. The purpose of this review would be to ensure the proper running of a system where the *prosecutor* makes the decisions, and (by the very fact that review is possible at the start of the trial, however difficult it may be to persuade the judge to review the decision or to stay the case) to encourage a culture of direct accountability in such cases. We should finally note that this review of prosecutorial discretion need not be regarded as 'satellite litigation', since the issues which would be relevant at the stage of review would not be relevant if the trial were to proceed. Nor should there be discretion as to the remedy if the exercise of prosecutorial discretion is found to be 'unlawful' under section 6 of the Human Rights Act 1998. Since in these cases the proper use of discretion is required in order for the slippery slope principle of criminalisation to be compatible with the Convention right, it should follow that the trial cannot proceed where discretion is exercised wrongfully. Thus, a court which were to give some lesser remedy to the defendant but proceed to trial would arguably act 'unlawfully' itself. This much seems to follow from the 7–2 decision of the House of Lords in *Attorney-General's Reference (No 2 of 2001)*[89] that to say that a prospective act is unlawful means that the relevant authority is not at liberty to do it. It may not instead proceed and then give a remedy for its own unlawfulness.

[88] It seems that whenever it is possible to seek judicial review of a decision to prosecute, it is also open for the defendant to plead abuse of process at the start of the trial. See *R v Uxbridge Magistrates's Court, ex parte Adimi* [2001] QB 667. This may be more convenient for him, and he would not need to seek leave in order to do so. But since he would be confining his remedy to having the trial stopped in the criminal courts, the defendant whose conduct engaged a Convention right would not be able simultaneously to claim damages for an 'unlawful act' (if that is what the decision to prosecute is held to be), as he might be if he had sought judicial review through the civil courts (see the Human Rights Act 1998 s 8).

[89] [2003] UKHL 68. This was *obiter*, however, since the same majority thought that it was not in fact 'unlawful' under s 6 (1) of the HRA to hold a trial which had been unreasonably delayed but with no prejudice to the accused.

Our conclusions thus far can be briefly summarised. Where the accused can rely upon a Convention right *in court* (as in the cases considered in the first part of this paper) he should generally do so and might only seek judicial review where the evidential test has been woefully misapplied. But in slippery slope cases, he cannot defend himself in court but might plead abuse of process, or seek judicial review, where the public interest in this prosecution has been unlawfully assessed. It is true that he will find it relatively difficult to succeed in that, but the solution in such cases is to campaign for legislative change to the slippery slope principle which lies at the root of his problems.

This thought prompts further questions. Is there not a danger that the courts will not be inclined to regard 'slippery slope' crimes as exceptional? Determining the necessity and proportionality of punishment in individual cases is undoubtedly challenging. It would be much easier (and slightly more familiar) for them to declare an offence to be a 'slippery slope' offence and to review the exercise of prosecutorial discretion where necessary. Certainly the reluctance to decide upon the necessity and proportionality of punishment in individual cases exists, as we shall see in the final part of this paper.

Judicial Attitudes and Deference to Parliament

In the first part of this paper, I argued that the normal way to give effect to a Convention right of the accused is to determine whether it is necessary and proportionate to punish him for exactly what he did. As the European Court of European Rights declared in *Handyside* [90] the court ought to be looking beyond the compatibility of the legislation itself and to be considering whether it is appropriately applied to the facts of the case before it;[91] and as the Divisional Court held in *Percy*, this requires a reasoned opinion from the court and not a mere statement that interference by the state is proportionate.[92] But it has to be said that one can find very few examples post *Percy* where a court has shown any commitment to doing this. Perhaps the root of the problem is the unfortunate coincidence that the first two House of Lords decisions in this area, namely *ex p Pretty* and *R v Shayler*, happened to be cases where the offence in question was one to which the 'slippery slope' principle of criminalisation applies. Unsurprisingly, however, their Lordships were not concerned to point out how unusual this

---

[90] n 6 above.
[91] The distinction between the two exercises was drawn clearly by the High Court in *Percy v DPP*, n 34 above, at para. 25. [92] Ibid.

was; it satisfied their purpose to identify the reasons for criminalisation, and to explain why the particular facts of *Pretty* and *Shayler* should make no difference. The upshot of this, however, is that Lord Bingham's *dicta* that 'Laws are not made for particular cases but for men in general. Second, to permit a law to be modified at discretion is to leave the community without law'[93] might be cited in cases where they are not appropriate.

But that is only part of the problem. The courts have not yet discovered a plethora of slippery slope offences, and we should be thankful for that. Even with the possibility of judicial review, they cause great hardship to defendants, especially if (as in the case of the Prettys) they want to plan their conduct in advance. It is true that anyone who wishes to rely upon a Convention right can usually only guess as to the likelihood of prosecution and conviction, but those who do not commit slippery slope offences can at least hope to argue the merits of their case openly in court. We might commend the reluctance of their Lordships to invoke the slippery slope principle in *Shayler*. Their Lordships discussed other ways of protecting national security and noted that alternative method of criminalisation had been considered in the Franks Report, but were rejected as being unworkable.[94] Even so, their Lordships made it clear that they were not *required* to accept that Parliament has got it right in deciding that the slippery slope principle should be applicable, and they would have been prepared to find the legislative blanket ban on the unauthorised revealing of state secrets to be incompatible with Article 10 had it not been for the fact that an automatic and inflexible refusal of authorisation could be effectively challenged on judicial review.[95] Thus, notwithstanding due deference, a court might yet form its own view contrary to that of Parliament on the notion that a slippery slope will cause horrible or arbitrary results, and when that happens it should be prepared to declare the legislation to be incompatible with the Convention right, if the offence cannot be read down under section 3 (1) of the Human Rights Act 1998.[96] But, substantial deference was rightly to be shown to Parliament on the matter of national security, and the House of Lords thought that the legislative solution in the Official Secrets Act 1989 was one which Parliament could reasonably reach.[97]

[93] n 60 above, at para. 29.   [94] Ibid; see para. 20 of Lord Bingham's opinion.
[95] n 75 above.
[96] The preparedness to find s 1 of the Official Secrets Act 1989 to be incompatible with Article 10 of the ECHR has been welcomed by F Klug, 'Judicial Deference under the Human Rights Act 1998' (2003) 2 European Human Rights Law Review 125 at 131.
[97] See *R v Shayler*, n 75 above, at para. 68. See too *Leander v Sweden* (1987) 9 EHRR 433. But some commentators have doubted whether our House of Lords needed to have been so deferential on the issues arising in *Pretty*. See R Edwards, 'Judicial Deference under

So, if the courts are properly restrained from finding new examples of slippery slope offences, then why have we not seen many discussions of the necessity and proportionality of punishment in individual cases? The answer seems to be that the courts have preferred to defer to general Parliamentary decisions about the necessity and proportionality of punishment (which are represented by the legislation which enacts the offence itself, without specific provision for defences which cover the circumstances of individual cases) as though these decisions are inevitably to apply even in individual cases. Thus, the court's decision in an individual case is circumscribed by the wider legislative judgement. In some contexts this reasoning can be plausible. One might agree with the Court of Appeal in *R v Taylor*,[98] where a Rastafarian was prosecuted for supplying cannabis which he said was essential to his worship, that a Crown Court judge should not have to hold his own inquiry to decide whether the amounts of cannabis possessed by the accused were sufficiently great to justify punishment (for the sake of deterring conduct which risks the health of others). Parliament is clearly the more appropriate forum for assessing the risks posed by the possession of cannabis, and the judge was entitled to defer to the legislative judgment (in addition to the United Kingdom Membership of international conventions on dealing with narcotic abuse)[99] that possession of *any* amount of cannabis was sufficiently serious as to justify punishment for the sake of protecting health.[100] This conclusion would similarly hold good for a prosecution of a multiple sclerosis sufferer who possesses cannabis for therapeutic purposes. Indeed, Parliament's judgement is all the more compelling here since the government has commissioned research into the possible therapeutic effects of cannabis and has not yet decided that it can safely be used.[101]

But at this point, we should remind ourselves that although the appropriate level of deference depends upon the subject matter, it should never quite be absolute.[102] There are certainly very good reasons to defer to Parliament's informed judgement where they are based upon empirical

the Human Rights Act' 65 MLR (2002) 859 at 877–8 and M Freeman, 'Denying Death its Dominion: Thoughts on the Dianne Pretty Case' 10 Med LR (2002) 245, 259.

[98] n 50 above, para. 31.

[99] The Single Convention on Narcotic Drugs 1961 and a similar United Nations Convention in 1988.

[100] See too the subsequent decision in *R v Andrews* [2004] WL 741779 at para. 21.

[101] *R v Quayle and Others* [2005] WL 1248402.

[102] 'In some contexts the deference is nearly absolute. In others it barely exists at all': *per* Laws LJ in *International Transport Roth GmbH v Secretary of State for the Home Department* [2002] 1 CMLR 52 (CA) at para. 75.

evidence, but all that we should be saying is that in the standard case of possession of drugs, we might properly defer to the generic judgment that even the possession of a small amount of drugs carries a substantial risk to health. The court should yet be alert to exceptional cases. It should still be possible to hold that a small quantity of drugs that is carefully used and well guarded (so that it might not be stolen, or distributed to other users) might not be the subject of criminal sanctions on account of the disproportionality in punishing the possessor (assuming as ever that a Convention right was thereby engaged). It is important to leave the door open to such exceptional cases rather than to say that deference to Parliament requires the court *never* to entertain such lines of defence. To say the latter is effectively to convert the possession of cannabis into a slippery slope offence. But it surely is not. To say that possession of cannabis is a slippery slope offence would mean that even the well-disposed offender who does not wish to pose a threat to health would be unable to assess the risks of so doing. That cannot be right. If it were to be determined that a certain level of cannabis *could* safely be possessed, then users would be fully capable of adjusting their conduct accordingly, and there would be no need to punish those who are careful to do so. The difficulties of measuring the quantity of drugs in one's own possession cannot be compared with the individual's difficulties in ascertaining the risk of assisting a person to commit suicide who is in fact not as willing to do this as might appear to be the case. Slippery slope offences exist where individuals, with the best will in the world, cannot be relied upon to reduce the risks to a vital state interest. They do not exist simply because the courts or Parliament are not ready to make fine distinctions for themselves. In the latter case, caution may be advisable, but an open mind should be kept for exceptional cases.

A similar concern might be expressed over the ever-prevailing judgment of the legislature that it is necessary to criminalise all consensual sexual activity with underage girls by males who know the age of the girl,[103] even if the male is himself under age and even where there is no suggestion of corruption or undue pressure being used by him. Again, one might readily agree that the conduct should be criminalised because of the potential for abuse, even among partners of the same age, but that is not to say that courts should refuse to listen in individual cases where the boy's right under Article 8 is engaged and where it is hard to conclude that it is proportionate to punish him for the sake of deterring other instances of the activity. That, however, is what the courts appear to be

---

[103] See Sexual Offences Act 2003 ss 9–10.

prepared to do.[104] The court's mistake, it is respectfully submitted, is to assume that it must be deferential in *all* cases. Yet there must be cases where, after the girl has given evidence, the court might conclude that the threat to her own rights (ie her sexual autonomy) was small or non-existent and that punishment serves no purpose. A further example of the tendency not to recognise that cases should depend upon the facts even if punishment will *normally* be necessary and proportionate towards protecting the state interest is the decision that an absolute ban on corporal punishment in schools is a proportionate measure to protect the rights of pupils.[105] In this case too, one can readily recognise the need to show deference to a Parliamentary judgment which has much outside support.[106] But can it really be said that a court is incompetent to say for itself that in some cases only a negligible risk to the child's psychological or physical health is evident?[107]

The point being made is this. One should not foreclose possible arguments on the absence of state justification simply because they would rarely be successful. No doctrine of deference requires a court to do this, and they have no mandate to do this. This result is only acceptable where the conduct in question is of a 'slippery slope' nature, in which case it is justified for the court to refuse to hear argument and to proceed automatically to conviction because it needs to give effect to Parliament's decision that individuals will not be able to assess the risks of their own conduct and need to be discouraged from acting upon their own assessments. But, as already mentioned, a slippery slope offence only occurs when well-disposed individuals cannot adjust their conduct accordingly to minimise risks to the state interest. One might reply that sexual activity with underage girls and corporal punishment of pupils are further

---

[104] *E v Director of Public Prosecutions* [2005] WL 62315 (CA). This is a case where one wishes that the court had heeded the warning in *Percy* not simply to declare that state interference is proportionate without offering reasons. The court's reasoning on state justification in *E* is contained in one sentence in para. 15. It might be noted that, if the Court of Appeal had found that any punishment of E would violate his right under Art 8, then it surely would have had to have found s 6(1) of the Sexual Offences Act 1956 itself to be incompatible with Art 8, because it is very hard to see how the section could possibly have been 'read down' so as to be made compatible. A similar fate would then have awaited s 9 of the Sexual Offences Act 2003.

[105] *R v Secretary of State for Education and Employment and Others* [2005] UKHL 15 (HL).

[106] Ibid, at para. 51, *per* Lord Bingham, at para. 85 *per* Lady Hale.

[107] Their Lordships recognised the difficulty in saying this, given the retention of a defence of chastisement for parents (the Children Act 2004 s 58). Moreover, one might assume that there is a greater risk of abuse in the family home than there might be at a school, assuming that in the latter cases procedures are adopted (including the consultation of parents) which minimise such risks.

examples of slippery slope offences: the boy might not know how much pressure the girl feels under from other sources to agree to activity, and the teacher similarly cannot be sure that he knows how much psychological torment is caused even by a single smack. Perhaps indeed it is true that these are slippery slope offences too. But if they are, then the courts need to be wary of the risks of so holding, and to ask themselves upon what basis Parliament might have decided that individuals cannot be expected to adjust their conduct accordingly.[108]

Conclusions

I might start this conclusion by summarising the paper. I have argued that where a person whose conduct engaged a qualified Convention right is prosecuted in order to protect a state interest, we must distinguish between cases where the prosecution is (from cases where it is not) required to prove that the conduct posed a risk to that state interest on the facts of the case. Where it is so required, then the court will have to decide whether punishment will be a necessary and proportionate way of protecting that interest in future. Much might depend upon the theory of punishment upon which the state wishes to rely, and we have drawn some distinctions here between punishment for specific deterrence and punishment for general deterrence. But where the 'slippery slope' princi- ple applies, the court has no equivalent function in determining the necessity or proportionality of imposing any punishment (though the *degree* of any punishment should, as always, be proportionate). But review of prosecutorial discretion on public interest grounds should be available during the trial, and the trial should be stopped for abuse of process if it is found wanting. It is important that there be a 'system' whereby the defendant is actively involved in the decision making process, though it is anticipated that this will be a less effective remedy than being able to challenge the prosecution on the merits of punishment in open court.

Now, this is the sort of structured approach which might be expected from an academic writer. If another should criticise it, then he or she will probably seek to replace it with a different one. However, structure seems

---

[108] This question was not asked in *R v Secretary of State for Education and Employment and others, ex parte Williamson* [2005] UKHL 15. Lady Hale at para. 80 noted the analogy with the blanket ban in *ex p Pretty* but did not note the important difference that in that case it was the individual (and not the courts) who was thought to be unable to assess the magnitude of risks to the state interest.

particularly important in this area of the law which is developing incrementally and where courts are only looking at cases with similar facts for guidance. There is not yet a recognition that the difficulties in justifying state interference with a qualified Convention right are common to a number of quite discrete areas of the criminal law (indeed, I started this paper with the quite dissimilar examples of sado-masochism and public order offences). Moreover, this structured approach is not contradicted by the (admittedly scattered) authorities to date. There is authority that the exercise of prosecutorial discretion which neglects the human rights arguments at the evidential stage can be an 'unlawful act' (*ex p Rusbridger*), and there is authority too that it is for the state to justify prosecution and punishment on the facts of a case where the conduct of the accused engages a right: (*Percy v DPP*). The contrary *dicta* in *ex p Pretty* have been distinguished because this is a slippery slope case, and although there is no authority yet for the judicial review of slippery slope prosecutions on public interest grounds, such a system can be argued to be required by reference to the Strasbourg jurisprudence.

The greatest obstacle to this academic structure is in fact the same tendency to defer to Parliamentary judgments as is capable of undermining all developments in human rights law. The wish to defer to Parliament on the risks posed by the possession of drugs is understandable, but when a court is similarly unwilling to hear an argument that there is insufficient state interest in punishing a boy for having consensual sex with a girl of the same age, then deference has been taken too far. The court should only ever decline to hear arguments on the facts of individual cases where Parliament intended an absolute ban on the basis that individuals could not be relied upon to adjust their conduct to minimise risks to legitimate state interests and need to be deterred in all cases from trying to do so. If we can agree upon this, then (even though deference might be appropriate in the general run of cases) we can look forward to a consistent development of principles in the future.

Rights Relating to Personality, Freedom of the Press and Private International Law: Some Common Law Comments

Robin Morse *

Introduction

Common law systems protect so-called 'rights relating to personality' (which is not a term of art in these systems)[1] in a variety of ways and through a variety of legal techniques amongst which are: defamation; malicious falsehood; invasion of privacy; the law relating to confidence; and the law relating to data protection. The scope of protection offered by these techniques (the first three of which involve the law of tort and the other two of which may involve equitable rights or tort and statute) may differ considerably as between different common law systems and, in the context of application to the press and other media, may be complicated by the impact of constitutional provisions[2] and/or human rights norms.[3] Translated into

---

* This is a revised and expanded version of a lecture delivered in the *Current Legal Problems* series at University College London on 21 October 2004. The contribution originally derives from a paper prepared for discussion at private meeting of the European Group for Private International Law (GEDIP) held in Tenerife on 18 September 2004. I am grateful to colleagues in GEDIP for their input. Thanks are also due to my colleague Dr Paul Mitchell who commented helpfully on a draft. Errors, omissions and imperfections are mine.

[1] cf Quebec Civil Code, Art 3: 'Every person is the holder of personality rights, such as the right to life, the right to the inviolability and integrity of his person, and the right to the respect of his name, reputation and privacy.' See Popovici, 'Personality Rights—A Civil Law Concept' (2004) 50 Loyola L Rev 349.

[2] The most obvious example is the First Amendment to the United States Constitution which has generated a vast amount of case law and literature in this context.

[3] The most obvious example in the United Kingdom is the European Convention on Human Rights, Art 10. Since the implementation of the Convention in domestic law in the Human Rights Act 1998, this provision has made regular appearances in the case law. For a notorious example see, in the context of defamation, *Reynolds v Times Newspapers Ltd* [2000] 2 AC 115.

the field of private international law, the issues may become increasingly complex, not least because of the increasingly global operations of traditional media and, of course, that most ubiquitous of creatures, the internet.[4]

This paper will deal with the impact of the law of defamation and the law relating to invasion of privacy on the freedom of the press and other media in the international context, principally from the standpoint of English law, though some consideration will be given to other common law systems. It treats selected issues and should not be regarded as an exhaustive consideration of all of the exotica to which this aspect of private international law may give rise. It begins by providing some background to the issues, before proceeding to consider aspects of the traditional questions of jurisdiction, choice of law and recognition of judgments.

Background

Defamation

London is often described as the 'libel capital of the world'[5] and, according to one authority, American journalists are prone to describe it as 'a town named Sue'.[6] Such extravagant descriptions are not prompted directly by private international law considerations, but rather by the pro-claimant character of the substantive rules of the English domestic law of defamation designed to protect a person's reputation.[7] These characteristics, it

---

[4] Consideration of the impact of the internet seems to have brought new life to American law reviews which are replete with articles on the matter, often carrying obscure, but catchy titles. For examples, in relation to the conflict of laws, see Beall, 'The Scientological Defenestration of Choice-of Law Doctrines for Publication Torts on the Internet' (1997) 15 John Marshall Journal of Computer and Information Law 361; Swire, 'Of Elephants, Mice and Privacy: International Choice of Law and the Internet' (1998) 32 Int'l Law 991.

[5] Robertson and Nicol, *Media Law* (4th edn, 2002), 70; Barendt *et al*, *Libel and the Media* (1997), p. 16; Vick and Macpherson, 'Anglicizing defamation law in the European Union' (1996) 36 Va. J Int'l L 933, 934; Penzi, 'Libel actions in England, a Game of Truth or Dare? Considering Recent Upjohn Cases and the Consequences of "Speaking Out" ' (1996) 10 Temple Int'l. & Comp. L. Q. 211; *Telnikoff v Matusevitch*, 702 A2d 230, 250–251 (1996).   [6] Robertson and Nicol, n 5 above.

[7] English law divides defamation into libel and slander, the former being a communication in permanent form, the latter being a communication in non-permanent form. Most communications through the media are regarded as being in permanent form and thus give rise to claims in libel. Accordingly, slander will not be separately considered in this paper. Libel, exceptionally, may give rise to criminal liability but this is now rarely, if ever, invoked and is not considered in this paper. This paper does not consider the possible effect of the E-Commerce Directive on the private international law of defamation. For some thoughts on the position in England, which is problematic, see Law Commission, *Defamation and the Internet, A Preliminary Investigation, Scoping Study No. 2* (2002), paras. 4.37–4.49;

has been said, attract 'many wealthy foreign forum-shoppers in search of favourable verdicts that they would not obtain at home, or in the home countries of publishers whose newspapers and magazines have an international circulation.'[8] Thus the English courts become a haven for those who are unable to claim against the relevant defendant in a court in the United States, or Europe, or some other country;[9] and while it is unsurprising that English based publishers are not safe from the law of England, it is important to note that foreign publishers are at risk as well.[10]

So what are the features of English libel law that make it so attractive? While this is not the place for a detailed discussion of substantive law the following may be briefly mentioned. First, liability is strict: there is no requirement on the claimant to prove fault. Second, the claimant is not required to prove the falsehood of the statement: if the defendant alleges the statement is true, the burden lies on the defendant to prove that fact. Third, libel is actionable without proof of special damage. Fourth, each publication of a statement is a separate tort. Fifth, unlike the position in the United States, there is no requirement that a claimant who is a public figure prove 'actual malice' on the part of the publisher.[11] Sixth, defamation claims are among the few civil claims in England which can be tried by jury and until recently juries were prone to award large sums by way of damages. This has now been corrected by guidance from the Court of Appeal[12] to the effect that libel awards should not be so large as to deter

Dicey and Morris, *The Conflict of Laws* (13th edn, 2000), *Fourth Supplement* (2004), 458–460. Further, it does not consider the proposal presented by the European Commission for a regulation of the European Parliament and of the Council on the law applicable to non-contractual obligations (COM (2003) 427 final). On the proposal, see House of Lords, European Union Committee, *The Rome II Regulation. Report with Evidence*, HL Paper 66 (2004).

[8] Robertson and Nicol, n 5 above, 101.

[9] Fifer and Sachs, 'The Price of International free Speech: Nations deal with Defamation on the Internet' (1997) 8 DePaul J. Art & Ent. Law 1, 4.

[10] See nn 27–38 below, and related text.

[11] 'Actual malice' requires knowledge that the statement was false or reckless disregard of whether it was false or not: *New York Times Co. v Sullivan*, 376 US 254 (1964), at 279–280. A 'private figure' claimant must prove that the defendant was at least negligent in publishing a false statement: *Gertz v Robert Welch Inc.*, 418 US 323 (1974).

[12] *Rantzen v Mirror Group Newspapers* [1994] QB 670 (claimant, well-known television presenter, awarded £250,000 by jury: award reduced to £110,000); *John v MGN Ltd.* [1997] QB 586 (claimant, rock star, awarded £350,000 by jury in respect of invented story about his eating habits: award reduced to £75,000). Earlier very high awards included: £500,000 to Conservative politician and popular novelist, Jeffrey Archer in respect of allegations in the *Star* that he had paid £2,000 to a prostitute to leave the country, and who, subsequently, as Lord Archer of Weston-super-Mare, was sentenced to four years imprisonment for fabricating evidence in support of his claim; a settlement of £1,000,000 in favour of Elton John against the *Sun*; a jury award of £600,000 to the wife of the 'Yorkshire Ripper' against *Private Eye*, the satirical magazine, a sum described by the Court of Appeal

investigative journalism, that juries should be given judicial guidance as to how to keep them in proportion, and that juries should be told of the level of damages awarded in personal injuries cases (which are generally much lower than the more exaggerated libel awards) since it is 'offensive to public opinion . . . that a defamation plaintiff should recover damages for injury to reputation greater, perhaps by a significant factor, than if that same plaintiff had been rendered a helpless cripple or insensate vegetable'.[13] A reduction in the size of awards may reduce the financial incentive to litigating in London, though it may well be that wealthy claimants are more interested in vindicating their reputations than in obtaining compensation.[14]

A variety of 'prominent' foreign residents have attempted to take advantage of these provisions so as to proceed against the English based media in cases which have raised no issues of private international law. These include: a claimant formerly responsible for the security services in Ghana;[15] the elder son of Colonel Gaddafi;[16] the ex-premier of the Republic of Ireland;[17] the second of the three wives of the Emir of Qatar;[18] Tom Cruise and Nicole

---

as unreasonable and excessive (see *Sutcliffe v Pressdram* [1991] 1 QB 153); £1.5m awarded by a jury against Count Tolstoy in favour of Lord Aldington whom the former had accused of being a 'war criminal' despite a direction by the judge that the jury should 'not deal in Mickey Mouse money, just reeling off noughts because they sound good', an award later described by the European Court of Human Rights as so disproportionate as to amount to a violation of Art. 10 of the Convention (see *Tolstoy Miloslavsky v United Kingdom* (1995) 20 EHRR 442).

13 *John v MGN*, n 12 above, 614.

14 Particularly if the claimant is anxious to preserve a business reputation with a view to continuing success: cf *Berezovsky v Michaels* [2000] 1 WLR 1004, 1010–1011 (HL). See also the *McDonald's* litigation described in [1995] 3 All ER 615. Defamation Act 1996, ss 8–10 enables the court to dispose summarily of a claim without jury trial if it appears to the court that there is no defence to the claim which has a realistic prospect of success, and that there is no other reason why the claim should be tried, but under this procedure damages awarded may not exceed £10,000. For a case considering the application of these provisions in the context of an alleged press libel having an international dimension, see *HH Sheikha Mouza Al Misnad v Azzaman Ltd.* [2003] EWHC 1783 (QB) (claimant sought summary disposal, resisted by defendant: claimant's application refused).

15 *Tsikata v Newspaper Publishing plc* [1995] EMLR 8 (claimant alleged to have masterminded abduction and murder of three Ghanaian High Court judges and a retired army officer).

16 *Gaddafi v Telegraph Group Ltd.* [2000] EMLR 431 (allegation that claimant had attempted through henchmen to lure journalist responsible for article in *Daily Telegraph* to Libya with a view 'to stringing him up from the nearest Tripoli lamp post'). See also *Gaddafi v Telegraph Group Ltd. (No. 2)* [2000] WL 1675142.

17 *Reynolds v Times Newspapers Ltd.* [2001] 2 AC 127 (allegation that claimant had lied to Parliament and deceived his coalition partner).

18 *HH Sheika Mouza Al Misnad v Azzaman*, n 14 above (allegation, *inter alia*, of abuse of power and interference in government affairs).

Kidman;[19] McDonald's;[20] the almost customary Russian 'oligarch;'[21] a prominent Saudi Arabian dissident, resident in London;[22] a Bulgarian company with subsidiaries engaged in a wide range of activities such as banking, commodity trading and manufacturing in various parts of the world;[23] two Australian actors in a popular Australian television series well known to an English audience;[24] and an Italian Prince.[25]

[19] *Cruise v Express Newspapers* [1999] QB 931 (allegation that their marriage a sham; newspaper apologised and paid damages; one year later claimants announced their divorce).
[20] eg *McDonald's Corp. v Steel* [1995] 3 All ER 615. In this case McDonald's Corp., incorporated in Iowa, USA and its wholly owned UK subsidiary, brought libel proceedings against an unemployed former postal worker and a part-time bar worker in respect of pamphlets alleging, *inter alia*, that McDonald's was destroying rain forests, producing litter in cities and causing cancer, heart disease and food poisoning. After the longest civil trial in English legal history at the time (313 days) and numerous interlocutory applications and appeals the claimants were awarded £40,000 in damages which they have little hope of recovering. McDonald's costs, which the company did not seek to recover from the defendants, have been estimated to be in the region of $10 million: see Nicholson, 'McLibel: A Case Study in English Defamation Law' (2000) 18 Wisconsin International Law Journal 1, 2 where the national proceedings are discussed. The European Court of Human Rights in a claim by the defendants against the UK found violations of Arts 6 and 10 of the Convention: see *Steel and Morris v United Kingdom* [2005] EMLR 314. See also the libel actions brought by the pharmaceutical company, Upjohn, in the mid 1990s, discussed by Penzi, n 5 above.
[21] *Loutchansky v Times Newspapers Ltd.* [2001] WL 98035 (allegation that claimant involved in international criminal activities of a most serious kind). This litigation has given rise to a plethora of applications and appeals. For a selection of reported outcomes, see *Loutchansky (No. 1)* [2001] EMLR 876; *Loutchansky (No. 2)* [2001] EMLR 885; *Loutchansky (No. 1)* [2001] EWCA Civ 536; [2002] QB 321; *Loutchansky (No. 4)* [2001] EMLR 898; *Loutchansky (No. 5)* [2001] EMLR 955; *Loutchansky (No. 2)* [2001] EWCA Civ 1805; [2002] QB 1805.
[22] *Al-Fagih v H.H. Saudi Research & Marketing (UK) Ltd.* [2001] EWCA Civ 1634; [2002] EMLR 215 (allegation that claimant had spread malicious rumours about another Saudi Arabian dissident and had said that the latter's mother had procured women to have sexual intercourse with him at his home). See also *Jameel v Times Newspapers Ltd.* [2004] EWCA Civ 983; [2004] EMLR 665 (allegation that claimant, a Saudia Arabian billionaire, was linked to Osama bin Laden).
[23] *Multigroup Bulgaria Holding AD v Oxford Analytica Ltd.* [2001] EMLR 737 (allegation by specialist information and research organisation on-line that claimant had engaged in corruption under the headings 'Power of Nomenklatura Businesses in Bulgaria' and 'Bulgaria: Red Conglomerates').
[24] *Charleston v News Group Newspapers Ltd.* [1995] 2 AC 65 (allegation under headline in *News of the World* 'Strewth! What's Harold up to with our Madge' accompanied by a photograph which appeared to show the actors who played the parts of a respectable married couple in *Neighbours* engaging in perverse sexual activity, the photographs having actually been produced by makers of pornographic computer games by superimposing faces of the plaintiffs, without their knowledge or consent, on the bodies of others).
[25] *Ruspoli v Associated Newspapers plc* (11 December 1992, CA) (allegation that what claimant said after fracas in New York restaurant meant that claimant was 'an arrogant snob who regards people who work for a living behind a bar as mere scum, and approves of violence being used against them'). Cf *Yousoupoff v MGM Pictures Ltd.* (1934) 50 TLR 581 (allegation that claimant, a Russian Princess, had been raped by Rasputin).

Doubtless the claimants in these cases may have been justified in their attempts to vindicate their reputations in an English court against English based media defendants who can hardly complain of being subjected to English jurisdiction and English law, in respect of publications which principally circulate in England. But the incentive to pursue the claims is undoubtedly, in many of these cases, the balance struck by English libel law between the protection of reputation and freedom of expression, a balance which clearly leans towards protection of the former and against the protection of the latter interest.[26]

This balance has also led (and this is of relevance from the standpoint of private international law) to foreign media defendants being sued for libel, by English and foreign based claimants, in the English courts. A sample of these cases is treated in more detail below but to set the context the following brief description may be helpful. In 1987 an English jury awarded to an English claimant £450,000 damages against a Greek news-paper and one of its journalists despite the fact that the paper was published in Greece and only 50 or so copies were sold in England.[27] Continuing with the Greek theme, Andreas Papandreou, a former Prime Minister of Greece, has sued *Time Magazine*, based in the United States, in London rather than in the United States or Greece.[28] More recently, the customary Russian 'oligarch' has proceeded against the American publishers of *Forbes* magazine in England.[29] In the last couple of years the English courts have been peppered with the following matters: an action by the leader of a Tunisian political movement against the printer, editor and publisher of an Arabic language newspaper circulated in Arab countries and in Europe;[30] an action by an Egyptian company and a businessman, apparently resident

---

[26] It is fair to say that many, if not most, of the cases referred to in the preceding notes established important points of the English substantive law of libel. See, in particular, *Reynolds*, n 17 above.

[27] See Douzinas *et al*, 'It's All Greek to Me; Libel Law and Freedom of the Press' (1987) 137 NLJ 609 for an account of this case. The claimant was a former British naval intelligence officer and the offending article concerned his alleged activities as a British intelligence agent in Greece during the period of the dictatorship between 1967 and 1974. See also William, 'Freedom of the Press' (1987) 137 NLJ 795.

[28] Vick and Macpherson, n 5 above, 935. Had he sued in the United States he would have undoubtedly fallen foul of *New York Times v Sullivan*, n 11 above. It has not been possible to locate any further formal records of the Papandreou case. According to a short squib in *The Independent* of 14 March 1989 the suit was brought in London rather than elsewhere because the procedures are less time-consuming in London than elsewhere. According to a Reuters press release of 30 July 1993, on 29 July 1993 Mr Papandreou accepted undisclosed libel damages from *Time* in respect of an article implying he was a party to embezzlement, bribery and blackmail. According to his solicitor, the damages were 'substantial': ibid.

[29] *Berezovsky v Michaels*, n 14 above, discussed below.

[30] *Ghannouchi v Houni Ltd*. [2002] EWHC 3070 (QB); [2003] EWHC 552 (QB) (allegation that claimant linked to Osama bin Laden).

in Paris and with joint Egyptian and French nationality against the al Jazeera Satellite Channel, based in Qatar, and one of the Channel's reporters;[31] an action by Harrods Ltd. (of department store fame) against Dow Jones, the American publishers of the *Wall Street Journal*, in respect of an article in the American edition of that newspaper which commented on a spoof (April fools' joke) statement on the website of Mr Mohamed Al Fayed, the chairman of Harrods;[32] an action by a bank incorporated in Saudi Arabia in connection with an article published in the *Wall Street Journal Europe*;[33] an action by two prominent British businessmen and several companies (some foreign) in which they had an interest, against Time Inc., the American publisher of the American and European editions of *Fortune* magazine;[34] an action brought by Don King, the well-known American boxing promoter, against Lennox Lewis (British former heavyweight boxing champion of the world, mainly resident in the United States), a Nevada company and a New York attorney representing Lennox Lewis, in respect of two articles on 'California based' boxing websites;[35] an action brought by a British television presenter against the present

[31] *Lakah Group v al Jazeera Satellite Channel* [2002] EWHC 2500(QB); [2003] EWHC 1231(QB); [2004] BCC 703; [2003] EWHC 1297(QB) (allegation that corporate claimant had a corrupt relationship with Egyptian Ministry of Health and its Minister and that individual claimant had bribed people in Minister's constituency to vote for him).

[32] *Harrods Ltd v Dow Jones & Co. Inc.* [2003] EWHC 1162 (QB) (under the heading 'The Enron of Britain', article stated 'If Harrods, the British luxury retailer, ever goes public, investors would be wise to question its every disclosure' and claimed by Harrods that, through the link to Enron, article meant that if Harrods was to become a public company it would prove itself to be Britain's Enron by deceiving and defrauding its investors on a huge scale). The article did not appear in the European edition of the *Wall Street Journal*. Dow Jones responded by bringing proceedings in a District Court in New York against Harrods and Mr Al Fayed seeking a declaratory judgment precluding the two last named from pursuing an action for defamation in England. Relief was denied and an appeal to the US Court of Appeals upheld the decision of the District Court. Rarely, if ever before, can an April fools' joke have provoked such consequences and the whole incident seems ludicrous! For further discussion, see below.

[33] *Al Rajhi Banking & Investment Corp. v The Wall Street Journal Europe SPRL* [2003] EWHC 1358(QB); [2003] EWHC 1776(QB); [2004] EWHC 667 (QB) (allegations (broadly) that claimant was, at the request of US authorities, being monitored by Saudi Arabian Central Bank as to its possible involvement in funding of terrorist activities). See also *Jameel v Wall Street Journal Europe SPRL* [2003] EWHC 2945(QB); [2004] 2 All ER 92 (allegation of links to Osama bin Laden).

[34] *Reuben v Time Inc.* [2003] EWCA Civ 6; [2003] EWHC 1430 (QB) (allegations (broadly) of disreputable business practices).

[35] *King v Lewis* [2004] EWHC 168(QB): [2004] ILPr 31, affd. [2004] EWCA Civ 1329; [2005] ILPr 185 (allegation that claimant, in calling the New York attorney a 'shyster lawyer', was anti-semitic). It appears that Mr King would have no cause of action under the law of New York: see [2004] EWHC 168(QB), [2004] ILPr 31 at paras. 36–37; [2004] EWCA Civ 1329 at paras. 40–42. The action was not brought against a media defendant as such but was in respect of statements appearing in the media. For further discussion see below.

Governor of California, his spokesman and a Hollywood publicist in respect of words contained in the hard copy and on-line copy of an edition of *The Los Angeles Times*;[36] and within the United Kingdom, an action brought by a well-known footballer, born in Northern Ireland, who plays for Celtic in Scotland,[37] against the publisher of the *Scottish Daily Record* in respect of an article in the latter newspaper.[38]

These various cases testify to the attraction to 'foreigners' of a London libel action and the consequent 'downside' for the foreign media defendant.

Invasion of Privacy

In contrast to the position with regard to libel, England is not so likely to be looked on as a forum of choice when it comes to claims for invasion of privacy. This is because English law does not recognise an 'overarching all-embracing'[39] right of privacy which, as such, can be protected by a civil action.[40] Nonetheless, protection of various aspects of privacy may be achieved through other causes of action and as has been recently pointed out this is 'a fast developing area of the law'[41] in England and in other common law jurisdictions, and is influenced in England, in particular, by the implementation of the European Convention on Human Rights in the Human Rights Act 1998.[42] Thus, for example, an action for breach of confidence may lie in a situation where the press misuse 'private

---

[36] *Richardson v Schwarzenegger* [2004] EWHC 2422(QB), affd. [2005] EWCA Civ 28 (allegation that claimant had concocted a story that she had been sexually assaulted or harassed by Arnold Schwarzenegger). In these particular proceedings Eady J., in a decision upheld by the Court of Appeal, refused to set aside service out of the jurisdiction on Sean Walsh, Arnold Schwarzenegger's gubernatorial campaign spokesman. Service has been effected in California on Governor Schwarzenegger and Sheryl Main, the Hollywood publicist, who have not, at the time of writing, made applications to have service set aside. The action was not brought against a media defendant as such but was in respect of statements appearing in the media.

[37] The claimant formerly played for Leicester City in England and was found to have a reputation in England and Scotland.

[38] *Neil Lennon v Scottish Daily Record and Sunday Mail Ltd.* [2004] EWHC 359(QB); [2004] EMLR 332 (allegation that article recounting that police were to question all members of Celtic team squad after members of the team emerged from a nightclub in Newcastle, England, and chased a *Daily Record* photographer, robbing him of £12,000 worth of camera equipment, meant that claimant would have been understood to be one of the guilty players or probably one of those players).

[39] *Campbell v MGN Ltd.* [2004] UKHL 22; [2004] 2 WLR 1322 at para. 11.

[40] *Wainwright v Home Office* [2003] UKHL 53; [2003] 3 WLR 1137; *Campbell v MGN*, n 39 above, at para. 11.

[41] *Campbell v MGN Ltd.* [2001] 2 WLR 1322 at para. 11.

[42] Protection of the right to privacy is well-known in the United States. For an account of the position in England, see, Markesinis, O'Cinneide, Fedtke and Hunter-Henin, 'Concerns and Ideas about the Developing English Law of Privacy (and How Knowledge

information'.[43] One such case which could have private international law implications is the saga (or soap opera) of Michael Douglas, Catherine Zeta-Jones and *Hello!* magazine which is discussed below.[44]

In Europe, a forum of choice for invasion of privacy is likely to be France.[45] The advantages of this jurisdiction were claimed by the reclusive Barclay brothers to proceed against the publishers of the English Sunday newspaper, *The Observer*, and the author of an article in that newspaper which concerned them.[46] The brothers, who jealously guard their privacy, were at the time found to be domiciled in the United Kingdom.[47] The court of first instance held that the French court lacked jurisdiction under Article 5(3) of the Brussels Convention since there was insufficient evidence of the distribution of the offending newspaper in France and the claimants had not stated the reasons why they were known in France or provided any explanation of the nature of the interests which they had in France which had been affected by the publication. The Cour d'Appel took a different view. It held that in the case of an invasion of privacy and infringement of the right to one's image by the press, the place in which the damage is suffered is the place where the publication is distributed. There was evidence which established that *The Observer* was sold systematically in France, particularly in Paris, Lyon and Marseille. The newspaper also featured in the list of titles distributed by les Nouvelles Messageries de la Presse Parisienne and Transports Presse accompanied by its price in French francs. The totality of these factors made it possible to draw the conclusion that this particular edition of *The Observer* was available for sale in France, and in particular in Paris. Additionally, it mattered little, for the purposes of determining jurisdiction, whether or not the claimants were known in France although that factor would be material to the substance of the claim.

of Foreign Law might Help)' (2004) 52 AJCL 133; Phillipson, 'Breach of Confidence as a Privacy Remedy in the Human Rights Act Era' (2003) 66 MLR 726. A readable account by a lawyer turned journalist will be found in Rozenberg, *Privacy and the Press* (Oxford University Press, 2004).

[43] *Campbell v MGN*, n 41 above. (Daily Mirror misused private information by publishing photographs and information relating to claimant's attendance at meetings of Narcotics Anonymous.)

[44] *Douglas v Hello! Ltd. (No. 2)* [2003] EWCA Civ 139; [2003] EMLR 585.

[45] Fifer and Sachs, n 9 above.

[46] *David Rowlat Barclay v John Sweeney* [1999] ILPr 288 (Cour d'Appel, Paris). A published picture of the brothers also formed part of the complaint. See also *Sola v La Tribune de Genève* [2000] ILPr 795 (Cour d'Appel, Paris (defamation)).

[47] Although they were resident in Monaco and are now said to be based in Brecqhou, one of the Channel Islands, which they purchased in 1993. Ironically, they have been reported to own a stake in the notorious tabloid, *The National Enquirer*: see *The Observer*, 24 September 1995 (Review, 1).

This was not the first time that an English newspaper had been sued in the French courts for invasion of privacy. In 1986 *The Mail on Sunday* had carried two articles written by its gossip columnist which concerned an unidentified 14-year-old prince.[48] The articles, apparently, gave details of his schooling and information about his father also, naturally enough, a prince. The report of the case does not reveal any argument about jurisdiction, but presumably son and father were able to bring the action against the publishers of the newspaper and the author of the article in the French courts because the paper was available in France, though it does not appear that the princes had any connection with France and, one suspects, *The Mail on Sunday* did not have a wide circulation in France, at least in 1986. The action was a conspicuous success with the little prince being awarded FFr 50,000 and the big prince (and his wife) the same amount against the publishers of the paper and the author of the articles.[49]

It appears to have been thought that the German law of privacy was less protective of an individual than its French counterpart. This did not, however, prevent the German Chancellor, Gerhard Schröder, from taking on *The Mail on Sunday* in the German courts in respect of an article linking him, in the romantic sense, with a well-known German television interviewer. A court in Hamburg granted an injunction forbidding the publishers from reporting on aspects of the Chancellor's private life even though that week's edition of the newspaper was not distributed in Germany, but rather was a story which the German press picked up from *The Mail on Sunday*. A spokesman for the court acknowledged that the injunction applied only in Germany, though the Hamburg court order stipulated that the publishers would face a penalty of €250,000 if the allegations were repeated.[50] The incident merely served to increase *The Mail on Sunday*'s already rampant Europhobia! Had the Chancellor sued in England, the more natural forum, he would have had to allege libel which would not be established if the allegations were proved to be true or breach of confidence (misuse, possibly, of private information) with an effective admission that the claims were true.

The German press, it is well known, has been vigorously pursued by Princess Caroline of Monaco with claims for violation of her privacy, often resulting from photographs taken in France but published not in France

---

[48] Rozenberg, n 42 above, at 230, points out that the only expatriate European prince born in 1972, the relevant year, was the Italian Prince Emanuele Filiberto of Savoy, son of Prince Vittorio Emanuele. Another commentator states that the relevant prince was Prince Karim Aga Khan: Korzenik, 'Libel and Privacy Suits Against US Media in Foreign Courts', 516 Practising Law Institute (PLI/Pat) 955, 980 (1998).

[49] *Societe Mail Newspapers plc v Prince X*, Cass. Civ 23 October 1990, Bull. Civ No. 222. An English translation of this case can be found at *www.ucl.ac.uk/laws/global_law*.

[50] This account is largely based on material contained in articles in *The Guardian* on 18 and 20 January 2003. See also Rozenberg, n 42 above, 232.

(where publication would be unlawful) but in Germany.[51] In the most recent bout of litigation, the Federal Constitutional Court recognised a right to restrain publication of photographs taken in a typically private place including a secluded table in the corner of a restaurant. However, the princess had to tolerate, as a 'figure of contemporary society *par excellence*' the publication of photographs in which she appeared in a public place even if they were photographs of scenes from her daily life (eg shopping) and not photographs showing her exercising her public functions. The public, so it was said, had a legitimate interest in knowing where the princess was staying and how she behaved in public.[52] The princess duly took Germany to the European Court of Human Rights, which, on 24 June 2004, found in her favour on the latter point.[53] Put very briefly, the court held that on the latter point her privacy was not adequately protected. The limited protection recognised by the German court might be appropriate for politicians but did not go far enough for individuals like the princess who did not hold any public office. Photographs of her going about her daily activities fell within the sphere of her private life and publication of them did not contribute to any debate of general interest to society. Writing in *The Times*, two experienced practitioners had this to say: 'The case makes clear that famous people have the right to be left alone, even when they are in public places. Before publishing photographs of celebrities doing their shopping the press must ask: what legitimate purpose does publication serve? A convincing answer may be hard to find. It is difficult to imagine a case where such pictures could be said to contribute to a debate on matters of public concern'.[54]

To the extent that this decision may bring about a change in German law so as to draw it towards the standards prevailing in French law, it may have the effect of making Germany a more attractive jurisdiction for at least some classes of privacy case. And for jurisdictions such as England, that afford relatively little protection, it might provide a warning that local law is not up to standard.

[51] Bundesgerichtshof, BGHZ 128, 1 51 November 1994; Bundesgerichtshof, 5 December 1995, NJW 1996, 984; Bundesgerichtshof, 12 December 1995, NJW 1996, 985 (claimant her 8-year-old son); Bundesgerichtshof, 19 December 1995, NJW 1996, 1128; Bundesgerichtshof, 29 June 1999 (claimant her current husband, Prince Ernst August of Hanover); Bundesverfassungsgerichts, 15 December 1999. English translations of these cases can be found on the website *www.ucl.ac.uk/laws/global_law*.

[52] Bundesverfassungsgerichts, 15 December 1999.

[53] *Von Hannover v Germany* (Application no. 59320/00) (24 June 2004); [2004] EMLR 21.

[54] H Rogers and H Tomlinson, 'Caroline Ruling Sounds Alarm for British Press', *The Times*, 29 June 2004. See also Tomlinson and Thomson, 'Bad News for Paparazzi—Strasbourg has Spoken' (2004) 154 NLJ 1040.

In none of the cases referred to above has foreign law been regarded as being of relevance to the substance of the claim and for the most part it is quite clear that the claimant chooses a particular forum because that forum will apply its own law. In England, this is so even where the media defendant is foreign and the substantial volume of the publication occurs abroad: provided there is publication in England and the claimant has some reputation in England, English law will be applied, at least in respect of the English publication, and the claimant or defendant need not rely or may not be able to rely in some circumstances on a foreign law. This means that the principal private international law issue which tends to arise in the English case law is that of the jurisdiction of the English court, an issue which is elaborated below. To understand that issue a preliminary point concerned with choice of law needs a mention.

Choice of Law: A Preliminary Point

Part III of the Private International Law (Miscellaneous Provisions) Act 1995 (hereafter 'the Act') generally places the English choice of law rules in tort on a statutory footing.[55] However, the new choice of law rules contained in the Act do not apply to claims for defamation[56] as defined in the Act.[57] The Bill on which the Act was based contained no provision excluding defamation claims from the scope of the Act. Earlier recommendations from the Law Commission had taken account of such matters by recommending that where a statement was published abroad and was simultaneously or previously published in the United Kingdom, the applicable law should be that of the relevant part of the United Kingdom.[58] This, so it was said, was intended to give effect to the public interest in free speech and in the proper functioning of public institutions: to protect that public interest it was not desirable that those who made statements in the United Kingdom should have their freedom of expression limited by the application of foreign law.[59] Concerns such as

[55] The principal rules are found in ss 11 and 12 of the Act. s 11 broadly establishes application of the law of the country in which the tort is committed or is to be taken to have been committed, as a general rule. s 12 establishes a rule of displacement whereby if it appears, in all the circumstances, from a comparison of the significance of the factors which connect the tort with the country whose law is applicable under the general rule and the significance of the factors which connect the tort with another country, that it is substantially more appropriate for the applicable law to be the law of the other country, the general rule is displaced and the applicable law is the law of the other country.   [56] ss 9(3), 10, 13.
[57] s 13(2).   [58] Law Com. No. 193 (1990), para. 3.33.
[59] Ibid, para. 3.31.

these and particularly the effect on freedom of the press, led to the preservation of the common law choice of law rules for defamation and related claims.[60] Those common law rules consist of the general rule of double actionability which is subject to a somewhat ill-defined exception which may permit sole application of the law of the forum or the sole application of the law of the country in which the tort is committed or (possibly) the law of some third country.[61]

Retention of that part of the general rule that requires that the act done in a foreign country be actionable as a tort by English domestic law preserves the barrier of the law of the forum so as, at least as a general rule, to prevent foreign liabilities in defamation and related claims being enforceable in English courts unless the events giving rise to those liabilities give rise to an actionable claim by English domestic law.[62] Retention of the common law preserved a further common law rule, to the effect that once it had been determined that a tort had been committed in England only English law applied and foreign law was entirely irrelevant.[63] This means that where a libel is found to have been committed in England, English libel law is exclusively applicable.[64]

The upshot of all this is that a combination of the pro-claimant character of English libel law, the choice of law rules applicable to defamation and the rules concerning the jurisdiction of English courts which are applied in this context means that the application of a foreign substantive law and, possibly (though this needs further consideration) a foreign law concerning invasion of privacy, is likely to be rare. Indeed, there appear to be only three reported cases where the choice of law rules for foreign torts have been seriously considered in the context of defamation.[65]

It is now proposed to consider specific jurisdictional issues raised in the case-law.

---

[60] ss 9(3), 10, 13. This was probably the most controversial feature in the passage of the Bill and was vigorously trumpeted by the very powerful press lobby: see Morse, 'Torts in Private International Law: A New Statutory Framework' (1996) 45 ICLQ 888, 891–893.

[61] See n 94 below, and related text.

[62] See the debate on the Bill at HL Deb., 1 March 1995, cols. 19–22.

[63] s 14(2) of the Act: see *Szalatnay-Stacho v Fink* [1947] KB 1 (a defamation case); *Metall und Rohstoff A.G. v Donaldson Lufkin & Jenrette Inc.* [1990] 1 QB 391.

[64] *Szalatnay-Stacho*, n 63 above. Whether invasion of privacy is excluded from the Act by s 13, as a defamation or related claim, is controversial: see n 172 below, and related text.

[65] *Machado v Fontes* [1897] 2 QB 231, overruled in *Boys v Chaplin* [1971] AC 356; *Church of Scientology of California v Commissioner of Police* (1976) 120 SJ 690; *University of Glasgow v The Economist* [1997] EMLR 495; cf *Szalatnay-Stacho*, n 63 above. More litigation was generated in Australia when the double actionability rule was accepted in that country (see Handford, 'Defamation and the Conflict of Laws in Australia', (1983) 32 ICLQ 452) which is no longer the case: see *John Pfeiffer Pty. Ltd. v Rogerson* (2000) 203 CLR 503; *Regie National des Usines Renault S.A. v Zhang* (2003) 210 CLR 491; and in the

Specific Jurisdictional Issues

Leaving to one side jurisdictional issues which arise under the Brussels and Lugano Conventions and Council Regulation No. 44/2001, assuming an English court does not have jurisdiction over a foreign media defendant because it is 'present' in England by virtue of doing business at a place of business in England,[66] jurisdiction will depend, in a defamation case on the exercise by the court of its power to give permission for process to be served on the defendant abroad pursuant to Civil Procedure Rule (CPR) r 6.20(8).[67] First, it must be shown that the damage was sustained in England or that the damage sustained resulted from an act committed in England. Second, it must be shown by the claimant that England is the *forum conveniens*.[68] Application of this rule is not without difficulty in the field of libel.

'A Gentleman of No Occupation'

In 1936 Mr Kroch, who described himself as a 'gentleman of no occupation', brought actions against the publishers of a Belgian and a French newspaper in respect of libel. He sought permission to serve, on those publishers, what was then called a writ, out of the jurisdiction, under the then equivalent of the CPR which required that there be a 'tort committed' in England. Since the newspapers were distributed in England, undoubtedly a tort had been committed there but the circulation there was minuscule in comparison with the circulation in Belgium and France. Nonetheless, the Court of Appeal declined to give permission for service abroad.[69]

context of defamation the important case of *Dow Jones & Co. Inc. v Gutnick* [2002] HCA 56; (2003) 210 CLR 575. The application of the double actionability rule to defamation cases is not further discussed in this paper. For the detail, see Dicey and Morris, n 7 above, paras. 35-120–35-149.

[66] Companies Act 1985, ss 690A–695 and Sch 21A; Civil Procedure Rules, Part 6: see *Harrods v Dow Jones*, n 32 above; *Reuben v Time*, n 34 above; *Lakah v al Jazeera*, n 31 above.

[67] Civil Procedure Rules (replacing RSC Ord 11, r 1(1)(f).

[68] Applying the principles established by the House of Lords in *Spiliada Maritime Corp. v Cansulex Ltd.* [1987] 1 AC 460 to the effect that the 'basic principle is that a stay will only be granted on the ground of *forum non conveniens* where the court is satisfied that there is some other available forum, having competent jurisdiction, which is the appropriate forum for the trial of the action, i.e. in which the case may be tried more suitably for the interests of all the parties and the ends of justice'. In CPR cases the burden lies on the claimant to show that England is the more appropriate forum. Where the claimant invokes the English jurisdiction as of right and the defendant pleads *forum non conveniens* the burden is on the defendant to show that there is another forum which is clearly or distinctly more appropriate than the English forum. See also *Schapira v Ahronson* [1998] ILPr 587.

[69] *Kroch v Rossell et Cie.* [1937] 1 All ER 725.

This was not so much because the circulation of the papers in England was small, but because there was no evidence that Mr Kroch had any reputation in, or, indeed any associations with England at all. As Slesser LJ put it:

He states that he is a gentleman of no occupation. A gentleman of no occupation, I think, if I remember my Blackstone rightly, means a person of certain means who can support the port and countenance of a gentleman, but does not necessarily mean he has any associates in this country.

Further affidavit evidence on behalf of one of the defendants stated that Mr Kroch 'has no permanent address in this country. The address given by him in the writ . . . is a place where he occupies one furnished room. He is an alien, having a domicile in Germany, and he is in this country only temporarily for the purpose of launching this and similar litigation.' There was no evidence that Mr Kroch knew anyone in England or had any interest in England. The latter proposition might be thought to ignore the potential monetary benefit to Mr Kroch which might have been afforded by English libel law had the court been prepared to take jurisdiction. *Kroch* offers an early example of cold comfort to forum shoppers in the libel game.[70]

'It's as if Lucky Luciano were Chairman of the Board of Chrysler'[71]

In an edition published on 30 December 1996, *Forbes* magazine contained an article the subject matter of which concerned two prominent Russian businessmen, Mr Boris Berezovsky[72] and Mr Nikolai Glouchkov.[73] The article, which contained, amongst other things, the words quoted above alleged that Mr Berezovsky was in fact a leader of organised crime in Russia and that Mr Glouchkov was one of his criminal associates. *Forbes* is an

[70] Slesser LJ clearly thought that this was an easy case but he went on to say that he had dealt with the case at some length 'because I think it is right that this foreign gentleman should know that his rights have been fully considered by the court, and his claim rejected upon a real consideration of the facts and sufficient reasons'!

[71] *Berezovsky v Michaels*, n 14 above, 1017, *per* Lord Nolan.

[72] Mr Berezovsky, at the time, had extensive interests in Russian businesses, including cars, oil, media and finance. Also a politician, in October 1996 he became Deputy Secretary of the Security Council of the Russian Federation, a senior post in the Russian Government, a post from which he was dismissed by President Yeltsin in November 1997. The case is concerned with his career as at 1996, but subsequently he was appointed Secretary of the Commonwealth of Independent States (by Yeltsin). In 1999 he was elected to the State Duma but after pressure from President Putin's authorities he left Russia, having earlier had a major falling out with Putin, and settled in England and France. In 2002, Russia sought his extradition from England on embezzlement charges but he was granted political asylum in England in September 2003.

[73] In December 1996, Mr Glouchkov was First Deputy Manager of Aeroflot, the Russian international airline. By 2000 he was Managing Director of Aeroflot.

influential American fortnightly business magazine which principally circulates in the United States. The circulation figures of the issue in question were as follows: United States and Canada, 785,710; England and Wales, 1,915; Russia, 13. There was an agreed estimate that this particular issue of *Forbes* would have been seen by about 6,000 readers in England. Both men decided to sue the defendants, respectively the editor of the magazine and its publisher, Forbes Inc, in England rather than in Russia or the United States[74] and to this end they applied for permission to serve their writs out of the jurisdiction under the then equivalent to CPR, r6.20(8).[75] The judge at first instance refused permission, holding that the plaintiffs' connections with the jurisdiction were tenuous and that they had failed to establish that England was the most appropriate jurisdiction for the trial. The Court of Appeal[76] admitted new evidence to the effect that the offending article was well known to executives of financial institutions and had deterred them from entering into or continuing London-based negotiations with companies with which the plaintiffs were associated. That court held that the judge had failed to take account of authority to the effect that, *prima facie*, England was the appropriate forum for the trial of any substantial complaint arising out of the English circulation of a foreign publication.[77] It then held that since both plaintiffs' connections with England were in fact significant they had a substantial complaint such as gave them a strong *prima facie* case for trial in England and since their connections with the United States were slight[78] and a trial in Russia,[79] though the place of their strongest connection, would nevertheless be unsuitable, England was the appropriate place for the trial of the action. By a majority of 3–2 the House of Lords affirmed the decision of the Court of Appeal.[80]

[74] A claim in the United States would almost certainly have failed on First Amendment grounds.　　　　[75] RSC Ord 11, r 1(1)(f) which was virtually identical to CPR, r 6.20(8).
[76] [1999] ILPr 358.
[77] *The Albaforth* [1984] 2 Lloyd's Rep. 91; *Schapira v Ahronson* [1999] EMLR 735. See also Case C-68/93 *Shevill v Presse Alliance S.A.* [1995] ECR I-415.
[78] Eg some newscuttings in a handful of newspapers referring to Mr Berezovsky and a newspaper article suggesting that Aeroflot was preparing to sell shares on the U.S. market. It was also said that an American jury was less well equipped than an English jury to assess the impact of an article in England and the appropriate measure of damages having regard to the extent of the damage caused to each plaintiff in England. The court explicitly rejected the juridical disadvantage referred to in the text accompanying n 81 below as affecting the issue at all.
[79] A Russian court would be ill equipped to make an assessment of damage suffered in England. The trial judge had also required the defendants to give certain undertakings if trial was to take place in Russia. The fact that he had found it necessary to do that indicated that Russia was an unsuitable forum.
[80] *Berezovsky*, n 14 above. The dissenters, Lords Hoffmann and Lord Hope, thought that it was not possible to say that the first instance judge had erred in law. There is much to be said for this view.

The plaintiffs had confined their claims for damages to the publication of *Forbes* within the jurisdiction through distribution of copies of the magazine and through publication on the internet.[81] This, first, seems to shift the focus on to publication in England rather than on to the totality of publication as a whole. Second, a well established principle of English libel law has it that each publication is a separate tort[82] and this seems to translate to the level of private international law in the form of a principle permitting the bringing of an action in England in respect of publication there.[83] Third, there is, therefore, no 'global cause of action'[84] or, if this is really different, 'one cause of action' arising out of a multi-national libel which should be incorporated into the *Spiliada* principles for the exercise of discretion.[85] If the latter concept was adopted it would usually favour trial in the home courts of the foreign publisher because the bulk of the publication would take place there. Counsel for *Forbes* argued that it was artificial for the plaintiffs to confine their claim to publication in England, but the House had no sympathy with the argument which was said to be contrary to a rule established in an elderly case to the effect that a plaintiff who seeks leave to serve out of the jurisdiction is guilty of an abuse if he seeks to include in the same action matters occurring elsewhere.[86] Fourth, all the constituent elements of the tort occurred in England. Fifth, the distribution in England of the defamatory material was significant. Sixth, the plaintiffs had significant connections with, and reputations to protect, in England.[87] And, where that was the case, seventh, it would be consistent with *Spiliada* principles to regard England as the place of the tort, as the natural forum for the trial. According to Lord Steyn, in 'such cases it is not unfair that the foreign publisher should be sued here'.[88]

The following comments may be made. First, it would appear that where the claimant sues a foreign publisher in England under the CPR the English court only has jurisdiction over the English publication and

---

[81] Ibid, 1008. In fact the majority did not find it necessary to deal with the internet issue: ibid, 1015.   [82] *Duke of Brunswick v Harmer* (1849) 14 QB 185.

[83] See critical comment by Briggs, 'Jurisdiction over International Defamation' (2000) 71 BYIL 440.

[84] *Berezovsky*, n 14 above, 1011. The approach taken in the United States in the Uniform Single Publication Act 1952 which provides in respect of a single publication only one action for damages' is maintainable (see also Restatement of the Law of Torts, Second 1997 s 577A and Prosser, 'Interstate Publication', (1953) 51 *Michigan L Rev* 959) was explicitly rejected by the Court of Appeal, a rejection endorsed by the majority of the House. It was said that the notion of a global tort was also inconsistent with the *Shevill* case, n 77 above.   [85] *Berezovsky*, n 14 above, 1012; *Spiliada*, n 68 above.

[86] Ibid. 1013. The case concerned is *Diamond v Sutton* (1866) LR 1 Ex. 130.

[87] Unlike the plaintiff in *Kroch*, n 69 above.

[88] *Berezovsky*, n 14 above, 1013; *Spiliada*, n 68 above.

any foreign publications cannot be relied on. This would seem to be a rule of law rather than a matter of pleading, although this is not entirely clear,[89] and in effect produces an outcome consistent with that reached by the European Court in *Shevill*.[90] Second, to justify an assertion of jurisdiction, a claimant must have significant connections with England and the volume of publication in England must be significant, though what is significant for these purposes is a matter of appreciation. Third, a claimant appears to be claiming for damage to 'English' reputation and it follows from this that he must have a reputation in England to protect. 'Location' of reputation in this manner may be thought by some to be rather fanciful. As Lord Hoffmann put it,

the notion that Mr Berezovsky, a man of enormous wealth, wants to sue in England in order to secure the most precise determination of the damages appropriate to compensate him for being lowered in the esteem of persons in this country who have heard of him is something which would be taken seriously only by a lawyer.... The common sense of the matter is that he wants the verdict of an English court that he has been acquitted of the allegations in the article, for use wherever in the world his business may take him. He does not want to sue in the United States because he considers that *New York Times v. Sullivan* (1964) 376 U.S. 254 makes it too likely that he will lose. He does not want to sue in Russia for the unusual reason that other people might think it was too likely that he would win. He says that success in the Russian courts would not be adequate to vindicate his reputation because it might be attributed to his corrupt influence over the Russian judiciary.... The plaintiffs are forum shoppers in the most literal sense. They have weighed up the advantages to them of the various jurisdictions that might be available and decided that England is the best place in which to vindicate their international reputations. They want English law, English judicial integrity and the international publicity which would attend success in an English libel action.[91]

Fourth, although *Berezovsky* is a case on jurisdiction, it is implicit, if not explicit, that once a court takes jurisdiction under the CPR, then it will apply English law and foreign law will be irrelevant.[92] Fifth,

---

[89] *Berezovsky*, n 14 above, 1008, 1016, 1017–1018, 1032.   [90] n 77 above.

[91] *Berezovsky*, n 14 above, 1023–1024.

[92] And see s 14(2) of the Private International Law (Miscellaneous Provisions) Act 1995: *Szalatnay-Stacho*, n 63 above (a defamation case); *Metall und Rohstoff*, also n 63 above. The *Berezovsky* litigation proceeded on the basis of English law: see *Berezovsky v Forbes Inc.* [2001] EWCA Civ 1251; [2001] EMLR 45. In a press release dated 6 March 2003, the claimants' law firm Carter-Ruck (according to *The Times* 'Britain's most feared firm of libel lawyers') announced a settlement in which *Forbes* accepted, in a statement read in the High Court, that the allegations were false, gave an undertaking not to repeat them and agreed to place a correction notice on its website: see *http://www.carter-ruck.com/recent-work/berezovsky-06mar03.html*. A press report indicates that the claimant was awarded no damages or costs: see *The Sunday Times*, 11 July 2004, 7. On 9 July 2004, the author of the

it seems to follow from this that the double actionability rule applicable to foreign publications can only become relevant in cases where the English court has direct (as opposed to 'long-arm') jurisdiction over the defendant.[93] And even here, it is, presumably, open to the claimant to limit his claim to any accompanying English publication, if such there be and such there will usually be.[94] The outcome of all this is that most libel actions properly brought in the English courts will be governed by the pro-claimant libel law of England.

'A Shyster Lawyer'

Victims of alleged defamatory statements are often sensitive souls. It is reported that a court in Paris threw out a defamation claim brought against Brigitte Bardot, ruling that the former film star had been provoked into calling the claimant, apparently the host of a French radio programme ironically named Radio Courtesy, 'a little jerk'.[95] Lawyers may be particularly sensitive in this regard. The Pennsylvania Court of Common Pleas was only recently compelled to hold that to call a lawyer a 'moron', an 'idiot' and 'incompetent' was not defamatory.[96] If it were to be ruled defamatory then, in the view of the court 'obeisance to the law would require ordinary individuals engaged in commerce, domestic matters, or casual acquaintances to communicate with antiseptic caution or in monkish silence'.[97] Conversely, as long ago as 1885, the Supreme Court of Minnesota held that it was defamatory to describe a lawyer as a 'shyster'.[98] According to the Supreme Court of Michigan, delivering a

article, Paul Klebnikov, an American-born journalist who was editor of the Russian edition of *Forbes*, was shot dead, allegedly by a contract killer, outside his Moscow office. The Russian edition, set up in April, 2004, had caused a stir in its May edition by publishing a list of Russia's richest people, claiming that there were more dollar billionaires in Moscow than in any other city in the world: see *The Sunday Times*, ibid; *The Times*, 10 July 2004, 23; *The Independent*, 10 July 2004, 26.

[93] *University of Glasgow*, n 65 above. [94] *Church of Scientology*, n 65 above.

[95] *The Independent*, 20 October 2004, 22.

[96] *Czech v Gordon*, 2004 WL 2426530 (Pa Com Pl). For an earlier episode in this saga, see *Czech v Gordon*, 2003 WL 22455078 (Pa Com Pl). See also *The Times*, 12 October 2004, s. 2, 15. [97] *Czech v Gordon*, n 96 above, 4.

[98] *Gribble v Pioneer Press Co.*, 34 Minn 342, 25 N W 710 (1885). See also *Bailey v Kalamazoo Publishing Co.*, 40 Mich 251 (1879) ('pettifogging shyster'); *Nolan v Standard Pub. Co.*, 67 Mont 212, 216 P 571 (1923); *Donovan v Standard Pub. Co.*, 67 Mont 226, 216 P 576 (1923) ('white livered shyster'); *Henderson v Evansville Press Inc.*, 127 Ind App 592, 142 NE 2d 920 (1957) (report of lawyer's behaviour as 'one of the lowest forms of shysterism'). Contrast *Rudin v Dow Jones & Co. Inc.*, 557 FSupp 535 (SDNY, 1983) (reference to lawyer as a 'mouthpiece' susceptible in principle of a defamatory meaning, indicating association of the lawyer with the underworld, but not in the circumstances of the particular case where the lawyer was described as 'Sinatra's mouthpiece').

judgment in 1879, such an epithet 'every lawyer and citizen knows belongs to none but unscrupulous practitioners who disgrace their profession by doing mean work, and resort to sharp practice to do it.'[99] On occasion, however, the lawyer's response to being called a 'shyster lawyer' may give the maker of the statement an opportunity to sue for libel in an English court.

In early 2004, a libel action was commenced in the English court by Don King against Lennox Lewis, Lion Promotions LLC and Judd Burstein.[100] The first named is a well known American boxing promoter, normally resident in the United States. The second named is the British former world heavyweight boxing champion, also mainly resident in the United States. The third named is a Nevada based boxing promotion company. And the fourth named is a New York attorney, normally resident in New York, who was representing Lennox Lewis and his company in litigation then pending in New York, in which Lewis and his associates battled with Mike Tyson and one of Don King's corporations. The allegations were said to be contained in two articles published on boxing websites,[101] located in California, one of which was written by Mr Burstein and the other of which, written by someone else, contained an interview with Mr Burstein in which the latter had alleged (as he had done in his own article) that Don King had called him a 'shyster lawyer' which indicated that Don King was anti-semitic.

Doubtlessly outraged by the allegation that he was anti-semitic, Mr King sought permission to serve process on the defendants outside the jurisdiction pursuant to CPR, r 6.20(8) (for present purposes it is enough to consider the application as against Mr Burstein, the author of the offending articles).[102] In this connection Eady J. began by considering 'a number of well known principles'[103] put forward on behalf of the claimant.

First, it has long been recognised that publication is regarded as taking place where the defamatory words are published in the sense of being heard or read.[104] In relation to internet posting, by analogy with the latter rule, the common law regards publication of an internet posting as taking place when and where it is downloaded. For this proposition, the learned judge cited two English authorities, *Godfrey v Demon Internet*

---

[99] *Bailey v Kalamazoo*, n 98 above, 3.   [100] *King v Lewis*, n 35 above.

[101] For the sites, see *www.boxingtalk.com* and *www.fightnews.com*.

[102] After the case had been heard in the Court of Appeal, but before judgment was given Don King discontinued the action against Lennox Lewis and Lion Promotions leaving Mr. Burstein as the sole defendant: [2004] EWCA Civ1329 at para. 5.

[103] *King v Lewis* [2004] EWHC 168(QB); [2004] ILPr 31 at para. 14.

[104] Ibid, para. 15. See *Bata v Bata* (1948) WN 366.

Ltd.[105] and *Loutchansky v Times Newspapers Ltd. (Nos. 4 and 5)*[106] though neither of theses cases squarely raised the issue in the context of the conflict of laws.[107] He also referred to the decision of the High Court of Australia in *Gutnick v Dow Jones Inc.*[108] where the point was extensively analysed by the court which came down in favour of the place of downloading[109] rather than the place of uploading, a view which tends to favour claimants over media defendants, and an outcome which has, predictably, been greeted by the media with a cacophony of protest.[110] Second, Eady J. emphasised that English law does not recognise a 'single publication' doctrine.[111] Third, English law recognises in the context of defamation generally that damage is presumed.[112] Fourth, the claimant was not permitted to complain (and did not do so) of publication of the defamatory words outside England.[113] Strictly speaking it follows, therefore, that he can only be compensated for injury to his reputation suffered in England. Fifth, the claimant is entitled to rely on what might be described as a general presumption that the natural forum in which to try the dispute is that of the jurisdiction where the tort is committed, as a weighty circumstance.[114] Sixth, the law regards the relevant claimant having a reputation to protect specifically in England as giving a significant dimension to a case not least because in such a case the English courts would appear to be the natural forum for achieving vindication and assessing compensation.[115]

Eady J. then went on to assess these principles in the light of the available evidence and concluded that permission for service out should be granted. That evidence disclosed that Don King had a substantial reputation in England as evidenced in frequent appearances on television, radio and other media and participation in advertisements on BBC television for the BBC's coverage of the F.A. Cup (a football competition!). Indeed there was evidence to the effect that he was the best known or at the very least one of the best known figures in boxing. He had a considerable financial and business connection with England having promoted several fights there or fights in other countries involving British

---

[105] [2001] QB 201.   [106] [2001] EWCA Civ 783; [2002] QB 783 at para. 58.
[107] The judge did not refer to the fact that the majority judgment in *Berezovsky* had left the point open: n 14 above.   [108] n 65 above, discussed below.
[109] This was the view which Eady J. had himself preferred in his earlier decision in *Harrods v Dow Jones*, n 32 above. See below.
[110] See eg House of Lords, European Union Committee, *The Rome II Regulation. Report with Evidence*, HL Paper 66, 55, (letter from Times Newspapers Ltd.).
[111] *Shevill v Presse Alliance SA* [1996] AC 959; *Berezovsky*, n 14 above.
[112] *Shevill*, ibid.   [113] *Diamond v Sutton*, n 86 above; *Berezovsky*, n 14 above.
[114] *Berezovsky*, ibid; see also *The Albaforth*, n 77 above.
[115] [2004] EWHC 168(QB); [2004] ILPr 31 at para. 20.

boxers which had generated tens of millions of dollars. He had many friends and associates there, including members of the Jewish community before whom he was anxious to vindicate his reputation.[116] Various witnesses gave evidence that the boxing websites involved are frequently accessed by fight fans in England and further it appeared that once news is placed on those websites it rapidly goes around the boxing community by means of telephone calls, word of mouth or by the information being forwarded on computers. In short these allegations against Don King became common knowledge in the boxing community very shortly after they were placed on the websites.

Eady J.'s decision was upheld by the Court of Appeal.[117] Describing the story, as revealed in the facts, as 'nothing if not colourful',[118] the court found nothing in the reasoning of Eady J. which amounted to an error of law. Further, the court felt required 'to don a hair shirt'[119] and to point out that the exercise of *forum non conveniens* discretion lay primarily in the hands of the first instance judge and an appellate court should be slow to interfere.[120] As the court emphasised the 'relative importance of the factors which must . . . be examined–the place of the tort, the parties' connection with this or that jurisdiction, the publishers' choice to go on the Internet–are not legal rules. They are matters which will inform the judge who must decide where the balance of convenience lies. We think it is a pity that there is so much learning about them. But it is a weakness of the common law that areas in which the litigants usually have ample resources with which to fund litigation tend to become too case-bound. That is what has happened here.'[121]

Three points made by the Court of Appeal merit emphasis. First, it was, apparently, accepted by the parties that a text on the internet is published at the place where it is downloaded.[122] Second, the court rejected the notion that in considering the appropriate forum in internet cases, regard should be had to whether the defendant intended to 'target' the publication at a particular jurisdiction in which the proceedings are brought: ' . . . it makes little sense to distinguish between one jurisdiction

---

[116] cf *Chada & Osicom Technologies Inc. v Dow Jones & Co. Inc.* [1999] ILPr 829.

[117] [2004] EWCA Civ 1329; [2005] ILPr 185.   [118] Ibid at para. 6.

[119] Ibid at para. 35. In saying this the collective judicial tongue must have left the judicial cheek literally bulging.

[120] Ibid at para. 36. Reference was made to Lord Templeman's explicit statement to this effect in *Spiliada*, n 68 above, 465 and to the similar sentiments forcibly expressed by Lord Hoffman in *Berezovsky*, n 14 above, 1021.

[121] [2004] EWCA Civ 1329; [2005] ILPr 185 at para. 36.

[122] Ibid at para. 2. In *Richardson v Schwarzenegger*, n 36 above, at para. 19, Eady J. stated that this was now a 'well settled principle'. See also *Dow Jones & Co. Inc. v Jameel* [2005] EWCA Civ 75; [2005] 2 WLR 1614.

and another in order to decide which jurisdiction the defendant has "targeted", when in truth he has "targeted" every jurisdiction in which his text may be downloaded. Further, if the exercise [of discretion] required the ascertainment of what it was the defendant had subjectively intended to "target", it would in our judgment be liable to manipulation and uncertainty, and much more likely to diminish than enhance the interests of justice.'[123] Finally, the court held that in exercising his discretion, Eady J. had not attributed too much weight to the fact that Don King would have been met with the *New York Times v Sullivan* defence had he sued in New York. This was not a point on which King had relied but rather was a point which, illogically and paradoxically, Burstein had raised to demonstrate that New York was a more appropriate forum![124]

In relation to this last point, this was, of course, an action by an American-based claimant against American-based defendants and it was clearly recognised that it could not be successfully mounted in New York where Don King would be regarded as a public figure, unless actual malice could be proved.[125] Although he may not have relied on the point, it seems fairly obvious that King and his advisers would have been aware of it. Thus they were equally aware, in effect, that the only place in which King could vindicate his reputation was England and given the publicity that will attach to any successful judgment he may receive, then in reality he is seeking to vindicate his reputation worldwide. It is of limited comfort to know that there was evidence that the websites were accessed here because, presumably, they would be accessed by fight fans in many other parts of the world as well and it may well be that should he secure a successful English judgment that fact would be posted on those very websites. Only on a charitable view was Don King not forum shopping, in the sense that there was no alternative forum in which he could successfully shop.[126] Nonetheless, the case demonstrates the pulling power of English substantive libel law[127] buttressed by the readiness of English courts to assert long-arm jurisdiction over foreign defendants in respect of claimants (usually the rich or famous or both) who can demonstrate possession of an 'English' reputation.

---

[123] [2004] EWCA Civ 1329; [2005] ILPr 185 at para. 34. Contrast the position taken in some American cases: eg *Griffis v Luban*, 646 N.W. 2d 527 (Minn. 2002). See also Borchers, 'Internet Libel: The Consequences of a Non-Rule Approach to Personal Jurisdiction', 98 *Nw U L Rev* 473 (2004).

[124] [2004] EWCA Civ 1329; [2005] ILPr 185 at para. 41.

[125] [2004] EWHC 168(QB); [2004] ILPr 31 at paras. 36–37.

[126] But see the point made at n 74 above.

[127] Counsel for the defendant had argued that the double actionability rule should apply on the basis that the relevant acts of the defendants took place in the United States. This was not accepted: see [2004] EWHC 168(QB); [2004] ILPr 31 at para. 41.

'Loof Lirpa'

Reasonable people might view some libel actions commenced in England as singularly lacking in merit. On 31 March 2002, Harrods, the London luxury department store issued a press release announcing a plan by its Chairman, Mr Al Fayed, to 'float' Harrods which indicated that anyone interested should contact Loof Lirpa at Harrods. The latter expression is, of course, 'April fool' spelt backwards and the press release was designed as a joke, no doubt to achieve publicity. The release was picked up by *The Wall Street Journal*, which published an article about it under the headline 'The Enron of Britain'. To cut a long story short, Harrods took the view that likening its business to Enron was defamatory and commenced proceedings against Dow Jones, the publisher of the *Journal*, in the English courts. Harrods' solicitor apparently accused the *Journal* of a 'sense of humour failure'.[128] A spokeswoman for the *Journal* described its piece as 'humorous comment on the bogus press release.... It is plainly light hearted commentary'.[129] Reasonable people might think that in the light of these comments further action would be superfluous and, indeed, even absurd. Nonetheless, Eady J. was called into action again to determine whether the English court had jurisdiction.[130] Having found that the defendant did not have a place of business in England, the learned judge had to determine whether permission for process to be served out of the jurisdiction under CPR r 6.20(8) should be granted.

By now the reader may not be surprised to learn that permission was granted. In customary fashion, Harrods limited its claim to publication in England.[131] The offending article was not contained in the European edition of *The Wall Street Journal* but in the American edition. The evidence was that only 10 copies of that edition are sent to subscribers in England, making the likely number of readers in England, as the judge so aptly put it, 'rather small'.[132] The article was also published in the online edition but the evidence disclosed a very small number of hits on the

---

[128] *The Independent on Sunday*, 6 June 2002, 6. According to press reports, the Harrods' press release or Mr Al Fayed's website (it is not clear which) even said that a Harrods store would be floated on a canal boat and not on the London Stock Exchange! See *The Guardian*, 18 February 2004, 19.

[129] Ibid. As the judge in the American litigation put it: 'At this point the lawyers entered. Promptly the face of comedy began to furrow and its smile to curl into what often becomes tragedy's first sour frowns and snarls: incipient litigation.' See *Dow Jones & Co. Inc. v Harrods Ltd. and Al Fayed*, 237 FSupp. 394 (SDNY, 2002) referred to below.

[130] *Harrods v Dow Jones*, n 32 above.   [131] Ibid, at para. 5.

[132] Ibid, at para. 4. The *Journal* has a national circulation within the United States of approximately 1.8 million: ibid.

article published on the web.[133] Despite this, of course, there was publication in England concerning an English trading company with a substantial reputation in England which it was seeking to vindicate. The judge was not aware of any actual damage suffered by the claimant, but that matters not on the issue of publication since under English libel law damage is presumed.[134] *Kroch*[135] mattered not since Kroch had no real connection with England in contrast with Harrods whose quintessential connections are with England, although it is also a 'world famous store'.[136] What was the point asked the judge, in the light of the technical nature of the publications, of allowing such litigation to go ahead involving, no doubt, considerable inconvenience and expense to parties outside England when it might be thought that the claimant had little to gain?[137] After all, any English judgment would be unlikely to be enforced in the United States.

Plenty of point apparently. The point was vindication of reputation, recognised as perhaps the main public policy consideration underlying the law of defamation and reflected as a legitimate consideration under Article 10(2) of ECHR.[138] For the claimant it was said that the defendant would not be put to inconvenience or expense since all the defendant would have to do is to acknowledge that it was not intending to draw a genuine analogy with Enron and had no basis for doing so. This option, suspected Eady J., would be 'unacceptable' to 'American citizens' since it 'would equate to "prior" or "previous" restraint'.[139] 'There is the impasse', he continued, 'the claimant wishes to pursue the action in order to demonstrate, as an objective matter of truth, and for the record, that the imputations reflected in its pleaded meanings are unjustified. It may be over-sensitive, but I believe as a matter of English law, and for that matter public policy, it is entitled to do so'.[140] And, finally, said the judge, 'I also take the view that these English publications relating to an English corporation, however limited and technical, are most conveniently dealt with in an English court. As a matter of fact, that seems to coincide with the view of the learned judge in the District Court in New York'.[141]

---

[133] Ibid. A press report put the number of hits at 12: see *The Guardian*, 18 February 2004, 19.

[134] He pointed out, however, that even if the claimant succeeded on liability, the damages recoverable might be nominal or very modest: ibid, at para. 39.

[135] n 69 above.

[136] So described in the press release which started this sorry saga: see [2003] EWHC 1162(QB) at para. 1. Perhaps Harrods was seeking to vindicate its worldwide reputation?

[137] Ibid, at para. 40.   [138] Ibid, at para. 41.   [139] Ibid, at para. 42.

[140] Ibid.   [141] [2003] EWHC 1162(QB), at para. 43.

In fact, Dow Jones had beaten Harrods to the litigational starting blocks. For after skirmishes by correspondence with Harrods, Dow Jones commenced proceedings in the District Court in New York against Harrods (and its Chairman, who was not a party to the English proceedings) five days before Harrods commenced its English proceedings. The New York proceedings requested the District Court to exercise its jurisdiction under the Declaratory Judgment Act (28 USCA s 2201) seeking a judgment that would declare any libel claim based on the article to be insufficient as a matter of (United States) law on the ground that the article contained no provably false statements of fact and represented only protected expressions of opinion and that Harrods could not prove that Dow Jones acted with actual malice or gross irresponsibility in publishing it. Moreover, by reason of the running costs it would continue to incur, and the perceived threat of restrictions on its continued publication of the article, Dow Jones requested an injunction barring Harrods and Mr Al Fayed from pursuing the English action or related litigation against Dow Jones in any other forum in the world.[142]

District Judge Marrero commenced his judgment with commendable irony: 'To the question "What is in a joke?", this lawsuit gives a decidedly wooden answer: a federal case'.[143] Some 48 pages later, the learned judge concluded, for reasons which are not central to this paper, that Dow Jones' action should be dismissed. Undeterred, Dow Jones appealed to the Circuit Court of Appeals for the Second Circuit, which, in a commendably short opinion of a page and a half, dismissed the appeal.[144]

So Harrods was free to go ahead with the English action, did so,[145] and lost.[146] According to press reports (there is no official information which has been discovered) a jury at the High Court threw out the claim and the judge ordered Harrods to pay £40,000 towards Dow Jones' legal costs, which were expected to be about £200,000.[147] The Chairman of Harrods issued a statement in which he is reported to have said: 'I was not concerned with winning damages in this case; I simply wanted the *Wall*

<hr />

[142] n 129 above, at 403.

[143] Ibid at 399. As he points out in a footnote it is a dispute over 'the exchange of not just one but *two* jokes, at least one of which arises from an April Fool's gag played in a foreign country, and which then raises the stakes to entail international consequences implicating the protection of speech under the First Amendment of the United States Constitution': ibid. To be fair, the judge conceded that the issues before the District Court did give rise to several serious legal questions.

[144] *Dow Jones & Co. Inc. v Harrods Ltd. and Al Fayed*, 346 F 3d 357 (2nd cir, 2003).

[145] *The Times*, 17 February 2004, 4.

[146] *The Times*, 18 February 2004, 10; *The Guardian*, 18 February 2004, 19.

[147] *The Guardian*, ibid.

Street Journal to accept its comparison was unwarranted and to apologise to me and to Harrods. It seems that the *Wall Street Journal* does not have the simple good manners to do this.'[148] The newspaper was reported as saying that it was 'delighted' to have won the case but is said to have added that the legal battle was a waste of time and effort. 'It seems ridiculous that Harrods, which could not sue in the US, has taken the time of an English court on an article with the most tenuous connection imaginable to England and with absolutely no evidence of any actual loss.'[149] No mention was made by the newspaper of the proceedings which Dow Jones had earlier instituted in the United States and of the unsuccessful appeal therefrom.

Everything to be learnt from this story, it is suggested, is sufficiently revealed by the telling of it.

Paparazzi, Privacy and Private International Law

Some segments of the press and their devoted readers have an almost lurid obsession with royalty and celebrity. An important tool of the trade in this regard is the paparazzo, armed with a very long-lens camera who is engaged to take pictures of 'unsuspecting' royals and celebrities in sensitive, humdrum, or even compromising situations. The activities of these characters provide some of the backdrop to the French and German privacy cases referred to above and have also provided factual scenarios in which the proper approach to privacy in English law has been considered.[150] The purpose here is to consider one such piece of English litigation which raised, though not perhaps as the major issue, a question of private international law.

One of the very many questions which arose in the litigation between Michael Douglas, Catherine Zeta-Jones and others, on the one hand, and Hello! Ltd and others, on the other hand, was whether one Philip Ramey was subject to the jurisdiction of the English court.[151] The litigation concerned the publication of photographs of the wedding of Mr Douglas and Ms Zeta-Jones (which took place in New York) in *Hello!* magazine, a 'celebrity magazine' edited in London, printed in Spain and published in

---

[148] Ibid.

[149] Ibid. Though see now *Dow Jones v Jameel*, n 122 above (allowing libel action to be struck out as an abuse of process where publication in England was minimal and had done no significant damage to claimant's reputation).

[150] One such case is a leading case: see *Campbell v MGN*, n 39 above.

[151] *Douglas v Hello! (No. 2)*, n 44 above. There are 10 reported *Douglas* decisions on various points.

the United Kingdom.[152] Hello! Ltd, an English company, was the distributor of the magazine and was the subsidiary of Hola SA, a Spanish company, which was the publisher of the magazine. Mr Ramey was a paparazzo photographer and photographic agent based in California,[153] who appeared to have been commissioned by *Hello!* to obtain photographs of the wedding, despite the strict security surrounding the event and an agreement between the claimants and the publisher of another English celebrity magazine *OK!* that the latter should have the exclusive right to take and publish photographs of the event. Mr Ramey had not, apparently, taken the photographs himself, but they had reached him via another paparazzo who had gained unauthorised access to the wedding and who had surreptitiously snapped the glittering couple.[154] The latter paparazzo had probably been put up to this by Mr Ramey.[155] The photographs were then transmitted digitally by Mr Ramey from New York to Hello! Ltd in London and from there to Hola SA in Spain. Six of the photographs were used in a 'spoiler' edition of *Hello!* which was printed in Spain, flown to London and sold there.

Various claims were made against the various defendants but only two of them need concern us here, namely a claim in tort for invasion of the right of privacy and a claim for equitable relief for breach of the duty of confidentiality. In relation to the former claim it was alleged that Mr Ramey was, along with the other defendants, a joint tortfeasor. In relation to the latter claim, it was alleged that he had 'conspired with' the other defendants to bring about the equitable wrong. In the context of leave to serve process out of the jurisdiction, the privacy claim fell within CPR r 6.20(8) which is referred to above. The breach of confidence claim fell within CPR r 6.20(15) which enables permission to be granted if 'a claim is made for restitution where the defendant's alleged liability arises out of acts committed within the jurisdiction'. The initial *ex parte* application was granted by a judge and proceedings were served on Mr Ramey in California. He then sought to have service set aside on the grounds (a) that there were no reasonable prospects of the claimants

---

[152] There is a Spanish version of the publication (*Hola!*) and a French version (*Oh La!*). In the UK the magazine is bought by an average of some 456,000 people a week leading to an estimated readership of 2.2 million people per week: see *Douglas v Hello! Ltd (No. 3)* [2003] EWHC 786(Ch); [2003] 3 All ER 996 at para. 11. This decision sets out fully the factual background to the case.

[153] He is, apparently, a most distinguished practitioner of his profession. As Lindsay J. put it, 'Mr Ramey . . . has a reputation of being able to get in where others were unlikely to be able to': ibid, at para. 8.

[154] This paparazzo is said to have been Mr Rupert Thorpe (ibid at paras. 66, 71), who is the son of the former leader of the Liberal Party in the UK, Mr Jeremy Thorpe.

[155] Ibid, at para. 71.

succeeding in their claim against him, (b) that the claimants had failed to make full and frank disclosure in the earlier application and (c) that the *forum conveniens* for the dispute was New York. This application was rejected by a Master whereupon Mr Ramey appealed to a judge, Laddie J, but only, interestingly enough, on ground (a), thereby conceding the *forum conveniens* issue in favour of the English court.[156]

It is well established that permission to serve out of the jurisdiction will only be given when the claimant can demonstrate 'a good arguable case' or a 'serious question to be tried'.[157] Thus in effect, Laddie J. had to make a preliminary determination of law to the level of this standard and this included the question of applicable law and for these purposes invasion of privacy was treated as a tort.[158] Privacy and breach of confidence were treated together. Laddie J. concluded that there was no reasonable prospect of either of these claims (or any other claim) against Mr Ramey succeeding and set service aside. His decision was reversed by the Court of Appeal for reasons which merit closer examination.[159] First, although it was not open to Mr Ramey to argue the point, the court emphasised that there was the necessary jurisdictional link with England to satisfy either CPR r 6.20(8) or 6.20(15). The essential act complained about which had invaded the rights of and harmed the claimants (at least Mr Douglas and Ms Zeta-Jones) had been publication of the photographs, and this occurred in England, and analogy was expressly drawn with libel.[160] It mattered not, for jurisdictional purposes, that there might well have been an earlier breach of the duty of confidentiality or invasion of the right of privacy when the photographs were first taken in New York, nor that such earlier wrongs may have been governed by the law of New York. For choice of law purposes, it was argued on behalf of Mr Ramey that the only possible wrongdoing (breach of confidence and invasion of privacy) was committed in New York where the photographs were taken. There was expert evidence before the court that there would be no liability under New York law because that law extends protection from liability in favour of 'newsworthy publications' which would cover the unauthorised photographs even if they were obtained by means of a

---

[156] [2002] EWHC 2560(Ch); 2002 WL 31599704.

[157] *Seaconsar Far East Ltd. v Bank Markazi* [1994] 1 AC 438.

[158] Although ultimately it was decided that there was no such tort and in this respect the court proceeded on the basis of breach of confidence.

[159] *Douglas v Hello (No. 2)*, n 44 above.

[160] Ibid, at para. 33, citing *Berezovsky*, n 14 above, and *The Albaforth*, n 77 above. The court pointed out that it had not been argued whether England was the natural forum, though the implication in para. 33 of the judgment, particularly because of the analogy with libel, is that it was.

trespass or other such wrongs.[161] This argument was rejected. First the 'newsworthiness' protection, the court understood from the expert evidence, applied only to publication in the State of New York.[162] Second, and more importantly, the court thought it to be well arguable that the claimants were entitled to rely on publication in England as the essence of their complaint so that there was a good case that New York law was irrelevant to the alleged causes of action. There was a good case that the law thereby applicable to the tort was English law either under section 11(1)[163] or 11(2)(c)[164] of the Private International Law (Miscellaneous Provisions) Act 1995.[165] Equally, there was a good case that the law applicable to the right in restitution for breach of the duty of confidentiality was English law on the basis of Dicey and Morris, Rule 200(2)(c) which provides that the proper law in such circumstances is 'the law of the country where the enrichment occurs'.[166]

Service on Mr Ramey in California therefore stood, but it was not possible to include him in the trial of the other five defendants.[167] At that trial, it was said that the claimants intended to move against him at a later date[168] but it is not known whether such a move has been actually made.

Although ultimately it was decided that English law did not recognise a claim for invasion of privacy, as opposed to one for breach of confidence,[169] the following comments may be made on the contribution of this case to the present debate, though bearing in mind that the court was only considering whether there was a good arguable case, one should beware of drawing dogmatic conclusions. First the drawing of the analogy with libel suggests that in the case of privacy-type liability arising out of publication, an English court may well be likely to assume jurisdiction under the CPR where publication takes place in England. Second, however, whereas in libel cases the English court treats English law as applicable without any choice of law analysis, in the two forms of liability here under discussion, application of choice of law

---

[161] *Douglas v Hello (No. 2)*, at para. 41.   [162] Ibid.

[163] Which provides that 'the general rule is that the law applicable to issues in tort is the law of the country in which the events constituting the tort occur'.

[164] Which provides that where the elements constituting the tort occur in different countries, the law applicable under the general rule in a case other than personal injury, death or damage to property is to be taken to be 'the law of the country in which the most significant element or elements of those events occurred'.

[165] [2003] EWCA Civ 139; [2003] EMLR 641 at para. 41.

[166] Ibid. See Dicey and Morris, n 7 above, paras. 34-032–34-041.

[167] n 165 above, at para. 7.   [168] *Douglas v Hello! (No. 3)*, n 152 above, at para. 5.

[169] Ibid, at para. 229.

rules is necessary to determine whether English law is the applicable law.[170] This, however, makes little practical difference, since if there is publication in England English law will normally be the applicable law[171] and if it is not, the court may well decline jurisdiction. The position in relation to breach of confidence and invasion of privacy claims is thus very similar to claims for libel so that a claimant will be able to rely on English law and there is little that a media defendant can do to protect itself by reference to foreign law. Third, it would appear that insofar as English law recognises, or in the future comes to recognise, claims for invasion of privacy, then for choice of law purposes, where those claims involve complaints arising out of publication they fall within the provisions of Part III of the Private International Law (Miscellaneous Provisions) Act 1995 and are not excluded from that Act as defamation and related claims. This is surely right since the respective interests protected by these liabilities are entirely different, at least in common law systems.[172] Fourth, while the limited protection currently given to privacy rights by English law does not threaten foreign media defendants in the same way as does English libel law, such defendants might become embroiled, nonetheless, in long and expensive jurisdictional battles.

Conclusion

The foregoing indicates that it is not entirely without justification to call London 'a town named Sue'. Indeed the cases referred to in the Background section of this paper which have been brought in the past few years suggest that what some call 'libel tourism'[173] is on the increase. Several of these cases involve actions brought by rich Saudi Arabians anxious to defend themselves against allegations that they have links with terrorism, al Quaeda, or Osama bin Laden.[174] In early 2004 it was reported that *The Mail on Sunday* had agreed to pay substantial damages to a Saudi Arabian businessman, Sheikh Khalid bin Mahfouz, over an article which suggested that he was the brother-in-law of bin Laden and helped to fund terrorism. The same report stated that the Sheikh is pursuing other libel actions against the French author, Jean Charles

---

[170] The new choice of law rules contained in Part III of the 1995 Act will apply even if the tort is committed in England: see s 9(6); Dicey and Morris, n 7 above, para. 35-019.   [171] Under s 11(1) or 11(2)(c) of the Act.

[172] Dicey and Morris, n 7 above, para. 35-123.

[173] *The Guardian*, 31 March 2004, 4.   [174] See nn 22, 30, 33 above.

Brisard, and the firms running his website.[175] And although the English
media may be fair game, foreign media defendants are at risk as well. The
approach taken to jurisdiction and applicable law in *Berezovsky, King,* and
Harrods, discussed above, suggests that private international law rules will
not protect foreign media defendants where there is publication in
England unless the subject of the publication has no reputation there,
which is unlikely to be the case in relation to the type of claimant who
brings these actions.

It is not only the press which is at risk. On 31 March 2004,
The Guardian carried an article which stated that Random House, the
American publishing firm, had suppressed the publication in the United
Kingdom by Secker and Warburg, its subsidiary, of the book by the
American writer Craig Unger entitled *House of Bush, House of Saud.*
The book focuses in part on Sheikh Khalid bin Mahfouz (above) and
possible Texas business links between the Bush 'circle' and the families of
the Sheikh and other rich Saudi Arabians. Random House said it could
not afford the risk of being sued for libel. Its Deputy-Chairman described
English libel law as 'ludicrous' and pointed out that a libel action was
immensely time consuming and potentially hugely expensive—'vastly
more than the publisher could hope to earn from the book'.[176] On 3 July
2004, it was announced that a small independent publisher, Gibson
Square Books, would take on the book which was eventually published in
England at the end of July. The head of this publishing house, very wisely
perhaps, apparently studied law at Oxford and Leiden. [177]

---

[175] *The Guardian,* 14 January 2004, 10.

[176] *The Guardian,* 31 March 2004, 4. See Robertson and Nicol, n 5 above, 76–79,
stating that in 2001 a contested two week defamation trial, including all the applications
which would precede it could easily cost each side £750,000, and the loser would have to
pay 75 per cent of the winner's costs, on top of damages which might amount to six figures.
Doubtless libel tourism contributes to the financial health of specialist solicitors and the
defamation bar. Costs for the media defendant may be very high indeed if the claimant has
a 'no win, no fee' arrangement with his lawyers. Should the claimant win, the lawyers are
allowed to 'uplift' their fees and the losing defendant may be liable to pay these fees as costs,
it being the general rule in England that the loser pays the winner's costs: see on this *King
v Telegraph Group Ltd.* [2004] EWCA Civ 613; [2005] 1 WLR 2282. It is worth noting that
the French Cour de Cassation has refused to enforce an English order for costs against a
French claimant who brought defamation proceedings in England against Times
Newspapers Ltd. on the ground that the amount of costs (£20,078, excluding VAT, with
interest) was set at a disproportionately high level which presented an obstacle to the
French claimant's access to justice, contrary to Art 6(1) of the European Convention on
Human Rights: *Pordea v Times Newspapers Ltd.* [2000] ILPr 763.

[177] *The Guardian,* 3 July 2004, p. 38. At the end of July 2004, a spokesman for
Amazon.co.uk announced that it was not currently listing the title 'for legal reasons': see
The Guardian, 30 July 2004, 5.

Enforcement of Judgments

As is pointed out above some libel claimants may be content to get a judgment in their favour from the English court so as to vindicate their reputation and are less concerned about increasing their existing wealth by being able to enforce an award of damages. This is particularly relevant when the media defendant is based in the United States where, as pointed out in *Berezovsky* and *Harrods*, English libel judgments are unlikely to be enforced. Not all claimants, however, may feel that way. It may therefore be helpful to consider briefly at this point two cases where attempts were made to enforce English libel judgments in the United States.[178]

Bachchan v India Abroad Publications Inc.[179]

The plaintiff, an Indian national, resident in England or Switzerland, obtained an English judgment against the defendant, the New York operator of a news service which transmitted reports only to a news service in India. The allegedly libellous story was written by a reporter in London and wired by the defendant to the news service in India which sent it to Indian newspapers. It was reported in two Indian newspapers, copies of which were distributed in the United Kingdom. The story was also reported in an issue of *India Abroad*, the defendant's New York newspaper.

---

[178] For discussion of the issue see Walters, 'Bachchan v. India Abroad Publications Inc.: these Clash between the Protection of Free Speech in the United States and Great Britain' (1993) 16 Fordham Int'l LJ 895; Sanders, 'Extraterritorial Application of the First Amendment to Defamation Claims against American Media' (1994) 19 N.C. J Int'l L. & Com. Reg. 515; Maltby, 'Juggling Comity and Self-Government: these Enforcement of Foreign Libel Judgments in U.S. Courts' (1994) 94 Columbia L Rev 1978; Devgun, 'United States Enforcement of English Libel Judgments: Exporting the First Amendment' (1994) 23 Anglo-Am L Rev 195; Stern, 'Foreign Judgments and the Freedom of Speech: Look Who's Talking' (1994) 60 Brooklyn L.Rev. 999; Enson, 'A Roadblock on the Detour around the First Amendment: Is the Enforcement of English Libel Judgments in the United States Unconstitutional?' (1999) 21 Loy. L.A. Int'l. & Comp. LJ 159; Kyu Ho Youm, 'Suing American Media in Foreign Courts: Doing an End-run around U.S. Libel Law?' (1994) 16 Hastings Comm. & Ent. LJ 235; 'The Interaction between American and Foreign Libel Law: US Courts Refuse to Enforce English Libel Judgments', (2000) 49 ICLQ 131; Rosen, 'Exporting the Constitution' (2004) 53 Emory LJ 171; 'Should "Un-American" Foreign Judgments be Enforced?' (2004) 88 Minn. L.Rev. 783. Compare *Yahoo! Inc. v La Ligue Contre Le Racisme et L'Antisémitisme*, 169 F Supp 2d 1181 (DC Cal, 2001), but see *Yahoo! Inc. v La Ligue Contre Le Racisme et L'Antisémitisme*, 379 F 3d 1120 (9th Cir, 2004); Van Houweling 'Enforcement of Foreign Judgments, the First Amendment, and Internet Speech: Notes for the Next *Yahoo v. Licra*' (2003) 24 Mich. J. Int'l. L. 697.

[179] *Bachchan v India Abroad Publications Inc.*, 54 Misc 2d 228, 585 NYS 2d 661 (Sup Ct, 1992).

An edition of *India Abroad* was printed and distributed in the United Kingdom by the defendant's English subsidiary. The wire service story which was transmitted by the defendant stated that *Dagens Nyheter*, a Swedish daily newspaper, had reported that the Swiss authorities had frozen an account belonging to the plaintiff to which money was transferred from a coded account into which 'commissions' paid by Bofors were deposited. Bofors was a Swedish arms company which some time before had been charged with paying kickbacks to obtain a large arms contract with the Indian government. The plaintiff's name had previously been mentioned in connection with this scandal in a variety of Indian and other publications.

The plaintiff brought the English action against *Dagens Nyheter* and the defendant. The former settled the claim against it by paying a sum of money and issuing an apology. The jury awarded damages of £40,000 against the American *India Abroad* defendant and it was this judgment that the plaintiff sought to enforce in New York under the New York Civil Practice Law and Rules which recognise foreign country money judgments.[180]

The defendant argued that the English judgment infringed the constitutional protections of the First Amendment and the New York Constitution and that the judgment was contrary to the public policy of New York which was a ground for refusing enforcement under the New York Rules.[181] As to the latter argument the public policy exception appears to be discretionary, on the words of the statute.[182] Judge Shirley Fingerhood held, however, that where a foreign judgment is repugnant to a policy embodied in both state and federal constitutions, the 'refusal to recognise the judgment should be, and is deemed to be, "constitutionally mandatory" '.[183] English libel law offended American constitutional standards in at least two fatal respects. First, it placed the burden of proving justification on the defendant rather than placing the burden of proving falsehood on the plaintiff as required under United States' law.[184] Second, English law was based on strict liability, whereas under United States' law even a 'private figure' plaintiff is required to prove that the publisher was negligent.[185]

Accordingly the court declined to enforce the English judgment.

---

[180] Implementing The Uniform Foreign Money-Judgments Recognition Act 1962.

[181] These provide, *inter alia*, that a foreign country money judgment 'need not' be recognised if the cause of action on which it is based is repugnant to the public policy of New York.

[182] See preceding note where the words are 'need not' rather than 'must not'.

[183] 585 N.Y.S. 2d 661, 662 (1992). See on the constitutional question, Enson, n 178 above; Van Houweling, n 178 above; Rosen, n 178 above.

[184] *Philadelphia Newspapers Inc. v Hepps*, 475 US 767 (1986).

[185] *Gertz*, n 11 above. The court found it unnecessary to address the question of whether the plaintiff was a public figure falling within the *New York Times v Sullivan* requirement of actual malice.

Telnikoff v Matusevitch[186]

After protracted litigation in London,[187] the plaintiff obtained a judgment against the defendant in respect of a libel, allegedly contained in an article and an exchange of letters published in *The Daily Telegraph*, which were said to accuse the plaintiff, *inter alia*, of racism and anti-semitism. He sought to enforce this judgment in the United States. After complicated manoeuvrings,[188] the case ended up in the Maryland Court of Appeals which decided, by a majority, that the judgment should not be enforced.[189]

At the time of the English proceedings, both plaintiff and defendant were Russian émigrés living in England, the publication complained of concerned the hiring practices of the BBC's Russian Service and no media defendant was involved in the case. Subsequent to those proceedings, the defendant had moved to Maryland and hence the Maryland enforcement proceedings. The question which was put to the court was not framed in First Amendment terms but, rather, as follows: 'Would recognition of Telnikoff's foreign judgment be repugnant to the public policy of Maryland?'[190] The court nonetheless took the view that the First Amendment and the freedom of the press clause of the Maryland Constitution[191] ought to be taken into account in the determination of the content of public policy. After a lengthy historical review of the history of the development of libel law in England and the United States, the court focused on the features of English libel law that had been referred to in *Bachchan* as indicating that enforcement would be inimical to the public policy of the State, including, also, in the 'list of defects', the absence of a public figure defence.[192]

Judge Chasanow delivered a vigorous dissent. Since some may think that his criticism of the majority view makes good sense, this opinion is worth some quotation. Judge Chasanow accepted the correctness of *Bachchan*, but did not regard the instant case as a freedom of the press case

[186] 37 Md. 561, 702 A. 2d 230 (1997).

[187] *Telnikoff v Matusevitch* [1992] 2 AC 952.

[188] *Matusevitch v Telnikoff*, 877 F Supp. 1 (DC Cir, 1995); 159 F 3d 636 (DC Cir, 1998).   [189] n 186 above.

[190] n 5 above, 236.

[191] Art 40 of the Maryland Declaration of Rights ('the liberty of the press ought to be observed': 'every citizen of the State ought to be allowed to speak, write and publish his sentiments on all subjects, being responsible for abuse of that privilege').

[192] The court concluded that Telnikoff was a public figure. The court applied the public policy exception under the Uniform Foreign Money-Judgments Recognition Act, as implemented in Maryland.

as no media defendant was involved. He continued:

> There is another public policy that should also be considered by this Court. That public policy, recognised by our legislature when it adopted the Uniform Foreign Money-Judgments Recognition Act is to give broad and uniform recognition to foreign judgments. The Act gives our courts discretion to subordinate our State's public policy. Our interest in international goodwill, comity, and *res judicata* fostered by recognition of foreign judgments must be weighed against our minimum interest in giving the benefit of our local libel public policy to residents of another country who defame foreign public figures in foreign publications and who have no reasonable expectation that they will be protected by the Maryland Constitution. Unless there is some United States interest that should be protected, there is no good reason to offend a friendly nation like England by refusing to recognise a purely local libel judgment for a purely local defamation. In the instant case, there is no United States interest that might necessitate non-recognition or non-enforcement of the English defamation judgment.[193]

And he concludes (perhaps somewhat extravagantly):

> The Court does little or no analysis of the global public policy considerations and seems inclined to make Maryland libel law applicable to the rest of the world by providing a safe haven for foreign libel judgment debtors.[194]

Choice of Law and The First Amendment

There are some early cases where American courts were prepared, in principle, to apply the defamation law of a foreign country as *lex loci delicti*.[195] However these cases are no longer reliable guides, first because of the increasing constitutionalisation of defamation law through the First Amendment as a result of *New York Times v Sullivan* and subsequent cases and, second, because of the considerable changes in the choice of law principles applied by American courts. The latter principles have become increasingly more flexible and have enabled courts to incorporate First Amendment protection into choice of law analysis where a potentially applicable law is that of a foreign country which does not provide that protection.

A variety of approaches to choice of law in defamation may be taken in the United States.[196] For present purposes, it must suffice to refer to the

---

[193] n 5 above, 257.   [194] Ibid, at 260.

[195] See *Philp v Macri*, 261 F 2d 945 (9th cir, 1958); *Gallegos v Union-Tribune Publishing Co.*, 195 Cal App 2d 791, 16 Cal Rptr 185 (1961); *Bakhshandeh v American Cyanamid Co.*, 211 F Supp. 803 (SDNY, 1962).

[196] See Note, 'The Choice of Law in Multistate Defamation—A Functional Apporach', (1963–1964) 77 *Harvard L.Rev* 1463; Rose, 'Interstate Libel and Choice of Law: Proposals

approach taken by the Restatement Second of Conflict of Laws of 1971. Section 149 provides as follows:

In an action for defamation the local law of the state where the publication occurs determines the rights and liabilities of the parties, except as stated in [section] 150, unless, with respect to the particular issue, some other state has a more significant relationship under the principles stated in [section] 6 to the occurrence and the parties, in which event the local law of the other state will be applied.

Section 150 (which was written prior to the advent of the internet) deals with multistate defamation and provides as follows:

(1) The rights and liabilities that arise from defamatory matter in any one edition of a book or newspaper, or any one broadcast over radio or television, exhibition of a motion picture or similar aggregate communication are determined by the local law of the state which, with respect to the particular issue, has the most significant relationship to the occurrence and the parties under the principles stated in [section] 6.

(2) When a natural person claims that he has been defamed by an aggregate communication, the state of most significant relationship will usually be the state where the person was domiciled at the time, if the matter complained of was published in that state.

(3) When a corporation, or other legal person, claims that it has been defamed by an aggregate communication, the state of most significant relationship will usually be the state where the corporation, or other legal person, had its principal place of business at the time, if the matter complained of was published in that state.[197]

for the Future' (1978–1979) 30 *Hastings LJ* 1515; Pielemeier, 'Constitutional Limitations on Choice of Law: The Special Case of Multistate Defamation' (1984–1985) 133 U. Pa. L.Rev. 381; Burnstein, 'Conflicts on the Net: Choice of Law in Transnational Cyberspace', (1996) 29 Vanderbilt J. of Transnational Law 75.

[197] Privacy is dealt with in ss 152 and 153. s 152 provides that the local law of the state where the invasion occurred determines the rights and liabilities of the parties, except as stated in s 153, unless, with respect to the particular issue, some other state has a more significant relationship under the principles stated in s 6 to the occurrence and the parties in which event the local law of the other state will be applied. s 153, dealing with multistate invasion of privacy provides that the 'rights and liabilities that arise from matter that invades a plaintiff's right of privacy and is contained in any one book or newspaper, or any one broadcast over radio or television, exhibition of a motion picture, or similar aggregate communication are determined by the local law of the state which, with respect to the particular issue, has the most significant relationship to the occurrence and the parties under the principles stated in s 6. This will usually be the state where the plaintiff was domiciled at the time if the matter complained of was published in that state.

The principles stated in section 6 include the following:

(a)　the needs of the interstate and international systems;

(b)　the relevant policies of the forum;

(c)　the relative policies of other interested states and the relative interests of those states in the determination of the particular issue;

(d)　the protection of justified expectations;

(e)　the basic policies underlying the particular field of law;

(f)　certainty, predictability and uniformity of result; and

(g)　ease in the determination and application of the law to be applied.

As can be seen sections 150(2) and (3) will normally lead to application of the law of the domicile of the victim of the alleged defamatory statement at least where the statement is also published in that state.[198] However, the position is complicated where the choice of law rule appears to point towards application of the law of a foreign country, by the potential impact of the First Amendment.

In *DeRoburt v Gannett Co. Inc.*[199] the plaintiff, the splendidly named Hammer DeRoburt, founding President of the Republic of Nauru, brought a libel action in the District Court of Hawaii against the defendants, Gannett Co. Inc., one of the largest newspaper publishers in the United States, and one of its subsidiaries, Guam Publications Inc., in respect of an article printed in the *Pacific Daily News*. Gannett was a Delaware corporation with its principal place of business in New York. Guam Publications was incorporated in Hawaii and had its principal place of business in Guam. The plaintiff claimed that the offending article accused him of committing serious crimes under the law of Nauru and of interfering in the internal political affairs of the Marshall Islands in violation of accepted standards of international diplomacy and relations. He sought compensatory damages of $1.5 million and punitive damages of $6 million. An initial question arose as to the applicable law, since the Supreme Court of Hawaii had not enunciated a choice of

---

[198]　See *Hanley v Tribune Publishing Co.*, 527 F 2d 68 (1975); *Franklin Prescriptions Inc. v The New York Times Co.*, 267 F Supp 2d 425 (EDPa, 2003) (legal person). Other choice of law theories tend to focus, eventually, on these connecting factors, eg *Elke Sommer v Zsa Zsa Gabor*, 40 Cal App 4th 1455; 48 Cal Rptr 2d 235 (1996); *Condit v Dunne*, 317 F Supp 344 (SDNY, 2004) (interest analysis). On occasion, the domicile principle is resorted to as a counsel of despair, eg *Rice v Nova Biomedical Corp.*, 318 F 3d 909, 916 (7th Cir, 1994), cert. denied, 514 US 1111 (1995) ('throwing up their hands in despair at the inoperability of modern conflicts laws, the Illinois cases say that in a multistate defamation case . . . the applicable law is that of the victim's domicile, period'). See also *Cook v Winfrey*, 141 F 3d 322 (7th Cir, 1998).　　　　　　　　[199]　83 FRD 574 (D Hawaii, 1979).

law rule for defamation cases. Accordingly the court had to apply the choice of law rule it thought most likely that the Hawaii Supreme Court would adopt.[200]

The plaintiff argued that the law of Nauru applied on the basis of the *lex loci delicti* principle which pointed to Nauru, since the greatest harm occurred there, at least with respect to publication which took place there. On the basis of the same principle, the defendant argued for the law of Guam because Guam was the place where publication, the last act necessary to cause liability, occurred. The defamation law of Nauru was based on English common law principles which would not include First Amendment protection for the defendant. In contrast, the law of Guam would include such protection. The court took the view that Hawaii would probably not adopt the *lex loci* principle which was rapidly going out of fashion in the United States at the time. Instead it was thought that Hawaii would adopt some form of interest-oriented choice of law analysis and seized upon two of the principles set out in section 6 of the Second Restatement. The first of these was the relevant policies of the forum. A fundamental policy of the forum (and of Guam) was the protection afforded by the First Amendment. With that exception, the court concluded that the policies underlying laws of defamation in Hawaii, Guam and Nauru did not appear to conflict:

The libel laws of the respective states represent a common commitment to protecting the reputations of their citizenries. Hence, application of the libel law of Nauru together with the First Amendment safeguards of *New York Times v Sullivan* and its progeny would provide a satisfactory accommodation of the relevant policies of this forum.[201]

Second, as to the expectations of the parties, the defendants could 'expect' the protection of the First Amendment but they could not 'expect', in other respects, the application of the law of Hawaii or Guam. Apart from the First Amendment, application of the law of Nauru was also supported by section 150 of the Second Restatement in that the plaintiff had suffered the greatest harm to his reputation there and was domiciled there.[202]

The conclusion reached by the court was that the law of Nauru should be applied to the extent that it was consistent with the First Amendment.

One suspects, however, that once First Amendment protection is injected into the choice of law question in this fashion, there will be very little of Nauru defamation law that will be left to apply. The plaintiff was undoubtedly a public figure and the critical question would therefore be

---

[200] A federal court sitting in diversity jurisdiction must apply the choice of law rule of the state in which it sits: *Klaxon Co. v Stentor Electric Mfg. Co.*, 313 US 487 (1941).

[201] n 199 above, 580.　　　[202] Citing Restatement Second, section 150, comment e.

whether he could establish actual malice within the meaning of *New York Times v Sullivan* and subsequent cases. As the court put it in a later case 'given the extensive modifications resulting from the imposition of first amendment safeguards, under *DeRoburt*, the (first amendment) exceptions swallow up the (foreign law) rule and the functional equivalent of American defamation law is applied'.[203]

The court which rendered the previous statement adopted a rather more sophisticated approach to the issue than did the court in *DeRoburt*. In *Desai v Hersh* Morarji Desai, a former Indian Prime Minister who had held many governmental posts in India, brought a defamation action against Seymour Hersh, the author of *The Price of Power: Kissinger in the Nixon White House*, claiming that allegations that he, while an official in the government of India, had sold Indian state secrets to the CIA, were defamatory.[204] The book was published in the United States, and to that extent, clearly fell within First Amendment protection, but the plaintiff also relied on the defamation law of India where, because Indian law derives from English law, no such protection would be available.

In this case the court adopted a technique somewhat different to that adopted in *DeRoburt*. It did not focus on traditional choice of law analysis, but rather posed the question as 'in what circumstances should the First Amendment be given extraterritorial application'.[205] The answer to this question was neither 'always' nor 'never'. A balance had to be struck. The rule ultimately adopted was stated as follows.

In cases where the plaintiff is a public official or figure and thus heightened first amendment protections, including the 'actual malice' standard, apply to domestic publication, these same protections will apply to extraterritorial publication of the same speech where the speech is a matter of public concern and the publisher has not intentionally published the speech in the foreign country in a manner consistent with the intention to abandon first amendment protections.[206]

---

[203] *Desai v Hersh* 719 F Supp 670, 679 (ND Ill, 1989). The truth of this is (perhaps unintentionally) recognised in a statement in *Ellis v Time Inc.* 1997 WL 863267 (DDC, 1997), at 13: 'The Court finds that applying English libel standards would violate the First Amendment's protection of free speech... United States courts must apply rules of law consistent with the Constitution, regardless of where the alleged wrong occurs. Principles of international comity do not dictate otherwise: it is the choice not the duty of the United States to acknowledge the laws of another nation... When it is contrary to its policy or prejudicial to its interests, the United States must not apply foreign law... This Court will not apply English libel law...'

After protracted litigation which went on until 1988, DeRoburt's claim was dismissed: see 859 F 2d 714 (9th cir, 1988).　　　　　　　[204] *Desai v Hersh*, n 203 above.

[205] In Europe the analogy can be drawn with mandatory rules of the law of the forum and the question of when the application of such rules is mandatory.

[206] n 203 above, 680–681. It is possible to construe this rule as a unilateral conflict rule.

It is probable that the 'public concern' aspect of this rule is likely to be satisfied in most cases of truly trans-national libel.[207] When a publisher will be taken to have intended to abandon First Amendment protection may be more difficult to judge, though the court gave some examples. Thus intentional publication in a foreign country which is substantial in comparison with domestic publication will indicate an intention to abandon,[208] though it is not made clear why this should be the case if there is other evidence indicating an absence of such an intention. Perhaps reference to intention here is unfortunate and a better question to ask may be whether in the light of the quantity of publication in the foreign country, it is reasonable to extend the protection of the Constitution to it. The court also suggested that where substantial publication resulted from the act of a third party only the third party will be taken to have abandoned protection and the author will retain protection even when the third party acts according to a contract with the author.[209] The court rejected the notion that principles of agency might be applied to third party republication so as to avoid the 'chilling' effect that would result from 'fear of sale of the speech to a third party who would, unbeknownst to the author and domestic publisher, introduce the speech into a foreign country'.[210] According to the court, 'avoiding this chilling effect justifies limiting potential liability under foreign defamation law to the actual person or entity responsible for foreign publication, even where the foreign distribution was a certainty.'[211] In the latter type of case the plaintiff may still recover under foreign law in the foreign court against the actual person or entity responsible for the foreign publication.[212]

In the instant case the court held that Seymour Hersh's book was a matter of public concern, but was unable to answer the question of abandonment and required the parties to produce evidence of Indian publication. It was held that the First Amendment would not apply in respect of the Indian publication if the plaintiff was able to establish that Hersh intentionally republished the book in India with a view to exploiting the Indian market.[213]

---

[207] Though that is not likely to be the case, eg where the defendant publishes only in India and a copy is taken back to the United States by a tourist so that the speech is perhaps of no, or only minimum, public concern to the American public: see ibid, at 676. Allegations that an Indian public official sold Indian state secrets to the CIA even if only published in India might be of more than minimum public concern to Americans. [208] Ibid, at 680.

[209] Ibid. [210] Ibid. [211] Ibid. [212] Ibid.

[213] Ibid, 679. It is not clear what the final outcome on the particular issue was, although a jury appears to have delivered a verdict in favour of Hersh: see 954 F 2d 1408 (7th cir, 1992), cert. denied 506 US 895 (1992).

Whilst the approach in *Desai* is capable of being interpreted to give less expansive effect to the First Amendment than that of *DeRoburt* the vagaries surrounding the definition of intentional abandonment of protection make it very difficult to predict that the former decision will actually have that effect, given the almost umbilical cord which binds the First Amendment and American courts. Foreign claimants are perhaps unlikely to have any more success in suing in United States courts in respect of publications in a foreign country where First Amendment protection does not apply than they will have in enforcing, in the United States, judgments emanating from courts in countries whose law does not supply such protection.

Choice of Law In Other Common Law Systems: Some Brief Remarks

This section offers some brief remarks on the position, as regards choice of law, in Australia and Canada.[214] Each of these countries has abandoned the common law double actionability rule, derived from English law, for all types of case.[215] The replacement rule involves, very generally speaking, reference to the *lex loci delicti*. The effects and scope of the change are still being worked out.

Australia

Dow Jones & Co. Inc. v Gutnick[216] is now a well known case. Once again the hapless Dow Jones was the 'fall-guy', this time in respect of its online edition of *Barron's* magazine (*Barron's Online*) which the plaintiff claimed

---

[214] Aspects of the position as regards choice of law and judgment enforcement in the United States are considered above. It may be noted in passing that English publishers and authors have been subject to defamation proceedings in Ireland in connection with published material concerning events in Northern Ireland: see *Ewins v Carlton UK Television* [1997] ILRM 223; *Hunter v Duckworth & Co. Ltd. and Louis Blom-Cooper* [2000] ILPr 229. According to Robertson and Nicol, n 5 above, 103, Irish defamation law is 'antediluvian'. See also the evidence of the Legal Manager of Times Newspapers Ltd. to the European Union Committee of the House of Lords considering an EU Commission proposal for a regulation on the law applicable to non-contractual obligations (Rome II), 'Dublin is regarded as the only other jurisdiction where you get a better crack of the whip than London': HL Paper 66 (2004), Evidence, 37.

[215] For Australia, see *John Pfeiffer v Rogerson*, n 65 above; *Renault v Zhang*, n 65 above; *Dow Jones v Gutnick*, n 65 above (all decisions of the High Court of Australia). For Canada, see *Tolofson v Jensen* (1994) 120 DLR (4th) 289 (a decision of the Supreme Court of Canada). The versions of the English common law rule formerly applied in these countries were not identical with each other or identical with the English approach.

[216] n 65 above. For discussion, see Rolph, 'The Message not the Medium: Defamation, Publication and the Internet in *Dow Jones & Co Inc. v Gutnick*' (2002) 24 Sydney L Rev 263;

contained an article which was defamatory of him.[217] The offending material was uploaded on to the defendants' server in New Jersey, USA. The material could be accessed by subscribers in many, if not most jurisdictions in the world. One such jurisdiction was the Australian State of Victoria, where resided the plaintiff, Joseph Gutnick. The plaintiff had his business headquarters in Victoria. Although he conducted business outside Australia, including in the United States, and made significant contributions to charities in the United States and Israel, much of his business and social life was focused in Victoria. There were more than 500,000 subscribers to *Barron's Online*, of whom approximately 1,700 were in Australia. The Australian High Court, affirming the decision of the Supreme Court of Victoria, held that the Victorian court had jurisdiction to deal with the plaintiff's claim under the Victorian rules for 'long-arm' jurisdiction, on the basis that a tort had been committed in Victoria. The High Court also held that the applicable law was the law of Victoria. The judgments of the court merit the closest attention, but the following points must suffice.

The policy underlying the defamation law of the Australian States is similar to that of English law and does not extend the protection to speech that is found in the United States. Although the plaintiff could have sued the defendant in the United States any proceedings there would no doubt have been met by the First Amendment. The defendant argued that the applicable law should be regarded as that of the jurisdiction in which the material was uploaded which would point to the law of New Jersey. Any other solution would expose the defendant to the possibility of suits in any country where the material was capable of being accessed and to the prospects of being found liable under the laws of these respective countries.[218] This argument, essentially supporting application of the law of the publisher's 'home state', was rejected, in favour of the place of downloading as elaborated in the majority judgment in the following passage:

In defamation, the same considerations that require rejection of locating the tort by reference only to the publisher's conduct lead to the conclusion that, ordinarily, defamation is to be located at the place where the damage to reputation occurs.

Fitzgerald, '*Dow Jones & Co v Gutnick*: Negotiating "American Legal Hegemony" in the Transnational world of Cyberspace' (2003) 27 Melbourne UL Rev 590; Kohl, 'Defamation on the Internet—Nice Decision. Shame about the Reasoning. *Dow Jones & Co v Gutnick*', (2003) 52 ICLQ 1049. See also *Macquarie Bank Ltd. v Berg* [1999] NSWSC 526; Kohl 'Defamation on the Internet—A Duty-free Zone After All?' (2000) 22 Sydney L Rev 119.

[217] Several foreign media organisations were given leave to intervene in these proceedings, including: Guardian Newspapers Ltd.; New York Times Co.; Reuters Group Plc; Time Inc.; Tribune Co.; The Washington Post Co.; Yahoo! Inc.; and the Internet Industry Association.   [218] The court rejected a single publication rule: ibid, 601–605.

Ordinarily that will be where the material which is alleged to be defamatory is available in comprehensible form assuming, of course, that the person defamed has in that place a reputation which is thereby damaged. It is only when the material is in comprehensible form that the damage to reputation is done and it is damage to reputation which is the principal focus of defamation, not any quality of the defendant's conduct. In the case of material on the World Wide Web, it is not available in comprehensible form until downloaded on to the computer of a person who has used a web browser to pull the material from the web server. It is where that person downloads the material that damage may be done. Ordinarily then, that will be the place where the tort of defamation is committed.[219]

The above is reminiscent of the references to publication and location of reputation in English case law. More generally, there is similarity with the English approach in that the plaintiff confined his claim to the damage he alleged was caused to his reputation in Victoria as a consequence of the publication that occurred in that state. And the majority continued, in terms reminiscent of *Berezovsky*: 'It is his reputation in that State, and only that State, which he seeks to vindicate'.[220]

So what of the defendant who may be exposed to actions in countries all over the world under the laws of countries all over the world? The majority had (some) words of comfort:

the spectre which Dow Jones sought to conjure up in the present appeal, of a publisher forced to consider every article it publishes on the World Wide Web against the defamation laws of every country from Afghanistan to Zimbabwe is seen to be unreal when it is recalled that in all except the most unusual of cases, identifying the person about whom material is to be published will readily identify the defamation law to which that person may resort.[221]

To put it slightly differently, Dow Jones must have known that Gutnick lived primarily in Victoria, that he had a Victorian reputation and that its publication could be accessed in Victoria. The broader argument, that of exposure to the world, is serious overkill. It would seem unlikely that Gutnick would seek to drag poor old Dow Jones before the courts or laws of Afghanistan or Zimbabwe or even those of any country in between, except those of the relevant Australian state, to wit Victoria. And Dow Jones was bound to know that New Jersey, USA was out of the equation because of the First Amendment.

It is perhaps the latter thoughts which prompted the somewhat more robust response of Callinan J. who concluded his judgment with the following.

---

[219] The court rejected a single publication rule: ibid, 606–607.   [220] Ibid, 608.
[221] Ibid, 609.

I agree with the respondent's submission that what the appellant seeks to do, is to impose upon Australian residents for the purposes of this and many other cases, an American legal hegemony in relation to Internet publications. The consequence, if the appellant's submission were to be accepted would be to confer upon one country, and one notably more benevolent to the commercial and other media than this one, an effective domain over the law of defamation, to the financial advantage of publishers in the United States, and the serious disadvantage of those unfortunate enough to be reputationally damaged outside the United States. A further consequence might be to place publishers in this country at a disadvantage to commercial publishers in the United States.[222]

In other words the Empire strikes back and rejects what is, in effect, an attempt by American media defendants to export the First Amendment.

Canada

Although the principle of the *lex loci delicti* has been accepted in Canadian law, its application has been considered in only a small number of cases mainly in the context of jurisdiction.[223]

Those who have punished themselves by reading this piece thus far will note that *Olde v Capital Publishing Ltd. Partnership*[224] has a familiar ring to it. American defendants had published an unflattering article about the individual and corporate plaintiff in a magazine, some of the issues of which were sold in Ontario, but the majority of which were sold in several

---

[222] Ibid, 653–654. Although the website in *Gutnick* was a subscription site no distinction is drawn in the judgments between subscription and non-subscription sites. Apparently the journalist who wrote the offending article has submitted a petition to the United Nations Human Rights Committee alleging that the decision in the case violates his right to freedom of speech under Art 19 of the International Covenant on Civil and Political Rights: see Kohl, 'Nice Decision', n 216 above, 1049, 1050.

[223] *Olde v Capital Publishing Ltd. Partnership* 1996 *CarswellOnt* 2959, affd. 1998 *CarswellOnt* 179; *Direct Energy Marketing Ltd. v Hillson* [1999] 12 WWR 408; [2000] ILPr 102 (not a press case); *Imagis Technologies Inc. v Red Herring Communications Inc.* 2003 *CarswellBC* 540; *Barrick Gold Corp. v Lopehandia* (2004) 71 OR (3d) 416 (not a press case); *Trizec Properties Inc. v Citigroup Global Markets Inc.* (2004) 72 OR (3d) 265 (not a press case); *Bangoura v Washington Post* (2004) 235 DLR (4th) 564. For a case concerned with non-recognition of a Texas libel judgment in British Columbia on the ground that the Texas court lacked jurisdiction, see *Braintech Inc. v Kostiuk* (1999) 171 DLR (4th) 46 (not a press case), discussed by Schafer, 'Canada's Approach to Jurisdiction over Cybertorts: *Braintech v Kostiuk*' (2000) 23 Fordham Int'l. LJ 1186. For a discussion of defamation issues in the light of the change in the law, see Martin, '*Tolofsen* and flames in Cyberspace: The Changing Landscape of Multistate Defamation' (1997) 31 *UBC L Rev* 127. For discussion in the context of the law before it was changed, see Castel, 'Multistate Defamation: Should the Place of Publication Rule be Abandoned for Jurisdiction and Choice of Law Purposes?' (1990) 28 Osgoode Hall LJ 153. And for two leading cases decided before the change, see *Jenner v Sun Oil Co.* [1952] 2 DLR 526; *Pindling v National Broadcasting Corp.* (1984) 14 DLR (4th) 391.   [224] n 233 above.

other jurisdictions. The individual plaintiff had some connection (but not much) with Ontario, in the form of a holiday home there, a current wife who hailed from there and former business dealings there. He was, however, an American citizen whose principal business dealings were in the United States and whose principal residence was in the Cayman Islands. The corporate plaintiff was an American corporation whose business was conducted in the United States. The plaintiffs claimed Can\$2 million for libel arising out of the article which related, principally, to the business methods they employed in the United States. The issue was whether the Ontario court had jurisdiction under the Ontario long-arm statute (tort committed in Ontario or damage suffered in Ontario) and on *forum non conveniens* grounds.[225] It was pretty clear that the plaintiffs would have no claim in the United States because of the First Amendment.[226]

Refreshingly, the court declined jurisdiction. While hinting that a tort might have been committed in Ontario through publication there, the matter of the case had no real and substantial connections with Ontario at all, not least because the plaintiff 'did not have his vocation in life here in Ontario. He lives here two months of the year. He does not have his place of business in here in Ontario. His corporation has no connection whatever with Ontario'.[227] The court also proffered the view that 'in cases involving magazines sold in a number of jurisdictions, it would make good sense at least in cases such as this where a very small number of the publications were sold in Canada, to name the place where the majority of the sales took place as the one where the action should be tried, *under the law thereof*.[228]

This decision was upheld by the Ontario Court of Appeal.[229] The Ontario court, at least, is prepared to send a forumshopper packing even if it means that the forumshopper will end up with nowhere to bring a successful claim.

The Ontario court has considered the question of jurisdiction in a defamation claim more recently in *Bangoura v Washington Post*[230] The plaintiff had worked in a senior capacity for the United Nations before settling in Canada and acquiring Canadian citizenship. At the time of the dispute he had lived in Ontario for two years and worked in that province. The articles he complained of, which related to his work for

---

[225] The judgment, which also concerns a constitutional point, is not very clear as to what the precise jurisdictional rule was in issue.

[226] 1996 *CarswellOnt* 2959, para. 4.   [227] Ibid, para. 11.

[228] Ibid, para. 15 (emphasis added).   [229] 1998 *CarswellOnt* 179.

[230] n 223 above.

the United Nations, appeared on the website of the *Washington Post* and were also to be found in the hard copy version of the newspaper. The *Washington Post* is operated by the Washington Post Co., a diversified media company incorporated in Delaware, with its head office in Washington, District of Columbia. The plaintiff sought to sue the *Post* and three of its journalists in Ontario and the question was whether the Ontario court had jurisdiction.

According to the defendants the *Post* had office space in Ontario which was used for the purpose of gathering news, but there was no wholesale distribution of the newspaper in Ontario or anywhere else in Canada. The only recipients of the *Post* in Ontario at the time of the publications complained of were agreed to be seven paid subscribers. At the time of the publication, the plaintiff was not in Ontario but he had no connections whatsoever with the United States. It would appear to be likely that if he brought a libel action in Washington, DC, it would fall foul of the First Amendment.

Applying the relevant principles, the court held that both the District of Columbia and Ontario were appropriate fora. In a judgment which is not of the greatest clarity the court appeared to approve of *Gutnick*[231] and found that the fact that an Ontario judgment might not be recognised in the United States (though 'an unfortunate expression of a lack of comity')[232] was not to be determinative of jurisdiction. It then reached a conclusion, which will doubtless send shivers down the spines of newspaper proprietors, that 'the *Post* is a newspaper with an international profile, and its writers influence viewpoints throughout the English speaking world. I would be surprised if it were not insured for damages for libel or defamation anywhere in the world, and if it is not then it should be'.[233] And on the question of applicable law, which is relevant in the jurisdictional inquiry, it could not reach a conclusion but said, instead, that if the *lex loci delicti* was based on publication the applicable law was that of the District of Columbia, whereas if it was based on damage and where reputation was affected the applicable law was the law of Ontario.[234] Accordingly since it could not be established that one forum was more appropriate than the other, the plaintiff's choice of the Ontario forum should prevail.[235]

It would be unwise to read too much into these two cases since each appears to be tentative and uncertain. They show, however, a pattern seen elsewhere in which a claimant is anxious to bring defamation proceedings

---

[231] See also *Barrick v Lopehandia*, n 223 above.
[232] Ibid, at para. 22. cf *Imagis v Red Herring*, n 223 above.   [233] Ibid.
[234] Ibid, at para. 29.   [235] Ibid.

in a jurisdiction which might, unlike the case with the United States, uphold the claim on the merits.[236]

The cases do not resolve the question of where the tort of defamation is to be regarded as committed for choice of law purposes[237] and this issue is likely to require further judicial attention. In the leading case of *Tolofson v Jensen* [238] which was not concerned with defamation, La Forest J. in the merest of *obiter dicta* said that in the case of a multistate libel 'the tort of libel should be held to take place where its effects are felt'.[239] It is possible that this points to the place where the claimant's reputation is located, an outcome which is consistent with the two Ontario cases described above. But it is also likely to be necessary that the offending material be published, at least to some extent, in that state as well.

'It is a Pain in the Neck'

When the European Union Committee of the House of Lords considered the European Commission's proposal for a regulation on the law applicable to non-contractual obligations ('Rome II'), there was a very interesting discussion between leading in-house media lawyers, who gave evidence to the Committee and the members of the Committee,[240] which picks up many of the tensions highlighted in this paper. Thus, for Mr Brett when *The Times* had been sued in England, he had only once come across a case in which it had been asserted that a foreign law might be applicable.[241] This perhaps reflects the media's favour of a country of origin choice of law rule, a choice of law rule that would secure the application of the law of the publisher's 'home state'. Such a rule is certain and, of course, is cheaper to comply with since the publisher need only take legal advice on the system in which it is established. Such a rule may also be practical, since the mechanics of daily newspaper production may

---

[236] Apparently Canadian libel law is similar to English libel law: ibid, at para. 22. The same pattern emerges in *Trizec v Citigroup*, n 223 above.

[237] In *Trizec*, n 223 above, which was also concerned with jurisdiction, it was said, at Para. 70 that the applicable law is the law of the jurisdiction where the publication was received and accessed though the decision also seems to require, for jurisdictional purposes (see para. 72), damage to reputation in that state.   [238] n 215 above.

[239] Ibid, 299.

[240] See HL Paper 66 (2004), Evidence, 36–37. The witnesses were Mr Alastair Brett, Legal Manager, Times Newspapers Ltd.; Ms Santha Rasaiah, Political, Editorial and Regulatory Affairs Director, The Newspaper Society; Ms Clare Hoban, Head of Public and Legal Affairs, Periodical Publishers Association; Mr Glenn del Medico, Head of Programme Legal Advice, BBC.

[241] Ibid, 36–38. This was the *Loutchansky* litigation.

make it impossible to seek legal advice as to the laws of all the countries into which the newspaper may find its way. For Mr Brett, being sued in a foreign country under foreign law was a 'pain in the neck' as illustrated by a complicated claim for invasion of privacy brought against *The Times* in France, where although small awards of damages may be given, the defendant will run up costs. Mr del Medico advised that the BBC was susceptible to actions all over the world.[242] And now there is the internet which is the real problem in the view of Mr Brett who, as the legal face of *The Times*, a leading newspaper in the town called Sue, can have the last word:

we only send hard copies within the EU and only a small number so the likelihood of it doing any serious damage is very remote, but the internet is a different animal altogether. We are used to living with liability where we send newspapers. If we flog newspapers in Northern Ireland and Dublin and everywhere else we are going to get sued—we know that and it is a reality of life—but what is really complicated now is if we are suddenly going to get sued in Serbia or another jurisdiction because somebody says "I was able to access you out there".[243]

---

[242] Ibid, 41.   [243] Ibid, 43.

When Systems Fail: Parents, Children and the Quality of Healthcare

Jo Bridgeman

My purpose in considering 'When systems fail' is to provide a feminist perspective on systems analysis, which has caught the attention of academics,[1] inquiry teams[2] and policy makers[3] as a mechanism for responding to failures in healthcare. On one level, I am seeking to support the development of systems analysis as a means through which to attain a more comprehensive understanding of what went wrong than can be secured through tort litigation.[4] However, a feminist analysis suggests that, as with tort law, unless the paradigms are challenged—that is, reconsidering the legal concept of the self, what harms that subject and how those harms may be remedied—the greater understanding sought through systems analysis will be partial. On another level, I am seeking to identify the limits of the response provided through the formal mechanisms of the law to one particular, scandalous failure within the healthcare system: the widespread removal at post-mortem and retention of human material from the bodies of children without parental knowledge or consent. Focus upon this one example does, I admit, make it easier for me to argue my central point which is the need to recognise, in the provision of quality healthcare and in the law which regulates it, responsibilities grounded in relationships. But, I argue, this example serves well to demonstrate the limits of the law, given its conceptual basis, to recognise and respond to failures in care.

---

[1] In the US, L Leape *et al*, 'Promoting Patient Safety by Preventing Medical Error' (1998) 16 *Journal of the American Medical Association* 280; in the UK, A Merry and A McCall Smith, *Errors, Medicine and the Law* (Cambridge University Press, 2001).

[2] Notably the Inquiry into the quality of the paediatric cardiac services at the Bristol Royal Infirmary: *The Report of the Public Inquiry into children's heart surgery at the Bristol Royal Infirmary 1984–1995: Learning from Bristol* (CM5207(I), July 2001) (the Kennedy Report).

[3] Department of Health, *An organisation with a memory, Report of an expert group on learning from adverse events in the NHS* (2000). The National Patient Safety Agency was established in 2001.

[4] Although there then needs to be separate consideration of how to meet the practical needs of those who are harmed as a consequence of failures in healthcare, as considered below.

The circumstances are well reported. In the course of providing evidence to the Bristol Royal Infirmary Inquiry—the public inquiry established to investigate the quality of care provided to children undergoing cardiac surgery at the Bristol Royal Infirmary between 1984 and 1995[5]—Professor Anderson (Professor of Paediatric Cardiac Morphology at Great Ormond Street Hospital) revealed that the retention of the organs of children who had undergone a post-mortem after their death for the purposes of education, research and medical archiving was not confined to Bristol—where it had already been exposed—but extended nationwide.[6] The Bristol Royal Infirmary Inquiry issued an Interim Report into the practice in Bristol and an independent inquiry was established into the removal, retention and disposal of human tissue and organs following post-mortem at the Royal Liverpool Children's NHS Trust (the Redfern Inquiry).[7] Subsequently, independent investigations were established into the retention of organs at hospitals in Manchester[8] and Birmingham.[9] In addition to these Inquiries, the shocking

[5] The Kennedy Report, n 2 above. The Inquiry was established under s 84 of the National Health Service Act 1977 to determine whether the care provided to children undergoing cardiac surgery at the Bristol Royal Infirmary between 1984 and 1995 was adequate and, in the light of conclusions reached about the adequacy of care and action taken in response to concerns raised, to make recommendations to improve the quality of care provided by the NHS in the future.

[6] The Inquiry into the management of care of children receiving complex heart surgery at The Bristol Royal Infirmary: Interim Report, *Removal and retention of human material* (May 2000), para. 6, identifying Alder Hey Children's Hospital, Royal Brompton Hospital, Great Ormond Street Hospital for Sick Children, Leeds General Infirmary, The Freeman Hospital Newcastle, Southampton General Hospital and the Royal Manchester Children's Hospital.

[7] *The Royal Liverpool Children's Inquiry: Report* (30 January 2001), chairman, Mr Michael Redfern QC. The Inquiry was established under s 2 of the National Health Service Act 1977 to inquire into the circumstances of the removal, retention and disposal of human tissue from children at the Royal Liverpool Children's NHS Trust, compliance with the Human Tissue Act 1961, professional practice and management and to make recommendations.

[8] This was established because of fears that there was a large collection of hearts which had been concealed or destroyed but found organ retention to a 'relatively restricted extent'. The Retained Organs Commission, *Organ Retention at Central Manchester and Manchester Children's University Hospitals Trust, Report of an Independent Investigation* (July 2002) concluded that there was widespread removal of organs following post-mortem in accordance with practice elsewhere for the purposes of proper examination. However, there was inadequate communication about the purpose and nature of post-mortems and insufficient information provided as to the findings. Some organs were used for teaching and research having been unlawfully retained following completion of the post-mortem examination and parents' enquiries were dealt with inadequately.

[9] Retained Organs Commission, *External Review of the Birmingham Children's Hospital NHS Trust, Report on Organ Donation* (November 2002).

nature of the revelations precipitated examination of the extent and nature of retention,[10] review of guidelines and the law and a range of responses by and to the individuals involved and affected.

The Chief Medical Officer organised a summit to provide a forum in which those involved and affected could express their differing perspectives upon the removal and retention of organs.[11] This was followed by advice from the Chief Medical Officer[12] recommending amendment of the Human Tissue Act 1961, a code of practice setting out standards for communication about post-mortems and a fundamental review of the law on the taking, storage and use of tissue from the living and the deceased to achieve an independent system of regulatory control and emphasis upon a gift relationship. Interim guidance on good practice was provided by the code of practice, model consent forms and information leaflets issued by the Department of Health.[13] A wide-ranging consultation on legislation governing human material[14] culminated in reform of the law in the form of the Human Tissue Act 2004. Following the Redfern Report, the Interim Orders Committee of the GMC suspended the registration of Professor van Velzen[15] and the Retained Organs Commission was established, amongst other things, to oversee the arrangements for the return of retained organs guiding NHS Trusts on good practice sensitive to the needs of relatives.[16] Inevitably, the revelations prompted a range of reactions amongst the parents and families of the children. A number of groups were established providing vital sources of support.[17] Mediation achieved a settlement for families of children

[10] CMO, *Report of a Census of Organs and Tissues Retained by Pathology Services in England* (DoH/DfEE/HO, January 2001).

[11] CMO Summit, 11 January 2001, *Proceedings* (published on *www.cmosummit.org.uk*, January 2001) (no longer available on this site).

[12] CMO advice, *The Removal, Retention and use of Human Organs and Tissue from Post Mortem Examination* (DoH/DfEE/HO, January 2001).

[13] DoH, *Families and Post Mortems* (April 2003).

[14] DoH, *Human Bodies, Human Choices: The Law on Human Organs and Tissue in England and Wales: A Consultation Report* (July 2002).

[15] The Interim Orders Committee suspended the registration of Professor van Velzen in February 2001 and he remains under a suspension order.

[16] A Special Health Authority established in April 2001. The Commission was also to act as an advocate and source of information for families and to advise the government on legislative reform which is considerate of the needs of relatives. Having completed its work, the Commission was closed on 31 March 2004.

[17] The National Committee relating to Organ Retention (NACOR) was established in response to revelations about retention of organs in Bristol but extended to provide support nationally. It ceased active work on 31 March 2004; Pity II (Parents who have Interred Their Young Twice) was established in response to revelations about retention at Alder Hey but extended to provide support nationally. Many local support groups were established nationwide.

whose organs were retained at the Alder Hey Children's Hospital (Royal Liverpool Children's NHS Trust).[18] The settlement included a letter of apology, a memorial to the victims, a donation to a charity chosen by the parents and a meeting with the parents to discuss changes at the hospital. Failure to reach a settlement with families affected nationwide led to civil proceedings to determine preliminary issues and three lead cases brought by parents who suffered psychiatric harm as a consequence of the retention of organs from their children.[19]

With these particular examples, the events may seem some time ago: 1984–1995 in the case of Bristol and 1962–2000 in the case of Alder Hey; the Inquiries reported and their reports were shelved; and the issues raised were exhaustively covered. It is my argument that there remain lessons to be learnt about the value of children and the role of parents in caring for them, beyond the specific question of the respect shown to the bodies of loved ones, of relevance both to the provision of high quality care and to the law which regulates their care. As an alternative to tort litigation, a systems analysis approach avoids blaming individuals, seeks a more comprehensive understanding of events and the learning of lessons of failures in care. But, in relation to healthcare, unless it is also appreciated that children (patients) are persons, situated in relationships with people who care, the understanding will be partial and lessons learnt limited.

To make this argument, drawing upon feminist analysis, I consider the conceptual boundaries of the law of tort as applied in the case of *AB and Others* in response to the harm caused by the failure to inform and obtain the consent of parents to the retention of organs from the bodies of their children. I then turn to consider the wider under-standing of this failure in care attainable through a systems analysis. My conclusion is that the development of systems analysis needs to give proper weight to the experiences of users of the healthcare system if lessons are to be learnt from failures in care in order to improve the quality of healthcare. In particular, there needs to be an understanding of persons—the nature of the subject and what harms them—derived not from abstract ideals but from the concrete experiences of those involved.

---

[18] A settlement was reached in the Royal Liverpool Children's Group Litigation totalling £5m with a payment of £5,000 and a hardship fund of £1.5m, BBC News, 31 January 2003. Parents who could not accept the settlement were permitted to join the nationwide group.

[19] *AB and Others v Leeds Teaching Hospital NHS Trust; Cardiff and Vale NHS Trust* [2004] EWHC 644, considered below.

The Response of the Common Law of Tort

Because, following a failure to achieve a negotiated settlement, they were recently considered in the context of tort law by Gage J. in *AB and Others* we know the way in which the parents had to (re)frame their responses to and the consequences of the removal and retention of human material from the bodies of their children without their knowledge or consent.[20] Gage J. considered four preliminary issues and three lead actions representing the 2,140 claims on the Nationwide Organ Group Litigation register. In all three of the lead cases, the basis of the claim was the discovery, some years after the death of their son or daughter, that organs had been removed at post-mortem and retained for examination whilst the child's body was returned to them and subsequently disposed of, and that this caused the mother—and although the judgment speaks of actions by parents, all three of the lead cases are brought by mothers[21]—to suffer psychiatric harm. Liability in two torts was at issue: negligence and wrongful interference with the child's body.[22]

Negligence

Questions of liability in negligence centred upon the failure of clinicians to inform and obtain consent to the removal and subsequent retention of organs when seeking consent to the performance of hospital post-mortems. This involved consideration of the familiar questions (in the context of negligence claims) of whether a duty of care arose; whether the claimants were primary or secondary victims; and whether the failure to inform about retention of organs was in breach of the duty of care. To put

[20] n 19 above; (Gage J.).

[21] M Chamallas and L K Kerber, 'Women, Mothers, and the Law of Fright: A History' (1990) 88 Mich L Rev 814–864 undertake a 'gendered history' of fright-based injuries in the US.

[22] It is unclear, following the House of Lords decision in *Wainwright and another v Home Office* [2003] UKHL 53, whether an action could have been based on the principle from *Wilkinson v Downton* [1897] 2 QB 57 that the doctors intentionally inflicted harm. Whilst accepting as a matter of principle that intentionally caused harm should attract a remedy, Lord Hoffmann considered that intention needed to be tightly defined, believing that Wright J in *Wilkinson* had 'sailed as close to negligence as he felt he could go' [para. 44]. According to Lord Hoffmann, it must be established that the defendant 'acted in a way which he knew to be unjustifiable and either intended to cause harm or at least acted without caring whether he caused harm or not' [para. 45]. Requiring on the part of the defendant knowledge of unjustifiable action would appear to necessitate conscious want of care, which would not be established in respect of doctors who failed to give any thought to the consequences of neglecting to inform parents about the retention of organs.

these issues into context, it is necessary to outline the circumstances of the two lead cases concerning the retention of organs following hospital post-mortems. Karen Harris's daughter Rosina was delivered at 28 weeks' gestation by caesarean section with severe abnormalities which resulted in her death at three days old. Her parents claimed that they had agreed to the post-mortem on condition that samples only were taken and all organs were returned to her body. The consent form which was signed by Rosina's father stated that he understood that tissue may be removed for treatment, education and research but he explained that he understood tissue to mean small samples and not whole organs. Her parents were informed, nearly 16 years later, in a letter from Southampton University Hospital, that her brain, heart, lungs and spinal cord had been removed, retained and subsequently disposed of. Denise Shorter's daughter Laura was stillborn at 40 weeks' gestation. She was informed, some 9 years later, that her daughter's brain had been removed at post-mortem, retained for examination and subsequently disposed of.

The first legal issue for determination was the question whether the clinicians who sought consent to the performance of a post-mortem owed a duty of care to the mothers. This turned upon the question whether a doctor/patient relationship existed, which was a question of fact and degree.[23] On facts such as those in the lead cases of Karen Harris and Denise Shorter, both recently delivered mothers, there was a continuing duty owed arising from the clinician's role in giving advice about future pregnancies for which information from the post-mortem was material.[24] Written consent to the performance of a post-mortem upon Rosina Harris had been given by her father, following discussion between the parents and the paediatric SHO who explained the importance of finding out if Rosina's condition was genetic. The senior obstetric registrar who obtained consent from Denise Shorter to the performance of a post-mortem upon her daughter, Laura, agreed that his duty included helping the mother of a stillborn child come to terms with her loss and find out the reasons for the child's death. However, the nationwide group also includes parents of older children upon whom post-mortems were performed following surgery, illness or accident when it would be unlikely that a doctor/patient relationship existed between the parents and the clinician who sought consent to a post-mortem.[25]

[23] n 19 above, para. 188. The requirements of proximity and whether it is fair, just and reasonable to impose a duty would be established where a doctor/patient relationship exists.   [24] Ibid, para. 203.

[25] *Powell & another v Boldaz and others* (CA 1 July 1997). Robert Powell died at the age of 10 from a rare undiagnosed disease, Addison's disease. The Health Authority admitted liability in respect of the failure to diagnose and treat Robert and damages paid in

As the harm at the basis of both claims was psychiatric, a second duty question arose which was whether the mothers were primary or secondary victims. Gage J. noted that the circumstances did not fit easily into the 'descriptions given to primary and secondary victims' but that he had to determine whether the claims fell into one or other category.[26] The claimants would not fulfil the limitations imposed upon secondary victims and, whilst they were never themselves at risk of physical injury, Gage J. concluded that the claimants were primary victims because:

(a) unlike the secondary victims in *Alcock*,[27] the claimants were readily identifiable before the event of obtaining consent to a post-mortem;

(b) the children were not primary victims (noting that Lord Oliver in *Alcock* appeared to assume that there has to be a primary victim for questions about liability to secondary victims to arise);

(c) where a doctor/patient relationship existed, the claimants were most appropriately placed within the first of Hale LJ's categories in *Hatton*. That is, primary victims 'at risk of foreseeable psychiatric harm because the circumstances are akin to those of primary victims in contract'[28] noting that the doctor/patient relationship is frequently compared to a contractual relationship.

Categorisation of the claimants as primary victims enabled them to avoid the hurdles placed by the arbitrary limitations imposed upon those categorised as secondary victims. The duty question thus became whether a reasonable clinician, at the time of securing consent to a post-mortem, would have foreseen that the claimant would have suffered psychiatric harm as a consequence of their failure to take care. On the facts, Gage J. concluded that the possibility that Karen Harris would suffer psychiatric injury upon discovering that her daughter Rosina's organs had been retained was not foreseeable by a reasonable paediatrician with Dr Clifford's knowledge of her at the time he obtained her consent to the post-mortem: '[S]he was a robust person and someone who Dr Clifford would have regarded as unlikely to collapse under the strain'.[29] Whereas, at the time, a reasonable consultant obstetrician would have foreseen that

settlement included a sum for the psychiatric illness of his mother. In separate proceedings centring upon allegations of a 'cover-up' after his death, it was held that the duty was owed to the child as patient, that after his death there is no doctor/patient duty with relatives unless the doctor treats them as patients.

[26] n 19 above, paras. 189–197.
[27] *Alcock v Chief Constable of South Yorkshire Police* [1992] 1 AC 310.
[28] *Hatton v Sutherland* [2002] 2 All ER 1.　　[29] n 19 above, para. 253.

Denise Shorter would suffer from psychiatric injury when she discovered that her daughter Laura's organs had been retained—a duty was owed to her as a primary victim.

Quoting extensively from *Sidaway*[30] and *Bolitho*,[31] Gage J. directed himself to the principle that the conduct of the clinicians had to accord with that of a competent body of professional opinion and to be both reasonable and logical in the circumstances. The failure of the clinicians in the lead cases to inform about the need to retain organs for proper post-mortem examination was 'an almost universal practice up to 1999/2000', motivated by a desire to save families further distress and a paternalistic view that parents might not want to know what was involved in a post-mortem. Looking at the issue from a common sense perspective and objectively, Gage J. considered that mothers of children who had recently died would want to know if their organs were going to be retained. Hospital post-mortems were a matter of choice and although the Human Tissue Act 1961 only required non-objection to a post-mortem, Gage J. took the common sense approach that this required the provision of some information about what they were being asked not to object to which meant information that organs may have to be removed and retained for proper post-mortem examination. Whilst accepting that there might be circumstances in which it was appropriate not to inform, the blanket adoption of this practice without consideration of the individual circumstances of the parent or family was not justified.[32]

From a tort lawyer's perspective, Gage J. could be considered to have reached a balanced judgment in his application of the elements of the tort of negligence. The pragmatic conclusion was reached that the parents were primary and not secondary victims in circumstances, as in *North Glamorgan*[33] and *Farrell*,[34] very different from the disaster situations in which the distinction emerged. Consequently, the parents were not denied a claim *merely* because they could not fulfil the arbitrary limits placed upon secondary victims in *Alcock*. Furthermore, the conclusion that the widespread and virtually unquestioned practice of removing and retaining organs without parental knowledge or consent was an unreasonable common practice, provides an example of post-*Bolitho*

---

[30] *Sidaway v Board of Governors of the Bethlam Royal Hospital and the Maudsley Hospital* [1985] 1 AC 871.   [31] *Bolitho v City and Hackney HA* [1998] 2 AC 232.

[32] *AB and Others*, n 19 above, paras. 206–238.

[33] *North Glamorgan NHS Trust v Walters* [2002] EWCA Civ 1792. The mother of a baby who died following negligent treatment in which there was a failure to properly diagnose and treat his liver condition was held to be a secondary victim.

[34] *Farrell v Merton, Sutton and Wandsworth HA* (QBD, 31 July 2000). The mother was a primary victim as the trauma of the birth of her son with severe disabilities due to the

willingness on the part of first instance judges to challenge accepted medical practice. Whilst some of the parents in the nationwide group, like Denise Shorter, will be able to establish a negligence claim against the clinician who failed to inform them of the need to retain organs at post-mortem for proper examination, many will not. For them, as for all families where the post-mortem performed was a coroner's post-mortem for which consent is not required so that a claim based upon negligence in securing consent did not arise, the issue is whether the tort of wrongful interference with a body had been committed.

Wrongful Interference with a Body

Susan Carpenter's son, Daniel,[35] died at the age of 17 months following surgery to remove a tumour round his brain stem performed at Southampton University Hospital. His mother considered that Daniel had received outstanding care during his treatment and, knowing the cause of his death, did not want him to undergo a post-mortem. However, she was told that Daniel's body would not be released by the coroner until a post-mortem had been carried out. Although she spoke to the coroner, she was not informed as to what was involved in a post-mortem or of the need to retain Daniel's brain for diagnostic examination. A letter, received some 14 years after his death, informed her that Daniel's brain had been removed at post-mortem, retained and cremated some six months later although the hospital still had wax blocks and slides containing tissue samples from his brain and brain stem.

In the absence of any case establishing the tort in English law, the claimants were required to establish that they had a duty or right to possess their child's body and that the defendant interfered with this duty/right without lawful authority by the retention and then disposal of organs. The starting point for determination was the accepted principle that there is no property in a dead body, although parts of the body may become subject to possessory rights if, by virtue of the application of skill, the part acquires different qualities.[36] On the agreed facts in the lead cases, the post-mortems were lawfully performed either under the authority of the coroner or, in the case of hospital post-mortems, with the consent of the parents, removing the organs for the purposes of diagnosis was lawful and they were lawfully

---

negligence of the defendant extended from the induction of labour through delivery by emergency caesarean to discovering the next day upon her transfer to another hospital where her son was in intensive care that he had severe disabilities.

[35] *AB and Others*, n 19 above.   [36] *R v Kelly* [1999] QB 621 (CA) 631 (Rose LJ).

in possession of the pathologist undertaking the post-mortem or subsequent histological examination. Although the parents had a duty to bury their child, Gage J. concluded that parents did not have right of burial and possession of *organs* lawfully removed at post-mortem and retained for the purposes of diagnosis after the burial of the child's body. Their duty to bury their child was discharged before investigations were complete, so there was no right to possession of *organs* lawfully retained for diagnostic purposes arising from the duty to bury. Leading to the conclusion that there was no action for wrongful interference with a body in the circumstances in which organs were retained—which was for the purposes of diagnostic examination—and then disposed of.[37] This leaves the question whether the tort would be committed if material were retained once diagnosis was completed or retained not for the purposes of diagnosis but for research or teaching. This conclusion denied an action in tort to many of the parents as the majority of post-mortems following the death of a child are, because of the nature of their death, coroner's post-mortems.[38]

The conceptual boundaries of the law of tort operate to deny that a tort was committed against many of the parents in the nationwide group by the actions of clinicians which failed to respect the relationship between parent and child and betrayed the trust parents had placed in professionals to care for their child as a unique individual. The focus of tort law is upon the individual clinician—whether the law imposed upon them an obligation to the claimant and whether they were at fault in their actions causing foreseeable harm—and not upon the context of the caring relationship or the impact of behaviour upon those affected. Gage J. declined the invitation of Counsel to use Articles 8 and 9 of the Human Rights Act 1998 'to shape the law, where it needs shaping, to provide a remedy for these claimants'[39] expressing both 'compassion and sympathy' for the families[40] and recognition that the clinicians sought to act in the best interests of their patients and according to what they

---

[37] *AB and Others*, n 19 above, paras. 128–161.

[38] The Bristol Inquiry Interim Report found that of the 265 post-mortems carried out in Bristol on children who had died following heart surgery or from a heart condition in the period covered by the Inquiry's terms of reference, 83% (220) were coroner's post-mortems, *Removal and retention*, n 6 above, 6.

[39] *AB and Others*, n 19 above, para. 113.

[40] Ibid, para. 114: 'There have been many sad cases arising out of organ retentions. I have no doubt that many families, although maybe not all, have been deeply distressed and angered by the revelation that a major organ or organs have been removed and retained from their child's body without their consent and knowledge. No one listening to the evidence in this trial, concerning as it does claims by three families, could feel anything other than compassion and sympathy for the claimants and families similarly affected.'

considered to be best practice.[41] The symbolic message of the application of the principles of the law of tort is that generally there is nothing wrong with the practice and, consequently, nothing to learn. To the parents the message was that they were not harmed, not in the way the law recognises, not in a way the law will remedy.

Feminist Critiques of Tort Law

Feminists analysing the law of tort have provided critiques of the principles and concepts of the discipline as well as the limits and the potential of tort in responding to gendered harms. In her recent lecture in the *Current Legal Problems* series, Joanne Conaghan explored the breadth of feminist analysis of tort within the UK, Australia, Canada and the United States. She provided a three-fold categorisation of feminist engagement with tort within this literature: instrumental analysis of the role of tort in perpetuating the subordination of women and its potential contribution to our liberation; tort law's construction of gender norms; and, analysis of ideas and concepts of tort such as personhood and autonomy.[42] The issues covered within this body of work include sexual harassment,[43] violence and abuse,[44] emotional distress consequent upon injury or death of a loved one,[45] wrongful conception,[46] and compensation for mass torts.[47] The primary focus of this work is upon the failure of the law (and tort's potential) to respond to the particular needs, values, priorities and harms of *women*

---

[41] Ibid, para. 115: 'On the other side these claims concern organs removed, retained and subsequently disposed of. They do not concern organs retained for the purposes of research. Whatever may have been said by some at or after the public inquiries the evidence from the doctors in this case, in my judgment, establishes that the clinicians and pathologists to whom I have listened have acted at all times sensitively and in good faith. I have no hesitation in stating that whether or not any of them have made mistakes I have been impressed by their obvious desire to do what they thought was in the best interests of their patients and families and conducted themselves according to what they believed was best practice. I am conscious of the fact that they are dedicated professionals and some, particularly the pathologists, feel aggrieved at the criticism and condemnation which has been heaped upon them since the scandal of organ retention was revealed in 1999.'

[42] J Conaghan, 'Tort Law and Feminist Critique' in MDA. Freeman (ed), *Current Legal Problems 2003* (Oxford University Press, 2004), 174–209.

[43] J Conaghan, 'Gendered Harms and the Law of Tort: Remedying (Sexual) Harassment' (1996) 16 OJLS 407–431.

[44] J Conaghan, 'Tort-Litigation in the Context of Intra-familial Abuse' (1998) 61 MLR 132–161. [45] Chamallas and Kerber, n 21 above.

[46] N Priaulx, 'Joy to the World! A (Healthy) Child is Born! Reconceptualizing "Harm" in Wrongful Conception' (2004) 13 Social & Legal Studies 5–26.

[47] L Bender, 'Frontier of Legal Thought III: Feminist (Re)Torts: Thoughts on the Liability Crisis, Mass Torts, Power and Responsibility' (1990) Duke Law Journal 848–912.

given that the principles of the common law of tort have developed according to an abstract ideal in a male image of a separate, boundaried, individual valuing freedom and fearing annihilation or, in Leslie Bender's words:

> Because tort law was created by men (as the only participants in its writing, thinking, and practice for many years), it is not surprising that an ethic of rights, which seems to be a controlling male ethical paradigm, dominates tort analysis. Because men devised tort laws to apply to themselves, because the ethic of rights involves an implicit assumption that others are the same as oneself, and because men frequently viewed people as separate but 'socially contracting' human beings, legal theorists looked for solutions to conflicts that respected separation and formalized, distanced interactions.[48]

Laws based upon these assumptions inevitably provide an inadequate response to harms arising from attachments, responsibilities and dependencies. But it is not only the harms experienced exclusively or more extensively by women which fall beyond the realm of the law of tort. The reality of parenthood confounds the separated, individualistic and self-interested ideal grounded as it is in inevitable connections, caring responsibilities and consideration of the needs of others as well as the self.

From this understanding, three aspects of the response of tort to the removal, retention and subsequent disposal of the organs of children without parental knowledge or consent are particularly deserving of attention: property or personhood in children's bodies; the concept of harm; remedies and responsibility.

Property or Personhood in Children's Bodies?

Wrongful interference with their child's body may initially appear to encapsulate the way in which the parents had been harmed. However, reasoning through the elements of this tort, Gage J. reached the conclusion that the parents had no rights to their child's body which had been unlawfully interfered with whilst, paradoxically, the pathologist gained possessory rights to the organs retained for examination. Furthermore, as Gage J. himself appreciated, having to frame a claim in terms of possessory rights and ownership in an attempt to secure recognition of the harm done might appear inappropriate, particularly to the parents and relatives.[49] Certainly, another example of the failure to grasp the reality of the harm done, compounding the practical failure to treat the child with dignity and respect with a symbolic one.

One of the debates within the academic literature prompted by the need to reform the law relating to the removal, retention and storage of human

---

[48] Duke Law Journal , 903–4.　　　　[49] n 19 above, para. 134.

material has been whether the law should be based upon a property model or a consent model. Although the position was, and remains, that consent is not required for coronal post-mortems and whilst the legislation governing hospital post-mortems at the time, the Human Tissue Act 1961, required merely 'non-objection', in practice parents were asked for 'consent' to the hospital post-mortem if not to the need to retain organs for diagnostic examination or the retention of organs for education, research or archiving. The legal obligation to obtain consent (requested after information has been provided) has developed as one of the foundational principles of healthcare law within England and Wales, to give legal effect to the principle of respect for autonomy. It is founded upon the right, in the absence of permission, to non-interference with the boundaries of our bodies. This betrays the origins of the legal concept of the self as a separate individual fearing invasion by others and influenced by liberal theory's separation of body and mind 'with the legal person conceived of as abstracted reason rather than as sensuous creature of the flesh'.[50] Within law, although personhood is attained at the moment of a live birth, in their early years when children lack the capacity for 'abstracted reason', children are too frequently treated as non-persons by virtue of their vulnerability and dependency. This legal notion of personhood is consistent with much philosophical thinking which likewise conceives of personhood narrowly around reason, rationality, capacity. John Locke considered a person to be 'a thinking intelligent being, that has reason and reflection, and can consider itself as itself, the same thinking thing, in different times and places'.[51] More recently, John Harris has located personhood in the individual's 'capacity to value life'.[52] In contrast, Eva Feder Kittay argues, in a philosophical piece inspired by her own daughter who has cerebral palsy and severe mental disabilities, that when personhood and, consequently, moral status are dependent upon reason and rationality those who through age, illness or disability lack these capacities are excluded.[53] She presents an alternative concept of personhood:

I propose that being a person means having the capacity to be in certain relationships with other persons, to sustain contact with other persons, to shape one's

[50] N Naffine, 'the body bag' in N Naffine and R Owens (eds), *sexing the subject of law* (Sydney: LBC Information Services, 1997).
[51] J Locke, *An Essay Concerning Human Understanding*, PH Nidditch (ed), (Oxford University Press, 1987) 1.27.11 quoted in E F Kittay, 'When Caring is Just and Justice is Caring: Justice and Mental Retardation' in E F Kittay and E K Feder (eds), *The Subject of Care: Feminist Perspectives on Dependency*, (Lanham, Boulder, New York, Oxford: Rowman & Littlefield Publishers, Inc., 2002), 262.
[52] J Harris, *The value of life* (London: Routledge and Kegan Paul, 1985) 17.
[53] Kittay, n 51 above, 263.

own world and the world of others, and to have a life that another person can conceive of as an imaginative possibility for him- or herself.... We do not become a person without the engagement of other persons—their care, as well as their recognition of the uniqueness and the connectedness of our human agency, and the distinctiveness of our particularly human relations to others and of the world we fashion.[54]

Eva Feder Kittay sketches an understanding of moral personhood which is strikingly different to the concept of legal personhood adopted by tort law: one that is based in relationships and admitting children.

After death, the legal requirement to secure consent based upon respect for autonomy and protection from non-interference with bodily integrity becomes problematic.[55] Furthermore, if giving consent gives effect to autonomy, relatives can assent or dissent but not consent to intervention upon the body of a deceased adult.[56] And, as the McLean Report recognised, it is hard to identify exactly how a post-mortem examination or retention of organs from the body of a child is in their best interests as required in order for parents to give a valid consent.[57] David Price argues that securing the consent of parents is appropriate in the case of the removal and retention of organs from children as to do so continues the responsibility which parents have for the care of their child during life.[58] Given the difficulties with a consent-based approach, the alternative which has been argued for is the property-based approach upon which the tort of wrongful interference with the child's body is founded.

Property rights give the proprietor control over the object exercisable against others. As Mason and Laurie state, paradoxically, the position that there is no property in the dead body may be due to a desire to continue to treat the body with dignity and respect by precluding

[54] Kittay, 266.

[55] J Harris, 'Law and regulation of retained organs: the ethical issues' (2002) 22 LS 527–549.

[56] J K Mason and G T Laurie, 'Consent or Property? Dealing with the Body and its Parts in the Shadow of Bristol and Alder Hey' (2001) 64 MLR 710–729, 718.

[57] Preferring the concept of authorisation, Scottish Executive, *Final Report of the Independent Review on the Retention of Organs at Post Mortem* (2001). And for this reason, John Harris argues that consent from parents is not required where there are greater person-affecting interests at issue, such as the benefits to be gained from the examination, use or research upon organs: Harris, n 55 above.

[58] D Price, 'From Cosmas and Damien to Van Velzen: The Human Tissue Saga Continues' (2003) 11 Med L Rev 1–47, 17. Dudley Knowles argues that 'agreement' of parents should be secured rather than consent to avoid the requirement for informed consent which may involve parents being provided with distressing detail they would rather not know about: D Knowles, 'Parents' Consent to the Post-Mortem Removal and Retention of Organs' (2001) 18 *Journal of Applied Philosophy* 215–227.

commercialisation.[59] However, a view of the dead body as belonging to no-one created the space which was filled with the medical perspective of the body after death as a resource for learning through training, education and research.[60] It contrasts with a very different perception of the value of the body of a loved one as the continued embodiment of the person they were. Neither children[61] nor the bodies of children who have died, must be treated by parents, professionals or within the law as items of property to be fought over for control. 'My child', 'our son', 'your daughter' is expressive not of ownership but of relationship. The retention of organs of children was an invasion not of parental property rights but of the person of their child who was, as a consequence, buried incomplete without the organs of 'life, love and his memories'.[62] The dissonance between the hospital's treatment of his daughter as no longer a person and his continuing relationship with her was expressed by Paul Bradley, father of Bethan:

[T]here was no appreciation of Bethan. It was as if she ceased to have any existence just because she had died. The retention of organs was a violation of her. The manner in which it was done, without reference to us, was an assumption that Bethan's body belonged to the Hospital to do with her as they wished. Yet to us, Bethan was still our daughter even though she had died.[63]

For parents, entrusted with the care of their child and decisions about his or her body in life, the body of the child continues to have value as their child. Death does not extinguish the relationship between parent and child through which they shape each other's worlds. So that, although it can't be argued that the child still has legal personhood, they are still a person to whom parents are attached and for whom they have responsibilities:

When a child dies that child is still the parents' child—not a specimen, not a case, not an unfortunate casualty of a failed procedure, but someone's baby, someone's child.[64]

[59] Mason and Laurie, n 56 above, 714. They argue for a combined consent/property model in which relatives are given 'interim—and delegable—property rights over the cadaver pending disposal of the body through the executor' (729). L Skene, 'Proprietary rights in human bodies, body parts and tissue: regulatory contexts and proposals for new laws' (2002) 22 LS 102 argues that inconsistencies within the law are the result of the different contexts in which the issue has arisen for determination and suggests personal rights to consent to removal, retention and use with proprietary rights of possession, control, use and commercial exploitation to institutions who lawfully acquire bodies, body parts and tissue.

[60] C Farsides, 'Body Ownership' in S McVeigh and S Wheeler (eds), *Law, Health and Medical Regulation* (Aldershot: Dartmouth, 1992) drawing on Locke's theory of property as part of the 'common stock' until value is given to it by mixing labour with it.

[61] J Montgomery, 'Children as Property?' (1988) 51 MLR 323–342.

[62] Written statement from Lorraine Pentecost, mother of Luke, *www.bristol-inquiry.org.uk*.

[63] Written statement from Paul Bradley, father of Bethan, *www.bristol-inquiry.org.uk*.

[64] CMO Summit, *Proceedings*, n 11 above, Bristol Heart Children's Action Group, 6.

If the concept of consent is problematic and property inappropriate, we should look to responsibility grounded in relationships to underpin the law.

The Concept of Harm

As Robin West has argued, legal constructions of harm have not been subjected to theoretical scrutiny. She points out that analysis of ways in which to respond to harm have proceeded with inadequate conceptualisation of the harm in question.[65] Where, as within tort law, the concept of harm is premised upon the harms caused to the abstract individual who values freedom and fears annihilation, physical safety and property have been protected whilst emotional and relational harms have not.[66] Harms arising from attachment, connections, valued intimacy, responsibility and care go unrecognised.[67] As Robin West has argued, the consequence of the failure of the law to recognise harm is that the law effects a second harm.[68] Where, as in this example, the harm is the failure to respect the close, intimate relationship between parent and child, the dignity of the child and the responsibility of the parent caring for the child, the law's response that no harm has been done is a further, compounding, failure to recognise relationships, dignity and responsibility.

Joanne Conaghan has demonstrated the *unrealised potential* of the law of tort in responding to the specific individual and social but gendered harm of sexual harassment[69] and the limitations of tort in recognising and providing a mechanism for redress of physical, sexual and psychological abuse, frequently of women and children, within the family.[70] In this work, the ability of tort to respond to gendered harm is assessed, that is, physical experiences of harm confined to women—for example, pregnancy—or harms to which women are more at risk—rape, or sexual harassment—occurring to individuals as part of the class of women within the context of power differentials. Robin West undertook to expose and analyse the ways in which women are harmed which differ from the ways in which the ideal upon which the law is based may be harmed, identifying the gendered harms of invasion, separation, private altruism and patriarchy.[71] The harm caused by the removal and retention

---

[65] R West, *Caring for Justice* (New York and London: New York University Press, 1997), 95.   [66] Chamallas and Kerber, n 21 above, 814.

[67] R West, 'Jurisprudence and Gender' (1988) 55 University of Chicago Law Review 1–72, 20–21.   [68] West, n 65 above, 96.

[69] Conaghan, n 43 above.   [70] Conaghan, n 44 above.

[71] West, n 65 above, ch. 2, 'The Concept of Harm'.

of children's organs without the knowledge or consent of their parents could be considered as an example of the law's role in producing gender norms—mothers who suffer psychiatric harm as a consequence of the treatment of their children based upon assumptions about the emotional fragility of women, particularly mothers. More fundamental is the failure to understand the harm arising from attachment, responsibility and care. In this context, Margaret Brazier has argued, drawing upon her experiences of talking to relatives in her role as Chair of the Retained Organs Commission, that the knowledge of the consequences of organ retention upon families (the hurt) raises questions about the harm which is recognised by law[72] stressing the importance of recognising the value attached to our loved ones, to the bodies of loved ones.

Exposing the ways in which the legal construction of harm fails to recognise relational harms raises, for feminists, the practical question of whether to eschew the law, because of a failure to understand the ways in which we are harmed, or to engage with it because of the potential it holds for responding to and remedying relational harms, admitting alternative understandings and as a tool for bringing about legal change. As US feminist academic Leslie Bender has argued, where people are treated in a way which harms them and this is not otherwise recognised, the law remains as an important forum in which to articulate what went wrong, to expose how they were treated.[73] This is the position identifiable in statements explaining why resort was made to litigation in the nationwide group:

'It is important to remember that these families have been through a deeply traumatic experience. They have received no formal apology and many felt that they had been left with no option than to pursue legal action.'[74]

'If families want to get involved in litigation [over organ retention] they will. There is still a lot of anger out there and the feeling is that the Government doesn't want to listen to the voices of the people most affected by these scandals.'[75]

Harms as they are experienced have to be explained in the legal forum if they are ever to become recognised within the legal construction of harm.[76]

---

[72] Contrasting their distress to the pinprick which as physical harm would attract remedy, M. Brazier, 'Retained organs: ethics and humanity' (2002) 22 LS 550–569, 567.

[73] Bender, n 47 above, 862.

[74] David Harris, senior partner, Alexander Harris, 'National Organ Retention case begins at High Court,' 26 January 2004, *www.alexanderharris.co.uk.*

[75] Steve Parker, Chairman, Bristol Heart Children's Action Group quoted in M Ribbeck, 'Organ families fight for millions', *Western Daily Press*, 11 April 2001.

[76] Conaghan, n 42 above, 431.

Remedies and Responsibility

As well as articulating what harms us, attention needs to be given to the remedy available when harm is recognised. Leslie Bender has explored how tort law has been developed to provide a remedy, principally through financial compensation and without reference to other things we value—attachments, relational responsibilities, children—adopting a concept of responsibility discharged in the currency of money. In a thought-provoking essay, Leslie Bender argues that we need to get imaginative about remedies. Using her example of mass torts caused by the negligence of corporations, she suggests that corporations, through the individuals of which they are comprised, need to take responsibility for those who suffer personal injuries through their carelessness by, for example, using laboratories for the development of remedies or undertaking the planning of care which usually falls upon family members. We know that legal proceedings in tort are brought for reasons other than securing financial compensation. Litigants may be seeking accountability, an explanation, acknowledgement or understanding of the harm done, an apology or to prevent harm being caused in the same way to another. For many parents the simple reality will be that money cannot begin to compensate for the violation of the personhood of their child and their responsibility of care. However, it is also the case that '[t]ort judgments are money judgments because we have not developed any other "coin" of worth or value in our society. This limited measure of value is a sad statement about all of us, not about the tort system.'[77] As Leslie Bender points out, if money is the only measure of value, claims have to be made for monetary compensation.

Whilst harm caused may result in needs which have to be met through financial support or services which have to be paid for—although the vagaries of tort law in doing so are well known—in some cases, other remedies may be sought as a more appropriate response to the harm caused. Responsibility here is contextual, focusing upon the needs of those harmed. Where, as in the example under consideration, the harm is irreparable violation of the personhood of a child and parental responsibility of care, the remedies sought might more appropriately be protection of cherished memories, taking responsibility for wrong-doing, acknowledgement of harm caused and enabling learning to prevent the same from happening to someone else? These are remedies which might better be achieved through mechanisms other than the common law of tort.

[77] Bender, n 47 above, 874.

Systems Analysis and How Systems Failed

The delivery of healthcare involves the provision of care by a team of professionals and failures in care can more readily be attributed to multiple causes than blamed upon the departure from common practice of one individual at one particular moment in time. Systems analysis rightly extends consideration beyond the limited purview of common law negligence; whilst an action in common law negligence is founded upon the search for an individual whose carelessness can be blamed for the harm and from whom a remedy in the form of financial compensation can be obtained, a systems analysis approach extends a wider reach placing the actions of individuals within the context of the systems in which they operate. Without denying that circumstances might require an individual to be held to account for their actions, the focus of systems analysis is broadened beyond the individual with the aim of understanding the range of factors contributing to a failure in order to learn the lessons, prevent a recurrence and improve the quality of care.

A systems analysis approach seeks to overcome the ideological premise of tort law that harm occurs in a 'random collision' caused by an incompetent individual by identifying the multitude of factors which brought it about. Whereas an action in tort involves a search for an individual at fault, thus focusing upon the actions of the individual at the final moment—the one at the sharp end, front line or holding the smoking gun—a systems analysis approach recognises that this is rarely the whole picture. Rather, that 'accidents in complex systems occur primarily through the concatenation of multiple small factors or failures, each necessary but only jointly sufficient to produce the accident.'[78] This involves a distinction between active failures—the unsafe acts of humans whether slip, lapse, mistake or violation—and latent conditions.[79] Systems analysis involves investigation beyond the active failure of the individual to assess the contribution of latent conditions including the way in which the service is resourced, organised, managed and led; the design and material conditions of buildings and equipment; the training, workload, support, morale and stress upon personnel; procedures; professionals working as a team and communicating with each other; and the culture of a service.[80]

An action in tort is a process of naming, blaming and shaming. The need to identify an individual responsible has the effect of making that

---

[78] L Leape *et al*, n 1 above, quoted in the Kennedy Report, n 2 above, para. 26.5.
[79] DoH, n 3 above, para. 3.9.   [80] Ibid.

individual the locus of blame. An appreciation of the wider context of contributory factors shifts the focus from blaming to understanding what went wrong. The Kennedy Report went as far as to argue that the current tort-based adversarial system of negligence liability supports a culture of blame and fear, encourages a code of silence and cover-up, whilst failing to hold the NHS to account or through deterrence prevent what happened from happening to someone else.[81] The recent book by Alan Merry and Alexander McCall Smith, *Errors, Medicine and the Law*,[82] presents a critique of tort as it operates in relation to errors within medicine. Informed by the psychology of errors, they seek to distinguish between institutional failures, unavoidable human error and blame-worthy conduct; between violations (involving choice and culpability) and errors (skill-, knowledge-, and rule-based). Their central point is that the focus of tort is upon identifying an individual to blame for harm and conclude that 'negligence, as it currently operates in tort law, does not always follow the contours of blame'[83] in failing to distinguish between being the cause of harm despite being morally blameless, unintentionally departing from expected standards, neglecting to attain expected standards, and recklessly and intentionally causing harm.

And third, a successful action in tort results in a sanction and remedy in the form of financial compensation. In contrast, a systems analysis approach seeks to learn the lessons of what happened so it can be explained and prevented from happening again. Understanding that harm or distress may have been caused even in the absence of negligence on the part of any individual, a systems analysis approach seeks to respond to the lessons learnt with changes to design, organisation and practice and thereby improve the quality of care.

Systems analysis has been employed to understand what went wrong in disasters such as the sinking of the *Herald of Free Enterprise*, the King's Cross Underground fire, the Hillsborough Stadium disaster, the Clapham Junction rail crash and the Piper Alpha oil rig fire.[84] It also framed the analysis of the Bristol Royal Infirmary Inquiry into the quality of care of the paediatric cardiac services in Bristol between 1984 and 1995

---

[81] Kennedy Report, n 2 above, paras. 24.24–24.31.　　　[82] n 1 above.
[83] Ibid, 151.
[84] J Reason, 'The human factor in medical accidents' in C Vincent, M Ennis and RJ Audley (eds), *Medical Accidents* (Oxford University Press, 1993) 3 referring to Mr Justice Sheen, *MV Herald of Free Enterprise, Report of Court No 8074 Formal Investigation* (London: Dept of Transport); D Fennell, *Investigation into the King's Cross underground fire* (London: Dept of Transport, HMSO, 1988); A Hidden, *Investigation into the Clapham Junction railway accident* (London: Dept of Transport, HMSO, 1989); Cullen, The Hon Lord, *The public inquiry into the Piper Alpha disaster* (London: Dept of Energy, HMSO, 1990).

which concluded that care provided was inadequate due to the organisation of care—a split site, poor management, heavy workload, a service provided without dedicated paediatric cardiac surgeons—and the prevailing culture—lack of leadership and teamwork, hierarchical divisions, a failure to reflect critically upon care. Crucially, the Inquiry concluded that the standard of care was not determined solely by the competence of the surgeons performing cardiac surgery:

[T]his is not an account of bad people, nor of people who did not care. It is certainly not an account of people who wilfully harmed patients. Rather, it is an account of how people who were well motivated, failed to work together effectively for the interests of their patients, through lack of insight, poor leadership, and lack of teamwork. It is an account of a hospital where there was an imbalance of power, with too much control in the hands of a few individuals. It is an account of a service offering PCS which was split between two sites, had no dedicated PCS nurses, had no dedicated paediatric intensive care beds at the BRI, and had no full-time paediatric cardiac surgeons. And it is an account of a system of hospital care which was poorly organised and beset with uncertainty from top to bottom as to how to get things done, such that when concerns were raised, it took years for them to be taken seriously.[85]

Systems analysis is not relevant only to mass disasters but provides a method of analysing all instances of failure in care including those occurring without negligence. Consider, for example, the understanding to be gained through looking beyond the actions of senior registrar, Mr Jordan, in the delivery of Stuart Whitehouse[86] or the systemic factors operating in *Bolitho v City and Hackney Health Authority*.[87] For the NHS as a whole, the National Patient Safety Agency (NPSA) has been established to learn the lessons of adverse events[88] and near misses.[89] The agency receives reports from healthcare staff and information from the complaints system and the National Health Service Litigation Authority (NHSLA) which is then analysed, action necessary to reduce risk is identified and this information fed back into the NHS. This system for analysis of

[85] Kennedy Report, n 2 above, para. 13.8. The events at Bristol are considered by O Quick, 'Disaster at Bristol: Explanations and implications of a tragedy', (1999) 21 *Journal of Social Welfare and Family Law* 307–326 and the conclusions and recommendations of the Kennedy Inquiry in J Bridgeman, ' "Learning from Bristol": Healthcare in the 21st century' (2002) 65 MLR 241–255.

[86] *Whitehouse v Jordan* [1981] 1 WLR 246.   [87] *Bolitho*, n 31 above.

[88] Defined as 'an event or omission arising during clinical care and causing physical or psychological injury to a patient': DoH, n 3 above, 81.

[89] Defined as 'a situation in which an event or omission, or a sequence of events or omissions arising during clinical care fails to develop further, whether or not as the result of compensating action, thus preventing injury to a patient': ibid.

adverse events must be coupled with a system for meeting the practical, everyday needs of those who are harmed by a systems failure. Currently, the NPSA co-exists with the common law of negligence although the Chief Medical Officer's Report, *Making Amends* recommended consigning tort law to the margins[90] with the establishment of an NHS Redress Scheme to respond to the individual harmed by coordinating an investigation, providing an explanation, developing and securing delivery of a care package and providing financial compensation where appropriate[91] following a complaint or a claim made to the NHSLA.

Understanding What Went Wrong

It was emphasised in the Bristol Royal Infirmary Interim Report that it was important not to mistake 'the language of shame and blame for the language of accountability. Of course, blame has a proper role where there is personal misconduct. But where, as here, it was a system which was responsible, and a system which needs to be changed, blaming any individual is not only unfair and unhelpful; it is positively counter-productive.'[92] The widespread removal and retention of organs from children without the knowledge and consent of their parents, considered in both the Bristol Inquiry Interim Report and the Royal Liverpool Children's Inquiry, can better be understood if the latent conditions are acknowledged. Here the conditions in which this widespread failure occurred were the lack of clarity as to the law, absence of professional training, lack of communication between professionals and the professional culture. As acknowledged in the Bristol Interim Report the law was 'complex and obscure'.[93] This gave professionals scope to interpret the law from their perspective—to serve the interests of the professional group through the retention of material for education, training and research. Referring to 'tissue' (terminology used in the legislation, familiar to medical science and repeated on consent forms) disguised the reality of whole organ

---

[90] Without removing the right to pursue litigation under existing principles, CMO, *Making Amends: A consultation paper setting out proposals for reforming the approach to clinical negligence in the NHS* (London: Dept of Health, 2003), Recommendation 5, 123.

[91] Ibid, Recommendation 1, 119 gives as criteria for payment that there were 'serious shortcomings in the standard of care', harm could not be avoided and was not due to natural progression of illness. In other words, anyone can secure an apology and explanation but only those 'harmed as a result of seriously substandard NHS hospital care' (115) would be eligible for financial compensation.

[92] Bristol Royal Infirmary, n 6 above, para. 57.   [93] Ibid, para. 59.

retention. Consent was usually sought by junior doctors who had no training—in the law,[94] in breaking bad news or in raising such a sensitive issue with parents who were, inevitably, distressed. A sense of failure made it difficult for professionals to cope with parents when their child had died so the information was withheld in a paternalistic gesture—that it was better to spare parents the details at a time of emotional upset but assuming that they would want professionals to learn from their loss and perhaps help another child in the future:

> The reasons offered are well-meaning: a desire to protect parents from the realities of post-mortem examination; a desire not to intrude further on the parents' grief. But these reasons are also, to a degree, self-serving to the profession. Pathologists and clinicians regarded post-mortems and all that followed to be an important activity, particularly in a teaching hospital. Therefore, the presumption was that they should be carried out and human material retained. Parents need not be involved. They might, after all, say no if they were told 'too much'. And, in any event, they would be pleased to know that research and education were being enhanced, if they ever found out. Their consent should be sought, because this was believed to be a legal requirement, but it need only be consent in form rather than in substance.[95]

Whilst the practice of removal and retention of organs for diagnostic purposes and subsequent storage was widespread, the concerns about the quality of care given to seriously ill children prior to their death provided a specific context to the revelations about organ retention at Bristol.[96] In Liverpool, the enquiries of parents for information following the revelation of an extensive collection were mishandled through poor crisis management. The task was a difficult one hindered by poor records but parents were provided with inaccurate information delivered piecemeal rendering necessary numerous funerals without any advice, counselling or support.[97] The Inquiry revealed the appointment of Professor van Velzen to a Chair in Fetal and Infant Pathology which was inadequately

---

[94] The Redfern Report noted that many professionals giving evidence informed the Inquiry that they had not read the Human Tissue Act 1961 prior to preparing to give evidence: n 7 above, para. 11.7.2.   [95] Bristol Royal Infirmary, n 6 above, para. 103.

[96] As expressed in the contribution of the Bristol Heart Children's Action Group to the Chief Medical Officer's Summit: 'To lose an elderly relative is a traumatic but sadly expected part of the life. To lose a child seems unnatural and is the most devastating of events to befit any parent. When that child should not have died, however, but did so as a result of poor medical practice it is unbearable. To take it further, imagine then finding out that you have not buried your child whole and that the hospital responsible for your child's death is also responsible for the removal and retention of their organs without your knowledge, your consent.' CMO Summit, n 11 above.

[97] Redfern Inquiry, n 7 above, Epilogue, para. 3.

resourced. The Report outlines his appalling conduct including the falsification of records, research applications and post-mortem reports; his failure to carry out his clinical duties and to complete histological analysis; disregarding conditions placed by parents upon post-mortem examination; failing to keep proper records of retained organs; and falsely representing deaths as Sudden Infant Death Syndrome when histological examination necessary for such a diagnosis had not been carried out thus rendering research invalid:[98] the horrific malevolent actions of a culpable individual clearly appropriate for censure. However, the Report stresses, management let him behave in this way. His department was inadequately resourced, he was not supervised, there was no audit and a failure to respond to complaints.[99] Furthermore, the systematic retention of organs by Professor van Velzen between 1988 and 1995 resulted in retention to a different degree, it was not viewed by the medical profession as a practice of a different order.[100] The question was posed in the Redfern Report:

While Alder Hey as a whole did not know the precise extent of the organs retained at Myrtle Street, it did know as a collective group that a substantial number of organs must be there, collected over a substantial number of years in a substantial number of cases. Why was there no outcry?[101]

The answer:

The simple fact is that the retention of organs was commonplace over the country. Doctors had been brought up to expect it. The doctors at Alder Hey no more considered the validity of the collection at Myrtle Street than they did of the Heart Collection in the ICH. . . . [T]he medical profession has exhibited a general ignorance of what the law requires and maintains a paternalistic attitude to the likely concerns of relatives. The attitude was that there were organs in every hospital. If Professor van Velzen had accumulated more than others it was not to them something to worry about unduly.[102]

Thus we can see the level of understanding achievable through looking beyond the actions of the individual to the context of the wider factors which contributed to an event, providing the perspective of the individual within the system. However, it is important to note that the Bristol

[98] Redfern Inquiry, Summary, para. 38.   [99] Ibid, Epilogue, para. 5.

[100] Ibid, paras. 1.1.3–1.1.4. Upon taking up his post Professor van Velzen instructed that the should be no disposal of human material, para. 8.2.10.1.

[101] Ibid, para. 8.8.17.4.

[102] Ibid, para. 8.8.17.5. A similar attitude prevailed in the information provided to parents by Alder Hey in response to enquiries about retention. Whilst the provision of correct information was hampered by poor records, parents experienced being 'drip-fed' information, in some cases discovering that more organs had been retained *after* a second burial.

Royal Infirmary Inquiry and the Redfern Report take systems analysis further than usual in academic writing or in practice through the NPSA. Systems analysis, developed out of responses of the aviation, nuclear power and transport industries has focused upon healthcare as a high-risk complex system and the need to learn the lessons from medical accidents,[103] errors[104] and mishaps.[105] However, there is another aspect to the provision of healthcare which is not currently addressed by systems analysis in academic writing or through the NPSA, focusing as both do upon technical failures resulting in physical or psychiatric harm to the patient. The National Patient Safety Agency, established in July 2001 as an organisation through which lessons can be learnt, is a welcome development but confined to learning the lessons of patient safety incidents and near misses from the perspective of the professional within the system. In contrast, the Inquiries took the process of understanding further by listening to the experiences of those harmed and seeking to gain a better understanding of how, from their perspective, the system failed. That is, that this complex organisation in which high-risk treatment may be provided, is dealing with sick children and their parents working in partnership with professionals to care for the child. Failures in the quality of care may cause harm beyond physical or psychiatric harm to the patient. The fuller picture secured through a systems analysis may position us to learn the lessons of what went wrong as understood from one perspective—that of the professional within the system—but, if we have moved away from blame and individual responsibility to learning and collective responsibility, do we not need to know what matters to those who were harmed by the failure in care? To respond to the accounts given by those affected by failures in care, not accounts retold according to the perspective of the individual professional or the professional within the system?

Parental Perspectives on How the System Failed

Whilst it is important to acknowledge that there is a plurality of feminist perspectives through which to undertake a critique of the law and not a single grand theory, feminist legal theory has exposed the way in which the law is based upon universal principles derived in the abstract about the

---

[103] Vincent, Ennis and Audley, n 84 above.
[104] Merry and McCall Smith, n 1 above.
[105] M M Rosenthal, L Mulcahy and S Lloyd-Bostock (eds), *Medical Mishaps: Pieces of the Puzzle* (Buckingham: Open University Press, 1999).

nature of the legal subject (autonomous, self-interested, boundaried), what it is that harms that subject (primarily physical harm to the person or their property) and how to remedy that harm (financial compensation). Choosing from amongst the rich variety of feminist critiques of the law, the legal regulation of healthcare is an obvious candidate for the application of feminist theories of care. Feminist theories of care direct us to consider the particular context, provide an understanding of the subject as situated in relationships and concerned to meet the needs of the other through attentiveness to them as a unique individual. A caring perspective is not limited to the question whether to care—whether we have obligations which must be fulfilled—but requires consideration of the question how to best meet caring responsibilities;[106] and for the law, raises the question of the role of the law in creating, fostering and supporting caring relationships.

Learning the Lessons

If lessons are really to be learnt from failings in care we need also to seek to understand the reality of those failures from the perspective of those affected. The scale of the retention of organs without parental knowledge or consent means that thousands of families were involved. The approach of the Inquiries which put parental experiences at the centre of their analysis and the support groups which acted as a forum for articulating the views of parents means that we have access to many accounts from parents—as to how, from their perspective, they were failed by the individual professionals and the healthcare system. The circumstances which led to the deaths of the children were varied: whilst the focus of the Bristol Inquiry was upon children who had died prior to, during, or following heart surgery, organs were retained nationwide from children who were stillborn, and after surgery, accident or illness. Clearly, there is a wide range of circumstances and individual responses but common themes do emerge from their accounts, told and extensively reflected in the Bristol and Alder Hey Inquiry Reports and, to an extent, Manchester and Birmingham investigations.

Numerous parents expressed their distress that their child had not been respected as a person; their feelings of being betrayed by the professionals to whom they entrusted care of their child; and, consequently, their guilt at feeling they had failed in their parental responsibility for their child.[107]

---

[106] G Clements, *Care, Autonomy and Justice: Feminism and the Ethic of Care* (Boulder Colorado and Oxford: Westview Press, 1996).

[107] M Maclean, 'Letting Go . . . Parents, Professionals and the Law in the Retention of Human Material after Post Mortem', in A Bainham, S Day Sclater and M Richards (eds), *Body Lore and Laws* (Oxford & Portland, Oregon: Hart Publishing, 2002) 80–81.

Parents expressed their anger and upset at the way in which their children were not treated with dignity and respect but were 'butchered',[108] 'abused'[109] or 'mutilated'.[110] The removal and retention of organs from the bodies of their children demonstrated a failure to respect the child as a person, an individual: a focus in medical treatment upon the disease or illness carried through into the post-mortem practice of removing the affected organ and, in some cases, other organs, as specimens. Parents spoke of a 'primal need to protect'[111] and their guilt arising from a feeling that they had let their child down.[112] Their ability to take responsibility and to act in the best interests of their child, as they had during their child's treatment, had been taken away from them by the failure to provide proper information about what was involved in a post-mortem. This was experienced as a failure to recognise the continuing attachment to their child and as disrespectful of their continuing sense of responsibility for them. They felt deceived: deceived because they were not told about the necessity for removal and sometimes retention but also by use of deceptive terminology: that 'tissue' included whole organs, complete systems. And not by the stranger of the paradigm tort case—they were deceived,[113] betrayed[114] and let down[115] by the professionals to whom they had entrusted their child but who failed to treat their child with dignity or respect. These parents provide a clear account of relational harm—harm to them as parents as a consequence of the way another, their child, was treated. Harm experienced as a consequence of a failure to treat with dignity and respect an individual to whom they were intimately attached, harm done to them through a failure to respect a valued relationship and harm done by another to whom they had entrusted the child they cared for.

Commonly parents expressed all three perspectives:

'[A]s a parent... she would have done anything and everything in her power to protect her child. That was what she was there to do even more so in death because it was the only thing she could do for her child at that stage. She had put her trust in the doctors, the midwives, the pathologists that they would respect her child and that they would deal with her in the way one would wish to deal with a dead person. They did not, they desecrated her. She feels let down. There

---

[108] The Redfern Report, in chapter 14 which outlines the parents' evidence, adopts the practice of giving the name, age and year of death of the child. This practice was adopted as a mark of respect and of the valuable contribution of the families to the Inquiry, whilst respecting their privacy: n 7 above, Laura, 410; Kirsten, 414.

[109] Ibid, Nicola, 427; Charlie, 437.   [110] Ibid, Stephen, 436.

[111] Ibid, Sean, 392.   [112] Ibid, Lindsay, 415; Sam, 425.

[113] Ibid, Claire, 424.   [114] Ibid, Kirsten, 414.   [115] Ibid, Nicola, 427.

was only one thing she could do and that was to protect her in death and she did not do it and she has to live with that.'[116]

'She feels her daughter has not been treated with the respect she deserved in death. She feels guilty that having loved her daughter so dearly in life she let her down when she needed her most, namely in allowing her organs to be retained without consent. Overall she feels let down, disgusted, angry, upset and betrayed.'[117]

'They now feel that they signed the consent because they were under pressure and lied to. Their child lost his dignity and was treated like a piece of meat in a butcher's shop. They feel let down. They feel that their child's dignity was taken away when his organs were retained . . . They feel guilty that they did not protect their child in death.'[118]

It is important to appreciate the context of parental experiences of the removal and retention of organs from their children following post-mortem. All children are dependent, reliant upon the care of their parents to which parents respond by taking responsibility for meeting their specific needs as individuals. Children who are injured, disabled or ill have 'magnified' needs and greater dependence upon their parents.[119] During times of illness, hospitalisation, injury, parental focus is upon their child as a unique individual to whom they are intimately connected and emotionally attached. Parents caring for a sick child respond to them as experts in their care developed through attentiveness to their child. Their role in caring for their child involves taking responsibility for decisions about medical treatment focused upon the specific needs of their child. Parents are, however, dependent upon the professionals who have the technical expertise to attend to the child's needs whether in treatment or (after death) the investigations necessary to gain an understanding of the reasons for their death: a dependency which inevitably involves vulnerability. Parents giving evidence to the Alder Hey Inquiry contrasted their role during their child's treatment—informed, involved and responsible for their child—with their exclusion once their child had died.[120] Parents at Bristol identified the way their child and themselves

---

[116] *Body Lore and Laws*, Alexandra, 408.   [117] Ibid, Lindsay, 415.

[118] Ibid, Jordan, 416.

[119] E K Feder, 'Doctor's Orders: Parents and Intersexed Children', in E F Kittay and E K Feder (eds), *The Subject of Care*, n 51 above, 297.

[120] Redfern Inquiry, n 7 above: Kathryn, 397; Nicola, 427; Jake, 403; Sam, 424; Philip, 426: 'Nobody told them that a post mortem examination was to be carried out. They should have been told what, if any, organs would be retained. They should have been informed of the result of the post mortem examination. They were fully informed of the details of all the operations their son had to go through. They consented to these operations. They should have had extended to them the same fullness of information at death as in life.'

as parents were treated after their child's death as consistent with the inadequate care provided during treatment.[121] Crucially, their accounts of how they were failed are expressive of attachments, responsibilities and dependencies in the provision of care continuing after the death of their child.

So what do we learn? The focus of tort is upon whether the law imposed an obligation upon the clinician to inform about the removal and retention of organs. Where a breach of legally imposed duties occurs through an unreasonable common practice causing reasonably foreseeable psychiatric harm, a remedy is available in the form of financial compensation. To embark upon a systems analysis approach is to place the actions of individual clinicians within the context of a focus upon a need for human material, lack of training in the law and in dealing with distressed parents over such a sensitive issue and a sense that parents would rather not know. A systems analysis approach seeks to understand from the perspective of professionals within organisations. The parents' perspective identifies the harm caused by a failure to respect their continued attachment to their child as an individual, continued sense of responsibility for their child and abuse of trust by professionals they depended upon. Neither tort law nor systems analysis as applied to healthcare are interested in the perspective of those harmed. Neither tort law nor systems analysis can provide an explanation, apology, or achieve the understanding necessary to prevent a recurrence unless consideration extends beyond the individual or the explanation within the system to the experiences of those involved. This, I think, needs to be understood if the harm caused is to be recognised and the lessons learnt.

Learning the Lessons of Caring Relationships

In relation to the specific issue of organ retention from children, the Human Tissue Act 2004 places consent[122] at the centre of removal, storage and use of human material balancing the 'rights and expectations of individuals and families' and the value of material for research, education,

---

[121] Written statements submitted by parents whose children underwent cardiac surgery in Bristol between 1984 and 1995 to the Bristol Royal Infirmary Inquiry, available from the Inquiry website, *www.bristol-inquiry.org.uk*: Jayne Cole, mother of Tanya; Sandra Curnow, mother of Laura and Rebecca; Rowena Cutter, mother of Scott; Aubrey Lewis, father of Kirsty; Timothy Powell, father of Jay.

[122] From a competent child or, if the child is not competent or does not wish to decide, from someone with parental responsibility or, if there is no-one with parental responsibility, one in a qualifying relationship, s 2(7). Qualifying relationship is defined in s 54(9).

training.[123] The 'consent' provisions within the Act do not apply to anything done under the authority of the coroner although it is now clear that material may not be retained without consent beyond that required for the purposes of the coroner's investigation.[124] The Human Tissue Act 2004, giving relatives the 'entitlement to say no',[125] could be seen as a considered response, learning the lessons of the 'organs scandal' and ensuring that it does not happen again. It is important, if the quality of care is to be improved, that the insights gained from the parental perspective inform the process of getting consent central to the Human Tissue Act 2004. Furthermore, their relevance is not confined to the issue of how post-mortems, the need to retain organs for diagnosis and the value of retaining organs for training, education and research should be approached in the future. I cannot imagine anything like the organ retention scandal coming to light—the scale of inadvertent disrespect makes it unthinkable. I can imagine children treated inadequately as a consequence of a failure to respect them as a person and without due recognition of the responsibility taken by parents in caring for their child with expertise gained through attentiveness to their needs, and resultant distress, anger, guilt and upset to parents let down by professionals they trusted as partners in care.

I started with when systems failed, I have covered parents and their relationship of responsibility for their child. I end with the quality of healthcare. Courts have tended to treat children as non-persons and parents as self-interested individuals, whose assessment of the best interests of the child is determined by their own interests, preferring medical judgment and thereby undermining equality in the partnership between parent and professional in caring for the child.[126] The parents' evidence challenges these assumptions, highlighting the importance of valuing the child as an individual, their role of caring responsibility and the trust placed in the professionals providing expert care throughout treatment as well as in the care provided after death. The parents' evidence suggests that consideration of attachments, responsibilities and dependencies

---

It will be an offence to carry out activities listed in s1 without consent (s 5) and unlawful to use donated material for purposes other than those listed in Sch 1, for medical treatment and diagnosis, decent disposal or for purposes specified in regulations made by the Secretary of State, s 8(4). The Human Tissue Authority will monitor compliance with the law, issue licences and issue a code of practice.

[123] House of Commons, Human Tissue Bill, Explanatory notes, para. 4.

[124] M Brazier, 'Human Tissue Retention' (2004) 39 *Medico-Legal Journal* 72, with changes to the coroner's rules expected.   [125] Brazier, n 72 above, 556.

[126] J Bridgeman, 'The Child's Body' in M Evans and E Lee (eds), *Real Bodies: A Sociological Introduction* (Basingstoke and New York: Palgrave, 2002), 96–114.

would have resulted in high quality rather than inadequate care of children undergoing cardiac surgery at the Bristol Royal Infirmary. It is my view that recognition of attachments, responsibilities and dependencies within the provision of care and the law which regulates it could have prevented the 'less favoured' treatment of children with Down's Syndrome whose parents were denied details of all the treatment options for their heart conditions at the Royal Brompton.[127] Would it have made any difference to the care provided to and the response of the court in relation to the treatment of *T*,[128] *C (HIV)*,[129] *David Glass*,[130] or *Charlotte Wyatt?*[131] Or to the response of the doctors providing care to mother and child in *North Glamorgan NHS Trust v Walters?*[132] Whether in decision-making or in the provision of care, should we not consider the parents' perspective of the particular value they place on their child as a unique individual, for whom they are responsible but whom they have to entrust to the care of others?

[127] Z Kmietowicz, 'Down's children received "less favourable" hospital treatment' (2001) 322 *British Medical Journal* 815; considering Department of Health, *The Report of the Independent Inquiries into Paediatric Cardiac Services at the Royal Brompton Hospital and Harefield Hospital* (London: Royal Brompton Hospital, 2001) (Ruth Evans, Chair).

[128] *Re T (A Minor) (Wardship: Medical Treatment)* [1997] 1 All ER 906.

[129] *In re C (A Child) (H.I.V. Testing)* [2000] 2 WLR 270.

[130] *Glass v United Kingdom* [2004] 1 FLR 1019.

[131] *Portsmouth NHS Trust v Wyatt & Others* [2004] EWHC 2247; *Wyatt v Portsmouth NHS Trust and Charlotte Wyatt* [2005] EWHC 693.   [132] n 33 above.

Feminist Fever? Cultures of Adversarialism in the Aftermath of the Woolf Reforms

Linda Mulcahy

Introduction

This paper considers some of the implications of the most radical reforms of the civil justice system to have been introduced in the last hundred years. In particular it analyses what has happened to cultures of adversarialism in the aftermath of the Woolf reforms. The issue is pertinent, as we watch the changes introduced bed down and practitioners calm down in the wake of a raft of reforms designed in part to ensure that civil procedure becomes cheaper and faster. More important, for present purposes, are the implications of the requirement that the various parties involved in litigation alter their expectations as to how they should behave in their quest for settlement or adjudication. A number of key issues arise from the analysis. Why is it that adversarial and uncooperative tendencies remain such a dominant part of the professional identity of lawyers? Is it the case that we are merely witnessing a transitional phase from a litigation system underpinned by the adversarial ideal to one based on more cooperation? Alternatively, could it be that there is something deep-rooted about adversarial tendencies that will serve to undermine the ethos promoted by the Woolf reforms? The issues raised are of particular importance for feminist debate about how marginalized voices can be heard in the civil justice arena. Can the shift towards cultures of cooperation ever be fully achieved whilst masculine ideology and methodology dominate legal practice and education?

The pace of change has been considerable and has left some of us struggling to come to terms with the difficulties of distinguishing between pragmatic responses to the reforms and genuine shifts in adversarial culture. The Woolf reforms were introduced at breakneck speed leading experts in the field to comment that we achieved in the UK in five years what it took the US litigation system at least 20 years to do. Senior Master

Turner has made clear that not even the Woolf team expected the dramatic changes that occurred in the first year after the introduction of the new *Civil Procedure Rules* (CPR).[1] It is difficult to overestimate the importance of these procedural reforms which have prompted a shift from a combative court system to a hybrid one that requires an increased level of understanding between competing sides in litigation and a much more interventionist role for the judiciary.[2] In short then, we have experienced a 'velvet revolution' which has prompted a level of change which would have been considered unlikely ten years ago and unthinkable 20 years ago.

My central thesis is that the reforms have the potential to feminize the process of dispute resolution in the civil litigation system but that resistance to the reforms can also best be understood as a resistance to the feminist epistemologies which Lord Woolf has unwittingly given life to.[3] I present my arguments in three sections. In the first I consider the adversarial ideal which has underpinned our civil justice system in recent centuries and the ways in which it has privileged 'masculine' philosophies of dispute resolution. I then go on to reflect on how that ideal has been challenged by the introduction of reforms which place considerable emphasis on cooperative lawyering and the mediation of disputes, both of which can be understood as an expression of a feminist ethic of justice. In the final section I look at reactions to the reforms; what such reactions tell us about societal resistance to feminist ideals; and the implications of this for practitioners and legal educators.

The Concept of Adversarialism

Adversarialism has traditionally been perceived as the cornerstone of procedures which built on the early English system of law, with no parallel outside common law jurisdictions.[4] Despite this common assertion, legal

---

[1] R Turner, 'New rules for the millennium' (2000) 150 (6919) NLJ 49. The shift towards mediation has also been encouraged by subsequent government reports such as the Better Regulation Task Force's *Better Routes to Redress* (London: Better Regulation Task Force, 2004).

[2] I consciously use the words 'cooperation' and 'competing' in the same sentence because their coexistence reflects an innate tension in the hybrid system with which litigators are working.

[3] Lord Woolf was kind enough to introduce my *Current Legal Problems* lecture and to engage in the discussion of my ideas. I hope he thinks it is fair of me to observe that he was rather surprised at being labelled as feminist, an attribute which many of us still consider to be praiseworthy.

[4] See for instance M Damaska, *Evidence Law Adrift* (London: Yale University Press, 1997); Royal Commission on Legal Services, Cmnd 7648, Chaired by Sir Henry Benson

historians have suggested that it is actually a relatively youthful organizing concept for civil procedure. Evidentiary rules which reflected this approach only began to crystallize in the late-eighteenth and nineteenth centuries when the judiciary began to abdicate its inquisitorial discretion.[5] Landsman[6] has argued that, in the early eighteenth century, the court functioned as an inquiring body in which judicial questioning, direction and control were seen as fundamental attributes of the system whilst the role of opposing counsel was marginal. It is, in his view, only since the beginning of the nineteenth century that the courtroom contest became strikingly more adversarial and advocates and their cross-examination of witnesses were placed at centre stage. Miller has gone so far as to suggest that 'an historian at some future date may look back and declare that the so-called English adversarial system was—to whatever extent it existed—a mere blip in the 900 year history of the common law system'.[7]

The adoption of an adversarial model of litigation has a number of practical implications, many of which have been challenged by recent reforms. Most notably, it is clear that the parties and their advisers are able to retain control over the gathering of information, the sifting and selection of evidence and the forms of inquiry to be used when interrogating the other side's evidence. It follows that witnesses are perceived to 'belong' to those who select, call and pay them. This is evident in the way that witnesses who could be of use to one side but are in danger of giving evidence that would be of benefit to the other side are termed 'hostile'.[8] Indeed the Court of Appeal found in *Abbey National v Key Surveyors* that, on occasion, the experts could become more adversarial than the parties themselves.[9]

The fact that the parties to litigation are conceived of as opponents means that they have had very few duties of candour or collaboration imposed upon them. Whilst out-of-court settlement has long been a feature of the English civil process and the vast majority of mature cases are

(London: HMSO, 1979); and the judgments of Lord Roskill in *Bremer Vulkan* [1980] 1 All ER 439 and Lords Fraser and Scarman on appeal [1981] 1 All ER.

[5] Damaska, n 4 above; F Miller, 'The Adversarial Myth' (1995) 145 No. 6696 NLJ, 734 and *http://web.lexis-nexis.com/professional/document 1–6.*

[6] S Landsman, 'The decline of the adversary system: How the rhetoric of swift and certain justice has affected adjudication in American courts' Buffalo Law Review, 1980, Vol 29, pp. 487–530.

[7] Miller, n 5 above, 734. Whilst it is clear that all legal systems have adversaries not all have an adversarial orientation. The term 'adversary' has a much longer heritage than the term 'adversarial' which appeared in the OED in relation to judicial proceedings as recently as 1972.

[8] By way of contrast, in most continental systems prior contact with a witness by lawyers is frowned upon. Lawyers play a much more limited part in gathering evidence. Instead they largely limit themselves to conveying investigative leads to the official in charge of proof-taking and nominate witnesses: Damaska, n 4 above.

[9] *Abbey National Mortgages plc v Key Surveyors Nationwide Ltd* [1996] EGCS 23.

concluded in this way, the incentive to settle has come about as a result of civil procedure rules on costs and 'payment in' rather than a culture in which cooperation was considered to have an innate value. On the contrary, Lord Woolf characterized certain types of civil proceeding prior to the implementation of his reforms as 'battlegrounds in which no rules apply'.[10]

As the parties and their advisers have increased their level of control the formal role of the judge has diminished with the result that the judiciary is relatively passive in the adversarial model. It is dependent on the evidence and witnesses produced by each of the parties and technically judges must rely only on what they 'hear'. Whilst judges will occasionally make their own inquiries of a witness, their intervention is comparatively limited since they are in danger of putting their own neutrality at risk. This contrasts with the inquisitorial model in which trial is preceded by an investigatory stage led by the judge and state bureaucrats. Under this system the exercise of judicial function is not limited to deciding contested facts or dependent on proof put forward by the parties. Possibly the best example of this alternative genre is that of the hearings described by Damaska in his important comparative study of adjudication, in which the judges in some socialist states had the discretion to reject the arguments of both sides and even to refer a civil dispute to a criminal court if the parties could be shown to have their own selfish needs rather than the economic interests of the community and state at heart.[11]

The Rise of the Adversarial Ideal

So how is it that adversarialism came to have such a hold on English litigation? It is clear that advocate-led legal proceedings are a relatively recent development in the history of English procedure and that judges were afforded a much more interventionist role in earlier centuries. The pivotal role of counsel took much longer to develop in the criminal sphere than the civil sphere. Defence counsel were virtually unknown in the sixteenth century because of the fear that they would slow proceedings down. It was assumed that the parties knew their case better than anyone else and could rely on a paternalistic judiciary for legal advice. The practice of having barristers in court became more usual towards the end of the eighteenth century, but was still not common, and counsel in

---

[10] Lord Chancellor's Department (LCD), *Access to Justice* (London: HMSO, 1996).
[11] Damaska, n 4 above.

criminal cases were not formally allowed to sum up on behalf of the accused until 1836.[12]

Various explanations have been advanced for the development of the advocate-led adversarial system in common law countries. The first of these relates to the reluctance of the lay judiciary to get involved in the intricacies of the case being argued. There has been a long-standing and widespread use of lay adjudicators in English courts in the form of the jury and magistrates. Indeed, Anglo-American theories of court procedure have glorified novice amateurs as fact-finders. But in parallel with this rhetoric there has also been a concern that lay adjudicators have difficulties dealing with technical or complex issues. Over time judges sought refuge from getting too deeply involved in the finer details of fact by allowing the parties to make their own case. As a result it became the job of the parties to bring out the facts by way of spasmodic argument in the courtroom. As Damaska has argued: 'It is therefore no wonder that the oldest and most widely accepted justification for distinctive Anglo-American evidence rules is the need to compensate for the alleged intellectual and emotional frailties of amateurs cast in the role of occasional judges.'[13] This devolution of responsibility for the technical aspects of cases gradually evolved into a procedure dominated by advocates and their cross-examinations.[14]

A second explanation of the growth of the trend towards adversarial procedures in the eighteenth and nineteenth centuries is that the shift reflects loyalty to a particular vision of the relationship between the citizen and state. It is no coincidence that increasing reliance on adversarial methods occurred in the same era as increasing adherence to the principles of utilitarianism and the glorification of the autonomous individual.[15] It was in the classic period of *laissez-faire* ideology that the adversarial genre of proceeding obtained quasi-constitutional backing from the

---

[12] C Graham, *Ordering Law: The Architectural and Social History of the English Law Court to 1914* (Aldershot: Ashgate, 2003). Graham notes that the extent to which representation increased during the late-eighteenth and early-nineteenth centuries and the role it was allowed to perform remain inadequately charted.

[13] Damaska, n 4 above, 28.

[14] This, Miller argues, means that the judiciary could just as easily revert to becoming more interventionist and inquisitorial without fundamental reform. Indeed, he argues that where the judge has knowledge of an area they are more likely to perform that role anyway. This is evinced in the commercial court as the judges become more familiar with modern technology: Miller, n 5 above.

[15] The influence of this approach has been considerable and long-lasting. Robin West refers to this idea as the 'separation thesis' of liberal and critical legal theory which sees distinctly individuals first and then relationships and cooperation: 'Jurisprudence and Gender' (1988) 55 University of Chicago Law Review 1.

assumption that civil justice cases were best seen as a dispute between two competent and autonomous individuals, each of whom had their own selfish motivations for presenting the most persuasive case. According to this scheme, the role of the state was that of a mere umpire and its responsibility was limited to providing dispute resolution mechanisms in order to retain peace and harmony in society and to enforce the rights of individuals. Viewed in this way, we can see the growth of adversarialism as the classic liberal impulse to keep the state, in the guise of the judiciary, at arms' length from the parties.

The third explanation depends on a feminist analysis of legal procedure. This is a theory of adversarialism which is less often mooted in legal journals and deserving of more attention as a result. Put simply, feminists have seen the orientation towards adversarialism as a masculine one. Indeed, it has been persuasively argued that it is masculine moral philosophy which has shaped not just our litigation system but also a much broader trend towards suppression of the feminist voice within contemporary legal culture.[16] Nowhere is this more apparent than in the courtroom where the hostile egotism of possessive individualism has been clearly marked. Brown has, for instance, characterized adversarialism as requiring 'high octane'[17] masculine values such as performance, control, security of transaction and standardization for its survival. These values are in complete opposition to feminine approaches to dispute resolution.

In their critique of adversarialism as an essentially masculine construct, feminist scholars have noted the goal of 'zero-sum' proceedings which produce one successful and one unsuccessful litigant. They have also drawn attention to the ways in which the parties are forced to construct opposing arguments which detract from the positive aspects of their relationship with the other party and their ongoing connection in pre-existing networks. In this way English civil procedure has been seen to repress the emotive and relational subject. Moreover, through the use of an extremely narrow range of remedies, it has come to view the link between the parties as a mere expression of economic obligation divorced from intimacy.[18] In short, according to prevailing concepts of adversaliasm,

---

[16] There is an extensive feminist literature on this point and the particular problems posed by ideas of objectivity and neutrality. For an excellent overview of these issues see R Graycar and J Morgan, *The Hidden Gender of Law* (Annandale, Australia: Federation Press, 2002).

[17] B Brown, 'Contracting Out/Contracting In: Some Feminist Considerations', in A Bottomly (ed), *Feminist Perspectives on the Foundational Subjects of Law* (London: Cavendish Publishing, 1996) 12.

[18] On this point, J Wightman, 'Intimate relationships, relational contract theory and the reach of contract' (2000) Feminist Legal Studies Vol 8, 93–131.

putting arguments in opposing positions is the only way in which individuals come to recognize the needs of others.

By way of contrast, feminist legal theorists drawing on the notion of the ethics of care have distinguished feminine forms of moral reasoning from the masculine forms privileged in the adversarial system. Rather than separating the 'legal' from the 'political' or 'moral', authors writing in this vein have explored the inevitability and desirability of connections between these concepts. According to this line of argument the ways in which the assertion that they can be separated draws on a particular 'masculine' epistemology which makes false claims to objectivity and truth. Drawing on the work of Gilligan[19] and others, writers in this school have argued that whilst feminine subjects prefer to focus on context, relationships and discretion in resolving disputes, masculine subjects prefer to work with predetermined and logical rules which, although inflexible, produce certainty.[20] Researchers have suggested that female subjects typically see disputes in terms of a narrative of relationship which extends over time. Their worlds are worlds of connection in which people recognize responsibility for one another.[21] Most significant for present purposes is the way in which this approach has been positioned as being opposed to a masculine model of justice. In the words of Gilligan:

> Women's construction of the moral problems as a problem of care and responsibility in relationships rather than as one of rights and rules ties the development of their moral thinking to changes in their understanding of responsibility and relationships, just as the conception of morality as justice (the masculine way) ties the development to the logic of equality and reciprocity.[22]

The implications of such assertions are wide-ranging. Not only do they suggest that there is such a thing as a feminine process of dispute

---

[19] Most notably C Gilligan, *In a Different Voice: Psychological Theory and Women's Development* (Cambridge, MA Harvard University Press, 1982). Gilligan's work, although still controversial, continues to have resonance in the present context because she is one of the only writers in her field to have specifically applied the idea of the ethics of care to the resolution of disputes. In my view she is wrongly identified as an 'essentialist' because the aim of her studies has been to observe how feminine subjects and masculine subjects reason rather than why they reason in particular ways. For a critique of her work see C MacKinnon, *Feminism Unmodified: Discourses on Life and Law* (Cambridge, MA: Harvard University Press, 1987).

[20] Like feminists, and relational contract theorists, mediation gurus recognize the interconnectedness of disputants rather than giving prominence to their separate and individual status.

[21] See for instance J Larrabee (ed), *An Ethic of Care: Feminist and Interdisciplinary Perspectives* (New York: Routledge, 1993).

[22] Gilligan, n 19 above, 73. Gilligan's work is not without critics who have been concerned that her emphasis on womanly virtues is undesirable—as they have traditionally been used to keep women in the private sphere—or that her work encourages an overly romantic simplification of women's moral personalities. See Larrabee, n 21 above.

resolution but that substantive outcomes achieved as a result are also more likely to satisfy feminine conceptions of what is fair. It is contended that a feminized legal system would privilege connection rather than competing rights and would result in a form of dispute resolution which valued diversity and inter-subjectivity. Frug's seminal discussion of feminist readings of the doctrine of frustration provides examples of how the dualism of masculine legal reasoning can be subverted when scholars begin to pay attention to the plurality of outcomes that are possible when serving justice in a particular case.[23]

I share the view of a number of feminists that the equation of certain methods of moral reasoning with the feminine can have a detrimental effect on the position of women in society because of the expectation that they behave in particular ways. Of course, this argument only holds if one equates the feminine with the biological woman. A closer reading of Gilligan's work makes clear that although female subjects in her empirical projects were much more likely to subscribe to an ethic of care, male subjects were also observed to use what has come to be seen as a 'feminine' form of legal reasoning. This leads us to the more important point that notions of femininity are best understood as culturally contingent.[24] Significantly, as Butler has convincingly argued, this does not mean that gender is a matter of choice. Instead it has been argued that there are, at any one time, considerable societal constraints upon the way gender is 'performed', resulting for instance in the characterization of effeminate men as deviant.

Viewed in this way, these generalizations about feminine values and ways of thinking and arguing can be understood as a masquerade which is socially constructed and transient rather then genetically anchored. However, this does not mean that they do not provide fertile ground in a critique of adversarialism as a masculine ideology. It is a sign of a patriarchal society that the values associated with masculine or feminine identities can change whilst patriarchy does not. Schroeder, for instance, has argued that European men in the Middle Ages understood as uniquely masculine certain values recognized as uniquely feminine by contemporary writers.[25] Similarly, it could be argued that the ethics promoted by some feminists were guiding principles in the pre-classical period of contract law.[26] But, whilst it is asserted that patriarchy does not depend for its existence on any

[23] M J Frug, *Postmodern Legal Feminism* (New York: Routledge, 1992).

[24] See, most notably, J Butler, *Gender Trouble: The Subversion of Identity* (New York: Routledge, 1990).

[25] J Schroeder, 'Feminism Historicized: Mediaeval Misogynist Stereotypes in Contemporary Feminist Jurisprudence' (1990) Iowa Law Review, 1136.

[26] See further J Feinman, 'The Meaning of Reliance: A Historical Perspective' (1984) Wisconsin Law Review, 1373.

one conception of masculinity or femininity, the argument that patriarchal societies such as our own privilege masculine values over feminine ones, whatever they happen to be, is the foundation upon which I build the argument I wish to pursue. I do not seek to claim that the feminine values identified by those interested in the ethics of care are necessarily superior to masculine ones at this juncture, although the argument appears to have much merit.[27] Instead, I seek to explore the implications of the Woolf reforms being conceived of as reflecting certain values which in our society have come to be associated with the feminine.

The Woolf Reforms of Civil Procedure

The purported aims of the Woolf reforms were to reduce the delay, complexity and cost of civil litigation. Lord Woolf did not propose the privileging of feminine over masculine values. Nor did he make explicit the fact that his reforms involved ideological shifts in addition to 'mere' procedural change. But the reforms have called into question a number of adversarial conventions described above. They have, for instance, heralded a shift towards single expert witnesses whose duty is to the court rather than to the party that pays them.[28] As the autonomy of the parties and their advisers to run a case as they see fit has diminished, the role of the judiciary has been strengthened. Since the introduction of the reforms, observers have witnessed much more pro-active case management by a judiciary which has been empowered and encouraged to be much more interventionist in the run-up to trial. Senior Master Turner is reported to have argued on the eve of the implementation of the new rules in 1999 that henceforth, 'the yellow and red cards of the judicial armoury will be used with fatal effect in appropriate cases', and we have since seen evidence of this approach.

But Lord Woolf has done much more than challenge existing conventions. He has attempted to replace them with something else. Pre-action

---

[27] Other writers have pursued this line of argument. See for instance N Noddings, *Caring: A Feminine Approach to Ethics and Moral Education* (Berkeley, CA: University of California Press, 1984).

[28] The Civil Procedure Rules enable the court to direct that, where expert evidence is necessary on a particular issue, it should be given by a single joint expert and all the pre-action protocols encourage the use of single experts. This change remains one of the most controversial of the post-Woolf era and an interesting body of case law on the matter has already emerged. Another Woolf innovation that the courts have taken to keenly is the use of written questions to experts. This reduces the need for cross-examination at trial: 'Witnessing the Change' (2001) *The Lawyer*, 20 August 2001, 33.

protocols now prescribe that the parties cooperate with each other in the preparation of their case by sharing key information at the earliest stages of disputes.[29] Even more radical is the way in which lawyers, disputants and the judiciary have been 'encouraged' to refer cases to mediation as an alternative to lengthy proceedings or trial. This has had a dual effect. In one sense it can be seen as heralding the 'privatization' of dispute resolution if cases which might otherwise have gone to trial are diverted to mediation instead. It is independent mediators, many of whom work for profit, who are providing these services rather than state officials or the judiciary.[30] Moreover, the discussions and negotiations which take place in mediation remain confidential between the parties. In another sense the reforms have legitimized the role of the mediator within the litigation process and in doing so exposed the adversarial contest to the influence of those who argue that different values should inform the dispute resolution process; values which I consider to be based on feminist ethics.

More than any other of the reforms introduced in the wake of the Woolf report, the official sanctioning of mediation has the potential to create a shift away from adversarial ways of resolving disputes. This form of dispute resolution has come to mean very different things to different people[31] but, despite cultural diversity and temporality, certain attributes could be said to underlie most accounts of the mediation process. These include a rejection of adversarial approaches to dispute resolution; emphasis on the importance of cooperation; a focus on self-determination

[29] Pre-action protocols have been labelled one of Lord Woolf's greatest achievements: T Goriely, 'The New Pre-action Protocol for Personal Injury Claims' (1998) 148(6861) NLJ 1547 and see also *http://web.lexis-nexis.com/professional/document*. During the course of his inquiry he brought lawyers together and asked them to develop guidelines on how to communicate more effectively. The hope was that by improving early communication cases could be settled more quickly, cheaply and fairly.

[30] Commentators have argued that in the final decades of the twentieth century, lawyers were subjected to an array of reforms which could be seen as heralding the retreat of law from society: C Corns, 'Reshaping the Judiciary' (2001) 18(1) *Law in Context* 1–11; N Poulantzas, *State, Power, Socialism* (London: New Left Books, 1978); but see P Fitzpatrick, *The Mythology of Modern Law* (London: Routledge, 1992). In this context, mediation can be seen as a contemporary example of an increasingly bureaucratic state which constrains lawyers' autonomy. The creation of pre-action protocols, recent case law on the consequences of unreasonable refusal to mediate, and reforms of legal aid are excellent examples of the increase in this regulatory culture.

[31] Commentators have classified the different varieties of resolution which claim to come under this banner in terms of the goals they seek to achieve, their evaluative, facilitative or transformative tendencies and the different epistemologies which underpin them. Others have categorized them according to their outcome orientation, with evaluative and facilitative models being seen as more settlement-oriented than transformative models, which focus on changes to ways of thinking and behaviour for the future. Elsewhere, the differences between extremes have been explained in terms of the drive to save costs and time and the more idealistic tendencies of those who talk of healing and repair.

and voice; and an insistence that disputes must be understood within their broader contexts and away from the narrow constraints of established legal doctrine. It becomes clear from this that mediation involves much more than an alternative process. It encompasses an alternative vision of how and why disputes need to be resolved and the role of opposing lawyers in dispute resolution: a process which I argue has the potential to feminize the litigation process.

Few feminist writers to date have discussed these links, although the suggestion that mediation reflects a feminist jurisprudence has been made.[32] In her work on feminist litigators, Cahn has argued that a feminized legal system would: make greater use of mediation; be more appreciative of different perspectives; be aware of the relational context to disputes; take account of the totality of the client's experience; and encourage less aggressive pre-trial tactics.[33] It should come as no surprise then that, in her review of the intellectual giants of alternative dispute resolution (ADR) it is to feminist scholars and practitioners that Menkel-Meadow predominantly refers.[34] But does the evidence suggest that there has been an ideological shift towards the acceptance of feminist dispute resolution goals or is change in legal behaviour no more than a pragmatic shuffling?

Reactions to Mediation

I have argued elsewhere that mediation poses a number of threats to lawyers and their sense of professional identity.[35] Many forms of mediation can and do take place without lawyers. Community and family mediation are excellent examples of this model and serve as reminders that law and lawyers are not symbiotic. Perhaps most significantly, mediation undermines the claim of lawyers to classify disputes, to define their parameters and to determine what constitutes successful process and outcome. The epistemological perspective of lawyers is a reductionist one in which the juridification of the client's account transforms the lawyer from the client's biographer to their autobiographer.[36] The epistemological perspective of mediators is an

---

[32] J Rifkin, 'Mediation from a Feminist Perspective: Promise and Problems' (1984) 2 Law and Inequality 21.

[33] N Cahn, 'Styles of Lawyering' (1992) 43 *Hastings Law Journal* 1039.

[34] C Menkel-Meadow , 'Will Managed Care give us Access to Justice?' in R Smith (ed), *Achieving Civil Justice: Appropriate Dispute Resolution for the 1990s* (London: Legal Action Group, 1996).

[35] L Mulcahy, 'Can Leopards Change their spots? An Evaluation of the Role of Lawyers in Medical Negligence Mediation' (2001) 8(3) International Journal of the Legal Profession, 203.

[36] W Felstiner and A Sarat, 'Negotiation between Lawyer and Client in an American Divorce' in R Dingwall and J Eekelaar (eds), *Divorce Mediation and the Legal Process*

expansionist one. Lawyers restrain clients from talking when they are likely to reveal too much about their case. Mediators encourage a certain level of catharsis. Distance from their clients and objectivity is a feature of lawyers' work which is thought to compare favourably with the unmanageable subjectivity of their clients. But the classification systems used by lawyers also reproduce an order which keeps the expression of lay narratives in check: the very lay narratives that mediators seek to focus upon.

Despite legal training and prevailing cultures, reactions to the Woolf reforms suggest that a number of lawyers have come to appreciate the benefits of mediated settlement. It would seem that there has been a genuine interest in mediation in the commercial sector. The Centre for Effective Dispute Resolution (CEDR) in London has claimed that referrals from the courts have risen sharply year on year: by 8 per cent in 1999–2000, 19 per cent in 2000–1 and 27 per cent in 2001–2.[37] Moreover, it reported in 2003 that it had handled 634 mediation cases—a 35 per cent increase on the previous year.[38] Individual lawyers have also demonstrated an increased readiness to undergo mediation training and we have been in the position for some time of having more lawyer-mediators than we have disputes to be mediated. At national level, elite members of the profession also appear to have embraced mediation enthusiastically. The Law Society, Bar Council and the Lord Chancellor have all pledged their support for this form of dispute resolution.[39]

There is also evidence from the legal press that certain aspects of the new approach of more cooperative working have been enthusiastically embraced for their intrinsic value. Perhaps the best example of this can be found in the form of the pre-action protocols which avoid tactical manoeuvring at a time when most experienced lawyers simply want to find out whether they have a case worth fighting. This has led some practitioners to celebrate the fact that the pervading adversarial approach has gone and that litigation has been taken from the battleground to the

(Oxford: Clarendon Press, 1988); L Mather and B Yngvesson, 'Language, Audience and the Transformation of Disputes' (1980–81) 15(3) Law and Society Review 775.

[37] They predict that, as the judiciary becomes more familiar and confident with the process, these figures will continue to rise: K Mackie (2002) 'Mediation—How is it Relevant to the Maritime Community?', *www.cedr.co.uk*.

[38] 'CEDR mediation figures reach all time high—24th February 2004', *www.cedr.co.uk*. There has been a corresponding reduction in the percentage of cases going through to trial and this is especially noticeable in the Queen's Bench Division. Judicial statistics for 2003 demonstrate that cases set down for trial fell by 32 per cent in the previous year. In the United States similar figures have prompted intense debate about the vanishing trial.

[39] By way of example, the Law Society recently launched *Disaster Litigation: Practice Guidelines for Solicitors* (London: Law Society, 2003) which included a requirement that mediation be considered before proceedings are issued.

negotiating table.[40] In the USA, where mediation has a much longer-standing relationship with litigation, the emergence of a number of 'collaborative lawyering' programmes also suggests a desire on the part of lawyers trained in the art of adversarialism to learn new skills and embrace new approaches to dispute resolution.[41]

In her evaluation of the county court pilot scheme, Genn found that despite knowing very little about mediation most lawyers had positive things to say about it. Take-up for this voluntary scheme was low but on the whole lawyers found it less formal than expected and the majority felt the settlement reached was fair. The primary motives of lawyers for taking a case to mediation remained speed and cost but those lawyers interviewed seemed to approve of many of the value-added aspects of mediation. They were particularly appreciative of the ability it gave their clients to state their case, think outside legal categories and focus on commercial realities rather than legal technicalities. They also recognized that occasionally it even gave the clients the opportunity to repair damaged business relationships.[42]

Despite this evidence, a certain level of scepticism is called for when discussing the plausibility of short-term cultural change. After all, the number of mediated settlements only increased after the reforms were introduced despite the fact that lawyers have always been free to refer cases to mediation. Do these shifts in behaviour reflect the embracing of the alternative ideology of mediation or a desire to buy time whilst lawyers renegotiate the jurisdictional boundaries of their professional world? Can these changes in behaviour be interpreted as acknowledgements that there are serious failings in the traditional litigation system or as the expression of a proprietorial interest in mediation as a way of maintaining case load and the professional status of lawyers? Is it more accurate to see such changes as a reaction to the new financial pressures to settle cases early, the requirement for more pro-active case management and judicial 'encouragement' to refer cases to a mediator, rather than evidence that a new culture of cooperation has been embraced?

Even with the encouragement of policy makers and the judiciary it would seem that in general the take-up of mediation has been much lower

---

[40] See for instance R Haliburton, 'Focus: Personal Injury' (1998) 95(39) LS Gaz 20 and see also *http://web.lexis-nexis.com/professional/document*. At a more pragmatic level others have celebrated the fact that the function of civil litigation and roles of the parties have never been so well defined: Turner, n 1 above.

[41] The idea of the scheme is that the two lawyers make a pact to settle a case. If they fail to do so, they receive much-reduced fees and are contractually bound to hand the case over to another lawyer to proceed to trial.

[42] H Genn, *The Central County Court Pilot Mediation Scheme Evaluation Report*, Research Paper No. 5/98 (London: LCD, 1998).

than originally anticipated by the architects of the reforms.[43] There is nothing unique in this. Evidence from a number of countries suggests that take-up remains low in the absence of compulsory referral and that much enthusiasm to embrace new lawyering skills is explained by the desire to preserve market share.[44] In a UK context it could be argued that the small increase in referrals since the introduction of the reforms can be attributed to judicial pressure as much as anything else. The judiciary has 'encouraged' more extensive use of mediation through a number of devices including imposing cost sanctions on litigants who unreasonably refuse to engage in mediation,[45] upholding the validity of mediated settlements[46] and enforcing contractual commitments to mediate.[47]

Although Lord Woolf has repeatedly emphasized the fundamental shift in thinking required in the new litigation climate, Goriely and colleagues[48] found in their work on the new fast-track procedures with personal injury and commercial lawyers that these groups underestimated the scale of the required transformation. Moreover, the inherently risky nature of litigation meant that they were very cautious about being more open or cooperative for fear of making a tactical mistake. The desire to circumvent new mediation initiatives was also evident during the medical negligence mediation pilot scheme in which the majority of lawyers involved in the scheme came to understand and give meaning to mediation as an *off-shoot* of the adversarial civil justice system rather than a genuine alternative to it. They considered referral to mediation to be

[43] L Mulcahy, with M Selwood, L Summerfield and A Netten, *Mediating Medical Negligence Claims: An Option for the Future?* (London: The Stationery Office, 1999).

[44] It is noticeable, for instance, that the support of the professional bodies has been contingent on lawyers playing a central role as mediators or representatives of the parties in state-sponsored schemes. Viewed in this way, support for such innovation can be seen as an attempt by some members of the legal profession to secure or colonize new areas of work and stake a claim to be the only legitimate occupants of it. The Law Society has, for example, claimed regulatory control over the conduct of solicitors when they are acting as mediators rather than advisers or advocates: Law Society of England and Wales (2001) *Criteria for Membership of the Law Society's Civil/Commercial Mediation Panel*, *http://www.lawsociety.org.uk/professional/accreditationpanels/civilandcommercial.law#detail*

[45] See *Dunnett v Railtrack* [2002] 2 All ER 850 and *Cowl v Plymouth City Council*, [2001] EWCA Civ 1935. *Neal v Jones* [2002] EWCA Civ 1757, *Leicester Circuits Ltd v Coates* [2003] EWCA Civ 333, *Virani v Manuel Revert* [2003] EWCA Civ 1651. But see, also, *Corenso (UK) Ltd v The Burnden Group plc* [2003] EWHC 1805 (QB) and *Halsey v Milton Keynes NHS Trust* [2004] EWCA (Civ) 576.

[46] See *Thakrar v Ciro Citterio Menswear plc* [2002] EWHC 1975, Ch in which the Vice-Chancellor reversed the effect of a Court of Appeal decision declining to authorize a settlement agreed at mediation.

[47] *Cable and Wireless v IBM* [2002] EWHC 2059, Comm Ct. See also the decisions in *Dunnett v Railtrack*, n 45 above *Hurst v Leeming* [2001] EWHC Ch 1051.

[48] Goriely, Tamara, F Butt and A Sherr, *Costing fast track procedures through hypothetical studies*, Research Series No. 4/98, Lord Chancellor's Department Research Secretariat, London.

appropriate only in the rare cases in which solicitors were not able to achieve settlement through pre-trial bilateral negotiations. At best then, lawyers preferred to see mediation as an adjunct of the courts and litigation system rather than a radically different tool in the lawyers' dispute resolution toolkit.[49]

Perhaps most significantly, empirical evidence from North America, where mandatory mediation has been a feature of the litigation process for much longer, suggests that it is unrealistic to expect lawyers trained in the art of the adversarial encounter to embrace an alternative dispute resolution philosophy. Studies suggest that, as mediation becomes firmly embedded within the litigation systems, lawyers are slowly introducing an adversarial culture into mediation and are playing a more prominent role in the process than was ever anticipated. Menkel-Meadow has drawn particular attention to the problem of 'mediation advocacy' and the plethora of courses in the US designed to teach attorneys how to 'win' at ADR—a concept she sees as fundamentally inconsistent with theories of mediation.[50] In a UK context, Miller has questioned the ability of the new procedural judges to 'squeeze a new culture out of their colleagues appearing before them—colleagues with whom they had in the past played all the games of strategy and moreover, with whom they may also have done all those so called despicable things which the new regime so deplores'.[51] It is to this issue of the more fundamental concept of litigation 'culture' that we now turn.

A Feminization of Dispute Resolution?

In the final part of this paper I would like to turn to consider whether the unidentified barrier to the acceptance of more cooperative approaches to conflict resolution is the subliminal rejection of what is an essentially feminist approach to the dispute resolution. In my view it is a feminist critique of these issues which has the greatest potential to help us understand the unease with which some practitioners have approached mediation and explain the tendency to introduce adversarial techniques into the process. My purpose here is not to discuss the ways in which mediation is, or is not, more sympathetic to women. Some of the best critiques of mediation to have come from a feminist perspective have drawn attention

---

[49] Mulcahy *et al*, 43 above. Somewhat ironically, given the cooperative ideology of mediation, there was some evidence that conducting settlement negotiations in front of clients in mediation encouraged solicitors to be *more* adversarial than they otherwise would be.

[50] Menkel-Meadow, n 34 above.   [51] Miller, n 5 above, 1179.

to the process dangers for women who are expected to behave in a certain way.[52] My focus is instead on the ease with which the gendered nature of dispute resolution can be played out or changed through choice. I would like to suggest that, if mediation is best seen as a feminized process, this is the most pervasive reason why it has not been more readily embraced, or indeed understood. It is for this reason that lawyers educated and trained within the masculine culture of law find the transition to cooperative working methods so difficult.

Research shows us that lawyers have been accepted much more easily in the profession when they suppress the feminine in their style of dress and working practices, practise in ghetto specialities or show themselves willing to play the role of the hired gun.[53] There is then, also something of an irony in our expectations that lawyers should feminize their practice at a time when cultures within law firms are more competitive and aggressive than ever before.[54] From this perspective, it becomes clear that it is something of an uphill struggle to change styles of thinking within the profession. These problems have been intensified by the conceptualization of feminist values as 'soft', or a mush of altruism.[55]

The competitive presentation of evidence by battling lawyers has been so successfully popularized around the world by novels, films and television that its association with English-speaking justice is now part of global popular culture which reflects and frames the identity work of lawyers. It has been argued that the most widely produced image of the lawyer is that of the hero, with litigators being the proto-hero.[56] Lawyers may be very uncomfortable with such images[57] but they continue to be powerful and pervasive. Most

[52] See particularly the work of: T Grillo, 'The Mediation Alternative: Process Dangers for Women' in M Freeman (ed), *Alternative Dispute Resolution* (Aldershot: Dartmouth Publishing, 1995); and Rifkin, n 32 above.

[53] V Drachman, *Sisters in Law: Women Lawyers in Modern American History* (Cambridge, MA: Harvard University Press, 1998); M Thornton, *Dissonance and Distrust* (Oxford University Press, 1996); C Wells, 'Women Law Professors—Negotiating and Transcending Gender Identities at Work' (2002) 10(1) Feminist Legal Studies 1.

[54] An article by Robert Mendick suggests how the pressure towards feminization is recognized and evaluated. Talking of his experience of interviewing the head of litigation at a leading law firm he offers the following: 'You cannot accuse Style of not being thorough, but then what do you expect of one of the City's leading litigators with a track record second to none. What is surprising, however, is how utterly nice he is.' He continues: 'Style may talk of alternative dispute resolution, arbitration and negotiation but, despite all the conciliatory words and the outer appearance of a very nice man, inside beats the heart of a deadly litigator': R Mendick, 'City Profile' (1999) *The Lawyer*, 13 December, p. 15.

[55] Wightman, n 18 above.

[56] L Moran, 'Heroes and Brothers in Love: The Male Homosexual as Lawyer in Popular Culture' (1998) 18 *Studies in Law, Politics and Society* 3–27.

[57] H Kritzer, 'Legal Practice in a Post-professional world' (1999) 33(3) Law and Society Review 713–59.

importantly they serve to both reflect and determine public expectations of lawyers. Significantly, research on images of female litigators within popular culture has intensified the equation of feminine values with weakness. Corcos[58] and Lamb[59] both found that film and television storylines typically focus on female lawyers' failed love affairs and soul-searching examinations of whether to continue to practise rather than their professional successes in the courtroom. Both these authors have also argued that it continues to be the case that it is much more common for women to be portrayed as victims or non-achievers in the legal system, whether as lawyers or clients.[60] In this context it is predictable that a finding which has consistently come out of empirical studies of mediation is that the offer to mediate, when unprompted by the court, is commonly perceived to be a sign of weakness.

The implication is that neither feminists nor mediators are likely to survive in the cut and thrust of 'hard' litigation cases and the real world. Feminist ethics have been undermined by the tendency to equate this cooperative perspective with a specific morality of self-denial and dedication to others, a fact that makes them unpalatable to the litigator interested in the discreet haggle. The vulnerable and dependent who have so often become the subjects of women's care in the family and sphere of work have in Sevenhuijsen's view fuelled the association of feminine values with 'weakness' and 'need' in a way which provides a stark contrast with the autonomous and independent actor of the adversarial process.[61] This equation of feminine values with self-sacrifice reflects a simplistic understanding of relationships and dispute resolution in which care is all too readily defined as servitude and subordination rather than reciprocity.

It is clear that the symbiotic relationship of masculine values and adversarialism develops long before the trainee lawyer attends their first trial. Legal academia like legal practice is a masculizing agency.[62] The perception that 'good' lawyers are adversarial, apolitical and competitive is perpetuated by us during the academic and practical stages of training in which the Socratic method is still widely used. Even the most impressive of clinical programmes tends to encourage students to concentrate on specific events and moments in time and to rely on linear modes of

[58] C Corcos, 'Women Lawyers' in R Jarvis and P Joseph (eds), *Prime Time Law: Fictional Television as Legal Narrative* (Carolina: Carolina Academic Press, 1998).
[59] S Lamb, *The Trouble with Blame: Victims, Perpetrators and Responsibility* (London: Harvard University Press, 1999). [60] Ibid; Corcos, n 58 above.
[61] S Sevenhuijsen, *Citizenship and the ethics of care: feminist considerations on justice, morality and politics* (London: Routledge, 1998).
[62] R Collier, 'Nutty Professors, Men in suits and New Entrepreneurs: corporeality, subjectivity and change in the law school and legal practice' (1998) 7 Social and Legal Studies, 27; R Hunter, 'Taking up Equality: Women Barristers and the Denial of Discrimination' (2002) 10(2) Feminist Legal Studies, 113.

reasoning. The student is taught that it is the job of the lawyer to translate the polyvocality of diverse human stories into one seamless legal narrative.[63] No wonder then that they feel unprepared for mediation and cooperative working. No wonder that new schemes involving training for collaborative lawyering have to teach listening skills and move beyond zero-sum calculations.

Numerous critics have argued that the traditional law school curriculum inappropriately privileges an adversarial approach to disputes and pays undue attention to the case-based method and masculine ideals at the expense of more holistic or contextualized understandings of grievances favoured by mediators and feminists.[64] In this way, legal training imbues graduates with an inappropriate fidelity to individualism, formal legality and abstract reasoning.[65] Traditional ways of teaching legal methods probably represented a conceivable educational objective when the ideal model was that of mooting as a preparation for a career as an advocate in an adversarial trial. But this model embodies only a small part of what a minority of graduates will end up doing in the post-Woolf environment of litigation. If one argues, as feminists do, that effective lawyering is probably more about listening, understanding context and motivation, counselling and preserving ongoing relationships, then the orthodox model is much less than satisfactory.

Conclusion

There is much to be discovered about the values which inform and underpin the behaviour of those involved in litigation. It may be, as some have suggested, that the story of cooperative lawyers has been suppressed and that there are many instances of cooperation and reciprocity within everyday practice which have been marginalized in public debate. This suggests that certain areas of legal practice are already more feminine than I have recognized or admitted. Lawyers are a far from homogeneous

---

[63] S Berns, *To Speak as a Judge—Difference, Voice and Power* (Dartmouth: Ashgate, 1999).

[64] D Bok, 'A Flawed System of Law Practice and Training' (1983) 3 Journal of Legal Education, 70; S Carr-Gregg, 'Alternative Dispute Resolution in Practical Legal Training—Too Little Too Late?' (1997) 10(1) Journal of Legal Education, 23–41; A Hunt, 'Critique and Law: Legal Education and Practice' in I Grigg-Spall and P Ireland (eds), *The Critical Lawyers' Handbook* (London: Pluto Press, 1992).

[65] D Kennedy, 'Legal Education as Training for Hierarchy' in Grigg-Spall and Ireland, n 64 above; R Abel and P Lewis, 'Introduction' in R Abel and P Lewis (eds), *Lawyers in Society: An Overview* (Berkeley: University of California Press, 1995).

group and there is conflicting evidence of their cooperative tendencies. Whilst it is clear that the individualistic approaches to adjudication encouraged by the common law have not prioritized cooperation or an ethic of care between litigants,[66] much less is known about the extent of common law lawyers' cooperative tendencies outside the court or litigation system. Yet we know that, for every trial or piece of litigation, many more cases are settled away from the public gaze.

The assertion that only lawyers with poor negotiation skills end up in court may be rather extreme but there has been a suspicion in socio-legal circles for some time that this difficult research topic is worthy of more attention and has the potential to challenge prevailing conceptions of what it is that lawyers do.[67] Walker and McCarthy concluded, in their empirical research into family disputes, that family law solicitors are generally cooperative.[68] One explanation for this is the holistic approach to dispute settlement promoted by family law legislation in recent decades and the consequent shift towards relational perspectives. Accounts of lawyers' negotiating tactics have also demonstrated that advocates *are* likely to be cooperative when faced with an opponent who is equally as experienced. It is only when the opposing lawyer is less experienced that the value of a more aggressive approach is mooted. But why have these stories of cooperation and contextualized thinking been marginalized? It seems to me that, until these barely told stories of cooperative lawyers are heard more loudly, there is no possibility of change or genuine debate about the assumptions which underpin the celebration of oppositional confrontation. As legal educators and students, I believe we have a crucial role to play in opening up these issues for discussion and dispelling the myth that there is just *one* legal method.

Assumptions about gender have informed the development of a variety of legal doctrines. They have also informed the design of gendered dispute resolution processes. Just as MacKinnon has argued in the context of the equality debate that men are the presumed standards against which the activity of women is judged,[69] it has become commonplace to assess the value of mediation against the standard of the traditional masculine and adversarial system of litigation. Whilst the masculine remains the standard reference point in debate about the relative value of adversarialism

---

[66] See most notably Genn, n 42 above.

[67] See for instance R Dingwall, 'Empowerment or Enforcement? Some Questions about Power and Control in Divorce Mediation', in Dingwall and Eekelaar, n 36 above.

[68] J Walker and P McCarthy, 'Picking up the pieces' (2004) *Family Law Journal* 34, p. 580.

[69] MacKinnon, n 19 above. A classic example of this in a UK context was the debate in the years following the passing of the Sex Discrimination Act 1975 as to whether it was appropriate to compare a pregnant female worker with a sick male worker.

and cooperation, it will remain difficult, if not impossible, to have a serious debate about the relative worth of these two approaches and the spectrum of approaches which lie between them.

I have consciously avoided entering into a discussion of whether the ethics of care are superior to the ethics of an adversarial approach to litigation, although many of my readers will consider the terms I have employed to be value-laden. It is difficult to circumvent this problem since many of the values associated with the ethic of care have long been cherished and celebrated in society and viewed as moral imperatives. It is somewhat ironic that patriarchal traditions have praised women for service to men, children, the sick and God and encouraged them to be caring and selfless. This has traditionally occurred in relation to debates which have idealized the home, the mother, nurse and the private sphere—unlike the arguments presented here. How is it that these values have become so discredited elsewhere? Is the average marriage any less tempestuous than the average contractual relationship? The point of this essay has not been to prescribe a better way of resolving disputes. Rather the aim has been to make transparent the connections between adversarialism, mediation and gender and to open up discussion about the implications of this. My own conclusion is that future possibilities are foreclosed by habitual presumptions about what constitutes the gold standard in the public sphere of law and legal process.

I do not believe that the process of mediation should be celebrated without question or intense scrutiny. Indeed, I have many reservations about the process: for example, I think it has the potential to exacerbate existing inequality between the parties to a dispute and suppress feminine voices.[70] If one lives in a society in which masculine values of independence, individuality and rationality are given precedence over others then it is rather too much to expect of a newly reified process that it address and challenge dominant assumptions about what constitutes appropriate behaviour. What has come to concern me most are the attempts by litigators to 'square the circle' of mediation by introducing adversarial techniques of dispute resolution into it. Is the threat of considering cooperation, context and the relational dimensions of disputes so abhorrent that they cannot be accommodated? Has the adversarial system served us that well?

---

[70] L Mulcahy, 'The Possibilities and Desirability of Mediator Neutrality—Towards an Ethics of Partiality?' (2001) Social and Legal Studies, Vol 10(4) 505.

Shifting Familiarity

Alison Diduck *

Some years ago Felicity Kaganas and I wrote that law's attempts to define family consistently reproduced the idea of the private heterosexual union.[1] In another context, I called that union the 'unmodified family'[2] and by that I meant that other family forms required a modifier of some sort to explain their deviance from a norm. Not so long ago, in other words, there appeared to me to be a particular version of family resting at the pinnacle of social, cultural and legal desirability. More than that, the conditions and terms of entry into this version of the 'traditional' family were clear, if often difficult to meet. Those relationships that did not meet the conditions were not real families—they were 'alternative' family forms, pretended families, broken families or even non-families. According to Patricia Morgan in 1995, for example, 'the one-parent family is the result of the break up of families, or procreation outside of family structures, not a new family form'.[3]

Our family practices,[4] however, our intimate, caring behaviour always belied this dichotomous real/not real categorisation. It did not matter whom we lived with or how we arranged our sexual, affective or reproductive lives; when we shared our lives with someone we thought of ourselves as a family and we made claims upon law and policy to recognise us this way as well. And then, with the *Fitzpatrick*[5] decision in 2000, which allowed that partners of the same sex could be considered 'family' for the purposes of succession to a tenancy under the Rent Act 1977, it seemed that law was finally taking notice of these claims. Since that landmark decision a number of other legal and policy reforms have occurred

---

* My thanks go to Davina Cooper, Michael Freeman, Felicity Kaganas, Reg Graycar, David Seymour and the anonymous referee of this paper, all of whom offered valuable comments and advice.

[1] A Diduck and F Kaganas, *Family Law, Gender and the State, Text, Cases and Materials* (Oxford: Hart Publishing Ltd., 1999).

[2] A Diduck, 'The Unmodified Family: the Child Support Act and the construction of legal subjects' (1995) 22 Journal of Law and Society, 527.

[3] P Morgan, *Farewell to the Family?* (London: IEA Health and Welfare Unit, 1995), 86.

[4] D H J Morgan, *Family Connections* (Cambridge: Polity Press, 1996).

[5] *Fitzpatrick v Sterling Housing Association* [2001] AC 27.

and, if *Fitzpatrick* did not actually change the legal meaning of family, one might legitimately argue that these more recent reforms have. In many ways new laws about the family, most of them in force only since 2000, have changed the legal status of our personal relationships in unprecedented ways and with astonishing speed. And it is not only that which we conventionally call 'family law' that has embraced our non-traditional intimate practices. Immigration law, human rights law, employment law and property law, for example, have also taken on board the diversity of our family practices. It is as though the 'family' club is not so exclusive anymore. We're all families now.

We seem to have moved in law from one meaning of familiarity with someone to another meaning of familiarity with them. Law may, in other words, have moved from one of the OED's modern definitions of 'familiar': 'intimately associated, well or habitually acquainted, having a close acquaintance or intimate knowledge' to another definition, which it calls rare: 'Of or pertaining to one's family or household.' In this shift, those with whom we were familiar have become our family. In part, the shift may be a consequence or reflection of law's new(ish) culture of equality and non-discrimination (illustrated most clearly in this context by the *Mendoza*[6] decision which applied human rights principles to designate same-sex partners as 'spouses' for the purposes of succession to tenancies), or it may be for other reasons entirely, but whatever the reason, it now seems that the category 'family' is open to all. The dividing line between us and them, between those of us who could (and therefore perhaps should?) assume the responsibilities of family and those who couldn't (or shouldn't?), seems to have shifted considerably.

These changes to the legal status attributed to intimate acquaintanceships that constitute a shifting familiarity of the personal are interesting in themselves, but their context and timing are also interesting. They are occurring at a time when increased social, economic and political as well as legal importance is attached to families and to family membership and are reflected in areas of law and policy thought to lie outside the traditionally separate sphere of the familial. In other words, the public or the social is becoming increasingly familialised and I suggest that these two trends (shifting familiarity of personal relationships and the familialisation of public ones) might point to a more generally emerging phenomenon. In contrast with, or at least in conjunction with, what many have identified as the *individualisation* of society, it seems to me that we may also be witnessing a *familialisation* of society. I shall, in the first part of this paper,

---

[6] *Ghaidan v Mendoza* [2004] UKHL 30.

outline some of the ways in which new legal rules operate to attach people to other people, in effect, to make new families. I shall then offer examples of legal changes that may point to a trend towards the familialisation of the public world, before I conclude by offering some observations about the potential implications of these phenomena. Is shifting personal familiarity simply all about non-discrimination and equality, pluralism and inclusivity? Is the new social and political familialisation that I postulate an exciting and robust example of law finally valuing non-traditional family practices and acknowledging that those practices cross the boundary from private to public? In this second part, I'll express some guarded scepticism about the extent and nature of the changes and also about their implications and potential consequences. If everyone can now be in a family, and if families are the foundation for a healthy society, then it becomes all too easy for 'can' to become 'should'. Family members have responsibilities, to each other and to society, and families as a unit have responsibilities, too. And so, familialisation might, intentionally or unintentionally, operate as an emotional and psychological corrective to individualisation, and its eager embrace by law means that more and more of us will now bear the *legal* responsibilities of family membership that are an important social and economic part of that corrective.

Part I

There is nothing new in the belief that stable relationships and stable families are the foundation for a healthy society. In 1998 the then-new New Labour Government made this official government policy its way in its *Supporting Families* document which was to be the blueprint for its 'joined-up' family policy.[7] Whilst eschewing the discredited 'back to basics' policy of its predecessors, marriage was still said in this document to provide the best basis for rearing children and for social stability, even though it was also conceded that 'there are strong supportive relationships outside marriage'. And then, in 2002, the Lord Chancellor's Advisory Group on Marriage and the Family published *Moving Forward Together* in which that sentiment was reiterated and reinforced.[8] In this strategy, marriage was again identified as the ideal basis for relationships, but there

[7] Home Office, *Supporting Families: A Consultation Document*, (London: The Stationery Office, 1998).
[8] Lord Chancellor's Advisory Group on Marriage and the Family, *Moving Forward Together: A Proposed Strategy for Marriage and Relationship Support for 2002 and Beyond*, (London: Department for Education and Skills, 2002), para. 2.1.

were also indications throughout that the Advisory Group acknowledged that not all family relationships were marital ones. In these two documents cracks were beginning to show in the boundaries of the 'official', unmodified family. In the later one, statements like 'family relationships are complex', 'relationship instability among adults is an increasing feature of modern life'[9], and 'family life is undergoing unprecedented change'[10] seem to suggest some readiness on the part of the Advisory Group to acknowledge that families come in different forms, shapes and sizes. Yet its focus on what it calls 'the couple relationship' makes it clear that any deviation from the norm would not be too great; monogamous conjugality, current, past or merely potential, is still central to the definition of family.

Having said this, however, there is some indication that those previously excluded from family, those who used to be undeserving of support as family, may now at least in policy terms, be allowed entry to the family fold. The document speaks of the importance of offering support to 'divorced families' and of the 'validity' of lone parent families. What were not so long ago broken families or non-families are now officially acknowledged as valid families and thus as legitimate targets for government intervention/support.

This policy of inclusion of the previously unfamilial is continued in the 2004 consultation document *Parental Separation: Children's Needs and Parents' Responsibilities.*[11] It states that government policy needs to reflect changing patterns in family life. Note that it is about changing patterns of family life, not about rebuilding broken families. Separation or divorce was once the mark of the end of the family, and policy was to encourage the former partners to go on to make new families. It seems that now separation or divorce is seen, if not as a normal part of changing family life, at least as an unremarkable one. The consultation paper refers throughout to the 'separated' or 'separating family'.[12]

In these documents 'family' transcends the boundaries of household and marital status, boundaries that previously were conclusive in determining family status. Their policy is implemented in procedural measures designed to achieve the 'good' divorce, now defined as one that creates the separate-but-continuing family. (The Child Support Act 1991, of course,

[9] *Moving Forward Together: A Proposed Strategy for Marriage and Relationship Support for 2002 and Beyond*, para. 2.2.   [10] Ibid, para. 4.1.
[11] Department for Constitutional Affairs, Department for Education and Skills and Department for Trade and Industry, *Parental Separation: Children's Needs and Parents' Responsibilities*, Cm 6273 (London: The Stationery Office, 2004).
[12] On the separate but continuing family, see also F Kaganas and A Diduck, 'Incomplete Citizens: Changing Images of Post-Separation Children' (2004) 67 MLR 959.

was an early effort to 'make new families' and in its newer versions continues to do so. By attaching unmarried fathers to children with whom they may never have cohabited, that legislation clearly sought to ascribe the responsibility of family to people across households. Importantly, it also familialised many who had never before experienced this type of responsibility and who may never have chosen it, at least according to the old rules.)

In addition to these directional signposts pointing toward the new inclusive view of family in government policy, overt changes in the law have also widened the family net. *Fitzpatrick* forged the way and *Mendoza*, coupled with the Civil Partnership Act 2004, carry on the journey for same-sex couples. The House of Lords in *Mendoza* highlighted the functions of a family, the care and support its members offer to each other and then, Lady Hale in particular, pointed to the importance to principles of dignity, humanity and equality of recognising that these roles could be undertaken regardless of the sex of the parties. The Department for Trade and Industry in sponsoring the Civil Partnership Bill also highlighted the familial roles undertaken by same-sex partners and the stability those partnerships provide for the individuals concerned as well as for society.[13] The Act assigns most of the rights and responsibilities of marriage to registered civil partners and so gives official recognition to the monogamous homosexual relationship. It thus offers some resistance to the heteronormative family and even to the co-resident family, as civil partners do not have to cohabit.[14] Finally, the Gender Recognition Act 2004 allows that those historically deemed to lack the capacity to contract the stable marriages they desired can, after meeting certain conditions, be deemed capable. In allowing gay men, lesbians and trans-sexual people entry into the 'family' club, in remaking their familiar relationships into familial ones, we see justice and equality and inclusivity. The pernicious 'pretended family units' of the Local Government Act have been well and truly consigned to history and the recognition formerly denied to one's lived experience as a man or woman and partner finally has been achieved.

We see similar moves to inclusivity when it comes to children. Adoption has always been about families, about the stability that a family can provide for individual children and that children can provide for couples: a child could convert a childless couple into a real family. But the

---

[13] Women and Equality Unit, Department for Trade and Industry, *Civil Partnership, A framework for the legal recognition of same-sex couples* (London: The Stationery Office, 2003).

[14] Separation and desertion, however, remain facts by which irretrievable breakdown of the partnership can be proved so as to warrant a dissolution order: Civil Partnership Act 2004 s 44(5)(b).

Adoption and Children Act 2002 takes these ideas further than that which was considered sacrosanct even five years ago. Government has set a target of increasing by 40 per cent at first, then if possible by 50 per cent, the number of looked-after children who are adopted[15] and section 49 of the 2002 Act provides for the joint adoption of children by unmarried cohabitants. While in the past, adoption by one party in an unmarried couple was permitted, acknowledgement in this way of cohabitants of the same or different sexes as acceptable co-parents gives their relationships with each other and with their children a stamp of legitimacy. In this way the Act allows for the familialisation of increased numbers of previously unfamilial children and adults. Children will be removed from public, insecure foster care into the more secure care of a private, 'real' family, and adults who cohabit without marriage (or now, civil registration) who were deemed unworthy of becoming family are now embraced within its bosom.

The Act does not ignore those children for whom adoption is not appropriate. First, it creates an entirely new legal relationship between adults and children (or, perhaps more accurately, resurrects a form of an old one: 'custodianship'), increasing the range and number of adults who can become legally attached to and therefore legally responsible for children and the number of children who can become subject to that responsibility. 'Special Guardianship' is intended to provide 'permanence' for children who, for example (according to the White Paper), are being cared for by their wider birth family, or who are members of ethnic communities that have religious and cultural difficulties with adoption or who are unaccompanied asylum seeking children.[16] These children, according to the White Paper, 'deserve the same chance as any other to enjoy the benefits of a legally secure, stable permanent placement that promotes a supportive, lifelong relationship with their carers'.[17]

Second, The Adoption and Children Act 2002 is also concerned to render previously unfamiliar men into familiar ones in new and different ways. It provides a simpler route for unmarried fathers to obtain parental responsibility for their children. Unlike the (admittedly easy) test for acquiring parental responsibility by court order—commitment, attachment and motivation[18]—unmarried fathers may now acquire parental responsibility without ever cohabiting with their children, caring for

---

[15] Department of Health, *Adoption—A New Approach: A White Paper*, Cm 5017 (London: The Stationery Office, 2000). See also J Eekelaar, 'Contact and the Adoption Reform' in A. Bainham, B Lindley, M Richards and L Trinder (eds), *Children and Their Families. Contact, Rights and Welfare* (Oxford: Hart Publishing, 2003).
[16] White Paper, n 15 above, para. 5.9.   [17] Ibid, para. 5.8.
[18] *Re H* [1991] FLR 214.

them or establishing any connection at all with them. In requiring simply joint registration of the child's birth with his or her mother, the Act requires the fathers to have a relationship only with the child's *mother* and in this way treats unmarried fathers like married ones. The Act also clears up the previously ambiguous role of step-parents, who, statistics show, are primarily stepfathers, by providing a simple route for them to acquire parental responsibility for their spouse's children. These parts of the Act exploit both biological and social connections to increase the number of men who can be legally connected to children by providing ways for them to familialise themselves and their children more easily. Finally, familialisation by parenthood is also open to same-sex parents as the Children Act will allow registered civil partners also to acquire parental responsibility in this way and the Civil Partnership Act 2004 creates financial obligations to a 'child of the family' in the same way the Matrimonial Causes Act 1973 does.[19]

Jurisprudence developed under the European Convention on Human Rights and the Human Rights Act 1998 has also contributed to changing the boundaries of the familiar. In recognising a family life, respect for which is worthy of protection, in an increasing variety of relationships, courts interpreting Article 8 of the Convention have played their part in changing the idea of what a family is. In developing a 'reality test' to determine if a family life exists for the purposes of Article 8, the courts assess the reality of the links between the family members; they look for evidence of close personal links such as a relationship of emotional (as opposed to merely economic) dependency between the parties.[20] This test has the potential to apply to a wide variety of different types of relationships and the European Court of Human Rights has, for example, found a family life to exist between divorced partners with children,[21] between a non-biologically related parent and his children (in the *X, Y and Z*[22] case it involved a post-operative trans-sexual parent), between a child and an unmarried parent[23] and between a child and a separated homosexual parent.[24] It has also recognised a family life as existing between extended family members such as grandparents with their children.[25] It is the UK domestic court, however, which appears to be pushing the boundary furthest, because while the European Court of Human Rights has not, as yet, recognised a family life between two cohabiting opposite

[19] Sch 5.
[20] H Salford, 'Concepts of Family under EU law—Lessons from the ECHR' (2002) 16 *Int'l Journal of Law, Policy and the Family* 410.
[21] *Berrehab and Koster v The Netherlands*, 11 EHRR 322.   [22] [1997] 2 FLR 892.
[23] *Keegan v Ireland* (1994) 18 EHRR 342.
[24] *Salgueiro da Silva Mouta v Portugal* (33290/96) [1999] ECHR 176 (21 December 1999).   [25] *Price v UK* (1982) 55 DR 224.

or same sex partners without children,[26] the Court of Appeal has. In *M v Secretary of State for Work and Pensions*[27] the court held, applying *Fitzpatrick* and *Mendoza*, that homosexual couples should enjoy the same protection of their family life under Articles 8 and 14 as heterosexual couples. The reality test, applied by the European Court and by the domestic courts has thus familialised increased numbers of relationships. In these Article 8 cases, the boundaries of the 'real' family have been pushed beyond cohabitation, marital status and biology.

Perhaps, however, the clearest examples of the boundaries of family being pushed in the European Court of Human Rights come from the *Goodwin* and *I* cases in which the court held that the UK's refusal to recognise legally the new gender of a post-operative trans-sexual person violated the individual's right to respect for private and family life under Article 8 and his or her right to marry and found a family under Article 12.[28] These cases are clear examples of law taking individual choice and family practices seriously. Whereas English law had always refused to acknowledge an individual's gender as changeable, the court in these cases said in the clearest terms that gender identity, and arguably therefore, familial identity, is as much a matter of individual choice, action and living as it is of biology or law. In the *I* case it said:

[T]he very essence of the Convention is respect for human dignity and human freedom. Under Art 8 of the Convention in particular, where the notion of personal autonomy is an important principle underlying the interpretation of its guarantees, protection is given to the personal sphere of each individual, includ-ing the right to establish details of their identity as individual human beings . . . [29]

Legal change in areas outside the realm of that which is considered family law has also shown shifts in familiarity. The new immigration rules,[30] for example, reassert official recognition as family of the previously unfamil-iar. They allow officers to grant leave to enter or to remain in the UK as the unmarried same-sex or opposite-sex partner of a person present and settled in the UK if the officer is satisfied that, among other things, the partners have the required intention to live together permanently in a relationship akin to marriage.

In these examples we see the law remaking familiar relationships into familial ones. This shift is interesting in itself, but it becomes even more

---

[26] *Mata Estevez v Spain*, Application No. 56501/00 ECtHR.
[27] [2005] 1 FLR 498, [2004] EWCA Civ 1343. This case has been set down for appeal in the House of Lords.
[28] *I v UK* [2002] 2 FLR 518; *Goodwin v UK* [2002] 2 FLR 487.
[29] *I v UK*, ibid, para. 70, 536.   [30] Immigration Rules 295AA–295L.

interesting when we see a correspondingly new importance attached to the familiar, to *the family*, in other areas of law and policy.

One example of the new social, or public significance of family are laws ascribing legal responsibility to parents for their children's criminal behaviour and those providing for parenting orders and parenting contracts as part of a young person's sentence.[31] These reforms provide evidence of a concern to familialise criminal law, or at least youth justice, in a new way by establishing clearly an expanded role for families to play to stabilise society. While families have always been thought to play a socialising role in creating productive citizens and thereby stable societies, families in these reforms are seen as differently important in influencing or deterring the criminal behaviour of their members; their role now extends to sharing responsibility for their members' criminal behaviour. They must now take responsibility for the behaviour after it has been committed as well as for preventing it. These changes also mean a subtle shift in the identity of the subject of this criminal law. He or she is no longer an autonomous free agent who can be held individually accountable for his or her own actions. On the one hand children are deemed, for the purpose of founding criminal liability, to be legally competent as autonomous individuals, but on the other they are now familialised: their identity, their legal subjectivity, includes being a part of a family which must, therefore, accept some responsibility for their criminal behaviour.

Changes in the Income Support rules regarding the New Deal for lone parents and in employment law[32] regarding maternity leave, paternity leave, and leave for family reasons, adoption of the working hours directive and of new rules for flexible working, not to mention recently published government plans for further extending maternity and paternity leave[33] and for universal, affordable breakfast and after school clubs,[34] also signal a new importance and recognition of family in the public sphere. And now that the Tories, the traditional party of the family, or the party of the traditional family, have even entered this discourse,[35] it appears to be accepted that workers, subjects who previously had no other identity (except, of course, for those trade union men historically who lobbied for payment of a 'family wage'), are now specifically recognised as

---

[31] See, eg, Crime and Disorder Act 1998 and Antisocial Behaviour Act 2003.

[32] Employment Act 2002.

[33] 'Blair puts focus on family friendly reforms', *The Guardian*, 28 February 2005.

[34] ' "Latchkey kids" to be thing of the past in Blair child care plan', *The Guardian*, 12 November 2004.

[35] 'Tories offer fathers share of baby leave', *The Guardian*, 11 November 2004.

family members, and attention is paid to them in ways that have not before been expressed. Here we see the language of family, the *importance* of family, being asserted even in employment law, the law that governs that area of life considered the antithesis of family—the public world of work. The familialisation of the worker and the criminal youth and the familialisation of work and youth crime suggest new roles for family as social stabiliser.

Finally, care giving, in many senses the *raison d'être* of family, has acquired a new public legitimacy by changes in 2002 to the ability of carers to qualify for Additional State Pension. Whereas before only employees could qualify for the additional state pension under the State Earnings Related Pension Scheme, since 2002 someone who earns less than the National Insurance lower earnings limit in any year because they care for a child under age 6 or for an ill or disabled person may now qualify for additional pension. Caring is thus attributed with both social and market value.

Even areas of the common law, including property rights that are in many ways the foundation of the common law and thus are firmly entrenched in it, also show signs of increasing familialisation. While this trend may have begun with Lord Denning's attempts in equity to protect deserted wives, *Fitzpatrick* and *Mendoza* are examples of law broadening the scope for interference with an individual's rights to property and in their regulation in the market. Further in the sphere of the market, where the interests of creditors and lenders have long been prioritised in law over the interests of family, usually by saying that that prioritisation was in the interests of society generally, there are signs that family life is becoming more important. The *Etridge* decision[36] about the responsibilities of mortgage lenders acknowledges not only that society's interests may not exclusively be economic, but also that one's familial self cannot be separated easily from one's rational, economic self. And two recent decisions, *Jackson v Bell*[37] and *Barca v Mears*[38], conceded that there might be an Article 8 case to argue even over the rights of a bankrupt's creditors. This concession is quite a departure from established principle in which eviction of the bankrupt's family from their home was considered unexceptional and simply 'one of the melancholy consequences of debt and improvidence with which every civilised society has been familiar'.[39] Now the 'value judgment' that courts must make in these bankruptcy

[36] *Royal Bank of Scotland v Etridge* [2002] AC 773.
[37] *Jackson v Bell and another* [2001] EWCA Civ 387, [2001] Fam Law 879.
[38] *Barca v Mears* [2005] BPIR 15, [2004] EWHC 2170.
[39] *Re Citro (A Bankrupt)* [1991] Ch 142, 157.

cases may be less clear; Article 8 may require reconsideration of the traditional view that 'a man's obligation is to pay his debts and pay them promptly, even if discharging this duty affects his duty to maintain his wife and family'.[40]

Finally, we also see some evidence of a concern on the popular agenda to familialise publicly the privacy of many family practices. In a curious Private Member's Bill that was only briefly before Parliament in November 2004, the rites of passage or traditional celebrations associated with the birth and development of children were not only to become matters of public celebration, they were to become a civic duty. While the Rite of Passage (Welcoming and Coming of Age) Bill stood no real chance of becoming law, it offers some glimpse into the potential social and political meaning, or social and political *importance*, that could attach to the every day practices of family living. The Bill proposed that those with parental responsibility for a child were to be required to arrange a civil welcoming ceremony for the child which was to include the signing of a responsibility to children agreement setting out the rights and responsibilities both of those with parental responsibility for the child and of the state (clause 2). It also would have required all people to take part in formal coming of age ceremonies, according to clause 3, which were to 'confer on the individual certain responsibilities and rights as prescribed by the Secretary of State; take place by the completion of Key Stage 3; and [ ] be linked to the undertaking and successful completion of learning within the scope of the National Curriculum for England (and Wales) and [ ] be specifically related to citizenship education'. While this bill failed, it can be read as an attempt both to discipline and to familialise publicly the privacy of family practices.

In addition, there appears to be some concern to recognise officially the individual and private role of the third generation in families—the elderly. First, we see a trend to acknowledge legally the unofficial role often played by grandparents in families, to familialise them anew after their special legal status was removed by the Children Act 1989. While many grandparents provide support and childcare to families, they were identified in the *Supporting Families* document as specific targets for government initiatives and the DTI is said to be considering paying them to provide childcare to single parents.[41] Second, there are increasing attempts to refamilialise elderly people who may be living alone or in care homes. While this policy began with the previous government, current

---

[40] *Re Bailey* [1977] 1 WLR 278, 284.

[41] G Douglas and N Ferguson, 'The Role of Grandparents in Divorced Families' (2003) 17 Int'l Journal of Law, Policy and the Family 41.

government initiatives have increased incentives to others to care for older people and for older people to care for others. In 2002 the 65 year age limit upon claimants of Carer's Allowance was removed and, by the Carers (Equal Opportunities) Act 2004, when the Local Authority undertakes an assessment of the carer for support it is bound to consider whether the carer works, undertakes any form of training or education, or wishes to do any of those things.

Part II

These examples of legal change seem to say that we all can, or should, be family members now. The legal barriers to family membership have broken down; there is no longer any excuse not to be in a family. More than that, however, they also say that our identities as family members have become important in new ways. Our 'new' personal familiarity means that our diverse intimate relationships have become legally and socially valued and the familialisation of our social relationships means that their significance clearly and legally crosses the public/private boundary. This crossing, or shifting, of the boundary is important. It adds a familial, moral, ethical and affective dimension to the public world and to the rational economic actor said to inhabit that world, and it gives legitimacy to lives and choices made in that more complicated reality. Not only are these results worth celebrating, but so is the rationale for their achievement. Many of the changes, for example, were made with the laudable aim of promoting the welfare of children and others were made in furtherance of principles of non-discrimination, equality and respect for individual dignity and individual choices about our loving, caring and sexual behaviour. The Civil Partnership Act 2004 and the consequent legal changes it compels to other statutory references to 'family' are perhaps the prime examples of the importance attached to equality and non-discrimination.

We also saw the application of principles of equality and non-discrimination in allowing that we have a family identity outside the privacy of the separate sphere in which that identity used to be confined. These changes also recognise and legitimise aspects of our personhood that law previously denied, in more than merely symbolic ways: for example, changes to employment law can allow for the possibility of reconfiguring traditionally oppressive gender and generational roles. We could say that the personal is finally becoming political.

But here is where I inject some caution into the celebration. Perhaps things really have not changed that much, or even where they have, the inclusivity for which we strove and which we seem to be winning, may have come about for less than agreeable reasons, and may have as many unwelcome consequences as welcome ones. First, it seems to me that the concern about children's welfare that is in part driving the shift in personal familiarity and social familialisation is not so much concern for their welfare today, for their happiness, health and well-being *as children*, but is rather a concern to control their potential to disrupt society now and in the future. It is about making children into good citizens. It is as much about children *as* risk as it is children *at* risk. And so, while many suggest that the link in the new normative family is no longer the link between adult partners, but rather is the link between parents and children,[42] it seems to me that it does not matter, the links perform the same disciplinary role. In the new familialised society, both attach people to others to make a new family which can then legitimately be ascribed the same responsibility—the privatization of both human and social welfare.

What about where there are no children? Can we see shifting familiarity between adults as an example of the successful application of principles of equality and respect for the dignity of those who identify as family to be called family or are these examples merely of old family norms being extended to greater numbers of people, as Smart[43] said, of the regulatory net of family spreading wider to capture more and more people? On the one hand, the inclusion of same-sex families into law marks a successful challenge to the heteronormativity of family, but on the other, as Boyd has said,[44] it means that the potentially far more disruptive gay or lesbian subject is absorbed back into familiar roles and his or her disruptive potential is displaced. The new families created by *Fitzpatrick, Mendoza* and civil registration are still some way away from the 'families of choice' described in Weeks'[45] research with non-heterosexual people and could be seen as having simply adopted the rhetoric of diversity while at the same time shoring up a vision of the 'traditional' family;[46] and diversity in its cultural sense seems not to be adverted to at all. Moves to include

---

[42] See, for example, F Williams, *Rethinking Families*, (London: Calouste Gulbenkian Foundation, 2004).

[43] C Smart, *The Ties That Bind* (London: Routledge and Kegan Paul, 1984).

[44] S Boyd, 'Family, Law and Sexuality: Feminist Engagements' (1999) 8 Social and Legal Studies 369.

[45] J Weeks, 'Elective Families: lesbian and gay life experiments' in A Carling, S Duncan and R Edwards (eds), *Analysing Families. Morality and rationality in policy and practice*, (London: Routledge, 2002).

[46] G Crow, 'Families, moralities, rationalities and social change' in Carling, Duncan and Edwards, ibid, 287. See also *Nutting v Southern Housing Group Ltd*, EWHC 2982 (Ch); [2005] 1 FLR 1066 in which Evens-Lombe J. held that to find that cohabitants, in this case of the same sex qualified as 'spouses' for the purposes of the Housing Act 1988's provisions

polygamous marriages as acceptable family forms in Britain go back at least half a century, yet the even the new diversified alternative families remain stubbornly monogamous.

And so, the new families created by immigration rules, civil partnerships and the courts regulate as much as they define by requiring even non-traditional partnerships to look 'as if they were' traditional marriages before they achieve the privileges that come with recognition. And in *I* and *Goodwin*, while the European Court of Human Rights allowed that sex/gender was changeable, rather than accept a fluid definition of marriage to account for that changeability, it required a choice to be made to fix identity within either one sex or its 'opposite' so that intimate partners could make an orthodox, heterosexual marriage. It was also clear that the basis for choice of gender identity remained, for the court, rooted in a medical or psychiatric dysfunction. It was seen to be an abnormality that could be remedied by law for the purpose of encouraging 'normal' traditional marriage. While we may indeed see a new politics of family practices and human rights in these cases, they remain safely ensconced within old family certainties and meanings.

The 'new' families of law thus look remarkably like the old ones. Coupledom and conjugality remain central. Indeed, as Cossman and Ryder[47] have said, it is ironic that at the same time as policy seems increasingly to be moving away from the view that marriage should be the only state-sanctioned intimate relationship, the test for others is the degree to which they are 'marriage-like'. Alternatives seem to remain incomprehensible. The Law Commission, reporting in 2002 on possibilities for reform of the legal rights of home-sharers, potentially another new family form, expressed its perplexity about them, perhaps about all non-conjugal families:

There is also an increasing problem concerning persons who are not in any sense 'a couple', but who live together for mutual support or caring. They may or may not be related, but their financial affairs become somewhat inextricably intertwined. This is not by any means a homogenous group.[48]

It could not decide what to do about this problem, but in fact by framing these relations in this way, as a problem, it restricted its range of available

---

for succession to tenancies, the important factors were whether the 'relationship' was an 'emotional one of lifetime commitment' (para. 9) that was 'openly and unequivocally displayed as such to the outside world' (para. 17).

[47] B Cossman and B Ryder, 'What is marriage-like like? The irrelevance of conjugality' (2001) 18 Canadian Journal of Family Law 269.

[48] The Law Commission, *Sharing Homes: A Discussion Paper*, Law Com No. 278 (London: The Stationery Office 2002) para. 1.31(4).

options. Its approach certainly differed markedly from approaches which accept some idea of families of choice and decentre conjugality entirely in familialisation. Let me offer one example. In 2001, the Law Commission of Canada[49] also observed the growing diversity in family life and it concluded that recognising and supporting the great variety of caring personal adult relationships is 'an important state objective'. It identified certain basic principles and values that the state must attend to when it devises a principled and comprehensive approach to the needs of all in relationships. It concluded that the state must value equality and autonomy, personal security, privacy, freedom of conscience and religion and coherence and efficiency. It further concluded that the distinction between conjugal and non-conjugal is inconsistent with the value of equality, since conjugality 'is not an accurate marker of the qualitative attributes of personal adult relationships that are relevant to practical legislative [and policy] objectives'. It said that 'the state's role should be neutral regarding the roles that people assume in their personal relationships'.

Instead, then, of simply arguing that some relationships currently excluded should be included in legal recognition, it proposed that we start from scratch and 'look at the way governments have relied upon relational status in allocating rights and responsibilities', and try to design a legislative regime that accomplishes its goals by relying less on whether people are living in certain kinds of relationships. Sometimes some characteristics of the relationship will be important, other times they would not be, but conjugality would never be important.

On the one hand this approach runs the risk of even broader familialisation, yet on the other, it eschews the word family completely in these contexts, and focuses on the variety of personal and caring relationships in which people live. Instead of being concerned about families, then, it is concerned about the individual rights and responsibilities that accrue from different relationships and about how law can help distribute them among people more equitably. For me the change in language is important. It allows us to think outside the 'family' box. It is, however, this more imaginative thinking that remains difficult if not virtually impossible as long as familiarity continues to shift as it has in Britain.

'[N]othing evokes emotion like the term family'[50], and few terms carry the ideological baggage of 'family'. Entrenched in the idea of 'family' are

---

[49] Law Commission of Canada, *Beyond Conjugality: Recognizing and supporting close personal adult relationships* (Ottawa: Law Commission of Canada, 2002).

[50] S D Walters, 'Breaking up is hard to do. Comments on Martha Fineman's *Cracking the Foundational Myths: Independence, Autonomy and Self-Sufficiency*' (2000) 9 Journal of Gender, Social Policy and the Law, 205, 205.

particular and ideological notions of conjugality, gender and generational roles. The legal irrationalities such as love, care or sacrifice that are fundamental to 'family' must be expressed according to those ideological notions in order to achieve legitimation in law, arguably even in society's 'new' families. On this view, the legal shift in personal familiarity is as limiting as it is liberating. While the range of potential family members has increased, the set of cultural, social and economic norms by which they must live has remained static. While we all can be in families now, we must also accept their roles, rules and responsibilities. Perhaps then, we shouldn't be surprised by recent legal shifts in familiarity. The more pressure there is from those on the outside to gain entry to family, the more it demonstrates the favour of the preferred model,[51] and thus provides law with a clear incentive to expand or re-order familiar relationships.

While it remains clear that law and policy must address the lived experience of intimate life which includes now, and indeed probably always has included, forms of group marriage, serial monogamy, cohabitation, lesbian and gay partnerships, non-co-resident intimate partnerships or living apart together, step-parenthood and or lone parenthood,[52] not to mention non-conjugal home-sharers and other household communities,[53] shifting familiarity and the familialisation of which it is a part provides only a limited means of doing so. Sociologists tell us that all these relationships are important to people in providing intimacy, care, and companionship and are central to people's core values but fit increasingly uneasily in the category family.[54] They also tell us that friendship practices are changing so that there may be a blurring of lines between friends and family.[55] Friends become lovers and lovers become friends, so that rather than the romantic love relationship being the basis for care, the sharing of lives and intimacy, these more fluid ones are. Roseneil[56] argues, for example, for taking friendship seriously in law and policy; for thinking beyond the conjugal, familial imaginary. Even relationships that may have begun on an economic basis, such as many long-term carer relationships, may also be open to revision as affection and intimacy grow. In all

---

[51] M A Fineman, *The Autonomy Myth: A Theory of Dependency* (New York: The New Press, 2004).

[52] A Carling, 'Family Policy, social theory and the state' in Carling, Duncan and Edwards, n 45 above.

[53] S Budgeon and S Roseneil, 'Editors' Introduction: Beyond the Conventional Family' (2004) 52 *Current Sociology* 127. [54] Ibid.

[55] S Roseneil and S Budgeon, 'Cultures of Intimacy and Care Beyond "the Family": Personal Life and Social Change in the Early 21st Century' (2004) *Current Sociology* 135; see also S Roseneil, 'Why we should Care about Friends: An argument for Queering the Care Imaginary in Social Policy' (2004) 3:4 *Social Policy and Society* 409.

[56] Ibid.

of these new caring practices, 'connectedness operates in more various ways than simply through conjugality, sexual intimacy and blood'.[57]

These ideas about changes in patterns of intimacy and care resonate with other research that demonstrates the ways in which people negotiate their sense of obligations to others. Finch and Mason,[58] for example have shown the ways in which people draw upon their histories and relationships with others in order to negotiate obligations to care. Taking these lived, personally negotiated intimate practices seriously might have far-reaching effects on law and policy. It might mean, for example, framing work-life balance policies 'in terms of the range of important personal relationships and commitments within which people live their lives, rather than narrowly with reference to family responsibilities'.[59] Sociologists say, therefore, that we should decentre family in the sociological imagination[60] and while shifting familiarity can provide the initial impetus to decentre it in the legal imagination as well, so far, it hasn't. Rather, it seems to have done the opposite.

Meanwhile, the familialisation of social relationships, while having great benefits, must also be treated with caution. 'Public culture constructs belonging to society through the love plot of intimacy and familialism'[61] rather than through wider stories of fluid intimacies and care or even aloneness. There are reasons for this, according to Fineman.[62] The family is an institution to which roles are clearly assigned and its primary role is the care of dependants. While carers are also dependent because they depend upon resources in order to undertake that care, those resources are assumed to be subsumed within the self-sufficient family. This privatisation means that individuals are expected to rely primarily upon family members, but also upon private employers and charity for economic support, rather than relying on the state or the larger community. As Adam says:

Relationship recognition is driven by men and women but also by exterior forces. When the social responsibilities of the welfare state are being peeled away, lesbian and gay men are voluntarily offering to take on the responsibilities of other men, women and children. The state interest in conscripting lesbians and gay men, along with the more usual targets of divorced fathers into the taking on the costs of family support has long been clear . . . .[63]

---

[57] Williams, n 42 above, 50.

[58] J Finch, and J Mason, *Negotiating Family Responsibilities* (London: Routledge, 1993).   [59] Roseneil, n 55 above, 415.

[60] Roseneil and Budgeon, n 55 above.   [61] Ibid.   [62] Fineman, n 51 above.

[63] B D Adam, 'Care, Intimacy and Same-Sex partnership in the 21st Century' (2004) 52 *Current Sociology* 265, 272.

The broader, social phenomenon of familialisation may thus be evidence of the state's retreat from sharing the costs of social reproduction. The blurring or redrawing of the boundary between public and private responsibilities in this way, so as to extend the space reserved for the 'family', may be part of a continuing process of privatising social reproduction and social responsibility. On this point, Fudge and Cossman say that a whole new set of assumptions about the role of government and the rights of citizens is emerging:

> In the new political and social order, governments are no longer responsible for the social welfare of their citizens but only for helping those citizens to help themselves. The social citizen is giving way to the market citizen who 'recognizes the limits and liabilities of state provision and embraces her obligation to . . . become more self-reliant.' This new market citizen recognizes and takes responsibility for her own risk and that of her family.[64]

The flip side, therefore, of recognising workers also as family members is that family members must also always be (potential) workers. New Deal and other family-friendly work practices, not to mention providing so-called equal opportunities for carers to enter work or training programmes, present parents and carers as partners with the state and with the market in new ways. In this new partnership, private self-reliance becomes one's social responsibility and founds one's claim to citizenship, and economic dependence becomes an individual failing that demands individualised solutions rather than social or structural ones.[65] The new private partners also have the responsibility of 'ensuring that their children behave responsibly and are sufficiently informed and educated to become citizen workers themselves'.[66] While familialisation and the privatisation of responsibility that it engenders may operate primarily 'at the level of the discursive', we have seen as Cossman says, that it is also 'embodied in legal and political institutions' and has 'real, material effects'.[67] And so while it is phrased in gender-neutral terms, this new partnership forged by familialisation frequently and profoundly affects women and the children in their care because structural conditions and the norms of family living encourage their continued mutual and economic dependencies.

---

[64] J Fudge and B Cossman, 'Introduction: Privatization, Law and the Challenge to Feminism' in J Fudge and B Cossman (eds), *Privatization, Law and the Challenge to Feminism* (Toronto: University of Toronto Press, 2002), 16, quoting J Brodie, 'Restructuring and the new citizenship' in I Bakkes (ed), *Rethinking Restructuring: Gender and change in Canada* (Toronto: University of Toronto Press, 1996).

[65] B Cossman, 'Family Feuds: Neo-liberal and Neo-conservative Vicious of the Reprivatization Project' in Fudge and Cossman, ibid, 172.

[66] Williams, n 42 above, 29.   [67] Cossman, n 65 above, 170.

There is also the possibility that reconfiguring the family, state, market relationship in this way may have the effect of *depoliticising* rather than politicising the reproductive and caring labour that takes place within the newly expanded familial sphere.[68] If society is becoming increasingly familial, public, political ideals of democracy and equality have the potential to become subordinate to familial ideals of privacy, sacrifice, exclusivity and loyalty. In other words, a consequence of 'family' becoming the model for life in the public sphere as well as the private may be that an increasing variety and an increasing range of social life will have to fit within its (unreconstructed) norms.

Finally, familialisation might *remoralise* society in a new way. In 2000, Day Sclater and Piper[69] wrote that they saw certain legal reforms in the spheres of family law and youth justice as part of a project of remoralising the family partly by attributing to it increased decision-making responsibility to produce good citizens and by inculcating personal responsibility for those decisions in its members. The remoralisation project had the aim, they said, of easing a perceived 'crisis' in the family. The broader phenomenon that I call the familialisation of society may be an extension of this idea: that is to say, the familialising of society may be part of a remoralising project as well, one aimed to ease a perceived crisis in *society*. If the individualism that is said to have overtaken society is perceived as corrosive, and if society cannot go back to demonising or marginalising new family practices, then this form of familialisation may be just what the doctor ordered. It engages with individualism's valuing of personal choice and its focus upon the subjective quality of individual life and relationships, but succeeds in reshaping those values within the contours of the traditional family, with all of the consequences this has for decisions about the responsibilities one bears or does not bear for self, family, community and 'others'.

Smart[70] suggests that efforts at divorce reform in the twentieth century were as much about efforts to achieve acceptable forms of governance and regulation of families as they were about divorce. From the Morton Commission's[71] post-war moral certainties about the duties contained within marriage to the reflexive or post-liberal individualism of the 1996

---

[68] L Philipps, 'Tax Law and Social Reproduction: The Gender of Fiscal Policy in an Age of Privatization' in Fudge and Cossman, n 64 above.

[69] S Day Sclater and C Piper, 'Re-moralising the family? Family policy, family law and youth justice' (2000) Child and Family Law Quarterly 135.

[70] C Smart, 'Divorce in England 1950–2000: A Moral Tale', paper prepared for CAVA Workshop, *Frameworks for Understanding Policy Change and Culture*, 1999.

[71] Royal Commission on Marriage and Divorce 1951–1955 (London: HMSO, 1956) Cmd 9678.

Family Law Act,[72] she sees a series of shifts 'away from the traditional method of controlling family life through restriction and limitation on movement and change, towards regulating it by providing directions for this movement and change'.[73] In a modern social and cultural context that includes respect for the individual and his or her choices, respect for the welfare of children and respect for (the myth of?) the stability and privacy of the 'family': the shifts in familiarity and familialisation that I have described may thus be evidence of a newly successful form of governance and regulation, a remoralisation of society that is peculiarly attuned to the plurality of moral constituencies with which a modern government must engage.

I'll end on a theme that has appeared frequently in my work. It is that of conflict and contradiction. The idea for this paper began by my being struck not only by the scope but also by the speed of the changes we have seen in the last five years or so to laws about families. On its face, English law seemed to be moving quickly and equitably in recognising the diversity of family practices. It seemed like the law wanted us all to be a part of a family and also to ensure that that family membership was acknowledged and valued in unprecedented ways. I was as curious about why this seemed to be happening as I was about how and to what effect. I hope I have shown here the how and the possible effects, and have at least raised some questions about why. Because I believe that legal change is rarely unreservedly either good or bad, I hope I have also shown the different meanings and consequences of this phenomenon that I have called familialisation, or at least that I have provided another example of the interaction between our chaotic family living and the laws that regulate it.

---

[72] H Reece, *Divorcing Responsibly* (Oxford: Hart Publishing, 2003).
[73] Smart, n 70 above, 7.

Mainstreaming Equality and Diversity in European Union Law and Policy

Jo Shaw *

Setting the Scene

This paper has twin objectives: (1) to consider how it is possible to give constitutional form and effect to the principles of equality and diversity, in the wider context of (2) delivering effective, transparent and legitimate governance in the European Union (hereinafter 'EU' or 'Union'). In the context of strategies for securing equality and diversity and in the context of the emergent EU constitutional system, it pays particular attention to the meanings and scope of the tool of 'mainstreaming'. By 'mainstreaming equality' is meant:

the integration of equal opportunities principles, strategies and practices into the every day work of Government and other public bodies from the outset, involving 'every day' policy actors in addition to equality specialists. In other words, it entails rethinking mainstream provision to accommodate gender, race, disability and other dimensions of discrimination and disadvantage, including class, sexuality and religion.[1]

This section sets the scene for the argument to be made that the Treaty establishing a Constitution for Europe,[2] if it is ratified by the Member

* My reflections on equality mainstreaming were originally triggered by a request to write a report on Article III-118 of the Constitutional Treaty by the European Network Against Racism. I am grateful for the funding provided by ENAR to support the writing of the Report. The Report, entitled *Mainstreaming Equality in European Union Law and Policymaking*, can be found on the ENAR website (*http://www.enar-eu.org/en/publication/mainstreaming_04_en.pdf*) (visited 8 August 2005). I am grateful for feedback given at the *Current Legal Problem* lecture on 28 October 2004, at which I delivered a first draft of this paper, and I am especially grateful to Tammy Hervey for giving me detailed written comments on a second draft.

[1] Text drawn from the website of the UK Equal Opportunities Commission: *http://www.eoc.org.uk/EOCeng/EOCcs/PolicyAndCampaigns/mainstreaming.asp* (visited 13 June 2005).

[2] Hereinafter referred to as Constitutional Treaty. Treaty establishing a Constitution for Europe [2004] OJ C310/1.

States, which now looks increasingly unlikely, could make an important contribution in this area where the EU's day-to-day governance challenges intersect with its broader constitutional framework, including the upholding of basic norms such as equality. It does so by considering—sequentially—the place of equality and diversity in the legal order of the Union and the nature and scope of the challenge of mainstreaming. The second section looks at constitutional and governance reform in the Union in more detail, with a particular focus on equality and diversity. The third section is concerned with better understanding how mainstreaming can and does operate as a policy tool. The fourth section then turns in a more practical bent towards the extent to which the promise of mainstreaming—within the framework of a culture of constitutionalism and good governance—could be achieved successfully through the implementation of the Constitutional Treaty, with a specific focus on Article III-118 CT.[3] Article III-118 CT would introduce a novel approach to equality into the existing constitutional toolkit of the Union, by providing that:

In defining and implementing the policies and activities referred to in this Part, the Union shall aim to combat discrimination based on sex, racial or ethnic origin, religion or belief, disability, age or sexual orientation.

The practical realisation of the challenges embedded in this provision provides the central empirical focus of this paper. It is important to stress, however, that even if the provision is not formally brought into force in the event that the Constitutional Treaty is not eventually ratified, the ideas which it embodies—in terms of constitutionalising the mainstreaming of equality and diversity—can still become increasingly influential for the development of governance in the EU.[4]

Equality and Diversity in the European Union

In one guise or another, the concept of equality has always been central to the evolving legal order of the European Union. So far as the Union is based on an international law system of treaties, it draws upon the

---

[3] The designation 'CT' refers to provisions of the Constitutional Treaty. References to provisions of the 'EC' and 'EU' treaties (or TEU—Treaty on European Union) are to the EC Treaty of 1957 and the TEU of 1993, as amended most recently by the Treaty of Nice which came into force in 2003.

[4] For example, in June 2005, the Luxembourg Presidency held a conference aimed at NGOs on *Mainstreaming diversity: opening the debate with the whole of society* (*http://www.fm.etat.lu/no_discr.htm*; visited 14 June 2005) which did not link the debate to the Constitutional Treaty as such, but rather to the task of developing the link between social policy making and wider civil society.

fundamental international law principle of the equality of sovereign states. Non-discrimination (or equal treatment) on grounds of nationality is a core principle of the single market, underpinning many aspects of the free movement of goods, services, persons and capital. Gillian More calls it, in that context, a 'market unifier'.[5] Gender equality—initially in the limited form of a guarantee of equal pay for work of equal value for women and men, and subsequently in the form of a more wide-ranging equal treatment principle applying to all aspects of employment and training, and most aspects of welfare—is deeply rooted in the EC and EU Treaties, in legislation, and in an extensive case law of the Court of Justice. The Court of Justice has recognised gender equality in its case law as a 'fundamental principle' of the Union legal order.[6] Gender equality has come to be widely viewed in the literature as a constitutionally embedded fundamental right under EU law.[7]

Since 1999 and the Treaty of Amsterdam, gender equality perspectives have been given an integrated constitutional basis in EU policy-making through Article 3(2) EC:

In all [its] activities . . . , the Community shall aim to eliminate inequalities, and to promote equality, between men and women.

The Treaty of Amsterdam also introduced into the EC Treaty a legal basis for the adoption of measures combating discrimination on grounds of sex, racial or ethnic origin, age, disability, religion and sexual orientation, and important directives have been enacted on the basis of this provision to prohibit discrimination on grounds of racial and ethnic origin, age, disability, religion and sexual orientation, as well as gender in fields outside employment (Article 13 EC). The Charter of Fundamental Rights, agreed on a declaratory basis in 2000,[8] contains a range of equality principles, from a formal principle of (individual) equality before the law to more pro-active principles seeking to promote substantive equality in areas such as gender and disability. Article 21 of the Charter of Fundamental Rights is not limited like Article 13 EC, and refers in an open-textured provision to the prohibition of *any*

---

[5] G More, 'The Principle of Equal Treatment: From Market Unifier to Fundamental Right?' in P Craig and G de Búrca (eds), *The Evolution of EU Law* (Oxford University Press, 1999), 517–53.

[6] Case 149/77 *Defrenne v SABENA (No. 3)* [1978] ECR 1365 at 1378.

[7] C Barnard, 'Gender Equality in the EU: A Balance Sheet' in P Alston (ed), *The EU and Human Rights* (Oxford University Press, 1999), 215–279.

[8] Charter of Fundamental Rights of the European Union, Solemn Proclamation by the Presidents of the European Parliament, the European Commission and the Council of Ministers, Nice, 7 December 2000, [2000] OJ C364/1.

discrimination on grounds *such as* 'sex, race, colour, ethnic or social origin, genetic features, language, religion or belief, political or any other opinion, membership of a national minority, property, birth, disability, age or sexual orientation'. However, this is not a prohibition which can currently be relied upon in the Court of Justice, because of the declaratory status of the Charter. In all these provisions, there has been a 'patchwork of models' of equality which have emerged in the context of EU equality law and policy.[9] These comprise three main strands: ensuring anti-discrimination in the formal sense, working towards substantive equality, and managing diversity. This has sometimes led to confusion about the extent and nature of the existing guarantees of equality within EU law. In the constitutional reform process which gripped the Union from 2000 onwards, occupying much time and effort on the part of key actors in the institutions and the Member States, and which became a central focus for commentators upon the Union's constitutional scene, the logical next step was to build on these principles and to bring equality fully into the 'mainstream' of Union law and policy within the constitutional texts.[10]

In contrast, the concept of diversity has played generally a much more hidden (and less intensively studied) role in the development of EU law. It is self-evident that the very foundation stone of the single market concerns the project of coping with national diversity in relation to regulation, customs and habits (of production and consumption), and the operation of markets. The case law of the Court of Justice on the free movement of goods has involved adjudication between the merits of centralisation, harmonisation and mutual recognition, and the preservation of local powers to regulate products and markets. Diversity is now explicitly recognised in the EC Treaty, specifically with a view to its protection and preservation. Thus the 'cultural and linguistic diversity' of the educational systems of the Member States is protected under Article 149 EC[11] against encroachment on the part of Union education and vocational training policies. Likewise under Article 151 EC, when the Union is called upon to contribute to the 'flowering of the cultures of the Member States', it is enjoined to do so whilst 'respecting their national

---

[9] M Bell, 'The Right to Equality and Non-Discrimination' in T Hervey and J Kenner (eds), *Economic and Social Rights under the EU Charter of Fundamental Rights. A Legal Perspective* (Oxford: Hart Publishing, 2003), 91–110.

[10] J Shaw, 'The European Union and Gender Mainstreaming: Constitutionally Embedded or Comprehensively Marginalised?' (2002) 10 Feminist Legal Studies, 213–26.

[11] The designation 'EC' is used to identify Treaty provisions which are cited as coming from the EC Treaty, as amended up to and including the Treaty of Nice.

and regional diversity'.[12] Article 174(2) EC requires the development of Union environmental policy to take into account the diversity of situations within the Member States. Beyond these instances of explicit recognition, it is safe to assume that this concept of diversity aimed at the Member States and—to some extent—at the regions and localities within the Member States, has been a central animating concept in the evolution of much Union policy. However, unlike the concept of equality, which has become increasingly attached under Union law and policy to the situations of individuals and social groups rather than those of the Member States and the regions, diversity has remained securely anchored at the collective and institutional level, rather than at the level of the individual. Diversity has been understood and applied in the Union context largely as a counterpoint to uniformity, rather than as a complement to equality.

Mainstreaming Equality and Diversity

This section of the paper examines the challenge of 'mainstreaming'[13] equality and diversity in the European Union's legal, institutional and constitutional framework. 'Equality mainstreaming' is a deceptively simple idea which involves 'the incorporation of Equal Opportunities issues into all actions, programmes and policies from the start.'[14] According to Christopher McCrudden, it is quite simply 'the principle that equality be seen as an integral part of all public policy-making and implementation, rather than something separated off in a policy or institutional ghetto.'[15] In other words, all policy fields must take account of a core principle, namely 'equality'. Picking this up and reformulating the principle as 'diversity mainstreaming' Olena Hankivsky, citing

[12] For an argument that policies have thus far failed fully to exploit these possibilities, see T Ahmed and T Hervey, 'The European Union and Cultural Diversity: A Missed Opportunity?' (2004) 2 European Yearbook of Minority Issues, 43–62.

[13] 'Mainstreaming' is a very difficult term, barely capable of translation into languages other than the English in which it originated in the documents such as those of the United Nations Development Programme and the Beijing Platform. References have been made to the concept of '*approche integrée*' in French, but this is as vague as 'mainstreaming' itself. One possible term in German is '*Gleichstellung als Querschnittsansatz*' (ie equality as a cross-cutting challenge), but more often than not—as in many other languages—the English term is used. For example, the title of a recent collection in German on gender mainstreaming is *Was bewirkt das Gender Mainstreaming?*, U Behning and B Sauer (eds), (Frankfurt: Campus Verlag, 2005).

[14] T Rees, *Mainstreaming Equality in the European Union: Education, Training and Labour Market Policies* (London: Routledge, 1998), 3–4.

[15] C McCrudden, 'Equality' in C J Harvey, *Human Rights, Equality and Democratic Renewal in Northern Ireland* (Oxford: Hart Publishing, 2001), 75–112, 75.

Rita Dhamoon, calls it a 'roadmap for policy with normative concerns for social justice'.[16] Obviously, these ideals are less easy to achieve than they are to state, not least because it is clear that several highly contested concepts (equality and diversity) are placed at the centre of the analysis.[17]

The 'turn to mainstreaming' as a 'new' approach to promoting equality and combating discrimination is not confined to the Union. In fact, mainstreaming originates in the sphere of international relations, in the area of development assistance, where the language of (gender) mainstreaming emerged in the context of the work of the World Bank and in decision making by the United Nations Development Programme. The language of mainstreaming infused the work of the United Nations Third World Conference on Women in 1985 and was adopted as a strategic objective by the United Nations in the Platform for Action agreed at Beijing in 1995.[18] According to Fiona Beveridge and Jo Shaw,

The recognition awarded to mainstreaming in the Platform for Action served both to reflect growing interest in the idea of mainstreaming and to encourage states and international organisations which had not already done so to adopt their own mainstreaming strategies and policies. It also signalled the widespread acceptance in the international community of the concept of mainstreaming as a 'new' approach to gender equality.[19]

Much important early reflective work took place in the context of the Council of Europe,[20] which likewise has given rise to an influential and much-cited definition which is widely attributed to Mieke Verloo.[21] This states that

Gender mainstreaming is the (re)organisation, improvement, development and evaluation of policy processes, so that a gender equality perspective is

---

[16] O Hankivsky, 'Gender Mainstreaming vs. Diversity Mainstreaming: A Preliminary Examination of the Role and Transformative Potential of Feminist Theory', forthcoming, Canadian Journal of Political Science, December 2005, 2 (page numbers refer to draft typescript), 3. The quotation from Rita Dhamoon is taken from private correspondence.

[17] S Walby, 'Gender Mainstreaming: productive tensions in theory and practice' (2005) 12 *Social Politics*, issue no. 3, forthcoming.

[18] On the development of gender mainstreaming in global governance see E Hafner-Burton and M Pollack, 'Gender Mainstreaming and Global Governance' (2002) 10 Feminist Legal Studies 285–98; E Hafner-Burton and M A Pollack, 'Mainstreaming Gender in Global Governance' (2002) 8 *European Journal of International Relations* 339–73; J True, 'Mainstreaming Gender in Global Public Policy' (2003) 5 *International Feminist Journal of Politics* 368–96.

[19] F Beveridge and J Shaw, 'Introduction: Mainstreaming Gender in European Public Policy' (2002) 10 Feminist Legal Studies 209–12, 209.

[20] J Lovecy, 'Gender Mainstreaming and the Framing of Women's Rights in Europe: The Contribution of the Council of Europe' (2002) 10 Feminist Legal Studies 271–83.

[21] Council of Europe, *Gender Mainstreaming: Conceptual Framework, Methodology and Presentation of Good Practices*, EG-S-MS (98) 2 rev., 1998, 15.

incorporated in all policies at all levels at all stages, by the actors normally involved in policy making.

Gender mainstreaming has since been applied in many national contexts,[22] both within the Member States of the Union[23] and elsewhere such as Canada[24] and Australia.[25] It is well established that mainstreaming may take different forms in different contexts, especially when the national/regional context is compared to the supranational/international context.[26] Gender mainstreaming is a relatively well-established, even if still quite poorly understood, governance technique to be found in the Commission policy toolbox available for ensuring equal treatment for men and women.[27] According to the European Commission, gender mainstreaming involves:

The systematic integration of the respective situations, priorities and needs of women and men in all policies and with a view to promoting equality between women and men and mobilising all general policies and measures specifically for the purpose of achieving equality by actively and openly taking into account, at the planning stage, their effect on the respective situation of women and men.[28]

This means that no matter what the *basis* for EU competence in a matter—whether exclusive, shared or complementary—and whether the

---

[22] For a review see F Mackay and K Bilton, *Learning from Experience: Lessons in Mainstreaming Equal Opportunities* (Edinburgh, Scottish Executive Social Research, 2003).

[23] F Beveridge, S Nott and K Stephens (eds), *Making Women Count. Integrating gender into law and policy-making* (Aldershot: Ashgate, 2000); A-M McGauran, *Plus ça change . . . ? Gender Mainstreaming of the Irish National Development Plan* (Dublin: The Policy Institute, 2005). For ongoing research on implementation at national level, including in the new Member States, see the Framework Five-funded project *Policy frames and implementation problems: the case of gender mainstreaming. http://www.iwm.at/mageeq/* (MAGEEQ) (visited 13 June 2005).

[24] Hankivsky, n 16 above, 6–7 for a short summary of Canadian initiatives.

[25] T Donaghy, 'Applications of Mainstreaming in Australia and Northern Ireland' (2004) 25 *International Political Science Review* 393–410.

[26] C Wank, 'Different Conceptualisations of Gender Mainstreaming in Different Institutional Settings: the specific interpretation of Gender Mainstreaming by the European Commission and the Goal of Gender Equality', Paper prepared for the ECPR Conference, Marburg, September 2003.

[27] See generally, S Mazey, *Gender Mainstreaming in the EU: Principles and Practice* (London: Kogan Page, 2001); A Woodward, 'European Gender Mainstreaming: Promises and Pitfalls of Transformative Policy' (2003) 20 *Review of Policy Research*, 65–88; F Beveridge and J Shaw, 'Gender Mainstreaming in European Public Policy', *Special Issue of Feminist Legal Studies* (2002), vol. 10, no. 3, 209–328; C Booth and C Bennett, 'Gender Mainstreaming in the European Union: Toward a New Conception and Practice of Equal Opportunities' (2002) 9 *European Journal of Women's Studies*, 430–46; M Pollack and E Hafner-Burton, 'Mainstreaming Gender in the European Union' (2000) 7 *Journal of European Public Policy*, 432–456.

[28] Commission Communication, *Incorporating Equal Opportunities for Women and Men into All Community Policies and Activities*, COM(96) 67, 2.

question concerns *internal* or *external* action, gender equality issues must be integrated into policy making. The principle of mainstreaming will apply whether the policy takes the form of 'hard' legislation adopted by the Union institutions and implemented at national level (eg in the environmental field), or of 'softer' forms of so-called 'new governance', where EU policy making is confined to setting recommendations or guidelines for national action, or to 'benchmarking' national policies in order to ensure gradual coordination or the transference of best practices between the Member States. Gender mainstreaming was given a constitutional basis in EU law through Article 3(2) EC.[29]

Not all commentators are optimistic about the state of gender equality policy and gender mainstreaming practices at the EU level, or contented with all of its results.[30] Jill Rubery and collaborators, for example, have highlighted mixed messages coming from the Member States in the context of the development of the European Employment Strategy, where gender has increasingly been airbrushed out.[31] There has been a fear that gender mainstreaming itself has been introduced at the expense of specific measures which focus on long-term, systemic and structural inequalities faced by women in the labour market. A good example is the threat which appeared to hang over the 'EQUAL' programme in the context of the mid-term review of the Structural Funds.[32] The original focus on gender mainstreaming is being replaced by a more generalised, but thus far rather unfocused attempt to mainstream equality. More seriously, it has been suggested that it would be (politically) preferable to mainstream equality into all the programmes horizontally, rather than having a specific programme such as EQUAL.[33] This may threaten the funds being directed at vulnerable groups who are women, especially ethnic minority women who face double discrimination.

[29] See n 7 above and related text.

[30] M Verloo, 'Mainstreaming Gender Equality in Europe. A Frame Analysis Approach', paper delivered to the Conference of Europeanists, Chicago, Il, 11–13 March 2004.

[31] See a series of articles in the *Industrial Relations Journal*: J Rubery, 'Gender Mainstreaming and gender equality in the EU: the impact of the EU employment strategy' (2002) 33 *Industrial Relations Journal* 500–22; J Rubery *et al*, 'Gender equality still on the European agenda—but for how long?' (2003) 34 *Industrial Relations Journal*, 477–97; J Rubery *et al*, 'The ups and downs of European gender equality policy' (2004) 35 *Industrial Relations Journal*, 603–28; J Rubery *et al*, 'How to close the gender pay gap in Europe: towards the gender mainstreaming of pay policy' (2005) 36 *Industrial Relations Journal*, 184–213.

[32] See the Commission's *Third Report on Economic and Social Cohesion*, 2004, where EQUAL does not appear in the summary of instruments and objectives in the Executive Summary.

[33] For information on EQUAL see the Commission's Website: *http://europa. eu.int/comm/employment_social/equal/index_en.cfm* (visited 14 June 2005).

Policy makers have experienced only limited success in applying the techniques of mainstreaming away from the field of gender. There have been mixed results in the field of policy on combating racism and xenophobia. From the date of the Amsterdam summit in June 1997 until the Laeken European Council in December 2001, the fight against racism and xenophobia always featured in the Presidency Conclusions issued at the end of each European Council meeting. This prominence for anti-racism policy coincided not only with the strengthening of the human rights and anti-discrimination provisions of the Treaty on European Union and the EC Treaty by the Treaty of Amsterdam (came into force: 1999), but also with the designation of 1997 as European Year Against Racism. The late 1990s were an important era for intensive policy-making in the anti-racism sphere. The mainstreaming of anti-racism figured prominently in policy rhetoric, especially after the adoption of the 1998 Action Plan against Racism.[34] This was followed up by further documents, such as the Commission Report in 2000 on the implementation of the Action Plan against Racism, entitled *Mainstreaming the fight against racism*,[35] as well as in documents prepared by the Commission before and since the Durban anti-racism Conference in 2001.[36]

In contrast, the 2000s appear to have been a period in which anti-racism policy-making has been watered down, even though the decade began with the adoption of the directive on racial equality which requires the Member States to make substantial amendments to national legislation,[37] and the adoption of the Action Programme which enables the Commission pro-actively to promote equality-focused activities. This loss of focus on the specific question of racism also appears to be signalled by the European Council initiative in December 2003 to replace the European Union Monitoring Centre concerned with racism and xenophobia (established at the conclusion of the 1997 Year against Racism)

---

[34] COM(1998) 183, 25 March 1998.

[35] Commission Report on the implementation of the Action Plan against Racism, *Mainstreaming the fight against racism*, January 2000.

[36] Commission Communication, *Contribution to the World Conference Against Racism, Racial Discrimination, Xenophobia and Related Intolerance*, Durban, South Africa, 31 August–7 September 2001, COM(2001) 291 of 1 June 2001; Follow-ups to the World Conference against Racism, Contributions from the European Commission, dated November 2002, June 2003 and December 2003. The documents mentioned in this and the previous footnote, along with other documentation on EU policies on anti-racism can be found on the Employment and Social Affairs DG Website of the Commission: *http://europa.eu.int/comm/employment_social/fundamental_rights/index_en.htm* (visited 14 June 2005).

[37] Council Directive 2000/43/EC implementing the principle of equal treatment between persons irrespective of racial or ethnic origin, [2000] OJ L180/22.

with a Fundamental Rights agency with a much wider vocation. The
EUMC has expressed serious concern that its transformation should not
detract from 'the urgent fight against racism'.[38] The Commission itself
admits that transforming the EUMC into a Fundamental Rights agency
raises 'delicate questions'.[39]

There have been some limited attempts to mainstream disability issues
into EU law and policy. According to the Commission's website, mainstreaming is one of the main objectives of policy on disability: 'When the
Commission creates or changes a policy it aims to consider the needs and
rights of people with disabilities. The Commission pays particular attention to disability aspects in its socio-economic policies, programmes and
projects'.[40] Finally, in the 2002 White Paper on *A New Impetus for
European Youth*, prepared by the DG for Education and Culture, reference
is made to the need for other policy areas to take account of youth. This
constitutes the seedcorn of a mainstreaming approach which takes into
account at least the 'youth' dynamic of the Article 13 EC ground of 'age'.

Thus far there has been no comprehensive programme of equality
mainstreaming cutting across various equality grounds,[41] although in the
January 2000 Report on mainstreaming anti-racism, the Commission
did refer to 'the possible extension of the "mainstreaming" concept to
include all the grounds for discrimination covered under Article 13 of the
EU Treaty...'.[42]

The story, in sum, of mainstreaming equality in the EU is incomplete
and in some respects a little incoherent.

From Scene-Setting to Argument

The question we need to ask is the following: (if the Constitutional Treaty
is ratified) does Article III-118 CT offer the possibility of a more
comprehensive and more comprehensible policy of mainstreaming
equality and diversity within the law and policy-making practices of the
EU? The argument to be made is that it does indeed, but only under

---

[38] EUMC Media Release, 15 March 2004, Issue: 194-03-04-03-01-EN, 'Future EU
human rights agency must not detract from urgent fight against racism, says EUMC'.
[39] *The Fundamental Rights Agency: Public consultation document*, SEC(2004) 1281,
Brussels, 25 October 2004, COM(2004) 693, 3. The EUMC is discussed in more detail in
'Implementing Article III-118 CT: Implementation and Enforcement' below.
[40] *http://europa.eu.int/comm/employment_social/disability/strategy_en.html* (visited 13
June 2005).
[41] See generally, J Shaw, *Mainstreaming Equality in European Union Law and Policy-
Making*, European Network Against Racism, Brussels, 2004.
[42] It should actually be the 'EC Treaty'.

certain conditions involving a fuller previous understanding of the meanings and methods of mainstreaming, of the conditions of effective mainstreaming, and of the relationship between this contested term and the broad notions and practices of governance in the multi-level system which is today's EU. For the purposes of this article, governance can be simply defined:

as the production of authoritative decisions which are not produced by a single hierarchical structure, such as a democratically elected legislative assembly and government, but instead arise from the interaction of a plethora of public and private, collective and individual actors.[43]

This definition tends to highlight the 'hard' quality of governance, rather than the 'softer' and more purely persuasive forms which are increasingly characteristic of much of what the EU actually does when it formulates and implements new policies. Recent years have seen the emergence of new styles of governance and policy making in the Union context. There has been a shift away from reliance upon 'traditional' legislation and regulatory measures towards softer techniques of governance based on persuasion rather than coercion. Moreover, there have been institutional initiatives, such as the European Commission's 2001 White Paper on Governance which have triggered more general debates about the future of governance in the Union. Finally, it is important to bear in mind the origins of Article III-118 CT in an ongoing and as yet incomplete constitutional reform process, the main outlines of which are sketched in the next section.

Thus that section ('Constitutional and governance reform') looks at the place of equality and diversity in the wider framework of constitutional and governance reform in the European Union. The section following ('Mainstreaming reconsidered') turns to mainstreaming and considers some aspects of the theory and the practice of mainstreaming. Given the wealth of material on concepts and practices of mainstreaming, the analysis in this paper can only sketch out in brief some of the main lines of argument, bringing out three questions in particular:

1. What message or messages are being mainstreamed?

2. What model or models of mainstreaming are being applied?

3. How is mainstreaming to be effected: ie what strategies of mainstreaming are being applied?

---

[43] T Christiansen, A Føllesdal and S Piattoni, 'Informal governance in the European Union: an introduction', in T Christiansen and S Piattoni (eds), *Informal governance in the European Union* (Cheltenham: Edward Elgar, 2003), 1–21, 6.

The third section also considers the call for a turn from gender mainstreaming to the mainstreaming of equality and diversity, the question whether mainstreaming can be a transformative political practice, and if so what the implications for law might be. Acknowledging the importance of the call to focus attention away from gender mainstreaming alone, the fourth section ('Implementing Article III-118 CT') considers how, in the light of the three practical questions highlighted here, the principles set out in Article III-118 could be implemented and developed, focusing on its constitutional and normative qualities, as well as upon its 'softer' governance dimensions. In particular, it is the challenge of the third question, namely that of strategy, which links back to the underlying themes of constitutional and governance reform.

Constitutional and Governance Reform in the European Union: The Place of Equality and Diversity

The Reform Process: Constitutionalism and Governance

The process of ongoing treaty reform in the European Union could be said to have started with the Single European Act in 1986, and certainly dates back to the Treaty of Maastricht in 1993. Indeed, one way to conceive that Treaty is as the first response of the Member States which took to the task of achieving a substantial realignment of the underlying legal structures of European integration in order to meet the challenges facing a post-Cold War Europe. This process, which has since acquired a distinctive constitutional clothing, was brought to an interim conclusion with the signature by the Member States of the Constitutional Treaty in Rome in October 2004, after political agreement was reached at an Intergovernmental Conference (IGC) in June 2004. This followed a lengthy process of reflection, deliberation and negotiation triggered at least in part by the Declaration on the Future of the Union appended to the Treaty of Nice when it was agreed at the end of 2000.[44] Much of that work took place in the Convention on the Future of Europe, which was established by the subsequent Laeken Declaration of December 2001.[45] The Convention met between 2002 and 2003 and was responsible for drafting the text of what has become Article III-118 CT, although in

[44] I have written elsewhere at greater length on constitutional reform, eg in 'Europe's Constitutional Future' [2005] Public Law, 132–151.
[45] This Declaration took the form of an appendix to the Conclusions of the European Council meeting of December 2001. The text can be found online at *http://europa.eu.int/ constitution/futurum/documents/offtext/doc151201_en.htm* (visited: 15 June 2005).

other respects the text which it put before the IGC was substantially changed by the Member States before they reached final agreement.

What is notable about these processes is that they have not 'just' been about treaty reform, but rather they have explicitly invoked the spirit and form of constitutions and constitutionalism—although to what extent that is reflected in the final product is a moot point as the negotiations leading to the conclusion of the Treaty in June 2004 increasingly came to resemble conventional intergovernmental diplomacy rather than deliberation about a constitutional text. In form, at least, the Constitutional Treaty is just that: a Treaty. Even so, the Union displays and has continued to develop certain key constitutional features. The Constitutional Treaty itself adds to this, but much of the underpinning structure has been constructed through the case law of the Court of Justice and has been codified in earlier Treaty amendments, such as those of the Treaty of Amsterdam which contributed much in the area of fundamental rights and equality. Ironically, the reform processes did not have a particularly 'constitutional' root. In many ways, these processes could be said to be a reflection of the emergence of a post-1989 consensus that for effective governance in an enlarged Union operating within a post-Cold War Europe there needed to be substantial institutional reform. The Treaties of Amsterdam and Nice groped—largely unsuccessfully—towards the project of reforming the institutions in view of the anticipated enlargement which finally occurred on 1 May 2004. The reform processes have also reflected a concern, which emerged particularly in the light of the difficulties associated with the ratification of the Treaty of Maastricht, that there was a growing legitimacy gap in EU governance under which citizens feel alienated from the institutions of government. While this is often true at the national level, it is doubly true at the Union level where the feeling is reinforced by the complexity and obscurity of what the Union institutions actually do. Rightly or wrongly, those who framed the Constitutional Treaty felt that a response which addressed some of the questions about legitimacy and democracy which are typically also addressed in *national* constitutions could usefully be adopted for the text they were preparing. This lies behind some of the important innovations it contains which pertain to the evolution of a constitutional framework for equality and diversity, as well as participatory democracy.

Effectiveness for Union governance has not always and only been sought through the medium of macro-level treaty change. There has also been an ongoing debate about governance reform in the Union which does not require treaty change, reflected in the Commission's 2001 White Paper on Governance[46] and other initiatives such as 'better

---

[46] *European Governance. A White Paper*, COM(2001) 428, 25 July 2001.

law-making'[47] (which includes the participation of civil society and increased transparency) and regulatory reform (which includes the simplification and consolidation of legislation). The White Paper bemoaned the failure on the part of the Member States to take political responsibility for EU decision-making, especially the tendency to say one thing in Brussels and something else for the consumption of the national media. It proclaimed five key principles of good governance: openness, participation, accountability, effectiveness and coherence. The Commission insisted upon the enduring qualities of the so-called 'Monnet' or 'Community' method. This comprises two articles of faith: the first concerns the role of *legislation* in the task of achieving the goals of the Union and the second concerns the institutional configuration originally established by the Treaty of Rome for the legislative process, and developed since then. This sees the Community legislature as comprising the Commission, the Council of Ministers and the European Parliament, in a form of institutional balance (which has evolved and changed over the years, notably as a result of the evolution of the European Parliament into an elected body with many decision-making powers which match those of the Council). Thus, the White Paper contains within itself a number of potential contradictions, with its focus on the Monnet method, as well as upon the virtues of empowering civil society within networks of governance.[48] Each year, the Commission publishes a Report on European Governance,[49] reviewing progress towards the grand ideas encapsulated in the White Paper.

At the micro level, governance reform concerns are reflected in the adoption of processes often associated with the discourse and practice of so-called 'new public management' such as the prior impact assessment of new legislative proposals and the move towards mechanisms of societal steering which rely much less upon the supposedly old-fashioned (hard) diktats of command and control and more upon (soft) coordination and persuasion. Many of these techniques indeed do depart from both tenets of the 'Monnet method'. Despite its failure to engage with many of the features of new governance in the White Paper, the Commission has none the less been forced to embrace the techniques and technologies of new

---

[47] For more details see the Commission's website: *http://europa.eu.int/comm/governance/governance_eu/law_making_en.htm* (visited: 15 June 2005).

[48] For commentary on the White Paper see C Joerges, Y Mény and J H H Weiler (eds), *Mountain or Molehill? A Critical Appraisal of the Commission White Paper on Governance*, Jean Monnet Working Paper No. 6/01 (*http://www.jeanmonnetprogram.org/papers/01/010601.html*, visited: 15 June 2005).

[49] See most recently, *Report on European Governance (2003–2004)*, SEC(2004) 1153, 22 September 2004.

governance in many fields of policy. This has not only been in order to press for more Union action in areas at the margins of existing Union competences, but also in order to challenge blockages in the legislative process at the level of the Council of Ministers. However, not all elements of new governance necessarily mean a departure from hard law, since governance techniques common in the Union such as comitology and the social dialogue, which can give rise to formally binding measures, can also be included under this heading. The whole topic of 'new governance' has infused the study of the law of the European Union in recent years,[50] and the practice of new governance has been studied in a number of policy spheres including economic policy,[51] employment policy,[52] social inclusion policy,[53] pensions policy,[54] health care policy,[55] immigration policy,[56] health and safety,[57] and—most recently—fundamental rights.[58]

[50] For a general review, see J Scott and D Trubek, 'Mind the Gap: Law and New Approaches to Governance in the EU' (2002) 8 European Law Journal, 1–18; G de Búrca, 'The constitutional challenge of new governance in the European Union' (2003) 28 ELR, 814–39.

[51] D Hodson and I Maher, 'The open method as a new mode of governance: the case of soft economic policy co-ordination' (2001) 39 *Journal of Common Market Studies*, 719–46.

[52] D Trubek and J Mosher, 'New Governance, Employment Policy, and the European Social Model', in J Zeitlin and D Trubek (eds), *Governing Work and Welfare in a New Economy. European and American Experiments* (Oxford University Press, 2003), 33–58; S Smismans, 'EU Employment Policy: Decentralisation or Centralisation through the Open Method of Coordination?' in R Toniatti, F Palermo and M Dani (eds), *An Ever More Complex Union. The Regional Variable as Missing Link in the EU Constitution* (Baden-Baden: Nomos, 2004), 291–312

[53] K Armstrong, 'Tackling Social Exclusion through OMC: Reshaping the Boundaries of European Governance' in T Börzel and R Cichowski (eds), *The State of the European Union. Vol. 6. Law, Politics and Society* (Oxford University Press, 2003), 170–94

[54] C de la Porte and P Nanz, 'The OMC—a deliberative-democratic mode of governance? The cases of employment and pensions' (2004) 11 *Journal of European Public Policy*, 267–88.

[55] T Hervey and J McHale, *Health Law and the European Union* (Cambridge University Press, 2004), 412–414.

[56] A Caviedes, 'The open method of co-ordination in immigration policy: a tool for prying open Fortress Europe?' (2004) 11 *Journal of European Public Policy*, 289–310. Using the so-called National Contact Points on Integration as a resource, as well as NGOs and other partners within civil society, the Commission has worked in conjunction with the Migration Policy Group (an NGO) to prepare a Handbook on Immigration and Integration for practitioners to draw together benchmarks for national policies and to promote the sharing of ideas. The handbook is available from the website of DG Justice and Home Affairs: *http://europa.eu.int/comm/justice_home/doc_centre/immigration/integration/doc/handbook_en.pdf* (visited 13 June 2005). For an introduction, see the Commission Press Release, IP/04/1349 of 19 November 2004.

[57] S Smismans, 'Towards a New Community Strategy on Health and Safety at Work? Caught in the institutional web of soft procedures' (2003) 19 International Journal of Comparative Labour Law and Industrial Relations, 55–84.

[58] N Bernard, 'A "New Governance" Approach to Economic, Social and Cultural Rights in the EU', in Hervey and Kenner, n 9 above, 245–68; G de Búrca, 'New Modes of

One of the most characteristic forms of 'new governance' is the so-called 'open method of coordination'. The phrase 'OMC' was first introduced at the Lisbon European Council meeting of Heads of State and Government in 2000, when it was applied specifically to suggesting how the Union could reach the strategic goal of becoming 'the most competitive and dynamic knowledge-based economy in the world capable of sustainable economic growth with more and better jobs and greater social cohesion.'[59] What is involved are systems of governance promoting mutual learning and closer policy coordination at the *national* and *sub-national* level, via benchmarking, exchanges of best practices, periodic monitoring and reporting, and recommendations. Common principles and objectives are established at the Union level but they are not formally binding. There is no single template for open coordination within the Union, but rather a set of 'family resemblances' which link together a number of governance mechanisms linked to the Lisbon objectives.[60] According to Stijn Smismans,[61]

these coordination procedures of national policies are called 'open' both because of their assumed openness to the participation of stakeholders, and because of their openness in terms of objectives and instruments, which can more easily be adjusted to changing needs than traditional regulatory policy based on legislative standards.

Kenneth Armstrong describes the 'parent' of the family of the various OMCs now under development as being the employment policy

Governance and the Protection of Human Rights' in P Alston and O de Schutter (eds), *Monitoring Fundamental Rights in the EU. The Contribution of the Fundamental Rights Agency* (Oxford: Hart Publishing, 2005), 25–36; S Smismans, 'How to be fundamental with soft procedures? The Open Method of Coordination and Fundamental Social Rights', URGE Working Paper 2/2005.

[59] For further details, see the Presidency Conclusions, Lisbon European Council, 23 and 24 March 2000, point 37: '(The) open method of coordination . . . involves: fixing guide-lines for the Union combined with . . . timetables for achieving the goals which they set in the short, medium and long terms; establishing, where appropriate, quantitative and qual-itative indicators and benchmarks against the best in the world and tailored to the needs of different Member States and sectors as a means of comparing best practice; translating these European guidelines into national and regional policies by setting specific targets and adopt-ing measures, taking into account national and regional differences; periodic monitoring, evaluation and peer review organised as mutual learning processes' (*http://ue.eu.int/ueDocs/ cms_Data/docs/pressData/en/ec/00100-r1.en0.htm*, visited 13 June 2003).

[60] K Armstrong, 'Inclusive Governance? Civil Society and the Open Method of Coordination', in S Smismans (ed), *Civil Society and Legitimate European Governance*, (London: Edward Elgar, 2005, forthcoming); available under the aegis of the ESRC Seminar Series on *Implementing the Lisbon Srategy: Policy Co-ordination through 'Open' Methods*, *www.laws.qmul.ac.uk/lisbon* (visited 13 June 2005).

[61] Smismans, n 58 above, 1.

coordination strategies constituting the European Employment Strategy, launched at the Luxembourg European Council meeting in November 1997 and formalised in Title VIII of the EC Treaty, as inserted by the Treaty of Amsterdam.[62] Gender mainstreaming has had quite a significant impact in this field, although Rubery has expressed the fear that that the open method of coordination could be just 'too open',[63] to make it an effective mechanism for securing equality. Equality concerns can end up slipping through the fingers, like sand. There are also doubts about the effectiveness of OMC[64]: does it actually bring about changes in relation to national policies and can it affect, for example, employer behaviour?[65]

Mainstreaming and the Constitutional Treaty

Reflected in both the macro level treaty/constitutional reform processes and many of the meso and micro level governance reform processes has been an increased concern with policy consistency and with ensuring that these policies are infused with the general or transversal principles which the Union, its institutions, and indeed its Member States, are supposed to observe. A number of examples can be found in the existing EC Treaty, including Article 3(2) EC, already referred to in note 7 above and related text.

In similar terms, Article 6 EC requires that 'environmental protection requirements must be integrated into the definition and implementation of the Community policies and activities referred to in Article 3, in particular with a view to promoting sustainable development'. These provisions could be said to establish principles of 'mainstreaming' within Union policies, namely the principle that all policies, laws and activities should reflect—bring into the mainstream—some deeper principle or value.

An important innovation of the Constitutional Treaty is that it greatly extends the range of these transversal principles, going beyond principles of gender mainstreaming and the mainstreaming of environmental requirements, which themselves are lifted more or less unchanged from the EC Treaty into the Constitutional Treaty (Articles III-116 CT and

---

62 Armstrong, n 60 above, 6 (page numbers refer to draft manuscript).

63 J Rubery, 'Gender mainstreaming and the open method of coordination: is the open method too open for gender equality policy', Paper prepared for the ESRC Gender Mainstreaming seminar, Leeds, October 2003.

64 See for example, C Radaelli, 'The Open Method of Coordination: A new governance architecture for the European Union', SIEPS Report, 2003/1.

65 K Grosser and J Moon, 'Gender Mainstreaming and Corporate Social Responsibility: Reporting Workplace Issues', No. 27–2005 ICCSR Research Paper Series, 1.

III-119 CT). There is a broadly drafted provision requiring the institutions to 'take into account' a widely defined range of requirements related to the social policy objectives articulated in Article I-3 CT (Article III-117 CT). The wording of Article III-118 CT is much stronger as it requires that 'in defining and implementing' its policies the Union should 'aim' at combating discrimination. Even then, however, the words are slightly weaker than those used in relation to gender equality, where the Union is mandated to 'eliminate inequalities'.

Article III-118 needs to be viewed against the wider background of the ongoing 'constitutionalisation' of equality in the European Union,[66] especially the significant strengthening of provisions aimed at combating discrimination not only in relation to sex, but also in relation to other grounds, under the Treaty of Amsterdam. This point was introduced in 'Setting the Scene: Equality and Diversity' above, but must now be developed in more detail. Article 13(1) EC, added by the Treaty of Amsterdam, provides:

> Without prejudice to the other provisions of this Treaty and within the limits of the powers conferred by it upon the Community, the Council, acting unanimously on a proposal from the Commission and after consulting the European Parliament, may take appropriate action to combat discrimination based on sex, racial or ethnic origin, religion or belief, disability, age or sexual orientation.

This provision does not encompass a principle of non-discrimination as such—certainly not one which binds the Union institutions or the Member States—but it does contain a legal basis for action, albeit of a limited nature, as any measures adopted require the unanimous consent of the Member States, and involves the European Parliament only marginally in the adoption of legislation, through the consultation procedure rather than co-decision. However, action after the entry into force of the Treaty of Amsterdam in 1999 was surprisingly swift, reflecting a high degree of sensitisation at that point in time amongst Member States especially regarding issues related to racism and xenophobia. A number of measures were adopted, notably a Directive establishing a general framework for equal treatment in employment and occupation,[67] a Directive specifically concerned with race discrimination in a wider range of areas[68] and a

---

[66] M Bell, 'The Constitutionalisation of the Principle of Gender Equality' in S Millns and M Mateo Diaz (eds), *The Future of Gender Equality in Europe* (Palgrave: Basingstoke, 2005, forthcoming); Shaw, n 10 above.

[67] Council Directive 2000/78/EC establishing a general framework for equal treatment in employment and occupation, [2000] OJ L 303/16.

[68] Council Directive 2000/43/EC implementing the principle of equal treatment between persons irrespective of racial or ethnic origin, [2000] OJ L 180/22.

programme of action for 2001–2006 to combat discrimination.[69] This latter instrument enables the Commission to direct funding to projects which seek to combat discrimination. More recently, a Directive concerned with equal treatment of men and women in relation to access to goods and services, which could not be validly based on other gender equality legal bases under the EC Treaty because it went beyond the field of employment and training, has been adopted on the basis of Article 13.[70] Reflecting concerns about the limitations of Article 13 as a legal basis, a second paragraph was added by the Treaty of Nice, to cover at least those aspects of Union action in this field which do not involve the harmonisation of national laws and to allow the use of the co-decision procedure involving the European Parliament and the Council of Ministers as co-legislators for such measures:

By way of derogation from paragraph 1, when the Council adopts Community incentive measures, excluding any harmonisation of the laws and regulations of the Member States, to support action taken by the Member States in order to contribute to the achievement of the objectives referred to in paragraph 1, it shall act in accordance with the procedure referred to in Article 251.

Article III-124 CT replicates Article 13 EC in the Constitutional Treaty, although there are very slight amendments to the legislative procedure. Measures under paragraph one, still to be adopted by unanimity in the Council of Ministers, require the consent of the European Parliament (as opposed to mere consultation at present). In other words, the European Parliament is co-legislator but measures are still vulnerable to veto by just one Member State. Measures under paragraph two are to be adopted in accordance with the ordinary legislative procedure under Article I-34 CT—that is, the co-decision procedure.

Article III-118 CT goes considerably further than Article III-124 CT/ex Article 13 EC in establishing a general obligation on the Union to 'aim to combat discrimination'. It should also be read in the light of the incorporation into the Constitutional Treaty, as Part II, of the Charter of Fundamental Rights of the European Union. If the Constitutional Treaty is ratified and comes into force, the Charter's provisions will be fully 'recognised' as part of the legal framework of the Union (Article I-9(1) CT). This means that the provisions of the Charter—subject to the qualifications imposed by the so-called horizontal provisions of the Charter on the scope and effectiveness of the provisions—will be treated as a binding

---

[69] Council Decision 2000/750 establishing a Community action programme to combat discrimination (2001–2006), [2000] OJ L303/23.

[70] Council Directive 2004/113/EC implementing the principle of equal treatment between men and women in the access to and supply of goods and services, [2004] OJ L373/37.

source of law within the new post-Constitutional Treaty Union legal order. The Charter contains a rather diverse but quite comprehensive set of provisions on equality, including a prohibition on discrimination on *any* ground, such as sex, race, colour, ethnic or social origin, genetic features, language, religion or belief, political or any other opinion, membership of a national minority, property, birth, disability, age or sexual orientation (Article II-81(1) CT). In some respects, therefore, with its fleshing-out of different concepts of equality, the Charter of Fundamental Rights provides some additional guidance about how to understand and how to apply Article III-118.

Article III-118 also needs to be read in the light of the Constitutional Treaty provisions on the Union's values and objectives. Article I-2 proclaims the Union's values, including equality and respect for human rights, values said to be 'common to the Member States in a society in which . . . non-discrimination . . . and equality between women and men prevail.' Article I-3 includes amongst the Union's objectives the combating of social exclusion and discrimination, the promotion of social justice and protection, and equality between women and men.

Turning to the question of diversity, the Constitutional Treaty has generated a proliferation of references to this concept, but as before the focus is largely on diversity expressed in relation to nations, regions, identities, languages and cultures, rather than in relation to the situatedness of any given individual or social group such as ethnic minorities. Fears about the (perceived) uniformity effects of a single constitutional document undoubtedly inspired much of this turn to the language of diversity. Departing from the *de facto* previous motto of 'ever closer union of the peoples of Europe', found in the Preamble to the Treaty of Rome, 'United in Diversity' will now become the Union's motto (Article I-8 CT). This phrase is referred to also in the Preamble. It is likewise an objective of the Union to preserve Europe's 'rich cultural and linguistic diversity'. There is also a reference in Article I-2 CT to 'respect for human rights, including the rights of persons belonging to minorities' as part of the Union's framework of values.

The references to diversity in Part III of the Constitutional Treaty are essentially the same as in the current EC Treaty, on which this Part is largely based, and as such they can be found, for example, in Article III-282 CT (education policy) and Article III-280 CT (cultural policy). In addition, there are a number of references to diversity in the Charter of Fundamental Rights (Part II of the Constitutional Treaty). The Preamble to Part II refers to 'the diversity of the cultures and traditions of the peoples of Europe' and Article II-82 CT guarantees cultural, religious and linguistic diversity. The possible role of Article II-82 in informing the implementation of Article III-118 will be explored further in the fourth section of this paper.

It is arguable that a new constitutional settlement in relation to policy on equality and diversity will be in place after ratification and entry into force of the Constitutional Treaty, and this new settlement will require a comprehensive rethinking of approaches to policy making in all fields at both the Union, and indeed the national, levels.[71] The move to strengthen and widen the transversal clauses, linked to more explicit concerns with equality and diversity issues in the Constitutional Treaty's preamble, provisions on values and objectives, and provisions on fundamental rights (Part II), adds force to this argument. However, it is a constitutional change which also implicates significant questions about the nature of Union governance, especially so-called 'new governance'. This is true notwithstanding the fact that the vast bulk of the Constitutional Treaty is concerned more with the traditional institutions and instruments of *government* than the more amorphous notion and concerns of *governance*. The aims of Article III-118 CT cannot simply be delivered through the application of the traditional 'Community' or 'Monnet' method of law-making, the adoption of directives and similar measures and their application within national law by legislatures, executives and even courts. This is not just because of the limitations of the relevant legal basis provisions already highlighted—Article III-124 CT/ex Article 13 EC—where Union action will always be restricted by the requirement to achieve unanimity in the Council of Ministers. The point is also evident from the previous experience of the Union institutions, notably the Commission, with gender mainstreaming, where there is already in place a much more comprehensive legislative framework to guarantee gender equality at the national level, yet this has not (so far) delivered even an approximation of substantive equality or even genuine equality of opportunities for women and men. Gender mainstreaming in the Union was always intended to go beyond the legal framework of equality guarantees, and now it is beginning to be studied explicitly in the context of the burgeoning sector of 'informal governance'.[72]

Moreover, mainstreaming is also aimed at the Union institutions themselves, as employers, as policy makers, and as guarantors of the principles contained in the Treaties, as well as at the Member States. It has necessitated changes to their internal working practices, as well as to the

---

[71] M Bell, 'Equality and the European Union Constitution' (2004) 33 ILJ, 242–60.
[72] A Woodward, 'Building velvet triangles: Gender and informal governance', in Christiansen and Piattoni, n 43 above, 76–93.

arrangements for formulating all types of policies, including those implemented through new governance arrangements, such as the Union's employment and social inclusion policies. In this context, new instruments have been developed such as the impact assessment of policy proposals.

Mainstreaming also demands a different culture of governance, with greater participation opportunities for those likely to be affected by policies, and here too the Constitutional Treaty could make a decisive contribution through its provisions on 'the democratic life of the Union' (Title VI of Part I), notably the explicit recognition now given to the principle of participatory democracy in Article I-47. It requires the institutions to give 'citizens and representative associations the opportunity to make known and publicly exchange their views in all areas of Union action', and to 'maintain an open, transparent and regular dialogue with representative associations and civil society'. As we shall see, this first step towards giving a constitutional status to civil society within a slowly emerging democratic settlement for the Union is potentially very important if mainstreaming is to be a transformative political practice.

This, then, is the primary constitutional background to the project of constitutionalising the mainstreaming of equality and diversity in Union law and policy making. It would be wrong to suggest that the development of a stronger and in some ways more explicit foundation for equality and diversity in the Constitutional Treaty is in any way the central *leitmotiv* of this highly complex and now very controversial document. On the contrary, much of the debate about the Constitutional Treaty in national politics during the increasingly fraught ratification debates which culminated in the Treaty's rejection in referendums in France and the Netherlands in 2005 was to the effect that the Treaty is insufficiently 'social' in orientation, and that its neo-liberal strands endanger certain aspects of the national and European 'social models'. However, the Constitutional Treaty does contain important proposed changes, which could set the frame for a different type of politics of equality and diversity in a future European Union. At the level of political culture, of course, those types of changes could doubtless come about without constitutional change if the political will were present, and indeed if the Constitutional Treaty is not ratified, this is the only way in which they could come about. We shall return to the question of the practical realization of the goals which I have read into Article III-118 CT in the fourth section of this paper and to the issue of Constitutional Treaty more generally in the conclusions. First, however, attention is turned to the task of reconsidering the concept of mainstreaming.

Mainstreaming Reconsidered

What is Mainstreaming?

Fiona Beveridge and Sue Nott speak of there being both a 'case for optimism' and a 'case for cynicism' in relation to gender mainstreaming.[73] They point out that gender mainstreaming has enjoyed a rapid ascendancy in many political institutions and states, but that this rapid growth has rendered the concept practically 'ownerless':

> no institution or body, international or national, has any authority to determine which efforts to adopt mainstreaming policies are 'true' as opposed to sham or misguided.[74]

Mainstreaming can also be vague, directionless, and lacking effective enforcement mechanisms. In terms of 'ownership', mainstreaming can become simultaneously the concern of all, and the responsibility of no-one. It may struggle to address issues such as the lack of political recognition of the groups whose interests are being 'mainstreamed' or questions of class and economic power. Despite the definition of the UK Equal Opportunities Commission with which I began this paper (which mentions class), issues of social class are in fact often airbrushed out of existence, with a clear preference for more neutral discourses of social inclusion and exclusion.[75] Mainstreaming can lead to the co-opting into political discourse of concepts such as 'gender equality' but only once their meaning has been 'transformed' and 'corrupted' in the service of other policy priorities such as economic policies.[76] The turn to mainstreaming has resulted in the undermining of specific focused programmes, such as positive action for under-represented or weaker groups. Its relationship to market mechanisms and a lack of political will, evidenced by a frequent lack of funding for the necessary institutions, have also been suspect dimensions. In principle, a mainstreaming approach should bring out a contrast between the short-, the medium- and the long-term impact of policies, suggesting corrective mechanisms that ought to be taken to balance the different temporal frames. On the other hand, in

---

[73] F Beveridge and S Nott, 'Mainstreaming: A Case for Optimism and Cynicism' (2002) 10 *Feminist Legal Studies* 299–311.

[74] Beveridge and Nott, n 73 above, 299.

[75] For an argument in favour of grounding laws against discrimination on social inclusion rather than equality, see H Collins, 'Discrimination, Equality and Social Inclusion' (2003) 66 MLR 16–43.

[76] M Stratigaki, 'The Cooptation of Gender Concepts in EU Policies: The Case of "Reconciliation of Work and the Family" ' (2004) 1 *Social Politics* 30–56.

practice, many so-called 'gender impact assessments' conducted on policy proposals appear to be little more than tick box exercises, generating public cynicism that this is all a marketing exercise for schools of 'new public management' or 'political correctness'. Is mainstreaming still dominated by the language of management, 'which is result-driven, requiring instrumental and rational measurement?'[77] Alison Woodward fears that it may be, and that there is insufficient attention paid to power relationships, which undermines the transformative potential of mainstreaming.

Even so, emphasising the case for optimism, Beveridge and Nott[78] conclude that

> the concept of [gender] mainstreaming has certain characteristics which provide the basis for optimism—the resonance between the mainstreaming concept and understandings about the pathology of gender-based inequalities and the non-essentialising quality of good mainstreaming practices. These characteristics give mainstreaming a transformative potential, which previous generations of equal treatment and positive discrimination strategies seem to lack.

How this might work out in practice requires a dissection of the main elements of mainstreaming. This means a focus on the messages, the models and the strategies of mainstreaming, highlighted at the end of the first section of this paper.

Mainstreaming, the Concept of Equality and the Evolution of Equality Laws and Strategies

One of the building blocks for conceptualising mainstreaming and ascertaining its *message* must inevitably be the concept of 'equality', which is a highly contested term.[79] Commentators often cite the basic dichotomy between formal and substantive equality.[80] Formal equality has its most traditional expression in Aristotle's notion of 'treating like as like'. The traditional Aristotelian 'likeness' standard is closely conceptually linked with the formal nature of law and legal norms. Legal norms find great difficulty incorporating differentiated standards based on 'treatment as an equal' rather than universalist standards of equal treatment. The problems with the approach of 'treating like as like' are manifest. Women are

---

[77] A Woodward, *Gender mainstreaming in European policy: Innovation or deception?*, WZB Discussion Paper FSI 01-03, Berlin, 2001, 29.

[78] Beveridge and Nott, n 73 above, 310.

[79] D Cooper, *Challenging Diversity: Rethinking Equality and the Value of Difference* (Cambridge University Press, 2004).

[80] G More, 'Equal Treatment of the Sexes in European Community Law: What does "Equal" Mean?' (1993) 1 Feminist Legal Studies, 45–74.

not necessarily 'like' men in the relevant sense or senses. The archetypal absurd question in the gender equality field has been whether a woman is 'like' or 'unlike' a man when she is pregnant. In the EU law context, the deployment of concepts of direct and indirect discrimination has made it possible for the EU gender equality law to begin to take account, for example, of women's double burden in the context of work and domestic labour.[81]

The sameness/difference dichotomy has meant, however, that where claims are made on the part of women or ethnic minorities for special treatment, especially to correct historical disadvantage or the effects of structural disadvantage in the labour market, these appear to contradict the highly valued formal principle of equal treatment. Hence, in the Union context, there has been a lively debate about extent of permissible positive action.[82] In its case law on positive action in favour of women as an under-represented sex in certain sectors of the economy, from *Kalanke*[83] to *Abrahamsson*,[84] the Court of Justice has taken an unsympathetic view of 'hard quotas', because these contravene the formal equality rights of disappointed (male) applicants. So-called 'hard quota' systems involve the automatic appointment of a member of the under-represented group to a particular post, providing she or he has the minimum qualifications, until a certain quota has been filled, regardless of the qualifications of members of the over-represented group. Only if there are appropriate savings clauses which protect members of the over-represented group in certain specified circumstances (such as cases of particular hardship) are quota systems permissible under EU law.[85] In the Union context, as has been suggested, 'the focus on market integration

---

[81] See generally T Hervey and J Shaw, 'Women, work and care: Women's dual role and double burden in EC sex equality law' (1998) 8 *Journal of European Social Policy*, 43–63.

[82] D Caruso, 'Limits of the Classic Method: Positive Action in the European Union after the New Equality Directives' (2003) 44 Harvard International Law Journal, 331–386.

[83] Case C-450/93 *Kalanke v Land Bremen* [1995] ECR I-3051.

[84] Case C-407/98 *Abrahamsson v Fogelqvist* [2000] ECR I-5539.

[85] The issue of positive action in favour of members of ethnic minorities (Article 5 of Directive 2000/43) has not yet come before the Court of Justice, given the novelty of the relevant legislative framework, but there is no reason to believe that the Court will not take a similarly formalistic view. Likewise, the Court may in the future be faced with the task of interpreting the positive action derogation in the general employment equality directive (Article 7 of Directive 2000/78). In relation to disability in particular it may be faced with the delicate task of interpreting the interaction between positive action and reasonable accommodation of the needs of disabled people by employers: Z. Apostolopoulou, 'Equal Treatment of People with Disabilities in the EC: What does "Equal" mean?', Jean Monnet Working Paper No. 9/04, *http://www.jeanmonnetprogram.org/papers/04/040901.html* (visited: 15 June 2005).

shapes the discursive terrain in ways which make it difficult to think of affirmative action as other than "preferential treatment" '.[86]

For disabled people, likewise, the concepts of direct and indirect discrimination are not helpful legal instruments to ensure full social inclusion through participation in the workplace or through access to services, facilities and premises. For such people, a concept of 'reasonable accommodation' discrimination is needed, as is provided for in Article 5 of the employment equality directive.[87] Taking into account the diversity of people seeking employment or access to services or facilities, what reasonable accommodations should an employer or service provider be required to make?

The sameness and difference approaches—notwithstanding their limitations—have each been associated with certain types of legal measures to promote equality and to combat discrimination, such as prohibitions on discrimination and measures to promote positive action, and the like. The limits to equality laws have been explored by commentators for many years, especially in the United States, but also more recently in the UK and elsewhere in the Union.[88] Emanuela Lombardo has expressed dissatisfaction with the practical effects on women of Union measures intended to promote equality for women in terms of the 'Wollstonecraft Dilemma', whereby such measures fail to benefit women because they do not escape from the patriarchal effects of the relevant 'gender regimes'[89] in which they are applied.[90] The same considerations can apply *mutatis mutandis* to laws enacted to combat discrimination on other grounds such as racial or ethnic origin, disability, age or sexual orientation.[91]

The difficulties of formulating and applying discrimination law are even greater if more than one ground of inequality is at issue. For example, black women frequently face multiple discrimination which cannot be

---

[86] C Bacchi, 'Policy and discourse: challenging the construction of affirmative action as preferential treatment' (2004) 11 *Journal of European Public Policy*, 128–146, 142.

[87] L Waddington and A Hendriks, 'The Expanding Concept of Employment Discrimination in Europe: From Direct and Indirect Discrimination to Reasonable Accommodation Discrimination' (2002) 18 *International Journal of Comparative Labour Law and Industrial Relations*, 403–27. *Mutatis mutandis* mainstreaming poses particular challenges in the context of combating discrimination on grounds of disability: S Witcher, 'Mainstreaming Equality: the implications for disabled people' (2004) 4 *Social Policy and Society*, 55–64.

[88] Eg N Lacey, 'Legislation Against Sex Discrimination: Questions from a Feminist Perspective' (1987) 14 Journal of Law and Society, 411–21.

[89] S Walby, 'The European Union and Gender Equality: Emergent Varieties of Gender Regime' (2004) 11 *Social Politics*, 4–29.

[90] E Lombardo, 'EU Gender Policy: Trapped in the "Wollstonecraft Dilemma?"' (2003) 10 *European Journal of Women's Studies*, 159–80.

[91] See the review of UK equality legislation published as B Hepple, M Coussey and T Choudhury, *Equality: A New Framework*, Report of the Independent Review of the Enforcement of UK Anti-Discrimination Legislation (Oxford: Hart Publishing, 2000).

simply treated on an additive basis as a combination of their gender *and* their membership of an ethnic minority.[92] On the contrary, their experience should neither be fragmented into separate experiences as a woman (compared with a man), or as a black person (compared to a white person), nor 'essentialised' and thus frozen in a reductive manner through an additive approach. Thus American scholars[93] have criticised the extrapolation:

- racism + sexism = straight black woman's experience
- racism + sexism + homophobia = lesbian black woman's experience

One of the dangers of this approach is that each 'experience' of discrimination or inequality can become isolated from each of the others, whereas often it is the intersection (eg the combination of racist, sexist and homophobic abuse in the workplace) which is the very core of the oppressive or demeaning experience that a person suffers.

For all these reasons, whether related to the limitations of traditional equality law, or the challenges posed by complex inequalities, it is important to see the struggle for equality and diversity not as a 'thing' or a 'concept', but more contextually as a process and a strategy. In that way it becomes possible to develop three linked strategies of equality all of which need to be given priority at different times and in different contexts[94]:

- a strategy of inclusion: under which the exclusion of groups such as women, ethnic minorities, disabled people or older people from the labour market is challenged, initially at least on the grounds of a claim for equal treatment—under this approach, the individual experience is at the core of challenge to exclusion;

- a strategy of reversal: under which the dominant culture (male, white, heterosexist, disablist) is problematised, and claims for positive action are made—under this approach, the status of the group is brought to the forefront, but equally is subject to the argument that this disadvantages individuals from within the dominant groups; and

---

[92] S Hannett, 'Equality at the Intersections: The Legislative and Judicial Failure to Tackle Multiple Discrimination' (2003) 23 OJLS, 65–86.

[93] For a review see S Sturm, 'Law, Norms and Complex Discrimination' in R Nelson and L B Nielsen (eds), *Rights and Realities: New Perspectives on Anti-Discrimination Law* (The Hague: Kluwer Law International, 2005, forthcoming); the practical application of intersectionality in relation to the discrimination faced by women migrant domestic workers through international human rights law is explored by M Satterthwaite, 'Crossing Borders, Claiming Rights: Using Human Rights Law to Empower Women Migrant Workers' (2005) 8 *Yale Human Rights and Development Law Journal*, forthcoming, *http://ssrn.com/abstract=680181* (visited: 14 June 2005).

[94] J Squires, *Gender in Political Theory* (Cambridge: Polity Press, 1999). Compare the more descriptive conclusion of Bell, n 9 above, referring to three 'strands' evident in the Union's approach to equality: ensuring anti-discrimination in the formal sense, working towards substantive equality, and managing diversity.

- a strategy of displacement, in which the very nature of the dichotomies of male/female, white/black, able-bodied/disabled, heterosexual/homosexual is challenged and a politics of diversity begins to be developed.

According to Judith Squires, this latter 'diversity perspective' is 'not located on either side of the equality/difference divide, but rather gains its definition from its commitment to deconstructing the division itself.'[95]

She argues that the diversity perspective is particularly useful for the purposes of conceptualising mainstreaming, in a way which is more likely to capture its full transformative potential. Before turning to this, and to the various approaches to understanding the mainstreaming of diversity which have been developed in the context of feminist theory and other critical social theories, it is interesting first to see that the private sector has picked up the diversity issue in a rather different way. This has taken the form of the so-called 'business case for diversity,' which is now incorporated into much management thinking.[96] Equality and diversity plans are now widely used as mechanisms for both affecting workplace demographics and addressing inclusive practices *vis-à-vis* employees and customers. They have become key instruments to enable companies to secure global competitiveness, and in this context diversity refers in particular to workplace demographics and to the need for inclusive behaviour.[97] In particular, addressing diversity is widely perceived as a necessary element of creating a positive and effective working environment via the insights that:

the workplace environment should be inclusive to all; that a wholesale change of culture is required to achieve this; and that concrete, imaginative and systematic innovation is necessary to reach these goals.[98]

In this context moral considerations are seen as essentially side issues.[99] Furthermore:

The diversity perspective deviates from the traditional legislative model in two main ways. First, despite taking the individual as the starting point, the diversity

---

[95] Squires, n 94 above, 124.

[96] L Barmes with S Ashtiany, 'The Diversity Approach to Achieving Equality: Potential and Pitfalls' (2003) 32 ILJ, 274–96; L Barmes, 'Promoting Diversity and the Definition of Direct Discrimination' (2003) 32 ILJ, 200–13.

[97] S Point and V Singh, 'Playing out Equality and Diversity on the Web across Europe', Paper 144 submitted to the SAM/IFSAM Conference, Gothenburg, 2004, available from *http://www.handels.gu.se/ifsam/* (visited: 14 June 2005).

[98] Barmes with Ashtiany, n 96 above, 275.

[99] See generally, *The Costs and Benefits of Diversity. A Study on Methods and Indicators to Measure the Cost-Effectiveness of Diversity Policies in Enterprises*, Report drawn up for the European Commission, October 2003, Executive Summary available at

perspective operates far less individualistically than the law. In practice . . . it takes a systemic approach. So organisational measures to achieve change are central. Individual complaints are not needed to initiate action and there is no necessity to engage with apportioning blame for past wrongs.

Second, the diversity perspective's emphasis on concrete steps to enhance inclusiveness, with the particular concern to accommodate difference, contrasts with the traditional legal model's resistance to any differentiation on a prohibited ground. In effect, the diversity perspective countenances differential treatment on grounds of race and sex, or in relation to other barriers to participation, so long as the objective is to promote diversity. In other words, the diversity perspective envisages positive action, in the sense of measures targeted to redressing difficulties faced by particular groups or individuals and always provided the steps taken do not give anyone an unfair advantage.[100]

The relationship with the law, however, can be a difficult question. According to Lizzie Barmes, law in fact could have the effect of 'chilling' the diversity approach. The limits of the diversity approach are set by the limits of (formal) equality law as presently interpreted, paying no particular regard to the circumstance that 'Employers who accept diversity ideas are voluntarily assuming positive obligations to promote equality.'[101]

The question remains why that might be so. Why are employers voluntarily accepting the diversity approach, not only in the United States where this approach originated, but increasingly in many European countries? The answer appears to be that diversity seems less confrontational than discrimination, and indeed positive obligations themselves can be put into a better light for employers than the rather negative task of avoiding discrimination. From many perspectives, therefore, diversity is about translating the 'quest for equality' into a theory of management, with its outputs being discernible on the balance sheet.[102] Ultimately, though, it is also about a (private sector) hostility to regulation.

Should one conclude from this, therefore, that regulators have given up on developing the role of law in the field of equality and diversity in favour of promoting market forces as drivers of change, or indeed that they are likely to do so in the near future? I would argue that this is far from the case, and evidence can be drawn from the case studies of the implementation of mainstreaming ideas discussed in the following section of this paper, especially the continuing endeavour to give constitutional force to equality in the context of the EU and the development

---

http://europa.eu.int/comm/employment_social/fundamental_rights/pdf/pubsg/costben_en.pdf (visited: 14 June 2005).

[100] Barmes with Ashtiany, n 96 above, 281.   [101] Ibid, 289.
[102] Ibid, 295.

of so-called positive duties on public authorities to promote equality, which are becoming increasingly commonplace in the United Kingdom, and may be extended in due course to the EU. In practice, much which now comes under the heading of 'mainstreaming' in the policy maker's toolkit concerns the challenge of producing innovative (and hopefully effective) legal solutions which harness some of law's normative power in order to promote equality, while avoiding most of the pitfalls of traditional individualistic equality laws. In other words, there has been a turn to more collective approaches and solutions, and these have used both traditional hard law approaches focused on legal duties as well as softer forms of 'new governance', such as those discussed in 'Constitutional and governance reform' above. This trend will be explored in more detail in the next section when we come to discuss the possible practical realisation of the challenges raised by Article III-118 CT.

Applying the Diversity Approach: Towards Mainstreaming

Thus far the argument has been developed that when considering which policy mechanisms or strategies are appropriate to the diversity perspective, for a variety of reasons, 'mainstreaming' appears to fit the bill—both as a theoretical approach and as a political strategy. Pragmatically, mainstreaming is attractive because it moves the focus from the results of discrimination towards its causes, and because it uses a variety of policy tools to achieve its goals.[103] On the other hand, there is no single definition of mainstreaming, and some fear that as a strategy it is too vague to be useful and presents a risk that those who become engaged in the process (eg NGOs, social partners) may find that they are being co-opted or that their objectives are being diluted. Mainstreaming may be more deception than it is innovation.[104]

There are also a number of theoretical issues which help to make mainstreaming an attractive option, and it is to these that we must now turn. Sylvia Walby argues that gender mainstreaming involves 'the re-invention, restructuring, and re-branding of a key part of feminism in the contemporary era'.[105] Hankivsky takes a more critical approach, arguing that:

the discursive effects of [gender mainstreaming] on constructions of gender and equality are not being interrogated. In particular, the potential of recent feminist theory for providing conceptual and analytical knowledge of the complex

---

[103] T Donaghy, 'Mainstreaming: Northern Ireland's participative-democratic approach' (2004) 32 *Policy and Politics* 49–62 at 50.
[104] Woodward, n 77 above.   [105] Walby, n 17 above, 2.

circumstances involving gender differences and intersectionalities, and multiple identities remains largely uninvestigated.[106]

In that respect, she echoes Verloo's concern that instruments to promote gender mainstreaming should have a 'dynamic connection to feminist academic knowledge'.[107] In fact, there is a slowly emerging critical and explicitly feminist critique of mainstreaming, one which precisely engages with the tensions which Hankivsky wishes to explore, in relation to the role of gender in the context of mainstreaming. Walby sees one of the main issues central to the analysis of gender mainstreaming as the relationship to other complex equalities.[108] Writing in 2002, Beveridge and Nott hinted that the time would soon be ripe for 'gender mainstreaming' to cede centre-stage in favour of a more generalised approach taking into account different grounds or inequalities. In other words, a more generalised approach of equality or diversity mainstreaming should replace the more limited approach of gender mainstreaming.[109] In their view, it is precisely the transformative potential of 'mainstreaming' as a model of politics which ultimately challenges the utility of a single-stranded *gender* mainstreaming approach and mandates the more generalised approach of mainstreaming equality and diversity. Far from diluting gender mainstreaming, the mainstreaming of equality and diversity more generally, and the challenge to deal with complex inequalities, precisely realises the transformative potential of gender mainstreaming and prevents it failing and disappointing.[110]

Likewise, Squires starts from the premise that 'equality can no longer be considered in isolation from diversity', with all the potential challenges which the diverse and sometimes conflicting claims of different social groups thereby entail.[111] Her analysis leads to some important conclusions about the messages and models of mainstreaming deriving from the threefold division of equality strategies highlighted earlier. She accepts, for example, the pragmatic conclusion that mainstreaming is not as such *only* a strategy of *displacement* rather than a strategy of inclusion or reversal. Although in some ways it goes beyond equality of opportunity

---

[106] Hankivsky, n 16 above, 2.

[107] M Verloo, *Another Velvet Revolution? Gender Mainstreaming and the Politics of Implementation*, IWM Working Paper No. 5/2001, Vienna, 2001, 17.

[108] Walby, n 17 above, 2.

[109] Beveridge and Nott, n 73 above, 310.

[110] Hankivsky, n 16 above, 21–22, seeks to demonstrate this through practical examples such as policy on HIV/AIDS and people trafficking.

[111] J Squires, 'Is Mainstreaming a Transformative Practice? Theorising Mainstreaming in the Context of Diversity and Deliberation' (2005) 12 *Social Politics*, issue no. 3, forthcoming (the page numbers refer to the draft typescript).

and positive action, it can also entail the incorporation of these two strategies. So long as the underlying premises of the legal and constitutional orders of the Member States and the European Union remain untouched, that will indeed be the only way in which a policy of mainstreaming will be able to operate effectively in the Union context. For they operate as liberal legal systems which privilege systems of formal legal rights and individual procedural justice. At the present time, the policy toolkit of mainstreaming, such as the techniques detailed in the next section of this paper, all build upon the premise of a liberal legal and constitutional order. At the present time, these premises are not fundamentally disrupted.

In any event, pragmatically, it is widely agreed that a clear legal status matters in order to make mainstreaming work effectively.[112] Moreover, as McCrudden comments, it is important to avoid 'over-fragmentation of equality policy, especially if it becomes an alternative to traditional anti-discrimination and other equality mechanisms'.[113] However, Squires' analysis of the transformative potential of mainstreaming is useful precisely because it highlights the potential of mainstreaming in terms of processes of decision-making, as well as outcomes. In other words, she links the *message* to be mainstreamed to the *model* of mainstreaming, through a concern with the question of democracy and—more specifically—democratic deliberation.

There have been two influential typologies of mainstreaming models. Rounaq Jahan distinguished in 1995 between the integrationist, agenda-setting and transformative models of mainstreaming.[114] Squires summarises these as follows:[115]

> The first approach is now fairly widely accepted to entail a focus on experts and the bureaucratic creation of evidence-based knowledge in policy-making, whilst the second model is perceived to entail a focus on the participation, presence and empowerment of disadvantaged groups . . . via consultation with civil society organisations . . . The features of the third, transformative model of mainstreaming are much less easy to discern in theory or in practice . . . The clear weakness of this model is its lack of specificity . . . [O]ne of [its] greatest strengths . . . is that it is best placed, of the three models, to address the emergent 'diversity' agenda.

More recently, Nott has drawn a related distinction between the so-called 'participative-democratic' and 'expert-bureaucratic' models of mainstreaming.[116] In brief, the expert-bureaucratic model

---

[112] McCrudden, n 15 above, 110.   [113] Ibid.

[114] R Jahan, *The Elusive Agenda: Mainstreaming Women in Development* (Atlantic Highlands: Zed Books, 1995), 126.   [115] Squires, n 111 above, 7, 11.

[116] S Nott, 'Accentuating the positive: alternative strategies for promoting gender equality', in Beveridge *et al*, n 23 above, 247.

relies heavily on a 'gender' expert(s) being located within the bureaucracy, such as a women's unit, and has been popular in countries such as Australia (both at federal and state levels), New Zealand and Canada. The participative-democratic model is the more recently developed (and tends to be the model which is most likely to incorporate multiple equality areas). It relies primarily on the participation of civic community groups through a consultation process. It has been popular in the UK and is epitomised in the Northern Ireland model.[117]

To put it another way, 'participative-democratic' mainstreaming is easier to see as 'real' mainstreaming, for it encourages transparency and full participation in decision-making as an indirect benefit.[118] It is also the only reasonable means for ensuring effective, legitimate and equitable trade-offs between sometimes competing interests. As McCrudden puts it:

It is intended to be anticipatory rather than retrospective, to be extensively participatory rather than limited to small groups of the knowledgeable, and to be integrated into activities of those involved in policy-making.[119]

Squires takes the analysis much further by distinguishing more clearly between the agenda-setting and transformative approaches, both of which seem, in some ways, to be collapsed together into Nott's model of participative-democratic mainstreaming. In particular, she distinguishes between the agenda-setting dimension of civil society participation (which is premised upon the culture of consultation and the politics of presence, but with the danger that there may be conflicts and tensions between different groups representing competing identities) and the possibilities of a transformative approach based on 'parity of participation' and impartiality in process. She cites Shane O'Neill,[120] who articulates the project of democratic deliberation as being the challenge

to conceive of how we might reflect critically, and impartially, on principles of justice without abstracting from concrete needs and interests that are particular to some social group or other . . . [suggesting that this will only be possible] if we can ground impartiality not in a hypothetical contract but rather in a conception of a reasonable yet open and unrestricted dialogue in the public domain.

Squires' conclusion is that 'mainstreaming is best understood as a transformative strategy when it is conceptualised as a means of pursuing complex equality via inclusive deliberation'.[121] Although it is now groping towards a culture of participatory democracy, the European Union is still

---

[117] Donaghy, n 25 above, 51. [118] McCrudden, n 15 above, 110.
[119] Ibid, 109.
[120] S O'Neill, *Impartiality in Context: Grounding Justice in a Pluralist World* (New York: SUNY Press, 1996), 56, 57. [121] Squires, n 111 above, 19–20.

hard to view in such terms, whether through conceptual vocabulary or practices of policy making. Returning to Nott's distinction, it is clear that the EU has a much stronger and longer experience with the 'expert-bureaucratic' model of mainstreaming than with the 'democratic-participative' model. Indeed, that has been no bad thing at certain points in the past history of equality policy, so far as it has given a 'kick start' to the whole project of policy making. Strategically positioned 'femocrats' within the Commission's bureaucracy have often been important triggers of change.[122] However, in terms of *strategies* of mainstreaming, Squires cites at least one mechanism with which the Union may be about to start experimenting in a post-Constitutional Treaty phase, namely citizens' initiatives under Article I-47(4) CT, allowing no less than one million citizens to present an initiative for a policy proposal to the European Commission. We return to this possibility briefly in 'Implementing Article III-118 CT: Implementation and Enforcement', below.

This section has shown clear inter-relationships between the different elements that go to make up the concept of mainstreaming, namely the messages, the models and the strategies. An increasingly important body of work seeks specifically to link mainstreaming to critical theories of difference and diversity, and to draw it away from the managerialist philosophies which often dominate the work of international organisations, including the European Union. What that means in practice is not, however, clear as yet. From the point of view of legal strategies to implement mainstreaming, stepping outside the familiar terrain of constitutional guarantees of equality, legislative frameworks to prohibit discrimination, and procedural structures which privilege individual over collective claims leads to uncertainty about exactly what might result if equality mainstreaming becomes a pervasive *leitmotiv* for the European Union. As Martin Loughlin presciently warned in 1992, the whole domain of so-called 'new public management' lacks a thorough-going 'legal and constitutional consciousness'.[123] Since that time, the European Union has matched other polities in pursuing what are now called new governance strategies with enthusiasm. In some cases, there have been attempts to link new governance to participatory democracy.[124] While the Constitutional Treaty undoubtedly does not contain any dramatic shift away from a liberal constitutional framework in its approach to providing the 'power map' of the polity,[125] it does open up some interesting

---

[122] C Hoskyns, *Integrating Gender* (London: Verso, 1996).
[123] M Loughlin, *Public Law and Political Theory* (Oxford University Press, 1992), 260.
[124] Armstrong, n 60 above.
[125] Ivo Duchacek famously called constitutions 'power maps': see *Power Maps: Comparative Politics of Constitutions* (Santa Barbara, CA: Clio Press, 1973).

possibilities for a new politics of equality and diversity which harnesses the potential of new governance strategies, without discarding the achievements of 'old governance'. It is therefore to the implementation of Article III-118 CT that we turn in the final substantive section of this paper.

Implementing Article III-118 CT: Mainstreaming Equality and Diversity in the Era of Constitutionalism and New Governance

The second section of this paper set out in brief some of the key steps taken towards the constitutionalisation of equality and diversity in the European Union, especially in the formal context of the negotiation and signature of the Constitutional Treaty. At the time of writing (mid 2005), it was no means clear whether that Treaty would be ratified by the Member States. However, the argument has proceeded on an 'as if' basis, assuming that ratification would occur, and in particular by identifying the potential offered by the new transversal mainstreaming provision due to be introduced into the legal framework of the Union by the Constitutional Treaty—Article III-118 CT. Furthermore, there has been much discussion about prospective and informal implementation of such uncontroversial aspects of the Constitutional Treaty as do not require formal Treaty amendment. The implementation of the promise of Article III-118 CT in relation to the mainstreaming of equality and diversity could be a case in point. As we noted at the very beginning of this article, this provision mandates the Union in its law and policy making to 'aim to combat discrimination based on sex, racial or ethnic origin, religion or belief, disability, age or sexual orientation.' At the present time, Article III-118 is largely an empty vessel. It is not clear what it adds to the status quo of EU law and policy on equality, given that no new competences or legal bases are established in this field under the Constitutional Treaty, and the existing legal bases such as Article III-124 CT (ex Article 13 EC) are largely retained unchanged, with a requirement of a unanimous vote under Article III-124(1) before any legislative measures may be adopted. Since the Treaty of Nice, it has already been possible for so-called incentive measures to be adopted under the existing Article 13(2) EC by qualified majority vote in the Council of Ministers, with the European Parliament acting as a co-legislator. Thus at first sight Article III-118 CT adds little more than a rhetorical flourish to the existing provisions.

A range of reflections, developments, reforms and experiments from studies and practices within the fields of European governance and constitutionalism can provide some clues as to how it might most effectively be implemented. This includes questioning whether the constitutionalisation of a principle of participatory democracy through Article I-47 CT can also make a contribution in this context. To this end, 'Constitutional and governance reform' above set out important background. What is also important is that this analysis of the potential of Article III-118 CT draws upon the ideational toolkit of mainstreaming, as it has developed in various contexts and jurisdictions, and its important links to theories of social justice and power, including feminism. Here we can draw upon the insights developed in 'Mainstreaming reconsidered' above. A broad definition of the types of strategies and practices which could fall within the general scope of the mainstreaming toolkit is taken. Hence, in this section we review a number of aspects of the effects and meanings of Article III-118 CT, such as its place within the constitutional system, which go the conventional route of mainstreaming practices, but which—it can be argued—nonetheless help to foster a culture of equality and diversity within policy making. Hence we begin with the question of the role of Article III-118 CT as a specifically *constitutional* text.

Article III-118 CT as Constitutional Text

In earlier work, I made the case for focusing on the constitutional inclusiveness of the European Union as an emergent polity, specifically by reference to the 'undoubtedly foundational character of constitutional law and discourse for any polity'. Constitutionalism is important not least because it offers 'a privileged frame of reference for questioning the boundaries, nature and purpose' of a polity.[126] Decisions as to where equality is located within the constitutional framework, what type of principle of equality is embodied in the text, and how it is protected are, therefore, all matters of intense legal and political interest. To the extent that the Constitutional Treaty embodies a clearer strand of social values and principles including equality and diversity throughout its constituent elements than the existing foundational treaties (EC Treaty and Treaty on European Union), it offers an interesting test case for the earlier argument, at least when it comes to the task of implementation and practical realisation. It is often argued that the impact on public authorities of a strongly worded obligation to engage in the mainstreaming of gender, or equality, with a clear legal basis, is fundamental to the success of mainstreaming endeavours, not least because it overcomes resistance on the

---

[126] Shaw, n 10 above, 215.

part of policy makers.[127] While acknowledging the arguments that the Constitutional Treaty is not (yet?) a 'real' constitution for the European Union, but rather perpetuates the hybrid mix of constitutional and international elements which underpin its founding order,[128] it is nonetheless hard to see a more authoritative expression of a public desire to eradicate discrimination than Article III-118 CT provides. On the other hand, the dangerously open terms of the text provide little in themselves. To that end, Mark Bell has expressed disappointment that the Member States did not decide to include a Protocol indicating how the transversal clauses are to be interpreted and applied, as they did in the case of the enhanced role given to national parliaments in the Union legislative process through the new Early Warning System, and in relation to the application of the principles of subsidiarity and proportionality.[129]

If the language of the constitutional texts is indeed a central matter of political and legal concern, what difference does it make that Article III-118 CT, like Article III-124 CT, is phrased in terms of 'combating discrimination' rather than 'eliminating inequality'? Does this mean that the practices of mainstreaming conducted under this provision must of necessity take on a different tenor to gender mainstreaming, where the constitutionally embedded provision (currently Article 3(2) EC; Article III-116 under the Constitutional Treaty) is phrased in terms of 'eliminating inequalities'? Alternatively, since the task of combating discrimination is in any event understood as including indirect as well as direct discrimination, and indirect discrimination is said to be more apt to foster substantive equality than direct discrimination alone, is the difference between the two wordings effectively elided? The legal test of 'discrimination' also dominates those texts of the Charter of Fundamental Rights which are concerned with equality questions. In that respect, Article III-118 CT echoes Article II-81 CT. However, the latter provision goes much further, in that it refers not just to a closed list of six grounds, but rather to the prohibition on discrimination on *any ground*, listing as examples not only the six grounds cited in Articles III-118 and III-124 CT, but also others such as social origin, genetic features, membership of a national minority and birth as part of an open list. This provision could potentially be used to argue that any project of equality mainstreaming developed by

---

[127] P Chaney, 'The post-devolution equality agenda: the case of the Welsh Assembly's statutory duty to promote equality of opportunity' (2004) 32 *Policy and Politics*, 63–77, 73.

[128] See further Shaw, n 44 above.

[129] Bell, n 66 above, 10 (page numbers refer to the draft typescript). The Protocol on Subsidiarity and Proportionality dates back to the Treaty of Amsterdam, but the Protocol on National Parliaments is new.

the Union cannot realistically be rigidly restricted in its focus, by reference to limitations drawn from the list of six grounds in Article III-118 CT alone. The argument can plausibly be made that any attempt to deal with complex inequalities cannot arbitrarily pick on some and ignore others.

Another way of widening the scope of Article III-118, especially in relation to its invocation of discrimination, is to read it in conjunction with Article II-82 CT. This provision of the Charter of Fundamental Rights mandates respect for cultural, religious and linguistic diversity. It is located in the section of the Charter expressly concerned with equality, and thus conceptually links the concepts of equality and diversity in a way which has not hitherto been achieved within the constitutional system of the EU. Chloë Wallace and I have argued elsewhere that this provision contains, along with the provision on education in the Charter (Article II-74), the possible seeds of a multicultural vision for the Union.[130] This vision is all the more plausible after the conclusion of the Constitutional Treaty, which includes the rights of persons belonging to minorities in Article I-2 CT, as part of the values framework of the Union. This addition creates a more complete vision, confirming what is implicit in the text of Article II-82—namely that it envisages the existence of and need for promotion of minority cultures which require respect.[131]

Despite this emergent vision, the concept of 'minority rights' remains highly controversial within EU law and policy.[132] It has been, in particular, a contested aspect of human rights conditionality applied to applicant states during the 1990s and 2000s.[133] The phrase 'rights of persons belonging to minorities' is a phrase drawn from international law on minority rights. However, such a phrase does not always resonate comfortably with the texts and values of all of the national constitutions. Notably, in France, it can come into conflict with the notion of the unitary nature of the human person, and the difficulty which this raises with the constitutional recognition of different groups, including ethnic groups.[134]

---

[130] C Wallace and J Shaw, 'Education, Multiculturalism and the Charter of Fundamental Rights of the European Union', in Hervey and Kenner, n 9 above, 223–246.

[131] Bell, n 9 above, 108.

[132] G Schwellnus and A Wiener, 'Contested Norms in the Process of EU Enlargement: Non-discrimination and minority rights', *Constitutionalism Web-Papers*, ConWEB, No. 2/2004 available from *http://www.qub.ac.uk/schools/SchoolofPoliticsInternationalStudies/Research/PaperSeries/ConWEB Papers/*.

[133] On that process, see C Hillion, 'Enlargement of the European Union—The Discrepancy between Membership Obligations and Accession Conditions as Regards the Protection of Minorities' (2003–2004) 27 Fordham International Law Journal, 716–40.

[134] Eg France has not yet signed the Council of Europe Framework Convention for the Protection of National Minorities, Feb 1 1998, ETS No. 157.

Thus the inclusion of a similar reference to minority rights in the preamble to the Charter of Fundamental Rights had previously been blocked by France during the Charter Convention.[135] However, from the perspective of the new (post 2004) Member States it is symbolically important for them to see the formal constitutional inclusion in the Constitutional Treaty of minority rights norms against which they have been held to account, in particular by the European Commission, during the course of the accession process.

The difficulty with applying this provision concerns the absence of a single European standard in relation to minority rights which the Member States all adhere to, in particular because there is a notable lack of guidance from the case law on the European Convention of Human Rights. Article 14 ECHR, although containing a reference to 'association with a national minority', does not establish a freestanding right to non-discrimination.[136] Moreover, it is not clear whether the Article I-2 CT refers only to so-called autochtonous 'national' minority groups, which are given special protections under a number of national constitutions in the Member States, including special electoral representation,[137] or whether it extends also to so-called 'new minorities', including the groups of non-EU nationals who have migrated to the Member States since the Second World War or indeed much more recently?[138] Does the text intend to confer rights, or merely to recognise rights conferred in other contexts?

It is not only at the level of the constitutional texts that there is a rather confusing array of different provisions regarding the various dimensions of equality and diversity. There is a lack of unity in relation to legislation on anti-discrimination which constrains the possibilities of formulating cross-cutting mainstreaming efforts. At present, Union legislation and action programmes are somewhat truncated with a mixture of specialist legislation on racial equality and gender equality and general framework legislation in respect of the other grounds, and separate action programmes for equality between women and men on the one hand, and for the other five grounds enumerated in Article 13 EC, on the other. This creates a patchwork at the EU level which is inevitably replicated at the

---

[135] Bell, n 9 above, 108.

[136] O de Schutter, *The Prohibition of Discrimination under European Human Rights Law. Relevance for EU Racial and Employment Equality Directives*, Study for the European Commission, DG Emp, 2005.

[137] Eg Danes in Germany and Italians in Slovenia.

[138] S Peers, ' "New" Minorities: What Status for Third Country Nationals in the EU System?', in G Toggenburg (ed), *Minority Protection and the Enlarged European Union: The Way Forward* (Budapest: Open Society Institute, 2004), 149–162.

national level where increasingly legislation is driven by the imperatives of Union harmonisation endeavours. In its 2004 Green Paper on Anti-Discrimination the Commission has begun to raise the question about whether the Union should put in place a comprehensive single approach to equality issues which covers gender issues, as well as the other grounds enumerated in Article 13 EC, as they are also in Article III-118.[139] However, this will require substantial legislative changes in the future to be brought to fruition. The current dispersed constitutional and legislative framework is therefore likely to impact upon the effects of Article III-118 for the foreseeable future.

Positive Duties

One plausible derivation from the constitutional status of Article III-118 CT is the argument that it sets out a basic framework for *positive duties* to pursue equality goals imposed upon public authorities.[140] Sandra Fredman highlights what she calls a 'new generation' of equality laws involving positive duties which may avoid some of the pitfalls associated with 'traditional' individually equality-focused anti-discrimination laws.[141] Such duties are treated by many commentators as part of the overall 'toolkit' of mainstreaming practices. As Fredman makes clear, this is a quantum step beyond the institutions of direct and indirect discrimination.[142] She argues that such 'fourth generation'[143] duties

move beyond the fault-based model of existing discrimination law, where legal liability only rests on those individuals who can be shown to have actively discriminated, whether directly or indirectly; and the remedy is to compensate the individual victim. At the root of the positive duty, by contrast, is a recognition that societal discrimination extends well beyond individual acts of racist prejudice. Equality can only be meaningfully advanced if practices and structures are altered proactively by those in a position to bring about real change, regardless of fault or original responsibility. Positive duties are therefore proactive rather than reactive, aiming to introduce equality measures rather than to respond to complaints by individual victims.[144]

---

[139] *Equality and non-discrimination in an enlarged European Union*, COM(2004) 379, 28 May 2004. The point is also made by the European Parliament in its response to the Green Paper, *Report on the on the protection of minorities and anti-discrimination policies in an enlarged Europe*, A6-0140/2005, 10 May 2005, approved in the European Parliament on 8 June 2005.   [140] See also Bell, n 71 above, 254–5.

[141] S Fredman, 'Equality: A New Generation?' (2001) 30 ILJ 145–68 at 163–164.

[142] S Fredman, 'Combating Racism with Human Rights: The Right to Equality', in S Fredman (ed), *Discrimination and Human Rights. The Case of Racism* (Oxford University Press, 2001), 9–44.   [143] A term used in Hepple *et al*, n 91 above.

[144] Fredman, n 141 above, 163–164.

A good example of a general positive duty is that enacted under the Race Relations (Amendment) Act 2000, requiring a specified list of public authorities in Great Britain to 'pay due regard' to a) the need to eliminate racial discrimination and the complementary positive obligations to b) promote equality of opportunity and c) good relations between people of different ethnic origins. A proportionality test is used by the Commission for Racial Equality in its guidance on the meaning of 'due regard': it states that this means that 'the weight given to race equality should be proportionate to its relevance to a particular function.'[145]

The positive duty on public authorities was enacted as a result of the recommendations of the Macpherson Report in the inquiry into the racist killing of a young black man, Stephen Lawrence, in London. Of significance was that Macpherson found that the Metropolitan Police in London was 'institutionally racist'. This did not mean that any blame attached to any identified individuals, but rather that structural factors mitigated against, in that case, an effective and equitable investigation into the murder of Stephen Lawrence, because he was black. The implementation of the positive duty approach in the racial equality field is still at a relatively early stage. What is quite clear already is the transformative potential of such an approach, relying as it does on the normative power of a statutorily enacted positive duty, with an institution—the Commission for Racial Equality—responsible for implementation and monitoring.

A similar provision has recently been introduced in relation to disability discrimination in the UK by virtue of the Disability Discrimination Act 2005,[146] and is under contemplation for the case of gender discrimination.[147] However, thus far, the only experience in the UK with cross-cutting duties where intersectional issues must necessarily be directly addressed has been in relation to the devolved assemblies and bodies in Scotland, Wales and London and, with much more substantial effects, Northern Ireland. This latter case is important, for if the mainstreaming of equality and diversity were to be introduced in the EU on the basis of Article III-118 CT, the challenge of intersectionality would be a prominent issue to be resolved.

---

[145] Commission for Racial Equality, *Statutory Code of Practice on the Duty to Promote Race Equality*, (London, Commission for Racial Equality, 2002).

[146] *http://www.hmso.gov.uk/acts/acts2005/20050013.htm* (visited: 14 June 2005). C O'Cinneide, 'A New Generation of Equality Legislation? Positive Duties and Disability Rights' in A Lawson and C Gooding (eds), *Disability Rights in Europe* (Oxford: Hart Publishing, 2005), 213–31.

[147] C O'Cinneide, 'Positive Duties and Gender Equality' (2005) 6 International Journal of Discrimination and the Law, forthcoming.

Northern Ireland has provided a beacon of policy change in the UK relating to the implementation of equality principles. The legislative framework in Northern Ireland dates back to the Fair Employment Act of 1989,[148] but the major turning point was the 1998 Good Friday Agreement seeking a resolution for the long-term conflict in Northern Ireland, which draws upon 'the best international and European practice, and which identified equality and human rights as a central element in a *new constitutional settlement*' [emphasis added].[149] The focus has become that of *positive duties*, namely duties on public authorities to have regard to equality considerations in all their activities. This is to be distinguished from *positive action* which is public policy action designed specifically to benefit particular groups. The two may in some circumstances be complementary.

What is interesting about the Northern Ireland model is that it has long gone beyond gender, focusing particular attention on the two 'religio-political communities' which have been at the heart of the conflict and the so-called Troubles.[150] Furthermore, it has a firm legal foundation and is, in a strong sense, 'constitutionalised', in the Northern Ireland Act. However, the shift to a system of positive duties on authorities was not a sudden change, but had been building since the 1980s, with legislation dating from 1989 (Fair Employment Act) focusing on compulsory compliance with mechanisms intended as much to address structural inequalities in the labour market as to deal with entrenched prejudice. This legislation itself was certainly innovatory for the United Kingdom. The so-called PAFT (Policy Appraisal and Fair Treatment) Guidelines from 1994 on 'equality proofing' were likewise novel. It was widely thought that these policy innovations were to some extent 'window dressing' in response to pressure from outside, especially from the United States, and little real change at the grassroots level could be seen. Subsequently, after a review had been conducted, a move to a statutorily based PAFT with more 'teeth' was mooted. A crucial document was a review prepared by McCrudden, which was commissioned by the trade union Unison.[151]

The innovation of the policy appraisal approach has offered the possibility of a 'new politics' in which mainstreaming equality can become an

---

[148] Donaghy, n 25 above T Donaghy, 'Mainstreaming Equality in Public Policy Making: A comparative analysis of Northern Ireland and Australia's mainstreaming strategies', IPSA Paper 2003; C McCrudden, 'Mainstreaming Equality in the Governance of Northern Ireland' (1999) 22 Fordham International Law Journal 1696–775.

[149] McCrudden, n 15 above 75.

[150] McCrudden, n 15 above 76; on mainstreaming as part of a package of 'justice in transition', see C. Bell, C Campbell and F Ní Aoláin, 'Justice Discourses in Transition' (2004) 13 Social and Legal Studies 305–28.

[151] C McCrudden, *Mainstreaming Fairness? A Discussion Paper on "Policy Appraisal and Fair Treatment"* (Belfast, Committee on the Administration of Justice, 1996).

important dimension in dealing with the deep-seated divisions within society. While this is not a panacea for all ills,[152] it nonetheless has some transformatory potential. The promise of the 'Good Friday Agreement' in 1998, which contained strong provisions on equality, was in turn translated into the Northern Ireland Act 1998. This established an Equality Commission for Northern Ireland, taking over the functions of the Fair Employment Commission, the Equal Opportunities Commission for Northern Ireland, the Commission for Racial Equality for Northern Ireland and the Northern Ireland Disability Council. Section 75 imposes an equality duty on all public authorities in Northern Ireland to have 'due regard to the need to promote equality of opportunity' across all the equality grounds, including sex, race and ethnic origin, disability, age, sexual orientation and also political belief, in carrying out their public functions. Also of interest is a duty to promote 'good relations' which is imposed in respect of race, religion and political belief. This 'hard law' duty was imposed in the wake of the failure of the 'softer' PAFT guidelines. As McCrudden comments, 'the Northern Ireland experience points to the inadequacy of a 'soft law' approach.'[153] All public authorities must submit to the Equality Commission equality schemes which show how they propose to fulfil its duties under Section 75. There is a complaints and investigations process. Of significance given the political difficulties with the peace process in Northern Ireland is that the Section 75 duty operates independently of the coming into force or maintenance in operation of the devolution arrangements.

Plans were made to introduce in Northern Ireland a Single Equality Act before the end of 2002. This has not happened, not least because of the difficulties of adjusting Northern Irish law in 2003 to the requirements of the new EU equality laws. Thus the framework of equality laws governing the different strands (as opposed to the public duty referred to in Section 75) remains both differentiated and complex, with varying standards applicable to the different grounds. In enforcing the duty, the Equality Commission has tended to use a 'name and shame' approach, using publicity to try to bring public authorities into line, rather than its formal enforcement powers. As for the response of those authorities subject to the positive duty, according to Colm O'Cinneide,[154] there has been

evidence of good practice in consultation, particularly in using joined-up approaches to consult across the different strands, but there was also evidence

---

[152] T Hutchinson, *Mainstreaming Equality as a Remedy for the Ills of Anti-Discrimination Law: Panacea or Placebo?* (Queen's University of Belfast Mimeo, 2000).

[153] McCrudden, n 15 above, 111.

[154] C O'Cinneide, *Taking equal opportunities seriously: the extension of positive duties to promote equality* (London: Equality and Diversity Forum, 2003), 53.

that the practice of some authorities of using mass mailing of consultation documents was producing consultation fatigue.

Many commentators agree that such positive duties represent a (generally good) example of the 'participative-democratic' approach in action.[155] Experience in Northern Ireland has been highly influential for the formulation of the commonly agreed criteria underpinning positive duties, which some commentators have argued[156] should be applied across the board in the UK. These criteria are:

- A clear positive statutory duty to promote equality of opportunity by public authorities across all areas of government policy and activities;
- The participation of affected groups in determining how this should be achieved;
- Assessment of the impact of existing and future government policies on affected groups;
- Consideration of the alternatives which have less of an adverse impact;
- The consideration of how to mitigate impacts which cannot be avoided; and
- Transparency and openness in the process of assessment.[157]

Can Article III-118 be seen as an embryonic positive duty applicable not only to the EU institutions, but also to the national (and sub-national) institutions, and capable of taking on board the diverse challenges highlighted by the checklist above? It is interesting to note that the EU already engages in many of the impact assessment and policy appraisal activities subsumed within the overall 'positive duty' approach as sketched here. These are discussed further in 'Implementation and Enforcement' below. Moreover, can the provisions of Article I-47 CT on participatory democracy be harnessed to this text to ensure the participative-democratic nature of the approach, by requiring the participation of civil society in relation to the assessment of impact on disparate groups, beyond the rather patchy state of consultation thus far? It is interesting to note that a rejected draft amendment to Directive 76/207 on equal treatment of men and women[158] would have come close to laying down such a positive duty at

[155] Nott, n 116 above; Donaghy, n 25 above.
[156] S Fredman, *The Future of Equality in Britain*, EOC Working Paper Series, No. 5, 2002.
[157] O'Cinneide, n 154 above, 43, quoting from the 'Hepple Report': Hepple *et al*, n 91 above.
[158] Council Directive 76/207, [1976] OJ L39/40.

least in relation to gender, and at least so far as concerns the role of the Member States. It provided that:[159]

Member States shall introduce such measures as are necessary to enable them actively and visibly to promote the objective of equality between men and women by its incorporation, in particular, into all laws, regulations, administrative provisions, policies and activities . . .

Instead what was finally adopted was much milder, and more generalised in nature. Article 1 of the 2002 Equal Treatment Directive, when it passes its implementation date in October 2005,[160] will add a new paragraph to the existing 1976 directive requiring that

Member States shall actively take into account the objective of equality between men and women when formulating and implementing laws, regulations, administrative provisions, policies and activities . . .

Furthermore, under the Equal Treatment Directive, as amended, the Racial Equality Directive and the Framework Equality Directive, Member States are now obliged to set up, under national law, public bodies with the role of promoting and monitoring equal treatment issues. However, it is much harder to envisage equality duties 'trickling down' any further than public bodies to affect employer behaviour as well as the behaviour of public authorities. As a start, at least, under the Equal Treatment Directive, as amended, Member States are enjoined to 'encourage . . . employers . . . to prevent all forms of discrimination on grounds of sex . . .' (Article 2(5)).

Implementation and Enforcement

There are no clear arrangements for the enforcement of the principles contained in Article III-118 CT. It is true that so far as prohibitions on discrimination apply to the Member States, the special procedure under Article I-59 CT (ex Article 7 TEU) could be triggered, leading to the suspension of rights resulting from Union membership, in the event that there is a 'a clear risk of a serious breach by a Member State of the values referred to in Article I-2'. However, this is only likely to apply in very exceptional cases.

As the guardian of the Treaties, a role which it preserves under Article I-25 CT, the Commission should clearly play some role in relation to the

---

[159] Proposal for a Directive of the European Parliament and the Council amending Council Directive 76/207, COM(2000) 334, 7 June 2000.

[160] Directive 2002/73 of the European Parliament and the Council amending Council Directive 76/207, [2002] OJ L269/15.

implementation and enforcement of Article III-118 CT. On the other hand, there are some respects in which it is the Commission's activities themselves which may be subject to scrutiny under the heading of equality mainstreaming. At the present time, there are no independent bodies established at Union level with a brief to watch over the implementation and enforcement of provisions such as Article III-118 CT. Since 1998, a very limited oversight role has been taken by the European Union Monitoring Centre on Racism and Xenophobia, established at the end of the European Year Against Racism, which was given the role of providing the Union and its Member States with objective, reliable and comparable information and data on racism, xenophobia, islamophobia and anti-Semitism at the European level in order to help the Union and its Member States to establish measures or formulate strategies to combat racism and xenophobia.[161] The powers of the EUMC were never great, although it has established the European Racism and Xenophobia Network (RAXEN), which helps it collect information and data. Its workings thus far have not been positively evaluated,[162] and in December 2003 the European Council made a proposal that it should be abolished and replaced with a more far-reaching Fundamental Rights Agency. The process of transformation is fraught with difficulties. There exists the danger, for example, of replicating the soft political oversight mechanisms already existing under international law under the aegis of the Council of Europe.[163] Moreover, the EU already has its own separate Network of Independent Experts on Fundamental Rights, whose work would seem likely to overlap with the work of the Agency. In addition, as part of the wider Social Policy Agenda, and with the explicit encouragement of the European Council, the Commission has proposed the establishment of another sectional body, a Gender Equality Institute.[164] The main role of this body would be to help combat the pervasive and persistent gender pay gap.[165] Its main task is to be the collection and pooling of information across the Union, the development of methodological tools

---

[161] Council Regulation 1035/97, [1997] OJ L151/1.

[162] Commission Communication, *Activities of the European Monitoring Centre on Racism and Xenophobia, together with proposals to recast Council Regulation (EC) 1035/97*, COM(2003) 483, 5 August 2003.

[163] *The Fundamental Rights Agency of the European Union—A Council of Europe Perspective*, Contribution by the Secretary General of the Council of Europe, SG/Inf (2004)34, 16 December 2004.

[164] Proposal for a European Parliament and Council Regulation establishing a Gender Equality Institute, COM(2005) 81, 8 March 2005.

[165] Commission Report on Equality between Women and Men, 2005, COM(2005) 44, 14 February 2005, 4–5.

and the dissemination of information. The story here is evidently one of mixed messages, with the Union institutions simultaneously concerned with the establishment of cross-cutting and single-strand bodies. There are bound to be concerns about synergies and overlaps between the bodies. Moreover, since the collection on a common basis across all Member States of comprehensive statistical data differentiated according to the various non-discrimination and equality grounds remains the most important task which such bodies can achieve, there remain uncertainties about the effectiveness of the current piecemeal arrangements.

A very different route to 'enforcement' is suggested by Article I-47(4) CT, which introduces the novelty of 'citizens' initiatives' into the EU legal framework for the first time:

Not less than one million citizens who are nationals of a significant number of Member States may take the initiative of inviting the Commission, within the framework of its powers, to submit any appropriate proposal on matters where citizens consider that a legal act of the Union is required for the purpose of implementing the Constitution. European laws shall determine the provisions for the procedures and conditions required for such a citizens' initiative, including the minimum number of Member States from which such citizens must come.

This text was introduced at the very end of the Convention's work in June 2003, and was not fully discussed by the Convention plenary, and the likely effects of such a clause are very uncertain. Some see this as a 'second chance for democracy'—a means to move beyond the type of popular dissatisfaction with party politics and electoral politics which challenges the legitimacy of the European Parliament as much as it does other parliaments, and to harness the increasingly widespread interest which citizens show in single issue politics and interest groups.[166] It is, of course, not the necessary corollary of the inclusion of such a clause in the Constitutional Treaty that it will always be used to pressure the EU institutions and the Member States to adopt progressive measures fostering social justice and equity between different social groups. In the current climate, it seems as likely to be used to bring pressure to bear in favour of measures to restrict immigration or reduce the likelihood of further

---

[166] D Wallis and S Picard, 'The Citizens' Right of Initiative in the European Constitution: A Second Chance for Democracy?', OSI/EUMAP: Monitoring human rights and the rule of law in Europe, *www.eumap.org/journal/features/2005/demodef/wallis* (visited 14 June 2005), March 2005. See also B Kaufmann and T Schilling, *Initiative for Europe: Into New Democratic Territory. Working Paper on the Options and Limits of Article 47.4 in the EU Constitution—The European Citizens' Initiative Process*, Initiative and Referendum for Europe, Working Paper, October 2004.

enlargement of the EU. However, in the longer term, in conjunction with an enhanced role for NGOs under the participatory democracy clauses of the Constitutional Treaty, it is possible to envisage this as a soft route to ensure compliance with Article III-118 CT.

Legislation and Article III-118 CT

Although new legislation is unlikely to result from Article III-118 CT, and although the failure to ease the conditions applicable to law making under Article III-124 CT (ex Article 13 EC) means that this is likewise unlikely to result in many new legislative initiatives, Article III-118 can nonetheless be expected to have an important role to play in relation to the quality and content of Union legislation, and consequently upon the quality and content of national law, so far as this is driven by Union legislation. This will be through the mechanism of impact and compatibility assessments of proposed legislation.

Pursuant to the commitments made by Commission President José Manuel Barroso at the time of the controversy over the proposed appointment Italian politician Rocco Buttiglione to the post of Justice and Home Affairs Commissioner, with responsibility for equal opportunities and fundamental rights, a firm proposal has recently been made to 'lock in' a 'culture of fundamental rights in EU legislation'.[167] Along with conceding on demands emanating from the European Parliament for the removal of Buttiglione from his team, Barroso also established a new Commissioners' Group on Fundamental Rights, Anti-Discrimination and Equal Opportunities, which he chairs. The first initiative of this Group was a new mechanism to ensure that all Commission legislative proposals 'are systematically and rigorously checked for compatibility with the Charter of Fundamental Rights'. However, the detail of the policy raises the question of how much of this is genuinely 'new', as opposed to being an exercise in consciousness raising or rebranding of existing practices. As the Commission itself acknowledges, it has already been submitting a declaration of compatibility with the Charter of Fundamental Rights with each proposal it makes, since 2001.[168]

Compatibility assessments comprise a one-off assessment—the judgment whether a particular proposal matches a standard set, in this

---

[167] Press Release, 'President Barroso proposes a new framework to "lock-in" a culture of fundamental rights in EU legislation', IP/05/494, 27 April 2005.
[168] SEC(2001)380/3, 13 March 2001.

case, by the Charter of Rights.[169] The Commission also has considerable experience with the practice normally termed 'impact assessment', or sometimes policy appraisal. This is a more ongoing process of reviewing policy throughout the process of preparation which is less susceptible to a yes/no answer, and implies more of a long term commitment to bring policy making closer to certain stated goals. So-called 'extended impact assessment' has been developed by the European Commission as a tool to:

[help] structure the process of policy-making. It identifies the problem at stake and the objectives pursued. It identifies the main options for achieving the objective and analyses their likely impacts. It outlines the advantages and disadvantages of each option as well as synergies and trade-offs.

Impact Assessment is an *aid* to political decision, not a substitute for it. (emphasis in the original)[170]

Impact assessment is concerned with what is sometimes called 'better lawmaking'. It is an approach which comes originally from the United States. It is now well established in the UK,[171] but it has transplanted less well into other jurisdictions, because of a lack of sensitivity to context.[172] In the UK, a Regulatory Impact Assessment (RIA) is required for any proposal for legislation (primary or secondary) which has an impact on business, charities or the voluntary sector. It is an analysis of the likely impact of a range of options for implementing a policy change. It must also set out the likely costs and benefits of each option.

Impact assessment can reflect usefully a diversity of perspectives and interests. A good example is integrated policy appraisal, as practiced in some parts of the UK executive. This is a further development of the 'impact assessment' idea with a view to developing a 'sustainable development'

---

[169] On the distinction between mainstreaming, compatibility assessments and impact assessment, see O de Schutter, 'Mainstreaming Human Rights in the European Union' in Alston and de Schutter, n 98 above, 37–72.

[170] A wide range of information can be obtained from the Commission's websites on impact assessment (*http://europa.eu.int/comm/secretariat_general/impact/index_en.htm* (visited: 15 June 2005)) and on sustainable development (*http://europa.eu.int/comm/ sustainable/index_en.htm* (visited: 15 June 2005)). The key policies and guidelines are contained in Commission Communication, *Impact Assessment*, COM(2002) 276, 5 June 2002; Commission report on *Impact Assessment: Next steps—In support of competitiveness and sustainable development*, SEC(2004)1377, 21 October 2004; and Commission, *Impact Assessment in the Commission. Internal Guidelines on the new Impact Assessment Procedure developed for the Commission Services*, October 2002, which are available on these websites.

[171] The framework for impact assessment and the broader topic of 'better regulation' is constantly in evolution; the current arrangements can be gleaned from the Cabinet Office's *Better Regulation Executive: http://www.cabinetoffice.gov.uk/regulation/* (visited: 15 June 2005).

[172] C M Radaelli, 'Getting to grips with the notion of quality in the diffusion of regulatory impact assessment in Europe', Paper presented at the *Conference on Regulatory Impact Assessment: Strengthening Regulation Policy and Practice*, Manchester, November 2003.

framework.[173] 'Integrated' policy appraisal allows a wider range of factors to be taken into account and integrated together. In the UK context it *does not* replace the separate assessments such as the RIA but offers evidence to the policy maker about which separate assessments should be made.

Environmental impact assessment has been a well established policy instrument in the EU context for many years. At the national level, construction or infrastructure projects must be subjected to the scrutiny of an assessment of their impact upon the environment. Article 6 EC, as introduced by the Treaty of Amsterdam, requires that

> environmental protection requirements must be integrated into the definition and implementation of Community policies and activities . . . , in particular with a view to promoting sustainable development.

Building on this, at the Cardiff European Council in 1998, the Heads of State and Government launched a process requiring the different Council formations to integrate environmental considerations into their respective activities. This was gradually extended to agriculture, transport, energy, industry, development, internal market, economic and financial affairs, trade and fisheries. Each of the Council formations must produce its own assessment of how it plans to integrate environmental concerns in its own work.[174] Most recently, the European Commission has adopted an approach of 'extended impact assessment' looking at social, economic and environmental impacts in the wider context of sustainable development, as a tool to improve 'the quality and coherence of policy development'.[175] This builds upon the European Council's commitment at its Gothenburg meeting to a sustainable development strategy, which includes measures to deal with important threats to wellbeing, such as climate change, poverty, and emerging health risks. It also draws upon the Commission's much derided White Paper on Governance which articulated the principle of the effective analysis of all policy proposals:

> Proposals must be prepared on the basis of an effective analysis of whether it is appropriate to intervene at EU level and whether regulatory intervention is needed? If so, the analysis must also assess the potential economic, social and environmental impact, as well as the costs and benefits of that particular

---

[173] See UK Government website on tools for delivery of sustainable development: *http://www.sustainable-development.gov.uk/what/tools.htm* (visited: 15 June 2005).

[174] More details at *http://europa.eu.int/comm/environment/integration/integration.htm* (visited: 15 June 2005) and *http://europa.eu.int/scadplus/leg/en/s15001.htm* (visited: 15 June 2005).

[175] Commission Communication, *Impact Assessment*, n 170 above. See S Dupressoir, 'The new impact assessment of Commission initiatives: a tool for sustainable development?', *TUTB Newsletter*, June 2003, 9–11.

approach. A key element in such an assessment is ensuring that the objectives of any proposal are clearly defined.[176]

Accordingly, the important step taken in the Commission's Impact Assessment Communication is to link the Gothenburg sustainable development objective to the Lisbon goals in relation to socio-economic development, to produce a template for impact assessment which covers economic, environmental and social impacts in specific sectors, and also distributional impacts on major interested parties.

At all levels of decision making, from the individual to the supra-national, sustainable development is now seen less as an abstract concept. Instead, it is generally considered as making common sense decisions, appraised from a variety of angles. At a practical level for the government and agencies this means evaluating decisions with an understanding of the impact they will have on other policy areas. For example, transport decisions may have implications for health spending (positive or negative), planning decisions may have a direct impact on water and energy networks, and agricultural spending may have implications for the environment and rural communities. This concept of Impact Assessment is being championed at European level.[177]

All major policy initiatives, including regulations, directives and also programmes have been subject to an extended impact assessment since 2004. This has been gradually introduced since 2003, and replaces as an integrated process all existing separate impact assessments previously used in the analysis of Commission proposals. Preliminary assessment enables the Commission to identify those proposals which require an extended assessment. Sections in the Work Programme for each year[178] as well as the Annual Policy Strategy,[179] which prepares the ground for the next Work Programme, now contain an indication of the programme of extended impact assessment.

There are a number of factors which are significant in giving extended impact assessment more than mere rhetorical force. These include the emphasis in the Commission's Communication on the culture of consultation with interested parties, and consequently the linkage with civil society and participatory democracy,[180] and the emphasis, in the

---

[176] Commission, n 46 above, 20.
[177] G Cook, *Sustainable Development*, SPICe Briefing, 03/64.
[178] See most recently COM(2005) 15, 26 January 2005, *Work Programme for 2005*.
[179] See most recently COM(2005) 73, 2 March 2005, *Annual Policy Strategy for 2006*.
[180] C George, C Kirkpatrick and S Mosedale, 'Participation in European Governance Reform: the role of sustainability impact assessment', Paper prepared for the conference on *Participation: From Tyranny to Transformation? Exploring New Approaches to Participation in Development*, Manchester, January 2003.

guidelines for Commission staff, that impact assessment is

not a 'fiche' to be filled in just before the Commission adopts a proposal. It requires you to think through the proposal's possible impacts from the beginning of the process and, in addition, to continue to review them until the final drafting of the proposal.

These are encouraging signs that impact assessment will not simply encourage a 'tick-box mentality' and could be very much part of a democratic-participative approach to mainstreaming. It should still be noted that at the present time what is known as 'extended impact assessment' pays *no particular attention* to the equality perspective. On the contrary, until the most recent attention given to the question of fundamental rights, it was 'competitiveness' which was being given the highest billing in reviews of the impact assessment strategies.[181] Given the signal failure to pay close attention to the question of gender in the Governance White Paper, there does seems to be a significant risk of gender issues being neglected.[182] There also remains a risk that, as with other aspects of the Lisbon process, within the tripartite relationship which links employment/social cohesion, sustainable development and innovation/competition, it is the latter group of goals which is given greater emphasis rather than the former two. In other words, social goals, including equality, might be sacrificed to economic expediency and to the primacy of *economic* policy coordination in the system of the EU. This could also see the corresponding subordination of (individual and group) rights.[183]

Article III-118 offers the possibility of placing the equity and social justice dimensions of impact assessment on to a firmer legal and constitutional footing than it is at present. In that context, not only does it promise thorough and effective review of the effects of proposed legislation, but also review which is not subject to fashions or whims, whether that be fundamental rights one week, or competitiveness the next. It offers the 'legal and constitutional consciousness'[184] for new public management tools called for by Martin Loughlin.

The Turn to 'New governance' and the Open Method of Coordination

Previous subsections have highlighted the limitations of a number of tools for developing EU policies and strategies in relation to equality

---

[181] COM(2005) 15, 11; Commission Staff Working Paper, 'Next Steps', n 170 above.
[182] J Shaw, 'European Union governance and the question of gender: a critical comment', in Joerges *et al*, n 48 above.   [183] de Búrca, n 50 above, 831–835.
[184] Loughlin, n 123 above, 260.

mainstreaming. They have focused on the possibility that there will be some normative constitutional resonance from Article III-118 CT, including a set of embryonic positive duties to promote equality and diversity, especially when it is viewed in combination with a newly constitutionalised Charter of Fundamental Rights, and that impact assessment tools may be developed into effective and ongoing participatory mechanisms to secure policy-making which is sensitive to equality and diversity issues. Even so, it seems most likely that mainstreaming will involve to a significant degree the harnessing of a range of so-called 'new governance' techniques, especially the open method of coordination. For example, if open coordination is to be increasingly an alternative to harmonisation of national laws, then it is important that equality issues are mainstreamed within these softer, vaguer and more diffuse arrangements just as effectively as they are within the process of formulating and implementing harmonisation legislation. Second, it may well be that policy makers will explore the use of open coordination techniques as a specific mechanism to promote convergence in national policies in areas directly concerned with equality policy at national level, to bring about a more holistic approach to the consideration of the range of fairness and equity issues implicated within the field of equality policy.[185]

'New governance' presents some constitutional conundrums and challenges, which Armstrong, adapting the terminology of Emilios Christodoulidis, describes in terms of 'constitutional optimism' and 'constitutional pessimism'.[186] Armstrong argues that[187]

viewed pessimistically, such new modes of governance may transfer decision-making to institutions beyond the normative embrace of traditional national democratic structures. In a transnational context, the setting of binding rules to be treated as a higher form of law may restrict (democratically-chosen) policy choices, while the processes by which such rules are agreed may themselves claim

---

[185] Similar arguments are being made regarding the relevance and application of OMC to fundamental rights. The concrete proposal came from the Union's Network of Independent Experts in Fundamental Rights in its Report on the Situation of Fundamental Rights in the European Union and its Member States in 2002, 31 March 2003, available at *http://europa.eu.int/comm/justice_home/cfr_cdf/doc/rapport_2002_en.pdf* (visited: 15 June 2005), 24. For commentary, see G de Búrca, 'Beyond the Charter: How Enlargement has Enlarged the Human Rights Policy of the European Union' (2003–2004) 27 Fordham International Law Journal 679–714, 704–8; O de Schutter, 'The Implementation of the EU Charter of Fundamental Rights through the Open Method of Coordination', Jean Monnet Working Paper, No. 07/04, *http://www.jeanmonnetprogram.org/papers/04/040701.html* (visited: 15 June 2005); de Schutter, n 169 above; Smismans, n 58 above.

[186] E Christodoulidis, 'Constitutional Irresolution: Law and the Framing of Civil Society' (2003) 9 European Law Journal, 401–32.   [187] Armstrong, n 60 above, 9.

little by way of democratic legitimation. On the other hand, new modes of governance open up the possibility for us to question how well 'old' modes of governance serve us in providing democratic and constitutional legitimacy as well as suggesting new possibilities for democratic and constitutional experimentation. From this more 'optimistic' perspective, the very value of new modes of governance lies in the fact that they do indeed trouble or transgress settled understandings of democracy and constitutionalism.

Gráinne de Búrca identifies six tensions which subsist between what she terms the 'traditional' hierarchical and top-down constitutionalism of the Union and some of the key features of new governance processes.[188] These exist

between legally limited competences and ever-expanding policy activities... between the depiction of a clear division of powers amongst levels of authority in accordance with a static version of the subsidiarity principle, and the actual fluid sharing of powers and responsibilities amongst different levels in a more dynamic way... between policy segmentation, privileging or ring-fencing, and the impetus towards policy integration and linkage... between a conception of fundamental human rights as representing binding, justiciable, negative constraints on the powers of the [Union], and a conception of human rights as the articulation of values which should positively inform and shape the conduct of all actors within the system of governance... between the emphasis on representative governmental institutions as the key to legitimacy, and the inclusion of a wider array of stakeholders, civil society actors and others in response to the dual concerns of democracy and effectiveness... [and]... between the intergovernmentalism/supranationalism dichotomy which has long characterized the political debate over federalism, and the less clearly theorized but descriptively powerful conception of multilevel governance.

Another way of putting this latter concern is to suggest that there has thus far been little indication about what constructive role a political principle of subsidiarity can play in relation to the evolution of new governance approaches, such as to lend substance to the rather vague conception of the governance of the Union as a multi-level but heterarchical exercise.

Linking these concerns back to the transformative potential of mainstreaming as a new mode of politics, it is clear that the key question is not just *whether* to engage in the coordination of national policies, but rather *how* to do so and how to do so in a manner which ensures the embedding of constitutional principles such as equality. In this context, it needs to be asked whether the perils of bringing in an unregulated and

---

[188]   de Búrca, n 50 above, 814.

perhaps unrepresentative civil society, and perhaps encouraging too much of an informal sphere of politics,[189] outweigh the chances that a participatory process will foster social justice through policies which spread costs and benefits more evenly because policy makers are better informed about the consequences of their choices. This is a field in which the Constitutional Treaty could have made an important contribution.

In fact, on the whole, the framers of the Constitutional Treaty did not choose to focus on the informal and 'new governance' spheres of Union politics. The main thrust of the reforms to the existing Treaties lies in areas such as the clarification of competences and the relationships between the Union and the Member States, the simplification of the legislative process and legal instruments, and the introduction of some elements to improve the effectiveness of the Union institutions. These are the traditional spheres of 'government' rather than 'governance'. Despite strong encouragement to do so, both from within the Convention membership and from commentators outside,[190] the Praesidium of the Convention chose not to put before the Convention's plenary a text which 'constitutionalised' OMC. OMC is not mentioned anywhere in the Constitutional Treaty, in particular not in Part I, which states the basic constitutional and governance principles of the Union. What does appear, in Article III-213 CT, is a descriptive text, not a definition. Article III-213 covers a wide range of social policy areas where the Commission is called upon to encourage cooperation between the Member States, and to facilitate the coordination of their action, including areas such as employment, labour law and working conditions, and social security. It then refers to how the Commission can organise 'initiatives aiming at the establishment of guidelines and indicators, the organization of exchange of best practice, and the preparation of the necessary elements for periodic monitoring and evaluation'. This is a phrasing picked up also in relation to policy on research and technological development (Article III-250 CT), public health (Article III-278 CT), and industry (Article III-279 CT). It draws to some extent upon established descriptions of the range of activities typically covered by open coordination, including the text of the existing Article 129 EC, which refers to exchanges of information and best practices in the field of employment policy, a text which is picked up again in Article III-206 CT. The coordination of national employment

---

[189] Christiansen, Føllesdal and Piattoni, n 43 above, 2–4.

[190] G de Búrca and J Zeitlin, 'Constitutionalising the Open Method of Coordination What Should the Convention Propose?' (2003), Centre for European Policy Studies Brief No. 31.

policies through the open method is, as was noted in 'Constitutional and governance reform: The reform process' above, the 'parent' of the wider spectrum of OMCs currently being developed under the aegis of the Union. To that extent, therefore, it can be extrapolated that these texts in Part III of the Constitutional Treaty represent a constitutional recognition of the existence of OMC, if not a formal constitutionalisation.

Although the text in Article III-213 in some way crystallises the practice of OMC, providing for the European Parliament to be kept informed, it does not go as far as many NGOs would have wanted in setting out the obligations of the Commission or the national governments. It does not specifically refer to the role of civil society in relation to these processes, and thus provides no real mechanism for ensuring the accountability of the actors involved. This remains an unsatisfactory outcome, therefore, for many of the actors most closely involved in the delivery of OMC at the national and, in particular, the regional level, as a new governance mechanism.

Conclusion

This article has sought to bring together two important constitutional concerns of the European Union at the present time, namely the task of giving constitutional form and force to principles of equality and diversity and the challenge of delivering effective, transparent and legitimate governance. The objectives of the Union now clearly include principles of equality and diversity, as well as strong references to the framework of non-discrimination as a legal approach to remedying social injustice or social exclusion. This was already the case, in many respects, before the Constitutional Treaty was ever contemplated, but is arguably strengthened by many of the texts discussed in this article, chief amongst which is Article III-118 CT.

However, this article was prepared in the shadow of the constitutional crisis generated by the rejection of the Constitutional Treaty by the French and Dutch electorates in May and June 2005. This cast very severe doubt over whether the Constitutional Treaty would ever be ratified by all Member States and whether it would ever enter into force in anything like the form which was agreed by the Convention in 2003 and by the IGC in 2004. One line of discussion which has emerged from this crisis concerns the possibility of salvaging specific parts of the Constitutional Treaty, especially those where there is no need for treaty amendments for changes to be brought into effect. This depends, of course, upon political will, but it is also based potentially upon flawed consent at the national level to the constitutional novelties of the Constitutional Treaty.

To the extent that the Constitutional Treaty has been concerned with giving a firmer constitutional grounding to other endeavours to deliver more effective and legitimate governance, it has operated as an ideas factory generating new possibilities for developing policy on equality and diversity which do not necessarily require the constitutional foundation which the Treaty would lend. To that extent, it could be said that Article III-118 CT only makes explicit that which is already implicit in the binding texts of the existing EC and EU Treaties, in secondary legislation and in case law, and in the non-binding text of the Charter of Fundamental Rights. It could be said, truly, to clarify and codify rather than to innovate as a text. Its innovatory potential, from that perspective, lies in the creation of a new political impetus towards the transformative politics promised by mainstreaming as an approach to policy-making, not in the existence (or non-existence) of the text itself. It is also significant that Article III-118 CT is just one of a cluster of transversal or mainstreaming clauses, concerned with a range of social justice and environmental issues. This clustering effect could be one of the most important contributions of the Constitutional Treaty if it is ratified. However, it would be a severe case of constitutional fetishism if we were to link all questions concerning the prospective development of a culture of mainstreaming equality and diversity into Union law and policy making exclusively to the evolution of constitutional texts.

The insight which this article has sought to offer is the importance of basing mainstreaming strategies not only upon political pragmatism, but also upon a better understanding of the politics of equality and diversity and of the challenges of legitimate and effective governance in a complex multi-level system such as the EU is at present. Many different mechanisms for assuring the practical realisation of the goals in relation to equality and diversity which I would argue underpin not only Article III-118 CT, but also the constitutional framework of the EU more generally, were canvassed in 'Implementing Article III-118 CT', above. The approach was premised upon taking a broad definition of what is included within the overall toolkit of mainstreaming, stretching from traditional normative constitutional concerns about rights and duties, to what appear at first sight to be the more 'bread-and-butter' questions about new governance approaches to achieving the EU's goals. One message is that nothing 'which works' (or which might work) should *a priori* be excluded from the toolkit of mainstreaming. The other clear message is that the vision of equality and diversity, on which is based much of the normative literature discussed in 'Mainstreaming Reconsidered', above, is not, as yet, firmly anchored in the EU's legal and institutional practices. Article III-118 CT would be but a start.

Decent Burials for Dead Concepts

James Penner*

Those who hate gardening need a theory. Not to garden without a theory is a shallow, unworthy way of life. (Leszek Kolakowski)**

'Theory', in the legal academy at least, seems to be a 'pro-word'. Indeed, one might plausibly say that the job of academic lawyers is to devise and assess theories of law, whether broad and general, about the nature of the law as a whole, or more particular, about specific areas of doctrine such as the law of contract or the criminal law. This, it is perhaps conventionally believed, is a good thing, for to theorise the law is to make sense of the law with rigour and system. By extension, to the extent that law commissions and judges and practicing lawyers draw upon these academic efforts, it may be plausible to suggest that they too are more or less engaged in this theoretical project. According to this portrayal, it is plausible to understand a change in the law of any particular region of doctrine as the consequence of a change in the reigning theory of that area of law; that is, the substantive law is thus regarded as susceptible to development by way of the movement from a now unacceptable theory of the law to a better one, and these theories are more or less abstract moral/political theories which try to capture some central philosophical concepts which underlie that area of law. Examples of theories which compete with others to best explain an area of law might be Fried's promissory theory of contract,[1] or Posner's economic theorisations of various areas of law.[2]

---

* Thanks to those who attended the public presentation of this lecture, in particular Hugh Collins, Nicola Lacey, Panos Kapotas, and Stephen Sedley, for instructive comments and questions. I also owe thanks to Hugh Collins, Duncan Horne, Nicola Lacey, Martin Loughlin, Richard Nobles, Mike Redmayne, Gabriel Segal and an anonymous reviewer for looking at the written version and giving me very instructive comments.

** L Kolakowski, 'The General Theory of Not Gardening' in *Modernity on Endless Trial* (Chicago: U of Chicago Press, 1990), 240.

[1] C Fried, *Contract as Promise* (Cambridge, MA: Harvard University Press, 1981).

[2] RA Posner, *Economic Analysis of Law* (5th edn, Boston: Aspen Law and Business, 1998). I do not mean to do an injustice to Professor Posner by suggesting that his work clearly bespeaks a belief that lawyers and judges do reason as economists, however unconsciously, or that the logic underlying the law, or the common law, is implicitly oriented to wealth

Here I will give reasons for thinking this picture of legal reasoning implausible, and point out some of the dangers that might attend embracing it. Indeed, this paper can be regarded as something of an anti-theory rant, or at least let me so characterise it for those who will strongly disagree with its central claim. Against theory I will claim that there is such a thing as non-theoretical critical reasoning, or 'plain old critical thinking'. I will argue that it is wrong simply to assume that whenever someone is critically weighing reasons and dealing with a number of beliefs in order to decide some issue they are also constructing, or assessing, or applying some theory, perhaps unconsciously or implicitly. I deny, therefore, that we lawyers are all 'theorists' of the law, whether we recognise it or not.

This is not simply a matter of words. If someone wants to say that any reasonably coherent collection of beliefs about something—dogs, wine, the weather, the law of trusts, anything—amounts to their 'theory' of those things, fine; this is not something over which I will rush to the barricades. Where I do take a stand in this paper is against the idea that such 'theories' count as theories in the way we typically understand scientific or philosophical theories. About those, I will argue, we apply critical standards which we would not dream of applying to plain old critical thinking, nor would the application of such standards be either appropriate or welcome. To repeat, I think lawyers are typically engaged in plain old critical thinking, not theorising, and so I will deny that the critical standards appropriate to true theory assessment apply to their considered judgments, though these judgments can be and often are thoughtful, analytic, and rigorous. Being thoughtful, analytic, and rigorous, does not mean *ipso facto* that one is a theorist.

Getting this wrong, characterising legal reasoning as theoretical when it is not, will not only impede our understanding of what we are up to, but does, I shall argue, compromise our understanding of legal change. Concepts which operate in our plain old critical legal thinking, but which are not embraced by the reigning theory of any area of legal doctrine, or which do not have a competing theory behind them, will not be regarded as respectable concepts to use in deciding cases or thinking about an area of law. Nevertheless, they will not have been killed off and 'buried' by the accepted theory if they continue actually to operate in the critical legal thinking of lawyers and judges. They will linger as what might be called 'undead' or 'zombie' concepts, which continue to play a role in legal

maximisation or economic efficiency. I cite the 'bible' of the law and economics school merely to provide a reference which shows the possibility of such a theoretical position.

reasoning but which cannot be acknowledged as doing so by theorists of the law, or even perhaps by lawyers or judges themselves when engaged in 'respectable' legal reasoning. Of course, one in favour of characterising legal reasoning as a kind of theoretical reasoning might acknowledge the continuing influence of these concepts in legal reasoning, but treat them as a source of *mistakes*. Such a one will hope that by more explicit and rigorous theorising of the law, these concepts will be exposed for the miscreants they are, and eradicated. This seems to me the right position for a pro-theory theorist of law to take. But it begs the issue of the character of legal reasoning in favour of the pro-theory perspective, and, as I hope to show, this is unwarranted; the arguments for taking legal reasoning to be theoretical are far less robust than I think is typically assumed. By taking critical, but not theoretical, legal thinking seriously, we will be able sketch a model of legal reasoning and legal change which shows how and when legal concepts that have had their day are decently buried, with appropriate tombstones to boot.

I

First, some stipulations. By 'theories' I mean explicit orderings of beliefs which hold themselves out to be judged by particular sorts of standards. A theory is not just a collection of beliefs. Having lots of beliefs about, say, tigers, does not mean that I hold any theories about tigers. To hold a theory of tigers, I would have to have what might be called 'second-order', 'explicit', 'authoritative' beliefs. I might, for example, believe that tigers are genetically more closely related to leopards than to lions. Such a belief is *second-order* because, if true, it helps explain and draw together other beliefs I have about tigers, their appearance, their instinctive behaviour, etc. Scientific theories explain or illuminate data, philosophical theories our intuitions or judgments, economic theories rational self-interested behaviour. Theoretical beliefs are *explicit* because they must be framed in such a way so as to be presentable to a certain sort of judgment. They must be couched in the proprietary vocabulary of the theoretical community whose theoretical interests they implicate. Finally, such beliefs are *authoritative* in the Razian[3] sense that the theoretical community, if it operates, coordinates the behaviour of theorists so as to make it more likely that the truth will be discovered than if people just individually puzzle things out

---

[3] See, eg, J Raz, *The Morality of Freedom* (Oxford: Clarendon Press, 1986), Part I 'The Bounds of Authority', 23–109.

on their own, and this justifies this theoretical community's place as the authoritative 'tribunal' in which theories are judged. A theory is meant to be usable so as to displace its user's own efforts to know the truth of the matter. This is not, to be clear, (just) a matter of standing on the shoulders of giants, but a point about explicitness and presentation. To varying degrees, non-theorists are expected to be able to apply or grasp theories or make use of their results, relying upon their validity, even if they are not themselves capable of deriving or justifying them from first principles.

Reasoning with theories occurs in two sorts of ways: one can *reason about* theories, testing their validity and so on, whether speculatively, creatively, or critically; and one can *apply* theories, explicitly following the dictates of a theory in one's reasoning, making use of a theory, as it were. This is an analytic distinction, not a cut and dried phenomenal one. In the course of reasoning with theories, we can alternate between one and the other, and can do both at the same time. Consider, by analogy, what Raz says about the distinction between making and applying the common law.[4] One both follows precedent and develops the law in the course of distinguishing cases; though there may be no identifiable moments when one just does the one rather than the other, this does not undermine the validity of the distinction.

What I shall call 'critical thinking', or 'mere critical thinking', or 'plain old critical thinking', is the application of one's general stock of beliefs to any particular issue. I deny that critical thinking always involves the consideration or application of theories as just characterised. And I will go on to argue that we must at least consider the possibility that much legal reasoning, perhaps the greatest part, is mere critical thinking. But first let me use some examples to prompt our familiarity with mere critical thinking, which will help make the distinction between critical and theoretical thinking a robust one.

People engage in critical thinking all the time, in matters as diverse as raising their children, coaching teams, writing, and cooking. This critical thinking may concern issues about which there is controversy and deep disagreement. But we are in danger of simply playing with words if we treat people so engaged as developing or applying or both developing *and* applying 'theories' of child-rearing, or football, or writing, or cooking, simply because they are critically so engaged.

Consider the case where one's daughter is very upset because she has had a terrible fight with a good friend. What, in the way of advice or comfort, ought one to offer? Any thoughtful parent would surely make

---

[4] J Raz, *The Authority of Law* (Oxford: Clarendon Press, 1979), 180ff.

such a decision based upon a number of considerations: the sort of child one's daughter is, whether she is normally emotionally tough or tends to be overly sensitive, what the friend is like and whether one thinks the friendship is likely to last for any length of time, the reasons for and circumstances of the fight and whether there is any serious issue of justice at stake, one's general experience of human affairs, in particular friendship, one's best recollection of what it was like to be a child of one's daughter's age, and, perhaps most importantly, one's direct experience of more or less similar cases and how they were, or were not, resolved. It seems impossible to deny that deciding on how one should comfort and advise one's daughter, if one takes the matter seriously, will require some genuine critical thinking. But nothing I have said in the way of doing this critical thinking makes any reference to any theory of childhood dispute resolution or, more broadly, to a theory of child raising. Of course, there are such theories. But it is clear that one can engage in this sort of task without making any reference to such things whatsoever (which is undoubtedly a good thing).

This first example raises an important aspect of the distinction I wish to draw. It is essential to the distinction that a mere collection of beliefs does not count as a theory, however well organised that collection of beliefs may be in the sense that one makes sensible connections between them, eg between one's own experience as a child and one's particular thoughts about one's daughter or her friend, and one's changing perspectives as one grows up, and so on. Merely knowing a lot about something is not the same thing as being a theorist of that thing.

This sort of example can easily be multiplied. It is true that I may have an explicit system which I use when I manage a football team, an explicit theory, if you will. But that I *can* rely on theory in this way when I manage a team does not entail that I must. As with advising a child, a team manager may draw upon a wealth of considerations in making managing decisions, assessing the strengths and weaknesses of his own and the other team's players, the style in which the teams tend to play, the weather, whether his team is at home or away and whether they usually react strongly to this factor, and on and on. It is unwarranted simply to assume that a manager must be applying some more or less well worked-out theory which incorporates these factors as parameters to generate a result.

Or consider writing. Think about all the ideas on good writing one has received or thought up oneself. 'Write in short, punchy sentences.' 'In general, don't start a sentence with a connective like "and" or "but".' 'Watch for unintentional rhymes.' 'Use terms derived from the Anglo-Saxon rather than imports from Romance languages where you can.' 'Avoid the use of the first person.' 'Use the first person as much as possible.' These various hints, rules of thumb, and bits of advice do not amount to a theory of writing. Of course some people do write according to some theory: these we call 'bad writers'. But no one would deny that writing often involves extremely demanding critical thinking.

Consider cooking, or learning to cook. This involves learning to attend to various things, to assess how flavours work together or not, to learn various tricks and techniques. I should consider this a kind of critical thinking, but again to say that in doing so one is applying one or other theory of cooking seems to mean no more than that one is bringing a complex of beliefs to bear in the performance of a more or less complicated task. But, as with writing, there are of course theorists of cooking. One *can* cook according to certain 'theories' of cooking, from *nouvelle cuisine* (though that involved much more than a mere theory) to the Atkins diet, but one needn't.

Now given the extent of theorising that occurs nowadays (perhaps most obviously in the case of scientific investigation, but also in terms of theories like psychoanalysis, game theory, economic analysis, to say nothing of 'spiritual' approaches to making sense of the world), it is likely that certain results or theses derived from theorising activities, couched in their proprietary vocabularies, will enter into the critical thinking I describe. One might ask oneself whether one's child is 'insecure', or 'hyper-active', and whether or not this bears on the matter. A team manager might have assimilated certain conventional truths about the relative merits of certain player formations and so on. One might assess whether one's writing is 'accessible', and so on. But again, it is false to take from this that the parent or manager or writer or cook are themselves applying a theory in any substantive way, much less engaging in the development or assessment of any theory. When one considers such ideas amongst others, one is neither assessing the truth of whatever theory gave rise to them, nor devising a new theory of one's own, nor following a theory in the sense of taking one's decisions to be subject to criticism as correct or incorrect applications of any particular theory. Often people employ generally accepted beliefs or reasons in their practical reasoning, and these generally accepted beliefs may have become part of the generally accepted stock of beliefs because, or partly because, they have been endorsed by theorists of certain kinds. But so long as they are employed in critical thinking *merely as* generally accepted beliefs, they are not being treated as authoritative theoretical norms; the individual reasoner is not putting forth his reasoning with them as an application of the theory answerable to the criticisms of the theorist.[5] If for example, I say Fred made a 'Freudian slip' when he said to Sally 'take off your clothes' when he intended to say 'take off your coat', it would be presumptuous and inappropriate for you to say that I said something false because Freud's theories are false, even though I am perfectly happy to agree that they are. You would come across as the same sort of person who objects to a conventional greeting like 'Dear...' in a letter, by muttering 'Why should I write "dear" if the person is not dear to me?' In using the term, I am not using or applying Freud's theory; rather, I am using Freud's terminology to refer to a phenomenon which exists independently of Freud's theory, but which was labelled by him. Perhaps if it weren't for Freud and his theory we wouldn't have a concept of this sort of phenomenon, and term which expresses it, so we might owe something to Freud. Fair enough. But that does not entail that I am a Freudian, nor that I am applying his theory simply because I draw on some of its proprietary vocabulary. Indeed, this example shows that it might well be the case that a fair amount of the proprietary vocabulary of many theories ends up as part of the common stock of expressions which are used regularly without any commitment to the theories from which they arise.

This leads to another point: one can no more apply a theory without knowing one is doing it than follow a rule without knowing one is doing it. In saying this, I am not denying that, having learned the rules of the road or of cricket, one is able more or less automatically to follow those rules without thinking of them. In these cases, however, one can, if asked, explain one's 'automatic' behaviour by citing the rule one is following.[6] The same thing goes for theories as I have characterised them. Theory application, assessment, or construction, are *kinds* of critical thinking, which only operate in reference to the idea that they are susceptible to theoretical issues, challenges, and questions. They are not identical with critical thinking, even if the latter occasionally or often draws on beliefs or concepts which originated with them.

---

[5] The distinction is essentially identical to the one drawn by Warnock between following the rules of cricket (following authoritative norms) and a team captain's changing the field settings when a fast bowler is replaced with a slow one (following the generally accepted reasons for rearranging one's players on the pitch): GJ Warnock, *The Object of Morality* (London: Methuen, 1971), 45–6. See also J Raz, *Practical Reason and Norms* (Oxford University Press, 1999), 53–57.

[6] I make no claims here about whether in certain domains, in particular the use of language, human intentional behaviour is best explained by positing the existence of rules or theories (whether innate or learned) which individuals subconsciously follow but to which the individuals themselves have no conscious access, and whether such 'rules' or 'theories' are rules and theories in the same way as those to which we have access in the sense of being able consciously to cite them to explain our or others' behaviour. As far as I know no-one says this about legal rules or theories of law.

The distinction can be sharpened by further considerations. First, consider what seems to be the case, which is that while it is native to humans to be critical thinkers, theory as I have distinguished it does not exist if the social conditions are not present. Consider science: people have always made observations about the natural world, acquiring knowledge in the course of doing so. But science as we know it, with its commitment to explicit methodologies and its institutions of discussion, assessment, and criticism, is an historical achievement. Similarly, philosophy, social theory, economics, and so on, as identifiable activities with their own proprietary vocabulary and modes of discussion and debate, are historical achievements, even though individuals from time immemorial have wondered about big questions, had views about human society, and engaged in market transactions.

While we do now live in a world where these practices are relentlessly engaged in, it does not follow that they have colonised all instances of human thought. At the drop of a hat we may start to theorise, that is, may frame our intellectual endeavours as attempts to postulate or consider abstract truths, understanding that such attempts are subject to a partic-ular sort of intellectual assessment and criticism. There is nothing in what I say which suggests that thinking about something might be an occasion not merely of critical thinking, but of theorising. And in the same way that, phenomenally, it is often difficult to distinguish theory application from theory development or assessment, there is no bright phenomenal distinction between thinking critically about something and speculating more or less abstractly about it so as to generate propositions which are fit for theoretical assessment.[7] But we needn't always theorise, and often we don't. For one thing, it may simply not be worth the time and effort. I presume that physics and physiology have something to say about what is involved in riding bicycles, but as one has no need of them in order to learn to ride one, why bother? For another, and more importantly, theorising generates goals and purposes of its own: theoretical interests are typically peculiar interests orthogonal to other interests. Think of this roughly as a difference between 'pure' and 'applied' science; there may be nothing of obvious or even very indirect utilitarian value in discovering how sex evolved, or whether the universe is expanding, or whether deconstruction ensures/permits/authorises the possibility of justice. I do not mean to say by this that theory is only a kind of game, one played for a certain kind of psychic amusement, as one might say of chess. What I do

---

[7] Though note, there *is* a phenomenal distinction between merely reasoning practically about something for a purpose and applying a theory to generate a result; see the text relating to n 5 above.

mean to say is that theorising about something does not comprise every way of acquiring knowledge about something or skill in an endeavour, but comprises acquiring knowledge or skill in a particular way, which way shapes, in part, its own ends. Theories, after all, have appeal as theories, in terms of their comprehensiveness, elegance, consilience and so on, quite beyond any instrumental punch they deliver.

It is now something of a commonplace in philosophy to refer to a more or less coherent constellation of beliefs that can be brought to bear by an individual as a 'theory'; for example in making sense of others, 'a theory of interpretation',[8] or a 'folk theory' of psychology.[9] Equivalently, if people in general say that they are applying their theory of child raising, team managing and so on, whenever they make use of their beliefs in a critical fashion to solve a problem or work towards a goal, so be it. It is never the right of the philosopher to reform language as he would like. The same goes if judges and lawyers say they are applying their theory of torts or whatever when they reason about the law. There is nothing to complain about in this usage, so long as we are not confused by it, equivocating between mere critical thinking and genuine theorising. The difference here is similar to the one between someone's 'philosophy of life', which usually consists of some more or less sedative platitudes about what really matters and what fulfilment amounts to, and Joseph Raz's *The Morality of Freedom*, which contains any number of superficially similar thoughts, but which cannot help but display the rigour, the peculiar questions, the institutional goals, and so on, of the practice we call moral and political philosophy.

What tends to darken our appreciation of the distinction even more, perhaps, is a tendency to equivocate between a theory *about* something, and a theory *of* that thing.[10] As a first approximation, the former accepts that there is such a thing as x, and makes claims about it; the second is an exploration of what an x essentially is, a theory about what the necessary features of x-hood are. In philosophy, the latter has often taken the form of 'conceptual' analysis, in the sense of elucidating what the concept of x applies to. In general, theorising *about* something is much more common than generating theories *of* something. I may know immense amounts about Persian rugs, how they are made, the shifting character of their

---

[8] See, eg D Davidson, *Inquiries into Truth and Interpretation* (Oxford: Clarendon Press, 1984).

[9] See, eg SP Stich, *From Folk Psychology to Cognitive Science: The Case Against Belief* (Cambridge, MA: MIT Press, 1983).

[10] This distinction will become more important later on, when I distinguish what I call 'doctrinal theory' from 'legal theory'; see text relating to n 51ff.

designs over time, and much more besides, which might put me in the position to spot fakes, for example. But having all this knowledge and the ability to make use of it does not in any way entail that I have devised a theory *of* Persian rugs, any kind of theory at all. Indeed, at first glance, trying to come up with a theory *of* Persian rugs seems like an idiotic project. What sort of theory would it be? I can of course, if I want, consider all sorts of theories *about* Persian rugs, or concerning Persian rugs, from Marxist theories about the development of the bourgeois taste for Persian rugs and the labour relations necessary for their production to historico-aesthetic theories about the development of the patterns and symbols woven into them, but it is worthwhile asking whether the knowledge *I* have about Persian rugs, which might be extensive, could itself be tied up in any way by a theory *of* Persian rugs. Theory, after all, is not some kind of magic. Theories have to be created, and there simply may not be anything in my collection of beliefs about Persian rugs which could generate, for example, a necessary-and-sufficient-conditions account or any other sort of account[11] of what Persian rugs essentially *are*. Now, one response to this might be to say, 'Well, look: you are able to distinguish Persian rugs from other things; indeed you said you have sufficient cognitive wherewithal to spot fakes; you clearly then have a *concept* of Persian rugs, and thus some beliefs about what makes Persian rugs what they are, some beliefs, that is, about the essential characteristics of Persian rugs. It follows, then, that you do have at least the *basis* for a theory of Persian rugs. Even accepting your own limitations on what makes belief theoretical, so long as you organise your beliefs about the necessary features of Persian rugs in a sufficiently abstract or philosophical way, then you would have a theory of Persian rugs.' This response seems perfectly correct, as far as it goes.[12] But this response alone does not give good grounds for thinking that one thereby has a theory of Persian rugs or anything else, much less establishes that that is so. It is purely a matter of historical fact whether my beliefs about what constitutes a Persian rug and what doesn't *could* be organised in a theoretically rigorous

---

[11]   Such as a 'family resemblance' account.

[12]   I am assuming for the sake of the argument that concept possession requires having certain beliefs of this kind (ie about what makes an *x* an *x*, that is beliefs about the essential features of anything we have a concept of); there is, however, a host of issues involved in accepting such a view uncritically. For brief discussions see J E Penner, 'The Semantic Sting, "Soft Positivism", and the Authority of Law According to Raz', ch 10 of J Penner, D Schiff, and R Nobles, *Jurisprudence and Legal Theory: Commentary and Materials* (London: Butterworths, 2002), 442ff; J E Penner, 'Legal Reasoning and the Authority of Law' in L H Meyer, S L Paulson and T W Pogge (eds), *Rights, Culture, and the Law* (Oxford University Press, 2003), 71–97, 90–91; see also J Fodor, *Concepts: Where Cognitive Science Went Wrong* (Oxford University Press, 1998).

fashion,[13] and another contingent matter whether I have ever sought
to do so, either as a first step in creating a 'philosophy of Persian rugs' or
in response to an already existing theoretical practice of the kind. Even
my theoretical beliefs *about* Persian rugs do not require me to be able to
establish or to have first established any theory of Persian rugs, for my
theories can still be meaningful even though I have not theoretically
explored the essence of Persian rugs or my application of the concept.
Such a thing happens all the time. Historians, sociologists, economists
and so on, can all come up with various theories about the law without
themselves having assessed in any genuine theoretical way their use of the
concept of law. While, of course, it might be a criticism of their theories
that their use of the concept is philosophically suspect, because it can be
shown for philosophically assessable reasons that their use of it is very
much out of whack with common or academic usage, that doesn't mean
for a minute that these theorists themselves have engaged in that project.
A theory about *x* can be perfectly meaningful though it relies upon an
everyday, common, rough and ready, understanding of what *x* is.[14]

There is, finally, a more general point to be made.[15] On pain of leading
ourselves into an infinite regress, we must distinguish between the critical
thinking that attends an activity, and theorising about that activity.
Assume we were to accept that the critical thinking that attends say, advising one's child, or managing a team, or writing, or cooking, amounts
to theorising that activity, or theorising about that activity. Well, we also take
it for granted that theorising is itself a kind of critical thinking. If so,
then if thoughtfully advising one's child amounts to theorising about
advising one's child, then theorising about advising one's child must
amount to theorising about theorising about advising one's child, and
so on. One must be careful here. This consideration does not merely
concern the distinction between critical thinking for a purpose and
theory *application*. The danger is a much more dramatic one, and leaps
from both critical thinking for a purpose and theory application in
precisely the same way. For critical thinking attends both the kind of
general application of knowledge to cases of advising a child or writing or
cooking that I have described, and also in many cases to *applying* a theory,

---

[13] It is the contention of 'ordinary language philosophy' that in some cases, at least, the
implicit beliefs which direct our application of words can be examined to provide a philosophically enlightening account of the concepts they express (for the *locus classicus*, see
J L Austin, 'A Plea for Excuses' in *Aristotelian Society Proceedings*, LVII (1956–57), 1–30),
but I don't think the claim has been made that this is possible for every concept we possess.

[14] Cf Raz's distinction between statements about the law and statements of the law:
J Raz, 'Legal Principles and the Limits of Law' (1972) 81 Yale LJ 823–54, at 828.

[15] A point I have made elsewhere: Penner, 'The Semantic Sting', n 12 above, 452.

as for example when one does a physics problem in an exam. I have argued above that a kind of critical thinking attends the former cases, but we would be foolish to deny that critical thought is also often required in order to apply the theoretical dictates of a theory, say of physics. Each time we tackle a new mechanics problem, we apply the formulae of physics to a new case; though we may be perfectly familiar with the rules, and capable of applying them, it is not the case that we do not need to attend, perhaps very closely, to what we are doing in order to get the correct result. So there is nothing in the distinction I draw between mere critical thinking and theory application which says that the latter does not involve critical thinking, is in some way mindless or unthinking or undemanding (though I shall say something further on about how its ambition is typically to deliver us from the sort of critical thinking I have described in the examples). My goal is to insist that the former can take place without the latter, not *vice versa*. The danger I mean to identify here is the one of assimilating any kind of critical thinking that attends doing *x*, from advising a child to cooking to applying the law, to a kind of theorising about, or 'theory-work' on, *x*. It is that which leads to the infinite regress.[16]

II

It is obvious from the foregoing that I think that much of what goes on in legal reasoning falls on the critical thinking side of the ledger, as opposed to the theory application/assessment side. To address the case of legal reasoning specifically, I want to begin by considering an analogy between scientific inquiry and legal reasoning that Dworkin employs to reveal the theoretical nature of the latter.

Dworkin claims that the law is 'theory-embedded', in this sense: where difficult cases arise there is always the possibility that judges will have to shift their reasoning to a more abstract level, employing more abstract

---

[16] Dworkin seems to me liable to this danger when he says: 'Any practical legal argument, no matter how detailed and limited, assumes the kind of abstract foundation jurisprudence offers, and when rival foundations compete, a legal argument assumes one and rejects others. So any judge's opinion is itself a piece of legal philosophy, even when the philosophy is hidden and the visible argument is dominated by citation and lists of facts. Jurisprudence is the general part of adjudication, silent prologue to any decision at law.' R Dworkin, *Law's Empire* (London: Fontana, 1986), 90. The claim seems to be that when a judge is 'doing law' he is *ipso facto* also necessarily doing the philosophy of law; but then presumably, doing the philosophy of law, he is also doing the philosophy of the philosophy of law, and so on *ad infinitum*.

concepts than the more concrete ones which one finds in the particular rules of law operating in that area. There is, therefore, the ever present possibility of what he calls 'justificatory ascent'.[17] In making this claim, Dworkin offers an analogy between the way in which Hercules, the ideal judge, does law, and the way that a goddess, Minerva, who has mastered all of physics, might build a bridge. The idea is that rather than ascending to higher scales of abstraction, in principle Hercules might work in the other direction. I quote:

[Hercules] might think, not inside-out, from more specific problems to broader and more abstract ones, as other lawyers do, but outside-in, the other way around. Before he sits on his first case, he could build a gigantic, 'over-arching' theory good for all seasons. He could decide all outstanding issues of metaphysics, epistemology and ethics, and also of morality, including political morality. He could decide what there is in the universe, and why he is justified in thinking that is what there is; what justice and fairness require; what freedom of speech, best understood, means, and whether and why it is a freedom particularly worth protecting; and when and why it is right to require people whose activity is connected to other people's loss to compensate them for that loss. He could weave all that and everything else into a marvelously architectonic system. When a new case arises, he would be very well prepared. From outside—beginning, perhaps, in the intergalactic stretches of his wonderful intellectual creation—he could work steadily in towards the problem at hand: finding the best available justifications for law in general, for American legal and constitutional practice as a species of law, for constitutional interpretation, for tort, and then, finally, [to the instant case].[18]

And a little further on:

There is no inconsistency in these two pictures—of Hercules thinking from outside-in and of the mortal lawyer reasoning from inside-out. I stress the compatibility of the two descriptions because many of the critics of an embedded approach to law make a point of saying that real judges are not Hercules. They do not mean only that judges are not superhuman creatures: they mean that my biographies of Hercules are beside the point. Analogies are always dangerous— almost as dangerous as metaphors—and I hope to keep the one I am about to make on a very short leash. But an analogy to science may help to show how an outside-in view of an intellectual domain can be helpful even to those who think within it from the inside-out. We think—or at least hope—that the body of knowledge we call, compendiously, science is very much of a seamless web. There

---

[17] R Dworkin, 'In Praise of Theory' (1997) 29 Ariz St L J 353, 356. It is not clear to me whether Dworkin thinks that difficult, controversial cases are *typically* met with justificatory ascent. More often, it seems to me, judges and lawyers pursue what might be seen as a more 'horizontal' investigation to see whether the logic of a position is sound, eg whether the conclusions flow from the premises, whether a fallacy like the fallacy of equivocation is revealed, whether there are mistakes in describing the cases, and so on.   [18] Ibid, 358.

are still seams, and scientists and philosophers worry about those seams. But we have no trouble with the ambition that our physics must be at least consistent with our chemistry, our cosmology, our microbiology, our metallurgy, and our engineering. We hope, indeed, for something more, which we believe we have partly realised—not only that each of these conventionally distinct bodies of knowledge is consistent with the others, but that they can be hierarchically arranged so that physics, perhaps, is taken to be the most abstract, and the others can be seen as drawn from it as progressively more concrete departments of thought. We might illustrate these theoretical and structural ambitions by imagining, in the style of Hercules, a goddess Minerva who spent the centuries necessary to master the biography of space and time and the fundamental forces of particle theory before she undertook to build a single bridge. Then, when someone asked her whether a particular metal would bear a certain weight, she could deduce the answer from her wonderful and complete theory. We understand that picture because it captures how we think about the body of our science.

But of course no scientist could even begin to follow Minerva's example. An engineer who builds a new kind of bridge works from the inside-out. She does not know what problems she will discover until she discovers them, and she cannot tell, at least until then, whether the problems she will inevitably discover will require her to rethink some principle of metallurgy, or whether, if they do, her excursion into metallurgy will require her—or someone else—to rethink particle physics. Minerva's story (grasping the possibility of that goddess's life) is one way of appreciating the basic assumptions that in turn explain the very different engineer's story—that explain why the ladder of theoretical ascent is always there, on the cards, even when no one is tempted to take even the first step up it. That is what I hoped to capture, for law, in the story of Hercules.[19]

Thus in the same way that engineering is concrete or applied physics, the law is supposed to be concrete or applied moral/political philosophy.

I believe that this is a bad picture of the relationship between physics and engineering, and if properly understood, that relationship shows that the comparison between Hercules and Minerva undercuts the case for justificatory ascent, rather than strengthens it. The argument can be summarised in this way: the unity of science demands that less basic sciences be compatible with more basic ones. Psychology must be compatible with neurology, neurology with biology, biology with chemistry, chemistry with physics. You cannot have an explanation of some chemical phenomenon that violates the more basic laws of physics. Similarly, you cannot explain a biological phenomenon in a way that violates chemistry. Or, at least, to do so, you must persuade us that this explanation is revolutionary in the sense that it requires us to revise the more basic science in order

[19] R Dworkin, 'In Praise of Theory' (1997) 29 Ariz St L J 359.

to account for it. But you cannot claim that biology is somehow independent of chemistry, so that, for example, you explain the operation of genes as some kind of miracle, on which our understanding of chemistry imposes no constraints.

But, and this is the crucial point, this kind of compatibility constraint does not require what I, following Fodor, will call 'reductionism', that every law of a less basic, or 'special' science must be *reducible* to some law of a more basic science or, as Fodor puts it, that 'every kind is, or is coextensive with, a physical kind.'[20]

That would entail that a phenomenon of biology, say, Batesian mimicry, ie the phenomenon of one species adopting the colouring of another species which is harmful or poisonous to predators without itself acquiring those harmful or poisonous traits, can be reduced to a causal relationship expressed in the proprietary vocabulary of physics, ie in terms such as force or mass, which seems implausible for the reasons Fodor gives:

The reason that it is unlikely that every kind corresponds to a physical kind is just that (a) interesting generalisations (eg counterfactual supporting generalisations) can often be made about events whose physical descriptions have nothing in common; (b) it is often the case that *whether* the physical descriptions of the events subsumed by such generalisations have anything in common is, in an obvious sense, entirely irrelevant to the truth of the generalisation, or to their interestingness, or to their degree of confirmation, or indeed, to any of their epistemologically important properties; and (c) the special sciences are very much in the business of formulating generalisations of this kind.[21]

As Fodor points out, these observations 'leap to the eye as soon as one [takes] the existence of the special sciences at all seriously.'[22] Consider a law of the social sciences, such as Gresham's law that bad money drives out good. I quote Fodor again:

Suppose, for example, that Gresham's law really is true. Gresham's law says something about what will happen in monetary exchanges under certain conditions. I am willing to believe that physics is general *in the sense it implies that any event which consists of a monetary exchange* (hence any event which falls under Gresham's law) *has a true description in the vocabulary of physics and in virtue of which it falls under the laws of physics.* But banal considerations suggest that a physical description which covers all such events must be wildly disjunctive. Some monetary exchanges involve strings of wampum. Some involve dollar

[20] J A Fodor, 'Special Sciences', ch 5 of *Representations* (Brighton: Harvester, 1981), 127–145, 132.   [21] Ibid, 133.
[22] Ibid, 133.

bills. And some involve signing one's name to a check. What are the chances that a disjunction of physical predicates which covers all these events... expresses a physical kind? In particular, what are the chances that such a predicate forms the antecedent or consequent of some proper law of physics? The point is that monetary exchanges have interesting things in common; Gresham's law, if true, says what one of those interesting things is. But what is interesting about monetary exchanges is surely not their commonalities under *physical* description. A kind like a monetary exchange *could* turn out to be co-extensive with a physical kind; but if it did, that would be an accident on a cosmic scale.[23]

To anthropomorphise the point, physics doesn't care what constitutes a monetary exchange, or how bridges are built, or what makes a better or worse bridge. Bridges are a practical human, functional kind, not a kind in physics. Similarly, there are no *laws of physics* that concern Batesian mimicry. Of course your engineering must be compatible with physics, as must your biology, but it needn't, and as far as we can tell from the success of the special sciences it doesn't, *reduce* to physics.

In short, the difference between special sciences and more basic ones is not merely a difference in degree, or the level of abstraction at which they take account of phenomena, but a difference in kind. Basic sciences are of necessity blind to the multiply-realised, functional orderings or organisations of matter in the world, at the level of biology, or psychology, orderings to which the special sciences are directed.

In the same way, even if, and this is a big if, even if the law can be analogised to a special science whose laws must be compatible with those of the more basic science of morality, it does not mean that law reduces to morality, is nothing more than 'applied' political morality, much less 'applied' moral/political philosophy. So, for example, if we think about the common law (in this case, 'equitable') device of the trust, one hopes that it isn't an *immoral* legal institution. But it is very implausible to suggest that one could ever read the trust off from even a 'completed' morality, given that civilian legal systems seem to have managed all these centuries without it. There are, it would seem, more legal ways than one to skin the moral cat.

---

[23] J A Fodor, 'Special Sciences', ch 5 of *Representations*, 133–34. See also J Fodor, 'Special Sciences: Still Autonomous After All These Years' (1997) 31 *Nous: Special Supplement: Philosophical Perspectives, 11, Mind, Causation, and World, 1977*, 149–63; D Davidson, 'Mental Events', ch 11 of *Essays on Actions and Events* (Oxford: Clarendon Press, 1980), 207–225. For a different argument against the possibility of reductionism, see N Cartwright, *The Dappled World* (Cambridge University Press, 1999), a theme of whose work is that while the laws of physics may well be true, they are 'local' rather than 'universal' in the sense that they are tied to 'model' situations, experimental or technological, in which they genuinely work.

If this argument is right, then Dworkin's analogy, rather than helping his case, undermines it. If Dworkin analogises the distinction between what Hercules does and what lawyers do to the distinction between what Minerva does and what bridge-builders do, then Dworkin, implicitly to be sure, seems to treat the law as a 'special science', and so that analogy gives no succour to his contention that the law can be reduced at a sufficiently abstract level to moral and political philosophy, so that the law is somehow just *applied* moral and political philosophy. That is all that I wish to establish here, *viz* that one argument for treating legal reasoning as theoretical reasoning fails, because it relies on an analogy between law/morality and science in which the relationship between the sciences is misconceived. One can only speculate on the extent to which Dworkin's more general claims about the Herculean nature of law are unsettled by the problems generated by his resort to this analogy.

To the extent, however, that Dworkin is correct in his implicit acceptance of law as something, at least, of a functional kind akin to the nature of bridge-building, we may, perhaps, celebrate a little. For if the law is not merely 'applied' moral/political philosophy, then the failure of judges to act like philosophers may not be the demerit Dworkin must think it.[24] If this is the way it is, it is much better to have an experienced judge to decide one's case, who perhaps has gained some thoughtful experience of critical thinking about human affairs and is adept on drawing on the decisions of others who have had to do the same, than a moral philosopher doing so by 'working inward from' his theory of justice. And anyway, who really thinks moral philosophers have a better grip on the morality of everyday conflicts? As Professor Brian Simpson once said to me discussing the behaviour of one of his colleagues: 'Just like a moral philosopher— doesn't begin to know the difference between right and wrong.'

III

I want now to consider a second way in which legal reasoning might be claimed to be theoretical, this time involving the idea of paradigm cases of a concept (more properly: paradigm cases of the thing a concept represents). The idea is that what is most theoretically interesting about x is equivalent to the most central or paradigmatic aspect of x. This, as I hope to show, is mistaken. If the idea were true, however, it would clearly make the theoretical consideration of the law most important to legal

---

[24] See, eg R Dworkin, *Freedom's Law* (Cambridge, MA: Harvard University Press, 1996), 304.

decision making and reasoning, for theory would reveal what elements of, say, the legal concept of contract, or of murder, were most fundamental; what elements, that is, would impose the most stringent constraints upon a lawyer or judge in making an argument or a decision concerning contract or murder. Moreover, we would see how legal change responded to changes in the reigning theory of any area of law, since with a change in a theory and what it determined to be most central or paradigmatic, our understanding, and practice, of the law would change in consequence.

Again we can draw on an example of Dworkin's. Dworkin considers a dispute between theorists of art, one holding that photography is a central, paradigmatic example of art, the other denying that photography is an art form at all.[25] Dworkin employs this example as part of his 'semantic sting' argument to try to show that those who adopt a paradigm case semantics for certain kinds of words cannot account for significant disagreements in respect of the nature of the phenomena they refer to.[26] The idea is that for certain concepts, like art, people who share the concept 'art' can disagree over what constitutes central paradigmatic instances of art; thus, in the example, Dworkin claims that while one theorist regards photography as a paradigmatic art form, the other denies it the status of art at all, yet the two are said to share the same concept of art. I have criticised this view elsewhere.[27] The thrust of that criticism is that Dworkin elides the idea of a paradigm case of a concept with the idea of a case pivotal for the truth of a theory about the concept. Just because it is pivotal for Smith's theory of art that photography counts as an art form in the fullest sense, does not make photography a paradigm case of art for Smith. That would depend upon how Smith applies the concept of art and teaches it, say, to her children; it depends on what Smith *does*, that is, in dealing with the concept. If it is truly the case that Smith treats photography as a paradigm case of art, eg teaching her children the word 'art' by pointing to photographs, it seems that she genuinely has a different (though related) concept of 'art' from Jones, who observes different paradigm cases (ie whose concept picks out different phenomena in the world) and who has substantially different beliefs about 'art'. Here I want to discuss the way in which mistakenly taking pivotal cases for the truth of a theory about *x* for paradigm cases of *x*, can blind one to the reality of *x*.

Consider a real life example from science, a dispute as to whether wolves are properly classed with dogs as members of the same species. According

---

[25] Dworkin, n 16 above 41–43.   [26] Ibid, 43ff.
[27] Penner, 'The Semantic Sting', n 12 above, 442–48.

to Patel, the essence of animal classes lies in their evolutionary history, particularly in the process of speciation (the way in which different species arise from common ancestors), and her test for membership of a species is whether a candidate member can interbreed with others of that class. It turns out that wolves and dogs interbreed, much more than was previously thought, and so according to Patel wolves *are dogs*, however surprising that sounds. On the other hand Singh, an animal behaviourist, would class together those animals that have a behavioural repertoire sufficiently alike. For him, the behaviour of wolves is distinct enough from that of dogs (understandable given the millennial co-evolution of dogs with humans) to show that wolves are not dogs. Now in their argument as to which of them has the better theory of animal classes, the status of wolves is a pivotal case. For whether we are willing or not to class wolves with dogs will be a crucial element of whether we adopt one theory or another. We might say, with Singh, that however informative the genetic interbreeding story is, it is an unsound way to classify animals, because it leads to the bizarre result that wolves are dogs. Or we might conclude with Patel, that focusing on behaviour provides an insufficiently rigorous classification scheme, and that whether or not animals interbreed (or can do) is a more essential criterion of their nature; on this score wolves really are dogs.[28] Now the point to notice about this case, where the status of wolves provides a pivotal case for the truth of these opposing theories, is that on neither theory do wolves count as paradigm cases of dogs. Neither Patel nor Singh would say that a wolf was a typical dog or start teaching his or her child the word 'dog' by pointing out a wolf. They would teach their children the word 'dog' as we all do, pointing out Labrador retrievers, for example. Paradigm cases of a word or concept are simply not the same thing as pivotal cases in a clash of theories about what the concept is a concept of, or what a word refers to. But, for obvious reasons, the case of whether wolves are dogs will result in the spilling of much more ink than any similar issue about Labrador retrievers. In consequence, it is appropriate to think of the issue of wolf doghood as getting at something very important about the nature of doghood *per se*. All that is well and good. But that the wolf question may reveal something important about doghood does not entail that this is a matter most fundamental or central to the nature of dogs. That dogs are

---

[28] Notice that both theories are equally 'externalist' about the semantics of 'dog'. Both tell a causal story—the interbreeding theorist says dogs and wolves are the same because he explains the traits of dogs via the causal processes underpinned by their genetic constitution; the animal ethologist says wolves are not dogs because their scientifically important traits are explained not by their genetic constitution, or not only by that, but also by their ecological niche and associated behavioural repertoire.

mammals, social, conscious, and so on, would seem to be features which, from a circumspect point of view, would trump this seemingly somewhat peripheral issue.[29]

Now consider a case closer to the province of this paper, that of a theory of murder and whether abortion is murder. For those anti-abortionists who claim that abortion is murder, abortion counts as a pivotal case for the truth of their theory of murder. In particular, the effective use of intra-uterine devices or morning after pills would have to be treated as examples of murder. Even so, it would be absurd for such a theorist to treat inserting an IUD or taking a morning after pill as a central or paradigm case of murder. Absurd but not impossible. It is conceivable, I suppose, that the anti-abortion theorist might do so, and might, for example, explain the concept of murder to a child by first explaining the evils of contraception and then, I suppose, go on to show how 'regular' murders like stabbings or shootings could be framed as peripheral cases of murder, as some kind of very, very, very late abortions. But in that case I would honestly say that this theorist's concept of murder was different from (though related to) mine—I really don't think I would have a sensible grasp upon such a concept, and we would have to express our disagreement about the moral significance of abortion in different terms. One can, I think, say similar things with respect to euthanasia. And, as with the example of wolves and dogs, I would not wish to deny that sorting out these sorts of issue tells us something very interesting about our concept of murder. But also, for the very same reason, this theoretical fascination with this topic should not be allowed to skew what is most essential or fundamental about murder, what might be called the 'trite law' of murder.

It is worth pausing to emphasise the idea of trite law. Learning the law in a common law system amounts, in large part, to examining those cases that press the boundaries of the law and for that reason are controversial. So inherent, one might say, in the common law itself is a tendency to emphasise the peripheral over the 'trite' law. But this tendency may be exacerbated by focusing not only upon what the common law itself finds difficulty with, but with what theorists of the law also find the most philo-sophically puzzling or theoretically challenging.

Consider the dominance of the law of negligence in the teaching of torts these days. A very recent phenomenon in common law timescales, negligence has achieved a prominence in the syllabus, and in the thinking of lawyers, which seems only to be explained because of the difficulty of

---

[29] Compare the same sort of issue arising with respect to whether definitions in terms of necessary and sufficient conditions reveal anything 'essential' or important about the term defined, eg man = featherless biped. See also J Raz, 'Two views on the Nature of the Theory of Law' (1998) 4 Legal Theory 249–82, 256–57.

making sense of it, its attraction as a theoretical project, to which the voluminous literature on negligence attests. Also, it is plausible to think that the prominent place it has been given conceals or marginalises what might be regarded as torts if any are, the intentional torts in particular. Let me retell (with minor modifications) a story of Professor Joe Thomson; he gives his tort students the following set of facts: You have invited me to dinner, but when I knock on your door at the appointed time, you do not answer. I see through the window that you are watching television. I break down the door to find you drunk in front of the television, obviously in no condition to serve me dinner. Enraged, I pick up the television and smash it to the floor, and when you rise from your chair, I knock you unconscious with one blow. He then asks: 'What is my liability to you', and depressingly often, he receives an initial response such as this: 'Well, the first thing we have to establish is whether you owe me a duty of care'.

My goal here is not to champion a bloodless, blackletter approach to legal study. My goal is simply to raise the possibility, perhaps probability, that we may be misled by our theoretical fascinations to misrepresent the law, by treating theoretically fascinating cases as the most doctrinally important ones. 'Easy cases' are not insignificant or unimportant cases for understanding the law as a whole.

IV

Where have we got to? I began by insisting on a less promiscuous use of the word theory, so that all that might be regarded as critical thinking does not amount to theorising willy nilly. I then considered two ideas, Dworkin's 'justificatory ascent', and the equation of paradigm cases of a concept/fundamental features of a concept with cases pivotal for the truth of a theory/issues drawing the most philosophical attention, which I found wanting as bases for the claim that theorising an area of law is illuminating. I want now to step back a bit, and try to work some of these ideas to show how, from a legal positivist's perspective, the idea that legal reasoning is critical, but by and large not theoretical, makes a kind of sense, and in doing so suggest a model for legal change which makes no reference to changes in reigning theories of the law.

I will not, therefore, take on here the large task of trying to show that the sort of theory I have been describing is atypical of legal reasoning. I have elsewhere sketched such a project,[30] and I will only cite the path-breaking work of Postema and Simpson for the proposition, which

---

[30] Penner, 'Legal Reasoning and the Authority of Law', n 12 above, 71–97.

they seem to establish fairly convincingly, that at least until the 20th century the ethos of judicial reasoning was very much that it comprised a critical, but 'artificial', functional, technical, kind of reason, not illuminated by moral philosophy.[31]

The model of the law that I am suggesting, which competes with the one which is more or less explicitly embraced by the 'theory' view, is of a law that is pre-eminently *practical*, which treats the institution of law as a social technology of collective practical reason. This is not to deny, by any means, that the law regards itself as an institution bound by morality, that seeks justice. But the model is one in which the justice delivered is 'justice according to law', an idea of justice shaped by a complex multiplicity of desiderata shaped by a host of social, economic, political and conceptual factors; in particular, such a model denies the legitimacy of a formulation of the law founded upon a religious, moral-philosophical, economic or any other kind of 'external' theory in so far as such a theory has the ambition of displacing the lawyer's own understanding of the way the rules work and what they mean (or worse, 'illuminating' the lawyer's understanding in such a way that he no longer recognises them). Why is this perspective positivist, beyond reflecting the crudely-put but roughly accurate positivist credo that what the law is is to be distinguished from what the law ought to be from the perspective of the moralist, or economist, or religious believer? It is positivist in the further sense that it characterises the law as authoritative and conventional in the ways variously elaborated by theorists such as Hart, Raz, and Marmor.[32]

From this positivist perspective, when I say that the law is technical, or functional, I do not mean to say that it is akin to reasoning about how to plumb a house or fix a car,[33] but rather that given either the truth of value pluralism, or the fact of unending controversy over the relative priority of various kinds of value, the law, both in legislation and in judicial decisions, will reflect the making of contestable choices but at the same time may be assessed by how the choices work together to generate a working system of rules, such as a working law of contract, a working criminal law, a working law of trusts. To make a contrast with 'theory', we might say the law of any particular area of doctrine has an 'ethos'; a general practical orientation which, to be sure, limits and constrains what counts as a good

---

[31] G J Postema, 'Law, Custom, and Reason', Part I of *Bentham and the Common Law Tradition* (Oxford: Clarendon Press, 1986), 3–143; A W B Simpson, 'The Common Law and Legal Theory' and 'The Survival of the Common Law System', chs 15 and 16 of *Legal Theory and Legal History* (London: Hambleton Press, 1987), 359–82, 383–402.

[32] See, eg, H L A Hart, *The Concept of Law*, 2nd edn., (Oxford: Clarendon Press, 1961, 1994); Raz, *The Authority of Law*, n 4 above; J Raz, *Ethics in the Public Domain*, (Oxford: Clarendon Press, 1994), 177–362; A Marmor, 'Legal Conventionalism' (1998) 4 Legal Theory 509–531. [33] Raz, *Ethics*, ibid at 318–319, 322–324.

reason for rendering a decision, but which is sensitive not to the shifting perceptions of what is theoretically sound, but to the changing social circumstances in which the law operates. This, to my mind, is reflected in the standard, bread-and-butter criticism to be found in case comments which criticise judicial decisions—that the judge simply failed to see how the decision upsets an area of law without properly realising and therefore assessing the consequences, the difficulties it may cause in advising clients in the future, in upsetting legitimate expectations, in leading to all kinds of changes required in the behaviour of subjects of the law to no worthwhile purpose. In the worst cases, one might claim that the judge actually gets the law *wrong*, showing that in some substantial way the judge did not know what he or she was talking about: ie that he or she simply failed to understand what the relevant cases and statutes stood for or aimed to achieve. It is often perfectly clear what mundane moral considerations weighed with a judge in rendering such a decision, ones that any critic might be in perfect sympathy with. The problem is that the judge did not properly think the case out, giving a decision that in some substantial way makes no sense.

It is the burden of this paper to suggest that this sort of problem is likely to be made worse by a faith in the efficacy of theorising areas of the law. I have already mentioned the way in which the theoretical fascination with negligence may more or less 'blind' students and lawyers to the way in which the law of torts also frames its actions in terms of the interests it protects, not the mode in which those interests are violated. A few further examples to illustrate the problem should strengthen the point.

To take a look at criminal law, consider the recent (in historical terms) rise of emphasis on the most general, abstract part of the criminal law, the so-called 'general part'. As Lacey shows, Blackstone reveals no real concern with a general part at all, and it is found only peripherally and insubstantially in the work of Stephen; it only arises in its full glory in Glanville William's *The Criminal Law: The General Part*[34] in 1953.[35] And it seems plausible to suggest that the focus on the general part coincides with the philosophical concern with the nature of moral responsibility. Clearly, Dworkin's picture of a seamless relationship of abstract to the concrete seems to fit perfectly here, as Gardner points out:[36]

[A] focus on the will provides an ideal way of factoring out, for moral purposes, the rich diversity of possible human actions. [This relates to a] restrictive view of moral agency, according to which the various apparently diverse particular

---

[34] London: Stevens & Sons, 1953.

[35] N Lacey, 'In Search of the Responsible Subject: History, Philosophy and Social Sciences in Criminal Law Theory' (2001) 64 MLR 350–71.

[36] J Gardner, 'On the General Part of the Criminal Law' in A Duff (ed), *Philosophy of the Criminal Law* (Cambridge University Press, 1998), 205–55, 217.

actions that people perform are, morally speaking, mere instances of more general actions. Moving the golf ball with one's foot is a mere instance of cheating, cheating is a mere instance of breaking trust, breaking trust is a mere instance of failing to respect others, and so on.

From this sort of perspective, it makes complete sense for the Theft Act 1968 to treat all instances where a person dishonestly acquires some economic advantage from another as the same offence, 'theft', for at some high level of abstraction these are the same crime. The focus is turned from the particular dishonesties of different sorts of acts, different types of theft distinguished by their *actus reus*, to an encompassing notion of 'dishonesty', which itself determines whether an act counts as an 'appropriation' of property for the purposes of the law.[37] It is, however, an understatement, I think, to say that the Act has not been notably successful in delivering a comprehensible and workable notion of what 'appropriation', as the *actus reus* of theft, amounts to,[38] as the 3:2 division in the House of Lords in the recent case of *R v Hinks*[39] reveals. It is notable that 28 years after the Act came into force Smith still begins his exposition of theft with an explanation of larceny, embezzlement, fraudulent conversion, and obtaining by false pretences.[40] These are perfect examples of what I would call 'zombie' concepts. While it would seem that they are no longer proper concepts in the criminal law, it seems we cannot do without them. While the reigning abstractions of 'dishonesty' and 'appropriation' would seek to replace them, so that no further reference need be made to them, they rise from their graves to influence our thinking and the way we reason through cases, as the criticisms of the post-Theft Act 1968 jurisprudence shows.[41] Adding to this picture is the perspective of Lacey *et al*, who convincingly point out that the notions of larceny, embezzlement, and so on, reflect what might be called the 'manifest criminality' of the offences, structuring legal consciousness and common sense notions of dishonesty to which juries seem to appeal.[42]

If I am right that 'zombie' concepts of this kind exist in the law, is that a good or bad thing? From my perspective, they are both. The existence of these zombies tends to undermine theoretical abstractions, and so their

---

[37] See, in particular, the criticism of JC Smith, 'The Sad Fate of the Theft Act 1968' in G Jones and W Swadling (eds), *The Search for Principle* (Oxford University Press, 1999).

[38] See ibid, and S Shute and J Horder, 'Thieving and Deceiving: What is the Difference?' (1993) 56 MLR 548–58.   [39] [2001] 2 AC 241.

[40] JC Smith, *The Law of Theft* (London: Butterworths, 1997), 5–7.

[41] Shute and Horder, n 38 above.

[42] N Lacey, C Wells, and O Quick, *Reconstructing Criminal Law: Text and Materials*, 3rd ed. (London: Butterworths, 2003), 350–83.

presence in the law reminds us that the dangers of treating law as a theoretical enterprise is real. If we take such concepts seriously, we may be in a position to unseat the influence of a bad theory and return to a more comprehensive understanding of the area of law they haunt, even though these concepts may not alone be sufficient to the task of delivering a workable justice. The sort of problems that a reliance solely upon the distinctions between larceny, embezzlement, and fraudulent conversion can give rise to are well known. The act of a shop assistant who dips into the till could be variously framed to count as any of the three. So the continuing presence of these zombies is also, typically, a bad thing, because we can assume that no theory whose aim was to replace them was given attention for no reason at all, but had appeared to be a solution to genuine problems to which their use had given rise. But it is plain that simply shifting to a higher level of abstraction which is intended better to reveal the core fundamentals of the moral wrong involved has not provided a solution to those problems. What is needed, rather, is an explanation which shows the value these concepts have for the law, to the extent they do, and how that value is both captured but made more complete by a new conceptual framework.

If the reader detects a Hegelian overtone here, he detects rightly. To my mind, Hegel's characterisation of historical moral development using the notion of *aufheben*, whereby the partial understandings of the past are both transcended and preserved in our current understanding, is attractive because of its characterisation of moral understanding and moral sensibility. Our first, partial understandings of the rights and wrongs of any situation are those to which we are prone; it is only by enriching our understanding with a fuller, more comprehensive understanding and sensibility that we are able to move forward, but this requires we retain a solid grasp of why our first impressions have the attraction they do, and what service they continue to provide in our moral reasoning. Reasoning about civil wrongs purely in terms of the various kinds of trespass is, we all now believe, insufficient. Paying attention to the mode by which an injury may be caused, eg negligence, makes us wiser, and better able to see situations where compensation may properly be required. But that doesn't mean that trespass to land or to the person are no longer categories of tort, and they continue to be torts for the very same reason they always were, whether or not some clever theorist claims to account for them by showing that the same legal decisions in trespass cases would 'fall out' of his theory if applied to the same sets of facts.

Consider now a couple of examples from the law of trusts. Several years ago, John Langbein ventured to assimilate the law of trusts to the law of contract, treating the trust as a particular sort of contract between the settlor and the trustee.[43] Now there is an obvious difficulty in treating the trust in this way, since the settlor and the trustee can be the same person. I can make what is called a 'self-declaration' of trust, declaring that I hold now property on trust for, eg, my children. This happens all the time; these are not by any means anomalous, rare, or peculiar trusts. But because they do not fit within Langbein's picture—one cannot contract with oneself, after all—he must relegate this sort of trust to the appendix of his article, the purpose of which seems to be to make these trusts seem as anomalous as possible.[44] I cannot think of a theory that more explicitly identifies a zombie concept guaranteed to come back and haunt the law, were the theory to be generally accepted. Now one might say this is simply a poor theory of trusts, and though I might agree with that, the example is directed to another point, which is the willingness of the theorist to treat the extant law so badly in this way; this illustrates one facet of the danger of 'theory' as I have characterised it.

Consider also the recent attempt by restitution lawyers who rely upon Birks's framework of events and legal responses to differentiate areas of law[45] to provide a 'taxonomic' structure for law,[46] to bring the law of 'knowing receipt' of trust property under the umbrella of the law of restitution for subtractive unjust enrichment. Now it is not our present concern that attempts to do so have run into problems internally, so to speak, eg in attempting to frame a plausible 'unjust factor' which serves to generate the claim for restitution.[47] Rather, as Smith has pointed out,[48] if this thesis is correct,

[T]he startling consequence is that not some but all of the cases on the subject are wrong. More recently, another line has been taken, to the effect that even if the claim in knowing receipt is based on wrongdoing rather than unjust enrichment, nonetheless there is no reason that a plaintiff cannot put to one side the claim based on wrongdoing, and sue instead in unjust enrichment. The consequences of this view are only slightly less startling: the cases may be right,

---

[43] J H Langbein, 'The Contractarian Nature of the Law of Trusts' (1995) 105 Yale LJ 625–75.

[44] 'In short, most usages of the declaration of trust are either non-trusts or way stations to real third-party-trustee trusts'. Ibid, at 672.

[45] P Birks, *The Law of Restitution* (Oxford: Clarendon, 1985) ch 2 'Differentiation'.

[46] P Birks, 'Rights, Wrongs, and Remedies' (2000) 20 OJLS 1–37; P Birks, 'Equity in the Modern Law: An Exercise in Taxonomy' (1996) 26 U. Western Australia LR 1.

[47] J E Penner, *The Law of Trusts*, 4th edn., (London: Butterworths, 2004), 433–35; W Swadling, 'A Claim in Restitution?' [1996] LMCLQ 63–66; ' "Ignorance" as a Ground of Restitution—Can it Survive?' [1998] LMCLQ 18–22.

[48] L Smith, 'Unjust Enrichment, Property, and the Structure of Trusts' (2000) 116 LQR 412–44, 412–13.

but all of the lawyers and judges involved failed to notice that there was another claim available to the plaintiff, and moreover one which would render otiose an inquiry into cognition.

Smith goes on to say that what seems to underlie this project is either a failure, or an unwillingness, to give effect to the trust as the legal device that it is. One finds a desire to abstract away from the distinct kinds of property interests one has as a legal owner and as a beneficiary under a trust, on the principle that like cases must be treated alike. While no-one would wish to deny the force of that principle, it is obviously not self-applying. The danger run here by applying the principle at a level of abstraction where the trust beneficiary is treated just as if he were a legal owner is that one falsely equates different things, and misses important distinctions.[49]

V

While I think these examples could be multiplied I must now leave it to the reader to ponder how extensively theory as I have characterised it operates in various areas of law with the deleterious consequences I have been warning of. I want to finish by responding to a couple of objections which these thoughts have provoked.

The first[50] is that while this analysis might be plausible with respect to the traditional common law areas of doctrine, it does not apply at all well to other vast stretches of the law, in particular those now heavily shaped by statute. Consider the Human Rights Act 1998, or consumer protection legislation which alters the common law of contract, or the Human Embryology Act 1990. In the context of these areas of the law, it may be claimed, lawyers and judges are actually intended to reason about cases trying to apply various theories of rights and justice, deriving from moral theories about rights, or economic theories about market failure, or moral theories about the sanctity of life, respectively. In such cases, to do law itself is to engage in the very sort of theorising I have characterised. In the first place, it is perhaps well to respond simply by agreeing, and to treat my analysis as one which applies only, or applies best, to the common law. But a little more can be said. While I accept the plausibility of the challenge, it is not proven, certainly. In view of the prominence of moral and political philosophy and economics, it is undeniable that they have had their

---

[49] Smith, n 48 above, 422ff.   [50] Put to me by Hugh Collins.

influence in shaping the sort of statutes which the objection identifies. But as I have said above, making use of theoretical insights in one's critical thinking does not alone make one a theorist oneself, or even mean that one is applying the theories from which the insights are drawn. It is, to put the point differently, not obvious that even in these areas of law judges and lawyers see themselves as presenting their reasons and arguments as answerable to some theoretical discourse or community that lies behind the statute, rather than as making practical, workable sense of the statute. I think that the objection may stem in part from the terms in which such statutes are couched, which are often identical to the very same terms which populate the theories, eg 'freedom of expression'. So it is true that the legal arguments deal in the 'proprietary' vocabulary of these theories, and in that sense at least draw close to them. As a result, it might well be the case that sometimes the legal discourse may draw very near to the theoretical, and sometimes may engage in theory *per se*. It would be foolish to say that this never happens. But, as I say, it is not proven that this typifies the legal discourse in these areas. A further question is whether it would be a good thing if lawyers reasoned like theorists, whether economists or moral philosophers or social scientists or theorists of some other kind. That is a very large question, and all I can offer here is a suggestion, which is that this should be explored domain by domain. Perhaps judges should reason like, or more like, economists in the domain of competition law, or criminologists in the domain of criminal law. But I can see no merit in striving for a general capture of critical legal thinking by theoretical think-ing, if only because there is no such thing as theory 'in general'; each kind of theory has its own provenance and its own claims, suitable in some areas of human experience and endeavour, but not in all.

The second objection[51] is that this analysis seems to undermine the entire project of legal theory. I would wish to deny this, and to do so I must refer back to the distinction I previously made between theories *of* and theories *about*.[52] The sort of theory I have been criticising are ones which claim to be a theories *of* contract, or tort, or criminal law. Call this a 'doctrinal theory', in that it purports to explain an area of doctrine because it purports to show its essential nature or features, in moral philosophical terms. Now we can consider two other sorts of theory that concern the law. The first, philosophy of law, is irrelevant to my considerations. Philosophers of law explore the philosophically interesting or puzzling questions the law raises. How do rules work to guide behaviour? Does law depend on sanctions? Is the law necessarily authoritative? and so on.

---

[51] Owing to Nicola Lacey.   [52] Text relating to n 10ff.

None of this has the least thing to do with doctrinal theories of areas of law.[53] The second, which might be called 'legal theory' *per se*, very much does. Socio-legal studies, feminist legal theory, legal history and so on, all very much concern themselves with particular areas of legal doctrine; and rather than wishing to unseat this sort of study, I would commend and encourage it, and this is so for one of the most basic features of our understanding of social phenomena like law.

Ever since Peter Winch wrote *The Idea of a Social Science and its Relation to Philosophy*[54] it has been widely understood that the nature of a social phenomenon cannot be appreciated without at the same time appreciating what the participants think they are up to. Chess is not moving pieces about a chequered board to make pretty patterns, but a game with goals the participants understand and which guide their behaviour. And as this is so, this leads to one of the most difficult aspects of the analysis of social phenomena, which might be called the 'moving target' problem. For example, if our views of marriage once were that it was a kind of contract, as much as between families as between the spouses, to afford a context for the issue of legitimate children and the distribution of wealth, but now we think of it as the legal recognition of a bond of affection and mutual support between two people, irrespective of their sexes, then not only has our 'concept' of marriage changed, but marriage itself is a different (though related) phenomenon. In the same way, if the law is (roughly speaking) a context-bound 'functional' kind of the sort I have described, then so are its concepts, such as property or contract or crime. Thus to describe legal change, and to purposely argue for legal development in the Hegelian fashion I have advocated, is in part to be informed by the meaning legal concepts have, evidenced both in the thinking and behaviour of legal officials and the law's subjects in history. I think it goes without saying that legal theories, theories *about* the law as I have described them, can hugely contribute to this understanding, without ever purporting to be 'theories' *of* the areas of law they consider, in the pejorative sense I have characterised them.

[53] Perhaps that is a bit strong. Richard Nobles suggests that the evolution of English constitutional law, particularly in the development of the doctrine of parliamentary sovereignty, is an area of doctrine which is properly examined by legal philosophy to reveal the nature of law, whether for example it is organised around the idea of authority rather than an idea of reason. Constitutional law doctrine may be somewhat special, however, in that it may more directly relate to and hence reveal any society's operative concept of law, and this of course is a proper object of legal philosophy, in so far as trying to understand such a concept gives rise to philosophical problems. See the text to n 54, below.

[54] London: Routledge & Kegan Paul, 1958.

Indeed, to my understanding, it is almost an ethos of *legal* as opposed to *doctrinal* theory that it doesn't purport to generate 'theories of' doctrine in this way, ie theories to be delivered to lawyers and judges to make their job easier by giving them a theory to apply. Rather, the goal is to deliver insights into the nature and working of law which, if powerful, might be brought to bear in the development of law. That the marital rape exception was overthrown[55] does not make the judges in that case feminist theorists of law. What feminist theory provided, however indirectly, was an understanding of the issue which allowed the judges both to recapitulate the basis upon which the exception once appeared to make sense, and to show why it was no longer a just and workable element of the law. To the extent they did so well, the marital rape exception was decidedly killed, given a decent burial, and the case, as a part of the law to which reference can always be made, serves as its proper epitaph.

The claim of this paper is that this model of conceptual burial, by which a concept can be shown to have had its day, plausibly typifies legal development. If this paper were to contain a plea, it would be for a much more thorough penetration by legal history into the study of law generally, by which I do not mean merely a better knowledge of the cases and statutes upon which areas of law are founded, though I must say that wouldn't hurt either, but a broader 'intellectual' history of the way the law operated in terms of the way it was understood by both the lawyers and the subjects of the law. For that would allow us to develop the law so as actually to refine it, and to write better epitaphs. It goes without saying that if and when we change our relationship to our social practices, and thus change those social practices themselves, it is better to do so knowledgeably, sensitively, and rationally, than ignorantly, crudely, and haphazardly, and 'theory' can very much contribute to that, so long as it knows its place.[56]

---

[55] *Regina v R* [1991] 1 AC 599.

[56] This is not meant to be understood as the claim that law should only change in a piecemeal, incremental fashion. Not in the least. To take an example, I have committed in print to the view that the entire doctrine of 'secret trusts' should be abolished by statute, on the basis that it grew out of a wrong turning in the law from which courts have not been able to extricate themselves. But if my argument is correct it is so, I think, only because I have fully explored the reasons why the law of secret trusts seemed and seems to be reasonable, and why it (incorrectly) continues to attract the allegiance of some lawyers and commentators.

Rights, Liberties and Duties: Reformulating Hohfeld's Scheme of Legal Relations?

*Vivienne Brown**

Introduction

A curious feature of contemporary debates about rights and duties is the conceptual distance between ordinary rights talk and academic legal and philosophical discourse. It might be expected that ordinary talk would lack the conceptual precision and refinement of academic discourse, but what is curious is that the ordinary understanding of a right and a duty is not available within legal and philosophical discourse based on Hohfeld's scheme of legal relations, a scheme that has provided the conceptual framework that is more or less accepted by many legal, moral and political philosophers.[1] The ordinary understanding of a right is that 'X's right to $\emptyset$' provides direct protection for X's action of $\emptyset$ing. Hohfeldian claim-rights, however, provide protection by virtue of the action required of the duty holder. To accommodate the idea that the right holder's action is being protected, it is necessary within this framework to say that X has a claim-right that Y does not interfere with or prevent X's action, but again the content of the right is expressed in terms of Y's action (or Y's omission of action) not X's action. Thus both 'positive' and 'negative' Hohfeldian claim-rights are denominated in terms of the action required

* I am grateful for the hospitality provided by the Sub-faculty, later Faculty, of Philosophy, Oxford, when I was a Visiting Philosopher for periods in 2000 and 2004 during which I worked on this paper. I am also very grateful to the Dean and Faculty of Social Sciences, The Open University, for financial support during the former period. I thank Jonathan Gorman for his comments and encouragement. I also thank Michael Freeman for providing encouragement. I am grateful to an audience at the Faculty of Laws, University College London, for discussion of an earlier version of the paper; I am especially grateful to Andrew Halpin for his written comments. I am also indebted to an anonymous referee for comments.
    1 W N Hohfeld, 'Some fundamental legal conceptions as applied in judicial reasoning' in W N Hohfeld, *Fundamental Legal Conceptions as Applied in Judicial Reasoning and other Essays* (ed) W W Cook (New Haven: Yale University Press, 1923).

of the duty holder.[2] On the other hand, an Hohfeldian 'privilege/liberty'[3] does refer to the right holder's action but it is not directly protected. X's action is not prohibited, but there is no direct protection for the action. Any protection for the action is indirect in deriving from the protective perimeter or ring fence provided by the claim-rights that the agent has, not from the privilege/liberty itself.[4] Thus it turns out that, in spite of its pervasive acceptance in ordinary rights talk, the notion of a directly protected 'active' right is not available within the most developed conceptual scheme for analysing rights.[5] The scheme contains only claim-rights, which provide direct protection but where the action referred to is not the right holder's action (passive right; direct protection), and privileges/ liberties, which do refer to the right holder's action but where any protection is indirect (active right; indirect protection).[6]

Similarly, the ordinary understanding of a duty—a duty that is not correlative to a claim-right—finds no place in Hohfeld's scheme. Just as claim-rights are logically correlative with duties in the Hohfeldian scheme, so all duties are held to be the logical correlative of a claim-right. This has led to protracted debate as to whether Hohfeld's scheme applies only to private law with its paradigm model of mutual relationships between agents. For example, some critics of Hohfeld's scheme argue that the notion of correlative duties does not apply to criminal or public law where this element of correlativity is either absent or can be accommodated only by strained attempts to identify putative correlative agents within the state's legal apparatus. They conclude that Hohfeld's scheme is of limited applicability and not appropriate to all areas of law. Defenders of Hohfeld's scheme have argued in response that, logically, duties are correlative to claim-rights, so that such correlative relations must be held to exist in practice. So, for example, they

---

[2] 'No one ever has a right to do something; he only has a right that someone else shall do (or refrain from doing) something', G Williams, 'The concept of legal liberty' (1956) Columbia Law Review, Vol 56 1145; cf 1138, n 11.

[3] Hohfeld used the term 'privilege' whereas Williams, n 2 above, proposed the term 'liberty'. I return to this below.

[4] J Finnis, 'Some professorial fallacies about rights' (1971–2) The Adelaide Law Review, 4: 377–88 at 378–9; H L A Hart, 'Legal Rights', in *Essays on Bentham: Studies in Jurisprudence and Political Theory* (Oxford University Press, 1982) 171–2; Williams, n 2 above, 1142–5.

[5] Although such rights talk is held to be 'loose and non-Hohfeldian', even defenders of Hohfeld find it hard to resist: 'though the urge to talk about someone's right to do something is probably irrepressible even among analysts of Hohfeld, we should recognise that such talk is in fact referring to an entitlement which requires that a *duty-bearer* forgo interference or afford assistance or provide remuneration', M H Kramer, 'Rights without trimmings' in Kramer, Simmonds and Steiner (eds), *A Debate over Rights: Philosophical Enquiries* (Oxford University Press, 1998), 14.

[6] That is, excluding the second-order legal relations of powers and immunities. In this paper I focus on the first-order legal relations of claim-rights and privileges/liberties, although in practice such relations might be 'bundled' with second-order ones.

would argue that the duties of the criminal law are correlated with claim-rights held by state officials. They conclude that identifying the correlative claim-rights, however complicated or abstract this may seem, is necessary for maintaining clarity and logical rigour in analysis of legal relations.[7]

Thus Hohfeld's scheme does not permit directly protected active rights or non-correlative duties. In this paper I shall question this outcome of Hohfeld's analysis by raising some questions about the internal coherence of the scheme.[8] Although my approach is critical of Hohfeld's analysis, I will attempt to show that additional conceptual resources may be identified by means of interrogating the scheme. The dialectical strategy of my argument here is thus to accept Hohfeld's argument in favour of analytical clarity and coherence in specifying the different legal relations and their logical properties, but to attempt to show that Hohfeld's scheme actually elides certain key notions and thereby compresses the range of rights and duties.

Legal Relations and Legal Concepts

Hohfeld argued that 'right' is a generic term and that the four different kinds of rights—claim-right, privilege, power and immunity—need to be analysed in terms of legal relations that are logically interlinked as opposites and correlatives of each other. In this paper I shall focus on the first-order rights of 'claim-right' and 'privilege/liberty'. These two rights with their correlatives and opposites are shown in Table 1 which clearly displays the internal symmetry of Hohfeld's scheme.[9]

In spite of Hohfeld's emphasis on the legal relations between agents, Table 1 does not include the agents. When the two agents are added,

---

[7] For explication and discussion of Hohfeld's scheme see eg S Coyle, 'Are there necessary truths about rights?' (2002) Canadian Journal of Law and Jurisprudence, XV, 21–49; Finnis, n 4 above; M D A Freeman, *Lloyd's Introduction to Jurisprudence*, 7th ed (London: Sweet & Maxwell, 2001) 355–8; J Gorman, *Rights and Reason: An Introduction to the Philosophy of Rights* (Chesham: Acumen, 2003) especially chs 7–8; A Halpin, 'Fundamental legal conceptions reconsidered' (2003) Canadian Journal of Law and Jurisprudence, XVI, 41–54; A Halpin, *Rights and Law: Analysis and Theory* (Oxford: Hart, 1997) especially ch 2; Kramer, n 5 above 7–60; P Mullock, 'The Hohfeldian legal opposite' (1962) *Ratio*, 4, 158–65; L W Sumner, *The Moral Foundation of Rights* (Oxford: Clarendon, 1987) especially ch 2; Williams, n 2 above.

[8] Theorists who are critical of Hohfeld's scheme have presented alternative analyses of rights, but this does not address the issue of the internal coherence of Hohfeld's scheme that I pursue here. Cf J Raz, 'On the nature of rights' (1984) *Mind*, XCIII, 194–214; J Raz, 'Legal Rights' (1984) OJLS, 4, 1–21.

[9] Hohfeld argues for a similar pattern of correlativity and opposition for the second-order rights of powers and immunities.

Table 1 Hohfeld's scheme of legal relations: claim-right and privilege/
liberty

	Claim-right	Privilege/liberty (no duty)
Legal opposite	No-right	Duty
Legal correlative	Duty	No-right

however, it turns out that, for the internal symmetry of the scheme to hold,
the agent holding the claim-right cannot be the same as the agent holding
the privilege/liberty. This switch in the right holder is not apparent
when the table is expressed without the agents but becomes obvious when
the agents are included.[10] In addition, as Glanville Williams argued in his
influential restatement of Hohfeld's doctrine in which he proposed the
term 'liberty' instead of 'privilege', Hohfeld failed to explain that a claim-
right of positive content is associated with a liberty of negative content.[11]
Including these two amendments gives Table 2 in the case of X's claim-
right of positive content and Y's privilege/liberty of negative content:[12]

Table 2 Hohfeld's scheme, amended to include agents X and Y, with
privilege/liberty of negative content[13]

	X's claim-right that $Y \emptyset$	Y's privilege/liberty not to $\emptyset$ (no-duty to $\emptyset$)
Legal opposite	X's no-right that $Y \emptyset$	Y's duty to X to $\emptyset$
Legal correlative	Y's duty to X to $\emptyset$	X's no-right that $Y \emptyset$

The table now appears internally consistent, although what we have is
not strictly a *comparison* of a claim-right and a privilege, as that would
require that the two rights are specified independently. We have seen that

---

[10] For a discussion of Hohfeld's interchanging of 'names' and 'variables' see Gorman,
n 7 above, 91–5.   [11] Williams, n 2 above. 1135–8.

[12] For the purposes of this paper, negative action is not differentiated from omission of
action.

[13] There is, of course, a second table, mirroring this, in terms of the negative of the
action/content of the right/duty; that is, the second table would be in terms of claim-right
of negative content and privilege/liberty of positive content. Thus an agent who, typically,
has a privilege/liberty both to $\emptyset$ and not to $\emptyset$ would be accommodated within this
approach by being deemed to hold both a privilege/liberty to $\emptyset$ and a privilege/liberty not
to $\emptyset$. Y's privilege/liberty to eat breakfast or not would be an example. See Williams, n 2
above, 1138, for such a double table. Halpin, 'Fundamental legal conceptions', n 7 above,
48, 53, however, argues that it is a weakness of Hohfeld's system that an agent's having

this is not the case here, in that the specification of the privilege/liberty as 'Y's privilege/liberty not to $\emptyset$' is determined by the specification of the claim-right, given the postulate of internal symmetry of the scheme. Perhaps the table needs to be interpreted, following Williams's interpretation of it, as 'explaining what happens when a right or duty is repealed or denied', since this would legitimate the switch from X as the claim-right holder to Y as the privilege/liberty holder, in that the repeal/denial of X's claim-right that $Y\emptyset$ results in Y's having the privilege/liberty not to $\emptyset$.[14] This interpretation underpins Williams's presentation of the scheme as a 2×2 array where the diagonal pairs—claim-right: no-right; and duty: liberty not (no-duty)—are legal opposites.

Some difficulties remain, however. If the purpose of the table is to trace the changes in the legal situations of the agents resulting from the repeal or denial of a claim-right or duty, the presentation of the table with legal opposites shown as diagonals is counter-intuitive if not misleading. If the second column is headed 'Their repeal or denial', as in Williams's table,[15] then the elements in the second column should be shown in horizontal alignment with the elements in the first column that they repeal/deny, not diagonally. Such a layout is shown in Table 3:

Table 3 Amending Williams's table: rights (of positive content) and their 'repeal or denial'

Rights of positive content	Their repeal or denial
X's claim-right that $Y\emptyset$	X's no-right that $Y\emptyset$
Y's duty to X to $\emptyset$	Y's no-duty to X to $\emptyset$ =
	Y's liberty not to $\emptyset$

Table 3 shows what happens when X's right of positive content (or Y's duty) is repealed or denied; that is, 'what happens' is shown by reading horizontally from left to right (or right to left). The vertical relation between the rows is that of correlativity. But such a table now seems some distance from Hohfeld's analysis which was meant to display the logical properties of the legal relations.

This raises a question concerning the congruence of a narrative account of 'what happens' in the scheme and a logical analysis of the scheme. Williams

a liberty not to $\emptyset$ is logically independent of whether the agent also has a liberty of positive action. See n 46 below.

[14] Williams, n 2 above, 1138. Finnis, n 4 above, 377, argues that if A no longer has a claim-right that B do (or not do) X 'the new (or asserted) situation will be such that B, *not now having that duty to A*, has a liberty not to do (or to do) X, while A now has [a] no-right that B do (or not do) X.' (emphasis added).   [15] Williams, n 2 above, 1138.

attempts to construe 'what happens' in repeal/denial by means of the logic of legal opposites.[16] He proposes a logical clarification of Hohfeld's legal opposites as 'contradictories' that taken together 'exhaust the relevant field (universe of discourse)'.[17] Williams thus treats 'what happens' in repeal/ denial as equivalent to logical contradiction. Interpreting legal opposites as contradictories seems to be correct, but there is a separate question of what Williams takes to be in contradiction here. Williams applies the logic of contradictories to the legal 'concepts' of rights and duties:

Reading diagonally towards the right, the tables state what happens when a right or duty is repealed or denied. In other words, the concepts connected by diagonal arrows are legal contradictories; each is a denial of the truth of the other.[18]

Here Williams interprets 'what happens' when a right or duty is repealed/ denied as a denial of the concept 'right' or 'duty'. A problem with this, however, is that it is not clear how concepts, such as 'right' or 'duty', can be contradictories. It is not clear how concepts can contradict or deny the truth of each other. In standard logic two propositions are contradictories if one must be true and the other must be false. Thus in standard logic it is propositions that can be contradictories, not concepts. Candidates for being contradictories in Hohfeld's scheme are thus the propositions that express the legal relations, not the concepts 'right/duty'; that is, it is the contradictory of the proposition expressing the legal relation that provides the legal opposite.[19] Thus, if we take '*Y* has a duty to *X* to *Ø*' as the legal relation, then the opposite is given by the contradictory of this, which is 'it is not the case that *Y* has a duty to *X* to *Ø*' or '*Y* does not have a duty to *X* to *Ø*'.

It follows that the negative of the concept 'duty', that is, 'no-duty', cannot be a contradictory and so cannot be a legal opposite within Hohfeld's scheme. Perhaps, however, all we need to do to retain the negative concept for the legal opposite is to set it in terms of the legal relation. This would give us '*Y* has a no-duty to *X* to *Ø*'. Logically, however, this is a 'contrary' of '*Y* has a duty to *X* to *Ø*', not the contradictory. Whereas two propositions are contradictories if one must be true and the other must be false, two propositions are contraries if both cannot be true although both could be false.[20] It now appears that we have two contenders for the

[16] For debate on 'legal opposites' see, for example, Halpin, *Rights and Law*, n 7 above, 35–43; Kramer, n 5 above, 7–60 especially 7–20; Mullock, n 7 above.

[17] Williams, n 2 above, 1135.   [18] Ibid, at 1138.

[19] Coyle, n 7 above, 28–9, and Gorman, n 7 above, 91–5, emphasise the importance of the distinction between the sentences/propositions and the concepts. Coyle also argues that contradiction applies to the propositions not the concepts; see, however, n 26 below.

[20] In terms of the traditional square of opposition, contradictories are given by the diagonal elements and contraries are given by the top horizontal elements.

opposite of '*Y* has a duty to *X* to *Ø*', ie '*Y* does not have a duty to *X* to *Ø*' and '*Y* has a no-duty to *X* to *Ø*'.[21] Logically, the difference between these two formulations is that the contradictory and the original relation together exhaust the relevant field (as stipulated by Williams), whereas a contrary and the original relation do not (it is possible that neither of the contrary propositions is true). Legally, the difference between the two formulations is that the contradictory refers to the negation of *Y*'s having the duty (negation of the legal relation), whereas the contrary refers to the negation of the duty that *Y* has (negation of the legal concept).

Does this distinction matter? Neither Hohfeld nor Williams discriminates between these two formulations. Williams writes: 'We may manufacture a compound noun "no-duty", meaning an absence of duty. No-duty is the contradictory of duty'; and 'a no-right means the absence of a right. Either *A* has a right in a particular respect or he has no right (a no-right); there is no third possibility'.[22] The argument above shows that there is a third possibility here within Williams's argument, not because there is a third term in a negation, but because there are two different items here that are capable of being negated: the legal relation (the agent's having the duty/right) and the concept 'duty/right' (the duty/right that the agent has). Williams thus conflates the two different 'negations', '*Y* does not have a duty/right' (negation of the legal relation) and '*Y* has a no-duty/no-right' (negation of the concept). And this conflation has continued ever since, perhaps reinforced by the tradition of presenting the scheme in terms of 'concepts' rather than legal relations between the agents.[23] In all this, however, Williams was simply following where Hohfeld had led the way. A root cause is that Hohfeld does not differentiate between the 'legal relation' and the 'legal conception'.[24] For example, Hohfeld writes:

That being so, if further evidence be needed as to the fundamental and important difference between a right (or claim) and a privilege, surely it is found in the fact

---

[21] In summary, for a legal relation such as '*X* has a claim-right that *YØ*', I differentiate between (i) its contradictory, ie 'it is not the case that *X* has a claim-right that *YØ* = '*X* does not have a claim-right that *YØ*', and (ii) various contraries where a term within the original relation is negated: (a) '*X* has a *no-claim-right* that *YØ* (negation of 'claim-right'); (b) '*X* has a claim-right that *Y not Ø*' (negation of the action or content of the claim-right); (c) '*Someone other than X* has a claim-right that *YØ*' (negation of the holder of the claim-right); and (d) '*X* has a claim-right that *someone other than YØ*' (negation of the agent against whom *X* has the claim-right). It is (i) that provides the legal opposite. Kramer, n 5 above, differentiates between (i) and (iib) at 19, n 7, but he neglects (iia).

[22] Williams, n 2 above, 1136, 1135.

[23] Although Sumner, n 7 above, 27, 30 presents the scheme in terms of legal relations between agents.

[24] Hohfeld uses the term 'conception'. I take this here as 'concept', without getting into debate about the relationship between 'concept' and 'conception'.

that the correlative of the latter *relation* is a 'no-right', there being no single term available to express the latter *conception*. . . .

In view of the considerations thus far emphasised, the importance of keeping the *conception* of a right (or claim) and the *conception* of a privilege quite distinct from each other seems evident; and, more than that, it is equally clear that there should be a separate term to represent the latter *relation*.[25]

In this passage Hohfeld slips from 'relation' to 'conception', and then from 'conception' back to 'relation', as if the terms were synonymous. Does this conflation of the legal relation and conception matter? Perhaps it might be thought that the 'conceptions' are simply a 'useful shorthand' for the legal relations, with no adverse implications attaching.[26] In principle there cannot be anything wrong with using a shorthand, as long as it is recognised that it *is* a shorthand. Trouble arises, however, if there are substantive implications of the 'shorthand' in conflating the legal relations with the right/duties that agents have.

Hohfeld's core message was that analytical clarity is essential for sound legal reasoning. This suggests that there is a *prima facie* case that the distinctions which I have just outlined should be taken into account for an understanding of rights and duties. It might be argued against this, however, that it is not apparent how these distinctions could have legal significance; or that the fact that neither Hohfeld nor Williams saw fit to make these distinctions is evidence that the distinctions are not significant. In the following section I address such objections by arguing that these distinctions are fundamental to an understanding of the category of privilege/liberty within Hohfeld's scheme.

The Category of 'Privilege/Liberty'

Hohfeld's scheme differentiates between claim-rights, with their correlative duties, and privileges/liberties where there is no correlative duty (the correlative is given by Hohfeld's neologism 'no-right'). Hohfeld provides many examples of mistakes in learned reasoning where this basic distinction is not recognised by the authorities cited. But it is a separate question as to whether the category of 'privilege/liberty' so formed is well defined. If the purpose of Hohfeld's analysis is simply to differentiate between

[25] Hohfeld, n 1 above, 39, emphasis added.
[26] As suggested by Coyle, n 7 above, 28–9. Unfortunately, Coyle goes on to argue that '*x* has a right wrt φ' and '*x* has a no-right wrt φ' are 'mutually contradictory', p 29, n 28. But these expressions are contraries (mutually exclusive) not contradictories. The contradictory of '*x* has a right wrt φ' is 'it is not the case that *x* has a right wrt φ' = '*x* does not have a right wrt φ'.

claim-rights and other (first-order) rights, then the category of privileges that he provides might need only to answer to this purpose. But Hohfeld's scheme is also interpreted as having a deeper analytical significance than this. It is interpreted as showing that, analytically, there are *only* two categories of first-order rights, claim-right and privilege/liberty; and that is a very different claim. It requires not only that the category of claim-right is well defined, but that the category of privilege/liberty is independently well-defined too. It has come to be accepted on the basis of Hohfeld's scheme that 'privilege/liberty', in not entailing protective correlative duties, constitutes a category of rights whose protection derives solely from the protective perimeter provided by any supporting claim-rights. This presupposes that the duties entailed by claim-rights are the sole source of protection.

Hohfeld's scheme establishes the category of privilege/liberty (of positive content) as the negation/opposite of a relation involving 'duty not'.[27] Two fundamental and interconnected questions are as follows. First, is this category of privilege/liberty well defined? Second, does the protection afforded to this category of privilege/liberty derive solely from the presence of a perimeter of supporting claim-rights?

These questions take us directly to the discussion in 'Legal relations and legal concepts' above. If a privilege/liberty is the negation/opposite of a relation involving 'duty not', then the agent's action is permissible in that the agent 'violates no rights of any of the parties' and 'commits no tort or crime or other legal wrong' thereby.[28] But we saw above that the negation/opposite of a relation involving a duty has two interpretations. This implies that there are two negations of 'Y has a duty not to $\emptyset$': the contradictory and a contrary of the legal relation, ie 'Y does not have a duty not to $\emptyset$' and 'Y has a no-duty not to $\emptyset$'. In both these cases Y's $\emptyset$ing is permissible. To the extent that the permissibility of the action is a defining feature of the category of privilege/liberty, to this extent both interpretations of the negative of a duty not are consistent with it. But these two interpretations show that there are two different senses of 'permissible' at work in Hohfeld's scheme. The first sense of permissible corresponds to negation of the legal relation ('Y does not have a duty not to $\emptyset$'). Here Y's $\emptyset$ing is not prohibited; Y's $\emptyset$ing stands outside the remit of the law and so it is not unlawful. The second sense of permissible corresponds to negation of the concept ('Y has a no-duty not to $\emptyset$'). Here what Y has is a no-duty not to $\emptyset$; that is, what Y has is an express permission (eg licence, abrogation of an otherwise existing duty not) to $\emptyset$, and

---

[27] Hohfeld, n 1 above, 38, 39.
[28] Hohfeld, n 1 above, 41; Williams, n 2 above, 1131.

so Y's Øing is made lawful.[29] Thus the two senses of negation of the legal relation provide two senses of permissible in Hohfeld's scheme—as 'not prohibited' (not unlawful) and 'expressly permitted' (lawful).

This can also be seen in the various examples that Hohfeld and Williams provide, which include both senses of permissible, although they do not differentiate between the two senses. Hohfeld's examples of the first sense, where the action is not prohibited and so is not unlawful, include: the liberty of a British subject 'to earn his living in his own way, provided he did not violate some special law prohibiting him from so doing, and provided he did not infringe the rights of other people'; and '*prima facie* it is the privilege of a trader in a free country, in all matters not contrary to law, to regulate his own mode of carrying them on according to his discretion and choice'.[30] Williams's examples include the liberty to get up in the morning, dress, take breakfast, and so on.[31] Hohfeld's examples of the second sense, where the action is expressly permitted and so is made lawful, include: the licence to eat someone else's shrimp salad; 'in the law of evidence, the privilege against self-crimination signifies the mere negation of a duty to testify,—a duty which rests upon a witness in relation to all ordinary matters'; and the privilege of self-defence such that, in the case of an attack on Y by X, 'the otherwise existing duty of Y to refrain from the application of force to the person of X is, by virtue of the special operative facts [of X's attack], immediately terminated or extinguished'.[32] Williams's examples include: the defence of privilege in defamation; substantive general defences in tort; and extensive discussion of licences which includes the comment that a legal liberty 'only makes an action lawful, which without it had been unlawful'.[33]

Williams also runs these two senses together in his discussion as to whether liberties are 'conferred by law', a question which he says 'is one of words'.[34] His prior discussion is as follows:

A liberty, as that word will be used in the following discussion, means any occasion on which an act or omission is not a breach of duty. When I get up in the

---

[29] This second sense is possibly recognised by Hohfeld in his reply to Pollock as to whether 'legal liberty' represents a 'true legal relation as such'. Hohfeld writes (n 1 above, p 48, n 59): 'A rule of law that *permits* is just as real as a rule of law that *forbids*; and, similarly, saying that the law *permits* a given act to X as between himself and Y predicates just as genuine a legal relation as saying that the law *forbids* a certain act to X as between himself and Y. That this is so seems, in some measure, to be confirmed by the fact that the first sort of act would ordinarily be pronounced "lawful", and the second "unlawful" '.

[30] Hohfeld, n 1 above, 42 (Lord Lindley in *Quinn v Leathem*); 47 (Baron Alderson in *Hilton v Eckerley*).   [31] Williams, n 2 above, 1129.

[32] Hohfeld, n 1 above, 41, 46, 32–3. Hohfeld's examples cover abrogations from otherwise existing duties, but express permission need not presuppose an otherwise-existing duty not. See n 38 below.

[33] Williams, n 2 above. The quotation, at 1133, cites Vaughan, CJ on the subject of licences to use land, but Williams states that this part of Vaughan's sentence 'expresses a legal liberty'.   [34] Williams, n 2 above, 1130.

morning, dress, take breakfast, and so on, I am exercising liberties, because I do not commit legal wrongs. Since the commission of legal wrongs is relatively infrequent, almost every act is the exercise of a liberty.

An example of a liberty appearing in legal works is the defence of privilege in defamation; also the (more or less) general defences in tort . . .

Most legal liberties are not to be found stated in law books, because there is generally no point in making these negative statements. It will not surprise the reader to know that there is no entry of 'breakfast, liberty to eat', in the index to *Corpus Juris*. If the law lays down no duty, it is generally indicated in legal works by making no reference to the subject. When a liberty is stated, it is generally by way of expressing the limits of a legal duty. Thus freedom of speech, which is a liberty, represents the limits of the duty not to utter defamation, blasphemy, obscenity, and sedition. Even so, we should not bother to proclaim liberty of speech unless this were regarded as a special value, to be jealously guarded.[35]

Williams then goes on to discuss the question whether liberties are conferred by the law, and in the course of answering it he again runs together the two senses of liberty:

It follows from what has been said that the question, sometimes mooted, whether liberties are conferred by law is one of words. If law is conceived as a system of rights and duties, liberties lie outside it; they are an 'extra-legal phenomenon', representing what is left of possible conduct after deducting the part regulated by rules of duty. However, it is often convenient to think and speak of liberties as being included in the law. The law, in this sense, includes rules denying duties as well as rules affirming duties. Considerable portions of law books are taken up with the denial of duties, that is to say the affirmation of liberties.

Liberties may be 'given' either by general rules of law (representing in reality the limits of legal duty) or by act of party; in the latter event a particular person has by law the power to dispense with the duty that would otherwise exist. Exercising this power, he confers a liberty. Liberties so given by act of party are generally termed licences. A clear example is the revocable licence to enter land.[36]

These passages suggest that there are two different interpretations of the question whether liberties are 'conferred by law' or are an 'extra-legal phenomenon'. One relates to legal process (eg abrogation of duty, defining the limits of a duty, giving a licence, repeal, and so on). According to this interpretation, as Williams argues, the question is one of words. But there is also an analytic interpretation of the question that is obscured in Williams's argument. In terms of the distinction I introduced above, one notion of liberty corresponds to the contradictory of the duty relation, '*Y* does not have a duty', and the other notion of liberty corresponds to a contrary of the duty relation, 'Y has a no-duty'. Thus, Y does not have a duty not to eat breakfast ($=$ has a liberty to eat breakfast) but if X gives Y a licence to enter X's land then Y has a no-duty not to enter X's land ($=$ has a liberty to enter). The answer to the analytic interpretation of the question whether liberties are an extra-legal phenomenon would be that, in the case of 'Y does not have a duty not to $\emptyset$', Y's $\emptyset$ing lies outside the remit of the law in not being prohibited, whereas in the case of 'Y has a no-duty not to $\emptyset$', Y's $\emptyset$ing lies within the remit of the law in being expressly permitted. It is for this reason that protection of Y's action in the former case is indirect whereas in the latter the protection is according to the terms of the express permission.

The category of 'privilege/liberty' is thus a hybrid category. There are two distinct notions of permissible at work in Hohfeld's and Williams's accounts, and these are equivalent to the two negations—of the legal relation and the legal concept 'right/duty'—discussed above. The significance of these two notions of permissible is that it is only in the case of the former, where the action is 'not prohibited', that protection is indirect. In the case of the latter, where the action is 'expressly permitted', there is direct protection deriving from the terms of the express permission. The category of 'privilege/liberty' as used by Hohfeld and Williams is thus not a well-defined category: although the category excludes direct protection from correlative duties, it does not exclude direct protection deriving from express permission.

The point here is not whether, in practice, Y may be equally protected whichever kind of 'privilege/liberty' Y has. Whether or not Y is, in practice, equally protected by the two different privileges/liberties is irrelevant to the analytic question of whether privileges/liberties can be directly protected in some way. Proponents and other interpreters of Hohfeld's scheme have insisted that privileges/liberties are protected solely by the perimeter of supporting claim-rights. Their argument, however, is based on conflating legal relations with concepts, and legal contradictories with contraries. The plausibility of such an argument has perhaps derived in some measure from the practice of construing the logic of negation in terms of a narrative account of 'what happens' to Y when X no longer has a claim-right against Y that $Y\emptyset$, since this puts Y's $\emptyset$ing outside any legal relationship (although within this narrative X is still construed as being the correlative agent, in spite of the absence of any legal relationship between X and Y with respect to Y's $\emptyset$ing), hence implicitly setting up the absence of a duty as the paradigm case of privilege/liberty, even though much of the discussion and many of the examples explicitly refer to express permissions of one sort or another.

This represents a profound challenge to the coherence of Hohfeld's scheme and to conventional understandings of the normative significance of the rights. Contrary to the standard interpretation of Hohfeld's scheme, it is not the case that no active rights are directly protected.[37] Active rights along with passive rights may be directly protected, although that protection derives not from the correlative duty laid upon a duty holder but from the terms of the express permission. What emerges from this analysis of Hohfeld's scheme is that the question of normative significance is an analytical question as well as a practical one: it involves not only the question of what Y may with impunity do, but also the question of what kind of protection Y has in acting with impunity. It is not only a question of 'what is it permissible for Y to do?', but also 'what kind of permissibility protects Y in doing what Y may?'.

To address these issues we need to differentiate within Hohfeld's scheme between the two different kinds of 'privileges/liberties'. To do this I shall have to introduce some additional terminology. I shall use 'simple liberty' where there is no prohibition against doing something. Thus 'Y does not have a duty not to $\emptyset$' = 'Y has a simple liberty to $\emptyset$'. For example, if Y does not have a duty not to eat breakfast, then Y has a simple liberty to eat breakfast in that Y's eating breakfast is not unlawful. And I shall use 'liberty-right' where the action is expressly permitted in law. In this case 'Y has a no-duty not to $\emptyset$' = 'Y has express permission to $\emptyset$' = 'Y has a liberty-right to $\emptyset$'.[38]

There is a question as to whether simple liberties and liberty rights are correlative.[39] In accounts of Hohfeld's scheme the other agent X remains on the scene in having a no-right after the repeal/denial of the claim-right against Y that X formerly had. But if Y has a simple liberty to $\emptyset$ why should there be any correlative? If Y's $\emptyset$ing isn't prohibited then there is no legal relationship between Y and any other agent with respect to Y's $\emptyset$ing. There may of course be legal relationships between Y and other agents with respect to claim-rights that Y has in relation to other agents' actions, but there is none with respect to Y's $\emptyset$ing; and if there is no legal relationship between Y and any other agent with respect to Y's $\emptyset$ing, then it is hard to see how there can be any correlative to Y's simple liberty.

---

[37] See n 2 and 5 above.

[38] In terms of Hart's explication of Bentham's analysis of liberty-rights (n 4 above, 165), this definition of 'simple liberty' is equivalent to Bentham's case (iii) where the law is silent, and this definition of 'liberty-right' is equivalent to Bentham's cases (i) active permission or countermand and (ii) inactive or original permission; although following Hohfeld both simple liberty and liberty-right are unilateral rights.

[39] In the discussion of the last few pages I have omitted the other agent when referring to duties. I now take this up.

Conflating the contradictory and a contrary of the legal relation, Hohfeld argued that X 'has a no-right', and this gives the impression that X does have a legal relation with Y of some sort. This is then easily extended to the notion that a liberty *tout court* is a liberty with respect to everyone. But the correlative of 'Y does not have a duty not to $\emptyset$' is 'there are not any rights with respect to Y's $\emptyset$ing' or 'no-one has a right with respect to Y's $\emptyset$ing'. In other words, there is no legal relationship with respect to Y's $\emptyset$ing. Identifying the conflation between negating the right and negating an agent's having of a right explains the absence of a correlative here. Thus 'Y has a simple liberty to $\emptyset$' is equivalent to 'Y does not have a duty not to $\emptyset$' only if 'duty' is construed non-correlatively. That is, this duty is not a duty owed to anyone. This duty is perhaps more like an 'ought' in specifying what the agent is to do (or not), but without any sense that the duty is owed to anyone. The notion of a duty as owed to another is thus a particular kind of duty. To differentiate between the two senses of duty I reserve the term 'obligation' for the correlative sort, and I use the term 'general duty' for the non-correlative sort.[40] According to this terminology, 'Y has a simple liberty to $\emptyset$' is equivalent to 'Y does not have a general duty not to $\emptyset$' or 'there is no prohibition against Y's $\emptyset$ing'.

Liberty-rights, however, may be correlative or non-correlative. For example, if X grants Y a licence to enter X's land then Y has a no-duty to X not to enter X's land. Here Y has a 'correlative liberty-right' against X to enter and there is a legal relationship between X and Y. On the other hand, if Y has a privilege against self-crimination then the liberty-right does not seem to be correlative. This would be equivalent to 'Y has a no-duty to self-criminate' (or Y has express permission not to self-criminate), without reference to a correlative agent. I term this a 'general liberty-right'. There are thus three kinds of liberty (adopting Williams's term, here, as the generic term), ie simple liberty, correlative liberty-right and general liberty-right.

'Liberty' and 'duty' are thus both generic terms.[41] Hohfeld's scheme of legal relations now needs reformulating so that the three different kinds

[40] This use of 'obligation' corresponds to an established legal terminology. I thank Andrew Halpin, without in any way implicating him, for kindly suggesting the term 'general' for 'not correlative'.

[41] Halpin, *Rights and Law*, n 7 above, 35–43, argues that Hohfeld has two distinct conceptions of privilege: one is 'no-duty' which is the negation of another concept; and the other, derived from Hohfeld's practical examples, is a protected right under which this protection takes the form of claim-rights with correlative duties. He concludes that neither of these conceptions is a fundamental legal conception, thus leaving claim-rights as the only form of rights. My argument is that both simple liberty and liberty-right are fundamental relations for Hohfeld's scheme.

of liberties can be identified separately. Following Hohfeld's analytic approach, we need to explore the opposites and correlatives (where relevant) of each of the four (first-order) rights relations in order to establish their logical properties. The internal symmetry of Hohfeld's scheme will be shown to dissolve but the benefit gained is the additional array of liberties and duties. The next section will reformulate the scheme of legal relations and it will also show how this can be used to construct a 'summary' scheme that goes some way towards retrieving something of the economy of Hohfeld's original table.

Reformulating Hohfeld's Scheme of Legal Relations

One way of presenting these four rights is to present them in two sub-tables, one containing the correlative rights (claim-right and correlative liberty-right), and the other containing the non-correlative rights (general liberty-right and simple liberty).

Table 4 presents the first sub-table which shows a claim-right and correlative liberty-right. Similarly with earlier tables, X is the holder of a positive claim-right and Y is the holder of the negative liberty-right:

Table 4 Reformulating Hohfeld's scheme: (i) correlative rights

	X has a claim-right that $Y \emptyset$	Y has a correlative liberty-right against X (permission) not to $\emptyset = Y$ has a no-obligation to X to $\emptyset$
Opposite (contradictory)	X does not have a claim-right that $Y \emptyset$	Y does not have a correlative liberty right against X (permission) not to $\emptyset = Y$ does not have a no-obligation to X to $\emptyset$
Correlative	Y has an obligation to X to $\emptyset$	X has a no-(correlative) liberty-right that $Y \emptyset$

In the first column, X has a claim-right that $Y \emptyset$. The opposite is the contradictory of this relation, ie 'X does not have a claim-right that $Y \emptyset$', and the correlative is 'Y has an obligation to X to $\emptyset$'. The legal opposite is thus clarified as the contradictory of the legal relation; it is not 'X has a no-right that $Y \emptyset$' as that is a contrary of the relation. And the legal correlative is clarified in that the two relations are here mutually entailing. This suggests that debate over the status of correlativity in Hohfeld's system stems either from a mis-statement of the legal relationship between X and

Y or from working with the conceptions rather than the legal relations, since the crucial point is that the action which is specified by the claim-right relation is the action which is required of the duty holder,[42] so this same action has to be registered in both statements of the legal relations.[43] Thus whether the relationship between *X* and *Y* is expressed in terms of *X*'s relation with *Y*, or in terms of *Y*'s relation with *X*, the action referred to (the content of the right/duty: *Y*'s action) remains unchanged.

In the second column, *Y* has a correlative liberty-right against *X* (permission) not to Ø; that is, *Y* has a no-obligation to *X* to Ø. *Y*'s not Øing is expressly permitted. For example, if *X* grants a licence to *Y* not to stay off *X*'s land, then *Y* has a correlative liberty-right not to stay off *X*'s land (or a no-obligation to stay off). This entails, correlatively, that *X* has a no-liberty-right that *Y* stays off. There is thus direct protection for *Y*'s not staying off, as provided by the licence.

The internal symmetry of Hohfeld's original table is now disrupted, however, even here where both relations are correlative and where *Y* is presented as the holder of the correlative liberty-right (cf Table 2 above). The opposite of a claim-right is no longer identical to the correlative of the liberty-right, because '*X* does not have a claim-right that *Y* Ø' is not identical to '*X* has a no-liberty-right that *Y* Ø'. In the former case there is no legal relationship between *X* and *Y*, whereas in the latter there is. In the former *X* cannot enforce *Y*'s Øing, whereas in the latter *Y*'s not Øing has some protection.

Furthermore, the opposite of the liberty-right is not identical to the correlative of the claim-right. This might appear counter-intuitive, in that it might be thought that '*Y* does not have a no-obligation to *X* to Ø' is identical to '*Y* has an obligation to *X* to Ø'. The intuition here might be

---

[42] As clearly stated by Williams, n 2 above: 'the conduct to which a right obliges is the conduct of the person under the duty', 1138, n 11.

[43] Even sophisticated interpretations of Hohfeld's scheme sometimes create problems for establishing correlativity by appearing to overlook this. For example in Coyle, n 7 above at p. 35 the action that is the content of the claim-right appears not to be that of the correlative duty. The correlativity of *x*'s claim-right and *y*'s duty is expressed formally by Coyle as 'Sophisticated Correlativity' thus: '$x \Delta \rightarrow \varphi(y) \Leftrightarrow y \nabla \rightarrow \varphi'(x)$', where '$\Delta \rightarrow$' is entitlement, '$\varphi(y)$' is *y*'s required action according to *x*'s entitlement, '$\nabla \rightarrow$' is duty, and '$\varphi'(x)$' represents '*x*'s project φ from the perspective of the duty-bearer rather than the right-holder' (n 39). Alternatively, Coyle moots a 'stronger' version of '$\varphi'(x)$' as '$\varphi(x)$' (n 39). But it is not clear why the content of *y*'s duty is not the same as the action required by *x*'s claim-right, which is '$\varphi(y)$'; the correlativity could then be expressed along the lines of: $x \Delta y \rightarrow \varphi(y) \Leftrightarrow y \nabla x \rightarrow \varphi(y)$, where '$x \Delta y \rightarrow$' is *x*'s entitlement against *y*, and '$y \nabla x \rightarrow$' is *y*'s duty to *x*. Coyle goes on to say that 'the axiomatisation based on Sophisticated Correlativity (SC) is not exhibitive of a *logical* system of relations among the various entitlements' (p. 36, original emphasis). But surely the point of Hohfeld's argument is to show how the legal relations *are* logically linked.

that the double negative in the former makes it identical to the latter. The problem, however, is that the two negatives in the former do not apply to the same item, which is what is required for a double negative to be identical to the positive.[44] Thus, logically, not having permission not to do something is not the same as having an obligation to do it. There may of course be circumstances where they amount to the same thing. The crucial distinction here is between the Hohfeldian scheme as displaying the logical properties of the legal relations, and the use of such a scheme to track a 'what happens' narrative. In using the logical properties of the relations to analyse a 'what happens' narrative, we are thus using logical differences to analyse changes in agents' legal relations. There is no problem with this as long as the distinction between the two interpretative stances is maintained. A possible source of confusion, however, is that in tracking changes the original legal relation might implicitly be taken as the default situation in a way that would not be valid as an interpretation of the logical properties of the relations.[45] Consider tracking a sequence thus: we start off with '*Y* has an obligation to *X* to *Ø*' (bottom cell, col. 1); then an express permission is granted to *Y* such that *Y*'s new situation is given by the top cell in col. 2 where '*Y* has a no-obligation to *X* to *Ø*' (this is a logical contrary of the original relation); and then this no-obligation lapses. What is *Y*'s final legal relation? This depends on what is taken as the default situation. If the default situation is taken to be the original relation of the narrative sequence, so that *Y* otherwise has an obligation to *X* to *Ø*, then, if *Y* no longer has the no-obligation the final relation amounts to the same thing as the original one. That is, for this sequence, with the supposition throughout that *Y* otherwise has an obligation to *X* to *Ø*, the final relation is equivalent to the original one. But this is not the same as saying that the final relation is logically identical to the original one; logically, the absence of permission to do something is not identical to an obligation not to do it. This may be illustrated by the case where the original relation does not function as the default situation. For example, the licence lapses and is not renewed because there is no longer an obligation to perform the action. Here there is no reversion to the original relation; *Y* does not have an obligation to perform the action even though *Y* does not have a no-obligation to perform it.

This shows, again, that we need to differentiate between the logical properties of legal relations and a 'what happens' narrative about a

---

[44] Williams, n 2 above makes this point at p. 1136 in connection with legal opposition and the negative of the content/action, that is, in connection with (i) and (iib) in n 21 above.

[45] This caveat applies even where the changes are simultaneous rather than sequential.

sequence of events. The former might be indispensable for understanding the latter—this is the theoretical core of Hohfeld's argument—but care needs to be taken when moving between the two forms of discourse. A further source of confusion here perhaps is the tendency amongst some commentators to refer to a legal relation as a legal 'position', as in Williams's usage. The term 'position' instead of 'relation' might seem to suggest that the entries in Hohfeld's scheme represent agents' situations in real time, rather than expressions of legal relations. Some theorists even seem to have thought that what ought to be described in the scheme is the agent's overall legal situation, so that it has been thought a weakness of Hohfeld's scheme that a single relation does not always achieve this.[46] But a legal situation for an agent may well be comprised of any number of legal relations (a bundle of rights, etc.), so it is not to be expected that a single relation can describe an agent's overall 'position'.

The practice of switching the right holder from X to Y, in construing the liberty-right as Y's liberty-right not X's, also contributes to this confusion between analysis of logical properties and a 'what happens' narrative about a sequence of events, as the only rationale for this switch is the construal of the scheme in terms of 'what happens' to Y when X no longer has a claim-right against Y. In view of this additional source of confusion, and in view of the fact that the purported internal symmetry of the table no longer holds even when Y is the liberty-right holder, there is no longer any rationale for continuing the practice of having Y as the holder of the liberty-right. I shall no longer follow this practice. Henceforth I shall adopt the same agent as right holder throughout (and positive content for all rights).

Table 5 presents the second sub-table. This shows the non-correlative liberty-right and simple liberty. X is the only agent and is shown as the holder of the liberty-right and the simple liberty. Both rights are given in terms of positive content.

In the first column we have a general liberty-right (permission) to $\emptyset$ such that 'X has a no-general-duty not to $\emptyset$'. The liberty-right thus derives from express permission for X to $\emptyset$. There is no mention of a correlative agent in the expression of the liberty-right and there is no correlative relation. Hohfeld's example of the privilege against self-crimination

---

[46] An example of this is provided by Halpin, 'Fundamental legal conceptions', n 7 above, 52–3: 'If we take, for example, a Hohfeldian liberty to enter Whiteacre, all that can be said from the Hohfeldian analysis is that this amounts to no duty not to enter. Hohfeld's analysis is incomplete, for we do not yet know whether the party enjoying this no duty not to enter is under a duty to enter . . . or also enjoys no duty to enter . . . We have seen that a Hohfeldian (half-)liberty is an incomplete analysis of a legal position'. But legal relations are not legal 'positions' in this sense. The legal position that Halpin seeks here would be described by liberty to enter and liberty not to enter. See n 13 above.

Table 5 Reformulating Hohfeld's scheme: (ii) non-correlative rights

	X has a general liberty-right (permission) to $\emptyset = X$ has a no-general-duty not to $\emptyset$	X has a simple liberty to $\emptyset$ = X does not have a general duty not to $\emptyset$
Opposite (contradictory)	X does not have a general liberty-right (permission) to $\emptyset$ = X does not have a no-general-duty not to $\emptyset$	X does not have a simple liberty to $\emptyset = X$ has a general duty not to $\emptyset$
Correlative	——	——

would seem to fall under this category. A more recent example might be the right of doctors under the UK Abortion Act 1967, to terminate pregnancies under certain conditions.[47] The Act states: 'Subject to the provisions of this section, a person shall not be guilty of an offence under the law relating to abortion [Offences Against the Person Act, 1861, ss 58–9] when a pregnancy is terminated by a registered medical practitioner . . .' s 1(1). The liberty-right to terminate (if that is what it is) thus specifies what doctors can under certain conditions do without committing a wrong. This would be a general liberty-right.[48]

The opposite of the liberty-right is 'X does not have a general liberty-right to $\emptyset$' or 'X does not have a no-general-duty not to $\emptyset$'. Again the question is raised as to whether the two negatives (in 'does not have a no-general-duty') logically constitute the positive, so that the opposite is identical to 'X has a general duty not to $\emptyset$'. (This would make the opposite of the general liberty-right identical to the opposite of a simple liberty.) The argument here is the same as that above concerning the opposite of a correlative liberty-right; and the caution against misreading a narrative sequence as entailing logical properties still holds. Again, logically the absence of permission is not identical to a prohibition against the action. I don't have a no-general-duty not to eat breakfast (I don't have express permission to eat breakfast), but it doesn't follow that I have a duty not to eat it.

In the case of a simple liberty such as X's liberty to eat breakfast, 'X does not have a general duty not to $\emptyset$'. Here X's action is not prohibited and it stands outside the remit of the law. The opposite of a simple liberty is 'X has a general duty not to $\emptyset$'. Again there is no correlative relation to the

---

simple liberty for the reasons given above. (It may be noted that general liberty-right and simple liberty are each a contrary of the opposite of the other.) This 'general duty' corresponds to the lay notion of a duty and is the non-correlative duty that a number of philosophers and legal theorists have argued for. Hohfeld's scheme has been taken to imply that all duties are the correlative of a claim-right. This result has been contested by those who argue that there are duties which are not correlative to any claim-rights; for example, it has been argued that various duties, such as those given by the criminal law, regulatory public laws, the duties of the state as given in public law, or the duties of moral or religious laws, are non-correlative duties. The analysis presented here shows that the category of 'general duty'—duties that are the opposite of simple liberties—answers to this notion of a non-correlative duty. This general duty provides another source of indirect protection for simple liberties; that is, X's simple liberty to $\emptyset$ may be protected by general duties laid on other agents as well as by X's claim-rights.

Tables 4 and 5 thus portray the categories of correlative and non-correlative rights/duties. They also show that the issue of 'protection' for these rights cross-cuts the two tables. X's claim-right is directly protected by the obligation on Y to perform some action. A simple liberty is an active right, which can be protected indirectly by a protective perimeter of X's claim-rights or by general duties on other agents. This leaves liberty-rights. These rights are active rights, denominated in terms of the right holder's action, yet they receive direct protection according to the express permission. This suggests that the distinction between correlative and non-correlative rights should not be seen as fragmenting the four rights into two entirely separate tables. Perhaps there is a way of recombining the two tables into one summary table. For claim-rights and correlative liberty-rights, what is important for their definition is the notion of correlativity. By contrast, for general liberty-rights and simple liberties there is no correlativity, although each one is a contrary of the opposite of the other. There is thus an inverse symmetry between the two sets of rights relations, in that correlativity is important for the definition of one set and opposition for the definition of the other. This may be displayed

---

'academics have freedom within the law "to question and test received wisdom, and to put forward new ideas and controversial or unpopular opinions" without fear of repercussions', p. 8. This 'academic freedom' might qualify as a general liberty-right. A difference between this and the right of doctors under certain circumstances to perform abortions, however, is that the latter abrogates an otherwise existing duty not to perform abortions under the stipulated circumstances, whereas in the former case there was no prior duty on academics not to question and test received truth, etc.

in a final summary table that provides a more economical way of presenting the results of this paper by combining what is important for the definitions of the two sets of rights relations. This table is achieved by amalgamating Tables 4 and 5 but omitting those relations that are not crucial for the definition of the right in question, and making X the right holder throughout (all rights are given in positive content). This final table is shown in Table 6:

Table 6 A reformulated scheme of rights

	X has a claim-right that Y Ø	X has a correlative liberty-right against Y to Ø	X has a general liberty-right to Ø	X has a simple liberty-right to Ø
Opposite (contradictory)	———	———	X does not have permission to Ø	X has a general duty not to Ø (X is prohibited from Øing)
Correlative	Y has an obligation to X to Ø	Y has a no-(liberty-)right that X not Ø	———	———

Table 6 suggests that Hohfeld's emphasis on the internal symmetry of opposites and correlatives for claim-right and privilege/liberty(not) derives from compressing four different kinds of right into two. Once the different kinds of rights are identified it can be seen that correlativity picks out an important element for two rights (cols. 1&2) while opposition picks out an important element for the other two rights (cols. 3&4). The issue of the protection of these various rights cuts across this distinction between correlative and non-correlative rights. Claim-rights (in col. 1) are directly protected by the correlative duty, and simple liberties (in col. 4) are protected indirectly by the agent's supporting claim-rights and by general duties on other agents. The liberty-rights (in cols. 2&3) are directly protected according to the terms of the express permission. Although there are more rights in Table 6 than in Tables 1 and 2, in one respect, however, the table is conceptually simpler because, without Hohfeld's postulated symmetries between opposites and correlatives, logically each column may now be read independently of the others.[49]

---

[49] This is not to suggest that there are only these four rights. These are the rights that are logically in play in Hohfeld's and Williams's accounts.

Some Implications and Applications

This paper has argued that Hohfeld's scheme needs to be reformulated and that the reformulated scheme displays a wider array of rights relations than has been recognised. Specifically the scheme now permits active rights which provide direct protection; it supplies a notion of 'liberty-right' that answers to lay perceptions of a right that is both active and directly protected, and it shows that this holds for both correlative and non-correlative versions of this liberty-right. The scheme now also permits a duty that is not correlative to a claim-right. The new scheme thus provides a more extensive conceptual framework for addressing the complexities of debates about claim-rights and liberties on one hand, and obligations and general duties on the other. The paper thus shows that philosophers and legal theorists have been unnecessarily constrained when discussing claim-rights and privileges/liberties in thinking that all cases must be shoehorned into just two rights.

The broader implications and applications of this reformulated scheme lie outside the scope of this paper and could well be developed in different ways, opening up debates about rights, liberties and duties in new directions. Yet some concluding comments might help to draw attention to some possible areas of development.

Theorists have debated the extent to which rights are essentially 'individualistic', but the rights in question in these debates have not included what I have outlined here as liberty-rights. These rights are 'active' and so might be thought to provide an exemplar of an individualist emphasis on autonomy and the agent's right to perform certain actions. This is true insofar as the right holder would not be dependent on an obligation holder for performance of the designated action. Yet there are other considerations which suggest that such a purely individualistic interpretation would be misleading. Liberty-rights rely on 'express permission' of some sort. Such rights are thus inconceivable except within a social/legal context where current norms, values, rules or law govern what individuals may do. The notion of an isolated individual expressing his/her will in absence of social, political or legal context, is thus misapplied in the case of liberty-rights. In repressive regimes liberty-rights (and simple liberties) would be restricted, and so resistance against such regimes would include campaigning against repressive prohibitions. In any regime, however, the liberty-rights that exist are the outcome of broader social, political, religious and legal arguments about their extent and compass.

Further, there has been considerable debate between the will/choice theory of rights and the benefit/interest theory of rights.[50] The former sees the purpose of rights in the independence and autonomy of the agent in exercising will and choice. The latter sees the purpose of rights as protecting the benefit or interests of the right holder, for example, by laying down duties (that is, obligations) which provide for that benefit or interest. Philosophers and legal theorists recognise that both theories seem to contribute something to an understanding of rights yet neither is without problems. For example, will/choice theories have faced difficulties where the beneficiary as right holder is not capable of exercising choice and lacks autonomy, for example, infants or the environment; and it has also been criticised in those cases where the correlative duty seems too important to be left to the exercise of the corresponding claim-right by the right holder, for example, the duty not to murder. Conversely, benefit/interest theories have been criticised for seeming unable to register the significance of claim-right holders' independence and self-sufficiency, and in failing to explain why benefits need to be carried by claim-rights. The reformulated scheme proposed above suggests that there might be another approach to this debate. Both theories have in common an acceptance that rights relations are theoretically homogeneous in that they all have to be explained by a single theory of rights; they see the law as having a single or unified purpose with respect to rights, and for this reason both theories have tried to redefine correlativity in terms of their own objectives.[51] But the greater array of rights relations put forward in this paper, together with the absence of internal logical symmetry proposed by Hohfeld, suggests that this theoretical homogeneity of rights might be an illusion fostered by the conceptual compression of Hohfeld's scheme. Correlativity is a logical property of some rights and duties and so is independent of construal by either of these theories. But, if some rights only are logically correlative, this suggests that different theories of rights might apply to different sorts of rights. Perhaps the will/choice theory of rights might be better suited to explain 'active' rights and general duties in terms of the legal or other endorsement of and limitation on the exercise of individual will and

---

[50] For a recent discussion from Hohfeldian perspectives see Kramer, Simmonds and Steiner, *A Debate over Rights*, n 5 above.

[51] As Simmonds summarises it: 'Crudely summarising a complex debate, we may say that the "will theory" claims that X possesses a claim-right when the enforcement of Y's duty is dependent upon an exercise of will by X. . . . The "interest theory", on the other hand, claims that a duty in Y is correlative to a claim-right in X when Y's duty was imposed by the law in order to protect X's interest', N E Simmonds, 'Introduction to W N Hohfeld', in D Campbell and P Thomas (eds), *Fundamental Legal Conceptions as Applied in Judicial Reasoning* (Ashgate: Dartmouth, 2001) p. xxi.

choice; whereas the benefit/interest theory of rights might be better at explaining claim-rights where the action required, which is of benefit to the right holder, is that of the obligation holder. If so, this would then raise questions as to which rights might be regarded as falling into one class rather than the other, and which (general) duties are properly so-called or are instead the obligations that are correlative to claim-rights.

Finally, the additional rights and duty relations outlined in this paper might have implications for understanding the history of rights in western European philosophy. Hohfeld's scheme of rights has been used to interpret past accounts of rights. The justification for doing so is that Hohfeld's scheme has been thought to be an accurate or 'true' analysis of rights, so that any coherent philosophy or history of rights needs to be congruent with it. Yet part of Hohfeld's argument was that previous commentators, including leading judges, had misconstrued the various rights. This suggests that it would be unlikely if earlier accounts of rights had sought and achieved just that degree of analytical clarity which Hohfeld criticised others for lacking; and to take an early twentieth-century legal analysis as a universally applicable scheme of rights relations for interpreting earlier work is itself anachronistic. If Hohfeld's scheme is the result of conceptual compression, as this paper has argued, its value as an interpretative frame for previous theories begins to look tenuous. Just two instances of application of Hohfeld's scheme to earlier theories might be mentioned briefly here. Aristotle's political theory has been interpreted in terms of Hohfeld's scheme of legal relations and this has generated philosophical debate, but there is a major question as to whether Aristotle's ethical and political writings are based on the correlative rights as laid out in Hohfeld's scheme.[52] John Locke's political philosophy is central to the modern development of secular rights, but there are difficulties in reconciling Locke's religious emphasis on God's power and donation to mankind with the idea of correlative claim-rights.[53] For example, if mankind owes duties to God and such duties are necessarily correlative, this implies that God has a claim-right against mankind. Yet God is held by Locke to be omnipotent, omniscient and the ultimate lawmaker—a being that is beyond finite human comprehension—so how can it be said that God is in a correlative relation with mankind or that he has a mere

---

[52] F D Miller, *Nature, Justice and Rights in Aristotle's Politics* (Oxford: Clarendon, 1994) proposed an Hohfeldian interpretation of Aristotle's political theory. See 'Aristotle's *Politics*: A Symposium' (1999), *The Review of Metaphysics*, 49, 731–907, especially the contributions by Richard Kraut and Malcolm Schofield; also V Brown, ' "Rights" in Aristotle's *Politics* and *Nicomachean Ethics*?' (2001) *The Review of Metaphysics*, 55, 269–95.

[53] For discussion see for example A J Simmons, *The Lockean Theory of Rights* (Princeton University Press, 1992) ch 2, especially 70–9.

'claim-right' against mankind for the performance of its duties?[54] By presenting a reformulated scheme with a more extensive range of rights and duties, this paper offers new potential for reconsidering the history of rights.

Conclusion

Hohfeld's analysis has been hugely influential in academic debates about rights and duties. This paper has argued that Hohfeld's analysis is in need of reformulation in order to differentiate the various rights, liberties and duties that have been conflated in Hohfeld's scheme. The outcome of the reformulation is a wider array of liberties and duties than Hohfeld's scheme seemed to admit. The end result is a more finely differentiated set of legal concepts and relations for philosophical, political and legal analysis of rights and duties, and for an understanding of their history and current political functions.

[54] For an interpretation of the figurative treatment of God in Locke's writing see V Brown, 'The "figure" of God and the limits to liberalism: a rereading of Locke's *Essay* and *Two Treatises*' (1999) *Journal of the History of Ideas*, 60, 83–100.

Who Should Make Corporate Law? EC Legislation *versus* Regulatory Competition

*John Armour**

Introduction

The beginning of the twenty-first century has brought with it an extraordinary set of stimuli for company law reform in the EU. A series of well-publicised recent scandals on both sides of the Atlantic have shaken faith in existing company law frameworks. Contemporaneously, in the wake of the ECJ's decisions in the *Centros* line of cases,[1] EU Member States are, for the first time, seemingly on the threshold of regulatory competition over the content of company law. The result has been protracted debates about the optimal 'model' for company law, informing an unprecedented volume of reform activity, both at EU and Member State level. A logically prior question concerns the allocation of jurisdiction to *make* the relevant reforms across the vertical, or 'federal', dimension—as between the EU and Member States.[2] This question is the subject of the current paper.

The analysis begins from the starting point that, given diversity amongst firms and national systems of corporate governance, a federal legislator cannot be sure which, if any, regulatory measures will be optimal. The paper's

---

* This paper is based on the text of a *Current Legal Problems* lecture given on 25 November 2004. I thank Brian Cheffins, Jens Dammann, Simon Deakin, Luca Enriques, Eilís Ferran, Martin Gelter, Barry O'Brien and especially Angus Johnston for helpful discussions and comments on earlier drafts and members of the audience at the lecture for their thoughtful questions. I am also grateful to Sir Gavin Lightman for kindly chairing the lecture and to Jane Holder for organising it so well. The usual disclaimers apply.

[1] Case C-212/97, *Centros Ltd v. Erhvervs-og Selskabsstyrelsen* [1999] ECR I-1459, [2000] Ch 446; Case C-208/00, *Überseering BV v Nordic Construction Company Baumanagement GmbH (NCC)* [2002] ECR I-9919; Case C-167/01, *Kamel van Koophandel en Fabrieken voor Amsterdam v Inspire Art Ltd* [2003] ECR I-10155.

[2] There is a second dimension, which may be termed the horizontal, or 'domestic', aspect. This concerns the selection of the appropriate body, within a given jurisdiction, for formulating the rules that govern the operation of corporate enterprise: namely, legislators, judges, regulators or private parties.

basic argument is that regulatory competition between Member States' company laws is likely to be a better way to stimulate the development of appropriate legal rules than is the European legislative process.

Whilst the theoretical possibilities for regulatory competition are now fairly well understood, a number of commentators have argued either that it is unlikely to be a significant force in Europe, or that if it is, it may be of the pathological, 'race to the bottom', variety.[3] My basic argument is that regulatory competition is likely to be both a significant and a beneficial mechanism for the development of European company law. A recurring theme will be that national diversity implies that the process will operate differently from the way it has done in the US: whilst there will be regulatory competition, no Member State will come to dominate as Delaware has done.

This argument will be developed in three stages. First, I will suggest that the EU is rapidly moving towards a framework within which companies will be both willing and able to locate their registered offices so as to secure a company law that is favourable to their requirements. For 'start-up' enterprises, this follows in the wake of recent landmark ECJ cases, and is motivated by entrepreneurs' desire to avoid barriers to entry created by capital maintenance rules. Moreover, it seems likely that EC legislation will soon also permit established companies to change their registered offices. For these firms, arbitrage will plausibly be motivated by a desire to ensure an appropriate 'fit' between ownership structure and the applicable governance regime. Most specifically, continental European companies which wish to shift from concentrated to dispersed ownership may find reincorporation in the UK to be an attractive option.

Second, I will argue that some Member States, and in particular the UK, will have incentives to engage in regulatory *competition* to attract companies, or to prevent them from being attracted elsewhere. For the UK, this will not be driven by tax revenues, as is the motivation for Delaware, but rather by professional services firms facing an increasingly competitive global environment. Other Member States are likely to respond with 'defensive' competition, either by removing inefficient rules or by further developing the complements of their systems. In the case of 'start-up' companies, recent and proposed legislative changes to

---

[3] See, eg, L Enriques, 'EC Company Law and the Fears of a European Delaware' (2004) 15 EBL Rev, 1259; M Gelter, 'The Structure of Regulatory Competition in European Corporate Law' (2005) 5 JCLS, 247; E M Kieninger, 'The Legal Framework of Regulatory Competition Based on Company Mobility: EU and US Compared' (2005) 6 German LJ, 740; T H Tröger, 'Choice of Jurisdiction in European Corporate Law: Perspectives of European Corporate Governance' (2005) 6 EBOR, 3.

European capital maintenance regimes provide evidence that this is already taking place.

My third claim is that the European regulatory competition will not result in a destructive 'race to the bottom'. In particular, proposed EU legislation governing the *process* by which established companies will be able to change their registered offices will give affected constituencies the ability to influence the outcome, so that arbitrage will be motivated by a desire to increase total value rather than the private interests of one group. The only way Member States will succeed in attracting such companies will be through providing company laws which enhance firm value. National legislators will therefore have incentives to engage in mutual learning: generally optimal rules will come to be adopted (and sub-optimal rules discarded); at the same time, particular national specialisations will tend to be enhanced.

Finally, I will extend the argument, rather more tentatively, to the case of corporate insolvency law. The better view is that Member States will not be able to preserve restrictive creditor protection rules from scrutiny under EC free movement law merely by characterising them as insolvency law, rather than company law. Moreover, I will suggest that the framework of the European Insolvency Regulation could permit a degree of regulatory competition to take place over aspects of corporate insolvency law— in particular, the nature of any 'corporate rescue' proceedings that may be available. It is sensible to consider their selection as part and parcel of the company law arbitrage, because the two may be complementary.

The rest of the paper is structured as follows. As a preliminary matter, the scene is set for the analysis by considering the scope of 'company law', the rationale for EU company law legislation, and the mechanisms of regulatory competition. The basic argument is then set out in the next part of the paper. Following this, the argument is extended to the case of corporate insolvency. The final part of the paper concludes with the suggestion that regulatory competition is likely to be superior than EC legislation for all aspects of company law on which there is no EU-wide consensus as to the appropriate regulatory choices.

Setting the Scene

What is 'Company Law', and What Does it Do?

In order to make sense of the issues, it is necessary to begin with a working definition of 'company law'. From a traditional domestic perspective, this may be thought to be obvious: that which is found in the companies legislation. Yet from a European perspective, this traditional answer is unsatisfactory, because the scope of 'company law' is understood differently in different jurisdictions.[4] It is therefore helpful to begin with a framework that is neutral across jurisdictions. For this purpose, a functionalist approach is useful.

A functionalist account of a particular set of legal rules or legal institutions focuses on the purposes served for society by the institution in question. Company law's role is to regulate and facilitate the operation of business firms. Thus, a functionalist explanation of the subject seeks to explain how the rules in question do this. A leading functionalist account of corporate law views the subject as doing two basic things:[5] establishing the structure of the corporate form (and in particular, property rules which partition corporate assets from the assets of individuals associated with the company),[6] and seeking to prevent opportunism within voluntary relationships between participants. All company laws view 'participants' as including shareholders and directors; most include, to some extent, creditors, and some—the German system, for example— also include employees.[7]

Thus company law establishes a fund of corporate property, and provides a set of rules to govern the voluntary arrangements between the individuals associated with the business. A contentious question at the level of domestic corporate law is whether the rules governing the 'terms' of these relationships—that is, the rules that seek to minimise opportunistic conduct—are adequate. The debate typically turns on whether such rules should be mandatory in their content, or whether 'default' terms will suffice, and in either case, what the preferred content of the rule should be.[8] In relation to each of the axes along which the law

---

[4] On differences in the scope of company law in other jurisdictions, see R Kraakman *et al*, *The Anatomy of Corporate Law* (Oxford University Press, 2004), 15–17. The proper scope of the subject has been extensively debated at the domestic level in the course of the UK's recent Company Law Review. See, eg, Company Law Review Steering Group (CLSRG), *The Strategic Framework*, URN 99/654 (London: DTI, 1999), 33–55; CLSRG, *Final Report, Vol I*, URN 01/942 (London: DTI, 2001), 41. See also DTI, *Company Law Reform*, Cm 6456 (London: TSO, 2005), 10.   [5] Kraakman *et al*, ibid, 1–31.

[6] H Hansmann and R Kraakman, 'The Essential Role of Organisational Law' (2000) 110 Yale LJ, 387; J Armour and M J Whincop, 'The Proprietary Foundations of Corporate Law', ESRC Centre for Business Research Working Paper, 299 (2005).

[7] Kraakman *et al*, n 4 above, 61–7. On employees, see H Gospel and A Pendleton, 'Corporate Governance and Labour Management—An International Comparison' in Gospel and Pendleton (eds), *Corporate Governance and Labour Management* (Oxford University Press, 2004), 1.

[8] F H Easterbrook and D R Fischel, *The Economic Structure of Corporate Law* (Cambridge, MA: Harvard University Press, 1991); B R Cheffins, *Company Law: Theory, Structure and Operation* (Oxford University Press, 1997), 126–262.

has an impact—shareholder-creditor, director-shareholder, shareholder-employee, and so on, it is possible to find a welter of academic and political opinion in either direction.[9] Moreover, it seems highly plausible that for any given regulatory issue, there may be no single 'best' approach for all European systems. Company law's regulatory choices complement other aspects of a corporate governance system and of the regulation of the economy more generally—including tax, labour, competition and pension regulation and corporate ownership structure. The diversity of national corporate governance regimes,[10] coupled with such complements, implies that different legal rules are likely to be best for different systems.[11] For the purposes of this paper, we need not engage in seeking answers for these debates, but may simply ensure that we keep their existence in mind by adopting, as an heuristic device, a perspective of 'regulatory agnosticism': that is, we can be sure of the desirability of neither rule nor content in any given case.

European Company Law

The European Community was established with the goal, *inter alia*, of forming a genuinely common market between Member States. This entailed the removal of barriers to trade and competition, and of other less direct distortions.[12] The variety of different national solutions to the

[9] For an impressionistic introduction, see (i) on manager-shareholder conflicts, P A Gompers *et al*, 'Corporate Governance and Equity Prices', NBER Working Paper No 8449 (2001) (weaker shareholder rights imply reduced performance); cf D F Larcker *et al*, 'How Important is Corporate Governance?' Wharton School Working Paper (2004) (corporate governance indicators poor explanators of performance); (ii) on shareholder-creditor conflicts, R la Porta *et al*, 'Legal Determinants of External Finance' (1997) 52 *Journal of Finance*, 1131 (relationship between debt finance and creditor protection ambiguous); Kraakman *et al*, n 4 above, 77–96 (different systems of creditor protection); and (iii) on employee-shareholder conflicts, B Frick and E Lehmann, 'Corporate Governance in Germany: Ownership, Codetermination and Firm Performance in a Stakeholder Economy' in Gospel and Pendleton, n 7 above, 122, 133–4 (evidence on codetermination inconclusive).

[10] O Fioretos, 'Varieties of Capitalism in the European Community' in P A Hall and D Soskice (eds), *Varieties of Capitalism* (Oxford University Press, 2001), 213–246; W Carlin and C Mayer, 'How do Financial Systems Affect Economic Performance?' in J A McCahery *et al* (eds), *Corporate Governance Regimes: Convergence and Diversity* (Oxford University Press, 2002), 325, 334–6.

[11] R H Schmidt and G Spindler, 'Path Dependence and Complementarity in Corporate Governance' in J N Gordon and M J Roe (eds), *Convergence and Persistence in Corporate Governance* (Cambridge University Press, 2004), 114–26; B Amable, *The Diversity of Modern Capitalism* (Oxford University Press, 2003), 54–66.

[12] See Preamble and Arts 2, 3 EC Treaty 1957 ('EC'); C Barnard, *The Substantive Law of the EU: The Four Freedoms* (Oxford University Press, 2004), 6 (citing Comité Intergouvernemental créé par la Conférence de Messina, Rapport des Chefs de Délégation aux Ministres des Affaires Etrangères, Brussels, 21 April 1956 (the 'Spaak Report') Mae 120 f/56, 14).

questions of company law formed the original impetus for the European company law programme.[13] In particular, there was concern that different national law structures might encourage harmful regulatory arbitrage, whereby companies were given incentives to relocate their operations or legal personality in other jurisdictions, not for sound economic reasons, but simply to avoid complying with domestic rules of company law. The plethora of different national law rules leads to a further distorting effect: namely, the increased transaction costs incurred by companies and their advisers when doing cross-border deals involving aspects of company law (for example, corporate finance or inward investment). The solution was to press for 'harmonisation' of national laws so as to minimise these costs.

The early years of the European project saw a consensus that the solution to these distorting effects of differences in national company law systems was to be found in the 'federal' (that is, EC-level) prescription of company law rules, which would ensure mutual compatibility.[14] This technique was employed in the early company law harmonisation efforts, such as the First and Second Company Law Directives on safeguards for third parties and share capital respectively.[15] As the European project has evolved, political consensus has become harder to find, with the result that progress has only been possible in the company law legislative programme by first focusing on specific areas.[16] From the early 1990s onwards, a range of less intensive techniques started to be employed, such as so-called 'framework' measures, which specify only general principles and leave Member States to specify the details at a later date. These less prescriptive measures have the manifest benefit of permitting greater adherence to the principle of subsidiarity, as well as being more politically feasible. The most interesting recent developments include the provision of a 'menu' of federal rules (as with the Takeover Directive),[17] and the 'comitology' process of devolution of legislative competence to a

---

[13] V Edwards, *EC Company Law* (Oxford University Press, 1999), 3–5.

[14] H C Ficker, 'The EEC Directives on Company Law Harmonization' in C M Schmitthoff (ed), *The Harmonization of European Company Law* (London: UNCCL, 1973), 66.

[15] First Council Directive 68/151/EEC [1968] OJ L 65/8; Second Council Directive 77/91/EEC [1977] OJ L26/1.

[16] J Wouters, 'European Company Law: *Quo Vadis?*' (2000) 37 CML Rev, 257, 268–76; S Grundmann, 'The Structure of European Company Law: From Crisis to Boom' (2004) 5 EBOR, 601; J A McCahery and E P M Vermeulen, 'Does the European Company Prevent the "Delaware-effect"?' (2005) TILEC Discussion Paper 2005-010, 10–18.

[17] Directive 2004/25/EC [2004] OJ L142/12. See J A McCahery and G Hertig, 'Company and Takeover Law Reforms in Europe: Misguided Harmonization Efforts or Regulatory Competition?', ECGI Law Working Paper No 12/2003.

committee of experts in relation to securities regulation.[18] A third, and even less prescriptive form of approximation, is what has been termed 'procedural' harmonisation.[19] This involves rules which, rather than seek to impose substantive solutions on Member States, aim instead to govern or influence the *process* by which legislation is passed.

In the wake of a series of high-profile corporate collapses, the European Commission announced in the summer of 2003 an 'Action Plan' for company law reform in Europe.[20] Much of the programme consists of measures for updating earlier EC legislation, but it contains a limited number of proposals for further substantive harmonisation. Most interesting for present purposes is the Commission's explicit recognition of the importance of national diversity, and the championing as part of the reform programme of measures which will allow companies to increase their jurisdictional mobility.[21] These measures, which will stimulate regulatory competition, can be understood as a form of procedural harmonisation—that is, regulation intended to influence indirectly the way in which Member States legislate by establishing an orderly framework within which regulatory competition can take place.

Regulatory Competition

As a third 'building block' for the argument that follows, we shall now consider what is meant by 'regulatory competition'. This may seem an obvious point, but it is one that is frequently misunderstood, or at least is used in different senses in different contexts. A brief scene-setting exercise may therefore be helpful.

Regulatory *competition* implies that national legislatures compete to attract firms to operate subject to their laws.[22] The preconditions for this occurring are as follows. First, firms must engage in regulatory

---

[18] E Ferran, *Building an EU Securities Market* (Cambridge University Press, 2004), 58–126.

[19] S Deakin, 'Regulatory Competition Versus Harmonization in European Company Law' in D Esty and D Gerardin (eds), *Regulatory Competition and Economic Integration* (Oxford University Press, 2001), 190, 209–13.

[20] EC Commission, *Modernising Company Law and Enhancing Corporate Governance in the European Union – A Plan to Move Forward* COM (2003) 284 final, Brussels 21.5.2003. See also K Hopt, 'Modern Company and Capital Market Problems: Improving European Corporate Governance After Enron' (2003) 3 *JCLS*, 221.

[21] EC Commission, ibid.

[22] See generally, Esty and Gerardin, n 19 above; D D Murphy, *The Structure of Regulatory Competition* (Oxford University Press, 2004). The classic model of regulatory competition responding to arbitrage by regulated parties is due to Tiebout: C Tiebout, 'A Pure Theory of Local Expenditures' (1956) 64 *Journal of Political Economy* 416.

arbitrage: that is, they select the law that governs their activities in a way that will minimise their costs of operation. In turn, this implies that firms are permitted to do so, and that the costs of switching jurisdictions are less than the savings thereby achieved. Second, even if such arbitrage occurs, for regulatory competition to follow, individual jurisdictions must have something to gain by firms conducting business subject to their laws (or lose by their not doing so). If both conditions are met, then jurisdictions will seek to enact laws designed to encourage firms to 'use' their regulations, as opposed to those in other jurisdictions. The key point is that the law reform process will come to be driven, at least in part, by the preferences of firms that are subject to the regulation in question.

Applied to company law, regulatory competition can operate with respect to the so-called *lex societatis*, where firms are able to select, freely as between different jurisdictions, the law governing a company's internal affairs. The US experience in this regard forms a well-known example.[23] It is worth considering in a little detail the institutional foundations of this case study. First, arbitrage. Federal conflicts rules rely on a 'place of incorporation' connecting factor in relation to the 'internal affairs' of a corporation, under which a US corporation's governance arrangements will be subject to the law of the state where it was formed. Moreover, almost all US states permit corporations (i) to reincorporate 'inwards' from another jurisdiction and (ii) to reincorporate 'outwards' in favour of another jurisdiction. These rules combine to permit a corporate entity to reincorporate in State B and have the laws of that state govern its internal affairs, even though the entirety of its business is physically located in State A, and its only connection with State B is incorporation there. It is not costly for firms to reincorporate, and a significant number of firms have chosen to do so, almost all in favour of the same jurisdiction: Delaware.[24]

Second, competition. Delaware is a small state, which derives a significant proportion of its tax revenues from charges levied on the grant of corporate charters.[25] It does not prohibit companies from switching out of Delaware once they have chosen to establish their registered office,

---

[23] R Romano, *The Genius of American Corporate Law* (Washington, DC: AEI Press, 1993); R Drury, 'A European Look at the American Experience of the Delaware Syndrome' (2005) 5 JCLS, 1.

[24] R Romano, 'Law as Product: Some Pieces of the Incorporation Puzzle' (1985) 1 *J L Econ & Org*, 225, 244 (82% of reincorporating firms chose Delaware); C Alva, 'Delaware and the Market for Corporate Charters: History and Agency' (1990) 15 Del J Corp L, 885, 887 (over 40% of NYSE listed firms and over 50% of Fortune 500 firms incorporated in Delaware).

[25] W L Cary, 'Federalism and Corporate Law: Reflections on Delaware' (1974) 88 Yale LJ, 663, 664; Romano, n 23 above, 15–16; M Kahan and E Kamar, 'The Myth of State Competition in Corporate Law' (2002) 55 Stanf L Rev, 679, 687–94.

should Delaware law cease to be attractive. Moreover, there is no viable alternative source of revenue to replace the charter dollars. Romano argues that the state's willingness to render itself vulnerable to the loss of this revenue, should it cease to satisfy its corporate 'customers', is part of its initial attractiveness. This is thus a 'hostage' given to them in order to signal Delaware's willingness to engage in continuous reform of its corporate law so as to reflect the preferences of firms that have incorporated there.[26] In addition, the Delaware bar are said to enjoy substantial revenues from the work they do in relation to firms incorporated in that state. As a well-organised and influential lobby-group, their concerns are thought to be taken seriously by the Delaware legislature.[27]

The process of regulatory competition is viewed with suspicion by some, who label it pejoratively as a 'race for the bottom'.[28] Indeed, the desire to avoid such an outcome was one of the original rationales for the European company law harmonisation project.[29] It is easy to show why this might be the case if it is assumed first that a particular variety of regulation is unequivocally in the public interest and, second, that compliance imposes a net private cost on regulated firms. If regulatory arbitrage occurs along the margin of minimisation of private costs by regulated firms, then regulatory competition will undermine the ability of such regulations to further the public interest.

However, both assumptions are unrealistic when applied to company law. First, 'regulatory agnosticism' implies that we cannot be sure about the relationship between regulatory provisions and the public interest.[30] Second, regulations which further the public interest will not necessarily impose net private costs on firms. In particular, regulations that seek to correct a market failure, if they work effectively, may result in a net *benefit* to firms that comply. This will be felt through the price mechanism of the market in question. For example, measures designed to ameliorate the costs of information asymmetries between shareholders and managers ('agency costs') may result in firms being able to lower their costs of corporate finance.[31] Where regulation seeks to correct market failure, and if the federal legislature has no privileged knowledge as to the 'best' type of

---

[26] Romano, n 23 above, 38.

[27] J Macey and G P Miller, 'Toward an Interest-Group Theory of Delaware Corporate Law' (1987) 65 Tex L Rev, 469, 472; Romano, n 23 above, 28–31; R Daines, 'The Incorporation Choices of IPO Firms' (2002) 77 NYU L Rev, 1559; Kahan and Kamar, n 25 above, 694–700.

[28] The phrase was first coined in relation to corporate law by Bill Cary, lamenting the 'Delaware effect' in the US: Cary, n 25 above, 666.   [29] Edwards, n 13 above, 3.

[30] See nn 9–11 above and related text.

[31] R K Winter, 'State Law, Shareholder Protection, and the Theory of the Corporation' (1977) 6 J Leg Stud, 251; Romano, n 24 above; Easterbrook and Fischel, n 8 above, 212–27.

regulation, then regulatory competition can act as a 'race to the top'. Under these assumptions, the 'market' for the regulatory provisions can act, in the fashion celebrated by Hayek, to stimulate innovation and to aggregate the information available to firms about regulatory effectiveness.[32] Similarly, if diversity of systems means that there *is* no global 'best' regulatory choice, but rather simply locally-optimal solutions, then a 'market' for regulatory provisions may result in greater specialisation, if states perceive the best way to attract incorporations as being to capitalise on complements.[33] Again, innovation and mutual learning may be expected. Under these preconditions, then, regulatory competition can promote the beneficial development of national company laws where a federal legislator is faced with regulatory agnosticism.

The crucial precondition for beneficial regulatory competition is that the price mechanism operate as a binding constraint on firms' choices. An extended and ultimately inconclusive debate on this point has taken place in relation to the case of Delaware. Critics of the US system point to the fact that reincorporation decisions are typically taken by a simple majority shareholder vote, responding to an agenda which will have been put forward by the board of directors.[34] Therefore, they suggest that there may be a tendency for companies to tend to select corporate laws that favour managers, for example through permitting the use of defensive tactics following hostile takeover bids.

The empirical literature, however, has not given strong support to the critics' claims. A number of studies have reported that reincorporation in Delaware appears to have a positive impact on a firm's stock price, suggesting that the move is viewed by the market as value-increasing.[35] Others have sought to examine factors which determine a decision to reincorporate in Delaware, as opposed to remaining in the initial 'home state'. Some found that firms are more likely to remain in their home state where this has adopted an anti-takeover statute, implying inefficient decisions.[36] Yet others have found weak evidence that firms *avoid* states

---

[32] Deakin, n 19 above 216–17; R Romano, 'The States as Laboratory: Legal Innovation and State Competition for Corporate Charters', ECGI Law Working Paper No 34/2005.

[33] S Choi, 'Law, Finance and Path Dependence: Developing Strong Securities Markets' (2002) 80 Tex L Rev, 1657, 1705–6; K Heine and W Kerber, 'European Corporate Laws, Regulatory Competition and Path Dependence' (2002) 13 *Eur JL & Econ*, 47.

[34] L A Bebchuk, 'Federalism and the Corporation: The Desirable Limits on State Competition in Corporate Law' (1992) 105 Harv L Rev, 1435.

[35] Eg R Daines, 'Does Delaware Law Improve Firm Value?' (2001) 62 *J Fin Econ*, 525. Earlier studies are reviewed by Romano, n 23 above, 16–24. However, see also G Subramanian, 'The Disappearing Delaware Effect' (2004) 20 *J L Econ & Org*, 32 (arguing that any beneficial effect on firm value of Delaware reincorporation has diminished over time).

with anti-takeover statutes,[37] and choose to incorporate in jurisdictions with more flexible corporate laws and better-quality judiciary.[38] However, it is unnecessary for present purposes to form a firm view on the merits of US regulatory competition. This is because, as we shall see, the process will operate differently in the EU, so that the concerns of the US critics are unlikely to be replicated.[39]

The Basic Argument

Following from these ideas, I shall now argue that as a general matter, regulatory competition in European company law can be both feasible and desirable.

To What Extent Does EU Law Permit Companies to Migrate?

Until recently, it was thought that the legal obstacles to regulatory arbitrage over company law within the EU were profound.[40] First, the conflicts of law rules of the vast majority of Member States made use of the so-called 'real seat' theory in determining the existence and proper law of a company. In contrast to the 'incorporation theory' used in the US, this applies the law of the place where the company has its main place of business or 'real seat'. When combined with rules on the recognition of the existence of corporate persons, it effectively prevented regulatory competition from taking place at all. For example, if a company incorporated in Member State A (which applied the incorporation theory) then carried on business in Member State B (which applied the real seat theory), the courts of Member State B would reason that the company's proper law would be that of Member State B, and consequently, because it was not incorporated under that law, it was not validly formed at all.

---

[36] G Subramanian, 'The Influence of Antitakeover Statutes on Incorporation Choice: Evidence on the "Race" Debate and Antitakeover Overreaching' (2002) 150 U Pa L Rev, 1795; L A Bebchuk and A Cohen, 'Firms' Decisions Where to Incorporate' (2003) 46 *J L & Econ*, 383.

[37] Daines, n 27 above, 1596–97; M Kahan, 'The Demand for Corporate Law: Statutory Flexibility, Judicial Quality, or Takeover Protection' (2004), NYU Law and Economics Working Paper No 04-015. [38] Kahan, ibid.

[39] See text relating to n 123 ff. [40] See, eg Cheffins, n 8 above, 426–31.

However, matters have changed dramatically following the ECJ decisions in *Centros, Überseering* and *Inspire Art*.[41] These cases relate to company law arbitrage at the point of *formation*. Each of the decisions concerned the treatment by Member State B of companies incorporated in Member State A, but having their 'real seat' in Member State B. The ECJ considered that the application of the real seat theory, so as to deny recognition of the existence of the company in Member State B because it was not validly incorporated, amounted to an interference with the company's freedom of establishment. Essentially, the Court ruled that as a matter of EC law, a company, once validly formed under the laws of *any* Member State, becomes a 'person' and is consequently entitled to exercise the Treaty Freedoms.[42] Moreover, the mere fact that the company was incorporated in Member State A solely to avoid laws which would otherwise apply, were it incorporated in Member State B, does not constitute an 'abuse' of that freedom. The consequence is that any laws of Member State B which tend to make the exercise of that freedom less attractive to companies incorporated in Member State A will therefore be struck down unless they satisfy the four-stage criteria set out in *Gebhard*:[43] that is, they

  (i)   are applied in a non-discriminatory manner;

 (ii)   are justified by imperative requirements of the public interest;

(iii)   secure the attainment of their objective; and

(iv)   are not disproportionate in their effect.

---

[41] n 1 above.

[42] A voluminous literature has grown up on the legal consequences of the *Centros* line of cases. See, eg E Wymeersch, '*Centros*: A Landmark Decision in European Company Law' in T Baums *et al* (eds), *Corporations, Capital Markets and Business in the Law* (London: Kluwer Law International, 2000), 629; E Micheler, 'The Impact of the *Centros* Case on Europe's Company Law' (2000) 21 Co Law, 179; K Baelz and T Baldwin, 'The End of the Real Seat Theory (*Sitztheorie*): the European Court of Justice Decision in *Überseering* of 5 November 2002 and its Impact on German and European Company Law' (2002) 3(12) German LJ; M Siems, 'Convergence, Competition, *Centros* and Conflicts of Law: European Company Law in the 21st Century' (2002) 27 ELR, 47; T Bachner, 'Freedom of Establishment for Companies: A Great Leap Forward' (2003) 62 CLJ, 47; C Kersting and C P Schindler, 'The ECJ's *Inspire Art* Decision of 30 September 2003 and its Effects on Practice' (2003) 4 German LJ, 1277; W-H Roth, 'From *Centros* to *Überseering*: Free Movement of Companies, Private International Law, and Community Law' (2003) 52 ICLQ, 177; E Wymeersch, 'The Transfer of the Company's Seat in European Company Law' (2003), ECGI Law Working Paper No 08/2003; J Lowry, 'Eliminating Obstacles to Freedom of Establishment: The Competitive Edge of UK Company Law' (2004) 63 CLJ, 331; S Rammeloo, 'At Long Last: Freedom of Establishment for Legal Persons in Europe Accomplished' (2004) 11 *MJ*, 379; D Zimmer, note on *Inspire Art* (2004) 41 CML Rev, 1127; W F Ebke, 'The European Conflict-of-Corporate-Laws Revolution: *Überseering, Inspire Art* and Beyond' (2005) EBL Rev, 9.

[43] Case C-55/94, *Gebhard v Colsiglio dell'Ordine degli Avvocati e Procuratori di Milano* [1995] ECR I-4165.

As the dust gradually settles from the ECJ's recent crusade in this area, it is coming to be appreciated that analyses of regulatory competition in European company law must consider the question in relation to two quite different contexts.[44] The first, heralded by the recent ECJ case law, is that of entrepreneurial 'start-up' companies, over which the competition will be for *formations*. The second context is that of established firms. Notwithstanding the developments in relation to 'start-up' companies, there remain a number of legal obstacles to *reincorporation* by established companies from Member State A in Member State B. First, and most obviously, the laws of many Member States (including the UK) do not permit such corporate 'emigration'.[45] The ECJ's ruling in *Daily Mail*,[46] as affirmed in *Überseering* and *Inspire Art*, seems to establish that this does not interfere with companies' freedom of establishment, for the Court has held that companies are 'creatures' of the national law under which they are formed and can exercise Treaty freedoms only consistently therewith. Second, many Member States impose 'exit taxes' on companies which seek to relocate either their registered or head office (again, as evidenced by the rule challenged in *Daily Mail*), which act as a financial disincentive to so doing.

However, it is my view that these legal obstacles to change of primary establishment by existing companies are unlikely to persist. At the national level, some member states—such as the UK—are proposing to change their company laws so as to permit free jurisdictional (e)migration.[47] At the European level, a limited power to reincorporate in another jurisdiction has already been introduced by the Regulation implementing the European Public Company, or *Societas Europaea* (SE).[48] SEs may be formed under the laws of any Member State by transformation from an existing public company, or through the merger of two or more such companies. Moreover, once established, an SE may subsequently change its jurisdiction of registered office.[49] More pertinently, the proposed Tenth Directive on

[44] Tröger, n 3 above; Gelter, n 3 above; Kieninger, n 3 above, 762–65.

[45] On the UK, see P Smart, *Cross-Border Insolvency*, 2nd ed. (London, Butterworths, 1998), 348–49.

[46] Case 81/87, *R. v H.M. Treasury and Commissioners of Inland Revenue, ex parte Daily Mail and General Trust plc* [1988] ECR 5483.

[47] DTI, *Company Law Reform*, n 4 above 48–9.

[48] EC Council Regulation 2157/2001 [2001] OJ L 294/1.

[49] Ibid, Art 8. However, the extent to which this may be used as a mechanism of regulatory arbitrage is limited by the requirement that the head office—that is, the 'real seat'—must always be in the same jurisdiction as the registered office: Art 7. See L Enriques, 'Silence is Golden: The European Company Statute as a Catalyst for Company Law Arbitrage' (2004) 4 JCLS, 77, 79–84 (arguing that SE statute may itself facilitate regulatory competition); McCahery and Vermeulen, n 16 above, 18–22.

Cross-Border Mergers,[50] and/or the draft Fourteenth Directive on Transfer of Registered Office,[51] are likely to introduce mechanisms by which a transfer of registered office may be achieved without necessitating a transfer of head office.

Turning to exit taxes, it seems most likely that, once companies are granted freedom to relocate by European legislation (thereby bypassing *Daily Mail*), such fiscal rules will come to be viewed as unlawful restrictions on the freedom of establishment which companies would otherwise be able to exercise: a sort of corporate equivalent of the recent *de Lastreyie du Saillant* ruling which outlawed exit taxes levied by French law upon a natural person.[52] In a similar vein, the Merger Tax Directive outlaws tax impediments to cross-border mergers.[53]

Table 1 summarises the current and anticipated position. Not only is it legally possible for 'start-up' companies to engage in company law arbitrage on formation, but it seems likely that it will also soon be possible for established companies to do so through reincorporation.

Even if Regulatory Arbitrage is Legally Possible, Will Firms Wish to Take Advantage?

For it to be legally *possible* for regulatory arbitrage to occur is, of course, only the starting point. If firms are actually to exercise this option, the benefits to them from doing so must exceed the costs. A number of scholars doubt whether this will be the case, at least on any significant scale. First, it is argued that there may be little legal benefit to be had from

[50] European Commission, 'Proposal for a Directive of the European Parliament and of the Council on Cross-Border Mergers of Companies with Share Capital' COM (2003) 703 final, 18.11.2003, Art 3 and p 6. The Tenth Directive received approval from the European Council on 25 November 2004 (see European Commission, 'Commission welcomes Council agreement on making cross-border mergers easier' Press Release IP/04/1405, 25.11.2004).

[51] European Commission, 'Proposal for a Fourteenth European Parliament and Council Directive on the Transfer of the Registered Office of a Company from one Member State to another with a Change of Applicable Law' (1997), doc no XV/D2/6002/97-EN REV.2, Art 2; European Commission, 'Company Law: Commission Consults on n the Cross-Border Transfer of Companies' Registered Offices', IP/04/270, 26.02.2004.

[52] Case C-9/02, *Hughes de Lastreyie du Saillant v Ministère de l'Économie, des Finances et de l'Industrie* [2004] 3 CMLR, 39.

[53] Council Directive 90/434/EEC [1990] OJ L 225/1. It is unclear whether the Merger Tax Directive applies to the formation of a SE by merger: see Enriques, n 3 above, 1261–62. However, an overwhelming majority of the respondents to the Commission's consultation as respects transfer of seat were in favour of the express application of the Merger Tax Directive: see European Commission, 'Public consultation on the outline of the planned proposal for a European Parliament and Council directive on the cross-border transfer of the registered office of a company' (2004), question 14.

Table 1 Current and anticipated legal framework for company law arbitrage

	Barriers	Removal
Formation: 'start-up' companies	Real seat theory	*Centros* etc: national laws must permit *immigration*
	Unnecessary and disproportionate measures failing *Gebhard* tests	Case-by-case challenge
Reincorporation: established companies	*Daily Mail*: no need for national law to permit *emigration*	10th, 14th Directives will shortly permit *emigration*
	Exit taxes commonly levied	Likely to fail *Gebhard* tests; prohibited by Merger Tax Directive; will probably also be prohibited by 14th Directive

'jurisdiction-shopping'. The existing harmonisation initiatives have reduced the differences between Member States' company laws, at least compared with those that existed between States' corporate laws in the US in the late nineteenth and early twentieth century, when Delaware developed its dominant position.[54] Moreover, litigation by minority shareholders being much rarer in Europe than in the US,[55] the expected benefits from switching to a more 'favourable' company law regime may be small.

A second factor concerns the nature of share ownership patterns. Unlike their Anglo-American counterparts, public companies in continental Europe typically have concentrated share ownership, with control being exercised by a single large blockholder or a coalition of blocks.[56] This alters the nature of the corporate law 'product' in which that such firms would be interested.[57] Rather than being concerned with protecting dispersed shareholders against the risk of managerial misbehaviour, shareholders in a blockholder system are more interested in the extent to

---

[54] Cheffins, n 8 above, 433; Enriques, n 3 above, 1269; Kieninger, n 3 above, 769.

[55] Enriques, ibid, 1262.

[56] R La Porta *et al*, 'Corporate Ownership Around the World' (1999) 44 *J Fin*, 471, 491–98; F Barca and M Becht (eds), *The Control of Corporate Europe* (Oxford University Press, 2001); M J Roe, *Political Determinants of Corporate Governance* (Oxford University Press, 2003).   [57] Romano, n 23 above, 136–8.

which a majority is able to exert control.[58] If, as is likely, corporate laws and ownership patterns have co-evolved over time in European jurisdictions, the two are likely to be strongly complementary.[59] Thus, it is argued, there will be little to be gained by a firm reincorporating under a different corporate law that will be likely to be maladapted to its particular governance requirements.[60]

Third, some argue that problems over litigation will act as a brake on regulatory arbitrage.[61] A company whose centre of business is located in Member State B but which has reincorporated in Member State A would then have to decide where disputes should be litigated. To do so in Member State A would, it is thought, be undesirable in many cases, because of the need to retain different lawyers, to follow a different procedural system, and to consider issues in a different language.[62] On the other hand, litigation in Member State B would have the obvious drawback of having judges in Member State B decide questions on the laws of Member State A, with accompanying problems of linguistic and conceptual translation. To be sure, jurisdiction or arbitration agreements could be used to structure matters in most cases so that the problem is minimised, but on issues relating to the validity of the corporate constitution and the acts of its organs, the exclusive jurisdiction rule of Article 22(2) of the Judgments Regulation[63] would mandate that litigation take place in Member State A.[64] Thus the problems could not be avoided entirely.

A fourth and closely related difficulty with regulatory arbitrage is thought to be the difficulties involved in getting appropriate legal advice both in relation to the possibility of making the change and in structuring affairs subsequently.[65] The languages of possible states of reincorporation are likely to be different from that spoken by the company's management. Moreover, any suggestion regarding change

---

[58] Kraakman *et al*, n 4 above 22, 53–4, 60–1.

[59] L A Bebchuk and M J Roe, 'A Theory of Path Dependence in Corporate Ownership and Governance' (1999) 52 Stanf L Rev, 127.   [60] Gelter, n 3 above, 23–29.

[61] J C Dammann, 'Freedom of Choice in European Company Law' (2004) 29 Yale J Int'l L, 477, 492–502; C Kirchner *et al*, 'Regulatory Competition in EU Corporate Law after *Inspire Art*: Unbundling Delaware's Product for Europe' (2004), working paper, Humboldt University, Berlin and University of Illinois, 23–35.

[62] Kirchner *et al*, ibid.

[63] EC Council Regulation 44/2001 [2001] OJ L 12/1. Art 22(2) grants exclusive jurisdiction to the courts of the Member State where the company has its 'real seat'. For jurisdictions using the incorporation theory, the 'seat' will be interpreted as meaning the place of incorporation. This rule is mandatory, and may not be ousted by a jurisdiction clause: ibid, Art 23(5).   [64] Dammann, n 61 above, 495.

[65] Dammann, ibid, 503–7; Enriques, n 3 above, 1264. These arguments are based on evidence from the US that the company's legal advisers are often key players in its decision to reincorporate or not : see Romano, n 23 above, 274; Daines, n 27 above, 1580–1.

is likely to encounter hostility from incumbent legal advisers. What lawyer would propose reincorporation in a different jurisdiction, if this will result in legal work being transferred to another adviser? If the company's existing legal team are unable to advise, it will be necessary to retain another law firm, which is likely to be based in the state of reincorporation, to advise instead. This may entail considerable risk, if the company does not have a good knowledge of the reputations of law firms in the new jurisdiction.

I shall suggest that the arguments of the pessimists are unconvincing, and particularly so if it is posited that the UK might be the jurisdiction of choice for reincorporation. Once more, it is helpful to divide the discussion into the separate cases of arbitrage by formation and by reincorporation. As far as formation is concerned, the driver of regulatory arbitrage by entrepreneurs is clearly the restrictive capital adequacy and maintenance requirements of many continental jurisdictions. As the Second Company Law Directive does not apply to private companies, there is considerable scope for variety between Member States' laws, and the UK undoubtedly has a more permissive regime than most continental European jurisdictions. Thus, for an entrepreneur wishing to form a company without complying with expensive minimum capital requirements, the UK is clearly likely to be the jurisdiction of choice.

To be sure, such a selection will entail increased legal risk owing to the need to litigate some issues in the UK, as opposed to local courts, and the need to obtain UK legal advice. There are reasons for thinking, however, that these costs are unlikely to act as a significant brake. First, there is likely to be little risk of litigation over the company's internal affairs in the UK if it is owned only by a small group of shareholders, who might bind themselves with a shareholder agreement for good measure. External affairs could be directed towards the jurisdiction of choice through jurisdiction clauses as part of the company's standard terms. As far as legal advice is concerned, it would appear that there is a market opportunity for lawyers serving the needs of such entrepreneurs to start to offer their services. An entrepreneur is unlikely to consult a lawyer frequently, and so the idea of 'incumbent lawyer resistance' is not particularly compelling. The indications are that specialist 'formation agents' are already targeting their services at continental European entrepreneurs in an attempt to win this business.[66] Further evidence comes from the recent dramatic

---

[66] A typical example of many such agents found by a Google search is Coddan CPM UK, which offers, via the internet, same-day incorporation of a UK private company for a fee of £42. The website has versions, explaining arbitrage opportunities, in Spanish and German. See *http://www.ukincorp.co.uk*.

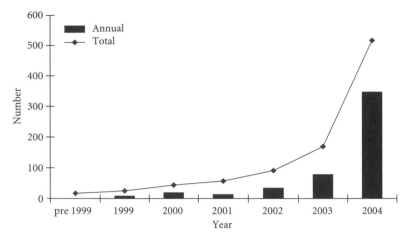

Figure 1. 'German' companies incorporating in UK.

increase in the number of companies located in continental Europe incorporating in the UK. To exemplify this, Figure 1 reports numbers of 'German' companies incorporating in the UK. These were identified by searching data from Companies House for companies with largely German-language names,[67] but ending with the word 'Limited'.[68] To be sure, the data are only impressionistic;[69] moreover, they respresent only a tiny fraction of the total number of companies incorporated in the UK.[70] What is significant about the figures is the way in which the rate of such incorporations surged after the *Überseering* and *Inspire Art* decisions in 2002 and 2003 respectively.

Turning to larger companies, the discussion necessarily becomes more speculative. However, if a typical listed company is taken as the paradigm, there are still good reasons for thinking that the UK may be an attractive reincorporation choice to many, notwithstanding the foregoing

[67] Companies House DVD-ROM Directory (April 2005 edition). The relevant companies were identified by searching for names including the following terms: 'AG', 'GmbH', 'Gesellschaft', 'und', 'mit' and 'handel'. This methodology follows Kirchner *et al*, n 61 above, 6–7, but by searching on a wider range of German words, a larger number of companies were identified. The results were checked manually to ensure that the names were in German.

[68] The suffix 'Limited' excludes firms incorporated in Germany but registered in the UK as an 'overseas company'.

[69] The data may be both under- and over-inclusive. On the one hand, the search methodology does not capture all German-language names. On the other hand, the data do not tell us whether these companies in fact carry on any business in the UK.

[70] There were over 2 million companies registered in the UK in 2003–4: DTI, *Companies in 2003–4* (London: TSO, 2004), 33.

objections. First, despite the early harmonisation efforts, many feel that the UK's company law still has a substantially more flexible character than the company laws of many other European jurisdictions.[71] To be sure, the difference is nowhere near as significant as the regulation gradient between Delaware and its competitors in the early twentieth century. Yet it is not simply the content of corporate law that makes reincorporation attractive. Commentators in the US have argued that a significant part of Delaware's advantage comes from the way in which adjudication is conducted. This includes the quality, expertise and 'business-friendliness' of its judiciary.[72] Thus it is notable that Delaware is the only state in the US to have a specialist court for the trial of corporate matters,[73] and Kahan's recent empirical study of incorporation decisions suggests that judicial quality is at least as important to firms choosing where to incorporate as the relative flexibility of key provisions in the corporate code.[74] Other related factors are the existence of a rich body of precedents accumulated over many years of judicial law-making, which enhance the certainty of legal rules, and the availability of high-quality legal advice through Delaware's specialist corporate law bar.[75]

Throughout Europe, the UK is perhaps uniquely positioned to capitalise on these procedural aspects of corporate law choice.[76] Similarly to Delaware, the UK has a specialist court list devoted solely to corporate matters.[77] This is presided over by judges who have spent many years in practice specialising in corporate matters, in contrast to the practice in many other Member States of appointing judges direct from law school.[78] In terms of certainty, it appears that English judges place even greater weight on precedents than their American counterparts.[79] This combination of legal flexibility and certainty permits UK companies to structure their affairs as they wish and with a low risk of legal challenge.

---

[71] CLSRG, *The Strategic Framework*, n 4 above, 96–8; Dammann, n 61 above, 525.

[72] Romano, n 23 above, 39–40; Kahan, n 37 above.

[73] Kahan and Kamar, n 25 above, 708–15.   [74] Kahan, n 37 above.

[75] Romano, n 23 above, 41; E Kamar, 'A Regulatory Competition Theory of Indeterminacy in Corporate Law' (1998) 98 Colum L Rev, 1908.

[76] Cheffins, n 8 above, 442–3.

[77] Rt Hon Lord Justice Brooke (ed), *Civil Procedure, Vol. 2* (London: Sweet and Maxwell, 2004), paras 1–143, 2G-14.

[78] M Shapiro, *Courts: A Comparative and Political Analysis* (Chicago: University of Chicago Press, 1981), 150; M Cappelletti, *The Judicial Process in Comparative Perspective* (Oxford: Clarendon Press, 1989), 220. However, it should be noted that many civilian jurisdictions provide for judicial specialisation in corporate/commercial matters.

[79] P S Atiyah and R S Summers, *Form and Substance in Anglo-American Law* (Oxford: Clarendon Press, 1987), 118–27; R Posner, *Law and Legal Theory in England and America* (Oxford University Press, 1996), 84–92.

However, for European companies considering reincorporating, these factors may be less salient than for their US counterparts, owing to the relatively low litigation rates in Europe.[80] Yet to focus on 'hard law' alone would be to miss entirely the juiciest part of the 'carrot' that will attract such firms. This is because much of what is important about the English approach to regulating the control of listed companies is not found in the companies legislation at all, but in the body of 'soft law' rules and codes that apply to companies listed on the London Stock Exchange. The most important of these are the UK Listing Rules and the City Code on Takeovers and Mergers. These deal with a range of matters that might equally well be regulated by company law,[81] including rules regarding substantive corporate governance,[82] and most obviously, takeovers.[83]

As compared with 'true' company law, these self-regulatory rules offer two key advantages in terms of functionality. First, they are capable of being continuously updated in response to developments in the market, and second, they are promulgated and enforced by people with relevant business and market expertise. Both the Listing Rules and the City Code originated as self-regulatory rules.[84] They owe their content and mode of enforcement largely to the preferences of UK institutional investors, who hold in excess of 60 per cent of the shares listed on the London Stock Exchange.[85] These institutions have sufficiently large interests to make it worthwhile to become involved both in setting up self-regulatory structures and lobbying government to avoid further encroachment of legislation.[86] The regulatory structures which have emerged are those

---

[80] See n 55 above, and related text.

[81] UK Listing Rules, rr 10.5, 10.37 (significant transactions requiring shareholder approval); ch 11 (related party transactions requiring shareholder approval); rr 4.16–21 (pre-emption rights); ch 15 (share repurchases); and ch 12 and Model Code (directors' share dealings).

[82] UKLA, *The Combined Code on Corporate Governance* (July 2003), available at *www.fsa.gov.uk/pubs/ukla/lr_comcode2003.pdf*.

[83] The Takeover Panel, *City Code on Takeovers and Mergers and the Rules Governing Substantial Acquisitions of Shares*, 7th ed. (Bowne International: London, 2002) plus updates. A regularly updated version of the City Code can be viewed at *www.thetakeoverpanel. org.uk*.

[84] The Listing Rules are now, of course, promulgated and enforced by the Financial Services Authority. The implementation of the Takeover Directive will see a statutory basis put in place for the Takeover Panel's jurisdiction, but will not, it seems, result in significant changes to the Panel's composition or mode of operating: see DTI, *Implementation of the European Directive on Takeover Bids* URN 05/511 (TSO: London, 2005), 11–24.

[85] M Becht and C Mayer, 'Introduction' in Barca and Becht (eds), *The Control of Corporate Europe*, 1, 26 (62%).

[86] B S Black and J C Coffee, 'Hail Britannia? Institutional Investor Behavior Under Limited Regulation' (1994) 92 Mich L Rev, 1997, 2034–41; G P Stapledon, *Institutional Shareholders and Corporate Governance* (Oxford: Clarendon Press, 1996), 55–153; Cheffins, n 8 above, 364–421; P Davies, 'Shareholder Value, Company Law, and Securities Markets

which these institutions consider serve their interests, as is most obviously the case with the Combined Code on Corporate Governance and the City Code on Takeovers. These codes are regularly updated by reviews which respond rapidly to changes in the way in which the market operates,[87] and invariably take into account the wishes of institutional investors.

It seems that the self-regulatory aspect of the UK system is in practice far more significant for companies than the content and enforcement of company law itself. To illustrate: during the year 2002/2003, the Takeover Panel were involved in advising on 305 transactions raising issues in relation to the Takeover Code, of which 108 resulted in published takeover or merger proposals.[88] Yet in the same period, there were only four cases decided in UK courts raising issues of company law involving listed companies.[89] This is not, however, to say that company law is irrelevant. Rather, it is a feature of the UK's *system of company law* that it permits such activities as takeovers to be regulated by the Code and enforced by the Panel as opposed to by the company law and the judiciary respectively.

The implications of this picture for our discussion are as follows. For a company with dispersed equity ownership, or which wishes to move towards it, the UK system provides an extremely attractive set of solutions to the managerial agency problem: hostile takeovers, shareholder control of related party and significant transactions, and pre-emption rights protection. This is combined with a system of company law that is relatively flexible, and is enforced by a highly specialist judiciary. At present it is possible for a company to opt into the Listing Rules by applying to join the UK Official List regardless of where its registered office or seat is located.[90] In contrast, it is not currently possible for a company that is not

---

Law: A British View' in K Hopt and E Wymeersch (eds), *Capital Markets and Company Law* (Oxford University Press, 2003), 261, 279–87; J Armour and D A Skeel, 'Who Makes the Rules for Hostile Takeovers, and Why?' working paper, University of Cambridge/University of Pennsylvania Law School (2005).

[87] Thus, the 'Combined Code' of corporate governance has been revised three times since its first incarnation as the 'Cadbury Code' in 1992 (following the Greenbury Report in 1995, the Hampel Report in 1998 and the Higgs Report in 2003). Similarly, the Code Committee of the Takeover Panel meets four times annually to review the workings of the City Code and propose revisions (see Takeover Panel, *Report on the Year Ended 31st March 2004*, 10–12).

[88] The Takeover Panel, *Report on the Year Ended 31st March 2003*, 14 (period from 1 April 2002 to 31 March 2003).

[89] *Criterion Properties plc v Stratford UK Properties LLC* [2002] EWCA Civ 1883, [2003] 2 BCLC 129 (validity of corporate transaction); *Chaston v SWP Group plc* [2002] EWCA Civ 1999, [2003] 1 BCLC 675 (financial assistance); *PNC Telecom plc v Thomas* [2002] EWHC 2848 (Ch), [2004] 1 BCLC 88 (whether notice of EGM served by fax valid); *Re Marconi plc* [2003] All ER (D) 362 (scheme of arrangement). These were identified using LEXIS. A further 12 cases involved issues of insolvency law relating to companies that had formerly been listed.   [90] Listing Rules, n 81 above, r 3.2.

'resident' in the UK—a test equivalent to the 'real seat'—to be subject to the Takeover Panel's jurisdiction. With the implementation of the Takeover Directive, however, this will change. The Takeover Panel will shortly take jurisdiction over offers in respect of any company with its real seat within the EU that is listed in the UK and which has a registered office in the UK.[91]

Such a system is, to be sure, most unlikely to be attractive to a continental company subject to stable control by a large blockholder.[92] Such a blockholder is likely to enjoy significant 'private benefits of control'.[93] Compliance with the UK Listing Rules would lessen their ability to enjoy these, through the one-share one-vote rules that outlaw complex and opaque ownership structures, and the restrictions on related party transactions. Moreover, the body of rules directed towards minimising managerial agency costs would be irrelevant for such a company, where the large blockholder will already be well-placed to keep management under careful scrutiny.

However, if such a blockholder wished to 'unwind' their holding, reincorporation in the UK would, by contrast, seem a much more attractive option to consider. This is because there is likely to be limited liquidity in any market for large blocks of shares.[94] Much greater liquidity could be obtained by breaking up the block and selling the shares to many small dispersed shareholders. To do so in a blockholder system would not, however, raise the maximum possible revenue. This is because, in a system which permits private benefits of control to be extracted, a dispersed ownership structure is unstable—that is, there are gains to be made by acquiring a controlling block and extracting the private benefits.[95] Shares generally would then trade at a discount in anticipation of the unfavourable possibility of being in the minority when control had been taken by a blockholder.[96]

Thus the argument is that controlling shareholders in continental European companies that wish to liquidate (or diversify) their holdings could do so most effectively through listing and reincorporating in the

---

[91] Takeover Panel, *Explanatory Paper: Implementation of the European Directive on Takeover Bids* (20 January 2005), 5–6.

[92] L A Bebchuk, 'A Rent-Protection Theory of Corporate Ownership and Control' NBER Working Paper No 7203, July 1999.

[93] For evidence relating to continental Europe, see K Gugler, 'Beneficial Block-Holders versus Entrenchment and Rent Extraction?' in K Gugler (ed), *Corporate Governance and Economic Performance* (Oxford University Press, 2001), 26.

[94] M Becht, 'European Corporate Governance: Trading off Liquidity Against Control' (1999) 43 *European Economic Review*, 1071.   [95] Bebchuk, n 92 above.

[96] Bebchuk and Roe, n 59 above, 142–53.

UK.[97] The extent to which such blockholdings will unwind is, of course, contentious. Nevertheless, there are strong reasons for thinking that significant numbers of blockholders in continental Europe will wish to make this transition. The value of the rents which a blockholder may extract are declining owing to European integration's enhancement of product market competition;[98] at the same time, reductions in capital gains taxes have eliminated a former penalty to divestment of blockholdings.[99] Consistently with these suggestions, the early evidence suggests that even within the strongly blockholder system of Germany, there has been a reduction in ownership concentration over the past 10 years.[100]

The preceding discussion does of course beg the question of whether blockholders wishing to avail themselves of opportunities for regulatory arbitrage will be able to obtain appropriate legal advice. Indeed, the idea of 'lawyer resistance' is one of the most heavily-pressed reasons for thinking that regulatory competition will not occur. However, it overlooks the transformation that has recently been effected in the European market for legal services. Large London-based law firms have aggressively expanded by merging with, or taking over, their continental counterparts.[101] Whilst the so-called 'magic circle' of London law firms have maintained offices in locations around the world for many years, these had until recently been little more than symbolic outposts. However, since the late 1990s, several of them have changed strategy in favour of practising 'local law'. As a result, they are now truly multi-jurisdictional in their orientation.[102] Table 2 shows the dramatic increase in the number of 'overseas' fee-earners in these firms over the period 1999–2005. This expansion in geographic scope has been mirrored by a similarly dramatic encroachment of their brand names upon continental European markets for legal services. For example, nearly all of the 'top 10' German firms in

[97] Another plausible scenario is that a private equity firm would purchase the blockholder's stake, and then having restructured the firm, seek to take the company public again in a way that would increase the value of the share price. See H Timmons, 'Private Equity Investors are Reshaping the Landscape of European Business', *New York Times*, 5 May 2005, C12.

[98] M J Roe, 'The Shareholder Wealth Maximization Norm and Industrial Organization' (2001) 149 U Pa L Rev, 2063.   [99] Frick and Lehmann, n 9 above, 123.

[100] D Wojcik, 'Change in the German Model of Corporate Governance: Evidence from Blockholdings 1997–2001' (2003) 35 *Environment and Planning A*, 1431; S Thomsen, 'Convergence of Corporate Governance during the Stock Market Bubble: Towards Anglo-American or European Standards?' in A Grandori (ed), *Corporate Governance and Firm Organization* (Oxford University Press, 2004), 297, 306–12.

[101] Linklaters, for example, merged in Germany, Belgium and Sweden (*The Lawyer UK 100*, 2004).

[102] International Financial Services London, *City Business Series: Legal Services* (London: IFSL, 1999, 2003, 2005).

Table 2 The international transformation of large 'London' law firms

Name	% fee-earners outside UK		
	1999	2003	2005
Clifford Chance	41	63	62
Freshfields Bruckhaus Deringer	50	61	66
Linklaters	n/a	52	55
Allen & Overy	35	48	53
Lovells	23	55	57

Source: International Financial Services London, *City Business Series: Legal Services, 1999–2005.*

2004 were organisations that had either merged with, or formed a 'strategic alliance' with, a foreign firm.[103]

This transformation has been driven by globalisation and consolidation in the financial services sector, with law firms growing in size as they seek to capture economies of scale associated with increased deal size.[104] The process of globalisation has brought with it increasingly direct competition from American law firms, which are able to draw upon work from deals generated by an economy approximately seven times the size of that of the UK. It seems a natural response for UK firms to seek to integrate the European market for legal services.[105] Thus these former 'London' firms are now pan-European, multi-jurisdictional and multi-language in their operations, and ideally placed to mediate between European jurisdictions.[106] Against this background, jurisdictional arbitrage is an obvious service offering.[107] If a particular

---

[103] *JUVE Handbook of German Commercial Law Firms 2004*, 'Ranking National Review', *www.juve.de.*

[104] R S Thomas *et al*, 'Megafirms' (2001) 80 NCL Rev, 115; A Hodgart, 'Globalization and the Future of International Law Firms—The Perspective of a Management Consultant' in J Drolshammer and M Pfeifer (eds), *The Internationalisation of the Practice of Law* (London: Kluwer Law International, 2001), 173, 194–202. On the historical background in London, see R G Lee, 'From Profession to Business: The Rise and Rise of the City Law Firm' in P A Thomas (ed), *Tomorrow's Lawyers* (Oxford: Blackwell, 1992), 31.

[105] However, the US firms are also competing aggressively throughout Europe: see C Griffiths, 'The UK firms are thinking global, but the savvier US practices are starting to act local', *The Lawyer Global 100*, 2004.

[106] E Wymeersch, 'Company Law in Turmoil and the Way to "Global Company Practice" ' (2003) 3 JCLS, 283, 286–7.

[107] Hence the marketing of English law to clients can credibly be seen as a means of saving the client money as opposed to maximising fee income ('rents') for the lawyers.

system of corporate law does offer cost advantages for large corporate clients (be they procedural or substantive), then these firms may be expected to offer this aggressively to their clients. The 'lawyer hostility' problem is greatly reduced where the incumbent and the new adviser are both within the same firm.[108]

To recapitulate: regulatory arbitrage is already occurring at the level of 'start-up' incorporations. Moreover, there are good reasons for thinking that once reincorporation becomes legally possible for large companies, continental firms that wish to shift from blockholder to dispersed ownership may wish to engage in regulatory arbitrage in favour of the UK, the system which offers the best-adapted legal and regulatory environment for this ownership pattern. In so doing, they will be able to obtain advice from international law firms.

Will Member States Have Incentives to Compete to Attract (Re)Incorporations?

Regulatory arbitrage is a necessary but not sufficient condition for regulatory competition. True regulatory competition requires that lawmakers respond to the threat or opportunity posed by firms' arbitrage activities so as to retain or attract incorporations. Once again, a number of scholars have voiced the opinion that such regulatory competition will not emerge to any significant extent within Europe. In other words, the necessary preconditions for the *supply* of corporate law in response to companies' preferences will not exist.[109] Unlike the position in the US, EU Member States are unable to derive significant amounts of revenue from 'charter taxes' levied on companies because these are prohibited by EU law, save in the Member State where the company has its real seat.[110] Moreover, it is thought that

---

[108] To be sure, there may be an inter-branch agency problem within such a firm. That is, lawyers in the branch in Member State B will naturally be loath to recommend to their local clients that they reincorporate in Member State A and thereby transfer their account to a different branch. This effect will be pitted against the firm's need to survive as a whole, which will depend upon successfully implementing its strategy. Lawyers in Member State B may therefore find their remuneration being structured so as to overcome such opposition, or being encouraged to retool in the law of Member State A. Future generations of lawyers in Member State B may indeed seek to qualify or learn the law of Member State A instead: Delaware's is the substantive corporate law taught at top law schools throughout the US.

[109] Romano, n 23 above, 133–4; Enriques, n 3 above, 1266–73; Dammann, n 61 above, 520–21; Gelter, n 3 above, 1, 259–264; Tröger, n 3 above.

[110] Council Directive 69/335/EEC [1969] OJ L 249/25 (prohibiting the levying of taxes or above-cost charges for the formation or registration of a company except in the case of prescribed 'capital duties' levied in the country where the company has its centre of management: arts 2(1), 10).

there is little prospect that the relevant Directive will be repealed, because business interest groups are likely to lobby against such change.[111]

There seems little doubt that the particular conditions which originally gave rise to Delaware's ascendancy at the turn of the twentieth century will not be replicated in Europe. Yet simply because no European state will have the same incentives as Delaware does not mean that regulatory competition cannot emerge. Once again, it is helpful to segment the analysis into law reforms that will make a jurisdiction attractive to incorporations, and those which will be relevant for larger, established companies. It appears that continental legislatures have already become concerned at the prospect of large-scale evasion of their legal capital requirements through incorporations in the UK. Some, such as France and Spain, have already relaxed their capital maintenance regimes;[112] others, such as Germany, are considering ways to respond.[113] The UK government, which has already acknowledged its desire to ensure English company law is internationally 'competitive',[114] has recently announced further deregulation of legal capital requirements in relation to private companies, including outright abolition of the prohibition on the giving of financial assistance by such a company for the acquisition of its own shares.[115] These sorts of changes are by definition, regulatory competition.

To be sure, once legal capital rules are relaxed for private companies by other Member States—as seems highly likely to happen—it seems unlikely that the UK's emergent 'competitive advantage' in this field will remain. With this obstacle removed at home, entrepreneurs will no longer have a compelling reason to incur the transaction costs of incorporating abroad. This will be more a case of 'defensive' regulatory competition than the 'active' version exhibited by Delaware, but it will be regulatory competition nevertheless.

Let us now consider the same issue in relation to the law relating to listed companies. I have suggested that the UK is likely to be the jurisdiction of choice for firms wishing to reincorporate so as to optimise their company law regime to a dispersed ownership structure. There are two reasons for thinking that the UK will have powerful incentives to adjust its company law environment so as to attract them, notwithstanding the lack of franchise taxes.

---

[111] G Hertig, 'Efficient Fostering of EU Regulatory Competition' (2004) SZW/RSDA 5 *Kurzbeiträge*, 369, 370.

[112] J Simon, 'A Comparative Approach to Capital Maintenance: France' (2004) 15 *EBL Rev* 1037; Kieninger, n 3 above, 768.   [113] Rammeloo, n 42 above, 409.

[114] CLSRG, *Final Report, Vol I*, n 4 above, xi, 6; DTI, *Company Law Reform*, n 4 above, 9.

[115] DTI, ibid, 41–3.

The first factor is the importance of legal services revenues to the UK economy. Having so much at stake, the UK-oriented pan-European law firms constitute a powerful interest group in lobbying for or against legal change that is likely to affect the competitiveness of English law.[116] The power of legal professionals' ability to drive regulatory competition has recently been demonstrated by Sitkoff and Schanzenbach's study of the dramatic evolution of tax-haven trust structures in the US, a practice which, given the function of these vehicles, is clearly not motivated by tax revenues derived by the states which are 'competing'.[117]

In this regard, it is worth pointing out that the UK's legal profession is also much better placed to spur regulatory competition than is Delaware's. Kahan and Kamar have argued that Delaware lawyers, as an interest group, are not a significant motor for regulatory competition.[118] On their analysis, the marginal revenues to lawyers practising in Delaware from legal business related to out-of-state incorporations attracted to Delaware are insignificant.[119] Yet the revenues of lawyers practising in Delaware are likely to be a small fraction of the total economic value derived from Delaware law by US legal practitioners. Most of the legal advice to listed firms incorporated in Delaware is not provided by lawyers practising in Delaware, but in large cities such as New York.[120] In contrast, a much larger proportion of the legal services revenues generated by UK company law would be captured by the UK. This is because London, the financial centre where many of the legal service providers are based, is geographically within the UK. As voters, taxpayers and experts, London lawyers may therefore be expected to be an influential interest group in the development of UK company law.[121]

The second reason for thinking that the UK company law environment will be highly responsive is closely related. It centres on the 'soft' or 'private' nature of crucial regulation such as the Takeover Code. Private legislatures

---

[116] Cheffins, n 8 above, 437–8.

[117] R Sitkoff and M M Schanzenbach, 'Jurisdictional Competition for Trust Funds: An Empirical Analysis of Perpetuities and Taxes', Northwestern Law & Econ Research Paper No 05-07 (2005).   [118] Kahan and Kamar, n 25 above, 694–8.

[119] Ibid, 698–9.

[120] Whilst leading New York M&A firms such as Cravath, Swaine & Moore, Davis, Polk & Wardwell, Simpson, Thacher & Bartlett, Sullivan & Cromwell and Wachtell, Lipton, Rosen & Katz do not have offices in Delaware, their practices encompass high-profile M&A transactions and associated litigation under Delaware law (source: law firm websites, consulted 1 May 2005).

[121] The Company Law Committees of the Law Society and the City of London Law Society are well-organised and powerful lobby groups that are in a position to offer effective arguments in for or against a change that will enhance or decrease the attractiveness of English law to their clients. See, eg responses to the DTI's 2002 White Paper, *Modernising Company Law* (Cm 5553), available online at *http://www.dti.gov.uk/cld/modern/index.htm*.

are able to capture a much greater proportion of the economic benefits of marginal revenues generated by 'users' of their laws than do public legislatures.[122] A public legislature is required to use tax revenues to provide public services, and so faces a steeply declining marginal utility curve from extra tax income. A private legislature, on the other hand, is effectively providing a service as a business and so derives a much greater marginal utility than its public counterpart from additional revenues generated by 'users'. It can therefore be expected to be much more responsive to the preferences of those who make use of it. This, coupled with the potential size of the professional services revenues, makes it likely that the UK has incentive enough to compete for reincorporations of listed companies.

Will Safeguards be in Place to Ensure a 'Race to the Top' Rather Than 'to the Bottom'?

My prediction is that, following the likely liberalisation of rules regarding transfer of registered office, there is real potential for a market in European company law to develop, and a significant possibility that the UK will be the favoured state of immigration for many continental listed companies. This in turn raises the question of whether this will be desirable. In other words, will the 'race' be to the bottom or to the top?

Once again, my suggestions will be sanguine. It is apposite to begin with the theoretical critique of regulatory competition in US state corporate law. Bebchuk and others argue that because shareholders have insufficient control over the reincorporation decision, choices are likely to be made in favour of jurisdictions that entrench managers, as opposed to maximising the value of firms. Under most corporate codes in the US, a decision to reincorporate may be made by a simple majority of the general meeting, following a proposal put by the board. Bebchuk's claim is that, in an environment of dispersed share ownership, a simple majority is too low a threshold to overcome the owner-manager agency problem.[123] Thus managements' proposals for reincorporation will tend to be biased towards jurisdictions with pro-manager provisions—especially laws that facilitate defences to hostile takeovers (as does Delaware).

Put more generally, the potential problem is this: laws that embody restrictions which will maximise value in the face of agency costs are unlikely to be adopted where the choice of law is itself pervaded by the

---

[122] G Hadfield and E Talley, 'On Public Versus Private Provision of Corporate Law', USC Law and Economics Working Paper No 04-18, USC CLEO Research Paper No C04-13 (2004).   [123] Bebchuk, n 34 above, 1459–61, 1470–75.

same agency problem. Indeed, it is possible that such agency problems could be present not just along the manager-shareholder axis, but also along shareholder-shareholder, shareholder-creditor and the shareholder-employee axes. The solution in each case is to ensure that procedural safeguards are in place so that the group who stand to be potentially disadvantaged by a change in corporate law will have been able to exercise genuine voice in the process. Thus Bebchuk argues that the perceived problem in the dynamics of US reincorporation could be solved by a federal rule that increases shareholder involvement in decisions about reincorporation, thus making it considerably more likely that the choice will benefit shareholders by enhancing the firm's overall value, as opposed simply to transferring wealth from shareholders to managers.[124] In the EU context, this sort of federal rule, which seeks to influence the *process* by which state law develops, as opposed to the *substance* of the rules themselves, has been termed by Deakin 'procedural harmonisation'.[125] Put most generally, this refers to rules intended to direct regulatory competition towards 'the top' rather than 'the bottom'.[126]

It seems highly likely that in the EU context, the opening of the road to regulatory competition in corporate law will be accompanied by the implementation of procedural safeguards to protect affected constituencies from proposed changes driven by opportunistic motives. Once again, it is helpful to distinguish the contexts of 'formation choice'—already permitted under EU law—and 'midstream reincorporation', which it has been argued will soon be generally facilitated by the proposed Cross-Border Mergers and Transfer of Registered Office Directives. Put at its most general, the difference is this: on formation, all parties are able to bargain for appropriate protection. Midstream changes, however, can be passed without unanimous consent of the affected parties, and so offer the possibility of opportunistic dilution of agreed protections.[127] For policy purposes, the analysis of a

---

[124] L A Bebchuk and A Farrell, 'A New Approach to Takeover Law and Regulatory Competition' (2001) 87 Va L Rev, 111, 152–3, 161–3; L A Bebchuk, 'The Case for Increasing Shareholder Power' (2005) 118 Harv LR, 833, 868–9.

[125] Deakin, n 19 above, 209–13.

[126] It should be noted that Bebchuk's pessimistic assessment is vigorously disputed by others in the US: see, eg Romano, n 32 above. For present purposes, it is unnecessary to take a view on the merits of the US debate. The discussion in the text is simply concerned to show that European regulatory competition will not result in a 'race to the bottom': this is done most effectively by demonstrating that the concerns of the US pessimists will not be replicated in Europe.

[127] L Bebchuk, 'Limiting Contractual Freedom in Corporate Law: The Desirable Constraints on Charter Amendments' (1989) 102 Harv L Rev, 1820 (arguing for restrictions on post-formation alterations of corporate constitution, owing to greater shareholder information costs).

company's choice of governing law is no different from the way in which any other aspect of a company's constitution might be selected.

Consider, first, competition over 'formation choice'. Here, every share-holder, creditor and employee has the opportunity to bargain with the new enterprise, and either to secure for herself terms that are satisfactory, or to decline to become involved. Provided adequate notice is given, then in principle any selected law should be value-maximising. To be sure, there may be problems of information asymmetry, or inequality of bargaining power. To the extent that such problems exist, they can be ameliorated either by substantively harmonised provisions, as has been the case with employment law rules and securities regulation, or by Member State national laws that are capable of satisfying the *Gebhard* criteria: that is, they are both 'effective and proportionate' at achieving the goal of ameliorating the market failure in question.

Now consider 'midstream changes'. The concern here is encapsulated by the following hypothesis: protections for a particular constituency (say, codetermination rights for the employees) are embodied in the company law of Member State B. Such provisions may be economically justified— for example, in relation to firms where employees are asked to make significant investments in firm-specific human capital. Entitlements to influence the firm's governance may reassure the employees that the firm will not renege on any implicit promises to share supracompetitive profits with the employees *ex post* in return for the latter's *ex ante* investments.[128] Regardless of whether this reasoning justifies mandatory (as opposed to default) protection for employees,[129] any such protection will be rendered entirely worthless if the firm has the option to renege on its commitments *ex post* simply by reincorporating in a jurisdiction where codetermination is not recognised.

This problem, in relation to employees, has long been a roadblock to negotiation of the Tenth and Fourteenth Directives. However, the solution agreed in respect of the *Societas Europaea* will probably form a blueprint for the final versions of the other two proposals.[130] For employees,

---

[128] See, eg M M Blair, *Ownership and Control: Rethinking Corporate Governance for the Twenty-First Century* (Washington, DC: Brookings Institution, 1995); G Kelly and J Parkinson, 'The Conceptual Foundations of the Company: A Pluralist Approach', [1998] *CFILR* 174; W Njoya, 'Employee Ownership and Efficiency: An Evolutionary Perspective' (2004) 33 ILJ, 211.

[129] Mandatory rules of a 'one size fits all' character are inappropriate where there exist a substantial number of firms for which the relevant rule is inappropriate. The extent to which firms rely upon firm-specific human capital is an empirical question, but it seems likely that in any system there will be many firms for which this rationale for employee-friendly governance rules is not present.

[130] European Commission, n 50 above, Art 14 (incorporating provisions of SE regulation and Directive in relation to employees); European Commission press release, n 51 above.

the principal protection is given through the provision for structured bargaining on formation of an SE.[131] This requires the management of pre-SE entities to engage in precursory negotiations with a body of employee representatives, with a view to agreeing employee participation rights in relation to the new entity.[132] If no agreement is reached after six months,[133] then as a default, a set of employee information/consultation and/or participation rights is put in place, the content of which is determined by the most employee-favourable of the regime(s) applying to the pre-SE entity or entities from which the European public company is formed.[134] The effect is to encourage an agreement that is no less favourable to the employees than their entitlements under the pre-SE entities.[135] Of course, if the employees can be persuaded to agree, then it is possible to abandon, or at least modify, the existing participation rights.[136] Thus the negotiation structure permits the parties to abandon participation rights if it is efficient to do so—that is, the benefits of such change exceed the costs to the employees, who will need to be compensated in order to induce them to agree.[137] The SE legislation, albeit complex, therefore provides a sound blueprint for the protection of employee interests.[138]

Moreover, it is quite plausible that, with such procedural protection in place, a certain amount of *specialisation* might occur in national corporate law structures. Thus, it has been argued that German codetermination structures provide a means of offering employees a 'credible commitment' that their investments in firm-specific human capital will be protected. Firms for which such commitments are valuable will have no incentive to renege upon them by reincorporating in jurisdictions such as the UK,

---

[131] See generally, P L Davies, 'Workers on the Board of the European Company?' (2003) 32 ILJ 75.

[132] Council Directive 2001/86/EC [2001] OJ L 294/22, Arts 3–5. See also V Edwards, 'The European Company—Essential Tool or Eviscerated Dream?' (2003) 40 CML Rev, 443, 459–62.

[133] The parties may consensually extend the negotiating period to one year: Directive 2001/86/EC, Art 5(2).   [134] Ibid, Art 7 and Annex.

[135] Davies, n 131 above, 84–90; Deakin, n 19 above, 212–3.

[136] C Teichmann, 'The European Company—A Challenge to Academics, Legislatures and Practitioners' (2003) 4 German LJ, 309, 319–21. An exception is where the SE is created by transformation of an existing public company, in which case the new entity must provide at least as much participation for employees as they enjoyed beforehand (Directive 2001/86/EC, Art 4(4)). However it would be simple enough to evade this requirement by creating an SE by merger into a shell company: Enriques, n 49 above, 5.

[137] On the use of bargaining levers to protect employee interests, see generally J Armour and S Deakin, 'Insolvency and Employment Protection: The Mixed Effects of the Acquired Rights Directive' (2003) 22 *Int Rev L & Econ*, 443, 448–62, 458–60.

[138] M Edbury, 'The European Company Statute: A Practical Working Model for the Future of European Company Law Making?' (2004) 15 EBL Rev, 1283.

which do not have codetermination rules. But the process rule model of the SE legislation would permit firms for which such codetermination is inappropriate to opt out by reincorporating, provided that the value realised in so doing is greater than the cost imposed on the employees.[139] By so protecting the interests of employees in any firm that seeks to switch 'out' of codetermination, the SE's structured bargaining mechanisms will ensure that this cannot be used as a tactic to undermine the credibility of such commitments.[140]

Similar safeguards can be put in place to protect shareholders from opportunistic transfer of governing laws by management. Again, the SE legislation provides an instructive model. Under the SE regulation, at least a supermajority (two-thirds) shareholder vote is required in order to transfer the registered office[141] or to form an SE by merger.[142]A similar rule would apply under the proposed Fourteenth Directive.[143] Under the proposed Cross-Border Mergers Directive, the 'general meeting' must approve the terms of any proposed merger, but the contours of the process which follows will be left to the national laws of the member states governing the companies concerned.[144]

As regards creditors, the SE Regulations and the proposals for the Tenth and Fourteenth Directives will leave the question of any safeguards prior to transfer of registered office to the national laws of the company concerned.[145] However, the treatment of creditors is complicated by the fact that many countries choose to protect them through corporate insolvency law, and so the discussion of the desirability of regulatory competition in relation to this constituency is postponed until the next section, where the question is tackled directly in relation to insolvency law.

---

[139] See nn 136–137 above and related text.

[140] Indeed, there is no legal reason why firms which are unable to offer such commitments under their governing law but would like to do so could not switch to German company law.

[141] Regulation 2157/2001, Arts 8(6), 59(1). Two-thirds is a mandatory floor, which may be raised if the relevant national law requires a higher majority.

[142] Ibid, Art 17(2) (incorporating by reference the approval procedure prescribed by the Third Council Directive, 78/885/EEC [1978] OJ L 295/36). See Edwards, n 132 above, 452–4. It is unnecessary to consider the other three methods of forming an SE, namely holding or subsidiary SEs and transformation of an existing public company, as these cannot bring about a change of registered office without subsequent invocation of the Art 8 procedure.   [143] Proposal for Fourteenth Directive, n 91 above Art 6.

[144] Proposal for Tenth Directive, n 50 above Art 6 ('the general meeting' shall approve proposed mergers); see also Art 2 (provisions of national law shall govern the decision-making process relating to the merger, save as otherwise provided in the Directive).

[145] Regulation 2157/2001, Art 8(7); Proposal for Tenth Directive, n 50 above, Art 2; Proposal for Fourteenth Directive, n 51 above, Art 8.

Table 3 Procedural protection for constituencies in company law arbitrage

	Formation	Reincorporation
Shareholders	• Initial bargain with firm	• Supermajority vote requirement
Employees	• 'Effective and proportionate' restrictions under national law (if any)	• Acquired rights' carried over or waiver agreed by employees

To summarise, this section has suggested that

  (i) regulatory competition is already occurring in relation to 'start-up' companies;

 (ii) the existing legal obstacles to regulatory competition in relation to company law for public companies are likely to be removed in the next few years;

(iii) the UK is likely to be the jurisdiction of choice for many such companies, although there will also be new possibilities for jurisdictional specialisation in particular 'models' of company law; and

 (iv) procedural harmonisation at the EU level (summarised in Table 3) will ensure that the 'race' is not to the bottom.

Extending the Argument: Insolvency Law and Creditor Protection

In the final part, the analysis turns to the extent to which regulatory competition may and should be permitted to operate in relation to Member State laws designed to protect creditors. The issue is considered separately because in many jurisdictions, the protection of corporate creditors is understood to be a matter of corporate insolvency law. This body of law is often treated separately from company law, typically being understood either as a procedural matter or as part of commercial law. This impression of partition is reinforced by the fact that jurisdiction and choice of law in European insolvency proceedings is governed by *sui generis* legislation, the European Insolvency Regulation (EIR).[146] Significantly for present purposes, the EIR is widely thought to be based upon connecting factors that bear more in common with the 'real seat' theory than the incorporation theory.

[146] EC Council Regulation 1346/2000 [2000] OJ L160/1. Jurisdiction over insolvency proceedings was specifically excluded from the Brussels Convention (now consolidated as EC Council Regulation 44/2001 [2001] OJ L12/1: see Art 1(2)(b)).

Two salient questions arise. First, can it be argued that corporate insolvency law constitutes an entirely separate regime from company law, such that the principles established in the recent ECJ corporate freedom of establishment cases do not apply to it? If so, then this might have the effect of stopping the nascent regulatory competition for 'start-up' formations dead in its tracks: in place of company law creditor protection rules that impede freedom of establishment, Member States could simply substitute identical rules located in their corporate insolvency law.

I will argue that no such presumptive partition can be supported. This is in keeping with the functional approach to the scope of company law which formed the first 'building block' for our analysis.[147] Corporate insolvency law supplies rules which govern companies experiencing financial distress, and so it is appropriate to consider it as being within the scope of a functional account of 'company law'.[148] In particular, insolvency law may complement other aspects of a country's corporate governance regime,[149] which implies that if it is desirable to permit companies to select a company law regime so as to achieve a better 'fit' with their corporate governance requirements, it is likely also to be desirable for them to be able to select the associated corporate insolvency law. This in turn leads on to the second question: to what extent might it be possible for regulatory arbitrage—and thence competition—to take place in relation to rules of insolvency law? In this regard, it will be suggested— contrary to the popular perception—that the EIR's scheme could indeed permit a significant and valuable degree of regulatory competition.

Is Insolvency Law a Constraint on Company Law Arbitrage?

To prepare the way for the discussion that follows, it is first necessary to give an overview of the EIR's operation. The Regulation establishes uniform rules for jurisdiction and choice of law in relation to international insolvencies occurring within the EU, and provides for their automatic recognition by the courts of other Member States.[150] Choice of law largely

---

[147] See nn 4–7 and related text.

[148] A point which has been emphasised by David Skeel: see D A Skeel, 'Rethinking the Line Between Corporate Law and Corporate Bankruptcy' (1994) 72 Tex L Rev, 471; 'Corporate Anatomy Lessons' (2004) 113 Yale LJ, 1519, 1550–62. See also Armour and Whincop, n 6 above, 25.

[149] D A Skeel, 'An Evolutionary Theory of Corporate Law and Corporate Bankruptcy' (1998) 51 Vand L Rev, 1325; J Armour *et al*, 'Corporate Ownership Structure and the Evolution of Corporate Bankruptcy Law: Lessons from the UK' (2002) 55 Vand L Rev, 1699.

[150] I F Fletcher, *Insolvency in Private International Law* (Oxford: Clarendon Press, 1999), 246–301; G Moss *et al*, *The EC Regulation on Insolvency Proceedings* (Oxford

follows the allocation of jurisdiction, so that the *lex concursus* (law of the jurisdiction where insolvency proceedings are opened) will govern most of the effects of the proceedings, both procedural and substantive.[151] Thus the rules concerning the allocation of jurisdiction are fundamental.

The EIR's jurisdiction-allocation scheme has two tracks. The first provides that 'main' proceedings shall be opened in the jurisdiction in which the debtor's 'centre of main interests' (COMI) is located.[152] Main proceedings are to have universal effect throughout the EU, except and insofar as a territorial 'carve-out' created by the second track is utilised. This provides that 'secondary' proceedings may be opened in any Member State (other than that of the COMI) in which the debtor has an 'establishment'.[153] Any such secondary proceedings are limited in their effect to the territory of the Member State in which they are opened and must be conducted in cooperation with the main proceedings.[154] Main proceedings may encompass either liquidation (that is, the sale of the debtor's assets and distribution of proceeds amongst creditors) or 'corporate rescue' (that is, a 'crisis governance' procedure seeking to preserve the company or its business from failure) proceedings. In contrast, secondary proceedings may only involve liquidation of local assets.[155] Table 4 summarises the key features of the foregoing discussion.

Table 4 Summary of the EIR's scheme

	Main proceedings	Secondary proceedings
Scope	Universal (EU-wide)	Territorial
Type of procedure	Rescue or liquidation	Liquidation only
Jurisdiction allocation	Centre of main interests (COMI)	Place(s) of establishment(s)

University Press, 2002); M Martinez Ferber, *European Insolvency Regulation* (Osterspai: Ditmar Weis, 2004); P Omar, *European Insolvency Law* (Aldershot: Ashgate, 2004).

[151] Reg. 1346/2000, Preamble para. 23, Art 4(2). To this principle there are a number of 'carve outs', including the effects of insolvency on:

(i) rights *in rem*, reservation of title claims, contracts relating to immoveables and rights of third-party purchasers of such assets (each governed by the *lex situs*: Arts 5, 7, 8 and 14);

(ii) rights of set-off (governed by the law applicable to the insolvent debtor's claim: Art 6);

(iii) contracts of employment (governed by the proper law of the contract: Art 10) and

(iv) rights subject to registration (governed by the law of the place of the register: Art 11).

[152] Ibid, Art 3(1).   [153] Ibid, Art 3(2).   [154] Ibid, Arts 16, 17, 27.

[155] Compare ibid, Annex A (proceedings which may be opened in COMI, including corporate rescue procedures) with Annex B (secondary proceedings, including only liquidation procedures). Both Annexes have recently been amended by EC Regulation 603/2005 [2005] OJ L 100/1.

We shall now consider whether the EIR's jurisdiction allocation scheme conforms to the 'real seat' or the incorporation theory. Given the centrality of the concept of the debtor's COMI to the scheme's operation, it is most unfortunate that its definition is shrouded in ambiguity, reflecting an ugly drafting compromise between Member States' preferences as between these two theories.[156] Thus, the preamble to the EIR provides that the COMI shall 'correspond to the place where the debtor conducts the administration of his interests on a regular basis and is therefore ascertainable by third parties.'[157] On the other hand, Article 3(1) raises a presumption in the case of corporate debtors that the COMI is the place of the registered office. The uncertainty concerns the degree of strength that should be accorded to this presumption. Member States' jurisprudence—even in the UK—has to date tended to treat the presumption as easily rebutted by factual evidence concerning where the debtor conducted business.[158] Thus, as currently interpreted in national case law,[159] the notion of COMI conforms more to the 'real seat' than the incorporation theory. Moreover, it is clear that even if a corporate debtor's COMI were not in the jurisdiction of its 'real seat', the debtor would nevertheless certainly have an 'establishment' there, so that secondary proceedings could be opened.

It follows that if a company is incorporated in Member State A, but carries on all its business in Member State B, then creditors who lend to it in Member State B can be assured that the insolvency law of Member State B will apply, at the very least to assets situated in that jurisdiction. This leads some commentators to suggest that corporate insolvency law should be treated as falling outside the scope of the regulatory competition recently ushered in by the ECJ.[160] If this view, which we might term the 'partition theory', were correct, it would follow that Member States wishing to preserve restrictive creditor protection rules should simply transfer them from 'company' to 'insolvency' sections of their civil codes. The only limit to such recycling would be a casuistic determination whether the rules in question were properly characterised as 'company

---

[156] Fletcher, n 150 above; 260–62; Omar, n 150 above, 97–9.

[157] Reg. 1346/2000, Preamble para. 13.

[158] See *Re Daisytek-ISA Ltd* [2004] BPIR 30 at [16]–[17] ('where the debtor enters into the majority of his financing arrangements'); see also *Re BRAC Rent-A-Car International, Inc.* [2003] EWHC (Ch) 128, [2003] 1 WLR, 1421 at [4]–[5]. For a thorough survey of other Member States' jurisprudence, see Martinez Ferber, n 150 above, 31–74.

[159] This understanding is questioned below, text relating to nn 168–171.

[160] Eg Kersting and Schindler, n 42 above, 1290; T Koller, 'The English Limited Company—Ready to Invade Germany' (2004) 15 ICCLR 334, 341–3; Martinez Ferber, n 150 above 86–111; Rammeloo, n 42 above, 403–6; Zimmer, n 42 above, 1137–8.

law' or 'insolvency law'.[161] The unappealing implications of this analysis may be seen by considering its application to the issues in *Inspire Art*. As will be recalled, that case concerned the application of the Dutch WFBV or 'law applicable to formally foreign companies', under which companies operating in the Netherlands but with only a nominal connection to their jurisdiction of incorporation were required to comply with minimum capital requirements consistent with those imposed upon companies incorporated domestically. Were the partition theory valid, then it could plausibly be argued that the WFBV's impact could be preserved by enacting an 'insolvency version' of the statute.[162] That is, to legislate that should a company that failed the relevant capitalisation requirements enter insolvency proceedings, the liquidator should have an action to make the directors liable to contribute the 'missing capital' for the benefit of the company's creditors.[163]

The better view is that the impact of *Inspire Art* cannot be constrained in the way suggested by the partition theory.[164] The EIR does not purport to govern the content of insolvency laws, merely the connecting factor for choice of jurisdiction and choice of law. The ECJ's judgment in *Inspire Art* is framed not in terms of connecting factors in company law, but of legal provisions that impede corporate freedom of establishment. Why should this apply any differently to rules formally characterised as 'corporate insolvency law' than to rules of 'company law'? The correct question, after *Inspire Art*, is not whether a rule is properly taxonomised as 'company' or 'insolvency', but rather whether its effect is to impede the exercise of corporate freedom of establishment, subject of course to the exception for provisions which satisfy the four-stage *Gebhard* test.[165]

---

[161] There is some relevant ECJ jurisprudence, albeit directed to the sibling question of the scope of the exclusion from the Brussels Convention for 'insolvency proceedings' (EC Council Regulation 44/2001). In *Gourdain v Nadler* (Case C-133/78, [1979] I ECR 733), the ECJ held that the French *action en comblement du passif* (loosely: failure by directors to take steps to initiate insolvency proceedings sufficiently quickly) was properly characterised as part of insolvency proceedings, on the ground that the action was open only to the liquidator, and that the proceeds went to enlarge the assets available to the creditors.

[162] As the Dutch legislature appear to have attempted: see Rammeloo, n 42 above, 407–8 and Lowry, n 42 above, 343 fn32.

[163] It would be at least arguable that such a provision could be brought within the ECJ's characterisation of 'insolvency proceedings' in *Gourdain v Nadler*.

[164] A point also made by Kieninger, n 3 above, 752–4.

[165] This can also be seen by considering the tax cases: in *de Lastreyie du Saillant*, the Court ruled that tax laws impeding individuals' freedom of establishment would be struck down; the reason for not so ruling in *Daily Mail* was on the basis of the court's peculiar conception of the 'status' of a company as governed by the provisions of its state of incorporation: see nn 45–46 above and related text.

Whether a rule that is characterised as part of the host state's 'insolvency law' would fail this test will depend upon the impact that (non-) compliance would have on the shareholders and/or directors of a foreign company that wishes to establish its business in that state. In terms of the ECJ's freedom of establishment jurisprudence, a rule that has such an effect which is more than 'indirect and uncertain' will fail this test.[166] It is the nature of insolvency proceedings that they only take place if the debtor is unable to pay their debts. Assuming that the company is solvent at the point it wishes to establish itself in the host state, most rules which operate in insolvency would be likely to be no more than 'indirect and uncertain' in their impact on the company's establishment decision, because of the small probability that they would ever apply.[167] Yet there are situations where the impact might be more direct. The most obvious would be where the insolvency code imposes retrospective liability for actions taken or omitted during the period of the company's existence which go beyond the obligations imposed by the home state company law during solvency and are excessive compared to the requirements of the debtor's home state. It seems that re-enacting the WFBV as 'insolvency law' would be precisely such a situation. It is not difficult to see that in such a case, shareholders and directors of companies such as Inspire Art Ltd would be deterred from establishing their company in the host state because of the risk that, had they failed to capitalise it in accordance with the WFBV, they would face concomitant liability to contribute to its assets in insolvency. They could only safely avoid such potential liability by incurring a significant cost at the time of (re)establishment. In contrast, insolvency liabilities for (in)actions immediately preceding entry to insolvency proceedings—such as, for example, for wrongful trading—would be unlikely to have a direct and certain impact, because they would only be incurred in relation to (in)actions during the 'twilight period', which would be no more than a distant possibility at the time of (re)establishment.

Could Regulatory Arbitrage in Corporate Insolvency Law be Possible?

The foregoing discussion suggests that insolvency law is capable of imposing only an indirect constraint on arbitrage (and hence competition) for company law. We now turn to the second question: that is, whether regulatory

---

[166] See, eg, Case C-19/92, *Kraus v Land Baden-Württemberg* [1993] ECR I-1663; Case C-190/98, *Graf v Filzmoser Maschinenbau GmbH* [2000] ECR I-493; Joined cases C-51/96 and C-191/97, *Deliège v Ligue Francophone de Judo et Disciplines Associées ASBL* [2000] ECR I-2549.   [167] This point is hinted at by Tröger, n 3 above.

competition in relation to corporate insolvency law itself would be feasible within the EU. Given the EIR's scheme, the answer will turn upon the proper interpretation of the notion of COMI. If this were tightly bound to a company's registered office, then a company which was registered in Member State A but which had its real seat in Member State B would thereby be able to engage in some arbitrage over corporate insolvency law as well as company law. However, the EIR's two-track scheme imposes an outer boundary on the extent to which such arbitrage would be possible. This is because, even if the company's COMI is in Member State A, the corporate insolvency law of Member State B will still be available for secondary proceedings conducted in that jurisdiction. The choice of COMI will therefore matter primarily for (i) the availability, and nature, of any corporate rescue proceedings (because the secondary proceedings under Member State B will be limited to liquidation); and (ii) the insolvency law rules applicable in third countries.

It is not implausible, notwithstanding the prevailing view in the national case law, that a corporate debtor's COMI could be interpreted as tightly bound to its registered office. As the concept is a creature of EC legislation, it will bear an autonomous meaning in European law. The ECJ has been called to rule upon the application of COMI in the pending case of *Bondi*.[168] There are good reasons for suggesting that the Court should treat the presumption created by Article 3(1), that a corporate debtor's COMI shall ordinarily be the state of its registered office, as a strong one. According to the Virgos-Schmidt Report, the unofficial interpretive guide to the Regulation, insolvency is a foreseeable risk to creditors, and therefore it is important that the jurisdiction in insolvency be one which they are able to predict easily.[169] *A priori*, it is hard to see how a test based on where business is in fact conducted renders creditors of international businesses more certain as to where insolvency proceedings will be conducted than a rule based on state of incorporation. This point is strengthened when it is borne in mind that local creditors will in any event be protected by the possibility of territorial secondary proceedings in any jurisdiction where business is carried on. Where a debtor conducts substantial business activities in more than one jurisdiction, the registered office will often be easier to determine than where the majority of the debtor's financial arrangements were conducted. What is worse, a purely geographic connecting factor is subject to change simply by the physical

---

[168] C-341/04, *Bondi v Bank of America NA*; application for urgent decision under the accelerated procedure refused, 15.09.2004.

[169] M Virgos and E Schmidt, *Report on the Convention on Insolvency Proceedings* (reprinted in Moss *et al*, n 150 above, Appendix 2), para. 75.

movement of the debtor, with the possibility that a transfer may be effected to a 'debtor-friendly' jurisdiction on the eve of insolvency.[170]

In contrast, tying COMI to the place of registered office would be readily ascertainable by creditors even where business is conducted in more than one state. Moreover, because the registered office is a legal rather than a geographic matter, corporate debtors could be prevented from 'switching COMI' to the detriment of their creditors through the simple expedient of a rule banning changes of registered office in contemplation of insolvency.[171] Most fundamentally, even in cases where such particular problems do not arise, equating COMI with registered office would promote certainty amongst creditors at least as well as the geographic location of business test in a day and age when all that is required to determine the relevant information is an internet search.

Would Regulatory Arbitrage in Corporate Insolvency Law be Desirable?

Were COMI interpreted in accordance with these suggestions, it would then become possible for companies to select the law which would govern any main insolvency proceedings in the same way as they can (or in the case of established companies, soon will be able to) do in respect of their company laws. It might be objected that having the law of Member State A (the home state) govern insolvency proceedings is impractical when the debtor's assets and business are located in Member State B (the host state). Yet it should be recalled that secondary proceedings could be opened in the host state. Rather, the only significant question which would be determined in this case by the COMI would be the availability, and nature of, any corporate rescue proceedings.

More fundamentally, it might be feared that permitting arbitrage over choice of insolvency law will lead to a 'race to the bottom', with companies incorporating in jurisdictions with weak insolvency laws so as to be able to benefit shareholders at the expense of creditors. To understand this, it is helpful to segment creditors into 'adjusting' and 'non-adjusting'

---

[170] See *Skjevesland v Geveran Trading Co Ltd* [2003] BPIR 924 at [4]; *Shierson v Vlieland-Boddy* [2004] EWHC 2752 (Ch), [2004] All ER (D) 420 at [13]–[23], esp. at [21]: '[T]he creditors are always at risk of such a change [of COMI], and they cannot safely make any assumptions as to the insolvency law which will apply in due course.' (*per* Mann J.).

[171] Such a rule would, on this paper's analysis, be a good candidate for EU legislation as a 'procedural harmonisation' provision.

categories.[172] The objection focuses upon the perceived plight of non-adjusting creditors—that is, those parties who extend 'credit' involuntarily (the paradigm case being tort victims), or in such small amounts that the transaction costs of becoming informed and adjusting their positions outweigh the benefits of doing so. The argument would assert that many Member States' insolvency regimes contain mechanisms designed to protect such creditors,[173] and that permitting companies to engage in regulatory arbitrage would allow them to undermine this protection.[174] Were this possible, shareholders would be able to benefit themselves at the expense of such creditors by selecting an insolvency law that would offer minimal protection. If this were unchecked, then it would clearly be an example of a 'race to the bottom'.

Yet such an outcome would not eventuate. First, under the EIR's scheme, insolvency priority rules designed to protect non-adjusting creditors would in any event be available to them through territorial proceedings in the jurisdiction in which they claim. Thus they will be made no worse off by permitting regulatory arbitrage over corporate rescue proceedings. Second, vulnerable creditors can be protected more effectively and precisely by mechanisms other than the reordering of priorities in insolvency.[175] If such regulatory requirements constituted *prima facie* restrictions on freedom of establishment, there seems little doubt that carefully-targeted provisions would satisfy the requirements of the *Gebhard* formula to be justified in the overriding public interest.

Thus, the limited regulatory arbitrage which the EIR could permit over insolvency law would not impose costs on non-adjusting creditors. Not only would it not *harm* these groups, but it would also bring significant benefits. To understand these, it is necessary to consider the way in which sophisticated—'adjusting'—creditors might be expected to

---

[172] The terminology is derived from L A Bebchuk and J M Fried, 'The Uneasy Case for the Priority of Secured Claims in Bankruptcy' (1996) 105 Yale LJ, 857. The possibility that the presence of non-adjusting creditors might distort firms' investment incentives so as to exploit them was first noted in J H Scott, Jr, 'Bankruptcy, Secured Debt and Optimal Capital Structure' (1979) 32 *J Fin*, 1.

[173] For example, the 'prescribed part' of floating charge assets which must be set aside for unsecured creditors in UK corporate insolvencies following the Enterprise Act 2002: see Insolvency Act 1986 s 176A.

[174] See, eg L LoPucki, 'Cooperation in International Bankruptcy: A Post-Universalist Approach' (1999) 84 Cornell L Rev, 696, 720–23.

[175] For tort victims and environmental claims, mandatory insurance or statutory guarantee requirements for those engaging in hazardous activities provide clearly-targeted incentives. For unsophisticated voluntary creditors, such as consumers, employees and trade creditors, credit insurance can be provided—either through statutory mandate or by market providers—by sophisticated creditors who then price the risk into their transactions with the debtor.

respond to such arbitrage.[176] They could be expected to adjust the terms of their credit transaction to reflect the effect of a debtor's choice of COMI. Where this is harmful to such creditors, the debtor will incur a higher cost of credit, or find it difficult to raise credit at all. Where the regime leaves gaps, such creditors may be expected to contract for protection in the form of loan covenants, security interests, and the like. If the costs of such contracting are high, then the debtor will have an incentive to select an insolvency regime which creditors would prefer. Member States wishing to attract, or not to deter, companies would respond by providing insolvency codes that offer the appropriate protection: regulatory competition resulting in a 'race to the top', rather than to the bottom.

As we have seen, the choice of COMI will matter, from creditors' point of view, principally in regard to corporate rescue proceedings. There are reasons for thinking that this area is one in which the operation of regulatory competition would be particularly fruitful.[177] The extent to which a legal regime should seek to foster 'rescue' of troubled companies, and the way in which control of the distressed company should be organised therein, are highly contentious matters. A vocal group of US scholars has argued that debtors should be permitted to design their own insolvency regimes by contract with their creditors, as opposed to being able to participate only in mandatory state-sanctioned insolvency procedures.[178] Permitting regulatory competition over insolvency laws would be an approximation to this result, with the added benefit that each regime on the 'menu' from which debtors could select would come with a ready-made body of case law interpreting and applying it, enabling the market to assess the likely consequences with confidence. Moreover, to the extent that corporate rescue regimes complement other aspects of a corporate governance system, permitting firms to opt into these as well as the other parts of the regime will further promote specialisation if this is indeed the direction taken by European regulatory competition. Thus corporate rescue procedures seem a prime candidate for a stance of regulatory agnosticism at the EU level, and for the forces of regulatory competition to be harnessed so as to permit a learning process as to the most appropriate legal regime.

---

[176] A T Guzman, 'International Bankruptcy: In Defence of Universalism' (2000) 98 Mich L Rev, 2177, 2180–81.

[177] Skeel, 'Rethinking the Line', n 148 above, 517–23.

[178] See, eg R K Rasmussen, 'Debtor's Choice: A Menu Approach to Corporate Bankruptcy', (1992) 71 Tex L Rev, 51; A Schwartz, 'Contracting About Bankruptcy' (1997) 13 *J L Econ & Org*, 127. The argument is extended to the context of international insolvencies in R K Rasmussen, 'A New Approach to Transnational Insolvencies' (1997) 19 Mich J Int'l L, 1.

To recapitulate: permitting regulatory arbitrage over corporate insolvency law to the extent which it could take place within the EIR framework would be a desirable step. The structure of the EIR means that it would principally affect the availability, and form of, any corporate rescue proceedings. This is a matter which adjusting creditors can be expected to take into account in pricing the firm's cost of credit, thereby forcing firms to internalise the impact of insolvency on creditors in their arbitrage decisions.[179] The position of non-adjusting creditors would be protected through territorial measures which are either given effect to in secondary proceedings, or which are necessary and proportionate in their impact—thus satisfying the *Gebhard* test. The EIR's jurisdiction-allocation scheme, if COMI is interpreted in accordance with the argument of this paper, would thus act as a form of procedural harmonisation in corporate insolvency law, so as to guide the process of the development of insolvency laws towards *beneficial* regulatory competition. The availability of secondary proceedings truncates the possibilities for a 'race to the bottom', leaving only opportunities for a 'race to the top' over corporate rescue proceedings.[180] Member States' regulatory responses could be expected to follow a pattern of mutual learning, permitting a beneficial evolution and the ultimate adoption of the most appropriate corporate rescue regimes.

Conclusion

The question this paper set out to address was whether European corporate law would in future best be made by 'federal' legislation or regulatory competition between Member States. As EC legislation carries with it well-known problems, the answer to the question depends on an assessment of the prospects for European regulatory competition in the field. If regulatory competition would be pathological, then EC legislation might be justified as a 'lesser evil'. Therefore, although 'crystal ball gazing' is a risky activity, I have sought—perhaps recklessly—to offer a view of the likely future development of European regulatory competition.

---

[179] This would be the case both for formation and reincorporation choices, as adjusting creditors could easily include loan covenants specifying that reincorporation without their consent would constitute an event of default.

[180] The structure is designed to protect local creditors, but not to permit them to stymie rescue proceedings. Thus the insolvency practitioner conducting main proceedings is empowered to stay secondary proceedings so as to effect a rescue, provided that adequate protection is offered for the interests of creditors in the secondary proceedings: Reg. 1346/2000, Art 33.

My conclusions on regulatory competition are generally optimistic. It seems plausible that regulatory competition will come to be a motor for the development of Member States' company laws and corporate governance systems. Arbitrage by 'start-up' firms is already legally possible, and this is starting to lead to responsive changes throughout Europe in laws applicable to private companies. For established companies, arbitrage will in all likelihood soon be facilitated by European legislation, in the form of the Tenth and Fourteenth Company Law Directives. This will not be attractive to all companies, because differences in ownership structure complement differences in national governance systems. However, it seems plausible that the UK, with a governance system adapted to dispersed ownership, will be an attractive destination for companies whose owners wish to exit blockholdings and shift to dispersed ownership. This process will be facilitated by the newly pan-European law firms. Hence the UK's professional services sector has a powerful incentive to ensure that the governance regime—most especially, the self-regulatory aspects—is kept attractive to firms thinking about moving there. Other Member States, faced with this apparent challenge, are likely to respond by 'defensive' regulatory competition. Precisely how this will develop is unclear, but it seems plausible that a likely strategy would be to enhance further those aspects of their systems which will complement firms with concentrated ownership. This would yield a process of path-dependent specialisation, rather than convergence.

Underpinning this process will be EC legislation governing how established firms will be able to make their reincorporation decisions. This 'procedural' regulation will ensure that affected constituencies are parties to the decision-making process, and so transfers of jurisdiction motivated by a desire to expropriate them will not succeed. This will reduce the prospect of a detrimental 'race to the bottom'.

Some Member States may seek to recharacterise creditor protection rules as part of their corporate insolvency codes, but the better view is that this will not insulate such rules from the possibility of being held to constitute unlawful impediments to corporate freedom of establishment. Indeed, perhaps my most radical suggestion is that the framework of the European Insolvency Regulation could actually permit a certain amount of arbitrage—and thence competition—over corporate rescue proceedings. As the relevant rules may complement other aspects of corporate law, it seems desirable that they should be subject to a similar process of development.

A positive assessment of regulatory competition makes the drawbacks of harmonised EC legislation all the more stark. Harmonised legislation runs two risks which are avoided by a process of benign regulatory competition. First, such legislation tends to encourage Member States to converge their laws on a central model, which may be inappropriate where one 'size' does not 'fit' all. Decentralised solutions can permit Member States to continue patterns of diversity, whilst regulatory arbitrage allows individual firms for which the national model is inappropriate to opt out. Second, harmonisation presupposes that the European legislator is able to specify the 'best' regulatory solution to any given problem. In an area such as company law, where the configuration of the optimal rules is hotly debated, regulatory competition can promote innovation and mutual learning between national legislatures.

In conclusion, then, the answer to our starting question is that the future of European company law-making would better be left with Member States than take the form of European legislation, save for areas in which a uniform consensus has emerged regarding the appropriate regulatory choice. This does not seem inconsistent with the thinking behind the European Commission's recent Company Law Action Plan, which recognises the benefits of national diversity and proposes EC legislation only in certain limited areas. It is to be hoped that time will be permitted to demonstrate the soundness of this approach.

Consumer Contract Law and General Contract Law: The German Experience

Reinhard Zimmermann *

Introduction

On 1 January 2000, the German Civil Code (BGB) became one hundred years old. It had been remarkably resilient throughout a century marked by catastrophic upheavals and a succession of fundamentally different political regimes.[1] Two years later, however, on 1 January 2002, the most sweeping individual reform ever to have effected the Code entered into force. This was the Modernization of the Law of Obligations Act.[2] It had been triggered by the necessity to implement the European Consumer Sales Directive,[3] but went far beyond what was required by the European Community. The then Minister of Justice had decided to use the tailwind from Brussels finally to implement an ambitious reform project dating

* This is the text on which my J A C Thomas lecture for the academic year 2004/05 was based; the lecture was delivered at University College, London, on 10 February 2005.

[1] On the German Civil Code and the development of private law in Germany in the twentieth century see R Zimmermann, 'Das Bürgerliche Gesetzbuch und die Entwicklung des Bürgerlichen Rechts', in M Schmoeckel, J Rückert and R Zimmermann (eds), *Historisch-kritischer Kommentar zum BGB*, vol. I (2003), vor § 1, nn 1ff; for an overview in English, Zimmermann, 'Characteristic Aspects of German Legal Culture', in M Reimann and J Zekoll (eds), *Introduction to German Law* (2nd edn., 2005),1ff.

[2] *Gesetz zur Modernisiesung des Schuldrechts*, 26 November 2001, *Bundesgesetzblatt* 2001 I, 3138. For the background of this Act, see W Ernst and R Zimmermann (eds), *Zivilrechtswissenschaft und Schuldrechtsreform*, (2001); R Schulze and H Schulte-Nölke (eds), *Die Schuldrechtsreform vor dem Hintergrund des Gemeinschaftsrechts* (2001); R Zimmermann, 'Modernizing the German Law of Obligations?', in P Birks and A Pretto (eds), *Themes in Comparative Law in Honour of Bernard Rudden* (2002), 265ff; for a general introduction to the new law, see P Huber and F Faust, *Schuldrechtsmodernisierung* (2002); S Lorenz and T Riehm, *Lehrbuch zum neuen Schuldrecht* (2002).

[3] Directive 1999/44/EC of the European Parliament and of the Council of 25 May 1999 on certain aspects of the sale of consumer goods and associated guarantees, OJ L 171/99, 12; for a commentary, see M C Bianca and S Grundmann (eds), *EU Sales Directive: Commentary* (2002); for comparative comment, see the contributions to (2001) 9 European Review of Private Law 157ff, and to M Schermaier (ed), *Verbraucherkauf in Europa* (2003).

back to the late 1970s.[4] It had led to the appointment of a Commission charged with the reform of the German law of obligations which had duly prepared a report and draft legislation.[5] That draft was used as the basis for a Discussion Draft of a Modernization of the German Law of Obligations Act which was published in September 2000.[6] Vehement criticism raised against the Discussion Draft[7] led to substantial revision but was no longer able to abort the reform project, or to confine it to the amendments required by the Consumer Sales Directive.[8] The most important aspect of the Act of 2002, from the point of view of legal practice, is the fundamental reform of the German law of (liberative) prescription.[9] Doctrinally the most remarkable feature of the revised BGB is the new regime concerning liability for non-performance in general[10] and for non-conformity in sales law in particular.[11]

More than by any other component of the reform process, however, the face of the BGB has been changed by the attempt to integrate into the Civil Code a number of special statutes aiming at the protection of consumers. The draftsmen of the new law have thus made an effort to streamline, or harmonise, general contract law and consumer contract law. This is the issue that will be discussed in the present paper. While it had been on the initial reform agenda of 1978,[12] it had no longer been

---

[4] H Däubler-Gmelin, 'Die Entscheidung für die so genannte Grosse Lösung bei der Schuldrechtsreform' [2001] *Neue Juristische Wochenschrift* 2281ff.

[5] Bundesminister der Justiz (ed), *Abschlussbericht der Kommission zur Überarbeitung des Schuldrechts* (1992).

[6] The text of the provisions has been printed in Ernst and Zimmermann, n 2 above, Appendix I, 613ff.; and see C-W Canaris (ed), *Schuldrechtsmodernisierung* 2002 (2002), 3ff (text of the provisions and motivation).

[7] See, in particular, the contributions to Ernst and Zimmermann n 2 above.

[8] For a proposal along those lines, see W Ernst and B Gsell, 'Kaufrechtsrichtlinie und BGB: Gesetzentwurf für eine "kleine" Lösung bei der Umsetzung der EU-Kaufrechtsrichtlinie', [2000] *Zeitschrift für Wirtschaftsrecht* 1410ff; cf also W Ernst and B Gsell, 'Nochmals für die "kleine" Lösung' [2000] *Zeitschrift für Wirtschaftsrecht* 1812 ff.

[9] On which see H-P Mansel, 'Die Neuregelung des Verjährungsrechts' [2002] *Neue Juristische Wochenschrift* 89ff; R Zimmermann, 'Das neue deutsche Verjährungsrecht—ein Vorbild für Europa?', in P Schlechtriem (ed), *Wandlungen des Schuldrechts* (2002), 53ff; Zimmermann, 'The New German Law of Prescription and Ch 14 of the Principles of European Contract Law' in A Vaquer Aloy (ed), *La Tercera Parte de los Principios de Derecho Contractual Europeo*, in preparation for 2005.

[10] For details, see R Zimmermann, 'Remedies for Non-Performance: The revised German law of obligations, viewed against the background of the Principles of European Contract Law' (2002) 6 Edinburgh Law Review 271ff.

[11] For details, see R Zimmermann, 'Liability for Non-Conformity: The new system of remedies in German sales' law and its historical context', 10th John Kelly Memorial Lecture' (University College Dublin, Faculty of Law, 2004).

[12] A Wolf, 'Weiterentwicklung und Überarbeitung des Schuldrechts' [1978] *Zeitschrift für Rechtspolitik* 253ff.

part of the brief of the Commission charged with the reform of the German law of obligations.[13] The Discussion Draft could not, therefore, be based on previous drafts or detailed academic discussion as to how such integration might be achieved. Nor was the incorporation into the BGB of the special legislation concerning consumer protection required by any *fiat* on the European level. On the contrary: European law is still itself confronted with the problem of coordinating general contract law and consumer contract law. The issue is very much on the agenda mapped out by the Action Plan for a more coherent European Contract Law[14] and it also still has to be considered by the draftsmen of the Principles of European Contract Law[15] who, while providing a blueprint for general contract law, have so far failed to take account of the *acquis communautaire* in the field of consumer contracts.[16] The debates conducted, and experiences gathered, in Germany may therefore also be instructive as far as the future development of European contract law is concerned.

Freedom, Equality and Social Responsibility at the Time of the Original BGB

Protecting the Weaker Party

One of the characteristic lines of development of contract law over the past four decades, both in Germany and internationally, is the rise of legislation aiming at the protection of consumers who are about to enter

---

[13] H A Engelhardt, 'Zu den Aufgaben einer Kommission für die Überarbeitung des Schuldrechts', [1984] *Neue Juristische Wochenschrift* 1201ff.

[14] COM (2003) 68, OJ 2003, C 63/1; the summary is printed in (2003) 11 *Zeitschrift für Europäisches Privatrecht* 656. On the action plan, see D Staudenmeyer, 'Der Aktionsplan der EG-Kommission zum Europäischen Vertragsrecht', [2003] *Europäische Zeitschrift für Wirtschaftsrecht* 481ff.; C von Bar and S Swann, 'Response to the Action Plan on European Contract Law: A More Coherent European Contract Law (COM (2003) 63)' (2003) 11 European Review of Private Law 595ff.

[15] O Lando and H Beale (eds), *Principles of European Contract Law, Parts I and II*, (2000); O Lando, E Clive, A Prüm and R Zimmermann (eds), *Principles of European Contract Law, Part III* (2003). For comment, see R Zimmermann, 'The Principles of European Contract Law: Contemporary Manifestation of the Old, and Possible Foundation for a New, European Scholarship of Private Law', in *Essays in Honour of Hein Kötz* (2005, forthcoming).

[16] This has repeatedly been criticized; see J Basedow, 'The Renascence of Uniform Law: European Contract Law and its Components' (1998) 18 LS 138ff; R Michaels, 'Privatautonomie und Privatkodifikation' (1998) 62 *Rabels Zeitschrift für ausländisches und internationales Privatrecht* 589; W Wurmnest, 'Common Core, Grundregeln, Kodifikationsentwürfe, Acquis-Grundsätze—Ansätze internationaler Wissenschaftlergruppen zur Privatrechtsvereinheitlichung in Europa' (2003) 11 *Zeitschrift für Europäisches Privatrecht* 729ff; H-W Micklitz, 'Verbraucherschutz in den Grundregeln des Europäischen

(or have entered) into contracts which may be (or turn out to be) against their own best interests. This legislation is widely regarded as unsatisfactory. It is obviously ill coordinated.[17] Moreover, a certain tension is often seen to exist between the approach embraced by the consumer contract legislation and the fundamental precepts of legal equality and private autonomy underlying the BGB.[18] Also, both the definition of, and focus on, the concept of 'consumer' have been criticized.[19] Does modern consumer law constitute a special branch of private law with its own distinctive features and policy considerations (and, some would say, ideology)? Does it deal with a specific type, or class, of persons who deserve to be protected? But Consumers do not constitute a class:[20] everyone can be a consumer, as long as he acts in a specific role.[21] The inexperienced housewife and the impecunious workman are as much 'consumers' as the wealthy entrepreneur or the distinguished law professor, as long as they buy a car, or book, or loaf of bread, or carpet, for their private use. Consumers are,

Vertragsrechts' (2004) 103 *Zeitschrift für vergleichende Rechtswissenschaft* 88ff; H Rösler, *Europäisches Konsumentenvertragsrecht* (2004), 137ff.

[17] See, for example, J Basedow, 'Das BGB im künftigen europäischen Privatrecht: der hybride Kodex' (2000) 200 *Archiv für die civilistische Praxis* 449ff; C Kirchner, 'Der punktuelle Ansatz als Leitprinzip gemeinschaftsrechtlicher Privatrechtsharmonisierung', in S Grundmann, D Medicus and W Rolland (eds), *Europäisches Kaufgewährleistungsrecht* (2000), 95ff; T M J Möllers, 'Europäische Richtlinien zum Bürgerlichen Recht' [2002] *Juristenzeitung* 121ff; T Pfeiffer, 'Die Integration von "Nebengesetzen" in das BGB' in Ernst and Zimmermann, n 2 above, 481ff; Rösler, n 16 above, 218ff.

[18] On the principles underlying the BGB, see J Rückert, 'Das BGB und seine Prinzipien: Aufgabe, Lösung, Erfolg' in Schmoeckel, Rückert and Zimmermann, n 1 above, vol. I, vor § 1, nn 1ff.

[19] See, for example, D Medicus, 'Wer ist ein Verbraucher?' in H G Leser (ed), *Wege zum japanischen Recht: Festschrift für Zentaro Kitagawa* (1992), 471ff; M Dreher, 'Der Verbraucher—Das Phantom in den opera des europäischen und deutschen Rechts?' [1997] *Juristenzeitung* 167ff. For a discussion of the issues involved on the European and German level, see W Faber, 'Elemente verschiedener Verbraucherbegriffe in EG-Richtlinien, zwischenstaatlichen Übereinkommen und nationalen Zivil- und Kollisionsrecht' (1998) 6 *Zeitschrift für Europäisches Privatrecht* 854ff; J Drexl, *Die wirtschaftliche Selbstbestimmung des Verbrauchers* (1998), 433ff; T Pfeiffer, 'Der Verbraucher nach § 13 BGB' in Schulze and Schulte-Nölke, n 2 above, 133ff; T Repgen, *Kein Abschied von der Privatautonomie: Die Funktion zwingenden Rechts in der Verbrauchsgüterkaufrichtlinie* (2001), 30ff; K Riesenhuber, *System und Prinzipien des Europäischen Vertragsrechts* (2003), 250ff; O Remien, *Zwingendes Vertragsrecht und Grundfreiheiten des EG-Vertrages* (2003), 238ff; Rösler, n 16 above, 101ff; K-U Wiedenmann, *Verbraucherleitbilder und Verbraucherbegriff im deutschen und europäischen Privatrecht* (2004), 134ff; B Heiderhoff, *Grundstrukturen des nationalen und europäischen Verbrauchervertragsrechts* (2004) 238ff; J Mohr, 'Der Begriff des Verbrauchers und seine Auswirkungen auf das neugeschaffene Kaufrecht und das Arbeitsrecht' (2004) 204 *Archiv für die civilistische Praxis*, 670ff.

[20] D Medicus, 'Schlussbetrachtung', in Ernst and Zimmermann, n 2 above, 607.

[21] On the notion of 'role' as a point of departure for legal consequences, see D Medicus, 'Eigenschaft oder Rolle als Anknüpfungspunkt für Rechtsfolgen', in H Honsell (ed), *Privatrecht und Methode: Festschrift für Ernst A. Kramer* (2004), 211ff.

however, protected only in specific situations against specific dangers which the law perceives to exist. Obviously, therefore, the law pursues a typological approach:[22] it attempts to grant protection to one contracting party who is considered to be in a weaker position, or at a specific disadvantage, *vis-à-vis* the other.

Consumer protection is thus a modern manifestation of a much broader concern. The tradition of legislation protecting weaker parties against disadvantageous contract terms is a long one; it reaches back to the maximum interest rates for loans,[23] the *senatus consultum Vellaeanum*,[24] and the *laesio enormis* of Roman law.[25] Commercial life in the Middle Ages was dominated by the prohibition of usury[26] and by countless regulations attempting to fix the *iustum pretium* for various commodities.[27] The aedilitian edict, issued in the early part of the 2nd century BC, essentially served the purpose of what would today be called consumer protection;[28] the generalized form of 'aedilitian liability' became part and parcel of the *ius commune* and also distinctively shaped national codifications in Europe.[29] The German Civil Code has often been criticized for unduly neglecting this protective dimension and with it, in the words of Otto von Gierke, the 'social task of private law'.[30] It is said to be based on an exaggerated individualism and on a formalistic concept of freedom and equality.[31] This evaluation does not, however, convey an entirely accurate picture of the broader legal position.[32] Contemporary lawyers were acutely aware of the limitations of freedom of contract.[33] At the same time, it

---

[22] T Duve, '§§ 1–14. Natürliche Personen, Verbraucher, Unternehmer' in Schmoeckel, Rückert and Zimmermann, n 1 above, vol. I, §§ 1–14, nn 78ff; Heiderhoff, n 19 above, 250ff; Wiedenmann, n 19 above, 113ff.

[23] R Zimmermann, *The Law of Obligations: Roman Foundations of the Civilian Tradition* (paperback edn., 1996), 166ff. [24] Ibid. 145ff.

[25] Ibid. 259ff. [26] Ibid. 170ff.

[27] H Kellenbenz, 'Preisbindung', in *Handwörterbuch zur deutschen Rechtsgeschichte*, vol. III (1984), cols 1886ff. Generally on the devices used in medieval and early modern Europe to provide what would today be called 'consumer' protection, see W Schuhmacher, *Verbraucher und Recht in historischer Sicht* (1981), 11ff.

[28] M Kaser and R Knütel, *Römisches Privatrecht* (17th edn., 2003), 270; E Jakab, 'Diebische Sklaven, marode Balken: Von den römischen Wurzeln der Gewährleistung für Sachmängel' in Schermaier, n 3 above, 27 ff.

[29] Zimmermann, n 23 above, 311ff, 319ff.

[30] O von Gierke, *Die soziale Aufgabe des Privatrechts* (1889); cf also, for example, R Sohm, 'Ueber den Entwurf eines bürgerlichen Gesetzbuches für das Deutsche Reich in zweiter Lesung' (1895) 39 *Gruchots Beiträge zur Erläuterung des deutschen Rechts*, 747.

[31] F Wieacker, *Privatrechtsgeschichte der Neuzeit* (2nd edn., 1967), 468ff; K Zweigert and H Kötz, *Einführung in die Rechtsvergleichung* (3rd edn., 1996), 147ff.

[32] Rückert, n 18 above revor § 1, n 96; Rösler, n 16 above, 50ff; Mohr, n 19 above, 660ff. For a comprehensive discussion, see T Repgen, *Die soziale Aufgabe des Privatrechts*, (2001).

[33] See, for example, G Planck, 'Die soziale Tendenz des BGB' (1899) 4 *Deutsche Juristenzeitung*, 181ff; Planck was one of the most influential draftsmen of the BGB. For

must be kept in mind that many of the problems with which we are faced today were only beginning to emerge.[34] They were not necessarily tackled by means of private law, and even where they were, the respective rules were enacted by way of special legislation rather than incorporated into the codification of general private law. The scene was thus set for the double-track approach which remained characteristic of German private law until 2002.

Economic Background

The German Civil Code was promulgated in 1896 and came into effect on 1 January 1900. Its preparation had taken 22 years, for the first, 'preliminary', Commission had been appointed in 1874.[35] This was a time when Germany was beginning to experience a period of rapid change. The population of the new *Reich* grew from 41 million in 1871 to 56 million in 1900.[36] More and more of that population lived in towns. While up to 1871 close to two thirds of all Germans had lived in the countryside, that number had sunk to less than half (45.6 per cent) in 1900.[37] The number of Germans living in cities (of over 100,000 inhabitants), on the other hand, had risen from 4.8 per cent in 1871 to 16.2 per cent in 1900; by 1910 Germany had 48 cities with over 100,000 inhabitants as opposed to merely 8 in 1871.[38] At the same time, there was a marked East–West migration; thus, in 1907, 24 % of those born in the three north-eastern provinces of Prussia lived in other areas of Germany, many of them in the mining area of the Ruhr.[39] During the last three decades of the nineteenth century Germany turned from a (predominantly) agrarian into a (predominantly) industrialized society. The coal output in the Ruhr area, for example, increased from 11.5 million tons in 1870 to 60.1 million tons in 1900.[40] Transportation facilities and capacities had been improved very considerably by the end of the century. In 1880, 10 per cent of the capital generated in the *Reich* was invested in the railways.[41] In

---

further discussion, and references, see Repgen, n 32 above, 24ff, 68ff; the revisionist view is also supported by S Hofer, *Freiheit ohne Grenzen?* (2001). For a comparative analysis, see J-L Halpérin, 'Quelle histoire pour le droit des consommateurs?' (2001) 23 *Zeitschrift für Neuere Rechtsgeschichte* 62ff; for Austria, see Schuhmacher, n 27 above, 34ff.

[34] The point is also emphasized by Rösler, n 16 above, 50ff.

[35] See the table prepared by S Stolte, 'Die Entstehung des BGB im Überblick mit Nachweis der Quellentexte', in Schmoeckel, Rückert and Zimmermann, n 1 above, vol. I (2003), xxviiff.

[36] T Nipperdey, *Deutsche Geschichte 1866–1918*, vol. I (paperback edn., 1998), 9ff.

[37] Ibid, 35.   [38] Ibid, 34.   [39] Ibid, 40.   [40] Ibid, 227.

[41] Ibid, 260.

1913 7,024 million letters were sent, compared with 269 million in 1867.[42] The invention of the telephone dramatically improved the speed of communication. In 1881 there had only been 1,400 telephone installations; by 1900, the figure had passed 1 million.[43] The years after 1870 saw the rise of the modern interventionist state. At the same time, it was a period of unparalleled economic growth; German national unification, in particular, stimulated the proverbial 'foundational boom'.[44] But there were also setbacks and recessions which highlighted the problems of an industrialized society.[45] An ever-larger percentage of the population worked as labourers in trade and industry[46] and thus depended for their livelihood on the smooth functioning and growth of these sectors of the economy. Trade unions and strikes for better work conditions became a feature of modern public life.[47]

The Drops of Social Oil

The law reacted to these challenges in various ways. Most famously, perhaps, Bismarck created the modern social security system in order to improve the welfare of the workers and, at the same time, to achieve an integration of the 'fourth estate' into the prevailing system of government.[48] The Emperor pronounced the promotion of the welfare of those in need to be one of the noblest tasks of every body politic.[49] The fathers of the BGB saw in the protection of the economically weaker party an important policy objective and emphasized the need for social sensitivity.[50] Within the code itself, these considerations manifested themselves in various ways. Thus, of course, there were the famous 'general provisions' like §§ 138, 226, 242 and 826 BGB. They have turned out to be highly pliable devices for the infusion of more than a few drops of social oil into the fabric of the BGB.[51] But there were also a number of other rules, most of them adopted in deviation from contemporary pandectist legal

---

[42] Ibid, 263.   [43] Ibid, 263.   [44] Ibid, 283ff.
[45] Ibid, 284, 336.   [46] Ibid, 291 ff.   [47] Ibid, 19ff.
[48] Ibid, 335ff; M Stolleis, *Geschichte des Sozialrechts in Deutschland* (2003), 52ff.
[49] Emperor's speech of 17 November 1881, as quoted by Repgen, n 32 above, 28.
[50] See the quotations from speeches by G. Planck before the Imperial Parliament, as quoted by Repgen, n 32 above, 70.
[51] Otto von Gierke had famously demanded that 'a drop of socialist oil' had to seep through the fabric of private law: Repgen, n 32 above, 12ff. On the pedigree of the oil metaphor (which had also, previously, been used by Bismarck, see Repgen, n 32 above, 4; cf also T Repgen, 'Was war und wo blieb das soziale Öl?' (2000) 22 *Zeitschrift für Neuere Privatrechtsgeschichte* 406ff. For a historical analysis of the application of §§ 138 and 226 BGB, see H-P Haferkamp in Schmoeckel, Rückert and Zimmermann, n 1 above, vol. I (2003), § 138 and §§ 226–231.

doctrine: sale does not 'break' lease;[52] the restrictions on the lessor's statutory pledge over objects brought on to the premises by the lessee;[53] continuation of payment of wages in cases where an employee is prevented from performing his services 'for a comparatively insignificant time' for a reason 'associated with his person' (such as sickness);[54] the protection of employees against excessively long employment contracts by means of a statutory right to terminate the contract after five years;[55] the judicial power to reduce 'disproportionately high' conventional penalties;[56] or the right of the debtor to terminate a loan after the lapse of six months if an interest rate in excess of six per cent has been agreed upon.[57] These are merely examples. Even the regulation of a technical area of the law not usually in the forefront of political discussion, such as 'extinctive' prescription, was based on social concerns including, particularly, protection of the debtor.[58] More important, however, is another point. The BGB was supposed to provide a general framework for parties to regulate their own affairs; it subscribed to the ideals of equal rights, freedom and self-determination. At the same time, it was not intended to advance the interests of particular groups, or classes, within contemporary society. Its draftsmen did not reject the legitimacy of specific policy concerns militating for special rules of a protective character. But these, by and large, were special concerns which required special legislation outside the general Civil Code.

The Act Concerning Instalment Sales

The most prominent example of such special legislation is the Act concerning Instalment Sales (*Abzahlungsgesetz*) of 16 May 1894.[59] Its origins

---

[52] § 571 BGB (old version) (now § 566 BGB); see Zimmermann, n 23 above, 377ff; Repgen, n 32 above, 231ff.

[53] §§ 559ff BGB (old version) (now: §§ 562ff BGB); for an extensive analysis, see Repgen, n 32 above, 250ff.

[54] § 616 BGB; on which see H Oetker, in Staudinger, *Kommentar zum Bürgerlichen Gesetzbuch* (revised edn., 2002), § 616, nn 1ff; cf also Repgen, n 32 above, 215ff.

[55] § 624 BGB; on which see U Preis, in Staudinger, n 54 above, § 624, nn 1ff.

[56] § 343 BGB; on which see R-P Sossna, *Die Geschichte der Begrenzung von Vertragsstrafen* (1993), 165ff.

[57] § 247 BGB (repealed in 1986); on the origin of which see P. Landau, 'Die Gesetzgebungsgeschichte des § 247 BGB: Zugleich ein Beitrag zur Geschichte der Einführung der Zinsfreiheit in Deutschland' in G Kleinheyer and P Mikat (eds), *Beiträge zur Rechtsgeschichte: Gedächtnisschrift für Hermann Conrad* (1979), 385ff; R Geyer, *Der Gedanke des Verbraucherschutzes im Reichsrecht des Kaiserreichs und der Weimarer Republik (1871–1933)*, (2001), 71ff.

[58] For details, see Repgen, n 32 above, 179ff; for the policy objectives pursued by the law of prescription cf also, in this context, R Zimmermann, *Comparative Foundations of a European Law of Set-Off and Prescription* (2002), 63, 77.

[59] *Reichsgesetzblatt* 1894, 450. Another very important special statute implementing a finely attuned model for protecting contractual parties perceived to be in a weaker

have repeatedly been analysed.[60] Mass production and improved distribution facilities had led to the opening up of new markets and a vastly increased range of potential purchasers. Instalment transactions enabled the members of the less affluent classes to obtain the goods required for their daily life (such as furniture) or the machinery required to earn their livelihood. By the middle of the 1880s, for example, more than half of the 500,000 sewing machines produced in Germany annually were sold by way of instalment sales; by 1892–3 the percentage even appears to have risen to between 80 and 90 per cent.[61] These sewing machines were bought, very largely, by female homeworkers. Instalment sales had thus become a very widespread type of transaction that was welcomed, in principle, from the point of view of both social policy and national economy. But it also entailed a number of specific risks and disadvantages. One of them was the so-called 'forfeiture clause' (*Verfallklausel*) on which instalment sellers used to insist:[62] if the purchaser failed to pay one of the instalments, the seller was entitled to take back the object and to keep all the instalments that had previously been paid. In the second half of the 1880s the problems associated with instalment sales became the subject of widespread debates. In 1891 they were examined at the annual meeting of the German Lawyers' Association, with the young Philipp Heck (subsequently to become one of the most influential German private lawyers and legal theorists) providing the key address.[63] By that time, close to 1,000 petitions had reached the *Reichstag*.[64] Only few of those who voiced their opinions questioned the necessity for intervention by the legislature. It was very widely agreed that commercial freedom had to be restricted in a situation where one party, as a result of his inferior economic position, was effectively required to accept the conditions fixed by the other:[65] in a situation, in other words, where the principle of *pacta sunt servanda* typically could not be relied upon in order to achieve

position is the Insurance Contract Act of 30 May 1908, Reichsgesetzblatt (as above) 1908, 263. For discussion, see W-H Roth, *Internationales Versicherungsvertragsrecht* (1985), 77ff.

[60] H-P Benöhr, 'Konsumentenschutz vor 80 Jahren: Zur Entstehung des Abzahlungsgesetzes vom 16. Mai 1894' (1974) 138 *Zeitschrift für das gesamte Handelsrecht und Wirtschaftsrecht*, 492ff; W Schubert, 'Das Abzahlungsgesetz von 1894 als Beispiel für das Verhältnis von Sozialpolitik und Privatrecht in der Regierungszeit des Reichskanzlers von Caprivi' (1985) 102 *Zeitschrift der Savigny-Stiftung für Rechtsgeschichte (Germanistische Abteilung)*, 130ff; Geyer, n 57 above, 48ff.

[61] Benöhr, n 60 above, 494; Geyer, n 57 above, 48.

[62] See, for example, Schubert, n 60 above, 146ff.

[63] P Heck, 'Wie ist den Mißbräuchen, welche sich bei den Abzahlungsgeschäften herausgestellt haben, entgegen zu wirken?', Gutachten, in *Verhandlungen des Einundzwanzigsten Deutschen Juristentages*, vol. II (1891), 131ff.

[64] E von Hippel, *Verbraucherschutz* (3rd edn., 1986), 193.

[65] See the references in Benöhr, n 60 above, 499ff; Geyer, n 57 above, 59.

acceptable results. The Act concerning Instalment Sales prohibited forfeiture clauses;[66] apart from that it introduced mandatory rules protecting purchasers in cases of termination of the instalment sale and in situations of default of payment.[67] Significantly, its range of application was not confined to 'consumers'; it was to cover, above all, small-scale professionals, such as poorly off seamstresses, craftsmen, or piano teachers.[68] This is why a negative formula was chosen: the Act did not apply, if the recipient of the object in question had been recorded as a merchant in the commercial register.[69]

The Act concerning Instalment Sales was prepared between 1890 and 1894, ie roughly at the same time as the Second Commission revised the draft BGB. The mere chronology of events, in other words, would not have prevented the incorporation of the Act into the BGB. A number of critics of the first draft of the BGB had in fact urged such inclusion.[70] Both the Department of Justice and the Second Commission, however, decided not to pursue this option.[71] Instalment sales had become both a mass phenomenon and an urgent problem. Since, in the early 1890s, it was not yet clear when the BGB would come into effect, a special Act could be, and was eventually, adopted considerably earlier. Equally important was probably another consideration which was expressed by Gottlieb Planck in reply to von Gierke. The BGB was supposed, by and large, to restate rather than change the existing law. Social innovation was to be left to special legislation, particularly if it was contemplated in response to very specific problems that had arisen comparatively recently with the result that the approach to be adopted was still a matter of political dispute and a well-established and time-tested set of rules that could be expected to last was not available.[72] The regulation of instalment sales, in other words, had not attained the level of doctrinal stability required for inclusion in a code envisaged to be something more than a permanent building site.

[66] §§ 1, 3, 5 *Gesetz betreffend Abzahlungsgeschäfte*.
[67] §§ 2, 4 II *Gesetz betreffend Abzahlungsgeschäfte*. § 4 I gave judges the right to reduce excessive penalty clauses; that rule was subsequently generalized: § 343 BGB.
[68] Geyer, n 57 above, 54ff.   [69] § 8 *Gesetz betreffend Abzahlungsgeschäfte*.
[70] H Jastrow, 'Wie ist den Mißbräuchen, welche sich bei den Abzahlungsgeschäften herausgestellt haben, entgegen zu wirken?', Gutachten, in *Verhandlungen des Zweiundzwanzigsten Deutschen Juristentages*, vol. I (1892), 285ff; W Hausmann, *Die Veräußerung beweglicher Sachen gegen Ratenzahlung (das sog. Abzahlungsgeschäft) nach dem Preußischen Allgemeinen Landrechte und dem Entwurfe eines bürgerlichen Gesetzbuches für das Deutsche Reich* (1891), 78ff; von Gierke, n 30 above, 16 and *passim*.
[71] For details, see Benöhr, n 60 above, 501 Geyer, n 57 above, 65ff; Duve, n 22 above, §§ 1–14, n 70.
[72] G Planck, 'Zur Kritik des Entwurfes eines bürgerlichen Gesetzbuches für das deutsche Reich' (1889) 75 *Archiv für die civilistische Praxis* 406ff.

Early 'Doorstep' Legislation

Instalment transactions have, in fact, remained a major policy concern; the relevant regulations have repeatedly been amended, and the protection of the purchaser has been extended in the course of time.[73] Another important issue on the modern consumer protection agenda has been doorstep sales (or, to quote the language of the relevant European Union Directive,[74] contracts negotiated away from business premises). It was prefigured, in the late nineteenth century, by the problems associated with contracts concluded with pedlars.[75] Once again, the matter was dealt with by special legislation: the Act concerning Trade and Industry.[76] When it came into effect, in October 1869, it was designed mainly to establish free trade.[77] But it also contained a number of provisions designed to protect the general public. Thus, pedlars had to obtain a licence, and were forbidden to sell several types of article.[78] The Act was repeatedly amended and, in particular, the range of excluded articles was considerably extended.[79] This was motivated by a desire to prevent the exploitation of purchasers who might be tempted to buy objects the value of which could not easily be assessed. In the course of the debate leading up to the amendments the term 'consumer' came to be used, increasingly, in the place of 'general public'.[80] Once again, the relevant provisions were not incorporated into the BGB. Special problems, it was felt, should be left to special legislation which could easily be amended and adapted to changing needs.[81] In addition, the Act concerning Trade and Industry was still wedded to the traditional idea of preventing abuses of contractual freedom by way of public law regulation rather than by granting potential or disappointed purchasers rights and remedies against the other party. The policing of lawful trade was seen as a matter for the State rather than the private parties to an individual transaction.[82] It was in the same spirit that innkeepers and bakers were required to tell the general public the prices for their goods and services by displaying notices.[83] Pawnbrokers were only allowed to carry out their business after obtaining

---

[73] See, eg n 118 below.

[74] Council Directive 85/577/EEC of 20 December 1985, OJ L 372/85, 31.

[75] For a detailed discussion, see Geyer n 57 above, 9ff.

[76] *Gewerbeordnung für den Norddeutschen Bund, Bundesgesetzblatt des Norddeutschen Bundes* (1869), 245; as from 1873 applicable in the German Empire.

[77] For general background, see H-P Benöhr, 'Wirtschaftsliberalismus und Gesetzgebung am Ende des 19. Jahrhunderts', 8 (1977) *Zeitschrift für Arbeitsrecht* 187ff.

[78] §§ 61, 56 *Gewerbeordnung.*   [79] For details, see Geyer, n 57 above, 15ff.

[80] Ibid, 21.   [81] Benöhr, n 77 above, 216.

[82] For historical background see Duve, n 22 above, §§ 1–14, nn 67ff.

[83] §§ 73ff *Gewerbeordnung;* for discussion, see Geyer, n 57 above, 79ff.

a licence.[84] The Trademark Acts of 1874 and 1894 can also be mentioned in this context: they were designed, in the first place, to protect businessmen from unfair competition but also, of course, had the effect of enabling purchasers to make better informed choices.[85]

Industrial Workers, Domestic Servants, Railway Engines

The 'social question' in the late nineteenth century, was, above all, the question of how to regulate the position of industrial workers. It was hardly touched upon in the deliberations leading up to the BGB and the main reason for what, from a modern point of view, appears to be a surprising lack of concern was the conviction that what needed to be done had been done, or was about to be done, by way of special legislation.[86] Once again, many of the matters to be dealt with were not regarded as falling within the domain of private law. This applied to the emerging rules concerning industrial relations as much as to the social security legislation above.[87] But it also applied to most of the rules contained in the Act concerning Trade and Industry. The Act was amended in 1891, in response to an initiative of the Emperor.[88] The most important innovations were: the prohibition of work on Sundays, the protection of women and children from work during the night and below ground, the duty to issue work regulations, and permission to establish workers' committees. The legal position of domestic servants and farmhands, incidentally, was also excluded from regulation in the BGB; the matter was left to legislation by the individual state within the German *Reich*.[89] The various *Gesindeordnungen* were only repealed after the First World War. The same pattern of development, based on the idea of a division of tasks between general private law codification and special legislation can, incidentally, be observed in other fields, most prominently that of liability law. From the 1830s onwards monstrous machines called railway engines had been steaming through the German countryside, pulling carriages for the transportation of goods and persons but also, occasionally, wreaking death and destruction around them. As early as 1838 Prussia had set a precedent by imposing a strict liability law regime on railway owners.[90]

---

[84] § 34 *Gewerbeordnung* (as amended in 1879).
[85] For discussion, see Geyer, n 57 above, 92ff.
[86] For a detailed discussion, see Repgen, n 32 above, 215ff.
[87] See n 48 above and related text.   [88] Repgen, n 32 above, 220, 228.
[89] For details, see T Vormbaum, *Politik und Gesinderecht im 19. Jahrhundert*, (1980).
[90] § 25 *Gesetz über die Eisenbahn-Unternehmungen*. The Act was introduced under the aegis of Friedrich Carl von Savigny; see T Baums, 'Die Einführung der Gefährdungshaftung durch F.C. von Savigny' (1987) 104 *Zeitschrift der Savigny-Stiftung für Rechtsgeschichte (Germanistische Abteilung)* 277ff.

It was a limited, and policy-based, deviation from the general principle of fault-based liability that was firmly entrenched in nineteenth century pandectist scholarship.[91] This pioneering piece of legislation was followed by similar statutes in other German states;[92] and when in 1871 the Empire was founded, the *Reichstag* followed suit almost immediately. The Imperial Liability Act[93] which, albeit under another name and in a substantially expanded form, is still in force today[94] provided for strict liability for harm to persons arising 'through the operation' of a railway. In a way, of course, this statute can be regarded, like the Act concerning Instalment Sales, as an early piece of consumer legislation; for specific protection was granted to those who travelled on the railway and who thus availed themselves (not of the goods but) of the services offered by the railway entrepreneur.[95]

Usury

There was one issue, however, that eventually prompted the *Reichstag* to amend the draft BGB. The protection of borrowers against excessive interest rates had been a major policy concern since time immemorial.[96] Until well into the nineteenth century, legislation imposing maximum rates had been in force but in 1867 all restrictions on contractual interest rates were lifted.[97] But in the economic crisis following 1873,[98] when small-scale traders, artisans and farmers increasingly required credit to be able to carry on their farms and businesses, it had become obvious that the lack of any restriction lent itself to abuse. Potential borrowers tend to be in urgent need of money and are not, therefore, normally in a position to negotiate the terms of the loan at arm's length. Characteristically, the *Reichstag* reacted by criminalising the objectionable conduct of money-lenders. The Act concerning Usury of 1880[99] amended the Criminal Code by introducing §§ 302a–d; in addition, however, it also made

---

[91] Zimmermann, n 23 above, 1033ff.

[92] J W Hedemann, *Die Fortschritte des Zivilrechts im XIX. Jahrhundert*, vol. I (1910), 88ff; R Ogorek, *Untersuchungen zur Entwicklung der Gefährdungshaftung im 19. Jahrhundert* (1975), 61ff.

[93] *Reichs-Haftpflichtgesetz* of 7 June 1871; on the origins of which see Ogorek, ibid, 98ff.

[94] *Haftpflichtgesetz* (as re-promulgated on 4 January 1978).

[95] Strict liability eventually came to be conceptualized as a second 'track' of extra-contractual liability, separate from fault-based delictual liability; see Zimmermann, n 23 above, 1130ff; N Jansen, *Die Struktur des Haftungsrechts* (2003), 14ff and *passim*.

[96] See n 23 above and related text.

[97] *Bundesgesetzblatt des Norddeutschen Bundes* (1867), 159; for background information, see Landau, n 57 above, 388ff.

[98] On which see Nipperdey, n 36 above, 284, 336.

[99] *Wuchergesetz* of 24 May 1880, *Reichsgesetzblatt*, 1880, 109.

usurious contracts invalid. In 1893 the policy adopted by the Act concerning Usury was extended to other types of contracts apart from money loans;[100] also, those engaged in the business of credit transactions became liable to render an annual account *vis-à-vis* their contractual partners.[101] A Commission of the *Reichstag* established in early 1896 to vet the draft BGB eventually decided to adopt what was to become § 138 II BGB.[102] Following the pattern of the provisions contained in the Criminal Code, this rule renders void any legal transaction that meets two conditions: there has to be a striking disproportion in value between the performances promised or exchanged between the two parties; and the transaction has to have been brought about by exploitation of the distress, gullibility or inexperience of the disadvantaged party. It was regarded as inappropriate to leave a rule so deeply affecting private law in a special statute outside the BGB.[103]

The rule of § 138 II BGB has to be read in the context of the time-honoured prohibition on contracts *contra bonos mores*,[104] as codified in its immediate vicinity: it merely specifies for one particular type of situation (disproportion in value between performance and counter-performance) what would otherwise have had to be deduced from the general standard contained in § 138 I BGB. Both §§ 138 II and 138 I are designed to keep commercial life, and legal relations in general, 'clean':[105] a legal system cannot countenance transactions which offend a just and fair-thinking person's sense of decency.[106] Compared to the clearly structured and restrictively worded § 138 II BGB, however, § 138 I BGB is notoriously uncertain and open to the dangers, and opportunities, of 'unlimited interpretation'.[107] It is hardly surprising, therefore, that the courts have fallen back on the latter provision when embarking on the process of

---

[100] § 302e Criminal Code (*Strafgesetzbuch*), as introduced in 1893.

[101] Art 4 *Wuchergesetz*, as introduced in 1893.

[102] Geyer, n 57 above, 46; generally on the history of usury legislation in the nineteenth century, see K Luig, 'Vertragsfreiheit und Äquivalenzprinzip im gemeinen Recht und im BGB', in *Aspekte europäischer Rechtsgeschichte: Festgabe für Helmut Coing, Ius Commune* (Special issue 17), (1982), 171ff; R Zimmermann, *Richterliches Moderationsrecht oder Totalnichtigkeit?* (1979), 145ff; cf also Haferkamp, in Schmoeckel, Rückert and Zimmermann, n 51 above, vol. I (2003), § 138, n 12.

[103] Geyer, n 57 above, 46; Zimmermann, n 102 above, 148ff.

[104] On which see Zimmermann, n 23 above, 706ff.

[105] See, for § 138 II BGB, Hedemann, n 92 above, 132.

[106] This is the prevailing formula used in Germany to describe the intention of § 138 I BGB: RGZ 48, 114, 124; RGZ 55, 367, 373; RGZ 79, 415, 418; see, today, T Mayer-Maly and C Armbrüster, in *Münchener Kommentar zum Bürgerlichen Gesetzbuch*, vol. I (4th edn., 2001), § 138, n 14.

[107] See the famous title of Bernd Rüthers' book: *Die unbegrenzte Auslegung: Zum Wandel der Privatrechtsordnung im Nationalsozialismus* (5th edn., 1997).

'materialising' German contract law that has been a characteristic feature of twentieth century legal development.[108] In particular, they have used this rule in order to protect what they regarded as the structurally disadvantaged party to the bargain.[109] This could be a main debtor's impecunious spouse or child asked to sign a suretyship contract;[110] or it could be a consumer who was charged an excessive interest rate by an instalment credit institution for a loan repayable by instalments.[111] Instalment credit transactions have provided German courts with an opportunity to establish what effectively amounts to a judicial price control. It was introduced for the protection of consumers, via § 138 I BGB, by side-stepping the restrictive requirements of § 138 II BGB. The relevant line of cases dates back to the late 1970s.

The Rise of Modern Consumer Legislation

The First Period: Until the End of the 1970s

Origins

By that time the issue of consumer protection had become the subject of a broadly based academic, political, and sometimes ideological, debate. That debate was one of the many manifestations of an atmosphere of departure generated by the student protests in 1968 and the change of government in 1969. But it had also been stimulated by international developments sparked off, most prominently, by President Kennedy's Special Message to Congress on Protecting the Consumer Interest.[112] 'Consumers, by definition, include us all', Kennedy had stated and had

---

[108] C-W. Canaris, 'Wandlungen des Schuldvertragsrechts—Tendenzen zu seiner "Materialisierung"' (2000) 200 *Archiv für die civilistische Praxis* 273ff; HC Grigoleit, *Vorvertragliche Informationshaftung* (1997), 64ff; Heiderhoff, n 19 above, 295ff; Rösler, n 16 above, 61ff; cf also Riesenhuber, n 19 above, 553ff (from a European perspective). For a general historical analysis of the interpretation of § 138 BGB over the last century, see Haferkamp, n 51 above, § 138, nn 1ff, 12ff (usury); for the use of this provision today, from a comparative and European point of view, Remien, n 19 above, 345ff.

[109] See, in particular, BVerfGE 89, 214, 232ff.

[110] M Habersack and R Zimmermann, 'Legal Change in a Codified System: Recent Developments in German Suretyship Law' (1999) 3 Edinburgh Law Review 272, 275ff; Haferkamp, n 51 above, § 138, nn 5ff; and n 111 below.

[111] V Emmerich, 'Rechtsfragen des Ratenkredits' [1998] *Juristische Schulung* 925ff; Mayer-Maly/Armbrüster, n 106 above, § 138, nn 117ff; and see following text.

[112] Easily accessible in von Hippel, n 64 above, 281ff. For an introduction to the historical development of consumer protection, see Duve, n 22 above, §§ 1–14, nn 67ff; Heiderhoff, n 19 above, 241ff; M Schmoeckel, in Schmoeckel, Rückert, and Zimmermann, n 1 above, vol. II (publication: 2006).

recognized a special obligation of the Federal Government 'to be alert to the consumer's needs and to advance the consumer's interests'. Moreover, he had specified four basic rights of all consumers: the right to safety, the right to be informed, the right to choose, and the right to be heard. In Germany, the government published two reports on consumer policy in 1971 and 1975 in which it undertook to improve the legal position of consumers.[113] That programme was implemented in a number of enactments starting with the Brokers Act of 1972:[114] brokers had to obtain a licence to carry on their trade, and such licence would be refused to those who were unreliable or in financial difficulties. In 1973, a duty was established for businesses to mark their goods with a price. In loan transactions the effective interest rate had to be stated.[115] In 1974 the law relating to food production and distribution was fundamentally reformed in order to protect consumers from health risks and deception.[116] The Production and Distribution of Pharmaceutical Products Act followed suit in 1976.[117]

Instalment Sales, Distance Teaching, Package Tours

In addition, the 1970s saw four important reforms affecting contract law. In the first place, the Act concerning Instalment Sales was amended so as to grant purchasers a right to revoke the contract within one week after having received a notice informing them about their right of revocation.[118] Second, distance teaching contracts were subjected to a comprehensive regulation.[119] Again, the customer was granted a right to revoke the contract, this time within a period of two weeks after having received his first batch of teaching materials.[120] A number of provisions often contained in distance teaching contracts were declared illegal, and advance payments were restricted to three months.[121] The Distance Teaching Act was necessitated by an increased desire of many Germans to improve their standard of education.

However, Germans of the 1970s did not only want to be better educated; they were also very keen on travelling. In 1978, 56.8 per cent of the German population above the age of 14 undertook one or several

---

[113] The second of these reports is reproduced in von Hippel, n 64 above, 295ff.

[114] *Maklergesetz, Bundesgesetzblatt* I, 1465.

[115] *Verordnung über Preisangaben, Bundesgesetzblatt* 1973 I, 461.

[116] *Gesetz zur Gesamtreform des Lebensmittelrechts, Bundesgesetzblatt* 1974 I, 1945.

[117] *Arzneimittelgesetz, Bundesgesetzblatt* 1976 I, 2445.

[118] § 1 b *Abzahlungsgesetz* (introduced by the *Zweites Gesetz zur Änderung des Abzahlungsgesetzes, Bundesgesetzblatt* 1974 I, 1169).

[119] *Gesetz zum Schutz der Teilnehmer am Fernunterricht (Fernunterrichtsschutzgesetz), Bundesgesetzblatt* 1976 I, 2525; for discussion, see von Hippel, n 64 above, 248ff.

[120] § 4 *Fernunterrichtsschutzgesetz.*

[121] §§ 2 II, III, IV, V, 10 *Fernunterrichtsschutzgesetz.*

holiday trips, predominantly abroad.[122] The rapid expansion of tourism was facilitated, particularly, by the availability of inexpensive 'package tours'. As in the case of distance learning contracts, the way in which package holiday contracts were drafted usually put customers, often ill informed about their destination, at a disadvantage. Again, therefore, the government intervened by introducing a set of unilaterally mandatory rules strengthening the position of customers *vis-à-vis* the organisers of package holiday tours.[123] The organisers were no longer allowed to claim that they had merely acted as agents for those who were to supply the individual services if they had created the impression of being something more than mere brokers.[124] Moreover, and particularly, their potential liability was considerably tightened: thus, for instance, the customer was granted a claim for financial compensation for the immaterial detriment of having his holidays spoilt.[125] As for instalment sales and distance learning it was, at first, envisaged to deal with package tours by way of special legislation; eventually, however, the relevant rules were incorporated into the BGB[126] where they constitute an appendix to the law relating to contracts for work to be done (*locatio conductio operis*).

Standard Terms of Business

A 'Page of Glory' in the History of Private Law Adjudication

The most important set of rules enacted in the field of contract law during the 1970s is that concerning unfair standard contract terms. This is in spite of the fact that the Standard Terms of Business Act of 1976[127] did not substantially change the law; nor was it, strictly speaking, a statute aiming at the protection of consumers. The use of standard contract terms has a long tradition. It dates back, at least, to Roman sales, and

---

[122] von Hippel, n 64 above, 255.

[123] §§ 651a–651k BGB, introduced by the *Reisevertragsgesetz, Bundesgesetzblatt* 1979 I, 505. By that time, however, the Federal Supreme Court had mapped out the future direction of the law relating to package holidays in a number of leading cases; cf, in particular, BGHZ 61, 267; BGHZ 60, 14; BGHZ 63, 98; and see K Tonner, 'Die Entwicklung des Reisevertragsrechts durch Rechtsprechung, Gesetzgebung und Verbandsverhandlungen' (1989) 189 *Archiv für die civilistische Praxis* 122ff. That the regime set out in §§ 651ff BGB is unilaterally mandatory follows from § 651k BGB (old version; now: § 651m BGB).

[124] § 651a II BGB.

[125] § 651f II BGB.

[126] For background information, see K Tonner, in: *Münchener Kommentar zum Bürgerlichen Gesetzbuch*, vol. IV (3rd edn., 1997), Vor § 651a, nn 20ff.

[127] *Gesetz zur Regelung des Rechts der Allgemeinen Geschäftsbedingungen (AGB-Gesetz), Bundesgesetzblatt* 1976 I, 3317. In this instance, again, the government did not decide to amend the BGB but tackled the problem of unfair standard terms of business by way of special legislation.

lease, and banking practice.[128] But it was only in the age of mass production following the Industrial Revolution that they started to present serious problems.[129] These problems resulted from the sheer frequency with which they were employed in legal practice and also from the fact that they were drafted no longer by an independent third party but by one of the contractual partners. Many of those who drafted standard terms of business could not resist the obvious temptation to tilt them in their favour and to displace the *ius dispositivum* contained in the BGB by a set of rules particularly favourable to their own interests. The courts reacted in a variety of ways. Thus, for instance, they availed themselves of the *contra proferentem* rule in order to resolve uncertainties in standard contract terms: the interpretation has to be adopted which is against the interests of the party who has drafted the terms and introduced them into the contract.[130] This was based, essentially, on a reasoning advanced by the Roman lawyers for their rule of *ambiguitas contra stipulatorem*: any ambiguity was attributable to the stipulator (ie the party who formulated the question which determined the content of the contract), for he could just as well have made it clear what he wanted the other party to promise to him.[131] In other cases the courts had argued that terms contained in a standard contract form could not be taken to have become part of the contract if they were 'surprising' to the other party.[132] To a considerable extent, of course, these rules of interpretation constituted covert tools for policing the substantive justice of standard terms of business.[133]

But in the course of time, the courts also arrogated to themselves a much more direct power to strike down unfair standard terms. Ludwig Raiser, the man who had written the first great monograph devoted to the topic,[134] referred to a 'page of glory' in the history of private law

---

[128] For references, see S Hofer, '§§ 305–310. Gestaltung rechtsgeschäftlicher Schuldverhältnisse durch Allgemeine Geschäftsbedingungen (Teil I)' in Schmoeckel, Rückert and Zimmermann, n 1 above, vol. II (forthcoming: 2006), n 2.

[129] R Pohlhausen, *Zum Recht der allgemeinen Geschäftsbedingungen im 19. Jahrhundert* (1978); Hofer, n 128 above, n 2.

[130] See, for example, RGZ 116, 198, 207; and see the analysis by S Vogenauer, '§§ 305–310. Gestaltung rechtsgeschäftlicher Schuldveshältnisse durch Allgemeine Geschafts bedingungen (Teil III)' in Schmoeckel, Rückert and Zimmermann, n 1 above, vol. II (2005).   [131] Zimmermann, n 23 above, 639ff.

[132] BGHZ 60, 353, 360; BGHZ 54, 106, 109.

[133] For the dangers inherent in such approach, see R Fischer, Review of Baumbach-Duden, *Handelsgesetzbuch*, 14. Aufl., 1961 (1963) 125 *Zeitschrift für das gesamte Handelsrecht und Wirtschaftsrecht* 202, 205ff; and, more generally, K Llewellyn, Review of O Prausnitz, *The Standardization of Commercial Contracts in English and Continental Law*, (1939) 52 Harvard Law Review 700, 703 ('Covert tools are never reliable tools').

[134] *Das Recht der Allgemeinen Geschäftsbedingungen* (1935).

adjudication in Germany.[135] At first, from 1906 onwards, the Imperial Court had only objected to unfair standard terms of business if one party had been able to impose them on the other as a result of abusing the position of a monopolist. The doctrinal peg was the *contra bonos mores* provision of § 138 I BGB.[136] Subsequently, the Court regarded it as sufficient that the party using the standard terms was carrying on an 'indispensable' trade and therefore, 'in a manner of speaking', had a monopoly.[137] The Federal Supreme Court in the first few years of its existence followed the same approach but then, from 1956 onwards, significantly extended its range of control by switching from § 138 I BGB to the good faith provision of § 242 BGB.[138] A standard business term was now regarded as invalid if, contrary to the precepts of good faith, it placed the other party at an unreasonable disadvantage. An unreasonable disadvantage was taken to exist, if the relevant term could not be reconciled with essential notions of justice and fairness, as expressed in the non-mandatory provisions of the German Civil Code from which the term proposed to deviate, or if the term restricted essential rights or duties arising from the nature of the contract. Very largely, the Standard Terms of Business Act of 1976 merely cast these, and a number of other, rules developed by the Federal Supreme Court in statutory form.[139] The power granted to the courts in § 9 openly to police the fairness of standard terms of business constituted its core component; it was specified by two long lists of individual contractual provisions that were to be regarded as objectionable.[140]

Consumer Protection?

In the years leading up to the Standard Terms of Business Act the pertinent political and academic discussions had been dominated by the notion of consumer protection. This specific perspective was due, largely, to the first report on consumer policy of 1971 where the Federal

---

[135] L Raiser, 'Vertragsfreiheit heute' [1958] *Juristenzeitung* 1, 7.

[136] RGZ 62, 264, 266.

[137] RGZ 103, 82, 83; cf. also, eg, RGZ 104, 308; RGZ 106, 386, 388; *Reichsgericht* [1925] *Juristische Wochenschrift* 1395; RGZ 132, 305.

[138] *Bundesgerichtshof* [1956] *Neue Juristische Wochenschrift* 908; *Bundesgerichtshof* 1957 *Neue Juristische Wochenschrift* 1065; BGHZ 41, 151, 154; BGHZ 54, 106, 109 f. For a comprehensive historical analysis and references to the pertinent case law and literature, see Hofer, n 128 above, nn 9ff.

[139] von Hippel, n 64 above, 121ff; J Basedow, in *Münchener Kommentar zum Bürgerlichen Gesetzbuch*, vol. I (4th edn., 2001), Einl. AGBG, nn 10ff; Hofer, n 128 above, nn 20ff.

[140] §§ 10 f AGBG. For comment in English, see O Sandrock, 'The Standard Terms Act 1976 of West Germany' (1978) 26 American Journal of Comparative Law, 551ff; 562ff.

Government had committed itself to provide 'effective protection of consumers against unreasonable contract terms which improperly serve to pursue unilateral interests'.[141] Protection of the weaker party was now taken to be the aim legitimating the policing of standard business terms. It is a view that has proved to be surprisingly long-lived: it is still widely held today. For it is often said that the consumer 'submits' to the terms presented to him in view of the entrepreneur's psychological, intellectual and, above all, economic superiority.[142] His unequal bargaining power is seen as the essential reason forcing the consumer to accept the contract on the basis of the other party's standard terms of business. It is a view, however, which is inconsistent with the fact that in exercising its power openly to control standard terms, the Federal Supreme Court had usually dealt with contracts concluded between two entrepreneurs.[143] Consumer protection had not, therefore, been the real reason supporting the courts' interventionist attitude. Consumers as well as businessmen tend to accept the proffered standard terms because they regard it as futile to invest time and money in studying a complex set of rules relating to rights and contingencies which do not usually materialize, in drafting alternative provisions, and in conducting long drawn-out negotiations; or in seeking out other firms whose terms may be more favourable to their own interests. If customers do not normally avail themselves of the opportunity to influence the standardized contents of the contract this is not because of the superiority of the entrepreneur, but because of the prohibitively high transaction costs involved in utilising any such opportunity. We are dealing, therefore, with a partial failure of the market which may legitimately be corrected by means of judicial intervention.[144] This is confirmed by the observation that no effective competition over standard contract terms exists. Competition, in other words, is not likely to lead, and has not led in the past, to the emergence of fairly balanced sets of standard contract terms.[145] Significantly, therefore, and contrary to the original proposals,[146] the German Standard Terms of Business Act was not confined to contracts concluded by consumers; it was also, at least in principle, made to apply to businessmen.[147] The case law concerning the

---

[141] *Bericht zur Verbraucherpolitik, Bundestags-Drucksache* 6/2724, 8.

[142] K Larenz and M Wolf, *Allgemeiner Teil des Bürgerlichen Rechts* (9th edn., 2004), §§ 43, nn 1, 7; H Köhler, *BGB Allgemeiner Teil* (26th edn., 2002), 259.

[143] The point is emphasized in Hofer, n 128 above, n 20 (fn 139).

[144] J Basedow, in *Münchener Kommentar zum Bürgerlichen Gesetzbuch*, vol. II a (4th edn., 2003), Vor § 305, nn 1ff; H Kötz, 'Der Schutzzweck der AGB-Kontrolle—Eine rechtsökonomische Skizze' [2003] *Juristische Schulung* 209ff.; Remien, n 19 above, 485.

[145] Basedow, n 144 above, Vor § 305, n 6.

[146] Basedow, n 144 above, § 24 ABGB, n 2.   [147] § 24 ABGB.

open fairness control under § 9 AGBG continued to be dominated by standard contract terms involving commercial transactions;[148] and if, according to § 24 I AGBG, the two lists of objectionable terms contained in §§ 10 and 11 AGBG were not to be applied to standard terms of business proffered by one businessman to another, this was not intended to mean that such terms could not be struck down under the general provision of § 9 AGBG. Subsequent court practice demonstrates that the indirect application, via § 9 AGBG, of §§ 10 and 11 AGBG also to standard terms accepted by businessmen has become the rule rather than the exception.[149]

Which 'Model of Society'?

Thus, by the end of the 1970s, consumer protection had made some advances; but the approach adopted was sector-specific. In the pertinent legislation, as far as it affected private law, the term 'consumer' was not used. Protection was granted not to consumers as such but to purchasers who had entered into an instalment contract, to customers of distance teaching enterprises, to travellers who had booked a package holiday, and to those who had accepted the other party's standard terms of business. With one exception,[150] these concerns were dealt with by way of special legislation, ie outside the BGB. The protective mechanisms that had begun to crystallize were intended, partly, to enable the customer to make a better informed choice; but they also included a right of revocation and an open fairness control. In addition, many of the new rules were of a unilaterally mandatory character, ie the parties were not allowed to change them to the disadvantage of the purchaser/customer/traveller/contractual partner of the person who had drafted the standard terms of business. Academic discussions had generated a considerable amount of literature. One of the key issues hotly debated was whether, for the protection of consumers, a special branch of private law with its own distinctive evaluations had to be developed which was based on a different 'model of society' (*Sozialmodell*) than the general private law. This view, forcefully propounded by some,[151] was equally forcefully rejected by others who regarded it as an assault on the legal foundations of a liberal market economy that was ultimately inspired by socialist ideals. Proponents of the

---

[148] Hofer, n 128 above, n 28 (fn 171).

[149] H E Brandner, in P Ulmer, H E Brandner, H-D Hensen and H Schmidt, *AGB-Gesetz* (9th edn., 2001), § 24, nn 19, 22ff.   [150] See n 126 above and related text.

[151] N Reich, 'Zivilrechtstheorie, Sozialwissenschaften und Verbraucherschutz' [1974] *Zeitschrift für Rechtspolitik*, 187ff; Reich, *Markt und Recht* (1977), 49ff, 193ff; U Reifner, *Alternatives Wirtschaftsrecht am Beispiel der Verbraucherverschuldung* (1979).

latter school of thought attempted to preserve the integrity of classical contract law as far as possible and to vindicate the model envisaged by the fathers of the BGB even within the modern consumer society: the law merely had to ensure that consumers were properly informed to make rational choices. This, in a nutshell, was the '*liberales Informations modell*' (liberal information model)[152]. Predominantly, however, it was realized that the supply of information alone would be unable to resolve all problems. Other devices of a genuinely protective character were required. However, they had to supplement rather than replace the mechanisms of the market.[153] But it remained unclear whether the relevant rules were of an exceptional character or whether, or to what extent, they could be reconciled with the basic principles underlying German private law. Thus, it remained equally unclear whether they should ideally be integrated into the BGB, or whether it was wiser to leave them where they were, ie predominantly outside the general code of private law.[154] What was clear was that the new rules did not, in themselves, constitute a coherent body of law. At the same time, they were not always as well drafted as rules of private law had traditionally been in Germany. §§ 651a–k, in particular, were widely regarded as an unfortunate stain on the BGB;[155] in the course of time, they have given rise to a host of difficult doctrinal problems.[156] The Standard Terms of Business Act, on the other hand, is generally

[152] See, in particular, B Dauner-Lieb, *Verbraucherschutz durch Ausbildung eines Sonderprivatrechts für Verbraucher: Systemkonforme Weiterentwicklung oder Schrittmacher der Systemveränderung?* (1983); cf also M Lieb, 'Sonderprivatrecht für Ungleichgewichtslagen? Überlegungen zum Anwendungsbereich der sogenannten Inhaltskontrolle privatrechtlicher Verträge' (1978) 178 *Archiv für die civilistische Praxis* 196ff; Lieb, 'Grundfragen einer Schuldrechtsreform' (1983) 183 *Archiv für die civilistische Praxis* 348ff and, more recently, W Zöllner, 'Zivilrechtswissenschaft und Zivilrecht im ausgehenden 20. Jahrhundert' (1988) 188 *Archiv für die civilistische Praxis* 91ff; Zöllner, *Die Privatrechtsgesellschaft im Gesetzes- und Richterstaat* (1996); P Hommelhoff, *Verbraucherschutz im System des deutschen und europäischen Privatrechts* (1996).

[153] See, for example, the discussion in HP Westermann, 'Verbraucherschutz' in Bundesminister der Justiz (ed), *Gutachten und Vorschläge zur Überarbeitung des Schuldrechts*, vol. II (1983), 1ff; F Bydlinski, *System und Prinzipien des Privatrechts* (1996), 708ff, 718ff; D Henrich, 'Verbraucherschutz: Vertragsrecht im Wandel', in V Beuthien (ed), *Festschrift für Dieter Medicus* (1999), 199ff; J Drexl, 'Verbraucherrecht—Allgemeines Privatrecht—Handelsrecht', in Schlechtriem, n 9 above, 97ff; Heiderhoff, n 19 above, 233ff; Wiedenmann, n 19 above, 49ff.

[154] For a summary of the arguments for and against these two options, see Pfeiffer, n 17 above, 481ff; W-H Roth, 'Europäischer Verbraucherschutz und BGB', [2001] *Juristenzeitung* 475, 484f.

[155] See, for example, H H Seiler, in *Erman, Bürgerliches Gesetzbuch* (10th edn., 2000), Vor § 651a, nn 7ff.

[156] For an overview of the system of remedies in case of liability for defects (§§ 651c–g BGB) and its relationship to the general rules on breach of contract under the old law, before the modernization of the German law of obligations, see Seiler, n 155 above, Vor §§ 651c–651g, nn 1ff.

considered to be a considerable achievement,[157] and the way in which it came to be accepted as an essential component of modern German private law can be accounted as a success story.[158] It has become the piece of legislation to which more commentaries have been devoted than to any other (including the BGB itself).

With the enactment of the new rules on package holidays in 1979, the German Government appeared to have lost its *élan* in the field of consumer legislation. The social-liberal regime was soon to collapse anyway, and the new conservative-liberal cabinet had different policy priorities. Thus, the field was left to the Commission of the European Union.

The European Community Takes Over

A Promising Field of Activity

At about the same time as the governments of the member states of the European Union, the European Union itself had discovered consumer protection as a promising field of activity.[159] In 1973 the Commission established an office for the environment and consumer protection which became an office for consumer protection in 1989 and was raised to the level of an independent directorate general (for health and consumer protection) in 1995. The significance of consumer protection within the common market was stressed by the European Court of Justice in 1979 in the case of *Cassis de Dijon*.[160] 'Compelling reasons of public interest', it was held, could justify an infringement of the freedom to trade (as well as the other market freedoms), and consumer protection was specifically mentioned as an example of such a compelling reason. In the meantime, it has become a 'community policy' to which an individual title within the third part of the EC Treaty is devoted. According to Article 153, the Community 'contributes' to the protection of the health, safety and economic interests of consumers and to the promotion of their right of

---

[157] Pfeiffer, n 17 above, 500ff; P Ulmer, 'Das ABG-Gesetz: ein eigenständiges Kodifikationswerk' [2001] *Juristenzeitung* 491ff.

[158] M Wolf, 'Vertragsfreiheit und Vertragsrecht im Lichte der AGB-Rechtsprechung des Bundesgerichtshofs' in C-W Canaris, A Heldrich *et al* (eds), *50 Jahre Bundesgerichtshof: Festgabe aus der Wissenschaft*, vol. I (2000), 111ff.

[159] For an overview, see von Hippel, n 64 above, 17ff; H-W Micklitz, in *Münchener Kommentar zum Bürgerlichen Gesetzbuch*, vol. I (4th edn., 2001), Vor §§ 13, 14, nn 23ff; W Berg, in J Schwarze (ed), *EU-Kommentar* (2000), Art 153, nn 1ff; B Lurger, in R Streinz (ed), *EUV/EGV* (2003), Art 153, nn 3ff; Remien, n 19 above, 121ff; Heiderhoff, n 19 above, 23ff. For a comprehensive discussion of the individual directives, see S Grundmann, *Europäisches Schuldvertragsrecht* (1999); N Reich and H-W Micklitz, *Europäisches Verbraucherrecht* (4th edn., 2003), parts II, III, and IV.

[160] C-120/78 [1979] ECR 649.

adequate information in order to safeguard 'a high level of consumer protection'. Some thirty directives have been issued since 1979 in the area of consumer protection,[161] about half of them affecting contract law, some of them tangentially, others profoundly. Unfair terms in consumer contracts, contracts negotiated away from business premises, consumer credit, distance contracts, contracts for the sale of consumer goods, package travel, timeshare agreements: the respective rules of German law are all based on European Community legislation. This entails, *inter alia*, that they have to be interpreted in conformity with the European directives[162] and that the European Court of Justice has attained, at least potentially, an important role in private law adjudication.[163]

The Beginning: Doorstep Selling, Product Liability, Consumer Credit

The German government, at first, followed the pattern established by the Act concerning Instalment Sales and kept the new rules locked in special statutory compartments. Thus, in January 1986 a Revocation of Doorstep Contracts Act came into effect which introduced a right for customers to revoke contracts concluded away from the business premises of the trader within one week. In view of the surprise element inherent in such transactions it was regarded as appropriate to grant the customer some time in order to assess the obligations incurred by him. Even though the term consumer was not used, the Act essentially aimed at his protection,[164] for customers who had concluded the 'doorstep' contract as part of their professional activity were excluded from the range of application of the Act.[165] The Act, therefore, attempted to establish

---

[161] See the list compiled by Lurger, n 159 above, Art 153, n 40.

[162] S Grundmann, 'Richtlinienkonforme Auslegung im Bereich des Privatrechts—insbesondere: der Kanon der nationalen Auslegungsmethoden als Grenze?' (1996) 4 *Zeitschrift für Europäisches Privatrecht*, 399ff; C-W Canaris, 'Die richtlinienkonforme Auslegung und Rechtsfortbildung im System der juristischen Methodenlehre' in H Koziol (ed), *Im Dienste der Gerechtigkeit—Festschrift für Franz Bydlinski* (2002), 47ff; Heiderhoff, n 19 above, 87ff.

[163] A number of important decisions concerning the consumer contract directives (*i.a.* *Dillenkofer, Dietzinger, Oceano Groupo, Heininger*) are listed in Lurger n 159 above, Art 153, n 41. For forceful criticism of national courts of law for not sufficiently frequently referring problems of interpretation to the European Court of Justice, see J Basedow, 'Die Klauselrichtlinie und der Europäische Gerichtshof—eine Geschichte der verpassten Gelegenheiten', in Schulte-Nölke and Schulze (eds), *Europäische Rechtsangleichung und nationale Privatrechte* (1999), 277ff.

[164] P. Ulmer, in *Münchener Kommentar zum Bürgerlichen Gesetzbuch*, vol. III (3rd edn., 1995), Vor § 1 HausTWG, n 1.

[165] *Gesetz über den Widerruf von Haustürgeschäften und ähnlichen Geschäften*, 16 January 1986, *Bundesgesetzblatt* 1986 I, 122; § 6 no. 1 HausTWG.

a new, substantive criterion in order to distinguish between those who deserved to be protected and those who did not deserve such protection.[166] Earlier enactments had focused on more formal criteria, particularly on whether the customer had been recorded as a merchant in the commercial register.[167] The scene was thus set for a considerable amount of debate surrounding the concept of 'consumer' underlying German consumer protection law; lack of conceptual clarity and uniformity became the subject of repeated criticism.[168] The Revocation of Doorstep Contracts Act had been preceded by more than ten years of discussion,[169] and it was passed a few weeks before the European Community issued its 'Directive to protect the consumer in respect of contracts negotiated away from business premises'.[170] The Directive, too, had been in the offing for many years,[171] and the discussions surrounding it had, of course, influenced the German debate. In fact, the German Act was regarded as an anticipated implementation of the Directive.[172] Certain differences in detail had to be taken account of by the way in which the provisions of the German Act were interpreted.[173]

Another important piece of European consumer legislation from about the same time—though not one affecting contract law—was the Directive 'on the approximation of the laws, regulations and administrative provisions of the Member States concerning liability for defective products'.[174] It was enacted in Germany, 18 months late, by means of the Product Liability Act of 15 December 1989.[175] Since the Act did not go beyond the level of protection afforded by the German Federal Supreme Court under the general law of delict to those who had been injured by defective products, it has not made a significant impact on German law.[176] The third significant initiative completed in the period before the Member States of the European Community changed gear by committing themselves to the establishment of the internal market

---

[166] Ulmer, n 164 above, § 6 HausTWG, n 2.

[167] Westermann, n 153 above, 66ff.

[168] See the contributions by D Medicus, n 19 above, and M Dreher, n 19 above; and see the evaluation by Duve, n 22 above, §§ 1–14, nn 78ff.

[169] For references, see Ulmer, n 164 above, Vor § 1 HausTWG, n 5.

[170] Council Directive 85/577/EEC of 20 December 1985, easily accessible in O Radley-Gardner, H Beale, R Zimmermann and R Schulze, *Fundamental Texts on European Private Law* (2003), 69ff.

[171] Ulmer, n 164 above, V or § 1 HausTWG, n 6.   [172] Ibid.

[173] Ibid, nn 8, 21.

[174] Council Directive 85/374/EEC of 25 July 1985, easily accessible in Radley-Gardner *et al*, n 170 above, 187ff.

[175] Gesetz über die Haftung für fehlerhafte Produkte, 15 December 1989, *Bundesgesetzblatt* 1989 I, 2198.

[176] See, for instance, D Medicus, *Bürgerliches Recht* (20th edn., 2004), nn 650ff.

(Single European Act of 1987)[177] was the Directive 'for the approximation of the laws, regulations and administrative provisions of the Member States concerning consumer credit' of December 1986,[178] implemented in Germany by the Consumer Credit Act of December 1990.[179] This enactment replaced the old Act concerning Instalment Sales. Applied beyond instalment sales, it applied to all consumer credit transactions and was designed at a time when the indebtedness of consumer debt had risen to a record level,[180] to provide consumers with adequate information on the conditions and cost of credit, on the content of the obligation they were about to incur,[181] and to protect them from disadvantageous conditions being imposed upon them concerning the discharge of their obligations and the consequences of their failure to discharge these obligations.[182] In addition, the consumer's right to revoke the contract within a period of one week, introduced into the Instalment Sales Act in 1974,[183] was not only preserved but extended to cover all consumer credit transactions.[184] This right of revocation, as well as a number of other details in the Act,[185] were not required by the Directive. The range of persons protected was defined in similar (though not identical) terms to the Doorstep Selling Act: it covered natural persons who did not receive the credit in the course, and for the purpose, of their professional activity. This time, the term 'consumer' was expressly used.[186]

Changing Gear: Developments up to the Consumer Sales Directive

Package Tours and Unfair Terms in Consumer Contracts

The Single European Act invested the Council of the European Union with a comprehensive power to adopt measures for the approximation of the laws of the Member States 'which have as their object the establishment and functioning of the common market' (Article 100a of the EC Treaty, now Article 95). All subsequent consumer protection statutes

---

[177] See Lurger, n 159 above, Art 153, nn 5ff.

[178] Council Directive 87/102/EEC of 22 December 1986, easily accessible in Radley-Gardner *et al*, n 170 above, 75ff.

[179] *Gesetz über Verbraucherkredite und zur Änderung der Zivilprozeßordnung und anderer Gesetze*, 17 December 1990, *Bundesgesetzblatt* 1990 I, 2840.

[180] For details, see Ulmer, n 164 above, Vor § 1 VerbrKrG, nn 7f.

[181] § 4 VerbKrG.   [182] §§ 11–13 VerbKrG.

[183] *Zweites Gesetz zur Änderung des Abzahlungsgesetzes* of 15 May 1974, *Bundesgesetzblatt* (as in n 165) 1974 I, 1169.   [184] § 7 VerbKrG.

[185] Ulmer, n 164 above, Vor § 1 VerbKrG, n 14.

[186] § 1 VerbKrG. The term 'consumer' had entered German statutory language in the Act on the Reform of Private International Law of 25 July 1986: see Art 29 EGBGB; Medicus, n 19 above, 478f.

were to be based on this new provision.[187] First came the Directive on package travel, package holidays and package tours (1990).[188] It required a number of amendments to §§ 651ff BGB. The most important one provided protection to the customer in cases of insolvency of the organizer of the package deal.[189] Apart from that, the legal position of the traveller was strengthened by the imposition of a comprehensive network of duties of information on the tour organizer, the details of which were not incorporated into the BGB but enacted by way of subordinate legislation.[190] The Directive on unfair terms in consumer contracts of April 1993[191] constituted a milestone in the history of EC contract law regulation. For even though it did not significantly change the face of German law, it brought home the clear message that the European Union was prepared to interfere with core areas of contract law. For some time, the introduction of a fairness control concerning all provisions contained in consumer contracts had even been considered, no matter whether they were standardized or not.[192] Vociferous protests, particularly from Germany, had forced the European Commission to back down in that respect.[193] If the German Standard Terms of Business Act could be left largely unchanged, this was due to the introduction of § 24a ABGB providing for an increased level of protection, in certain respects, for consumers faced with not individually negotiated terms contained in a contract concluded with an entrepreneur. Consumer protection had thus become a second important policy objective underlying the German Standard Terms of Business Act.[194] At the same time, three different levels of protection were now envisaged by the Act: a lower level, as far as standard terms of business used *vis-à-vis* a business person

---

[187] The standard formulation at the beginning of the pertinent directives is: 'Having regard to the Treaty etablishing the European Community, and in particular Article 100a (or now: Article 95) thereof . . .'.

[188] Council Directive 90/314/EEC of 13 June, easily accessible in Radley-Gardner *et al*, n 170 above, 149ff.

[189] § 651 k BGB; for comment, see Seiler, n 155 above, § 651k, n 1ff.

[190] §§ 651a III–V *Bundesgesetzblatt* and *Verordnung über die Informationspflichten von Reiseveranstaltern* of 14 November 1994 (BGBl 1994 I, 3436); the text is printed in Seiler, n 155 above, § 651a, n 38.

[191] Council Directive 93/13/EEC of 5 April; easily accessible in Radley-Gardner *et al*, n 170 above, 49ff.

[192] Proposal for a Council Directive on Unfair Terms in Consumer Contracts, OJ C 243/2.

[193] P Hommelhoff, 'Zivilrecht unter dem Einfluss europäischer Rechtsangleichung' (1992) 192 *Archiv für die civilistische Praxis* 90ff; C-W Canaris, 'Verfassungs- und europarechtliche Aspekte der Vertragsfreiheit in der Privatrechtsgesellschaft', in P Badura (ed), *Wege und Verfahren des Verfassungslebens: Festschrift für Peter Lerche* (1993), 873ff, 887ff.

[194] Basedow, n 144 above, § 24a AGBG, nn 5f; H Heinrichs, in *Palandt, Bürgerliches Gesetzbuch* (61st edn., 2002), Einführung, n 6; Remien, n 19 above, 491.

were concerned; a higher level for consumer contracts; and the standard level for the remaining, but practically much less significant situations, such as the one of standard terms used in transactions between two consumers.[195]

Timeshare Agreements and Cross-Border Credit Transfers

Next came the Timeshare Agreements Act of December 1996[196] which was based on the Directive on the protection of purchasers in respect of certain aspects of contracts relating to the purchase of the right to use immovable properties on a timeshare basis.[197] Following a trend established in the United States, timeshare agreements had, in the course of the 1980s, become an increasingly popular proposition on the expanding holiday market, particularly in cross-border situations involving Southern European holiday resorts.[198] Aggressive sales methods and misleading advertising had induced holidaymakers impressed by Southern sun and sand, to enter grossly disadvantageous contracts. The principal devices employed by the Directive (and, consequently, the German Act) in order to protect purchasers in this situation were: an insistence on the supply of adequate information prior to the conclusion of the contract; the granting of a right of revocation within 10 days after conclusion of the contract; and a prohibition on advance payments.[199] Both the Directive and the Act used a neutral term ('purchaser', *Erwerber*) which, however, they defined in a way that approximated the concept of consumer. The Directive on cross-border credit transfers of January 1997[200] was not confined to consumers in whatever sense of the word. It was intended to improve cross-border credit transfer services and thus to promote the efficiency of cross-border payments. Significantly, this Directive was not implemented by way of special legislation but by amending the BGB. At the same time, the new §§ 676a–k BGB went far beyond what was required by the Directive in that their range of

---

[195] D Coester-Waltjen, 'Änderungen im Recht der Allgemeinen Geschäftsbedingungen' [1997] *Jura* 272ff.

[196] *Gesetz über die Veräußerung von Teilzeitnutzungsrechten an Wohngebäuden, Bundesgesetzblatt* (as in n 165) 1996 I, 2154.

[197] Directive 94/47/EC of the European Parliament and the Council of 26 October 1994, easily accessible in Radley-Gardner *et al*, n 170 above, 197ff.

[198] M Martinek, 'Das Teilzeiteigentum an Immobilien in der Europäischen Union' (1994) 2 *Zeitschrift für Europäisches Privatrecht*, 473ff.

[199] For trenchant criticism of the German Act, see M Martinek, 'Das neue Teilzeit-Wohnrechtsgesetz—missratener Verbraucherschutz bei Time-Sharing-Verträgen' [1997] *Neue Juristische Wochenschrift* 1393ff.

[200] Directive 97/5/EC of the European Parliament and of the Council of 27 January 1997, easily accessible in Radley-Gardner *et al*, n 170 above, 159ff.

application was not confined to cross-border credit transfers within the EC; these provisions were made to cover all cross-border credit transfers as well as all domestic credit transfers.[201] This may have been a reason prompting the German government to include the respective provisions into the BGB. Also, we are dealing here with a special type of transaction which can be added, relatively easily, to the other types of transactions regulated by the BGB. The same approach had, previously, been adopted with regard to package tours.[202]

Distance Contracts
The implementation of the Directive on cross-border credit transfers, though not geared towards consumer contracts, was to establish a pattern affecting the development of German consumer contract law. This became apparent when the Directive on the protection of consumers in respect of distance contracts of May 1997[203] was implemented in June 2000. For even though a special piece of legislation relating to distance contracts was enacted,[204] the German government also decided to change the BGB in certain respects. This was done in an attempt to provide a nucleus of general rules concerning consumer contracts and to establish consumer contract law as part of general contract law.[205] Thus, in particular, the lengthy new provision § 361a BGB dealt with the details of the right of revocation granted to consumers not only by the Distance Contract Act but also by the Distance Teaching, Doorstep Selling, Consumer Credit and Timeshare Agreements Acts. It attempted to provide uniformity, as far as that was possible in view of the requirements established by the pertinent EC Directives in each specific context. Thus, the period within which the right of revocation may be exercised was standardized (two weeks). Where a contract is concluded on the basis of a sales prospectus, the right of revocation is usually replaced by a right of return. § 361b BGB regulated the circumstances in which this is permissible and how the right of return may be exercised.[206] Another provision

---

[201] For a critical evaluation of the new regime, see D Einsele, 'Das neue Recht der Banküberweisung' [2000] *Juristenzeitung*, 9ff.

[202] See n 126 above and related text.

[203] Directive 97/7/EC of the European Parliament and of the Council of 20 May 1997, easily accessible in Radley-Gardner *et al*, n 170 above, 91ff.

[204] *Fernabsatzgesetz* of 27 June 2000, *Bundesgesetzblatt* 2000 I, 897; for comment, see H Roth, 'Das Fernabsatzgesetz' [2000] *Juristenzeitung*, 1013ff.; C Wendehorst, in *Münchener Kommentar zum Bürgerlichen Gesetzbuch*, vol. II (4th edn., 2001), 2117ff.

[205] P Ulmer, in *Münchener Kommentar zum Bürgerlichen Gesetzbuch*, vol. II, 4th edn., (2001), § 361a, n 7; Wendehorst, n 204 above, Vor § 1 FernAbsG.

[206] The differences between a right of revocation and a right of return are explained in Ulmer, n 205 above, § 361b, nn 11ff.

(§ 241a BGB) was introduced in order to deal with the delivery of unsolicited goods or the supply of unsolicited services by a business person to a consumer. Most importantly, however, the BGB was now amended to contain a definition of the key terms 'consumer' (*Verbraucher*) and 'entrepreneur' (*Unternehmer*). Consumers are all natural persons effecting a legal act the purpose of which cannot be attributed to their trade or independent professional activity;[207] entrepreneurs are natural persons, or legal entities, or partnerships possessing legal personality, who in effecting a transaction act in pursuit of their trade or independent professional activity.[208] As a result of the reform of June 2000, the BGB thus, in a way, contained several 'anchors'[209] to which the special rules outside the BGB could intellectually be tied. Core features of the Distance Contract Act itself were the provisions requiring suppliers to give adequate information prior to the conclusion of the contract and granting the consumer a right of revocation. While, therefore, the consumer was to be placed in as good a position as possible to make an informed choice, this did not change the fact that a consumer engaging in a distance transaction does not actually see the product or ascertain the nature of the service before concluding the contract. This was the reason advanced by the draftsmen of the Directive in support of the right of revocation.[210]

Late Payments, Electronic Signatures, E-Commerce

In June 2000, a Directive on combating late payment in commercial transactions was enacted.[211] It was intended to improve the position of businesspeople faced with increasingly slack payment habits on the part of their debtors and had nothing to do with consumer protection. Nonetheless, it affected a core component of the traditional rules relating to breach of contract: the concept of *mora debitoris*. Barely two months before the enactment of the Directive an Acceleration of Due Payments Act[212] had come into force in Germany pursuing exactly the same aim and amending § 284 BGB.[213] This Act was heralded as an

---

[207] § 13 BGB.   [208] § 14 BGB.

[209] H Dörner, 'Die Integration des Verbraucherrechts in das BGB', in Schulze and Schulte-Nölke, n 2 above, 181ff.

[210] See recital 14 of the Distance Contracts Directive.

[211] Directive 2000/35/EC of the European Parliament and of the Council of 29 June 2000, easily accessible in Radley-Gardner *et al*, n 170 above, 59ff.

[212] *Gesetz zur Beschleunigung Fälliger Zahlungen*, 30 March 2000, *Bundesgesetzblatt* 2000 I, 330.

[213] For detailed comment on the new § 284 III BGB, see U Huber, 'Das neue Recht des Zahlungsverzugs und das Prinzip der Privatautonomie' [2000] *Juristenzeitung* 743ff; cf also W Ernst, 'Deutsche Gesetzgebung in Europa—am Beispiel des Verzugsrechts' (2000) 8 *Zeitschrift für Europäisches Privatrecht* 767ff.

anticipated implementation of the Directive. A comparison between the new § 284 III BGB and the requirements of the Directive, however, immediately revealed that they were incompatible.[214] A reform of the reform was, therefore, necessary and it was implemented on 1 January 2002, in the course of the modernisation of the German law of obligations.[215] The Directive on a Community framework for electronic signatures of December 1999[216] had no specific consumer orientation; its implementation in Germany, however, necessitated both a special act (the Signature Act of May 2001)[217] and the introduction of two new provisions into the BGB.[218] The same approach was adopted with regard to the Directive on certain aspects of information society services, in particular electronic commerce, in the Internal Market of June 2000:[219] It was implemented, partly, by the Legal Framework for Electronic Commerce Act of December 2001[220], and partly by the introduction of § 312e into the BGB;[221] the latter step was taken as part of the modernisation of the German law of obligations. § 312e BGB aims to protect both entrepreneurs and consumers from the risks inherent in using 'information society services' in order to buy goods or obtain the supply of services, but consumers enjoy a higher level of protection. Consumer protection can, therefore, be regarded as one of the purposes pursued by the new provision.[222] The risks from which customers engaging in e-commerce are to be protected are (i) entry into the contract without having been supplied with adequate information, and (ii) placing a different order to the one intended by them, or placing the same order several times as a result of the way in which the 'information society service' has been programmed.

---

[214] U Huber, 'Das Gesetz zur Beschleunigung fälliger Zahlungen und die europäische Richtlinie zur Bekämpfung von Zahlungsverzug im Geschäftsverkehr' [2000] *Juristenzeitung* 957ff.   [215] See the new § 286 BGB.

[216] Directive 1999/93/EC of the European Parliament and of the Council of 13 December 1999; easily accessible in Radley-Gardner *et al*, n 170 above, *Fundamental Texts* 33ff.

[217] *Gesetz über Rahmenbedingungen für elektronische Signaturen* of 16 May 2001, *Bundesgesetzblatt* 2001 I, 876.   [218] §§ 126a and b BGB; cf also § 126 III BGB.

[219] Directive 2000/31/EC of the European Parliament and of the Council of 8 June 2000; easily accessible in Radley-Gardner *et al*, n 170 above, 3ff.

[220] *Gesetz über rechtliche Rahmenbedingungen für den elektronischen Geschäftsverkehr* of 14 December 2001, *Bundesgesetzblatt* 2001 I, 3721.

[221] As far as the duties of information contained in Arts 10 and 11 of the Directive are concerned, see § 3 *Verordnung über Informationspflichten nach Bürgerlichem Recht* of 5 August 2002, *Bundesgesetzblatt* 2002 I, 3002.

[222] C Wendehorst, in *Münchener Kommentar zum Bürgerlichen Gesetzbuch*, vol. 2a (4th edn., 2003), Vor § 312b, n 5 and § 312e, n 3.

Consumer Sales

Finally, then, the Directive on certain aspects of the sale of consumer goods and associated guarantees of May 1999[223] which brought about the culmination of the new approach. For not only was the Directive used as the political trigger to implement a far-ranging modernisation of the German law of obligations including, particularly, a reform of the law of prescription, breach of contract, and liability for non-conformity;[224] it was also taken to provide the appropriate opportunity for integrating a range of special statutes into the BGB. Since all of these statutes concern the protection of consumers, this step (which was not necessitated by the Consumer Sales Directive) must be seen as an expression of the German government's desire to integrate consumer law and general law, as far as possible.[225] The statutes affected are the Standard Terms of Business, Doorstep Selling, Consumer Credit, Distance Contracts and Timeshare Agreements Acts. They have all been replaced by provisions contained in the BGB. Somewhat surprisingly, two other important consumer protection statutes, ie the ones on Distance Teaching and Product Liability, have remained untouched.

Incorporation: The Law as It Stands Today

Definitions, Unsolicited Performances, Standard Terms of Business

The new consumer protection provisions have been spread over the first two books of the BGB in an attempt to find appropriate niches within the BGB system. That system, as is well known, proceeds from the general to the specific: general part for the BGB as a whole (book I), general part of the law of obligations (book II, sections 1–6) and particular obligations (book II, section 7; this is a section split into 25 titles, ranging from sale to delict). The general part of the BGB has been amended by the two definitions of the terms 'consumer' and 'entrepreneur' (§§ 13 and 14 BGB) mentioned above.[226] These definitions certainly belong together

---

[223] Directive 1999/44/EC of the European Parliament and of the Council of 25 May 1999, easily accessible in Radley-Gardner *et al*, n 170 above, 107ff.

[224] See n 126 above and related text.

[225] See 'Diskussionsentwurf eines Schuldrechtsmodernisierungsgesetzes', in Canaris, n 6 above, 66, 95; 'Begründung der Bundesregierung zum Entwurf eines Gesetzes zur Modernisierung des Schuldrechts', in ibid, 601f; 'Bericht des Rechtsausschusses', in ibid, 1067f.   [226] See n 207 above and related text.

since consumer contracts are defined as contracts between an entrepreneur and a consumer.[227] So, for example, protection is not granted to a consumer who has concluded a contract with another consumer. This has, incidentally, led some commentators to suggest that the entire subject matter should be regarded as a special branch of business law.[228] All the other consumer protection provisions have become part of the law of obligations. The new § 241a BGB on unsolicited performances has been mentioned;[229] it has obtained a prominent position within the provisions dealing with the 'subject matter of obligations'. The substantive provisions of the Standard Terms of Business Act have been slotted in, *en bloc*, by way of a new section 2 on 'the shaping of contractual obligations by means of standard terms of business' (§§ 305–310 BGB). The text of the new rules does not differ much from those contained in the old statute. There has been some rearrangement, and the number of provisions has been reduced from fourteen to ten. § 307 I 2 BGB now provides that an unreasonable advantage (as a result of which a provision in standard terms of business may be regarded as invalid) may also result from the fact that that provision is not clear and comprehensible. This is, however, nothing new since it is merely a statutory restatement of the transparency requirement developed by the courts under the old law.[230] The fairness control has been extended to employment contracts governed by the rules of labour law (§ 310 IV 2 BGB; but 'appropriate regard must be had to the special features of labour law').[231] The most important change, however, is not reflected in the text of the new rules. It results from the fact that the Modernization of the Law of Obligations Act has reformed, *inter alia*, the law relating to prescription, non-conformity in contracts of sale, and breach of contract in general,[232] and these reforms are bound to affect the standard for evaluating whether a provision contained in standard terms of business places the contractual partner at an unreasonable disadvantage.[233] For, according to § 307 II no. 2 BGB an unreasonable

---

[227] § 310 III BGB.

[228] S Grundmann, *Europäisches Schuldvertragsrecht* (1999), *passim*; Grundmann, 'Europäisches Handelsrecht—vom Handelsrecht des laissez faire im Kodex des 19. Jahrhunderts zum Handelsrecht der sozialen Verantwortung' (1999) 163 *Zeitschrift für das gesamte Handelsrecht und Wirtschaftsrecht* 635, 665f, 669ff.

[229] See n 206 above and following text.

[230] BGHZ 104, 82, 92; BGHZ 106, 42, 49; BGHZ 106, 259, 264; BGHZ 108, 52, 57; BGHZ 115, 177, 185; Heinrichs, n 194 above, § 9 AGBG, nn 15ff.; Basedow, n 144 above, § 9 AGBG, nn 28ff.; Ulmer *et al*, n 149 above, § 9, nn. 87ff.; and see Art 5 of the Directive on unfair terms in consumer contracts.

[231] For details, see Basedow, n 144 above, § 310, nn 87ff.

[232] See n 5 above, plus related and following text.

[233] J Hennrichs, in *Anwaltkommentar, Schuldrecht* (2002), § 307, n 13; Heinrichs, in *Palandt, Bürgerliches Gesetzbuch* (63rd edn., 2004), § 307, n 26; A Stadler, in Jauernig (ed),

disadvantage is to be presumed to exist, if a provision 'cannot be reconciled with essential notions of justice underlying the statutory provision from which it deviates'. In particular, it remains to be seen whether, or to what extent, the new rules of German sales law which relate to the sale of consumer goods or which, even if they apply to contracts of sale in general, originate from the *consumer* sales directive[234], will be taken to embody such essential notions of justice.

Particular forms of Marketing

Section 3 ('Contractual obligations'), title 1 ('Creation, subject matter and termination') now contains a new subtitle on 'particular forms of marketing'. Here we find a regulation of the specificities concerning doorstep transactions, distance contracts and e-commerce, particularly the granting of a right of revocation in the case of doorstep transactions (§ 312 BGB) and distance contracts (§ 312 d BGB), the right of return as an alternative to the right of revocation in distance contracts (§ 312 e BGB), a general provision concerning information to be given to consumers in the case of distance contracts (§ 312 c BGB), and another concerning the duties (including the duties of information) of an entrepreneur using a television or media service for the purpose of concluding a contract for the delivery of goods or the supply of services (§ 312 e BGB). All the rules contained in this subtitle (ie also the right of revocation concerning doorstep transactions)[235] now apply to consumer contracts, except for § 312 e BGB, where the two parties are referred to as 'entrepreneur' and 'customer'. All of these rules (including § 312 e BGB) are unilaterally mandatory, ie they may not be derogated from to the detriment of the consumer/customer. The common denominator of the three types of transactions covered in this subtitle is that they constitute forms of direct marketing.[236] Thus, it is not their content which puts them apart from other transactions but the manner in which they are concluded.

Right of Revocation (General Rules)

Another new subtitle introduced into the general part of the law of obligations provides general rules on the right of revocation in consumer

Bürgerliches Gesetzbuch (11th edn., 2004), § 307, n 10; W-H Roth, n 154 above, 475, 486f, 489; H P Westermann, 'Das neue Kaufrecht einschliesslich des Verbrauchsgüterkaufs' [2001] *Juristenzeitung* 530, 535f.

[234] Zimmermann, n 11 above, 29f.   [235] See n 165 above and related text.
[236] P Ulmer in *Münchener Kommentar zum Burgerlichen Gesetzbuch*, vol. IIa (4th edn., 2003), Vor §§ 312, 312a, n 8.

contracts.[237] It covers the rights of revocation granted in the case of doorstep transactions (§ 312 I 1 BGB), distance contracts (§ 312d I 1 BGB), timeshare agreements (§ 485 I BGB), consumer loan contracts (§ 495 I BGB), instalment supply contracts (§ 505 I 1 BGB), and distance teaching contracts (§ 4 I Distance Teaching Act), and it is based on §§ 361a and b BGB which had been introduced 18 months before the enactment of the Modernization of the Law of Obligations Act[238] in order to replace the previously prevailing chaotic coexistence of different rules and approaches[239] with as uniform a regime as possible.[240] Thus, for example, the right of revocation is now regarded as a special instance of a statutory right to terminate the contract.[241] This means that, until the consumer exercises his right of revocation, the contract is valid.[242] Revocation, like termination, has the effect of transforming the contract into a winding-up relationship.[243] Save where otherwise provided, the provisions on statutory termination apply *mutatis mutandis*.[244] Notice of revocation has to be given to the entrepreneur within two weeks after the consumer has been informed clearly and by way of a text supplied to him about the details of his right of revocation. No reason has to be given for exercising the right of revocation.[245]

The new law also provides for a standardized period of six months from conclusion of the contract, after which the right of revocation ceases to exist.[246] As regards doorstep transactions, this rule is not in conformity with the relevant European Community Directive.[247] This is why only a few months after the enactment of the new § 355 BGB its third paragraph was amended[248] by a sentence stating that, irrespective of § 355 III 1 BGB, the right of revocation does not cease to exist, if the consumer has not been duly informed about his right of revocation.[249] This very largely deprives the six month period of its practical effect, and that not only for

---

[237] §§ 355ff BGB. This subtitle also covers the right of return, insofar as it is available to a consumer; see n 251 below and related text.

[238] See n 206 above and related text.   [239] Heinrichs, n 194 above, § 361a, n 3.

[240] For comment, see Ulmer, n 205 above, § 361a, nn 1ff.

[241] Ulmer, n 236 above § 355, n 9; Stadler, n 233 above, § 355, n 3.

[242] For an extensive discussion of this approach, in comparison with the legal position prevailing before June 2000, see P Mankowski, *Beseitigungsrechte* (2003), 33ff.

[243] Ulmer, n 236 above, § 355, n 33.   [244] § 357 I 1 BGB.

[245] § 355 I 2, II 1 BGB.   [246] § 355 III 1 BGB.

[247] Art 4 (3) of Directive 85/577/EEC; ECJ Decision of 13 December 2001 (C-481/99) *Heininger v. Bayerische Hypo- und Vereinsbank AG* [2001] ECR I-9945.

[248] This happened as part of a statute reforming the right of appearance of lawyers before Regional Supreme Courts: *Gesetz zur Änderung des Rechts der Vertretung durch Rechtsanwälte vor den Oberlandesgerichten* of 23 July 2002, *Bundesgesetzblatt* (as in n 165) 2002 I, 2850.   [249] § 355 III 3 BGB.

doorstep transactions but also for all other rights of revocation where such a step would not have been required under EC law. Thus, in many situations there will be no temporal limitation at all for the right to revoke, and the existence of the contract can be in jeopardy for a long time. This is hardly desirable.[250] Where a contract has been concluded on the basis of a sales prospectus, the right of revocation can sometimes be replaced by an unrestricted right of return.[251] Details concerning this right of return are specified in §§ 356ff. BGB. It is a formalized type of revocation which follows very similar rules.[252] In particular, as for the right of revocation, the provisions on statutory termination apply *mutatis mutandis*.[253] Often a consumer will only be able to finance the goods to be delivered, or the services to be performed, by way of concluding a consumer loan contract with the entrepreneur offering the goods or services, or with a third party, ie typically a bank. As a result, he will be exposed to two creditors. §§ 358 and 359 BGB are designed to provide protection in cases where the loan serves to finance the other contract and where both contracts constitute an economic unit.[254] If the consumer has a right of revocation against the businessperson, and has exercised this right of revocation, he also ceases to be bound by the contract of loan.[255] The same also applies the other way round: if the consumer has revoked the loan transaction (this is possible under § 495 BGB), he also ceases to be bound by the contract for the supply of goods or services. The legal consequences of revocation of the one contract, in other words, are extended to the other contract. Details concerning the winding-up relationship now also existing with regard to the 'linked' contract are provided in § 358 IV BGB. § 359 BGB also deals with linked contracts, though not with rights of revocation: the consumer may also raise defences available to him under the contract financed by the consumer loan transaction against the party with whom he has concluded that consumer loan transaction. All the provisions

---

[250] Ulmer, n 236 above, § 355, nn 56ff; Heinrichs, n 233 above, § 355, n 22; S Timmerbeil, 'Der neue § 355 III BGB—ein Schnellschuss des Gesetzgebers?' [2003] *Neue Juristische Wochenschrift*, 569ff.

[251] §§ 312 I 2, 312 d I 2, 503 I BGB. That the right of revocation can only be replaced by a right of return if the contract has been concluded on the basis of a sales prospectus, is not apparent from these rules themselves but follows from the reference in these rules to § 356 BGB: cf, eg Ulmer, n 236 above, § 312, n 8; Wendehorst, n 222 above, § 312 d, n 112. On the significance of the term 'unrestricted' (right of return), see Ulmer, n 236 above, § 356, n 15.

[252] Formalized, insofar as it can only be exercised 'by return of the thing or, if it cannot be dispatched as a parcel, by a demand for collection': § 356 II BGB.

[253] § 357 I BGB

[254] For background information, see Ulmer, n 236 above, § 358, nn 1ff.

[255] § 358 I BGB.

contained in the subtitle on rights of revocation and return in consumer contracts, with two small exceptions,[256] are unilaterally mandatory. This has not been specifically stated but may be gathered by way of interpretation.[257]

Sale of Consumer Goods

The regulation of 'Particular types of obligations' commences with the contracts of sale and exchange (section 8, title 1). Here we find a new subtitle on the 'sale of consumer goods' (§§ 474–479). The label (in German *Verbrauchsgüterkauf*) is misleading in view of the fact that the provisions in this subtitle do not deal with the sale of a specific type of goods but with the sale of movables by an entrepreneur to a consumer in general.[258] Obviously, §§ 474ff BGB constitute a set of special rules implementing the Consumer Sales Directive. Since, however, the regulatory model contained in that Directive has largely found its way into the new *general* law of sale,[259] only a few additional rules were necessary for 'consumer sales'. Most importantly, § 475 BGB declares the provisions of general sales law on the seller's liability for non-conformity, as well as the provisions relating to consumer sales themselves, to be unilaterally mandatory in favour of the purchaser/consumer.[260] In addition, there is a presumption that an object, which turns out to be defective within six months after it has been handed over to the purchaser, was already defective at the time when it was handed over, unless such presumption is incompatible with the nature of the object or of the defect.[261] There are special provisions for warranties, for the seller's right of recourse against the entrepreneur from whom he himself had previously bought the object, and on the prescription of these rights of recourse.[262] Title 1 ('Sale, exchange') is now followed by a new title 2 devoted to timeshare agreements (§§ 481—487 BGB). It serves the purpose of incorporating the provisions of the Timeshare Agreements Act into the BGB. A definition of the concept of 'timeshare agreements' is followed by provisions

---

[256] §§ 356 I 1, 357 II 3 BGB.

[257] Ulmer, n 236 above, § 355, n 4; Stadler, n 233 above, § 355, n 2.

[258] F Faust, in HG Bamberger and H Roth (eds), *Kommentar zum Bürgerlichen Gesetzbuch*, vol. I (2003), § 474, n 3.   [259] Zimmermann, n 11 above, 29ff.

[260] For details, see Faust, n 258 above, § 475, nn 3ff.

[261] § 476 BGB. Nature of the object: for objects the durability of which does not come close to six months (food), see 'Motivation to the Discussion Draft of the Law of Obligations Modernization Act', in Canaris, n 6 above, 296; nature of the defect: for diseases in animals that have been sold, see Faust, n 258 above, § 476, n 4.

[262] §§ 477–479 BGB.

imposing the duty on an entrepreneur who offers a timeshare agreement
to issue a prospectus containing detailed information, specifying the language of the contract and of the prospectus, imposing a form requirement
for timeshare agreements, granting the consumer a right of revocation,
and establishing a prohibition on advance payments. All provisions of
this title are unilaterally mandatory.[263]

Credit Transactions

The Consumer Credit Act used to be one of the most important
consumer protection statutes. Its incorporation into the BGB provided
the government with a welcome opportunity to revise the entire law relating to credit transactions, particularly contracts of loan. The old rules,
contained in §§ 607ff BGB, were regarded as outdated,[264] particularly
since they still appeared to perpetuate, conceptually, the Roman notion
of a 'real' contract:[265] a contract which comes into existence with the
handing over of an object (or, in this case: a sum of money).[266] The
history of the reform was brief but turbulent. The Discussion Draft had
contained a set of rules which was widely regarded as entirely unsatisfactory;[267] for example, the Discussion Draft had failed to provide for
contracts for the loan of an object.[268] As a result of the criticism a number
of changes were made which have led to the following pattern of regulation. Provisions covering loan contracts are now split between contracts
for the loan of a thing (§§ 607–609 BGB) and contracts of loan
(meaning: contracts for the loan of a sum of money; §§ 488–498 BGB).
The latter have become part of a new title 3 on 'Contracts of loan; financing aids and instalment supply contracts between an entrepreneur and
a consumer'. Loan brokerage contracts between an entrepreneur and a
consumer have found their new place in §§ 655a–655e BGB, as part
of title 10 on brokerage contracts. The new rules on contracts for the loan of
a sum of money constitute a modernized version of the old rules on
contracts of loan in general (§§ 488–490 BGB). They are supplemented

---

[263] § 487 BGB.

[264] See the 'Motivation to the Government Draft of the Law of Obligations
Modernization Act', in Canaris, n 6 above, 884.

[265] D Medicus, *Schuldrecht II* (12th edn., 2004), n 287; J Köndgen, 'Modernisierung
des Darlehensrechts: eine Fehlanzeige', in Ernst and Zimmermann, n 2 above, 457ff.

[266] Zimmermann, n 23 above, 153ff, 163ff.

[267] Köndgen, n 265 above, 457ff; P Bülow, 'Kreditvertrag und Verbraucherkreditrecht
im BGB', in Schulze and Schulte-Nölke, n 2 above, 153ff.

[268] See the criticism raised by Teichmann, U Huber and Koller at the Regensburg meeting
of German professors of private law: Ernst and Zimmermann, n 2 above, 479.

by a number of provisions specifically dealing with consumer loan contracts (ie loan contracts made for remuneration between an entrepreneur and a consumer). Here we find, *inter alia*, a form requirement,[269] detailed duties of information on the part of the businessperson *vis-à-vis* the consumer,[270] a regulation of the legal consequences of non-compliance with the form requirement,[271] the consumer's right of revocation,[272] and provisions on the treatment of default interest, the attribution of part performance and repayment of the entire loan in the case of loans payable in instalments.[273]

A new subtitle is devoted to financing aids (extension of time for payment and other financing aids).[274] Most of the rules concerning consumer loan contracts apply *mutatis mutandis*.[275] Special rules have been enacted for instalment payment transactions (ie the most important form of 'extension of time for payment') and finance leasing contracts (ie the most important form of 'another financing aid').[276] Instalment supply contracts between an entrepreneur and a consumer are covered by § 505 BGB. In the tradition of § 1c of the Instalment Sales Act and, subsequently, § 2 Consumer Credit Act, the consumer is granted a right of revocation even though we are not dealing with a credit transaction. All the provisions just mentioned, with the exception of those on contracts for loan of a thing and on contracts of loan in general, are unilaterally mandatory.[277] The provisions of §§ 491–506 BGB do not just apply to consumers in the sense of § 13 BGB, but also to those to whom a loan, extension of time for payment or other financing aid is granted for the taking-up of a trade or self-employed professional activity, or who conclude an instalment supply contract for that purpose, unless the net amount of the loan, or the cash price, exceeds €50,000.[278] This extension of the protection granted to consumers is based on a provision of the Consumer Credit Act; it was not required by the Consumer Credit Directive.[279]

Package Tours

Finally, of course, there is the codification of the package travel contract in §§ 651a ff BGB. The respective subtitle was incorporated into the

---

[269] § 492 I 1–3 BGB.   [270] § 492 I 5 BGB.   [271] § 494 BGB.
[272] § 495 BGB.   [273] §§ 497, 498 BGB.   [274] §§ 499–504 BGB.
[275] § 499 I BGB.   [276] § 499 II in connection with §§ 500–504 BGB.
[277] §§ 506, 655e BGB.   [278] § 507 BGB.
[279] C Möller and C Wendehorst, in H G Bamberger and H Roth (eds), *Kommentar zum Bürgerlichen Gesetzbuch*, vol. I (2003), § 507, nn 1, 3.

BGB in 1979[280] and amended, as a result of the package travel directive, in 1990[281]. Further amendments were made in July 2001 (Second Package Travel Provisions Amendment Act) and yet again, in November 2002 (Modernization of the Law of Obligations Act).[282] All provisions concerning package travel (with one exception)[283] are unilaterally mandatory.[284] Even today the person to whom protection is granted is referred to as the 'traveller', ie §§ 651a ff BGB have not been tied to the consumer concept of § 13 BGB.

General Comments

Consumer Contract Law and the EC

This, in brief outline, is the law as it stands today. A few comments may be apposite.

In the first place it is open to doubt to what extent the European Union, which has dominated the development of consumer contract law over the past 25 years, is competent to regulate this area of the law. All the Directives mentioned above have been based on Article 95 EC Treaty (ie Article 100a, under the old numbering); or, more precisely, and in the words of the Directives themselves, 'in particular' Article 95.[285] In its decision on the Tobacco Advertising Directive, the European Court of Justice has emphasized, however, that the European Community may only adopt measures for the approximation of the laws prevailing in the Member States if they aim at improving the functioning of the internal market.[286] This can only be the case if the divergence of the respective national rules constitutes an impediment to free trade or leads to noticeable distortions of competition.[287] In view of these strict standards, many provisions of the consumer protection directives rest on fragile foundations. For it is less than obvious, to mention one example, that the

---

[280] See n 126 above and related text.   [281] See n 190 above and related text.

[282] For details of the rules that were amended on both occasions, see H Sprau, in *Palandt, Bürgerliches Gesetzbuch* (63rd edn., 2004), Einf. v. § 651a, n 2.

[283] §§ 651g II BGB (extinctive prescription).   [284] § 651m BGB.

[285] See n 187 above; cf also Heiderhoff, n 19 above, 223ff. On the phenomenon of 'competence creep', in the present context, S Weatherill, 'Why Object to the Harmonization of Private Law by the EC?' (2004) 12 European Review of Private Law 634ff.

[286] ECJ Decision of 5 October 2000, *Germany v European Parliament* (C-481/99) [2000] ECR I-8419; generally on the role of the European Court of Justice see, most recently, Heiderhoff, n 19 above, 94ff.

[287] *Germany v European Parliament*, n 286 above.

introduction of a right of revocation in doorstep sales—ie the introduction of a legal device *hampering* direct marketing—should be able to remove trade barriers between the Member States of the EU.[288] Moreover, the Member States are not usually prevented from adopting or maintaining more favourable provisions for the protection of consumers.[289] This is an indication that the real aim pursued by the EC is the promotion of a certain minimum level of consumer protection across all Member States rather than the removal of supposed trade barriers resulting from a diversity of levels of protection in the Member States. Also, noticeable distortions of competition are often more pretended than real; in doorstep selling situations, for example, they can hardly arise given the fact that all traders compete, on equal terms, under the conditions prevailing in the respective markets. According to Article 5 of the Rome Convention on the law applicable to contractual obligations, the mandatory rules of the law of the country in which the consumer has his habitual residence are applicable to these types of consumer contract.[290] The Consumer Sales Directive, apart from stating, but not making plausible, that 'competition between sellers may be distorted' as a result of the fact that the laws of the Member States concerning consumer sales 'are somewhat disparate',[291] also evokes the notion of the confident consumer when it states that 'the creation of a common set of minimum rules of consumer law, valid no matter where goods are purchased within the Community, will strengthen consumer confidence and enable consumers to make the most of the internal market'.[292] Consumers, in other words, can be prevented from entering into cross-border purchases because they may be faced with different and unfamiliar legal rules. If this consideration were taken to constitute a valid basis for legal harmonization, it would provide the EC with the competence to harmonize the entire law of contract (as well as adjacent areas of the law, such as the rules on unjustified enrichment):[293] a conclusion which is usually not accepted today.[294] Whether, and to what extent, future Directives in the field of consumer contract law may be based on

---

[288] Roth, n 154 above, 475, 477.

[289] The problem of harmonization on the basis of a minimum standard is discussed, in the present context, by H Heiss, 'Verbraucherschutz im Binnenmarkt: Art 129a EGV und die wirtschaftlichen Verbraucherinteressen' (1996) 4 *Zeitschrift für Europäisches Privatrecht* 637ff; Heiderhoff, n 19 above, 38ff.

[290] Roth, n 154 above, 475, 477f.   [291] Directive 1999/44/EC, third recital.

[292] Ibid, fifth recital.   [293] Roth, n 154 above, 475, 478f.

[294] For the interpretation of Art 95 in the light of the decision of the ECJ on the Tobacco Advertising Directive see, along these lines, W-H Roth, 'Die Schuldrechtsmodernisierung im Kontext des Europarechts' in Ernst and Zimmermann, n 2 above, 231ff; Riesenhuber, n 19 above, 135ff; Rösler, n 16 above, 284ff; but see Reich and Micklitz, n 159 above, 1.21ff; Heiderhoff, n 19 above, 29ff, 220ff.

Article 153 rather than Article 95 EC Treaty remains to be seen. It depends, essentially, on whether such Directives can be understood as 'measures which support, supplement and monitor the policy pursued by the Member States' in the field of consumer protection; for Article 153 (3)b specifically empowers the Community to adopt such measures in order to 'contribute' to the attainment of 'a high level of consumer protection'.[295]

Being Caught by Surprise

If, in the course of the 1980s and 1990s, German lawyers had become used to the idea that the development of German consumer contract law was ultimately determined in Brussels, that one directive after another had to be transformed into national law, and that, as a result, a patchwork of special statutes had been added to the tapestry of private law, they were caught off-guard by the decision of the *German* government to incorporate these statutes into the BGB.[296] In hindsight, of course, they might have been alerted by the way in which the government had started to place 'anchors' for consumer protection statutes into the BGB in the course of implementing the Distance Contracts Directive.[297] But that had been in June 2000, a mere fifteen months before the Discussion Draft for a Modernization of the Law of Obligations Act was published. The *one* surprise contained in the Discussion Draft was the decision to use the Consumer Sales Directive, and the necessity of implementing it, as a vehicle for fundamentally reforming the German law of obligations; for the Directive could have been implemented by a few, relatively marginal, changes to the then-current German law of sale.[298]

Of course, it was well known that a blueprint exited for a reform of the German law of obligations; it was contained in the final report of the Commission charged with the revision of the law of obligations.[299] That report had been published in 1992. But the scope of the reform envisaged by the Commission was confined to the law of breach of

[295] Lurger, n 159 above, Art 153, nn 34f; Heiderhoff, n 19 above, 28f; Wiedenmann, n 19 above, 48. Art 153 (3)a EU Treaty does not provide the EU with competency to regulate consumer affairs; W Berg, in J Schwartze (ed), *EU-Kommentar* (2000), Art 153, n 14; but cf also Lurger, n 159 above, Art 153, nn 32f.

[296] B Dauner-Lieb, 'Die geplante Schuldrechtsmodernisierung—Durchbruch oder Schnellschuss' [2001] *Juristenzeitung*, 8ff.; H Honsell, 'Einige Bemerkungen zum Diskussionsentwurf eines Schuldrechtsmodernisierungsgesetzes', [2001] *Juristenzeitung*, 18ff; R Zimmermann, 'Schuldrechtsmodernisierung?' [2001] *Juristenzeitung*, 171ff.

[297] See n 209 above and related text; Micklitz, n 159 above, Vor §§ 13, 14, nn 1 refers to 'kind of revolution' in this respect.   [298] See n 8 above.

[299] See n 5 above.

contract, liability for non-conformity in contracts of sale and contracts for work, and extinctive prescription. This, then, was the *second* surprise hidden in the pages of the Discussion Draft: the Government had decided to revive an issue that had initially been on the reform agenda but had, in the meantime, been dropped:[300] the incorporation of consumer protection legislation into the BGB. The report of the Reform Commission was thus amended accordingly. The main problem associated with this way of proceeding was, however, that the matter had hardly been discussed; and since barely 18 months were left before the reform was to enter into effect, not many of the issues could now be subjected to close scrutiny.[301] It is obvious that the quality of reform has suffered from this lack of time for reflection.

A Newly Gained Transparency?

The incorporation of the consumer protection legislation into the BGB has not been comprehensive. The Distance Teaching and Product Liability Acts continue to exist (as does the Product Safety Act of April 1997).[302] There is a Duties of Information in Private Law Regulation[303] which specifies the duties of information in the case of distance contracts (§ 1), timeshare agreements (§ 2), e-commerce (§ 3), and package travel contracts (§§ 4–11); in addition it details the duties of information of credit institutions vis-à-vis their clients concerning the transfer of payments (§§ 12ff). Procedural aspects of consumer protection are dealt with by an Injunctions Act, as promulgated in August 2002.[304] Certain associations are given the right to sue those who use, or recommend for use, standard terms of business infringing the provisions of §§ 307–309 BGB, or who contravene in any other manner provisions which serve to protect consumers. The Act contains a list of statutes which are to be treated as serving the protection of consumers,[305] and it specifies the range of associations which may bring an action.[306] The action aims at putting to an end objectionable practices as effectively as possible. Consumers,

---

[300] See n 13 and related text.

[301] For the main contributions to the debate, see Roth, n 154 above, 225ff; Pfeiffer, n 17 above, 481ff; J. Schmidt-Räntsch, H Dörner, H-W Micklitz and P Ulmer, all in: Schulze and Schulte-Nölke, n 2 above, 169ff; Roth, n 233 above 475ff; Ulmer, n 157 above, 491ff.   [302] *Produktsicherheitsgesetz, Bundesgesetzblatt* I 1997, 934.

[303] *Verordnung über Informations- und Nachweispflichten nach bürgerlichem Recht, Bundesgesetzblatt* I 2002, 3002.

[304] *Gesetz über Unterlassungsklagen bei Verbraucherrechts- und anderen Verstößen, Bundesgesetzblatt* 2002 I, 3422.   [305] § 2 UKlaG.

[306] § 4 UKlaG.

therefore, cannot gauge how far, and in what respect, they enjoy legal protection by glancing through the BGB; they have to refer to a number of other statutory instruments.

The transparency of consumer protection under the BGB also leaves much to be desired. Thus, for example, §§ 355ff BGB are designed to provide uniform rules concerning rights of revocation and return in consumer contracts; yet a number of modifications concerning the legal consequences of revocation and return are contained in special rules, such as § 495 II 1 BGB, § 485 V BGB and § 4 III Distance Teaching Act. The reader is alerted to these modifications by the phrase 'save where otherwise provided' contained in § 357 BGB. But there are also special provisions establishing additional, or different, requirements for the right of revocation under § 355 BGB, even though that rule does not contain a similar proviso. § 4 I 2 Distance Teaching Act and §§ 312d, 312e III 2 and 485 IV BGB have to be mentioned in this context. Contrary to the somewhat simplistic expectations of the draftsmen of the reform legislation the assessment of a consumer's legal position still requires a considerable amount of legal skill. Also, so far § 13 BGB has failed to achieve conceptual uniformity, for both the Distance Teaching Act and §§ 651a ff BGB are consumer protection statutes[307] but continue to use their own terminology to define the range of those to be protected. Persons taking up a trade or self-employed professional activity are treated as consumers in the context of the transactions described in § 507 BGB.

The New Provisions and the System of the BGB

One of the characteristic features of a codification is its systematic nature.[308] It is based on the belief that the legal material does not constitute an indigestible and arbitrary mass of individual rules and cases but that it can be reduced to a rational system. Codification thus promotes the internal coherence of the law and facilitates its comprehensibility. The German Civil Code used to be a showpiece for the truth of this assertion. The draftsmen of the reform legislation have attempted to preserve the system of the BGB and to find appropriate systematic niches for the new consumer contract provisions. But they have only been partly successful.[309] The provisions that used to be contained in §§ 1–11 Standard Terms of

[307] § 2 II nos 1 and 3 UKlaG.
[308] R Zimmermann, 'Codification: History and Present Significance of an Idea' (1995) 3 European Review of Private Law, 95ff; J Basedow, 'Das BGB im künftigen europäischen Privatrecht: Der hybride Kodex' (2000) 200 *Archiv für die civilistische Praxis* 465ff.
[309] See, for example, the criticism in Wiedenmann, n 19 above, 34ff.

Business Act can now be found in §§ 305–310 BGB. They deal with a number of different issues. They concern themselves with the question how standard terms of business can become part of a contract,[310] they include rules of interpretation,[311] they regulate the consequences of non-incorporation and invalidity (and, in the process, deviate from the general rule on partial invalidity in § 139 BGB),[312] and they determine standards for the policing of unfair standard contract terms.[313] Systematically, these issues need to be related to §§ 145ff. (formation of contract), §§ 133, 157 BGB (interpretation), § 139 (partial invalidity), and either § 138 (contracts *contra bonos mores*), § 242 (good faith) or possibly even §§ 315ff BGB (unilateral determination of performance). The German government, however, decided to preserve the integrity of what used to be the Standard Terms of Business Act without preserving the Act itself. The provisions were thus shoved, lock, stock and barrel, into one place, and the place chosen for this purpose was the one immediately following the rules on *mora creditoris* (and immediately preceding a section of the code entitled 'contractual obligations': as if standard terms of business were part of non-contractual obligations). There is no good reason at all to deal with standard terms of business at this specific place; and the only reason that can possibly be advanced is that a convenient space could relatively easily be created by dropping, removing, or compressing the rules previously located here. As a result, the new §§ 305–310 seem like a piece of pop music tossed into the second movement of a classical symphony: a *corpus alienum* without intellectual connection to its surroundings. The incorporation of the Standard Terms of Business Act into the BGB, in other words, has been a purely formal exercise; it has not led to anything that could be called an integration into the fabric of the BGB.[314]

Another example of an unhappy form of integration is provided by § 241a BGB, the rule on unsolicited performances.[315] It sits awkwardly between two of the most fundamental rules of the German law of obligations,[316] and there is no apparent reason for this choice of place, not even,

---

[310] §§ 305, 305a, 305c I BGB.
[311] §§ 305b, 305c II BGB; cf also § 306a BGB.   [312] § 306 BGB.
[313] §§ 307, 308, 309 BGB.
[314] As has been mentioned above (see n 230 above and related text), §§ 305ff BGB contain a statutory restatement of the transparency requirement developed by the courts under the old law. The new § 307 I 2 BGB has, however, been placed in the wrong position, given the internal system of what used to be the Standard Terms of Business Act: see Basedow, n 144 above, § 307, n 51.   [315] See text following n 206 above.
[316] § 241 BGB (ie the rule with which book II of the BGB on the law of obligations is introduced) defines the duties arising under an obligation), whereas § 242 BGB is the famous general good faith provision.

in this case, a *lacuna* in the numbering of the BGB provisions. Werner Flume regards this as 'monstrous',[317] and one of the standard commentaries refers to an 'unparalleled legislative blunder'.[318]

Occasionally, the draftsmen of the new law attempted to patch up a systematic awkwardness. The first section of book I (General Part) of the BGB deals with persons. It is subdivided into two titles, the one dealing with natural persons, the other with legal persons. The definitions of the terms 'consumer' and 'entrepreneur' have been added to the first title as if that title contained a random collection of definitions. An 'entrepreneur', as § 14 BGB itself makes clear, can be a natural or legal person; Hence the change of the heading for title one; it now reads 'Natural person, consumer, entrepreneur'. Still, however, this is an uneasy compromise given the fact that title 2, now as previously, deals with 'legal persons'.[319] Also, the definitions contained in §§ 13ff BGB are relevant only for the law of obligations; they should, therefore, have been placed into the general part of the law of obligations rather than into the general part of the BGB. That loan contracts in general (including consumer loans) and contracts for the loan of a thing have been dealt with in two different corners within section 8 ('Particular kinds of obligations')[320] can also only be attributed to the vagaries of the new law's drafting history.

'Throw-away' Legislation

The new provisions amending the BGB are easily recognizable in view of the fact that they tend to be long-winded, badly drafted and also, not rarely, ill-considered. The quality of modern legislation has often been deplored. Dieter Medicus has remarked, with characteristic understatement, that those responsible for legislation have 'not rarely been infelicitous' in their efforts.[321] Others have used stronger language. The piece of legislation relating to credit transfers has been characterized as *monstrum horribile*,[322] the act on distance contracts has prompted a respected practitioner (the former Vice-President of the Supreme Court of Appeal for the State of Hamburg) to remark that 'one might like

---

[317] W Flume, 'Vom Beruf unserer Zeit für Gesetzgebung' [2000] *Zeitschrift für Wirtschaftsrecht* 1428.
[318] H-P Mansel, in: Jauernig (ed), *Bürgerliches Gesetzbuch* (11th edn, 2004), § 241a, n 1.
[319] See, for example, Flume, n 317 above, 1427f; Duve, n 22 above, §§ 1–14, n 89.
[320] See text following n 263 above.
[321] D Medicus, 'Entscheidungen des BGH als Marksteine für die Entwicklung des allgemeinen Zivilrechts' [2000] *Neue Juristische Wochenschrift*, 2927.
[322] Flume, n 317 above, 1430; cf also Einsele [2000] *Juristenzeitung*, 9ff.; H H Jakobs, 'Gesetzgebung im Banküberweisungsrecht' [2000] *Juristenzeitung*, 641ff.

to cry',[323] and the change effected in anticipation of the Directive on combating late payment in commercial transactions has been described as 'infinitely ill-conceived and inappropriate'; the consequences for commercial life were predicted to be 'disastrous'.[324] Rolf Knütel has devoted a thirty page article to the Consumer Credit Act as the paradigmatic example of a 'statutory failure',[325] while Christiane Wendehorst has characterised the quality of the German rules for e-commerce as 'extremely bad' and as having descended to the level of the respective EC Directive.[326] Hans Hermann Seiler generally speaks of the phenomenon of 'throw-away' legislation.[327] In summary, I think, it is safe to say that the incorporation of the *ius novum* into the BGB has not enhanced its technical quality. It is a fitting testimony to the fast food approach to legislation that some areas of the law have been the subject of repeated change over the past few years[328] and that even a number of rules that had been put in place by the Modernization of the Law of Obligations Act at the beginning of 2002 had to be amended shortly afterwards. These amendments have sometimes been necessary as the result of the fact that the European Court of Justice held the respective rules to be incompatible with EC legislation. One example has been mentioned above: it concerns the question when the right of revocation of doorstep transactions ceases to exist (§ 355 III BGB).[329] The same decision of the ECJ also prompted a fundamental revision of § 312a BGB concerning the relationship of a right of revocation or return under § 312 BGB (doorstep transactions) with other rights of revocation or return which might be applicable in the same situation.[330] At the time of preparation of the Modernization of the Law of Obligations Act, the case was pending before the ECJ; the decision was handed down on 9 December 2001, a mere 13 days after the Act had been promulgated and about three weeks before it came into force.[331]

---

[323] H-D Hensen, 'Das Fernabsatzgesetz oder: Man könnte heulen' [2000] *Zeitschrift für Wirtschaftsrecht* 1151f.

[324] W Ernst, 'Deutsche Gesetzgebung in Europa—am Beispiel des Verzugsrechts' (2000) 8 *Zeitschrift für Europäisches Privatrecht*, 767, 769; cf also U Huber, 'Das neue Recht des Zahlungsverzugs und das Prinzip der Privatautonomie' [2000] *Juristenzeitung*, 743ff.

[325] R Knütel, 'Das Verbraucherkreditgesetz als misslungenes Gesetz', in U Diederichsen and R Dreier (eds), *Das missglückte Gesetz* (1997), 62ff.

[326] Wendehorst, n 222 above, § 312e, n 5.

[327] H H Seiler, 'Bewahrung von Kodifikationen in der Gegenwart am Beispiel des BGB' in O Behrends and W Sellert (eds), *Der Kodifikationsgedanke und das Modell des Bürgerlichen Gesetzbuches (BGB)* (2000), 110.

[328] For examples, see nn 215 and 282 above and related text.

[329] See n 248 above and related text.

[330] Ulmer, n 236 above, § 312a, nn 2ff; Stadler, n 233 above, § 312a, n 1.

[331] ECJ Decision, *Heininger*, n 247 above.

The problem of whether § 5 II of the Doorstep Selling Act (§ 312a BGB old version) was compatible with EC law had been the subject of academic discussion[332] but the draftsmen of the Modernization of the Law of Obligations Act did not take the opportunity to examine the matter: time was too short for subtleties of this kind.[333]

Many details of the new rules immediately became the subject of dispute: because these rules are conceptually unclear, because they are ill-adjusted to each other or to other areas of the law, because they are the result of an obvious mistake,[334] or because they do not correctly implement the provisions of a European Directive. § 241a I BGB does not say what it intends to say.[335] Moreover, it is one of those rules that have created more problems than they have solved, for the issue tackled by it has not constituted a problem under the old law.[336] Even the key definition of 'consumer' in § 13 BGB is defective in that it wrongly insinuates that only someone who normally engages in an independent professional activity or trade, but does not do so in the present context, can be regarded as a consumer;[337] and in that it is confined to natural persons 'concluding a legal act' which cannot be attributed to their independent professional activity or trade.[338] Whether the concept of 'consumer' can be taken to

---

[332] See the references in Stadler, n 233 above, § 312a, n 1.

[333] Ulmer, n 236 above, § 312a, n 2.

[334] For an example, see Wendehorst, n 222 above, § 312c, n 6.

[335] The rule states that the delivery of unsolicited goods—or the supply of other unsolicited services—does not give rise to a (contractual) claim (for the purchase price, or remuneration) against the consumer. This is self-evident. What § 241a BGB meant to prevent is a consumer who does not return the goods supplied to him being taken to have accepted a contractual obligation; see E A Kramer, in *Münchener Kommentar zum Bürgerlichen Gesetzbuch*, 4th edn., vol. 2a (2003), § 241a, n 11.

[336] Heinrichs, n 233 above, § 241a, n 1. § 241a BGB excludes all claims against the consumer, even those based not on contract but on unjustified enrichment or ownership: Kramer, n 335 above, § 241a, n 13; Heinrichs, n 233 above, § 241a, n 4; Mansel, n 318 above, § 241a, n 5. This is intended to be a sanction for what essentially constitutes an objectionable marketing practice. *Contra*: R Schulze, in: R Schulze and H Dörner, *Bürgerliches Gesetzbuch, Handkommentar* (3rd edn., 2003), § 241a, n 7. According to Flume, n 317 above, 1429, § 241a BGB is to be treated as *pro non scripto*. Cf also the criticism by C Berger, 'Der Ausschluss gesetzlicher Rückgewähransprüche bei der Erbringung unbestellter Leistungen nach § 241a BGB' [2001] *Juristische Schulung* 649ff; P Krebs, in *Anwaltkommentar, Schuldrecht* (2002), § 241a, n 5; Heiderhoff, n 19 above, 385ff.

[337] Flume, n 317 above, 1427 f.; Repgen, n 19 above, 30f; see also Medicus, n 21 above, 216; Wiedenmann, n 19 above, 137ff. For comparative comment as to the distinction between private and professional activities, see Remien, n 19 above, 248ff.

[338] It is generally agreed that, contrary to the wording of § 13 BGB, a consumer need not be a (natural) person who concludes a contract but can also be someone to whom unsolicited services are supplied (§ 241a BGB), or to whom legally relevant information has to be given (§§ 312c, 482 BGB), etc: O. Jauernig, in Jauernig, n 233 above, § 13, n 5; Heinrichs, n 233 above, § 13, n 5; Duve, n 22 above, §§ 1–14, n 82. See also Medicus, n 21

relate to associations which do not constitute a juristic person (ie private law partnerships) is disputed.[339] The exclusion of all legal persons (ie also those that do not constitute a business enterprise, such as non-profit organisations) is widely criticized.[340] The definition of a 'consumer' contained in Article 29 EGBGB is slightly different from that in § 13 BGB; also, the official heading of Article 29 EGBGB ('Consumer contracts') does not correspond to the definition of consumer contracts provided in § 310 III BGB. Whether, or to what extent, a transaction can be regarded as a consumer contract which can only partly be attributed to the independent professional activity, or trade, of the consumer, is controversial.[341]

Excessive Implementation

Where the German government has had to implement European Directives, it has often decided to go beyond what was required by the Directive. Thus, most importantly, the system of remedies provided in the Consumer Sales Directive has become the model for sales contracts in general,[342] and, as a result, the subtitle dealing specifically with consumer sales only contains a few additional rules.[343] Even here, the draftsmen of the new German law, however, did more than would have been necessary under EC law. If a consumer, on account of a defect in the object sold, successfully sues the seller, the seller, in turn, will seek recourse against his supplier. According to § 478 IV 1 BGB, the seller's rights against the supplier are, effectively, mandatory.[344] This constitutes an unprecedented

---

above, 214ff who points out that the combination of the words 'to conclude' and 'legal act' is inappropriate since, while contracts are 'concluded', legal acts (which include unilateral acts, such as the giving of notice or the declaration of set-off) are 'effected' rather than concluded. For an unconvincing attempt to justify the choice of terminology see J Schmidt-Räntsch, in H G Bamberger and H Roth (eds), *Kommentar zum Bürgerlichen Gesetzbuch*, vol. I (2003), § 13, n 11.

[339] See the references in Jauernig, n 233 above, § 13, n 2; Heinrichs, n 233 above, § 13, n 2; Micklitz, n 159 above, § 13, n 16; Medicus, n 21 above, 214. According to BGHZ 149, 80, 84f private law partnerships can be 'consumers'. But see ECJ Decision of 22 November 2001 [2002] *Neue Juristische Wochenschrift* 205.

[340] W Faber, 'Elemente verschiedener Verbraucherbegriffe in EG-Richtlinien, zwischenstaatlichen Übereinkommen und nationalem Zivil- und Kollisionsrecht' (1998) 6 *Zeitschrift für Europäisches Privatrecht*, 854, 864; Flume, n 317 above, 1428; Pfeiffer, n 19 above, 138; Duve, n 22 above, §§ 1–14, n 82; cf also Micklitz, n 159 above, § 13, nn 12ff; Remien, n 19 above, 247ff. But see also Wiedenmann, n 19 above, 171ff.

[341] O Jauernig, 'Verbraucherschutz in "Mischfällen"', in I Schwenzer (ed), *Festschrift für Peter Schlechtriem* (2003), 569ff; Medicus, n 337 above, 216ff; Wiedenmann, n 19 above, 190ff.   [342] See n 224 above and related text.

[343] See n 259 above and related text.

[344] This includes the prescription of these rights (§ 479 BGB). It does not, however, apply to the claim for damages: § 478 IV 2 BGB.

interference with the private autonomy of one entrepreneur *vis-à-vis* another.[345] The German rules on standard terms of business also have a scope of application extending far beyond consumer contracts. This was the approach adopted in the Standard Terms of Business Act of 1976 and it was retained at the time when the Directive on Unfair Terms in Consumer Contracts had to be implemented.[346] The implementation was effected by appending a provision to the Act (§ 24a Standard Terms of Business Act; now § 310 III BGB) modifying some of its provisions for consumer contracts.[347]

Outside the area of consumer law, the Directive on cross-border credit transfers has become the model for the regulation of credit transfers in general (including, in particular, domestic credit transfers).[348] A right of revocation has been introduced into German law for consumer credit transactions[349] even though this was not required by the Consumer Credit Directive. Consumers are also granted a right of revocation in the case of instalment supply contracts;[350] again, this was not necessitated by EC legislation. § 241a BGB on the delivery of unsolicited goods and the supply of unsolicited services is based on Article 9 of the Distance Contracts Directive; it exceeds the requirements of the Directive in that it not only protects the recipient/consumer from any obligation to pay for the unsolicited goods, or services, but even excludes any duty to return the object.[351] The right of revocation in consumer contracts does not cease to exist, at the latest, six months after the conclusion of the contract if the consumer has not been duly informed about that right of revocation.[352] Under EC law this kind of rule was required only for rights of revocation in the case of doorstep transactions.[353] Nonetheless, the German Government decided to generalize it so as to apply to the other rights of revocation covered by § 355 BGB.[354] Other individual instances of an implementation exceeding the requirements of EC law could be mentioned.[355] In many of these situations the question will arise whether the provisions of German law need to be interpreted in conformity with

---

[345] For criticism, see S. Lorenz, ' "Unternehmer—Unternehmerlein—Verbraucher": Ein neues Leitbild?' [2004] *Recht der internationalen Wirtschaft* issue 10, "Die erste Seite". On the complex problems arising under § 478 BGB, see M Jacobs, 'Der Rückgriff des Unternehmers nach § 478 BGB' [2004] *Juristenzeitung*, 225.

[346] See n 137 above and related text; and n 183 above and the following text.

[347] For full details, see Basedow, n 144 above, § 310, nn 18ff.

[348] See n 201 above and related text.   [349] § 495 BGB.   [350] § 505 BGB.

[351] See, for example, Krebs, n 336 above, § 241a, n 3; Heiderhoff, n 19 above 385 f.

[352] § 355 III 3 BGB.   [353] Art 4 of the Doorstep Selling Directive 85/577/EWG.

[354] See n 249 above and related text.

[355] See, for example, Wendehorst, n 222 above, § 312c, n 4.

the relevant Directive only so far as they are required by that Directive or so far as they constitute instances of an excessive implementation. From the point of view of EC law, national courts are under no duty to follow the second alternative.[356] Considerations concerning the systematic coherence of the national legal system, however, should normally prompt the courts to avoid a split interpretation as far as that is possible.[357] As a result, considerable parts of German contract law will have to be interpreted in conformity with some EC Directive or other, most notably a range of provisions of the general law of sale and the rules on standard terms of business. Many individual questions are disputed, as is the associated question to what extent German courts may (or perhaps even must) refer the relevant cases to the European Court of Justice.[358]

The Decision to Incorporate: An Evaluation

General Background

Freedom of Contract and Self-Determination

Has the decision to incorporate the consumer statutes into the BGB been right? An answer to this question has to take account of the fact that the development of consumer contract law reflects changes of perception affecting German contract law more generally. Of course, contract law is, and remains, based on freedom of contract.[359] But it has long been recognized that freedom of contract is not an end in itself: rather, it must be regarded as a means of promoting the self-determination of those who wish to conclude a contract. More than hundred years ago Rudolf von Jhering emphasized that he could not think of a more fatal mistake than

---

[356] U Büdenbender, 'Die Bedeutung der Verbrauchsgüterkaufrichtlinie für das deutsche Kaufrecht nach der Schuldrechtsreform' (2004) 12 *Zeitschrift für Europäisches Privatrecht* 36ff.

[357] See, apart from Büdenbender, ibid., M Habersack, 'Die überschiessende Umsetzung von Richtlinien' [1999] *Juristenzeitung* 913ff; P Hommelhoff, 'Die Rolle der nationalen Gerichte bei der Europäisierung des Privatrechts', in Canaris, Heldrich *et al*, n 158 above, vol. II (2000), 914ff.; Y Schnorbus, 'Autonome Harmonisierung in den Mitgliedstaaten durch die Inkorporation von Gemeinschaftsrecht' (2001) 65 *Rabels Zeitschrift für ausländisches und internationales Privatrecht* 654ff; C. Mayer and J. Schürnbrand, 'Einheitlich oder gespalten?—Zur Auslegung nationalen Rechts bei überschiessender Umsetzung von Richtlinien' [2004] *Juristenzeitung* 545ff.

[358] As far as the provisions on standard terms of business are concerned, see Basedow, n 144 above, Vor § 305, nn 45, 50.

[359] Canaris, n 193 above, 873ff; H. Kötz, 'Freiheit und Zwag im Vertragsrecht', in *Festschrift für Ernst-Joachim Mestmäcker* (1996), 1037ff; Drexl, n 19 above, 218ff; Heiderhoff, n 19 above, 295ff.

to imagine that any contract could justly claim the protection of the law, as long as its content was not illegal or immoral.[360] But his statement was of a prescriptive rather than descriptive character, for it did not correspond to the approach adopted by contemporary courts and writers towards general contract law. This approach, in turn, was rooted in a desire to prevent the state from tampering with the freedom to establish and carry on trade or industry—a freedom which had only just been secured with the enactment of the Trade Act of 1869.[361] Judicial control is a type of state control, and thus it was bound to appear as an undue interference with the private sphere of the individual citizen. The core of contract law, as it was to be embodied in the Civil Code, was to be kept free from such interference; it was to be based on the principles of freedom and equality.[362]

This view began to be challenged, towards the middle of the last century, by a theory focusing upon the conditions for the proper functioning of the market.[363] Contracts are supposed to bring about, without any interference on the part of the State, a 'just' result in a specific situation. This expectation is based upon the way in which a contract is concluded. The selfish will of one party alone does not ensure any correspondence between what that party wants and the precepts of substantive fairness. A proper balance is achieved only as a result of the other party having to agree: a requirement which allows that other party to bring his own interests to bear upon the content of the contract.[364] If the parties manage to reconcile their antagonistic interests, the balance established by them may be accepted as being just for them under the prevailing circumstances. If, on the other hand, the parties fail in this endeavour, a contract does not come into existence. This entails that no 'unjust' contract is concluded, ie a contract which fails to take account of the interests of both parties concerned. This model, however, is based upon certain preconditions. A contract cannot be the means of bringing about a just regulation in situations where one of the parties is typically deprived of his freedom of choice: for example, where he cannot make do without what is offered by the other party, or where he is in some other way dependent upon the

---

[360] R von Jhering, *Der Zweck im Recht*, 1877–1883, vol. I, 107ff.

[361] See n 76 above and related text.

[362] See generally Rückert, n 18 above, vol. I (2003), vor § 1, nn 39ff and *passim*.

[363] W Schmidt-Rimpler, 'Grundfragen einer Erneuerung des Vertragsrechts' (1941) 147 *Archiv für die civilistische Praxis* 130ff. Today see, among many others, M Habersack, 'Richtigkeitsgewähr notariell beurkundeter Verträge' (1989) 189 *Archiv für die civilistische Praxis*, 403ff; Heiderhoff, n 19 above, 300ff; L Fastrich, *Richterliche Inhaltskontrolle im Privatrecht* (1992) 29ff, 51ff.;

[364] Schmidt-Rimpler, n 363 above, 130, 151ff; cf also von Jhering, n 360 above, 103.

goods or services to be supplied by the latter. Nor can the contract fulfil its normal function where, for any other reason, a proper evaluation and balancing of the consequences of the transaction does not normally occur on the side of one of the parties concerned.[365] If, therefore, the legal community accepts a contract as the product of the self-determination of two parties, it has to exercise some kind of control as to whether a contract can in fact be regarded as the proper expression of the self-determination of both of these parties.[366]

A Combination of Criteria

This is the intellectual background for the Federal Supreme Court's use of § 242 BGB as a means of policing the substantive fairness of standard terms of business. These standard terms have been formulated in advance by one of the parties and, therefore, typically only reflect that party's interest. The other party, in turn, even if he is a businessman, does not usually regard it as worth his time and trouble to enter into negotiations about the content of these terms.[367] This is why judicial control is not limited to consumer contracts. The Federal Supreme Court's approach towards standard contract terms clearly illustrates one very important point: it is not the substantive unfairness of the contract term *per se* that justifies judicial interference, but the substantive unfairness in combination with another consideration explaining why the normal mechanisms of the market fail to bring about a just result. This specific combination of criteria, incidentally, merely develops the evaluations embodied in a key provision of the original BGB: § 138 II, the rule on 'usury'.[368] For it is not the excessive interest rate, or the exorbitant purchase price, as such that justifies the verdict of invalidity but only the striking disproportion in value between a performance and the pecuniary advantage paid, or promised to be paid, for it, plus an exploitation of the distress, gullibility or inexperience of the other party.[369] It is clear that, under these circumstances, the contract cannot be regarded as an expression of the self-determination of *both* parties concerned and as having led, typically, to a fairly balanced result.

---

[365] Schmidt-Rimpler, n 363 above, 130, 133f, 157f, 179ff; cf also Schmidt-Rimpler, 'Zum Problem der Geschäftsgrundlage' in R Dietz and H Hübner (eds), *Festschrift für Hans Carl Nipperdey zum 70. Geburtstag* (1965), 16ff; H Hübner, 'Zum Vertragsproblem', in F Baur, J Esser and F Kübler (eds), *Funktionswandel der Privatrechtsinstitutionen: Festschrift für Ludwig Raiser zum 70. Geburtstag* (1974), 12ff.

[366] A modern theory of consumer protection legislation along these lines has been developed by J Drexl, n 19 above. [367] See n 144 above and related text.

[368] See n 102 above and related text.

[369] The point is emphasized, particularly clearly, by Bydlinski, n 153 above, 753f and Canaris, n 108 above, 280f.

Close Family Members of the Main Debtor as Securities

Similar considerations have, more recently, induced German courts to tighten the control of contracts of suretyship concluded by close family members of the main debtor.[370] This development was initiated by a spectacular decision of the Federal Constitutional Court[371] enjoining the Federal Supreme Court, when applying open-ended provisions such as §§ 138 I and 242 BGB, to pay due attention to the guarantee of the autonomy of private individuals, as enshrined in Article 2 I of the Basic Law (*Grundgesetz*).[372] Such autonomy, the Court held, is not properly safeguarded by a regime of unrestricted freedom of contract. On the contrary, the civil courts are bound to control the content of contracts which are unusually burdensome for one of the parties and which result from a structural inequality of bargaining power. In this context, the Federal Constitutional Court pointed out that the parties engaging in private transactions are fundamentally equal, as regards the protection of their fundamental rights enshrined in the first part of the Basic Law. This fundamental equality would be disregarded if the right only of the more powerful party were to prevail. Where one of the parties dominates to such an extent that he can, for all practical purposes, unilaterally determine the content of the contract, the autonomy of the other party is replaced by a state of heteronomy. Of course, the maintenance of legal certainty makes it impossible for each and every contract to be scrutinized as to whether it is based on an inequality of bargaining power. In typical situations, however, where one party is in a structurally inferior position, the legal system has to come to his rescue in order to maintain private autonomy and to comply with the requirements of social responsibility.[373]

This decision of the Federal Constitutional Court has led to a far-reaching reappraisal of the German law of suretyship on the part of the Federal Supreme Court.[374] The doctrinal peg chosen for policing suretyship

---

[370] Habersack and Zimmermann, n 110 above, 272ff; Bydlinski, n 153 above, 760ff; Drexl, n 19 above, 263ff, 505ff; Remien, n 19 above, 356ff; for an overview of the more recent developments, see Heinrichs, n 233 above, § 138, nn 37ff; Stadler, n 233 above, § 765, n 4.

[371] BVerfGE 89, 214ff; cf also *Bundesverfassungsgericht* [1994] *Neue Juristische Wochenschrift* 2749f; *Bundesverfassungsgericht* [1996] *Zeitschrift für Wirtschaftsrecht* 956ff.

[372] Art 2 I GG, in spite of its more restrictive wording, has consistently been interpreted to establish 'a general right of freedom of action'. Of fundamental importance, in this respect, is the Elfes-decision of the Federal Constitutional Court: BVerfGE 6, 32ff; more recently, see BVerfGE 80, 137, 154ff ('Reiten im Wald' = horse riding in the forest).

[373] BVerfGE 89, 214, 233f; and see previously BVerfGE 81, 242, 255. On the principle of Germany as being a state with social responsibility (*Sozialstaatsprinzip*), see D P Currie, *The Constitution of the Federal Republic of Germany* (1994), 20ff.

[374] See, for example, *Bundesgerichtshof* [2002] *Neue Juristische Wochenschrift* 747.

transactions was § 138 I BGB: invalidity of contracts *contra bonos mores*. Significantly, the contract of suretyship concluded by a close relative of the main debtor is not to be regarded as void merely in view of the extent of the obligation incurred and the resulting condition of overindebtedness. For the Federal Supreme Court regards a striking discrepancy between the obligation incurred and the financial potential of the surety as only *one* of two elements sustaining the verdict of invalidity; there have to be additional circumstances indicating that the surety's ability to reach a free and responsible decision was impaired, thereby creating an intolerable imbalance between the contracting parties.[375] This is the case, for instance, if a spouse or descendant of the main debtor complies with the latter's wish in a situation of psychological distress, or as a result of lack of business experience. Essentially, in these cases, German courts have to have recourse to the general *contra bonos mores* provision for lack of a modern civilian notion of undue influence (or, as the lawyers of the earlier *ius commune* used to put it, *metus reverentialis*).[376]

Excessive Interest Rates

These decisions concerning suretyship contracts can be contrasted to another line of cases dating back to the late 1970s and involving loans repayable by instalments and granted by instalment credit institutions to consumers.[377] Such loans may be *contra bonos mores*, according to the Federal Supreme Court,[378] if there is an obvious disproportion between the obligations of the bank and of the borrower, and if the bank displayed a reprehensible attitude, either by deliberately exploiting the weaker economic position of the consumer, or by grossly negligently failing to realize that the latter entered into the contract only because of his precarious situation. This 'subjective' component, however, is of an almost fictitious character, since the courts are prepared to draw inferences from the objective circumstances of the contract (especially the disproportion in values) without requiring specific evidence as to whether the conduct in question was wilful or grossly negligent. Of central importance, therefore, is the interest rate charged by the bank, and here the rule has been

---

[375] Habersack and Zimmermann, n 110 above, 272, 281ff.

[376] J du Plessis and R Zimmermann, 'The Relevance of Reverence: Undue Influence Civilian Style' (2003) 10 Maastricht Journal of European and Comparative Law 345ff.

[377] V Emmerich, 'Rechtsfragen des Ratenkredits' [1988] *Juristische Schulung*, 925ff; Mayer-Maly/Armbrüster, n 106 above, § 138, nn 117ff; Heinrichs, n 233 above, § 138, nn 25ff; Jauernig, n 338 above, § 138, n 16.

[378] *Bundesgerichtshof* [1979] *Neue Juristische Wochenschrift* 805; *Bundesgerichtshof* [1979] *Neue Juristische Wochenschrift* 2089; BGHZ 80, 153, 160.

established that the effective rate of interest must not exceed the current interest rate by more than 100 per cent (relatively) or 12 to 13 per cent (absolutely). The Federal Supreme Court has based these pronouncements on the *contra bonos mores* provision of § 138 I BGB, thereby sidestepping the additional, restrictive requirements contained in § 138 II BGB. It has effectively established a thinly veiled interest control for consumer loans. This is incompatible with the basic evaluations of German contract law and the existing economic order, and it cannot be justified by merely pointing out that the borrower is a consumer and, as such, finds himself always and necessarily in a weaker position.[379] More plausible, as a point of departure for interfering with excessive interest rates in consumer credit situations, would have been the impairment of the consumer's ability to reach a free and responsible decision resulting from the lack of transparency that used to be associated with instalment credit transactions: for the way in which these contracts were drafted tended to make it difficult for inexperienced customers of instalment credit banks to gauge the effective annual rate of interest charged to them. The problem has subsequently been taken care of by § 492 BGB (previously § 4 VerbrKrG) in that the document containing the consumer loan contract (which has to be signed by the borrower) must indicate, *inter alia*, the effective interest rate, including all charges applicable to the loan, and also the costs of insuring the outstanding balance of the loan. Thus, the notorious transparency problems can no longer be used as an explanation for the judicial control of an interest rate agreed between a credit institution and its fully informed customer. Apart from that, the borrower's right of termination according to § 489 (previously § 609a) BGB provides the consumer with an opportunity to extricate himself from charges which he subsequently considers to be too burdensome.

Consumer Protection

The legitimacy of specific rules concerning consumer contracts has to be assessed in the light of these developments. Such rules should not, from the outset, be denounced as constituting inappropriate infringements of the freedom of the parties to make their own contractual arrangements. Rather, they may be seen as legitimate attempts to sustain private autonomy by providing mechanisms which aim at preventing contracts from coming into existence, or from being enforced, which cannot be regarded as the result of acts of self-determination of *both* parties concerned.[380]

---

[379] H Koziol, 'Sonderprivatrecht für Konsumentenkredite?' (1988) 188 *Archiv für die civilistische Praxis* 197ff; Canaris, n 108 above, 300ff.

[380] See recently, above all, Drexl, n 19 above; Drexl, n 153 above, 109ff.

These rules can therefore make an essential contribution towards the proper functioning of a market economy based on freedom of contract. However, they can only be accepted as legitimate to the extent that they are indeed suitable to remedy the impairment of a contractual party's self-determination. In the interests of legal certainty, of course, the law has to typify; it cannot intervene in each individual case where such impairment has occurred or is impending. Nor should the law use indeterminable criteria such as whether one party is in an economically weaker, or inferior, position compared to the other. And, above all, it may not object to contract terms merely because they are unduly burdensome to one of the parties concerned. Of central importance is the inquiry whether, for some reason or other, that party has not been able to influence the content of the contract in a way which can lead the legal community typically to accept it as representing a just balance of both parties' interests.

The Main Devices for Protecting Consumers

The main devices used by German law, in this context, are the imposition of duties of information on the entrepreneur, the granting of a right of revocation to the consumer, the establishment of mandatory rules of law, or even contractual regimes, and, of course, the notion of 'consumer'.[381]

Duties of Information

The imposition of duties of information is the mildest form of legal intervention.[382] It does not constitute an interference with the principle of

---

[381] There are, of course, other devices such as the establishment form requirements (see §§ 484, 492, 655b BGB; the former two are based on EC Directives; generally on form requirements contained in EC Directives: see P Bydlinski, 'Formgebote für Rechtsgeschäfte und die Folgen ihrer Verletzung' in R Schulze, M Ebers and H C Grigoleit (eds), *Informationspflichten und Vertragsschluss im Acquis communautaire* (2003), 141ff; Rösler, n 16 above, 148ff); or the reversal of the onus of proof (see, for example, § 476 BGB); or the right, granted to consumers who have taken up a loan in order to finance another contract, to raise defences available to them under the contract financed by the consumer loan transaction against the party with whom they have concluded the consumer loan transaction, provided both contracts can be regarded as 'linked contracts' (*verbundene Geschäfte*): § 359 BGB. The first two devices are well known outside the area of consumer contract law; see, for example, the form requirements introduced by the draftsmen of the original BGB in §§ 313 (old version), 518 and 766 for contracts for sale of land, donation, and suretyship (for comment, see Zimmermann, n 23 above, 85ff), and the reversal of the onus of proof effected by the courts in order to cope with the problem of product liability (see, for example, Medicus, n 176 above, nn 650ff). The rule in § 359 BGB, deviating from the well-established principle governing *exceptiones ex iure tertii*, essentially constitutes a codification of the rules developed by the German courts on the basis of § 6 AbzG (prohibition of evading the provisions of the Act concerning Instalment Sales); on which see H P Westermann, in *Münchener Kommentar zum Bürgerlichen Gesetzbuch*, vol. III/I (2nd edn., 1988), § 6 AbzG, nn 23ff.

[382] See, for example, Bydlinski, n 153 above, 741ff.

pacta sunt servanda but attempts to ensure that both parties' decision to contract rests on firm foundations. Duties of information, therefore, can be regarded as a means of strengthening adherence to *pacta sunt servanda*. Over the years, a host of very specific duties of information has been laid down, first in various consumer protection statutes, now in the BGB and the Duties of Information in Private Law Regulation.[383] They relate to transactions typically involving an informational deficit on the part of the consumer *vis-à-vis* the entrepreneur: because they are of considerable complexity (eg timeshare agreements), entail the use of new technologies and the specific risks associated with it (e-commerce), do not provide the consumer with an opportunity to see the product or ascertain the nature of the service before concluding the contract (distance contracts, package holidays), are notoriously non-transparent (consumer credit), etc. The information provided by the entrepreneur is designed to place consumers who are about to embark on these types of transactions in a position to make a free and responsible choice.[384] This is, in principle, an excellent idea. At the same time, however, it is vaguely reminiscent of some of the utopian ideals of the Age of Enlightenment. In the first place, many people are resistant to any form of forced instruction: they simply do not read lengthy standard business documents presented to them. Second, and more importantly, the amount of obligatory information descending upon the consumer does not always lead to an exemplary state of transparency: a consumer faced with an information overload can be as unable to take a well-informed decision as one who has not been informed at all.[385] The imposition of duties of information on the entrepreneur, in other words, does not always remedy the informational deficit of the consumer.[386]

Consumer contracts are transactions between an entrepreneur (ie a person who acts in his professional capacity) and a consumer (ie a person

---

[383] See n 303 above and related text.

[384] See, eg Dauner-Lieb, n 152 above, 62ff; R. Kemper, *Verbraucherschutzinstrumente* (1994), 33ff, 186ff; B. Lurger, *Vertragliche Solidarität*, (1998), 14ff; Repgen, n 19 above, 90ff; Riesenhuber, n 19 above, 292ff; Remien, n 19 above, 270ff.; Heiderhoff, n 19 above, 366ff; Rösler, n 16 above, 142ff. For an analysis of the concept of the informed consumer and its implementation in the primary and secondary EC law, see H Fleischer, 'Vertragsschlussbezogene Informationspflichten im Gemeinschaftsprivatrecht' (2000) 8 *Zeitschrift für Europäisches Privatrecht*, 781ff; S Grundmann, 'Privatautonomie im Binnenmarkt: Informationsregeln als Instrument' [2000] *Juristenzeitung*, 1133ff; Repgen, n 19 above, 31ff.

[385] Cf also Martinek, n 199 above, 1393, 1395f, 1399, concerning the Timeshare Agreements Act: 'Crushing masses of information which threaten to choke the consumer . . .'; generally H Roth, 'EG-Richtlinien und Bürgerliches Recht' [1999] *Juristenzeitung* 533 ('inflationary use' of duties of information); Bydlinski, n 153 above, 758f.

[386] For further discussion, see Rösler, n 16 above, 151ff.

who is not professionally involved in transactions of this kind). Thus, they can reasonably be taken to constitute typical situations of imbalance in the level of information available to the contracting parties. But they are not the only situations. The rules on the avoidance of contracts for mistake and fraudulent non-disclosure[387] as well as the rules on non-conformity[388] can be seen as attempts to cope with informational imbalances on a more general level. Moreover, the past decades have seen a significant expansion of differentiated duties of disclosure under the label of *culpa in contrahendo*[389] inspired, ultimately, by an increased sensitivity for the requirements of good faith.[390] One of the great challenges posed by these developments consists in an intellectual coordination of the general and the specifically consumer-oriented duties of information on the level both of policy and legal doctrine. This, presumably, will be a two-way process. For just as it should be possible to domesticate the jungle of informational requirements concerning individual consumer contracts, so these requirements can act as pointers as to what is owed, more generally, in situations of an informational imbalance.[391] At the same time, it is clear that the issues raised pertain to the core of contract law and should be discussed in that context.

Right of Revocation

'Being Caught Off-Guard'

An informational asymmetry is not the only potential source of objectionable imbalances in contracts concluded between consumers and entrepreneurs. Another situation where consumers may be tempted to enter into contracts which are detrimental to their own interests and which therefore, upon sober reflection, they subsequently regret, is the one where they are caught 'off their guard'. This typically happens where the contract is negotiated away from the business premises of the entrepreneur: particularly where the entrepreneur visits the consumer at his house, or place of work, without having been asked to do so, but also

---

[387] For full details, see H Fleischer, *Informationsasymmetrie im Vertragsrecht* (2001), 244ff, 336ff.   [388] Ibid, 469ff.

[389] See the detailed analysis in ibid, 416ff; Grigoleit, n 108 above, 50ff. The doctrine of *culpa in contrahendo* as a tool for 'materialising' contract law is also discussed by Canaris, n 108 above, 304ff.

[390] For a succinct overview, see Mansel, n 318 above, § 242, nn 19f Fleischer describes the existence of duties of information at the pre-contractual stage as a core element of (modern) European private law: 'Vertragsschlußbezogene Informationspflichten im Gemeinschaftsprivatrecht' (2000) 8 *Zeitschrift für Europäisches Privatrecht*, 772; cf also H Kötz, *European Contract Law* (1997) (tr. T. Weir), 198ff.

[391] See, along the same lines, Fleischer, n 387 above, 207f, 570ff.

where the entrepreneur uses the opportunity of a chance encounter on the street, or in a bus or subway, in order to talk the consumer into the contract, or where the parties have met at a social event.[392] In all these situations the consumer is unprepared for the negotiations, and also usually unable to compare the quality and price of the offer with other offers. Thus, it is the surprise element which puts the consumer at a specific disadvantage.[393] Here it appears to be reasonable to allow for a 'cooling-off period', in the form of a right subsequently to revoke the contract.[394] The period within which this right may be exercised has been increased, in the course of the modernization of the German law of obligations, from one week to two.[395] An informational component has been incorporated by providing that the period only begins when the consumer has been informed by a clearly formulated notice of his right of revocation.[396]

Obviously, the granting of a right of revocation is a more serious interference with the freedom of the parties to regulate their own affairs than the imposition of specific duties of information.[397] After all, it entails a qualification of the principle of *pacta sunt servanda*. Compared to other qualifications of that principle (right of termination in case of breach of contract, right of rescission on account of fraud or threats, *clausula rebus sic stantibus*) it is entirely novel in that the consumer does not have to adduce any reason for revoking the contract. He may exercise his right of revocation simply because he regrets the transaction. On the other hand, however, we are still dealing here with a procedural device for coping with a potential source of contractual imbalance.[398] The contract, in a way, has to be treated as if it had been subjected to a resolutive condition. There is, at first, a state of pendency, at the end of which the contract either remains effective exactly as it has been concluded, or it fails altogether. In particular, therefore, the granting of a right of revocation avoids any necessity for judicial interference with the substance of the contract. Also, it can be

---

[392] For the range of situations covered by the German term 'doorstep transaction' (*Haustürgeschäft*), see § 312 I nos 1–3; and see Ulmer, n 236 above, § 312, nn 33ff.

[393] Canaris, n 108 above, 346ff; Ulmer, n 236 above, Vor §§ 312, 312a, n 1; Wiedenmann, n 19 above, 242ff; Mankowski, n 242 above, 224ff.

[394] § 312 BGB.

[395] See § 355 I 2 BGB, as opposed to § 1 I HaustürWG; for criticism, see Drexl, n 153 above, 124f.   [396] § 355 II BGB.

[397] Henrich, n 153 above, 204ff ('. . . the most serious interference with the prevailing principles of contract law'); Remien, n 19 above, 334. Remien (328ff) draws attention to the fact that the granting of a right of revocation can be regarded as an alternative to the establishment of a form requirement; he even refers to the right of revocation as the 'ordinary man's form requirement' (328). Kemper, n 384 above, 220ff also deals with form requirements and rights of revocation under the same heading.

[398] Canaris, n 108 above, 344f; Rösler, n 16 above, 172ff.

argued that it constitutes a more efficient means of protecting the consumer than having recourse to general devices such as invalidity under § 138 I BGB, or restitution in terms of *culpa in contrahendo*, since, while the consumer will usually be unaware of his legal position in general, he has to be informed about his right to revoke which he must then exercise within a relatively short period of time.[399]

Even if the right of revocation is a novel addition to the remedial armoury available, in certain situations to certain types of disappointed customer, the substantive concern motivating the introduction of this right is not novel at all. If someone uses a situation where another person is unable, for some reason or other, properly to collect his thoughts and evaluate his legal position, in order to secure a contract which is disadvantageous to that other person, the contract can be regarded as *contra bonos mores* and, therefore, void.[400] Alternatively, a person who has been caught off-guard can be granted protection against an unwelcome contract concluded in this situation by means of a claim based on *culpa in contrahendo*.[401] Once again, therefore, the problem is of a more general nature and does not lend itself to an isolated regulation in a consumer contract code. Characteristically, in his report on a possible codification of the law relating to *culpa in contrahendo*, Medicus included the problem of protection against unwelcome contracts and proposed a general rule granting a right of revocation to every person who has been 'caught off guard' in the conclusion of a contract.[402] This was to be followed by a number of provisions containing details of the right of revocation and granting a claim for compensation in other situations of *culpa in contrahendo*.[403]

Other Policy Considerations

German law, following European Community law in that respect, not only provides for a right of revocation in doorstep selling (and similar)[404] situations, but also with regard to timeshare agreements and distance

---

[399] Canaris, n 108 above, 345; cf also Remien, n 19 above, 330.

[400] See, for example, D Medicus, 'Verschulden bei Vertragsverhandlungen' in Bundesminister der Justiz (ed), *Gutachten und Vorschläge zur Überarbeitung des Schuldrechts*, vol. I (1981), 520; *Bundesgerichtshof* [1997] *Neue Juristische Wochenschrift* 1980.

[401] See, for example, S Lorenz, *Der Schutz vor dem unerwünschten Vertrag* (1997), 445ff; Lorenz, 'Vertragsaufhebung wegen unzulässiger Einflussnahme auf die Entscheidungsfreiheit: Der BGH auf dem Weg zur reinen Abschlusskontrolle?' [1997] *Neue Juristische Wochenschrift* 2578ff.; Stadler, n 233 above, § 311, n 62; V Emmerich, in *Münchener Kommentar zum Bürgerlichen Gesetzbuch* vol. 2a (4th edn., 2003), § 311, n 116.

[402] Medicus, n 400 above, 519ff, 531, 548; cf also Kemper, n 384 above, 255.

[403] Medicus, n 400 above, 548ff. It must be borne in mind, in this respect, that compensation has to be made, in the first place, 'in kind'; ie the aggrieved party has to be restored to his former position: § 249 BGB.   [404] See n 392 above and related text.

contracts.[405] In addition, there are rights of revocation concerning consumer credit transactions,[406] instalment supply contracts,[407] and distance teaching contracts,[408] none of them based on EC law. What is the justification for jeopardizing the principle of *pacta sunt servanda* in such a variety of individual instances? The right of revocation with regard to doorstep contracts, as we have seen, is 'situation-specific'.[409] It is granted because the consumer has been caught off-guard and needs an extra-period for cool reflection. The same argument cannot be advanced to justify the right of revocation in the case of consumer credit transactions. Here it is maintained that the consumer requires the extra-period in view of the great economic significance as well as the considerable complexity of this type of transaction.[410] A careful examination of the obligations incurred by him will often lead the borrower to have second thoughts and to reconsider his decision to take up the loan; moreover, he may be able to find credit institutions offering more favourable terms. These arguments, however, are hardly convincing. The consumer has been under no pressure to rush into the contract; he could easily have assessed the obligations to be incurred by him before concluding the contract. This is so even if the relevant information only has to be provided in the contract form which must be signed by the borrower/consumer:[411] he is entirely free to take that document home for close scrutiny before signing it. It is not clear why the consumer should need another two weeks after conclusion of the contract. Also, an extra-period of two weeks does not appear to be a suitable means to achieve the aim for which it has been granted. It is usually much later that the borrower begins to feel how onerous the obligations undertaken by him actually are and that he may have overestimated his ability to meet them.[412] A right of termination such as the one granted in § 489 I no. 2 BGB is both more suitable and quite sufficient to meet these concerns.

Timeshare Agreements

The right of revocation in consumer credit transactions can be regarded as 'type-of-transaction-specific' as opposed to 'situation-specific'; the policy

---

[405] §§ 312d I 1, 485 I BGB.   [406] § 495 I BGB.   [407] § 505 I 1 BGB.
[408] § 4 I FernUSG.

[409] For the distinction between 'situation-specific' and 'type-of-transaction-specific' rights of revocation, see Mankowski, n 242 above, 222ff; Canaris, n 108 above, 346ff; a similar, though more refined, typology has been proposed by Lurger, n 384 above, 33ff; S Kalss and B Lurger, 'Zu einer Systematik der Rücktrittsrechte insbesondere im Verbraucherrecht' [1998] *Juristische Blätter* 153ff.

[410] P Ulmer in *Münchener Kommentar zum Bürgerlichen Gesetzbuch*, vol. III (4th edn., 2004), § 495, n 2; Mankowski, n 242 above, 239ff.   [411] § 492 I 5 BGB.

[412] Medicus, n 400 above, 524; Lorenz, n 401 above, 191; and see Kemper, n 384 above, 255ff; Remien, n 19 above, 335 for further critical comment.

considerations supporting it, however, are unconvincing. The right of revocation concerning timeshare agreements is often granted under both heads.[413] For, on the one hand, the complexity of these transactions, and the associated lack of transparency, are widely advanced as arguments supporting the granting of an extra-period for sober deliberation:[414] the consumer has to be protected against the danger of precipitately rushing into the contract. On the other hand, attention is drawn to the aggressive marketing methods often pursued by timeshare salesmen and aimed at customers charmed by the attractions of southern holiday resorts.[415] The former consideration focuses on the type of transaction, whereas the latter aspect is a situative one. Once again, however, the former consideration is unconvincing, both in itself and in the way in which it is implemented. The advantages deriving from a timeshare agreement, and the burdens associated with it, often become apparent only after a considerable period[416] and not within two weeks after the consumer has received notice of his right of revocation (which normally happens when the contract is concluded). Even if such two-week-period were meaningful, account would have to be taken of the fact that the consumer cannot realistically be expected to unravel the details of the transaction, to ponder its financial consequences, and possibly to exercise his right of revocation, until after his return home.[417] The second, situative, aspect is much more plausible but does not require the introduction of a right of revocation for timeshare agreements: it is quite adequately taken care of by the provisions concerning contracts negotiated away from business premises.[418]

Instalment Supply Contracts, Distance Contracts, Distance Teaching Contracts

Instalment supply contract are another type of transaction with regard to which consumers have been granted a right of revocation.[419] The specific

---

[413] M Franzen, in *Münchener Kommentar zum Bürgerlichen Gesetzbuch* vol. III (4th edn., 2004), § 485, n 1; cf also Riesenhuber, n 19 above, 329ff; but see Mankowski, n 242 above, 241f.

[414] See, for example, Heinrichs, n 233 above, § 485, n 1; Mankowski, n 242 above, 241f.

[415] Franzen, n 413 above, Vor § 481, n 12, and § 485, n 1; cf also Martinek, n 199 above, 1393.   [416] This is conceded also by Mankowski, n 242 above, 241.

[417] Martinek, n 199 above, 1393, 1397; the same point is made, in a different context, by Drexl, n 153 above, 124. Martinek also argues that the establishment of a form requirement (the execution of a notarial instrument) would have been more in tune with the German legal system and would, moreover, have offered better protection to the purchaser: n 199 above, 1393, 1396; cf also Remien, n 19 above, 329.

[418] The sales methods of timeshare salesmen are often covered by § 312 BGB; see Franzen, n 413 above, § 485, n 6; Riesenhuber, n 19 above, 331. According to § 312a BGB, however, if a doorstep transaction also falls within the scope of the provisions on timeshare contracts, only the latter provisions prevail.

[419] It dates back to § 1 b AbzG; see n 118 above and related text.

temptation arising from the fact that the consumer is immediately able to use an object which he only has to pay for later, which has been noted for a long time,[420] does not change the fact that a right of revocation which has to be exercised (normally) within two weeks after conclusion of the contract is hardly a suitable means for protecting consumers from yielding to this temptation.[421]

The right of revocation in § 312d BGB (distance contracts) is supposed to take account of the fact that the consumer, prior to concluding the contract, does not have an opportunity to see the goods to be purchased and to assess their quality.[422] Here it may be argued that the consumer, when using one of the means of distance communication, and particularly those provided by the new technologies, must be quite aware of these disadvantages. Thus, it can hardly be maintained that his right of self-determination is impaired in any way. On the other hand, however, the right of revocation may be seen as a legitimate incentive for entrepreneurs to enhance the quality of their goods so as to minimize the return of these goods as a result of the contract being revoked.[423] The right of revocation, in other words, counteracts the temptation inherent in distance contracts to land customers with products which are unfit for their intended use, in that it places the customer, as far as possible, in the same situation as if he had bought the object in a shop. It is in tune with this rationale that the two-week period does not start to run until the goods reach the recipient.[424] At the same time it must be said that the right of revocation will usually fail to serve a meaningful function when it comes to the supply of services by way of distance contracts[425] as, under § 312d III BGB, the right of revocation expires if the entrepreneur has begun to provide the service with the consent of the consumer before the end of the revocation period.

The right of revocation granted by § 4 Distance Teaching Act can be justified with the same argument, as for distance sales, particularly in view of the fact that the two-week period does not commence before the first instalment of the distance teaching material has been received by the customer.[426]

---

[420] See, as early as 1890, P Heck, *Verhandlungen des Einundzwanzigsten Deutschen Juristentags* (1891), vol. II, 148. Today, see Canaris, n 108 above, 348ff; Wiedenmann, n 19 above, 243ff. [421] Medicus, n 400 above, 524ff.

[422] Wendehorst, n 222 above, § 312d, n 1; Mankowski, n 242 above, 235f; Wiedenmann, n 19 above, 238ff; cf also Riesenhuber, n 19 above, 326ff; Kalss and Lurger [1998] *Juristische Blätter* 155ff; Rösler, n 16 above, 173ff.

[423] Mankowski, n 242 above, 236ff. [424] § 312 d II BGB.

[425] Wendehorst, n 222 above, § 312d, n 2.

[426] Mankowski, n 242 above, 238ff; but see the criticism advanced by Medicus, n 400 above, 523ff.

Every right of revocation has to be based on a convincing policy consideration,[427] otherwise the path will inevitably lead to a generalized right of revocation in consumer/entrepreneur relationships, as has indeed been proposed.[428] This, in turn, would tend to set consumer law apart from the concerns of general contract law. Recognition of the 'complexity' or 'economic significance' of a transaction as bases for a right of revocation[429] are unfortunate steps in that direction.

Unilaterally Mandatory Rules of Law

Specific Protective Rules

Another hallmark of modern consumer protection legislation is the establishment of mandatory, or rather unilaterally mandatory, rules of law.[430] These are rules which may not be departed from to the detriment of the consumer, though the parties remain free to agree upon a legal regime more favourable to the consumer.[431] This is no longer a merely procedural device but one that substantially impinges upon the freedom of the parties to regulate the content of their contract. At the same time, it is a very familiar device. The BGB in its original form contained a number of mandatory rules that were designed to ensure a minimum level of decency in business life,[432] that were intended to guard against the dangers associated with specific types of transaction[433] or that were aimed to protect a weaker party from being taken advantage of.[434] Even the establishment of legal regimes that were unilaterally mandatory was not

---

[427] The point is emphasized also by Canaris, n 108 above, 345 and Remien, n 19 above, 341 (who calls on the EC to re-examine the existing rights of revocation and develop a convincing general scheme).

[428] H-W Micklitz, 'Perspektiven eines Europäischen Privatrechts' (1998) 6 *Zeitschrift für Europäisches Privatrecht* 265.

[429] See n 410 above and related text. The same point is made by Kemper, n 384 above, 256.

[430] See, most recently, J Drexl, 'Zwingendes Recht als Strukturprinzip des Europäischen Verbrauchervertragsrechts?', in M Coester (ed), *Privatrecht in Europa: Vielfalt, Kollision, Kooperation—Festschrift für Hans Jürgen Sonnenbergers* (2004), 771ff. Generally on the role of mandatory rules of contract law, see Remien, n 19 above, 461ff and *passim*.

[431] See § 312f BGB (concerning §§ 312ff BGB on doorstep transactions, distance contracts and e-commerce); § 475 BGB (covering consumer sales); § 487 BGB (concerning §§ 481ff on timeshare agreements); § 506 BGB (concerning §§ 491ff on consumer loans, financing aids, and instalment supply contracts); § 651m BGB (concerning §§ 651a ff on package travel contracts); § 655e (concerning §§ 655a ff on loan brokerage contracts). In other cases the unilaterally mandatory character has to be established by way of interpretation; see Ulmer, n 236 above, § 355, n 4 (concerning §§ 355ff on the right of revocation).

[432] See, for example, §§ 138, 276 II, 443, 476, 540, 637 BGB.

[433] See, in particular, the form requirements in §§ 313, 518, 766 BGB (sale of land, donation, suretyship).

[434] See, for example, §§ 247 I, 248 I, 343, 559 3, 617–619, 624 BGB. In earlier nineteenth century legislation we also find mandatory rules; see Repgen, n 19 above, 14, 80f.

unknown: § 225 BGB which used to allow the parties to facilitate prescription, especially by providing for a period that is shorter than the statutory one, while it refused to recognize agreements rendering prescription more difficult, particularly by extending the statutory period, provides an example.[435]

In modern consumer legislation, of course, the protective purpose of mandatory rules of law prevails; this also explains why we are dealing with unilaterally mandatory rules. The rules elevated to this status are, in the first place, the ones already discussed in the preceding sections: those imposing duties of information on the entrepreneur and granting rights of revocation to the consumer. If they are considered necessary in order to ensure that a contract concluded between consumer and entrepreneur can typically be regarded as the proper product of the self-determination of both parties, it appears reasonable to prevent the parties from sidestepping the protection by way of private agreement (though this may be questionable in cases where that agreement itself can be regarded as the proper product of the self-determination not only of the entrepreneur but also of the consumer). Second, there are other rules specifically aiming at the protection of the consumer which are of a unilaterally mandatory character: the form requirements concerning timeshare agreements or consumer credit contracts,[436] the provision dealing with the remuneration of the contractor under a loan brokerage contract,[437] etc.

Policing Types of Contract

But German law, following (or anticipating) the respective European Community Directives, has gone much further: it has converted either the entire regime governing the details of specific types of contract, or large parts of it, to a (unilaterally) mandatory status. In some ways, this comes close to the comprehensive control established for standard terms of business in §§ 307ff BGB (and the respective provisions of the Unfair Terms in Consumer Contracts Directive)[438]. The BGB contains two

---

[435] A large number of unilaterally mandatory rules can also be found in the Insurance Contract Act of 1908; see Roth, n 59 above, 79, 503.   [436] §§ 484, 492 BGB.

[437] § 655 c BGB.

[438] W-H Roth, therefore, deals with all three sets of rules under the heading 'control of the contractual content': n 233 above, 475, 481; cf also Drexl, n 153 above, 125ff. On the relationship between the control of unfair standard terms and mandatory law (*ius cogens*), see Remien, n 19 above, 469ff; cf also Fastrich, n 363 above, 5ff, who draws a distinction between control of the contractual content in a wide and a narrow sense. There is, of course, one crucial difference in that mandatory rules of law cannot be derogated from even by individually negotiated agreements; their interference with the freedom of the parties, formally conceived, to conclude their own contract is thus even more serious than the control of unfair standard terms. German law, therefore, today distinguishes between *ius*

types of contract of this kind. One is the consumer sale, the other the package travel contract.[439] In the one case, large areas of general contract law as well as the specific rules on consumer sales cannot be departed from,[440] in the other case the entire statutory regime governing package travel contracts has become unilaterally mandatory.[441] Again, however, we are dealing here with an issue that cannot be separated from the development of contract law in general. §§ 307ff BGB provide the best confirmation for this assertion, for the policing of unfair standard terms of business is not confined to consumer contracts but covers, in principle, all types of transaction.[442] Before the introduction of the Standard Terms of Business Act in 1976, the courts had arrogated to themselves the power to strike down unfair standard terms under the general provision of § 242 BGB.[443] Also, the key decisions subsequently enshrined, in statutory form, in §§ 651a ff BGB, were arrived at by the Federal Supreme Court under general contract law.[444] In the meantime, there are other instances where the courts have started to control the content of specific types of transaction: be it on the basis of § 138 I BGB (as in the case of matrimonial property agreements)[445] or even of § 242 BGB (as in the case of contracts concluded on the basis of standard provisions preformulated by a notary).[446] At the same time, incorporation of the provisions on consumer sales and package travel contracts into the BGB serves as a reminder to always check very carefully whether, or to what extent, new rules are justifiable within a general body of law characterized by the notion of freedom of contract.

---

dispositivum (which is, of course, still the rule in contract law), rules of law which are mandatory *vis-à-vis* standard terms of business, and rules of law which are mandatory *vis-à-vis* individually negotiated agreements: Remien, n 19 above, 471ff and, generally, D. Medicus, *Schuldrecht I, Allgemeiner Teil* (15th edn., 2004), nn 86ff.

[439] A third type of contract with regard to which German law has, very largely, established a mandatory regime is the lease of residential accommodation; for the justification of which, see Fastrich, n 363 above, 109ff. The respective body of law which has developed around the cornerstones of notice protection and rent control has been built up, after the Second World War, by way of special legislation, ie outside the BGB. In the summer of 2001, it has largely been incorporated into the BGB (*Mietrechtsreformgesetz, Bundesgesetzblatt* (as in n 165) I, 1149; see, today, §§ 549ff BGB). Distance teaching contracts and loan transactions are two other areas of the law dominated by mandatory rules; cf § 9 FernUSG and §§ 491ff BGB.

[440] § 475 I BGB.   [441] § 651m BGB.

[442] See n 142 above and the following text; n 193 above and the following text.

[443] See n 134 above and related text.   [444] See n 123 above and related text.

[445] See, for example, G Brudermüller, in *Palandt, Bürgerliches Gesetzbuch*, 63rd edn., (2004), § 1408, nn 7ff; cf also I Schwenzer, 'Vertragsfreiheit im Ehevermögens- und Scheidungsfolgenrecht' (1996) 196 *Archiv für die civilistische Praxis* 111ff (arguing for the application of § 242 BGB).

[446] BGHZ 101, 350, 353 and G H Roth, in *Münchener Kommentar zum Bürgerlichen Gesetzbuch* vol. 2a (4th edn., 2003), § 242, n 436. For criticism, see D Medicus, *Zur*

It has been argued, above, that duties of information and the introduction of rights of revocation can serve as legitimate tools to strengthen the self-determination of both parties and thus effectively to fortify the notion of freedom of contract.[447] The same can be said about the judicial control of unfair contract terms[448] as well as for a variety of mandatory rules of law.[449] Whether the unilaterally mandatory regime for consumer sales and package travel contracts also meets this standard is much more doubtful.[450] So, for example, there does not appear to be any good reason why a consumer should not be able, by way of individually negotiated agreement (!), to buy a second-hand car on the basis of a complete exemption of the entrepreneur/seller from his liability for latent defects, in return for a reduced purchase price.[451] In fact, it has been argued that under the new regime some people may no longer be able to afford to buy a car.[452] The imposition of mandatory rules of law can also be prejudicial to private autonomy in view of the schematic approach necessarily adopted by them. It is not easy to see why a pastor or sports club, organising a day trip, should be subject to the doctrinal corset tailored by §§ 651a ff BGB. Again, however, it must be said that many mandatory rules of law not specifically motivated by consumer concerns meet with a similar objection. It hardly appears to be appropriate, for example, for a widow letting a flat within her house to a solicitor to have to draw his attention, in her letter giving notice of termination, to the possibility of filing an objection against such notice, and to the form in which, and

---

gerichtlichen Inhaltskontrolle notarieller Verträge (1989); Fastrich, n 363 above, 94ff Today § 310 III BGB will largely prevail in these cases; see Heiderhoff, n 19 above, 428ff.

[447] See pp. 471ff.

[448] See n 142 above and the following text. For a general theory of the phenomenon of judicial control of individually and not individually negotiated terms, see Fastrich, n 363 above, 29ff, 215ff.

[449] The point is made by Kötz, n 359 above, 1037ff; Repgen, n 19 above, 9ff and *passim*; Drexl, n 430 above, 780ff.

[450] For particularly forceful criticism, concerning consumer sales, see Canaris, n 108 above, 362ff; cf. also Drexl, n 430 above, 786ff; contra: Repgen, n 19 above, 98ff. Generally, see Fastrich, n 363 above, 117ff; Riesenhuber, n 19 above, 490ff. The Consumer Sales Directive attempts to justify the far-reaching restriction of private autonomy by pointing out that 'the legal protection afforded to consumers would be thwarted', if they were able to restrict or waive the rights granted to them (recital 22). This, however, is no more than a restatement of the assertion for which a good reason would have had to be advanced; see Canaris, n 108 above, 362f; Drexl, 153 above, 126. Heiderhoff, n 19 above, 326 even quite generally asserts that freedom of contract is neither the basis nor the aim of European community legislation.

[451] S Lorenz, in *Münchener Kommentar zum Bürgerlichen Gesetzbuch*, vol. 3 (4th edn., 2004), § 475, n 9; K Adomeit, 'Das Günstigkeitsprinzip—jetzt auch beim Kaufvertrag' [2003] *Juristenzeitung* 1053ff; Drexl, n 430 above, 778.

[452] Canaris, n 108 above, 363.

period within which, the objection has to be raised.[453] Moreover, it should also be borne in mind that individually negotiated agreements are hardly of great importance with regard to package travel contracts, distance teaching contracts, and probably also consumer sales; and that the necessity of so strictly regulating these types of transactions can be seriously questioned in view of the control devices contained in the Standard Terms of Business Act.

The Definition of 'Consumer'

Who is to benefit from the various protective devices so liberally spread across the new German law of obligations? Essentially, the legal system has two options. It can either attempt to establish a flexible system which would allow for a supple levelling-out of structural, or situative, imbalances (concerning information, freedom of choice, etc.) between two parties to a contract.[454] While such an approach would have the advantages of being based, directly, on the substantive concern motivating the introduction of rules of law of a protective character, and of targeting only those who actually deserve to be protected, the disadvantage necessarily associated with it is equally obvious: a considerable lack of legal certainty. Both European law and German law have, therefore, understandably pursued the second option: by focusing on the concept of 'consumer' they have endeavoured to tie the application of the relevant body of law to specific criteria which can be applied easily in practice. They have, in other words, adopted a typological approach.[455] At the same time they have had to accept the inevitable drawback of occasionally offering protection to parties who do not deserve to be protected—the professor of law who buys a book, the car mechanic who acquires an exhaust pipe for his private vehicle, the bank director who takes up a loan in order to buy a family home[456]—and of occasionally not offering protection to parties who deserve to be protected.

These examples also demonstrate that German law does not attempt to conceptualize the term consumer as a kind of legal status:[457] a certain

---

[453] § 568 II BGB (previously § 564a II BGB old version). The rule, in spite of its wording, is of a mandatory character: W Weidenkaff, in *Palandt, Bürgerliches Gesetzbuch* (63rd edn., 2004), § 568, n 3.

[454] See, along these lines, Bydlinski, n 153 above, 766ff who wishes to recognize a 'control principle'. Cf also Medicus, n 19 above, 485ff; Dreher, n 19 above, 170; H Koziol, 'Verbraucherschutz als Selbstzweck oder als Mittel sachgerechter Interessenwahrung?', in B Eccher (ed), *Verbraucherschutz in Europa: Festgabe für Heinrich Mayrhofer* (2002), 201ff; Koziol, 'Bankrecht und Verbraucherschutz' in W Wiegand (ed), *Banken und Bankrecht im Wandel* (2004), 129ff. [455] See n 22 above and related text.

[456] Canaris, n 108 above, 348; Mohr, n 19 above, 675ff.

[457] This is a criticism sometimes levelled at modern consumer protection; see, very pointedly, H Hattenhauer, *Grundbegriffe des Bürgerlichen Rechts* (2nd edn., 2000), 23;

range of persons deserves to be protected because specific attributes (or perhaps rather, the lack of specific attributes) can typically be ascribed to them.[458] Such an approach would have more than a faintly discriminatory flavour in that it appears to insinuate that consumers, unguarded and unguided, lack the ability to engage in legal transactions. It would place consumers in close proximity to infirm persons who need to be taken care of.[459] The BGB, in turn, commendably, I think, subscribes to what may be called both a functional and a 'situative' approach to consumer protection.[460] In the first place, it defines as consumers all natural persons effecting a legal act the purpose of which cannot be attributed to their trade or independent professional activity (§ 13 BGB). The infelicities surrounding the definition as it is today enshrined in the BGB have been pointed out above.[461] But, in principle, this approach appears to be both plausible and practicable, for it can realistically be assumed that a person will typically be more alert, more inclined to look at his own advantage, and better informed, in his professional than in his private sphere.[462] Second, consumers, so defined, are not protected at random. They are protected only *vis-à-vis* an entrepreneur, ie a (natural or legal) person who in concluding a transaction *does* act in pursuit of his trade or independent professional activity. Hence, the key term for the application of the rules of consumer protection is not so much that of the 'consumer', but of the 'consumer contract', ie a contract between a consumer and an entrepreneur.[463] Undoubtedly, the mere fact that one party acts in his professional capacity whereas the other does not creates an imbalance between them. But it is not, *per se*, an imbalance which the legal system needs to redress. The crucial factor justifying legal interference is the impairment of

H Ehmann and U Rust, 'Die Verbrauchsgüterkaufrichtlinie' [1999] *Juristenzeitung* 864 (who refer to 'the danger of a new, deep class division').

[458] For critical discussion, see Bydlinski, n 153 above, 718ff; Micklitz, n 159 above, Vor §§ 13, 14, nn 62ff; Duve, n 22 above, §§ 1–14, n 79. On the distinction between 'role' and '(personal) attribute' as the starting point for legal consequences see, in the present context, Medicus, n 21 above, 211ff.   [459] §§ 1896ff BGB.

[460] See Pfeiffer, n 19 above, 27ff; Pfeiffer, n 17 above, 495ff; Micklitz, n 159 above, Vor §§ 13, 14, nn 65f; Duve, n 22 above, §§ 1–14, n 80; Drexl, n 153 above, 120ff, 128ff; Riesenhuber, n 19 above, 250ff, 260ff; Heiderhoff, n 19 above, 261ff; Wiedenmann, n 19 above, 152ff; Rösler, n 16 above, 46ff.   [461] See n 337 above and related text.

[462] Canaris, n 108 above, 360; and see K J Hopt, 'Nichtvertragliche Haftung außerhalb von Schadens- und Bereicherungsausgleich' (1983) 183 *Archiv für die civilistische Praxis* 645ff; Riesenhuber, n 19 above, 256ff; Wiedenmann, n 19 above, 115ff. *Contra*: Remien, n 19 above, 259ff.

[463] See the definition now provided in § 310 III BGB. The point is also emphasized by Pfeiffer, n 19 above, 139ff; Drexl, n 153 above, 113; M Becker, 'Verbrauchervertrag und allgemeines Privatrecht', in *Aufbruch nach Europa: 75 Jahre Max-Planck-Institut für Privatrecht* (2001), 85ff.

the consumer's freedom to take a free and rational decision.[464] Such impairment, of course, only exists in specific situations, and not merely because a person acts in the role of consumer. This is why the law attempts to identify the situations (complexity of the transaction, being caught off-guard, etc.) where a consumer faces the real danger of concluding a contract which reflects the interests of the entrepreneur rather than those of both parties. At the same time, this is the touchstone for determining whether the legal system may not occasionally have gone too far in the execution of a policy which is, in principle, in tune with a market economy based on freedom of contract.

Again, incidentally, there is nothing special in the legal system's endeavour to protect persons who act in a specific role *vis-à-vis* other persons acting in a different role.[465] German law also protects employees *vis-à-vis* their employers,[466] tenants of residential space against their lessors,[467] and those who are faced with standard terms of business *vis-à-vis* those who have introduced these terms into the contract.[468] In all these cases the question may legitimately be asked whether, and to what extent, the protective devices are both necessary and appropriate to remedy a situative, or perhaps even structural, imbalance. That, however, is a general question,[469] since it has to be addressed in terms of every person's right of self-determination which the legal system has to safeguard.[470]

Possible Objections

This, then, is the most important reason why of the three imaginable solutions to dealing with the question of consumer contracts—piecemeal legislation, the drafting of a separate code of consumer contract law, or incorporation into the general Civil Code—the third one has to be preferred:[471] both general contract law and consumer contract law are

[464] See n 365 above and related text; n 380 and following text.

[465] D Medicus, 'Schutzbedürfnisse (insbesondere der Verbraucherschutz) und das Privatrecht' [1996] *Juristische Schulung*, 761ff; Medicus, n 21 above, 219ff.

[466] Particularly by granting them protection against termination of contract; see, for an overview, Mansel, n 318 above, § 622, nn 7ff.

[467] For an overview, see Medicus, n 265 above, nn 237ff.

[468] §§ 305ff BGB; on which see n 143 above and the following text; n 230 above and related text.

[469] Consequently, German law has now re-integrated the rules on standard terms of business as well as the 'social lease law' into the framework of the BGB.

[470] See the references to Drexl, n 380 above; cf also Repgen, n 19 above, 70ff (with many references); Rösler, n 16 above, 71ff.

[471] This view is shared by Bydlinski, n 153 above, 718ff; Pfeiffer, n 17 above, 494ff; W-H Roth, n 154 above, 475, 484ff; Drexl, n 153 above, 117ff; Duve, n 22 above, §§ 1–14, nn 84ff; Rösler, n 16 above, 269ff; *contra*, most recently, Wiedenmann, n 19 above, 267ff and *passim* (who argues in favour of a consumer contract code). A consumer code (comprising not

designed to serve the same aim. It would be fatal for the integrity of the legal system if general contract law were seen to be the domain of a very formal conception of freedom of contract while consumer contract law were informed by loosely defined social concerns. The notion of freedom of contract has to be the lode-star for the entire law of contract; but at the same time, a contract may only be accepted by the legal community if it can typically be regarded as reflecting both parties' right of self-determination. The latter consideration cannot simply be relegated to a separate part of contract law but has to (and does in fact) permeate contract law as a whole. The process of 'materialising' German contract law[472] over the past hundred years has gone too far, and has been too pervasive, for what then used to be called the accomplishment of the 'social task of private law'[473] to be left to special legislation. It has become a concern of central significance.

In comparison with this central line of reasoning, most of the arguments advanced in favour of a separate Consumer Contract Code pale into insignificance. Thus, it has been argued that, since German consumer contract law is based on European Community law, the European dimension of this body of law (including, particularly, the need to interpret German law in conformity with the respective Directives) would become more apparent; at the same time, the conceptual devices of European Community law could be transformed into German law in an undistorted form, ie without the necessity of an adjustment to the conceptual world of the BGB. Also, the detailed style of legal drafting

---

only contract law) has existed in France since 1993; it is sharply criticized by C Witz and G Wolter, 'Das neue französische Verbrauchergesetzbuch' (1995) 3 *Zeitschrift für Europäisches Privatrecht*, 35ff; for a somewhat more positive evaluation, see D Heuer, *Der Code de la consommation: Eine Studie zur Kodifizierung des französischen Verbrauchsrechts* (2002). Austria also has a Consumer Protection Act; it dates from 1979 and is neither comprehensive nor systematic; see H Koziol and R Welser, *Grundriss des bürgerlichen Rechts*, vol. II (12th edn., 2001), 372ff. On the Greek Consumer Act of 1994, see E Alexandridou, 'The Greek Consumer Protection Act of 1994' [1996] *Gewerblicher Rechtsschutz und Urheberrecht International* 400ff. Incorporation into the general Civil Code has been the path pursued in the Netherlands; see E Hondius, 'Niederländisches Verbraucherrecht—vom Sonderrecht zum integrierten Zivilrecht', 1996 *Verbraucher und Recht* 295ff; Houdius, 'European Contract Law: The Contribution of the Dutch', in H-L Weyers (ed), *Europäisches Vertragsrecht* (1996), 62ff; for Italy, integration has recently been advocated by P Sirena, 'L'integrazione del diritto dei consumatori nella disciplina generale del contratto' (2004) 50 *Rivista di Diritto Civile*, 787ff. For comparative discussion, see E Hondius, 'Consumer Law and Private Law: Where the Twain Shall Meet', in L Krämer (ed), *Law and Diffuse Interests in the European Legal Order—Festschrift für Norbert Reich* (1997), 311ff; M Tenreiro, 'Un code de la consommation ou un code autour du consommateur? Quelques reflexions critiques sur la codification et la notion du consommateur', in ibid, 339ff; Rösler, n 16 above, 275ff; and the contributions to the volume F Osman (ed), *Vers un Code Européen de la Consommation*, (1998).

[472] See above, pp. 465ff.   [473] n 30.

prevailing in the institutionalized Europe could be preserved without conflicting with the more elegant and economical approach traditionally preferred in German law.[474] But then it has to be taken into consideration that the European Community has also enacted a number of Directives pertaining to contract law, though not specifically to consumer contract law: on combating late payment in commercial transactions, cross-border credit transfers, a Community framework for electronic signatures and, partly at least, electronic commerce. These Directives have been transformed into German law by amending the BGB.[475] The same is true of the Directives on the implementation of the principle of equal treatment for men and women as regards access to employment, vocational training and promotion, and working conditions,[476] and on the safeguarding of employees' rights on transfers of undertakings, businesses or parts of undertakings and businesses.[477] The BGB, in other words, cannot remain, and has in fact not remained unaffected (or, some would say, untainted), by the development of European Community law, even if consumer contract law is not taken into consideration. Some form of adjustment is inevitable, anyway. And as far as the prolix nature of European Community legislation is concerned, it will sometimes be possible to place a doctrinal anchor within the BGB and to leave the details to subordinate legislation; this has in fact happened with regard to the duties of information imposed on the entrepreneur in a number of contexts.[478] At the same time, it must be said that the BGB has been sullied on many occasions and in many ways by the German legislature even without any prompting from Brussels.[479] The modern German style of legal drafting is not what it was one hundred years ago. Also, it should be remembered that a general code of contract law would be a pretty poor thing were it not to cover consumer contracts. It could hardly claim to be comprehensive. Nor could it achieve its task of promoting the internal coherence of the law, of facilitating its comprehensibility, and of providing the intellectual and doctrinal fulcrum for the further development of the law.[480] Such development would very largely occur outside of its

[474] See the discussion by Roth, n 154 above, 485.
[475] See n 212 above and the following text; n 200 above and the following text; n 216 above and the following text.
[476] Council Directive 76/207/EEC of 9 February 1976; easily accessible in Radley-Gardner *et al*, n 170 above, 119ff.
[477] Council Directive 2001/23/EC of 12 March 2001, easily accessible in Radley-Gardner *et al*, n 170 above, 127ff.
[478] See n 303 above and related text; and see Henrich, n 153 above, 209.
[479] See the examples discussed by Seiler, n 327 above, 105ff.
[480] For these aims of codification, see n 308 and the following text.

parameters. A Consumer Contract Code, on the other hand, would either provide a mere collection of additional rules which have to be read against the background of the BGB; then it would increase the complexity of the law and disappoint the expectations engendered not rarely by law reformers that such a code would provide an easily comprehensible statement of a consumer's rights and duties. Or it would aim to be comprehensive, in which case it would have to duplicate many of the provisions contained in the BGB, and that would be equally problematic.[481]

Building Site or Museum?

There is one argument against the incorporation of consumer contract law into the BGB the truth of which can hardly be disputed. Consumer contract law is not yet an area with stable doctrinal structures. It will remain unsettled and subject to further change and amendment. Recently, the Commission of the European Union has announced its intention to review the existing consumer *acquis* in order to assess whether it achieves 'the key goals . . . to enhance consumer and business confidence in the internal market through a high common level of consumer protection and the elimination of internal market barriers and regulatory simplification'.[482] At the same time, it intends to develop, first, a 'common frame of reference'[483] and, subsequently, possibly also an 'optional instrument' of European contract law.[484] The optional instrument will effectively constitute a model code (at least) of general contract law.[485] But even the common frame of reference will provide common fundamental principles of European contract law, definitions of key concepts, and model rules of contract law; thus, the 'possible structure of the common frame of reference' suggested in Annex I to the communication[486] closely follows that of the Principles of European Contract Law drafted by the Lando Commission.[487] As a result, the focus of European Community consumer contract legislation will have to move away from the establishment and functioning of the internal market. For while it is obvious that this goal has hitherto inspired the relevant Community Directives,[488] consideration of contract law at large is bound to reveal

---

[481] Roth, n 154 above, 485ff.

[482] Communication from Commission of the European Communities to the European Parliament and the Council: *European Contract Law and the revision of the acquis: the way forward* of 11 October 2004, COM (2004) 651 final, p. 3.

[483] Ibid, 2ff.   [484] Ibid, 8ff.

[485] For details, see Annex II to the Communication, ibid, 17ff.   [486] Ibid, 14ff.

[487] See n 15 above and related text.

[488] See, most recently, the analysis by Heiderhoff, n 19 above, 265ff, 318ff. As far as the community's competence to regulate consumer contract law is concerned, see n 285 above and related text.

that it cannot sensibly be conceptualized as a mere instrument for the constitution of markets but that it has to reflect fundamental concerns such as freedom and responsibility, good faith, and the protection of reasonable reliance.[489] In particular, freedom of contract will have to be perceived as a means of self-determination. A number of the regulatory excesses presently disfiguring German contract law[490] are symptomatic of the partial clash of orientation between national German contract law (of which consumer contract law only forms an integral part) and European Community consumer contract law.[491] As things stand, German lawyers may question the wisdom of much that has to be implemented; but they cannot change the necessity of implementing it as well as that is possible. The impending large-scale revision instigated by the European Commission offers the chance of a re-orientation and of a more coherent contract law[492] not only on the European but also on the national level.

What does this mean, as far as the German Civil Code is concerned? The decision to incorporate consumer contract law has effectively converted the BGB into a permanent building site.[493] But then it may be said that a building site bristling with the cheery voices of craftsmen and artisans may be a more appropriate metaphor for a modern code of private law than a museum in which only the weary murmurs of the occasional tourist group can be heard.

---

[489] That point was made by the editors of *Zeitschrift für Europäisches Privatrecht* as early as 1993, in the founding editorial of that journal.

[490] See example above, pp. 482f.

[491] For a detailed substantiation of this statement, see Heiderhoff, n 19 above, 238ff; cf also B Heiderhoff, 'Vertrauen versus Vertragsfreiheit im europäischen Verbrauchervertragsrecht' (2003) 11 *Zeitschrift für Europäisches Privatrecht* 769ff.

[492] See the title of the Action Plan of 2003 (see text to n 14 above) on which the new Communication is based.   [493] Roth, n 154 above, 488.

The Mark as Expression/The Mark as Property

Michael Spence

Legal doctrines develop in the interplay of *topoi*, commitments to ideas about the law, none of which is wholly accurate, that have a shaping influence on the development of doctrine. These are often commitments to ideas, more or less fully articulated, about the fundamental purpose of an area of law. Thus, it is neither wholly accurate to say that contract is the law of promise, nor that it is law protecting justified reliance, but both these ideas have been powerful in shaping doctrine. It is neither entirely true that tort is a system of compensation for harm, nor that is a system for correcting wrongs, and yet both these ideas have had an important role. It is neither wholly true that administrative law merely operates to keep decision makers within the bounds of their appropriate authority, nor that it is a mechanism for ensuring good administration, but both these ideas have been formative. In different historical periods, different *topoi* will be in the ascendency in a given legal field, usually reflecting in some way the dominant mood in contemporary moral or political philosophy. The advocates of the *topos* in ascendancy will squeeze the complexities of the relevant legal doctrines into a shape for which it can account. Aspects of those doctrines that do not fit, they will either criticise or relegate to the category of the exceptional. And in each historical period there are advocates for some *topos* not in the ascendency, desert prophets who either call the law back to what is often represented as its 'classic' commitments or who show that some unfashionable *topos* is far richer, and has far more explanatory power, than is often allowed.

In this paper, I want to assume the role of the desert prophet. I want to suggest that the law of trade marks, wanders between the *topos* of 'property' and the *topos* of 'speech' and unashamedly to act as an apologist for the latter. The law of trade marks is undoubtedly part of the law of intangible property. But trade mark law also restricts what people may say about themselves and other people, and about their own and other people's goods and services. I believe that a description of trade mark law as a system for the regulation of speech is able to account for far more of the current law than might initially be thought, and is normatively far more attractive than a description that focuses upon its operation as a system of property rights. I believe that it also provides a satisfactory way through some of the dilemmas that have beset modern trade mark law.

Before beginning, however, I should emphasise that these *topoi* of property and speech make very odd companions. The enforcement of property and the regulation of speech characteristically involve quite contrasting foundational assumptions. Those different foundational assumptions have potentially very powerful consequences for the shape that the law is likely to take.

To say that something is 'property' is usually by presumption to legitimise control of its use by an individual owner. It is to require that any limitation of that control be justified. As Singer puts it:

> If ownership means presumptive control by an owner, and if the existence of ownership rights is a good thing, then limitations on the rights of the owner must be justified by sufficiently strong reasons to overcome the presumption of legitimacy. . . [L]ibertarians, or liberals, or communitarians, they all tend to frame the issue in the same way: How much community control should be imposed on individuals?[1]

Of course, very few proprietary rights entail that full control over their subject matter for which some would reserve the word 'ownership'. However, those that do represent the core case of the legal concept of property. The rhetorical power of the 'property' *topos* is the implication that such control is a given: invoking the 'property' *topos* challenges those who would derogate from the owner's presumptive right of control to make their case. If this is right, and trade mark law is at its very heart a system for the protection of certain types of property, then the trade mark owner has the whip-hand in disputes about the use of particular signs.

By contrast, to say that something is 'speech' is usually by presumption to suggest that it ought to be the subject of minimal regulation, that it ought to be free. Of course, almost all types of speech, and particularly commercial speech of the type that trade mark law often restricts, are in fact subject to regulation. But the rhetorical power of the 'speech' *topos* is that it establishes the freedom to say what we want as a starting point, and challenges those who would restrict our speech to make their case. If this is right, and trade mark law is at its very heart a system for the regulation of speech, then the person whose speech trade mark law would restrict presumptively has the whip-hand.

---

[1] J W Singer, *Entitlement: The Paradoxes of Property* (New Haven: Yale UP, 2000), 4.

But, though they are very different and might shape the law in very different ways, both these *topoi* of 'property' and 'speech' have long been commonplace in the law of trade marks and in commentaries upon it. So the first edition of Kerly's *Law of Trade-Marks*[2] opens with the a claim that the law of trade marks is law regulating deception, that is a kind of law regulating speech, and cites as the 'leading principle' of the law a passage from the decision of James LJ in *Singer Manufacturing Co. v Loog*:

No man is entitled to represent his goods as being the goods of another man: and no man is permitted to . . . [enable a] purchaser to tell a lie or to make a false representation to somebody else who is the ultimate customer. That being, as it appears to me, a comprehensive statement of what the law is upon the question of trade-mark or trade-designation, I am of the opinion that there is no such thing as a monopoly or a property in the nature of a copyright, or in the nature of a patent, in the use of any name.[3]

Kerly then goes on to assert, without any attempt at reconciling the claim with his leading principle, that there had been property in trade-marks in Equity from *Millington v Fox*[4] in 1838, and also effectively at Law from the time of the Judicature Acts. Of course, by the time Kerly was writing in 1894 there had been a lot of worrying about what it meant to speak of property in a trade mark, in cases such as the *Leather Cloth Company v American Leather Cloth Company*[5]. But the competing notions of a trade mark action as an action to restrain a type of wrongful speech, and a trade mark action as an action to protect property, have been a part of the law from the beginning.

What these early judges and commentators were struggling with, and the danger that besets any account of trade mark law that focuses upon trade mark as a property regime, is that the object of the property rights recognised by the law of trade marks is very peculiar. There is no doubt that trade mark is a property regime. It says in section 22 of the Trade Marks Act 1994 that 'a registered trade mark is personal property'. Trade marks are assigned a value by accountants like other forms of property, a value that in the case of the Coca-Cola mark is estimated at US$63,394,000,000.[6] But like the associated form of property 'goodwill', if goodwill can rightly be called property at all,[7] property in a trade mark is a very peculiar form of property indeed.

---

2 D M Kerly, *The Law of Trade-Marks, Trade-Name, and Merchandise Marks* (London: Sweet & Maxwell, 1894).   3 (1880) 18 Ch D 395 at 412.
  4 (1838) 3 My & Cr 338, 40 ER 956.
  5 (1863) 1 H & M 271, 71 ER 118; (1863) De GJ & S 137, 46 ER 868; (1865) 11 HLC 523, 11 ER 1435.
  6 'The Global Brand Scoreboard', *Business Week*, 9–16 August 2004.
  7 Compare J E Penner, *The Idea of Property in Law* (Oxford: Clarendon, 1997), n 18 and F H Lawson and B Rudden, *The Law of Property* (3rd edn., Oxford: Clarendon, 2002), 42–43.

In order to understand what it means to claim that a trade mark is property, we need to understand something about the nature of property in intellectual property generally. Harris has claimed that intellectual property is property in the subject matter to which intellectual property rights attach: for copyright in the relevant work; for patent in the relevant invention; for trade mark in the mark itself.[8] However, it is clear that this cannot be the case for reasons that Penner has emphasised, adopting a concept of property of which ownership is the core case. Indeed, Penner calls the suggestion that intellectual property is property in the subject matter to which it attaches 'idiotic fiction'.[9] Intellectual property rights do not exclude others from the enjoyment of the relevant subject matter, but only from its use in one of a broadly or narrowly defined range of ways. Take the trade mark 'Coca-Cola'. I can meditate upon this mark; I can discuss it with my friends; I can sew it on to my T-shirt or on to the T-shirt that I give my daughter for her birthday; I can refer to it in writing a song or a novel or making a film. I simply cannot use it use in one of the ways specified in section 10 of the Trade Marks Act 1994. What I own when I own intellectual property, is not the subject matter of the intellectual property right, but the intellectual property right itself. It is the right itself over which I enjoy the usual incidents of a property claim. All this is clearer in the copyright and patent legislation than the trade mark legislation: whereas it speaks loosely of property in the registered trade mark, they speak of property in the copyright or patent, not in the work or invention.[10] Penner adopts the language of monopoly to describe the object of an intellectual property rights. Such rights, he says, are property in a 'monopoly'.[11] I find that language unhelpful because the word monopoly implies a certain relationship between a supplier of goods or services and a market, a relationship that may or may not be established by the recognition of an intellectual property right. I would prefer to say that an intellectual property right is a right that can be treated as property, to control particular uses of a specified type of subject matter. This property right might look like a *chose in action*, but of course it is not. Until there has been infringement, the holder of an intellectual property right has no right of action to recover money or property, yet it is clear that there is property in an intellectual property right that has never been infringed.[12]

---

[8] J Harris, *Property and Justice* (Oxford: Clarendon, 1996), 42–47.

[9] Penner, n 70 above 118–120.

[10] Copyright, Designs and Patents Act, 1988 s 90, Patents Act, 1977(PA 77)s 30.

[11] Penner, n 7 above 118.

[12] This point was the subject of a well-known debate in the *Law Quarterly Review* at the turn of the twentieth century: see HW Elphinstone, 'What is a *Chose in Action*?' (1893) 9 LQR 311; C Sweet, '*Choses in Action*' (1894) 10 LQR 303; F Pollock, 'What is a Thing?'

The distinction between property in subject matter and property in the right to control particular uses of subject matter may seem like academic sophistry. To the businesswoman it makes more sense to say that this is 'my work', or 'my invention' or 'my mark'. In relation to some types of intellectual property regime, the distinction is indeed rather fine. Patent grants such broad rights to control the use of an invention, that the distinction between property in the invention and property in the right to control particular uses of the invention may seem academic. Copyright gives the owner of copyright in a work control over all its most commercially significant uses. This is a point that Penner underestimates.[13] But in relation to trade marks, the distinction between property in subject matter and property in the right to control particular uses of subject matter has, at least traditionally, been very important indeed. This is because the control that the trade mark owner was traditionally given over the use of the mark was very limited. In the United Kingdom, it was—until the Trade Marks Act 1994 and with the exception of infringement by importing a reference under the Trade Marks Act 1938—limited to the right to prevent others from using the mark in a way that would deceive or cause confusion. Moreover, until the Trade Marks Act 1994, the circumstances in which trade mark rights could be assigned or licensed were controlled so as prevent the trade mark itself effectively constituting a misrepresentation or, as it was put, a 'fraud upon the public'. In other words, trade mark was a right that could be treated as property to prevent a certain type of potentially misleading speech by a trade competitor. This is a long way from what the businesswoman means when she speaks simply of the mark as 'hers'.

Of course, the law has moved on in the last decade. It is now possible to assign and license trade mark rights in the same way as any other personal property.[14] Moreover, many would claim that the scope of trade mark protection has so expanded as to make the difference between trade mark and other forms of intellectual property less profound and, indeed, to render it more meaningful to speak of property in trade marks themselves. This expansion has occurred in two ways. First, there has been a broadening of the circumstances in which consumer confusion sufficient to establish infringement is likely to be found. Second, infringement can now also be found in certain circumstances in which there has been, not *confusion*, but merely *allusion* by a competitor to the owner's mark. That is, the owner of the mark can use it to prevent others not only making

(1894) 10 LQR 318; S Brodhurst, 'Is Copyright a Chose in Action?' (1895) 11 LQR 64; C Sweet, '*Choses in Action*' (1895) 11 LQR 238. Perhaps for this reason section 30 PA77 specifically provides that neither a patent nor a patent application is a thing in action.

13 Penner, n 7 above, 120.   14 Trade Marks Act 1994 (TMA 94) ss 22 and 28.

what are effectively misrepresentations, but also making perfectly true statements that allude to the owner of the mark or her goods or services. This type of protection had been available under the Trade Marks 1938 in the limited guise of protection against importing a reference to a trade mark, but under the Trade Marks Act 1994 it is potentially much more widely available. This is fairly extensive control over the use of a mark. In a legal environment in which the language of property is predominate, and the slippage is so easy between property in the right to control certain uses of the mark and property in the mark itself, the presumption all too soon becomes that the owner of a trade mark ought, absent good reason to the contrary, to control all its potential uses. The law seems to reflect the claim of the businesswoman that a particular mark is hers, far more closely than it used to do.

However, the precise extent of the control over a mark allocated to its owner by modern European trade mark law is far from settled. It is not clear how far the shift from the speech *topos* to the property *topos* has gone. Both the language of speech and the language of property continues to echo in cases at all levels. In one sharp contrast the OHIM Third Board of Appeal recently said that a trade mark is 'not only a sign affixed to a product to indicate its business origin, but is also a vehicle for communicating a message to the public [MS: all speech talk], and itself represents financial value [MS: classic property talk].'[15] The European Court of Justice has seen a string of cases about the scope of trade mark protection in the last seven years, as they try to make sense of the directive underlying the Trade Marks Act 1994.

I would argue that perhaps the best justification for the expanded scope of protection available under the Trade Marks Act 1994, or at least for protection against allusive uses of a mark, is not to be found in theories of property, but in free speech theory itself. This is surprising claim. Free speech is usually thought of as only limiting, and not grounding, trade mark rights: practitioners think that free speech issues are only relevant when, to adopt the facts of a recent American case as an example, Mattel wants to prevent an artist from using the 'Barbie' trade mark in a protest work.[16] But I hope to show that free speech, or at least a respect for expressive autonomy, is the best justification for the scope of the trade mark protection against allusive use afforded by section 10 of the Trade Marks Act 1994. I hope to show that it is the best justification for Mattel's own claim to limit certain allusive uses of the Barbie mark. If this is right,

---

[15] *Hollywood S.A.S. v Souza Cruz S.A.* (Case R 283/1999-3) [2002] ETMR 64 at para. 67.   [16] See 353 F3d 792 (9th Cir. 2003).

it has some unexpected consequences for trade mark law, but also an ability to resolve some of the dilemmas that trade mark law is facing in a normatively satisfying way. If it is right, trade mark continues to be a regime concerned, at its heart, with the regulation of speech and that has very important consequences for the interpretation of the legislative schema.

The reason that I will focus on expanded protection against the allusive use of a mark is worth emphasising. Protection of this type is often heralded as signalling the progression of trade mark law from protection against certain types of potentially deceptive speech, to protection of a type of intellectual property in the fullest sense of the term. I want to show that this progression is not inevitable, even under the Trade Marks Act 1994, and that it is not desirable.

As for expanded protection against confusion, I shall make just two comments in passing. The first is that protection against confusion is clearly justifiable both in light of the wrongfulness of misleading conduct and its potential economic consequences. Trade marks reduce consumer search costs and create incentives for investment in competition on the basis of product quality and price, by facilitating the repeat purchase of experience goods. I may not be able to tell which washing powder really works until I try a few but, having found one that works, I need to be able to identify it with certainty in order to make a repeat purchase. Protection against confusing commercial speech is both easy to justify and easy to reconcile with the claim that speech should be free. My second comment about expanded protection against consumer confusion is that the jurisprudence of 'global confusion' developed by the European Court of Justice since the decision in *Canon Kabushki Kaisha v Metro-Goldwyn-Mayer Inc.*[17] makes almost no sense to me. It is not merely that a bicycle is no more similar to a bottle of soft drink because it is labelled 'Coca Cola' than it would be if it were labelled 'Smiths'. It is also that the recent jurisprudence assumes that consumers are more likely to be confused by the use of signs only slightly different to well-known marks than they are by the use of signs only slightly different to less well-known marks (that they will be more confused by a soft drink calling itself 'Poca Pola' than they will by a similarly close variant on a less well-known mark). This is simply counter-intuitive and driven by the desire to protect marks of greater value more strongly, a desire reflecting the corollary of the property *topos* that investment should be protected.

As for expanded protection against allusive uses of a mark, it has come about in two ways, the first of which turns on the interpretation of section

[17] [1999] RPC 117.

10(1) of the Trade Marks Act 1994 and the second of which turns on the interpretation of section 10(3) of that Act. In commenting on these sections, I shall assume that authorities concerned with sections 5(1) and 5(3) dealing with relative grounds of refusal, are also good as authorities concerning the scope of sections 10(1) and 10(3).

Section 10(1) of the Trade Marks Act 1994 provides that:

A person infringes a registered trade mark if he uses in the course of trade a sign which is identical with the trade mark in relation to goods or services for which the trade mark is registered.

This protection of the mark is said to be 'absolute' in the Recitals to the Trade Marks Directive and is justified by reference to the function of the trade mark as an indication of origin.[18] However, it was appreciated early on that such absolute protection could extend beyond that which was justified by the protection of a trade mark as an indication of origin. In particular, the section could be used to prevent merely allusive uses of the mark. But preventing uses of a mark that, though they identified an owner or her goods or services, did not suggest any association with them, seemed more than was necessary to protect the trade origin function. The first of the UK cases concerned the trade mark 'Wet, Wet, Wet' registered for books and other classes of goods. The question in the case was whether it could be used to prevent the publication of a book entitled *A Sweet little Mystery—Wet, Wet, Wet—The Inside Story*.[19] It might be thought that preventing such uses is difficult to justify on the grounds that a mark should operate as an indication of origin. The trade mark might appear to be used in a way that, if anything, reinforces and does not undermine the association between the mark and its owner. These are issues to which we shall return. In the case of the 'Wet, Wet, Wet' mark, it was held that the use did fall within the ambit of section 10(1), but that it was protected by a defence in section 11 of the Trade Marks Act 1994 exempting purely descriptive uses from liability for infringement. A series of subsequent decisions, including the complex litigation in *Arsenal Football Club Plc v Reed*,[20] have approached this problem either on the basis of the section 11 defence,[21] on the basis of whether the challenged use is use 'as a trade mark' (that is, use to indicate the trade origin of goods),[22] or on the somewhat

---

[18] First Council Directive of 21 December 1988 to approximate the laws of the Member States relating to trade marks (89/104/EEC).   [19] [1996] FSR 205.
  [20] [2001] RPC 922; [2003] RPC 144; *Arsenal Football Club Plc v Reed (No. 2)* [2003] CMLR 13; [2003] RPC 696.
  [21] *Bayerische Motorenwerke AG v. Deenik* (Case C-36/97) [1999] All ER (EC) 235.
  [22] *Hölterhoff v. Freiesleben* (Case C-2/00) [2002] All ER (EC) 665; *Arsenal (No. 2)* [2003] 1 CMLR 13; *R v. Johnstone* [2003] 1 WLR 1736.

more elusive basis of whether it might damage the ability of the trade mark to operation as an indication of origin.[23]

These different approaches have led to sometimes surprisingly divergent results. In *Arsenal Football Club Plc v Reed (No.2)*[24] the Court of Appeal followed the direction of the European Court of Justice in holding that the football club Arsenal could prevent the use of its trade mark name on unauthorised souvenirs, even if no-one thought that the Club was the trade origin of those souvenirs. In doing so it held that the decision of the European Court of Justice, a decision that we shall consider in greater detail further on, was that the issue of trade mark use is irrelevant in determining infringement under section 10(1). Just one day later, the House of Lords held that the effect of the European Court of Justice in the *Arsenal* decision was to render non-trade mark use outside the scope of section 10(1) and that the use of the trade mark name of the pop singer Bon Jovi on bootleg CDs did not constitute infringement because purchasers would believe that the name referred to the contents of the CD and not its trade origin. In this latter case, *R. v Johnstone*, Lord Walker claimed that the relevant law is 'in . . . a state of disarray'.[25] What does seem clear after *Arsenal*, however, is that some purely allusive uses will be caught by the current interpretation of section 10(1).

Section 10(3) of the Trade Marks Act 1994 provides that:

A person infringes a registered trade mark if he uses in the course of trade, in relation to goods or services, a sign which is identical to or similar to the trade mark where the trade mark has a reputation in the United Kingdom and the use of the sign, being without due cause, takes unfair advantage of, or is detrimental to, the distinctive character of the repute of the trade mark.

This history of this section has been tortuous. It originally applied only to the situation in which a sign similar or identical to a registered mark was used on goods dissimilar to those for which it was registered. But following two decisions of the European Court of Justice in 2003, it was amended to be of more general application.[26]

The section protects a mark against at least two types of allusion. The first is allusion that leads to dilution by loss of distinctiveness. The example often given is drawn from some classic American cases in which the jeweller Tiffany was able to prevent the use of that name by a motion picture

---

[23] *Arsenal (No. 2)* [2003] RPC 696.   [24] [2003] 1 CMLR 13.
[25] *R v Johnstone* [2003] 1 WLR 1736, 1761.
[26] The section was amended by the Trade Marks (Proof of Use, etc.) Regulations 2004 (SI 2004/946), Reg 7(2)(b) as a consequence of *Davidoff & Cie SA v Gofkid Ltd* (Case C-292/00) [2003] All ER (EC) 1029 and *Adidas—Salomon AG v Fitnessworld Trading Ltd* (Case C-408/01) [2004] Ch 120.

company,[27] a bar in Boston,[28] and a perfume company.[29] The damage entailed in dilution by loss of distinctiveness is that the mark gradually loses its ability to identify the activities of the registered owner. In the language of Peircean semiotics, the danger is that a mark such as 'Tiffany' ceases to operate primarily as a symbol with the activities of the jeweller as its reference and begins to operate primarily as an index with generalised associations of quality, luxury and prestige.[30] The second type of allusion caught by section 10(3) is that which leads to dilution by tarnishing.[31] The example often given of such dilution is again based on the facts of a classic American case. In that case the cheerleaders of the Dallas Cowboys were able to prevent the use of a uniform similar to their own in a pornographic film.[32] The damage entailed in dilution by tarnishing is that the mark is unable to be used free of the unpleasant associations that its allusive use has created. Section 10(3) is clear in not requiring confusion for protection. It prevents, not confusion, but allusion to a registered mark, its owner or her goods or services.

Three reasons are sometimes given for this expansive protection of trade marks against not only confusing, but also allusive, use. I want to deal with them quickly, because I do not regard any of them to be satisfactory. I will then mount a case for such protection on the basis of respect for the trade mark owner's expressive autonomy.

A first possible reason for an expanded protection of trade marks is the one that arguably underpins the decision of the European Court of Justice in the *Arsenal* case. This is that situations of dilution, though apparently offering protection against *allusion* to a mark, are really situations in which the signalling ability of the trade mark is being preserved against possible *confusion*, in which one of two possible expanded understandings of confusion is adopted.

The first of these is post-sale confusion. The European Court of Justice in the *Arsenal* case was concerned that 'some consumers . . . if they come across the goods [bearing the Arsenal mark] after they have been sold by Mr Reed and taken away from the stall . . . may interpret the sign as designating Arsenal FC as the undertaking of origin of the goods'.[33] Protection against this type of confusion is not difficult to justify. Landes

---

[27] *Tiffany & Co. v Tiffany Productions, Inc.* 262 NY 482 (Ct App 1933).
[28] *Tiffany & Co. v Boston Club, Inc* 231 F Supp 836 (DC Mass, 1964).
[29] *Tiffany & Co. v L'Argene Products Co.* 324 NYS 2d 326 (NY Sup 1971).
[30] CS Peirce, *Collected Papers of Charles Sanders Peirce*, C Hartshorne and P Wiess (eds), (Cambridge, MA: HUP, 1960), Vol 2 at 156–173.
[31] Also known as 'dilution by tarnishment'.
[32] *Dallas Cowboy Cheerleaders, Inc v Pussycat Cinema Ltd* 604 F2d 200 (2nd Cir, 1979).
[33] *Arsenal* [2003] RPC 144 at 172.

and Posner make an argument based on the complementary view of advertising, the view that brands can be regarded by consumers as themselves complementary goods for which they are willing to pay.[34] Their argument is that protection against post-sale confusion facilitates the creation of markets in what they call reputation capital, the prestige that comes from association with particular goods. In fact, this problematic argument is unnecessary. Protection against post-sale confusion can be justified on a similar basis to confusion at the point of sale. The ability of the trade mark system to create incentives for investment in product quality and price and to facilitate repeat purchases must depend upon a consumer being able to identify the goods of a particular producer in whatever context she encounters them. Moreover, the control of what amount to potentially damaging misrepresentations must be as compatible with a commitment to free speech whether the misrepresentation occurs at the point of sale or later. However, though justified, protection against post-sale confusion does not require that the law prohibit merely allusive uses of a mark. *Some* such uses may give rise to post-sale confusion, but there is no reason to suggest that *all* or even *most* will do so. The likelihood of post-sale confusion should be assessed in exactly the same way as confusion at the point of sale. The law ought not simply to assume that allusive uses will give rise to this potential damage, with which they have no necessary nexus.

An alternative expanded concept of confusion thus also makes its way into the decision of the European Court of Justice in the *Arsenal* decision. This is the notion that use can sometimes damage the ability of a mark to signal the origin of goods, even if that use does not entail confusion of the type traditionally required for trade mark infringement. The only way in which this could happen, it is submitted, is if a consumer, either at the point of sale or afterwards, subconsciously associates goods bearing the potentially infringing sign with the trade mark owner, even though, when asked a direct question as to their trade origin, she can identify that this association is mistaken. This must clearly be a possible scenario. We often make hasty subconscious assessments which we, even unawares, correct when focusing our minds more clearly. This subconscious confusion is the expanded concept of confusion upon which dilution protection is sometimes said to be built. However, this concept cannot be a satisfactory basis for protection against dilution. The law cannot remedy the chaos of our subconscious minds. We will see later on that there may be good

---

[34] W M Landes and R A Posner, 'The Economics of Trademark Law' (1987) 78 *Trademark Rep.* 267, 305.

reasons for using a sign that is very similar to an existing brand. If someone who is not the trade mark owner does so in a way that will not confuse the average consumer, it is difficult to know how much responsibility she should bear for the disorder of a consumer's unconscious.

Another possible justification for dilution protection therefore abandons the concept of confusion and mirrors a common justification for the other intellectual property regimes. This is the suggestion that incentives should be offered for the creation and efficient exploitation of trade marks. Richardson claims that trade marks enrich our culture, 'entertain us' and 'help us to express ourselves in relation to our world'. She says that '[i]f there is any policy justification for protecting copyright works as the products of intellectual and innovative activity . . . it extends to . . . expressive trade marks'. The policy justifications to which she points are those concerning incentives to create and exploit such resources.[35] However, it is difficult to argue that the market failure-based arguments regarding incentives to create and exploit the subject matter of the intellectual property regimes apply in the context of trade marks. Whether investment in branding is desirable, far less appropriately the object of legal incentive, has long been a disputed issue of welfare economics. For those who subscribe to a persuasive view of advertising, the creation of brand associations can distort consumer preference and create barriers to entry for competitors.[36] Landes and Posner summarily dismiss this position.[37] It is true that other views of the economic effect of advertising are current (including the informative view of advertising in which investment in brands can be desirable because it provides important signals of a concern for the quality and price of experience goods and facilitates entry,[38] and the complementary view of advertising to which I have already referred[39]). But even if the persuasive view is wrong, and

---

[35] M Richardson 'Copyright in Trade Marks? On Understanding Trade Mark Dilution' [2000] IPQ 66, 80 and n 13.

[36] See, for example, D Braithwaite, 'The Economic Effects of Advertisement' (1928) 38 *Economic* J. 16, E Chamberlin, *The Theory of Monopolistic Competition* (Cambridge MA: Harvard UP, 1933), N V Kaldor, 'The Economic Aspects of Advertising' (1950) (195) 18 *Review of Economic Studies* 1, and A Dixit and V Norman, 'Advertising and Welfare' (1978) 9 *BellJ. of Econ.* 1   [37] Landes and Posner, 34 above, 277

[38] See the classic work of Nelson: P Nelson, 'Information and Consumer Behaviour' (1970) 78 *J. of Political Economy*, 311; 'The Economic Value of Advertising' in Y Brozen (ed), *Advertising and Society* (New York, NYU Press, 1974), 43; 'Advertising as Information' (1974) 82 *J. of Political Economy*, 729; 'The Economic Consequences of Advertising' (1975), 48 *J. of Business*, 213; 'Advertising as Information Once More' in D. G. Tuerck (ed), *Advertising: The Economics of Persuasion* (Washington, American Institute for Public Policy Research, 1978), 133

[39] See, for example, G J Stigler and G S Becker, 'De Gustibus Non Est Disputandum', (1977) 67 *Am. Econ. Rev.*, 76; L M Nichols, 75 'Advertising and Economic Welfare' (1985)

the creation of such incentives is not economically deleterious, Landes and Posner themselves agree that it may be economically unnecessary. There is always an incentive to create and exploit new marks, the incentive to succeed in the market for the goods to which they are attached. Landes and Posner conclude that 'we do not need trademark protection [let alone protection against allusive use] just to be sure of having enough words, though we may need patent protection to be sure of having enough inventions, or copyright protection to be sure of having enough books, movies and musical compositions.'[40] The market failure justification does not seem to apply.

A third approach to justifying dilution protection focuses upon two other common justifications for the intellectual property regimes. These are that dilution protection remedies the unjust enrichment of those who allude to trade marks or recognises the desert of those who create brand reputations. At least the first of these arguments seems reflected in the language of section 10(3) when it speaks of taking 'unfair advantage' of the reputation of the mark. However, it has often been shown that these justifications for intellectual property law generally are vacuous. They are even more so as justifications for trade mark protection. As for the unjust enrichment argument, we are all regularly enriched by the innovative and creative activities of others. The claim that we stand on the shoulders of giants is platitudinous because it rings true. But if we are all regularly enriched by the innovative and creative activities of others, the question is when that enrichment will be unjust. This is the question that those who speak of 'reaping without sowing', a phrase that draws its rhetorical power from a New Testament source in which the behaviour is neither lauded nor condemned,[41] have been unable to answer. As for the desert arguments, there is no clear reason why someone who has built a successful brand reputation is particularly deserving. As Advocate General de Lamonthe pointed out in *Sirena SRL v. Eda SRL*[42] in a passage later taken up by the European Court of Justice:[43] 'from the point of view of humanity, certainly the debt that society owes to the "inventor" of the name "Prep Good Morning" is not of the same order (this is the least that may be said) as that which humanity has contracted with the "inventor" of penicillin.' Moreover, it has never been made clear why the creator of any intangible asset deserves control over its use and not some other form of reward,

---

Am. Econ. Rev., 213; and G S Becker and K M Murphy, 'A Simple Theory of Advertising as a Good or Bad' (1993) *Q. J. of Econ.*, 942.

[40] Landes and Posner, 34 above, 275.   [41] Luke 19:22.

[42] [1971] CMLR 260, 264–265.

[43] *SA Cnl-Sucal NV v Hag CF AG* (Case C-10/89) [1990] 3 CMLR 571.

particularly in contexts such as that of a successful brand when reward may already have come in the form of a market advantage.

Having rejected, therefore, the three most commonly advanced justifications for dilution protection, the ability of a trade mark to prevent allusion to her mark, I want to turn to a reason that will, at least initially seem very surprising. This is also a justification that is sometimes mounted for copyright and moral rights regimes. It is that the expressive autonomy of a trade mark owner might require that she be given some control over allusion to her mark by others.

I began this line of thought with a consideration of the 'Barbie' case to which I have already referred, *Mattel Inc v Walking Mountain Productions*.[44] This involved the work of the artist Tom Forsythe and his series of photographs 'Food Chain Barbie'. These showed 'Barbie' dolls mutilated in various ways by common kitchen appliances. According to Forysthe's website, the point of the pictures is to reveal the 'continuity of the commodity machine',[45] though to the untrained eye the impression they create is one of unbridled misogyny. The Court of Appeals for the Ninth Circuit was keen to ensure that Mattel could rely upon neither American copyright, nor trade mark, nor trade dress, protection to limit Forsythe's freedom of speech. However, I began to wonder whether adequate account had been taken of Mattel's expressive autonomy. In fact, I would support the result in the case, but I began to wonder whether I would do so in all cases in which there had been allusion to a trade mark and that allusion either implicated the owner of the trade mark in the expression of a message from which she would wish to be disassociated or altered the ability of the mark to carry its owner's primary message. I began to wonder whether my concern for the expressive autonomy of the trade mark owner was entirely misplaced. I do not believe that it was. I believe that trade mark owners have a good claim, grounded in respect for their expressive autonomy, to protection against some allusive uses of their marks.

This argument begins with a recognition that a mark is a form of speech. Trade mark owners work hard to ensure that their mark communicates, not only the trade origin of goods, but also a whole range of associated values. The meaning of the 'Pepsi' mark is not only that the relevant soft drink has been produced by, or under the licence of, PepsiCo International, but includes all the values associated with the 'Pepsi Generation'. The company's website argues that the development of the concept of the 'Pepsi Generation' was 'one of the most significant

---

[44] See 16 above.   [45] *http://creativefreedomdefense.org/biography.htm*.

demographic events in commercial history.'[46] The brand Polo not only signifies a connection with the Polo Ralph Lauren Corporation, it signifies what the company's website calls 'an entire world', telling 'a story and [encouraging] customers to participate in . . . [a] lifestyle.'[47] The trade mark 'Maxim' is intended to signify not only a magazine for men published by Dennis Publishing, but also a range of values culminating in the campaign by the American edition of the magazine to have 'man' listed as an endangered species with the United States Fish and Wildlife Service.[48] Kant drew a distinction between books on the one hand and pictures and symbols on the other. He claimed that only the former could count as speech.[49] However, it is hard to see why this is the case. Both word and picture marks operate to express a whole range of meanings with which they are invested by their owners. Trade mark owners are constantly speaking through their marks.

An important corollary of the right to free speech is the right to refrain from speech. This can also constitute a right to control the meaning of speech, particularly ongoing speech such as a mark. In the free speech jurisprudence of the United States, this right against compelled speech has been given a variety of different expressions. For example, in *Pacific Gas and Electric Company v Public Utilities Commission of California*,[50] it was relied upon to prevent the compelled distribution with utility bills of a newsletter expressing views which the utility company did not endorse. In *Hurley v. Irish-American Gay, Lesbian and Bisexual Group of Boston*,[51] it was relied upon to prevent the compelled inclusion of a gay rights group in a St Patrick's Day parade organised by a war veterans group. In *Boy Scouts of America v Dale*,[52] it was used to justify the dismissal of a Boy Scout leader who was openly gay on the basis that his retention would 'force the organization to send a message, both to the youth members and the world, that the Boy Scouts accepts homosexual conduct as a legitimate form of behaviour.'[53] Finally, in *United States v United Foods Inc*,[54] it was used to prohibit compelled contributions by growers to a mushroom advertising fund. This right to resist compelled speech is usually justified, not on the basis that free speech is essential to maintaining

---

[46] *http://www.pepsiworld.com/help/faqs/faq.php?category=ads_and_history&page=highlights*.   [47] *http://about.polo.com/default.asp*.
[48] *http://www.endangeredman.com/source/homepage.html*.
[49] I Kant, 'On the Wrongfulness of Unauthorized Publication of Books' in *The Cambridge Edition of the Works of Immanuel Kant: Practical Philosophy*, M J Gregor (ed), (Cambridge University Press, 1996) 27, 30 and *The Metaphysics of Morals*, M J Gregor (ed), (Cambridge University Press, 1996), 71.   [50] 106 S Ct 903 (1986).
[51] 115 S Ct 2338 (1995).   [52] 120 S Ct 2446 (2000).   [53] Ibid, 2454.
[54] 121 S Ct 2334 (2001).

a healthy marketplace of ideas, but on the basis that affording control over when and how a person expresses herself, including control over when and how she refrains from doing so, is an important part of protecting her personal autonomy.

If this is right, then the implications for trade mark dilution should be clear. When someone uses a sign that alludes to a mark, they may be involved in compelling speech. This consists either in forcing the trade mark owner to participate in speech with which she would disagree or in making her mark subsequently bear a meaning from which she would be disassociated. This can be demonstrated on the facts of the well-known American trade mark case *Girl Scouts of the United States of America v Personality Posters Manufacturing Co.*,[55] though in the case itself the dilution claim of the Girl Scouts was unsuccessful on the basis that New York law was said then to require a showing of confusion for a successful dilution claim. The case concerned a poster with a picture of a pregnant Girl Scout wearing the uniform of the organisation and marked with its trade mark. Her hands were clasped above her abdomen and next to her hands was the Girl Scouts' motto 'Be Prepared'. If forcing the Boy Scouts to retain a gay Scout Leader constituted forcing them to express a message with which they might disagree, is it not conceivable that this use of the motto of the Girl Scouts also entailed a type of compelled speech? First, the Girl Scouts were effectively conscripted to express a message about sexual activity with which they might have disagreed. Second, were this poster widely distributed, the Girl Scouts would have been forced either to abandon the use of their motto, a type of silencing, or to contend with the fact that they no longer controlled the message that it conveyed. It would be difficult having seen the poster ever to hear the motto again in quite the same way. The claim against trade mark dilution then becomes a claim grounded in preserving autonomy of expression.

Before considering the important qualifications to such a claim and the way in which this understanding of the justification of dilution protection might be given effect in a reading of section 10 of the Trade Marks Act 1994, I want to deal with four of the most obvious objections to it.

The first of these objections is that in each of the American speech cases to which I have alluded it is the government that is responsible for compelling speech. In the trade mark dilution situation, I am claiming that the private person who uses the mark allusively is compelling speech. In fact, it is hard to see why this distinction is of any importance. A government that is committed to expressive autonomy bears a responsibility

---

[55] 304 F Supp 1228 (DCNY 1969).

to uphold it both in its own actions and in the actions of private parties that it permits and prohibits.

The second objection is that a trade mark is commercial speech and, in the usual course of events, the trade mark owner will be a corporation. The American cases dealing with compelled speech, and with corporate speech more generally, have been the subject of powerful criticism on this basis.[56] However, the fact that speech is commercial is not a reason for it to be denied protection altogether, although it may impact on the level of protection that it is given.[57] Let us assume that the cases concerning compelled speech are at least in part about the protection of personal autonomy. Such protection must surely entail protecting the way in which a person chooses to be presented in inviting commercial transactions to at least some extent, given the importance of commercial transactions to our community life. But this reasoning, though it may justify the protection of commercial speech, highlights the difficulty regarding the corporate identity of most trade mark owners. It makes sense to protect the personal autonomy of natural persons, but does it make sense to protect the personal autonomy of legal persons? This is an important question for many areas of the law, a full consideration of which is outside the scope of this paper. But a robust defence of the attribution of rights to corporations, including rights grounded in autonomy, can be made. For example, Finnis mounts a defence of the attribution of rights to corporations on the basis of the rights of the individuals who use a corporate vehicle to achieve their collective aims.[58] In doing so he builds upon classic arguments made by Hohfeld.[59]

The third objection to my argument is that infringement of a trade mark, whether infringement by causing confusion or infringement by dilution, can only be constituted by the use of a sign 'in the course of trade.'[60] The meaning of this phrase suggested in *Arsenal* is that the use

---

[56] See, for example, R P Bezanson, 'Institutional Speech' (1994–1995) 80 Iowa L. Rev 735; A Hirsch and R Nader, ' "The Corporate Conscience" and Other First Amendment Follies in *Pacific Gas & Electric*' (2004) 41 San Diego L. Rev, 483; and C E Baker, 'Paternalism, Politics, and Citizen Freedom: The Commercial Speech Quandary in *Nike*' (2004) 54 Case W. Res. L. Rev, 1161. For an opposing position see M H Redish and H M Wasserman, 'What's Good for General Motors: Corporate Speech and the Theory of Free Expression' (1997–1998) 66 Geo. Wash. L. Rev., 235.

[57] *Central Hudson Gas & Electric Corporation v Public Service Commission of New York*, 109 SC 2343 (1980).

[58] J Finnis, 'The Priority of Persons' in J Horder (ed), *Oxford Essays in Jurisprudence (Fourth Series)* (Oxford: Clarendon, 2000), 9–11.

[59] W Newcomb Hohfeld, 'Nature of Stockholders' Individual Liability for Corporation Debts' (1909) 9 Columbia L. Rev., 285.

[60] TMA 94 ss 10(1), 10(2) and 10(3).

must have been 'in the context of commercial activity with a view to economic advantage and not as a private matter.'[61] If the law of dilution is best understood as protection against a type of compelled speech, why ought that protection only to be available in these particular circumstances? A mark can be used in an enormous variety of expressive acts from which its owner would wish to be disassociated, and its meaning altered in an enormous variety of ways. Indeed, long before he began his artistic work, the 'Barbie' mark had come to bear some of the meanings upon which Tom Forsythe relied. The mark was certainly not the unaltered speech of its owners. Most of the ways in this had happened could not have constituted use 'in the course of trade' and would not have been actionable as trade mark infringement. Moreover, it is appropriate that this should be the case. The law cannot, and should not, try to control all the ways in which vehicles of expression such as trade marks are used and acquire new meanings. Respect for the expressive autonomy of the trade mark owner does not require that the law give her so complete control over her ongoing speech. However, it may well be an appropriate way of evincing that respect to remove a powerful incentive for using and altering the meaning of speech, the incentive of potential economic advantage. It is the contention of this paper that, subject to the qualifications outlined below, this is an appropriate alternative to offering the trade mark owner either no control, or complete control, over the meaning of her mark. If that is right, then the function of the requirement that an infringement occur 'in the course of trade' is evident.

The fourth objection to my argument is arguably the most powerful and can be expressed in one of two similar ways. First, it can be said that, in situations where it is clear that the use of the sign is merely allusive, the sign is the speech of the party making the allusion and not the speech of the trade mark owner. Alternatively, it can be said that allusion to a mark involves no more than a type of comment, favourable or unfavourable, on the trade mark, its owner or the goods or services to which it is attached, and not a type of compelled speech. These arguments are sometimes made by those who claim that, even if someone has a right to control the way in which her expression is used grounded in her expressive autonomy, any 'transformative' use of that expression renders it the speech of the party responsible for the transformative use and not that of the original speaker. Bezanson takes such a position regarding claims grounded in expressive autonomy for control over the use of copyright works, whether the relevant transformative use involves what he calls 'substantive transformation'

---

[61] [2003] RPC 144 at 170.

(an alteration in the meaning of the work by someone who is clearly not the author) or merely transformation by avowal (its adoption by such a person for purposes of which the author may or may not approve).[62]

However, I would argue that these objections are unfounded and that excluding just any transformative use from the control of the trade mark owner, even if we might want to exclude some, is not an appropriate approach to limiting the scope of dilution claims. I will mount this argument by considering in greater detail the two ways in which I think allusion to the mark might involve compelled speech.

First, as Wasserman emphasises and as I have suggested earlier, the problem with compelled speech is not that it involves a misrepresentation (that some audience will be confused as to the identity or message of the speaker), but that it forces the speaker to participate in an expressive act with which she would disagree and is, in that way, an affront to her autonomy.[63] This is, for example, why the American cases prevent forced financial contributions to expressive activity even though no-one might be confused that an individual required to contribute endorses the relevant expression: in *United States v United Foods Inc*[64] the criterion for contribution was simply that the person levied was a commercial handler of fresh mushrooms. In speaking of fair use exceptions in copyright, Madison claims that allowing access to a work can be forcing its author to 'subsidize, with raw material, the speech of [the] . . . second user.'[65] Talk of 'subsidy' seems unfortunate because, of course, it assumes the right to control use of the material, but Madison's point is the same as that of Wasserman. I prefer to put the relevant wrong as forcing the participation of the trade mark owner in speech to which she may object. When I use the 'Mickey Mouse' mark to sell T-shirts that protest the foreign policy of the United States, I am not necessarily commenting upon either 'Mickey Mouse' or the Disney Corporation. I may simply be conscripting them to participate in a political cause that the corporation has no desire to join; I may be doing so even if those who observe my protest know that there is no connection between me and the Disney Corporation. We shall see that permitting such forced participation may sometimes be essential to protecting the expressive autonomy of the party wanting to allude to the mark, including her ability to comment upon, or even identify, the trade mark, its owner or her goods or services. But it may not always be so.

[62] R P Bezanson, 'Speaking Through Others' Voices: Authorship, Originality and Free Speech' (2003) 38 Wake Forest L. Rev., 983.

[63] H M Wasserman, 'Compelled Expression and the Public Forum Doctrine' (2002–2003) 77 Tulane L. Rev. 163, 191–193.   [64] See n 54 above.

[65] M J Madison, 'Complexity and Copyright in Contradiction' (2000) 18 Cardozo Art & Ent. L. J. 125, 166.

Second, the allusive use of a mark may effectively change its subsequent meaning even if there is no confusion about whether the owner of the mark has authorised the allusive use. It may do this by changing the way in which the mark can subsequently be received. The compelled speech may consist in forcing a mark to bear a meaning with which its owner would want to be disassociated in the way that we saw with the *Girl Scouts'* case. Of course, criticism of a mark, or its owner or her goods or services may also have this effect, but it does not do so by the recoding of the actual speech itself. To be criticised is one thing. To have the meaning of my own words effectively transformed, robbed of their ability to communicate my primary message, is another. Of course, again I affirm that permitting allusion to the mark may be entailed in respect for the expressive autonomy of the party wanting to make the allusion, especially where it is necessary for successful criticism of the mark, its owner or her goods or services. But it may not always be so. In circumstances in which it is not necessary, there may be good reason grounded in the expressive autonomy of the trade mark owner for preventing it.

If my answers to these four objections can be accepted, there seems to be good reason, grounded in the expressive autonomy of the trade mark owner, for permitting some control over allusive uses of the mark. The question that now arises is how that control ought to be limited. It is at this point that the expressive autonomy of the party wanting to allude to the mark becomes relevant and a very important way of limiting the availability of relief for dilution. I believe that there are two situations in which allusion to the mark ought to be permitted despite the expressive autonomy claims of the trade mark owner.

The first of these is the situation in which it is necessary to allude to the mark in order adequately to comment upon, or even identify, the mark, its owner or her goods or services. It is reasonable to allow allusion to the mark for this purpose because there may be no other effective way in which to make such comments than to use, and sometimes to alter the meaning of, the mark. Moreover, using a mark for this purpose does not undermine, but recognises the nexus between the mark and its owner. A speaker cannot object to compelled participation in an argument about her own activities.

Existing trade mark law includes partial provision for this problem. We have seen that it has been prepared to allow purely descriptive uses of a mark and the Trade Marks Act 1994 includes a much more generous provision for comparative advertising than its predecessor.[66] However, I would argue that the courts have not been sufficiently willing to allow

<hr />

[66] TMA 94 s 10(6).

allusive uses of the mark for this purpose. In particular, the courts seem suspicious of allowing allusive uses of a mark for one of the most commercially important purposes, that of signalling the substitutability of a product to consumers. The *Arsenal* decision is instructive here. There is undoubtedly a market for Arsenal souvenirs. That market is defined by a very low cross-price elasticity of demand. Arsenal souvenirs would need to become very expensive indeed in order for Arsenal fans to buy Chelsea souvenirs. Within that market, the *Arsenal* decision gives a powerful monopoly to the football club. It does so by preventing the use of the word 'Arsenal' to signal the substitutability of unauthorised souvenirs, even unauthorised souvenirs where no possibility of post-sale confusion arises. If branding is not to become the powerful barrier to entry that persuasive advertising theorists claim, new entrants must be allowed to allude to trade marks to signal the substitutability of their products for those of the market leaders. I have already suggested that if I sell Poca Pola, no-one is going to be confused, either at the point of sale of subsequently, that I am selling Coca Cola. But consumers may be led to believe that my product is an appropriate substitute for Coca Cola and it may be that this is the only way in which I can effectively inform them of that claim. This is an allusive use of the mark that should be permitted, even if it involves the forced participation of the Coca Cola Company in the speech of its competitors.

The second situation in which it might be necessary to limit the expressive autonomy claim of a trade mark owner to prevent allusive uses of her mark is more problematic. We have already seen that dilution protection can help in preventing a mark from losing its primary value as a symbol and operating as an index of some broader set of associations. However, if a mark has already acquired an important indexical function, it may be essential that it be available to other speakers. 'Barbie' as a index for a particular understanding of womanhood is an example much discussed in the literature. In the United States it has been the subject' not only of the litigation in *Mattel v Walking Mountain Productions*[67] but also of the case *Mattel v MCA Records Inc*[68] concerning the song 'Barbie Girl' by the Danish group 'Aqua'. Indeed, Mattel themselves recognise the indexical status of Barbie. When 'Barbie' turned thirty-five, the company supported the production of one hundred images of the doll, most of which exploited its indexical function in some way (perhaps none more amusingly than the image entitled 'Put Another Shrimp on the Barbie, Mate').[69] Many did so in ways not too dissimilar from those over which

---

[67] See n 16 above.   [68] 296 F 3d 894 (9th Cir 2002).
[69] C Yoe (ed), *The Art of Barbie* (New York: Workman, 1994), 72.

Mattel took action in *Mattel v Walking Mountain Productions*. If there genuinely exists no satisfactory alternative index for an idea or set of ideas—as there may not be in the case of 'Barbie'—then the mark itself should be available for use. To put it another way, the mark may have become a kind of public forum. It may have become a space for debate rather than a contribution to debate. This type of thinking seems to underpin the law of trade mark genericide, although that law is arguably inadequate to protect the relevant free speech interest. In particular, genericide happens when a trade mark shifts from being a symbol with one particular referential function (that of identifying the supplier of goods or services) to being a symbol with a different referential function (that of signifying a whole type of goods or services). However, if a mark has already acquired an important indexical function in the way that the 'Barbie' mark has, there may be just as good a reason for protecting it less strongly as there is for denying protection altogether to a mark that has become generic. In particular, there may be good reason for only protecting these marks against confusion and not dilution. In the case of a limited range of marks which have become important cultural indices, such a response seems justified by a commitment to protecting the expressive autonomy, not only of the owner of the mark, but also those who would allude to it.

We turn back, then, to the language of the statute. Even if I am right and protection against allusions to a mark is best both justified, and limited, by a concern for expressive autonomy, how can that conceptual framework be used in interpreting section 10 of the Trade Marks Act 1994? In relation to section 10(1) it would mean that the judgment of the European Court of Justice in *Arsenal* should be interpreted to recognise a requirement of trade mark use, as it was interpreted in *R. v Johnstone*.[70] Such protection against post-sale confusion as is warranted should be available under section 10(2) and 10(3). It does not require absolute protection against merely allusive uses of a mark under section 10(1). The concept of an allusive use which damages the origin function of the mark, though it is not a trade mark use, should be abandoned by the European Court of Justice.[71]

In relation to section 10(3), the important statutory question is when allusive uses of a mark will 'without due cause, . . . [take] unfair advantage of, or [be] . . . detrimental to, the distinctive character or repute of

---

[70] See n 22 above.
[71] There is now some indication that this might be possible: see *Anheuser-Busch Inc. v Budějovický, národní podnik* (Case C-245/02) 16 November 2004, Grand Chamber, European Court of Justice (unreported) at paras. 60–63.

the mark.' In a commercial context, almost all allusive uses of a mark will either take advantage of, or be detrimental to, its distinctive character or reputation. The person making the allusion will be either using a reference to the mark, its owner or her goods or services as a point of departure of her own activities (that is, taking advantage of them) or criticising them (that is, potentially causing them detriment). Attention must be paid, therefore to the qualifiers that the advantage taken must be *unfair* and the detriment caused *without due cause*. While in theory the phrase 'without due cause' applies also to taking unfair advantage, it was recognised in *Premier Brands UK Ltd v Typhoon Europe Ltd*[72] that the phrase will operate primarily in relation to causing detriment. In decisions of the OHIM Boards of Appeal, 'without due cause' has been interpreted to mean the party who is not the registered owner 'cannot reasonably be required to abstain from its use.'[73] In the High Court it has been interpreted to mean that the context of the use is one in which the owner 'of the protected mark should be required to subordinate his own interests to those of the defendant in relation to the use of the sign in question.'[74]

It is at this point that the relevance of the interpretive framework that I have proposed will become clear. A trade mark owner should be able to insist on maintaining the distinctive character of her mark, her expression. The concept of distinctive character is arguably broader than, and inclusive of, the reputation of the mark. A trade mark owner should be able to insist on maintaining the distinctive character of her mark because that is entailed in respect for her expressive autonomy. However, she should not be able to do so wherever allusive use of the mark is necessary comment upon the owner, her goods or services, or where allusion to the mark is essential because it has become indexical of something else. In other words, a speech-based approach to section 10 would ensure a generous reading of both the protection that it offers and the exclusions to that protection for which it provides. This is more satisfactory than a property-based approach which is likely to afford strong protection to the trade mark owner, without sufficiently protecting the expressive autonomy of the person alluding to the mark.

In offering this reading of section 10(3), there is one requirement that I have omitted. This is the requirement that the protected mark has a reputation. At first sight this may seem incompatible with my reading of the

---

[72] [2000] FSR 767 at 791–792.
[73] *Aktieselskabet af 21 November 2001 v TDK Kabushki Kaisha (TDK Corporation)* (Case R-364/2003-1) OHIM First Board of Appeal, 7 October 2004, unreported at para. 18 relying on *Hollywood*, n 15 above, at paras. 98–103.
[74] *Electrocoin Automatics Limited v Coinworld Limited* [2004] EWHC 1498 at para. 103.

section as one protecting the expressive autonomy of the owner. Surely this is an indication that the section prioritises investment in marks, a classic feature of a property-oriented approach to their protection. Interestingly, however, this does not seem to be how the requirement will be treated by the courts. In *General Motors Corporation v Yplon* the European Court of Justice said that a mark would be regarded as having a reputation wherever there is a 'sufficient degree of knowledge of the mark that the public, when confronted with the later trade mark may possibly make an association between the two trade marks'.[75] In other words, the requirement that a mark have a reputation is not a requirement that it has been the object of sufficient investment to be worthy of protection, but merely a requirement that the potentially infringing sign will be recognisable as an allusion to the mark. If it is not so recognisable, then it cannot have a direct impact on the trade mark owner's ability to control the meaning of her own expression.

In beginning with the idea of a legal *topos*, I wanted to make it clear that I am not suggesting that trade mark law can only be presented as law regulating speech. But it is often claimed that protection against allusive uses is a sign of how deeply embedded the idea that a trade mark owner owns her mark has become. I have shown that this need not be the case, that perhaps the best justification for protection against allusive use is grounded in a commitment to upholding expressive autonomy and not in a commitment to property. If this is right, then it has some important repercussions for trade mark law. I will close with just one example.

My example concerns the lawfulness of the parallel importation of trade marked goods (that is, whether a trade mark owner can use her trade mark rights to prevent the importation into the United Kingdom of goods to which the mark has legitimately been applied outside the European Economic Area). This question is often treated as equivalent to the question of the whether a copyright or patent owner can use her intellectual property rights to prevent the parallel importation of goods in which they are embodied. However, if trade mark is ultimately a system for the private regulation of speech, then these issues could barely be more dissimilar. I said at the beginning that there might be good reason for not worrying too much about the difference between property in a work or invention and property in the right to control particular uses of a work or invention. Part of that reason is that we want to encourage investment in works and inventions and permitting price discrimination is a good way of giving incentive to investment in both their creation and efficient

---

[75] *General Motors Corporation v Yplon Sa* (Case C-375/97) [2000] RPC 572, 577.

exploitation. But if property in a trade mark is property in a right to control someone else's speech, and if we have no real interest in encouraging investment in trade marks and their efficient exploitation, then there is no good reason for permitting price discrimination. On the contrary, encouraging a trade mark owner to use her mark to send different messages in different jurisdictions might undercut the effectiveness of the trade mark system as a system for the regulation of speech.

The differences between a law of trade marks conceived of as a system for the regulation of speech and a law of trade marks conceived of as a system for the protection of property are sometimes subtle, but nevertheless real. Like all *topoi* in the law, the speech and property *topoi* are both accurate and misleading. But the question of which is to predominate as European trade mark law develops, is a question of not only legal, but also economic and cultural, importance.[75]

---

[75] At proof stage I became aware of an argument for dilution as useful 'to preserve the expressive capacity of trade marks and protect their status as effective instruments of culural dialogue'. (J Bosland, 'The Culture of Trade Marks: An Alternative Cultural Theory Perspective' (2005) 10 Media & Arts Law Review 99). Such an argument arguably comlements the rights-based approach to dilution of this paper and I am grateful to Cesar Ramirez-Monkes for drawing my attention to it.

Rethinking the Personal Work Contract

Mark Freedland

Introduction

It was an honour to have been invited to give this lecture, and a considerable pleasure to deliver it; and the opportunity to publish it in the annual *Current Legal Problems* volume is a welcome one. In order to explain why that is the case, I need to engage in a moment of autobiography, and to explain how my interest in the subject of 'rethinking the personal work contract' is specially associated with the Faculty of Laws, University College London, and indeed with the *Current Legal Problems* series in which this lecture figures. I hope I will be forgiven for having largely retained in the published version of this lecture the obviously dialectical style of the lecture as delivered; I have regarded that as permissible by reason of the particularly personal odyssey, both past and intended for the future, which it describes.

Just under 40 years ago, in the academic year of 1965/1966, I was a law student in my final year at UCL, and had made the unusual choice of studying the optional subject of Industrial Law, the title of the course which would later generally be known as labour law, and now increasingly often styled as employment law. During that year, the teacher of that course, Roger Rideout, delivered an extremely influential lecture on the Contract of Employment in that year's *Current Legal Problems* series[1].

In the course of that year, and not least by reason of Roger's teaching, I acquired what was to be a career-long interest in employment law in general and the law of the contract of employment in particular. I was dispatched to Oxford to undertake doctoral research with Otto Kahn-Freund, who had himself quite recently before that gone from the London School of Economics, where almost all of his British career had been spent, to the Chair of Comparative Law at Oxford. I wrote a thesis on the termination of the contract of employment, and later enlarged it into a general treatise on the English law of the contract of employment

---

[1] (1966) 19 *Current Legal Problems*, 111–127.

which was published in 1976.[2] In 1977, I myself delivered a *Current Legal Problems* lecture on 'The Obligation to Work and to Pay for Work'[3] in which I sought to develop one aspect of the law of the contract of employment somewhat further.

Now I am here again, having published in 2003 an enlarged and updated counterpart of my treatise on the contract of employment,[4] and with the purpose of describing what is now decidedly a late-career project of 'rethinking the personal work contract', and sketching out one small aspect of it in slightly more detail. I hope that I can persuade you that the topic is not just my own perpetual Current Legal Problem but also one of continuing general interest and importance.

My attempt to do this takes the following form. First, I will describe the work which I think remains to be done in 'rethinking the personal work contract', and I will give a sense of how I hope to begin to carry out that work. This will involve referring to the work which has been done and is being done in the field by a succession of distinguished writers, and locating my own intended work in relation to that existing output.

Second, as a preliminary part of my own project, I will try out some tentative ideas about the further analysis of the concept of the employer as it figures in the law of personal employment contracts.

Rethinking the Personal Work Contract—the Task Ahead

Let me start by explaining the origins and aims of the work that I was trying to do on the contract of employment in the 1960s and 1970s, and what has become of those aims and ambitions in the intervening time. My starting points, as I have indicated, were the approaches which Otto Kahn-Freund and Roger Rideout had taken to the English law of the contract of employment. They had both fully recognised the centrality of the contract of employment to British labour law, and had both been in the business of decrying it. For Kahn-Freund, the individualism of the law of the contract of employment amounted to a denial and suppression of what for him was the essential collectivism of relations between labour and capital.

At the same time, Kahn-Freund, as I have hinted elsewhere,[5] had made something of a Faustian pact with the English law of the contract of

---

[2] M R Freedland, *The Contract of Employment* (Oxford: Clarendon Press, 1976).
[3] (1977) 30 *Current Legal Problems*, 175–189.
[4] M R Freedland, *The Personal Employment Contract* (Oxford University Press, 2003).
[5] In a biographical chapter on 'Otto Kahn-Freund (1900–1979)' in J Beatson and R Zimmermann (eds), *Jurists Uprooted: German-speaking Émigré Lawyers in Twentieth Century Britain* (Oxford University Press, 2004), 314–315.

employment; for he had come to see it as the vehicle by which his conception of collective *laissez-faire* might be driven into the framework of British labour law. This was the masterly accomplishment of his chapter on the legal framework in the symposium on 'The System of Industrial Relations in Great Britain' which Flanders and Clegg put together in the early 1950s.[6] It was there that Kahn-Freund so memorably deployed the notion of 'crystallised custom' in order to endow the standard-setting provisions of collective agreements with legal effect in favour of individual workers, while maintaining the not legally enforceable character of those agreements as between the collective parties to them.[7]

Kahn-Freund was bound to feel a mixture of antipathy for and yet some indulgence towards this institution of English law which could thus in his own skilled hands be adapted to deliver the goods of a legal accounting for the collective voluntarism which he so admired in British industrial relations. I think that tension is evident in the rather conflicted historical evaluation which he much later offered in his Blackstone Lecture of 1977, under title of 'The Contract of Employment: Blackstone's Neglected Child'.[8]

Rideout, writing as I have said in the mid-1960s, had a rather different bone to pick with the law of the contract of employment. For him, the trouble was the way in which it provided a shaky and distorted set of foundations on which to build an edifice of general legislative protections and positive rights for the worker, such as was starting to be constructed at that period. In his view, those defects would continue to undermine the whole conceptual structure of the legal analysis of the employment relationship unless and until that relationship was understood more as a status than as a contract.[9]

I suppose that with the optimism, and perhaps the arrogance, of youth, I embarked upon work on the English law of the contract of employment in the belief that a careful rationalisation of the, at that time still rather sparse, case law might contribute to the formation of a more robust and satisfactory analytical structure for the law of the employment relation than had previously been believed to exist.

It must have displayed the even more considerable folly of middle age to return to that task in 1999, embarking on labours which issued forth in the work on *The Personal Employment Contract* which was published in 2003.[10]

[6] A Flanders and H A Clegg (eds), *The System of Industrial Relations in Great Britain: Its History, Law and Institutions* (Oxford: Basil Blackwell, 1954).   [7] Ibid, 58–60.

[8] (1977) 93 LQR 508.

[9] See especially (1966) 19 *Current Legal Problems*, 122–127.

[10] Freedland, n 4 above.

I had become convinced, after a long absence from direct concentration on the contract of employment, that a coherent work could be produced by updating and somewhat enlarging the scope of the earlier treatise. My difficulties with that undertaking were the genesis of the further project with which this lecture is concerned, from which you will gather that my ardour has still not been dampened for work in this area: truly, a triumph of hope over experience.

As I began work in earnest on updating my book on *The Contract of Employment* during two terms of sabbatical leave at the beginning of the year 2000, I realised that there were really three fundamental evolutions going on in the law of the contract of employment, interlinked but distinguishable, and that the task of doing justice to all three of them had become quite a daunting one. There was and is also a fourth evolution coming into view. I shall touch briefly on each of these evolutions in turn.

The first evolution consists of an exponential elaboration of the law of the contract of employment as a conceptual apparatus and substructure for an itself ever-elaborating body of employment legislation. A great wave of elaboration occurred in the 1970s and 1980s, as employment legislation wrapped itself into an apparently simple but actually deeply arcane set of notions about termination of the contract of employment, whether by lawful dismissal, as the result of wrongful dismissal, or by other means.[11] A most valuable analysis of this set of issues was carried out by Steve Anderman in his article, published in 2000, on 'The Interpretation of Protective Employment Statutes and the Contract of Employment'.[12] Another wave now starts to roll ashore as post-1997 legislation regulating minimum wages and, even more especially, working time, reveals the true hideous complexity of the wage–work bargain, and the inadequacy of the legal accounting for it in the law of the contract of employment.[13]

The second evolution consisted in the growth of an increasingly urgent awareness that the law of the contract of employment did not extend to or account for the situation of sections of the labour force working under arrangements not coming within that legal category; this was an awareness, moreover, that those sections were growing in significance by reason of the swing to 'marginal', 'atypical' or 'flexible' forms of employment from the early 1980s onwards. Harbingers of the growth of this concern were the major articles written by Bob Hepple in 1986 on 'Restructuring Employment Rights',[14] and by Hugh Collins in 1990 on 'Independent Contractors and the Challenge of Vertical Disintegration to Employment

---

[11] Compare Freedland, n 4 above, 291–298. [12] (2000) 29 ILJ 223.
[13] Compare Freedland, n 4 above, 86–98. [14] (1986) 15 ILJ 69.

Protection Laws'.[15] By now, there is a genre of writing which focuses upon the personal scope of employment law; Sandra Fredman provided an important addition to it with her piece on 'Labour Law in Flux: The Changing Composition of the Workforce', published in 1997.[16] Perhaps the most far-reaching contribution to it has been the report prepared for the European Commission by Alain Supiot and his colleagues, published in English translation in 2001 under the title *Beyond Employment: Changes in Work and the Future of Labour Law in Europe*.[17]

The third evolution has consisted in a new debate among the judges and the commentators upon their case law as to whether the implied or default provisions of the contract of employment might develop in radically worker-protective directions, especially so as to provide workers with a set of claims in respect of avoidable psychological damage resulting from their situation during employment or on the termination of employment. The main though not the sole focus for this evolution was the articulation and development of the implied obligation as to mutual trust and confidence. Among the commentators, it has been Douglas Brodie who in a series of seminal articles[18] has done most to pursue this development. What had appeared to be a steadily rising tide of judicial development turned abruptly with the decision of the House of Lords in 2001 in *Johnson v Unisys Ltd*[19] that the implied obligation did not apply in respect of dismissal. Less dramatic but also highly significant has been the judicial containment of the claim to damages for stress-related psychological damage caused by the employee's treatment during the continuance of the employment relationship, for which the crucial decision is that of the Court of Appeal in 2002 in *Hatton v Sutherland*.[20] In this evolution, the question was whether the common law of the employment relation was going to provide a parallel and supplementary set of claims and remedies to reinforce and supplement the legislation on unfair dismissal and on health and safety; and the judicial answer, after some serious flirtation with such possibilities, seems to be a broadly negative one.

On the other hand, we may be embarking on a fourth evolution in which the legislators, judges, and commentators work out a state of alignment between the contract law of the employment relation and the

---

[15] (1990) 10 OJLS 353 (see also below at n 61). [16] (1997) 26 ILJ 337.

[17] (Oxford University Press, 2001).

[18] Especially 'The Heart of the Matter: Mutual Trust and Confidence'(1996) 25 ILJ 121, and 'Legal Coherence and the Employment Revolution' (2001) 117 LQR 604.

[19] [2001] ICR 480.

[20] [2002] ICR 613; the principles enunciated were later upheld by HL sub nom *Barber v Somerset CC* [2004] ICR 457.

statute law articulating the set of fundamental human, social and economic rights which public policy sees fit to attach to that relation. The question here is whether and how far those rights, for example those incorporated into British law by the Human Rights Act 1998, will be derogable or malleable by contract. This is the subtle form of the debate between *jus cogens* and *jus dispositivum*, absolutely binding law and negotiable law; Gillian Morris has done much to launch that debate in the employment context in the article which she published in 2001 on 'Fundamental Rights; Exclusion by Agreement'.[21]

It is notable, though when one thinks about it unsurprising, that these evolutions have contributed to a sense that the law of the contract of employment is in a state not merely of ferment but also of crisis. Kahn-Freund and Rideout, as we have seen, were anticipating this in the 1950s and 1960s; by the early 1980s, Bill Wedderburn and Jon Clark were pronouncing there to be a 'crisis of fundamental concepts';[22] Lizzie Barmes—I think the latest, and very welcome, UCL entrant into the lists to joust about the contract of employment—has recently written about 'The Continuing Conceptual Crisis in the Common Law of the Contract of Employment'.[23] The seat of the crisis shifts from time to time; while Wedderburn and Clark were mainly concerned with my first two sets of critical evolutions, Barmes is more concerned with the third and fourth ones; but the underlying sense of a system in turmoil and dysfunction is a common one.

It was this crisis or set of crises with which I felt I was confronted when I set out in 1999 to revise my work on the contract of employment. This presented itself as a millennial task in more senses than one. My idea was to enlarge the conceptual category under consideration from that of the contract of employment to that of the personal work contract at large, and to comment critically upon the way in which an updated version of my mid-1970s exegesis might apply across that extended board. As in due course I acknowledged in the Conclusion to the new version, that emerged as an enormous undertaking for which I could really only present an account of 'work in progress' in 2003.

Last year, Paul Davies and I published, in the *Liber Amicorum for Bob Hepple* which Catherine Barnard, Simon Deakin and Gillian Morris have so successfully put together,[24] an essay on 'Changing Perspectives Upon

---

[21] (2001) 30 ILJ 49.

[22] In 'Modern Law: Problems Functions and Policies', their chapter in K W Wedderburn, R Lewis and J Clark (eds), *Labour Law and Industrial Relations: Building on Kahn-Freund* (Oxford: Clarendon Press, 1983).   [23] (2004) 67 MLR 435.

[24] C Barnard, S Deakin and G Morris (eds), *The Future of Labour Law: Liber Amicorum for Sir Bob Hepple QC* (Oxford and Portland, OR: Hart Publishing, 2004).

the Employment Relationship in British Labour Law' which was meant to delineate a broad canvas within which further work on the law of the employment contract or relationship could be undertaken. We called for reconsideration of that body of law from three critical aspects, those of the worker, the employer, and the relationship between them. At that time, it was far from clear how much if any time either of us would have available in the succeeding years to pursue those concerns. Since then, the Trustees of the Leverhulme Foundation have given me a precious three-year opportunity to do some at least of that work, from October 2005 onwards, and the purpose of this lecture is to describe some preliminary thinking about how to make further progress during that time. The remainder of this lecture will be concerned, firstly, with establishing the methodology for that project, and finally with beginning to apply that methodology to the concept of the employer.

The Task Ahead—Settling the Methodology

In my work on the personal employment contract, I identified and sought to develop a methodology of 'Expansion and Restatement'.[25] In my Leverhulme proposal I used the terminology of 'Reframing'; and in the title to this lecture, I spoke of 'Rethinking'. Nothing much turns on the difference between those terms, but I am now proposing a some-what adapted methodology from that which was used in *The Personal Employment Contract*.

In the course of working on that book, and reviewing that work in hindsight, my feeling has been that I needed to develop both a better-defined normative stance, and if possible a more searching analytical method. But perhaps the most important single methodological innova-tion was to seek a clearer separation between the normative and the narrative or descriptive. Let me address those three issues in turn.

With hindsight then, I think that my writing in *The Personal Employment Contract* could be improved by a stricter separation between the descriptive and the prescriptive. Perhaps I was getting stuck in a tradition of writing about labour law in which those two elements are truly inseparable. The formation of that tradition was understandable on the part of those who had to *invent* British labour law, and who were concerned that it should in its very nature be 'good' labour law, as formed, and not just as performed, to draw on the terminology of illegality in

[25] Freedland, n 4 above, 1–12.

contracts. We still of course have that concern; but we no longer have to invent British labour law (even if we still wish continually to improve it). So it now seems to me that there is scope for improving both the narrative and the normative elements of a discourse about the law of personal employment contracts by disentangling the two. The work which I would hope to produce from this project would consist of narrative sections and evaluative sections separate from, though alongside, each other.

I therefore have the task of articulating a distinct and distinctive normative or critical stance, and equally, an analytical method by which to operate on the basis of that stance. I shall have to engage in a good deal of further reflection about this; the main task is to escape from a simplistic set of assumptions that it is the role of the law of employment contracts to become more worker-protective in each and every particular, and therefore the task of analysts to scrutinise the law for any shortcomings in this respect. There is a rich body of recent and current literature on which to draw for the purpose of refining the analysis. Some of it is organised around the idea of labour or employment law being transformative of labour or employment practice, such as the symposium edited by Joanne Conaghan, Richard Fischl and Karl Klare on *Labour Law in an Era of Globalisation; Transformative Practices and Possibilities* published in 2002,[26] or around the associated idea of labour law as itself being in a state of rapid transformation away from its mid-twentieth-century paradigm, such as the very recent symposium on *The Future of Labour Law* edited by Barnard, Deakin, and Morris to which I referred earlier.[27]

But I anticipate wishing to draw more specifically upon a developing sub-genre of labour law writing which concentrates upon the rationales for the regulation, in the interests of public policy as from time to time perceived, of the employment relation or the labour market. Paul Davies and I worked in the early 1990s on the post-war history of labour legislation and public policy, publishing a work on that subject in 1993,[28] and we are continuing to labour in that vineyard. But I have particularly in mind here some more recent work, for instance, the symposium put together by Collins, Davies and Rideout in which were published in 2000 a number of papers from the 1999 WG Hart Workshop on *Legal Regulation of the Employment Relation*.[29] I also had the great privilege of reading in draft the work of Simon Deakin and Frank Wilkinson on

---

[26] (Oxford: Oxford University Press, 2002).
[27] Barnard, Deakin and Morris, n 24 above, and associated text.
[28] *Labour Legislation and Public Policy: A Contemporary History* (Oxford: Clarendon Press, 1993).
[29] (London: Institute of Advanced Legal Studies and Kluwer Law International, 2000).

The Law of the Labour Market: Industrialisation, Employment and Legal Evolution,[30] clearly a major addition to that literature. I expect that, like Supiot's *Beyond Employment* report to which I referred earlier, this work will help to develop a normative stance which locates the law of employment contracts within the whole context of social policy and provision, thus assisting in the evolution of something which is more truly Social Law in a continental European sense, corresponding to the notions of *droit social* or *Sozialrecht*.

Within that context, it seems to me important to try to develop a broad notion of optimal regulatory impact, which might form the basis of a more refined critical analysis of the law of employment contracts than is offered from a narrowly and remorselessly worker-protective standpoint. It is I admit much easier to postulate a notion of optimal regulatory impact than to sketch out its content, but I have in mind an idea which is more extensive and searching than the one which underlies the regulatory impact assessments which now accompany governmental proposals for legislation, those assessments sometimes amounting to no more than a rather superficial cost/benefit analysis concentrated on the immediate costs to the public purse of implementing the proposed measures in question.

A particular demand which I shall make of myself in trying to develop in more detail a notion of optimal regulatory impact will be that this notion will be capable of being applied in a critical way not only to legislative regulation of the employment relation, but also to judicial regulation in the form of judicial articulation of definitions, rules, and principles with regulatory effects or implications. So, to take an example from earlier in this discussion,[31] the doctrinal ruling in *Johnson v Unisys* would be a prime candidate for such scrutiny.

That in turn brings me to the issue of analytical method, both for the narrative and the normative elements of the work. Here again, much more development will be needed; but I have in mind three lines of development which I think might be promising. Those three lines of thought can be identified in terms of, first, multi-functionality, second, structural regulation, and third, intra-European comparison; I will enlarge on each of them in turn.

The idea of multi-functionality is the following one. It starts from the observation that legal rules, or definitions, or principles often have not just one regulatory function, but a multiplicity of them; and that the law

---

[30] (Oxford: Oxford University Press, 2005).
[31] See [2001] ICR 480 and associated text.

of employment contracts is especially full of such multi-functional principles, definitions and rules. Nowhere is this more famously the case than with the distinction between employees and independent contractors or self-employed persons. We all know that one of the reasons why that distinction is such a fraught one is that it has to be drawn for such a wide variety of disparate purposes, from attributing vicarious liability to delineating the personal scope of employment rights, to assigning working persons to different income tax or social security regimes and so on.

However, this is only one of a host of examples of multi-functionality in this body of law, many such examples being more or less undetected or concealed ones. The whole idea of 'termination of employment' is another good illustration. Workers may wish to claim that their employment has been terminated for one purpose, such as entitlement to remedies for unfair dismissal, but that it remains in being for other purposes, such as entitlement to continuing remuneration. So the impulse to be protective of workers, even if we respond to it in a single-minded way, pulls in different directions when we define 'the termination of employment'. My proposed analytical method seeks to tease out and recognise the huge regulatory significance of this kind of multi-functionality.

My second idea is to focus on structural analysis. This is the idea of being especially aware of the way in which legal rules, or definitions, or principles serve to create perceptions about the *structure* of employment relations. Again, this capacity for structuring, or structuralism, is a specially marked feature of the law of employment relations and contracts, by comparison with the law of other contracts; and, again, it is sometimes very obviously present but sometimes less obvious or indeed concealed. Thus the structural dimension is very evident, for example, when we consider the development of the doctrine of mutuality of obligations in contracts of employment, or the inter-relatedness of the obligations to work and to pay for work. It is less obvious but strongly present when we consider the evolution and interpretation of concepts such as 'payment in lieu of notice' or 'garden leave'. My idea is to concentrate on that structural dimension, and to identify how central it is to the regulatory impact of this body of law.

My third idea is to use inter-European comparison as a principal analytical method. So although my narrative will be about English law, the normative analysis will be conducted partly by means of comparison with other European systems of law of employment contracts or relations. My suggestion is that comparison with other employment law systems in general, and with other European systems in particular will be helpful in developing the notions of multi-functionality and structuralism which I have just elaborated. Let me seek to illustrate that with one line of comparison with US employment law, and another line of comparison with some other European employment law systems.

The line of comparison with US employment law is with its doctrine of employment at will. There has been endless debate about the exact way in which to formulate this doctrine, and about its significance in US employment law; suffice it in the present context for me to refer to Clyde Summers' authoritative statement and assessment of it in his article, published in 2001, on 'Individualism, Collectivism and Autonomy in American Labor Law'.[32] I would myself formulate the employment-at-will doctrine thus: it is to the effect that the default assumption of US employment law is that, in the absence of indications to the contrary, an employment relationship is to be construed as being terminable by the employer without notice and without good cause shown. I want to draw attention both to the multi-functionality and to the structural significance of this doctrine.

The principal function of that doctrine has been thought to be the obstacle which it has historically placed in the path of development of the kind of protection of workers against contractually wrongful and unfair dismissal which has developed in European employment law systems. However, I would see that as perhaps less important than its ubiquitous if less specific influence elsewhere in US employment law. Even those who think that the doctrine no longer prevails in the face of development of notions of unfair discharge in US employment law would I think accept that the idea of employment at will rules from the grave in other areas. For instance, a recent article by Karen Eltis convincingly argued that it was still shaping 'The Emerging American Approach to E-mail Privacy in the Workplace', dictating a mentality in which employer prerogative was paramount.[33]

Even more interesting than its multi-functionality is the structural character of the 'employment at will' doctrine. My suggestion is—and I think that too little attention has been paid to this—that the doctrine has represented a whole way of thinking about the structure of the employment relation which is in radical contrast to the way in which English law thinks about it. For whereas English law insists upon conceptualising that relation in contractual terms, the employment-at-will doctrine provides an analysis of the employment relation which is either

---

[32] (2001) 5 Employment Rights and Employment Policy Journal, 453.
[33] (2003) 24 Comparative Labor Law and Policy Journal, 487.

not contractual at all, or in such a weak sense as to fall below the horizon of English contractual employment law. There is a splendid irony in the fact that employment at will, though the default paradigm for employee status in US employment law, is actually excluded from employee status in English employment law, because by definition it fails to satisfy the requirement of continuing mutuality of obligation as in recent years articulated by the House of Lords in *Carmichael v National Power Plc.*[34] It is little short of revelatory to realise the extent to which an employment law system which has its origins in English common law can manage to think about the employment relation in terms which are not primarily or strictly contractual, given the extent to which we have come to regard the contract of employment as the 'cornerstone of the edifice' in a conceptual or structural sense.

This takes me on to the question of inter-European comparative method. My idea is that, given my interest in the multi-functional and structural elements in the rules, definitions and principles of the law of the employment relation, I might expect to find especially interesting comparisons and contrasts with other European employment law systems. That is perhaps because of the underlying differences between common-law-based and civil-law-based employment law systems; but perhaps it is even more because of the different way in which many other European employment law systems handle and understand the difference between employment relationships and employment contracts.

I am coming to the view that English employment law, while very non-prescriptive as to the range and variety of employment relations which may be recognised as contractual ones, has great difficulty in understanding and handling non-contractual employment relations, simply relegating them to a sort of legal outer darkness in which their shapes remain vague and ill-defined. (This, as we have just seen, may be in contrast to US employment law, which does seem well accustomed to the non-contractual or weakly contractual relation of employment at will.) In some continental European employment law systems, the approach may be different again. They seem very prescriptive about the conditions on which employment relations are admitted to the contractual fold, imposing a set of fairly rigid standard contractual paradigms. But I think they may be readier than English law to recognise and handle non-contractual employment relations outside those standard contractual paradigms. (That incidentally may help to explain why EC employment law measures bring in the notion of 'employment relations' when it is

---

[34] [1999] ICR 1226.

wished to extend them to a wider category of workers than those with contracts of employment, as for example in the case of the Part-time Work Directive.[35] Clause 2.1 of the Agreement which that Directive enacts states that 'This agreement applies to part-time workers who have an employment contract *or relationship* as defined by the law, collective agreement or practice in force in each Member State.')

Extreme and illustrative in this respect is the Italian Legislative Decree 276 of 2003, (implementing the White Paper of which the architect was our much-lamented colleague Marco Biagi). Articles 33–40 of that Decree introduce a new contract of '*lavoro intermittente*' often referred to as '*lavoro a chiamata*' probably best understood as an 'on-call contract'; the workers under such contracts, the shape and conditions of which are quite rigidly framed by the legislation, receive some labour law protections. My sense is that this marks a transition to a new type of labour contract from an employment relation which was legally *recognisable* even if outside the labour law fold. It is that kind of functionality and legal structuring of employment relations which I think it will be fruitful to compare in depth with the way in which English employment law approaches such issues.

Deconstructing the Concept of the Employer

Having I trust given some sense of the approaches I hope to bring to my further work in this field, I propose to devote the remainder of this lecture to the further exploration of one part of the conceptual edifice which is still (I think) in a ramshackle condition, that of the notion of the employer in the law of employment relations and contracts. This exploration will turn out to have significant implications for the other two parts of the structure, that is to say the notions of the worker and of the relation between the worker and the employer. So let me embark on some deconstruction of the concept of the employer. In the course of doing so, I shall look first at some issues about multilateral employment and the multi-agency employer, and I will then devote the rest of my attention to the concept of the single employer. Finally I will consider how inter-European comparative method might assist with the reconstruction which this exercise in deconstruction demands.

[35] Council Directive 97/81/EC of 15 December 1997 concerning the framework agreement on part-time work concluded by UNICE, CEEP and the ETUC [OJ 1998 L14/9].

Multilateral Employment and the Multi-agency Employer

So I begin my deconstruction of the concept of the employer with multi-lateral employment and the multi-agency employer. In recent years, theorists of labour law and employment relations have been quite well aware of the need to reconsider their concept of the employer. The main focus of this awareness has been on situations of multilateral employment, where more than one legal entity is involved on the management or employing side of the employment relationship. Davies and I concentrated on those situations in our discussion of the concept of the employer in our contribution to the symposium on *The Future of Labour Law* to which I referred earlier.[36]

We distinguished between two main varieties of such situations, looking first at the case of employers within corporate groups within which there is unified management, and second at the case of multilateral employment involving multiple legal entities on the employing or management side which are not under unified management and where there is therefore dispersed management of the employment relation.

We identified the first of those two kinds of situation as posing the older of the two sets of problems about multilateral employment. It resulted from the tendency of private sector capital to structure or restructure itself not just into corporations but into complex corporate groups, a tendency latterly replicated in the public sector too, for example in the ways that the rail network has been restructured and the National Health Service is in the course of being restructured.[37] Charlotte Villiers, John Armour and Simon Deakin provided, in two linked commentary pieces,[38] a very useful study of the employment law implications of one such private sector restructuring exercise, that by which, in the year 2000, the Rover Group car manufacturing enterprise centred on Longbridge was transferred from BMW to the Phoenix consortium, a salvage operation of which the endgame is currently being played out in negotiations with potential Chinese corporate purchasers.

We could—indeed we are invited by those writings to—think of the problems posed by this kind of situation as an elaborate variant on the basic regulatory problem, addressed by successive Acquired Rights

---

[36] Barnard, Deakin and Morris, n 24 above, 134–145.
[37] Compare ibid, 136; (2001) 30 ILJ 49 and associated text.
[38] C Villiers, 'The Rover Case (1) The Sale of Rover Cars by BMW—The Role of the Works Council' (2000) 29 ILJ 386; J Armour and S Deakin, 'The Rover Case (2) Bargaining in the Shadow of TUPE' (2000) 29 ILJ 395.

Directives[39] and TUPE Regulations,[40] of maintaining the continuity of the employer's responsibilities and liabilities upon the transfer of business undertakings. This is a regulatory task the successful execution of which ultimately depends on devising and maintaining a coherent concept of the employing undertaking or separable and continuing part thereof.

The second kind of situation, that of multilateral employment where management is dispersed, is actually no new one, but has become much more prominent and perceived as much more problematical for employment law by reason of the very considerable increase in recent times of employment through intermediaries such as sub-contractors, franchisees, and employment agencies or businesses. There has been an increasing perception of significant issues of legislative policy and judicial interpretation as workers within such structures cast about to establish whether they have employment rights against either the end-users of their services or the intermediary enterprises. The risks that workers might fall between two or more stools in this respect were starkly revealed by the decision of the Court of Appeal in *Montgomery v Johnson Underwood Ltd*,[41] and have been only partially reduced by their later decisions in *Frank v Reuters Ltd*[42] and *Dacas v Brook Street Bureau (UK) Ltd*.[43] Proposals for legislative responses seem hopelessly stalled both at national and equally, it must be said, at European Community level, despite some recent gentle blowing on the embers by the European Commission in their newly announced Social Agenda.[44]

The theorists have not been behind-hand in appreciating the way in which this expanding category of multilateral employment casts doubt upon our traditional conception of the employer. In 2001, Deakin wrote a commentary piece drawing attention to 'The Changing Concept of the "Employer" in Labour Law'.[45] In 2002, Jill Earnshaw, Jill Rubery and Fang Lee Cooke published a valuable study entitled *Who is the Employer*,[46] in which they charted 'the rise of multi-employer or multi-agency relationships'. At the end of last year there was published Guy Davidov's article on 'Joint Employer Status in Triangular Employment Relationships'.[47]

---

[39] Currently Directive 2001/23/EC consolidating the original Directive 77/187/EEC and the subsequent amending Directive 98/50/EC.
[40] The Transfer of Undertakings (Protection of Employment) Regulations 1981 (SI 1981/1794) as since amended on various occasions in various respects.
[41] [2001] ICR 819.   [42] [2003] ICR 1166.   [43] [2004] ICR 1437.
[44] See *http://europa.eu.int/comm/employment_social/news/2005/feb/social_agenda_en. html.*
[45] (2001) 30 ILJ 72.
[46] (The Institute of Employment Rights, London 2002).
[47] (2004) 42 *British Journal of Industrial Relations*, 727.

I do not need or propose to add much to that particular body of theoretical work, because my focus is mainly on issues arising within the conception of the single employer rather than upon the conception of the employer in multi-agency relationships. However, I might in passing draw attention to some very interesting forms of concealed or emergent multi-agency employment which are starting to present themselves, and which may wreak further havoc upon our concept of the employer.

One form of concealed multi-agency employment which I had imagined as a possibility was the situation in which an employing enterprise brings in a firm of management consultants to advise closely upon or carry out its human resource management. This it seemed to me could amount to an effective contracting out of the employment functions of the enterprise in question. That possibility is being fully and quite dramatically realised in practice, in the shape of the outsourcing by BT of its human resources management to Accenture. Let me relate this story in a little bit of detail and reflect on its implications for the present discussion.

Accenture is a multinational management consultancy, I believe based in the USA, with more than 110 offices in 48 countries. Its website declares that 'Accenture is a global management consulting, technology services and outsourcing company. Committed to delivering innovation, Accenture collaborates with its clients to help them become high-performance businesses and governments'.[48] There is a long history of restructuring and reorganising BT, going back to its separation from the Post Office, then a civil service department, in 1969. A significant recent episode in that history was the partial outsourcing by BT of its human resources management activity to Accenture, by means of a five-year joint venture contract made in the year 2000. In February 2005, this arrangement was renewed and extended into a ten-year contract, reported to be worth £306m, for the world-wide provision of human resources management to BT by Accenture. The Accenture website proudly declares of the first five years that, 'BT transformed its in-house Human Resources capability from 14,500 people to fewer than 600 HR Business Partners with HR transactional needs now provided by Accenture HR Services'. Accenture has published a 'Client Success Story' of its relations with BT which I commend to your attention.[49]

How is all this relevant to the theme of this lecture? In various ways, as will appear. My immediate point is that the effect of this HR outsourcing is to create a situation in which the conduct of employment relations at

---

[48] *http://www.accenture.com/xd/xd.asp?it=enweb&xd=aboutus\about_home.xml.*
[49] *http://www.accenture.com/xdoc/en/services/hp/hrservices/case/case_bt.pdf.*

BT has become an activity integrally shared with Accenture HR Services; I assume this includes decisions about hiring and firing, reward and promotion, and job specifications. I would imagine that workers at BT have what is in substance a multilateral employment relationship. Yet I am sure that the law would still regard BT as their employer; certainly as their contractual employer. This is a perfect case of concealed multi-agency employment.

I hinted there at the possibility of divergence of analysis as to the employer in contractual terms and the employer in terms of employment law more generally. We can now start to observe that possibility becoming quite a difficult reality. I can illustrate this in one of the very significant locations of partial or emergent multilateral employment, that of local authority schools of which the management is delegated to the head teacher and governing body of each school. The very recent decision of the Court of Appeal in *Murphy v Slough Borough Council and the Governing Body of Langleywood School*[50] exemplifies this situation and its acute difficulties.

Langleywood School is a maintained community school with a delegated budget under the School Standards and Framework Act 1998. Mrs Murphy was or is a teacher there who suffers from a congenital heart disorder making it dangerous for her to go through a pregnancy. So she and her husband arranged for a surrogate mother in the USA to give birth to their child, and she requested paid maternity leave so as to be able to bond with the child once it was born. The Governing Body decided that the school budget could not support paid leave. The Head Teacher sought additional funds from the LEA contingency fund, but this was refused. Mrs Murphy, who would have been entitled to statutory paid maternity leave if she had borne her child herself, claimed that she had been the subject of disability discrimination.

The issues were whether her claim was against the LEA or the school, and whether the budgetary justification for refusing paid leave was to be judged as against the school budget alone, or as against the LEA budget too. The latter situation might have been more favourable to the claimant; but it was held that the claim lay only against the school, and was to be judged only as against the school budget, so that the claim and Mrs Murphy's appeal from the EAT had to fail.

It was not in doubt that Mrs Murphy's contract of employment was with the LEA; so she had a single contractual employer and that was the LEA. But the Secretary of State for Education had made a statutory order that for various statutory purposes, among them those of the Disability

---

[50] [2005] EWCA Civ 122 (16 February 2005).

Discrimination Act 1995, the governing body of the school 'acting in the exercise of their employment powers' was to be 'included in any reference to an employer'.[51] That enactment, as construed and applied by the EAT and the Court of Appeal, produced the effect that Mrs Murphy had one employer for contractual purposes, and another one for statutory purposes. But surely this was in truth a situation which had emerged as one of multi-agency employment, in the sense that a multiplicity of agencies had emerged from what had previously been a single agency. (I am glossing over here the very interesting development by which the governing body is being treated as if it were a distinct legal entity, when that is in truth highly doubtful.) This was a situation for which neither of the two proposed single-employer analyses was at all adequate.

Let me permit myself one further, and I hope not too extravagant, example of concealed or emergent multilateral employment relationships. This concerns workers in the informal economy; it refers in particular to the practice of employment of immigrant workers in and on dangerous and exploitative conditions by gangmasters, of which the grievous illustration was the sad death of the Chinese cockle-pickers at Grangemouth in February 2004. The modest but still under-remarked exercise in statutory regulation which resulted from the concern about this event, the Gangmasters (Licensing) Act 2004, deserves our attention. It was realised that in order to control these abusive practices, it was necessary to recognise the way in which the 'respectable' suppliers, manufacturers and retailers of the food products in question might be indirectly responsible for the employment of those who harvested those products. So offences were created, not only of acting as unlicensed gangmaster,[52] but also of entering into arrangements for the supply of workers or services by unlicensed gangmasters.[53] This recognises an underlying multilateral employment relationship. Of course, it would never occur to anyone to suggest that those entities further down the supply chain were the *contractual* employers of the workers in question.

So I would like to add these instances and problems of concealed, partial, and emergent multilateral employment into the melting-pot of debate about triangular or multilateral employment relationships. But my purpose now is to pursue my task of deconstruction into the heart of the employer concept, that is in the situation where the employment relation is conceived of quite simply as a bilateral one between a single worker and a single employer.

[51] Education (Modification of Enactments Relating to Employment) Order 1999, SI 1999/2256 para 3(1)(a).   [52] Ss 6, 12.
[53] Ss 13–14.

Deconstructing the Single Employer

My attempt at deconstruction of the legal concept of the single employer will consist first of a depiction of it as a largely fictitious perpetuation of the old notion of the 'master' in the Law of Master and Servant. Secondly I will revisit the notion of 'vertical disintegration of production'. Thirdly I will consider the emergence of project or network employment.

The Persistent Fiction of the Master in Employment Law

My first line of attack on the legal concept of the single employer in employment law, especially but not solely the law of employment contracts, is a provocative one: I want to suggest that it constitutes so distorted a vision of reality as to amount almost to a legal fiction. It is as if the notion of the Master in the Law of Master and Servant has been prolonged, albeit under a more polite name, until the present day.

Let me be more precise; my complaint is that the use of the terminology of the employer evokes the notion of employment by a single human being almost as surely as the terminology of the Master used to do.

I am quite ready to admit that the term 'employer' is a less strongly gendered one than the term 'master'. I concede that although employment legislation still persists in referring to the employer as 'he' (for example as recently as in the Employment Relations Act 2004),[54] the employer could equally be referred to as 'she', as some American writers now prefer to do,[55] without causing any special feeling of incongruence (except among those who are suspicious of anything smacking of 'political correctness', among whom I do not count myself).

But substituting 'she' for 'he' does not meet my objection at all, for my objection is not to the masculinity of the term 'employer', which is very slight, but to its anthropomorphism, its reference to the human being, which is very intense. It is a terminology which fits a single human being much better than it fits an institution or an organisation. You can test this against your inbuilt sense of linguistic correctness in the English language. It does not sound incongruous for an employer to be 'he' or 'she', but it sounds thoroughly incongruous to refer to an employer as 'it'. By contrast, it is incongruous to refer to a company as 'he' or 'she' but natural to refer to a company as 'it'.

---

[54] For instance in the course of s 3 'Duty of employer to supply information to union'.
[55] For example K. Eltis in 24 Comparative Labor Law and Policy Journal, 487.

This inbuilt anthropomorphism is seriously distorting of reality. It is a very pre-industrial construct to think of the employing enterprise as a single human being. It is a very long time since the majority of workers were employed by single human beings rather than by legal entities representing organisations, often complex ones. The pure Wooster and Jeeves employment relation or contract is now quite a rarity. By a nice irony, in the one such relation to be encountered in recent case law, that of the super-model Naomi Campbell and her personal aide Pamela Frisbee, the contract between them was carefully dressed up as a contract for services, not a contract of employment at all.[56]

Now it may be thought that I am tilting at windmills, or imaginary enemies, like Don Quixote. In fact it might even be thought that I am insulting the intelligence of employment lawyers. It will be said that they—we—understand perfectly well that 'the employer' is most likely to be a legal entity, the legal proxy for a business organisation, rather than a single human being. So be it. But why then does employment law, especially the law of employment contracts, display so little awareness of 'the employer' as a complex organisation? I truly think that a misleading terminology and a one-dimensional analysis go hand-in-hand-together at this point. Let me try to substantiate that grave charge.

In my work on *The Personal Employment Contract* I sought to demonstrate how difficult it has seemed to be for the law of the contract of employment to get to grips with problems of hierarchies within employing enterprises, because of this particular flattened-out conception of the employer as a single person.[57] I cited cases such as that of *Laws v London Chronicle Ltd,*[58] where the issue was whether a secretary was properly dismissed without notice for 'disobedience' in following her immediate superior out of the room in defiance of his superior with whom he was having an argument. This was decided as a question of whether this worker had 'intended to repudiate her contract'; it was held that she had not. But this was really to sidestep the problem that it was unclear to *which* of the managers in the hierarchy this worker was expected to report and defer.

I argued that this problem of, and failure in, analysing internal hierarchies and responsibilities within the employing enterprise, presented itself even more acutely in working out the notion of the implied duty of mutual trust and confidence as accepted by the House of Lords in the leading case of *Malik v Bank of Credit and Commerce International.*[59]

---

[56] *Campbell v Frisbee* [2003] ICR 141.   [57] Freedland, n 4 above, 51–52.
[58] [1959] 1 WLR 698.   [59] [1997] ICR 606.

It will be recalled that the decision was that the Bank as employer could in principle be regarded as having acted in breach of that implied duty in that its business had been run in such a corrupt manner that when it collapsed, its employees found it difficult to obtain other employment in banking or financial services. The application of that ruling to individual employees was seen as presenting immense problems of causation, requiring further high-level litigation to resolve them.[60] But to see the issues as ones of causation was to sidestep a greater difficulty, namely that there was no analytical apparatus with which to work out the implied obligation within a complex managerial hierarchy, or therefore to decide where in that hierarchy the perpetrating 'employer' stopped and the victimised employee began.

It is that difficulty which points out or points up the way in which a crucial reality is obscured by trying to impose on to a complex employing enterprise a simple antithesis and contractual relationship between 'the employer' and his or her employees. That crucial reality is that most employing organisations today are staffed from bottom to top by persons who stand in the legal relationship of workers with their employing organisation. The chief executive is as likely as the office cleaner to be an employee of the employing enterprise—in fact quite a bit more likely so to be, because the office cleaner may well be employed by a sub-contractor, or may lack a continuing contract of employment with any organisation at all.

The more one thinks about it, the more unsettling of established employment law thinking this perception becomes. If Napoleon could say of his army that every soldier carried a field marshal's baton in his knapsack, it can be said, to the contrary, of today's army of workers in business organisations that every senior executive carries a worker's contract in her briefcase. The serious point is that the categories of 'managers' with employing functions and 'employees' with working functions are strongly overlapping ones. The overlap covers almost the whole of the upper echelons of many employing enterprises, and tends to extend itself as more and more occupations or functions are transformed from operative ones into wholly or partly managerial ones— a transformation which has been hugely dynamised by technological development, formerly in the nature of physical automation and latterly in the nature of computerisation of mental tasks. It means that there are extensive cadres of people in dual employer/employee roles. I seriously suggest that we are only just beginning to think about the deep implications of this set of developments for employment law.

[60] See *BCCI v Ali (No. 2)* [2002] ICR 1258 (CA).

Vertical Disintegration Revisited

My next step in the deconstruction of the concept of the employer is to look further at this dynamic towards the expansion of dual employer/ employee roles, and to suggest that we can understand it better by revisiting the idea of vertical disintegration of production. This is a notion whose importance to employment law Collins identified in his justly celebrated article, published in 1990, on 'Independent Contractors and the Challenge of Vertical Disintegration to Employment Protection Laws'.[61] In that article he was concerned with the way in which the historical process (strongly associated with industrialisation and, as we would now tend to say, with Fordism) of the integration of small businesses linked by commercial contracts into large single organisations was being reversed by a disintegration of production through sub-contracting, franchising, concessions and outsourcing. His focus was on the tendency of this disintegration to place workers outside what he described as the 'complementary paradigm form of employment in vertically integrated production: employment which is full-time, stable, and for an indefinite duration' and thereby also to place them beyond the range of employment protection laws.[62]

Collins' concern was therefore with the way in which vertical dis-integration of production was affecting the legal concept of the employee, or relocating workers outside that concept. I think it is useful to revisit vertical disintegration with an eye upon the way it in which that process equally redesigns, or at least should redesign, our understanding of the concept of the employer. The original process of vertical integration of production was above all one of attaching small *organisations* into large ones; it was building big complex *employers* by absorbing small employers with their workers. It was I think the turning of 'little masters' and 'butty-men'[63] and gangleaders into foremen and line mangers which was the really transformative aspect of vertical integration. Those previously external or independent contractors became, in terms of my earlier analysis, dual role employer/employees within integrated organisations. They contributed to the complexity of such organisations, thus further fictionalising the notion of the single employer.

Sometimes those sub-contracting systems remained remarkably intact within apparently integrated employing organisations. This can still

---

[61] (1990) 10 OJLS 353 (see above at n 15).   [62] Ibid, 353.
[63] See a description of the butty system at *http://www.healeyhero.info/rescue/history/ butty.htm.*

present interesting problems for employment law, as in the fascinating case of *New Century Cleaning Co Ltd v Church*[64] which concerned window-cleaners employed in teams, within each of which there was a gangleader who distributed within the team the sums allocated to the team as a whole for particular work assignments. The issue was whether those allocated sums constituted 'payable wages' before they were distributed by the gangleader, so that a reduction in the tariff of those sums would count as a 'deduction from wages' for each individual worker, of which that worker could complain if it was unauthorised by prior agreement. The Court of Appeal, Sedley LJ dissenting, held that the workers had no such entitlement, thus in effect denying the workers the benefit of the integration of the teams into the employing organisation.

More normally, of course, these internal sub-contracting systems disappeared completely from view; indeed, it was of the essence of vertical integration that they should do so. But the vertical disintegration of production which Collins described tended to reverse that process; and, symmetrically with vertical integration, I think it began to reintroduce various forms of sub-contracting, not only in the obvious forms of outsourcing and franchising, but also in less obvious forms of partly or even fully internal sub-contracting. I have in mind here the ways in which employing enterprises, especially the larger ones, have tended to use their job specification and reward systems to create separately managed and accounted profit centres or consultancies within the organisation. Those entrusted with the management of such sub-centres are placed precisely in dual employer/worker roles, and may become in a sense partially detached from the employing enterprise even if nominally still holding full employee status within it.

At the risk of over-working one example—though I need not apologise given its central practical importance to one of the country's largest employing enterprises—may I return to the case of the outsourcing of BT human resources management to Accenture? This precisely illustrates the kind of complex refashioning of the 'employer' which I have in mind when I refer to partial forms of vertical disintegration. Consider if you will the situation of the 14,500 people originally employed within the HRM department of BT. Some of them will have been the subject of 'natural wastage' or 'downsizing'; some of them of them will have been transferred, or 'transitioned' as the Accenture literature puts it, into work for Accenture HR Services; but let us concentrate for a moment on the fewer than 600 people who remained as the in-house HR personnel. You

---

[64] [2000] IRLR 27 (CA).

may have noticed that they were referred to, in the description I quoted earlier, as 'business partners'.

This suggested to me that the agenda of vertical disintegration might have been applied to them. Further scrutiny of the Accenture literature confirmed this hypothesis. The system is described as follows:-

Here's how it works. The new service delivery model enabled through outsourcing releases the productive energy of the retained HR employee who is now relieved of the burden of routine administrative work. Once liberated, HR personnel can become more effective 'business partners,' directing their energies more fully towards implementing strategies that align the workforce with the needs of the business.[65]

And, even more tellingly in another place:

Transforming the Retained Workforce

Realizing the value from the outsourcing arrangement requires a focus on the retained HR workforce to be considered in parallel with the outsourcing decision. The role of retained HR staff will need to be re-defined to strategically drive workforce performance *much like a consultant would.*[66]

In those concluding words you can see in a nutshell the sort of disintegration to which I refer, and also the way in which it redesigns not only the employment relation but also the very structure of the employing enterprise itself.

The Transition to Network and Project Employment

There is yet a further sense in which the latter structural transformation takes place, and it is to that sense to which I shall refer in conclusion of my discussion of this theme. This is the transition to network and project employment. In what I promise will be the last episode in my paper of the BT/Accenture human resource management story, may I use that story to illustrate the emergent paradigm which I have in mind. Consider how the HRM activity of BT is now constituted as the result of the transformation which has taken place. Some of those engaged in that activity are employed by BT; some of them are employed by Accenture HR Services; all of them are regarded as forming a team or project or consultancy, mostly working in a dual employer/worker role within a multilateral network of enterprises.

In that model, the organisation of the employing enterprise itself has been deeply transformed; it is scarcely possible to identify a single

[65] *http://www.accenture.com/xd/xd.asp?it=enweb&xd=industries/Communications/ Capabilities/Cht_hr_conundrum.xml.*
[66] *http://www.accenture.com/xdoc/en/services/hp/ideas_solution.pdf.*

employer in the sense in which employment law, and the law of employment contracts in particular, expects there to be one. It is deeply remote from the Master and Servant paradigm; and although I have drawn heavily upon my BT/Accenture case-study, I am confident that it represents a emerging paradigm which will be of widespread occurrence.

In fact that whole development has been charted and analysed by a group of contributors to the 2003 World Congress of the International Industrial Relations Association on the theme, *Beyond Employment: Network*, the papers from which appeared in a special issue of the *British Journal of Industrial Relations* published in December 2004.[67] Specially relevant to my present theme is a paper by David Marsden on 'The "Network Economy" and Models of the Employment Contract'[68] in which, to quote from his abstract, he argues and shows that 'the development of the "network economy" and project-based work challenge established methods of regulating employment relationships'. He contends further that 'there appears to be an unsatisfied demand for the greater use [of these forms of economic activity], especially among employers, *and this may be blocked by the lack of suitable contractual forms*' (emphasis added).

That brings me to the very nub and conclusion of my lecture. That last contention lays down a challenge to employment lawyers which I wish to accept and to try to meet. That challenge is to identify and to try to repair some functional deficiencies in our law of employment contracts. Problems arise in all three elements of the employment relationship, but not least, in fact I think now most prominently, in the way in which employment law conceptualises the employer, but fails accurately or adequately to do so.

I am optimistic that my proposed inter-European comparative legal methodology, as I have sought to outline it, may be helpful in that respect. A number of the papers contributed to the symposium on *Labour Law in the Courts: National Judges and the European Court of Justice* edited by Silvana Sciarra and published in 2001[69] show, in the context of discussion of the jurisprudence of interpretation of the Transfer of Undertaking Directives,[70] how some continental European employment law systems have been able to conceptualise the employing undertaking in a way which breaks free of the single employer paradigm and imagines a continuing *entreprise/organisation*, or, even more radically, a continuing

---

[67] (2004) 42:4 BJIR. [68] Ibid, 659–684.
[69] (Oxford and Portland Oregon: Hart Publishing, 2001).
[70] Council Directives 77/187/EEC and 98/50/EC, since consolidated into 2001/23/EC.

entreprise/activité. Marsden in his article points to various possible continental starting points for development of contractual forms for project or team employment.[71] So I hope to be able to return in due course with some trophies and fruits from the journey which I have sought to map out in prospect in the course of this paper.

[71] (2004) 42:4 BJIR, 675–6, 677–8.

Biotechnology, Biodiversity and International Law

Catherine Redgwell*

Introduction

Whilst on the one hand the development of biotechnology[1] and the conservation of biodiversity may be viewed as mutually supportive and compatible, closer analysis of their interaction reveals several areas of tension and conflict. These tensions exist at the practical level, in the extent to which biotechnology poses risks to biodiversity through, for example, the release of genetically modified organisms (GMOs)[2] and the consequent adulteration of natural habitat. Potential conflict plays out at the theoretical level as well, in the different dynamics for regulation of biodiversity and of biotechnology. Integration of biotechnology and biodiversity into sustainable development concerns is a current challenge in international law.[3] This is in order to achieve both intragenerational

* This paper is a revised and updated version of 'Biodiversity, Biotechnology and Sustainable Development' in F Francioni and T Scovazzi (eds), *Biotechnology and International Law* (Oxford: Hart Publishing, forthcoming 2005). I am grateful for the comments on the text from participants at the 2004 Siena Conference 'Biotechnology and International Law' and at public lectures delivered at the University of Edinburgh and University College London in 2005.

[1] Defined in Art 2 of the 1992 Convention on Biological Diversity (CBD): ' "Biotechnology" means any technological application that uses biological systems, living organisms, or derivatives thereof, to make or modify products or processes for specific use'.

[2] The 2000 Biosafety Protocol to the CBD uses the term 'LMO' which is defined in Art 3 thereof: ' "Living Modified Organism" means any living organism that possesses a novel combination of genetic material obtained through the use of modern biotechnology'. 'Modern biotechnology' means the application of *in vitro* nucleic acid techniques, or fusion of cells beyond the taxonomic family, 'that overcome natural physiological reproductive or recombination barriers and that are not techniques used in traditional breeding and selection'. This paper will use 'LMO' and 'GMO' (genetically modified organism) interchangeably.

[3] *The Report of the Secretary General on the Transfer of Environmentally Sound Technologies and the Sound Management of Biotechnology*, ECOSOC E/CN.17/2001/PC/11, 6, para 31 raises some of these issues. The Report was prepared for the Commission on Sustainable Development in its capacity as the Preparatory Committee for the 2002 Johannesburg World Summit on Sustainable Development ('Rio + 10').

544 Catherine Redgwell

equity, that is, equitable distribution of the benefits and burdens of biotechnology *within* the present generation, and intergenerational equity, which also raises questions of equitable distribution of the benefits and burdens of biotechnology, but *between* rather than only within generations. Intergenerational equity also includes responsibility to future generations for the conservation and sustainable use of biodiversity. Owing to the diverse range of factors involved in GMO regulation, perhaps the single most important issue in resolving conflict over such regulation is to develop 'reliable information and analysis' in a multidisciplinary range of fields—biology, ecology, law, economics, ecosystem management, and social policy.[4] This suggests that the international regulatory[5] challenge transcends 'sound science' alone and relies on a range of factors for risk assessment and risk management.[6] Nonetheless science remains a crucial cross-cutting issue, a characteristic which biotechnology and biodiversity share with many other contemporary environmental problems, whether it is determining the human causes of greenhouse gas emissions or setting sustainable harvesting quotas for fish stocks.

The confluence of rapidly developing new technologies and the role of non-State actors in the process are further complicating factors for the development of international legal rules for the regulation of biosafety and biodiversity. As the International Union for the Conservation of

[4] IUCN—The World Conservation Union, *Genetically Modified Organisms and Biosafety: A background paper for decision-makers and others to assist in consideration of GMO issues* (August 2004), 5. It identifies three, often disconnected, strands in GMO discourse, namely: (i) science; (ii) economics; and (iii) socio-cultural issues.

[5] Given the requirement for national implementation found in Art 1 of the 2000 Biosafety Protocol, and the general tendency to use regulatory techniques in assessing and managing risk, it is unlikely that the solution to the problems posed here will lie in voluntary agreements or other forms of self-regulation by non-State actors. This is not to eschew a role for public-private partnerships, especially in indigenous capacity building and for technology transfer. In 2000, the IUCN noted in connection with GMOs and biotechnology that '[a]chieving positive results will test the world's collective creativity in public-private partnerships, governance and international scientific and legal regimes': IUCN, *Stepping into the new millennium* (2000), 5. Nor is private sector involvement excluded under the Biosafety Protocol, Art 22(1) of which, for example, explicitly envisages such involvement in capacity building.

[6] For recent discussion see C Hilson, 'Beyond Rationality? Judicial Review and Risk Perception in the EU and WTO', (manuscript, 2005). He points to two camps in the literature on risk regulation: (i) the 'rationalists' who emphasise the benefits of objective cost-benefit analysis and risk assessment based on scientific principles; and (ii) the 'populists' who stress the importance of public perceptions of risk assessment, and the input of such perceptions into the risk assessment process, as part of good governance in a democratic society. He provides as an example of the former C Sunstein, *Risk and Reason: Safety, Law and Environment* (Cambridge University Press, 2002) whilst an example of the latter is ESRC Global Environmental Change Programme, *The Politics of GM Food: Risk, Science and Public Trust*, Special Briefing No. 5 (Brighton: University of Sussex, 1999).

Nature's (IUCN) recent background paper on *Genetically Modified Organisms and Biosafety* observes, one of the regulatory challenges for States in this area is that the 'technological capacity to act has moved significantly faster than the governmental (and in some cases the technical) ability to oversee and regulate it' leading to regulatory lag and gaps.[7] Also, like other 'strategic technologies', biotechnology has been driven by commercial considerations with often substantial capital investments required for product development and approvals. Such investment has come principally from the private sector, with resulting innovations likewise in the private domain and protected by proprietary (intellectual property) rights and hence often practically unobtainable by many developing State actors. Very limited technology transfer has occurred in the health and agriculture fields, but a recent UN report, *Transfer of Environmentally Sound Technologies and the Sound Management of Biotechnology*, concludes that the impact for economic and social development has been limited.[8] It identifies that 'the major challenge now is to find the means to develop biotechnology-based public goods while maintaining corporate incentives for biotechnology innovation'.[9] International regulation is further complicated (one might even say undermined) by the non-participation of a key GMO-exporting State, the United States, in the CBD/Biosafety arrangements and in the absence of well-developed customary rules to fill the consequent treaty gap.[10]

In order to highlight these areas of conflict and congruence, this paper will first briefly analyse the development of international legal regulation of biodiversity and biotechnology, focusing on the provisions of the 1992 Convention on Biological Diversity[11] and the 2000 Cartagena Protocol on Biosafety.[12] This is not to suggest that other instruments are not pertinent—most notably the *Codex Alimentarius*,[13] the International Plant Protection Convention,[14] and certain of the WTO covered agreements,[15]

---

[7] IUCN, n 5 above, 4.   [8] n 3 above, 5, para 29.   [9] Ibid, 6, para 30.
[10] For discussion of the applicable general rules of international law, see F Francioni, 'International Law for Biotechnology' in Francioni and Scovazzi, introductory note above. Of course, this is not to suggest that adequate regulation of the transboundary movement and environmental impact of GMOs could be adequately regulated by customary international law alone, since much of the technical regulation required is not of a sufficiently norm creating character to generate custom, even assuming consistent state practice.
[11] 1992 Convention on Biological Diversity, in force 29 May 1994, available at (1992) 31 *International Legal Materials*, 818.
[12] 2000 Cartagena Protocol on Biosafety, in force 11 September 2003, available at (2000) 39 *International Legal Materials*, 1027.
[13] See *http://www.codexalimentarius.net*.   [14] See *http://www.ippc.int*.
[15] In particular the Agreement on the Application of Sanitary and Phytosanitary Measures ('SPS Agreement'), the Agreement on Technical Barriers to Trade ('TBT

but these are addressed only in passing.[16] I will then turn to examine four issues in the context of the international regulation of biosafety:

  (i) the role of 'advanced' informed agreement in decision-making under the Protocol and the interplay of precaution and risk assessment;

  (ii) the role of civil society in decision making in the biosafety field;

  (iii) the role of 'sound science' in such decision making; and

  (iv) the relationship between the Biosafety Protocol and other international legal rules, including trade rules.

I have chosen these four areas as best exemplifying the current pressure points in the regulation of biosafety; clearly there are other issues which might be addressed, such as the difficulty in elaborating liability rules to address environmental damage caused through the use of GMOs and the adoption of compliance procedures under the Protocol to address the failure by states to fulfil their Protocol obligations,[17] but these are beyond the scope of the present paper.

The Development of the Biodiversity Concept

Christopher Stone[18] suggests that human concerns for 'the planet's biological capital' may be traced back as far as pre-Roman times, citing

Agreement'), and the General Agreement on Tariffs and Trade ('GATT'), in World Trade Organization, *The Legal Texts: The Results of the Uruguay Round of Multilateral Trade Negotiation* (Geneva: WTO, 1994). See also *http://www.wto.org*.

  16 In the context of agricultural biotechnology in particular, there are further linkages with, for example, the work of the UN Commission on Human Rights' Special Rapporteur on the Right to Food, and the FAO Panel of Eminent Experts in Ethics on Food and Agriculture, discussed in R Mackenzie, 'The International Regulation of Modern Biotechnology' (2002) 13 Yearbook of International Environmental Law, 97–163. See also M Footer, 'Agricultural biotechnology, food security and human rights' in Francioni and Scovazzi, introductory note above.

  17 Art 34 of the 2000 Biosafety Protocol expressly contemplates the conclusion of a compliance mechanism after its entry into force, while Art 27 provides for the negotiation of rules and procedures on liability and redress. At their first meeting in February 2004, the Parties to the Protocol adopted Decision BS-I/7 on the 'Establishment of procedures and mechanisms on compliance under the Cartagena Protocol on Biosafety': for background, and the text of the decision, see *http://www.biodiv.org/biosafety/issues/compliance2. aspx*. In addition, an Ad Hoc Working Group on Liability and Redress was established pursuant to Decision BS-I/8 and held its first meeting in May 2005: see *http://www.biodiv. org/biosafety/issues/liability2.aspx*. For background on the key liability and redress issues, see the *Report of the Technical Group of Experts on Liability and Redress in the Context of the Cartagena Protocol on Biosafety* UNEP/CBD/BS/TEG-L&R/1/3, 9 November 2004.

  18 C Stone, 'What to do about Biodiversity: Property Rights, Public Goods, and the Earth's Biological Riches', (1995) 68 Southern California Law Review, 577.

Hammurabi's Code which included eleven sections on agriculture.[19] One illustration he recounts is the Hittites' punishment for illicit second sowing of a field: a horrible death was prescribed, with the malefactor placed between two oxen and pulled apart.[20] International law utilises less distressing methods for addressing non-compliance—where it is able to deal with it at all. But the point Stone clearly wishes to make is that, notwithstanding the relatively recent conclusion of the first international treaty to address the conservation of biological diversity in 1992, humankind's concerns regarding human impact on the natural environment may be traced back thousands of years. Certainly the international regulation of wildlife and habitat protection may be traced to the nineteenth century.[21]

Indeed, scholars of international law and the environment traditionally divide consideration of international regulation into several phases,[22] the first being the nineteenth century approach of which these treaties formed a party, being principally concerned to preserve wildlife and habitat for anthropocentric reasons, usually to protect a common property resource such as fish from overexploitation. The second arises with the development of environmental law in the United Nations era, with a significant turning point being the 1972 United Nations-sponsored Stockholm Conference on the Human Environment. This produced a non-binding 'Declaration of Principles' which contain some brief reference to safeguarding the natural resources of the earth, especially representative samples of natural ecosystems, and to humankind's 'special responsibility to safeguard and wisely manage the heritage of wildlife and its habitat which are now gravely imperilled by a combination of adverse factors'.[23] However, while of clear significance in the genesis of modern international environmental law, there is little

---

[19] Ibid, 578, relying on H S F Saggs, *Civilisation Before Greece and Rome* (London: Batsford, 1989), 158. This work is now in its second edition (1999).

[20] Saggs, ibid, 168.

[21] And even earlier: see P Birnie and A E Boyle, *International Law and the Environment* (Oxford: Oxford University Press, 2nd edn, 2002), 554.

[22] See, generally, Birnie and Boyle, ibid; P Sands, *Principles of International Environmental Law* (Cambridge University Press, 2nd edn., 2003); F Francioni, 'Developments in Environmental Law from Sovereignty to Governance: The EC Environmental Policy' in B Markesinis (ed), *The Gradual Convergence: Foreign Ideas, Foreign Influences, and English Law on the Eve of the 21st Century* (Oxford: Clarendon Press, 1994); M Fitzmaurice, 'International Protection of the Environment', (2001) 293 *Recueil des Cours de l'Academie de Droit International*, 13; and C Redgwell, 'International Environmental Law' in M D Evans (ed), *International Law* (Oxford University Press, 2002; 2nd edition forthcoming 2006).

[23] Declaration of the UN Conference on the Human Environment, Stockholm, 5–16 June 1972, UN Doc. A/CONF/48/14/REV.1.

sign of the biodiversity concept as such at Stockholm. This was to emerge in full force in the second UN-sponsored conference on the environment, the 1992 Rio Conference on Environment and Development, where the 1992 Convention on Biological Diversity was opened for signature, and which ushered in the current phase of international environmental law. This current phase[24] is characterised by an holistic, ecosystem approach to environmental protection and seeks to marry such protection with economic development—the theme of the 1992 Rio Conference and one which was carried through to the third such event a decade later, the World Summit on Sustainable Development held in Johannesburg in 2002.

In the meantime, following on from the 1972 Stockholm Conference, the biodiversity concept was gaining ground in international law and policy. In 1980 three bodies—IUCN, the United Nations' Environment Programme (UNEP), which was established after the Stockholm Conference, and the World Wide Fund for Nature (WWF)—set out an ethical basis for preserving biodiversity in their *World Conservation Strategy*.[25] With its underlying theme of sustainable development, this is widely considered to have set the 'real foundation' for the biodiversity concept in international law. The Strategy sets forth three fundamental objectives of living resources conservation, namely:

(a) to maintain essential ecological processes and life-support systems;

(b) to preserve genetic diversity; and

(c) to ensure the sustainable utilisation of species and ecosystems.

The second of these objectives, the preservation of genetic diversity, captures the essence of the biodiversity concept later developed.[26] Another striking feature of the 1980 World Conservation Strategy is the emphasis upon the practical, utilitarian values of wildlife conservation, seeking to demonstrate that environmental protection and economic development are not only reconcilable but that the former is a prerequisite for the latter. Economic development is dependent on the continued viability of natural systems and the availability of resources, especially

---

[24] It may be questioned whether we are not indeed embarking upon a further phase in the development of international (environmental) law, against the backdrop of processes of globalisation, technological innovation, democratisation and privatisation. See, generally, P Sands, 'Turtles and Torturers: The Transformation of International Law' (2000) 33 New York University Journal of International Law & Policy, 527.

[25] IUCN/UNEP/WWF, *World Conservation Strategy* (Gland, 1980).

[26] Indeed, the WCS was revised in 1991, whilst negotiation of the CBD was reaching its conclusion, and explicitly calls for the protection of biodiversity as an important element in sustainable living: IUCN/UNEP/WWF, *Caring for the Earth: A Strategy for Sustainable Living* (Gland, 1991). Explicit linkage of biodiversity and legal principle is

consumables. Thus sustainable development, the *rapprochement* of environment and development at the heart of the 1992 Rio Conference at which the Biodiversity Convention was opened for signature, is therefore central to this Convention.[27] It was one of two major treaties celebrated at Rio, the other being the 1992 Climate Change Convention. Like Stockholm in 1972, the 1992 Rio Conference also produced a non-binding Declaration of Principles,[28] and an Action Plan, titled 'Agenda 21: Earth's Action Plan'.[29]

It is in this last that we find perhaps the greatest congruence of bio-diversity conservation and biotechnology development at the level of policy and principle, embraced within the concept of sustainable development.[30] Chapters 15 and 16 of Agenda 21 are devoted to Conservation of Biological Diversity and to Environmentally Sound Management of Biotechnology, respectively. Whilst cautioning that biotechnology by itself 'cannot resolve all the fundamental problems of environment and development', Chapter 16 nonetheless strikes an upbeat note in the preamble's recognition that biotechnology 'promises to make a significant contribution in enabling the development of, for example, better health care, enhanced food security through sustainable agricultural practices, improved supplies of potable water, more efficient industrial development processes for transforming raw materials, support for

made in the 1987 Report of the World Commission on Environment and Development, *Our Common Future* (Oxford University Press, 1987), the Legal Experts Group of which proposed 'Legal Principles for Environmental Protection and Sustainable Development', the third of which provides: 'States shall maintain ecosystems and ecological processes essential for the functioning of the biosphere, shall preserve biological diversity, and shall observe the principles of optimum sustainable yield in the use of living natural resources and ecosystems.' G Munro and D Lammers (eds), *Environmental Protection and Sustainable Development* (London: Graham & Trotman, 1986).

[27] The objectives of which, in Art 1, have been referred to by Boyle as a trade-off between conservation and economic equity unusual for an international environmental agreement: A E Boyle, 'The Convention on Biological Diversity' in L Campiglio, L Pineschi, D Siniscalco and T Treves (eds), *The Environment After Rio* (London: Graham & Trotman, 1994), 38; see also D M McGraw, 'The CBD—Key Characteristics and Implications for Implementation', (2002) 11:1 Review of European Community and International Environmental Law, 17.

[28] Declaration of the UN Conference on Environment and Development, Rio de Janeiro, 3–14 June 1992, UN Doc. A/CONF.151/26/Rev 1, Vol I, Annex II (1992).

[29] Agenda 21, Report of the United Nations Conference on Environment and Development, Rio de Janeiro, 3–14 June 1992, UN Doc. A/CONF.151/26, Vols I–III, (1992).

[30] The concept was first articulated in the 1987 Brundtland Commission Report *Our Common Future* and is reflected in the focus of the 1992 Rio Conference on Environment and Development. The Brundtland Commission defined sustainable development as development which meets the needs of the present generation without jeopardising the ability of future generations to meet their needs. The precise international legal contours of the concept remain imprecise, however. For further discussion, see P Sands, 'International

sustainable methods of afforestation and reforestation, and detoxification of hazardous wastes'.[31]

With relation to biodiversity, Chapter 16 of Agenda 21 explicitly acknowledges both the benefits and the risks of biotechnology development. On the one hand, biotechnology may assist with the transformation of biological resources to serve the needs of sustainable development and assist in the _ex situ_ conservation of biological diversity.[32] The downside is the need to develop environmentally sound biotechnologies based on risk assessment and management, and to avoid developing countries in particular becoming ' "testing" or "dumping" grounds for potentially harmful technologies and products',[33] as has occurred in the past with hazardous wastes, chemicals and pesticides. Indeed, as will be discussed shortly below, the structure of the Biosafety Protocol owes much to the instruments regulating transboundary movement of hazardous wastes and pesticides,[34] as well as building on a number of soft law initiatives.[35]

The 1992 Convention on Biological Diversity [36]

As I indicated earlier, the Convention on Biological Diversity (CBD) was opened for signature at the Rio Conference on Environment and Development in 1992 and entered into force in 1995. Today it has

Law in the Field of Sustainable Development', (1994) 65 _British Yearbook of International Law_, 303 and D French, _International law and policy of sustainable development_ (Manchester: Manchester University Press, 2005).

[31] 'Agenda 21', n 29 above para. 16.1.   [32] Ibid.
[33] Mackenzie, n 16 above, 97.
[34] C Redgwell, 'Regulating Trade in Dangerous Substances: Prior Informed Consent under the 1998 Rotterdam Convention' in A Kiss, D Shelton and K Ishibashi (eds), _Economic Globalization and Compliance with International Environmental Agreements_ (The Hague: Kluwer Law International, 2003).
[35] For example, UNEP's _International Guidelines for Safety in Biotechnology_ (1995) and UNIDO's _Voluntary Code of Conduct for the Release of Organisms into the Environment_ (1992).
[36] On the CBD see, generally, F McConnell, _The Biodiversity Convention: A Negotiating History_ (1996); M-A Hermitte, 'La Convention Sur La Diversite Biologique' (1992) XXXVIII Annuaire Francais De Droit International', 844; F Burhenne-Guilmin and S Casey-Lefkowitz, 'The New Law of Biodiversity' (1992) 3 Yearbook of International Environmental Law 43; the _Convention on Biological Diversity Handbook_ (CBD Secretariat, 2001) available at _http://www.biodiv.org_; C de Klemm and C Shine, _Biological Diversity Conservation and Law: Legal Mechanisms for Conserving Species and Ecosystems_, IUCN Environmental Policy & Law Paper Series No. 29 (Gland: IUCN, 1993); C Redgwell, 'The Protection of Biological Diversity' in K Koufa (ed), _Protection of the Environment for the New Millenium, Thesaurus Acroasium_, Volume XXXI (Thessaloniki: Sakkoulas

an impressive 188 States Parties bound by its terms—only a few less than the current number of States members of the United Nations—with only a handful of states including Brunei, Iraq, Somalia and the United States (a signatory only) outside the regime.[37] Thus it enjoys near universal membership. Its primary objectives are the conservation of biological diversity, sustainable use of its components and fair and equitable sharing of the benefits arising from the utilisation of genetic resources (Article 1). The reference to 'sustainable use' of the components of biological diversity is a clear indicator that this Convention is not concerned primarily with the preservation of biodiversity but 'assumes human use and benefit as the fundamental purpose for conserving biodiversity, limited only by the requirement of sustainability and the need to benefit future generations'.[38] Conservation obligations are reflected in the provisions on adoption of national strategies, plans or programmes (Article 6) and in the provisions on *in situ* and *ex situ* conservation, eg through protected areas in states, or in zoological and plant collections abroad (Articles 7 and 8). There is a very significant emphasis on national implementation, and upon national identification of significant biological diversity for protection. This is because unlike, say, the 1972 World Heritage Convention[39] or the 1973 Convention on International Trade in Endangered Species,[40] the Biodiversity Convention does not adopt a listing or designation approach, so it does not contain international lists of biologically significant animals, plants and habitat which states are obliged to protect.

In the 11 years since the entry into force of the CBD, the international community's approach to biodiversity has continued to evolve, with biological diversity now considered an essential part of efforts to eradicate poverty and achieve sustainable development. In the immediate run-up

Publications, 2002), 355–96; and two special issues of the *Review of European Community and International Environmental Law* (1997, Vol 6:3 and 2002, Vol 11:1). For the wider background see, generally, M Bowman and C Redgwell (eds), *The Conservation of Biological Diversity* (The Hague: Kluwer Law International, 1991).

[37] Andorra, the Holy See and Timor-Leste are also outside the CBD.

[38] Boyle, n 27 above, 115. 'Sustainable use' is defined in Art 2 as 'the use of components of biological diversity in a way and at a rate that does not lead to the long-term decline of biological diversity, thereby maintaining its potential to meet the needs and aspirations of present and future generations'. At COP V (2002, Decision V/24), sustainable use was adopted as a cross-cutting issue under the Convention, and at COP 7 (2004) the Addis Ababa Principles and Guidelines for the Sustainable Use of Biodiversity were adopted. See further *http://www.biodiv.org*.

[39] 1972 Convention for the Protection of the World Cultural and Natural Heritage, in force 17 December 1975, available at (1972) 11 *International Legal Materials*, 1358.

[40] 1973 Convention on International Trade in Endangered Species of Wild Fauna and Flora, in force 1 July 1975, available at 993 *United Nations Treaty Series* 243.

to the 2002 World Summit on Sustainable Development (WSSD) in Johannesburg, the 2002 Hague Ministerial Declaration of the Conference of the Parties to the CBD recognised 'that biodiversity underpins sustainable development in many ways; poverty eradication, food security, provision of fresh water, soil conservation and human health all depend directly upon maintaining and using the world's biological diversity and therefore sustainable development cannot be achieved without the conservation and sustainable use of biological diversity'.[41] Recommendation 1B of the WSSD accordingly recognises the contribution of the CBD to the sustainable development process, and to poverty eradication in particular. The need to integrate the objectives of the CBD in global, regional and national sectoral and cross-sectoral programmes and policies—the 'mainstreaming of biodiversity'—is seen both as contributing to the sustainable development process whilst also ensuring full implementation of the Convention.[42]

Biosafety in the Convention on Biological Diversity

It will be recalled that in seeking to 'operationalise' sustainable development in the biodiversity and biotechnology spheres, Agenda 21 enthusiastically embraces the possibilities of biotechnology for sustainable development of biological and other resources in developing states in particular. In the event, two provisions of the 1992 Biodiversity Convention are specifically addressed to biotechnology and to biosafety (Articles 8(g) and 19). It strikes a more cautionary note in the provisions on *in situ* conservation, which require that '[e]ach Contracting Party shall, as far as possible and as appropriate establish or maintain means to regulate, manage or control the risks associated with the use and release of living modified organisms resulting from biotechnology which are likely to have adverse environmental impacts that could affect the conservation and sustainable use of biological diversity, taking into account the risks to human health' (Article 8). This obligation is not geographically limited under the Convention, so it applies not only to components of biological

---

[41] Para. 5. The Declaration calls upon the World Summit on Sustainable Development to recognise and to promote these strong linkages (see para. 15(c)).

[42] Contribution of the Convention on Biological Diversity to Implementing the Outcomes of the Johannesburg Summit, *Report of the [CBD] Executive Secretary to the Commission on Sustainable Development*. The marginalisation of biodiversity issues is perceived as one of the principle obstacles to full implementation of the CBD (para. 6).

diversity within the limits of national jurisdiction, but also to processes and activities, regardless of where they occur, which are carried out under its jurisdiction and control.

Transboundary movement of LMOs is also addressed in the Convention, which requires information regarding use and safety regulations in respect of the organisms to be provided to the contracting party where the organisms are to be introduced, and any available information on the potential adverse impact of the specific organisms concerned (Article 19(4)). Because the Biodiversity Convention reflects the balance indicated above, and is not a prohibitionist charter, but rather an instrument based on sustainability, it further recognises the need to promote and advance priority access on a fair and equitable basis, especially by developing country parties, to the results and benefits arising from biotechnologies based on their genetic resources. This is all the more compelling given the reference in Agenda 21 to the variety of purposes biotechnology might serve particularly with respect to human health, food security, and poverty alleviation.

The Convention also expressly recognises the need to develop further international regulation of the transfer and use of LMOs which may have adverse effect on the conservation and sustainable use of biological diversity.[43] This was started shortly after the entry into force of the Biodiversity Convention and in January 2000, the text of the Cartagena Protocol on Biosafety was adopted. It entered into force on 11 September 2003 and, while it has not yet acquired the widespread participation of its parent Convention, with recent ratifications by Azerbaijan and the Democratic Republic of the Congo there are now 119 States and the EC bound by the Protocol.

As this brief history suggests, the origins of international biosafety regulation may be found in the late 1980s and early 1990s. National biosafety regulation in many states also predates the Biosafety Protocol, not least owing to the obligations of the parent Biodiversity Convention already indicated.[44] Even the core decision making principle of the Protocol— 'advanced' informed agreement—is trailed in the parent Biodiversity Convention, though of course leaving much left to be negotiated.

---

[43] Art 19(3). McGraw, n 27 above, 19, refers to criticisms of this choice as reflecting an absence of 'sound science'—why not a Protocol on the traditional knowledge or on alien species, for example?

[44] See discussion of eg Egypt's biosafety regime in P Kameri-Mbote, 'The Development of Biosafety Regulation in Africa in the Context of the Cartagena Protocol: Legal and Administrative Issues' (2002) 11:1 Review of European Community and International Environmental Law, 62.

The 2000 Cartagena Protocol on Biosafety [45]

The focus of the Biosafety Protocol is upon the transboundary movement of LMOs which may have adverse effects on biological diversity and human health. 'Living modified organism' is defined as 'any living organism that possesses a novel combination of genetic material obtained through the use of modern biotechnology'.[46] In fact the Protocol addresses two general categories of LMO: (i) those intended for release into the environment (eg seeds for cultivation or animal breeding stock); and (ii) those intended for use in food or feed, or for processing (eg corn, cotton and soy). The latter was of particular concern to the United States as the chief exporter of genetically modified crops.[47] In the event the Protocol distinguishes between these categories, subjecting organisms intended for direct use as food or feed, or for processing, to a less onerous regime (Article 11) than that applicable to LMOs intended for direct release into the environment (Articles 7–10). This distinction in regulatory approach reflects a perception of the higher degree of risk posed by non-contained LMOs to the natural environment and, in particular, to the conservation of biological diversity, whilst not ignoring the potentially adverse effect of contained GMOs on human health and the environment.

'Advanced' Informed Agreement under the Protocol

A marked feature of the Protocol is its overtly precautionary approach, with Article 1 making express reference to the precautionary approach contained in Principle 15 of the 1992 Rio Declaration, and using the

---

[45] For coverage of the final negotiating session see (2000) 9:137 *Earth Negotiations Bulletin*, 1-11; see also *http://www.iisd.ca/process/biodiv_wildlife.html* for the full negotiating history, and CBD/UNEP, *The Cartagena Protocol on Biosafety: A Record of the Negotiations* (Montreal: CBD, 2003). On the Protocol generally, see P E Hagan and J B Weiner, 'The Cartagena Protocol on Biosafety: New Rules for International Trade in Living Modified Organisms' (2000) 12 Georgetown Environmental Law Review, 697; S W Burgiel, 'The Cartagena Protocol on Biosafety: Taking the Steps from Negotiation to Implementation' (2002) 11:1 Review of European Community and International Environmental Law, 53; and R McKenzie *et al*, *An Explanatory Guide to the Cartagena Protocol on Biosafety*, IUCN Environmental Policy and Law Paper No. 46 (Gland: IUCN, 2003).   [46] Art 3(f).

[47] See further Hagen and Weiner, n 45 above. Although not a party to the CBD the United States participated in the negotiation of the Protocol in which, notwithstanding the compromises contained in, *inter alia*, Art 11, it is unlikely to participate for the foreseeable future.

implicitly precautionary language '*may* have an adverse effect' on biodiversity and/or human health. The chief regulatory technique employed is the 'advanced informed agreement' (AIA) procedure set out in Article 7, which is designed to ensure that Contracting Parties are provided with the information necessary to make informed decisions before agreeing to the import of LMOs into their territory. AIA marks the Protocol out from the 'prior informed consent' procedures of the 1989 Basel and 1998 Rotterdam Conventions,[48] which are based on prior multilateral agreement on the hazardous substances to be regulated and lists of which are set out in annexes. Prior informed consent has been applied where substances have already been judged hazardous; it is an example of an *ex ante* procedural mechanism for avoiding, managing and resolving conflict[49] which is deployed in the environmental field particularly where the transboundary movement of hazardous and dangerous substances is involved. It is closely linked with the obligation to consult under international law, an obligation that is found in a wide range of existing environmental treaties.[50] The primary purpose of the Biosafety Protocol is to facilitate early assessment by *each contracting party* of the potential risks in accordance with the Protocol. As Stoll observes, the Biosafety Protocol's 'unique combination between import State control and risk assessment results from the fact that it does not contain an agreed definition of materials that the importing State may refuse without condition or even

[48] 1989 Basel Convention Convention on the Transboundary Movement of Hazardous Wastes and their Disposal, in force 5 May 1992, available at (1989) 23 *International Legal Materials* and the 1998 Rotterdam Convention on Prior Informed Consent, in force 24 February 2004, available at (1999) 38 *International Legal Materials*, 1. The latter expressly excludes LMOs from its scope, thus eliminating the possibility of conflict arising between it and the Biosafety Protocol.

[49] For more general discussion see F L Kirgis, *Prior Consultation in International Law* (Charlottesville: University Press of Virginia, 1983). On the function of prior informed consent in dispute avoidance, see J Collier and V Lowe, *The Settlement of Disputes in International Law: Institutions and Procedures* (Oxford University Press, 1999), Ch. 1 and, specifically in the environmental context, Sands, n 30 above, 838 and Birnie and Boyle, n 21 above, 126–29.

[50] See, for example, the 1991 Espoo Convention on Environmental Impact Assessment in a Transboundary Context, in force 10 September 1997, available at (1991) 30 *International Legal Materials*, 802 and the 1992 OSPAR Convention for the Protection of the Marine Environment of the North East Atlantic, in force 25 March 1998, available at (1993) 32 *International Legal Materials*, 1068. The current litigation between the United Kingdom and the Republic of Ireland regarding the nuclear reprocessing facility at Sellafield has raised issues including access to information under Art 9 of the OSPAR Convention and the proper conduct of an environmental impact assessment and the obligation to cooperate under the 1982 United Nations Convention on the Law of the Sea (in force 16 November 1994, available at (1982) 21 *International Legal Materials*, 1261). See further R Churchill and J Scott, 'The MOx Plant Litigation: The First Half-Life', (2004) 53:3 International and Comparative Law Quarterly, 643.

an agreement that the substances that it regulates are "undesirable" '.[51] Indeed, the flexibility of the rules under the Protocol has led to suggestions that it represents a form of 'treaty-based environmental unilateralism'; that it is a 'prototype of minimum harmonisation legislation'.[52] It establishes principles and procedures to guide national decision making based on risk assessment and risk management, without mandating a particular outcome.

The AIA procedure set forth in Article 7 is buttressed by provisions addressing notification[53] and decision procedures (Articles 8–10). The import of LMOs may be approved, with or without conditions; prohibited; or additional information may be requested. Silence in response to an initial notification from the party of export does not imply consent to transboundary movement (Article 9(4)). There is also provision for review of decisions in the light of new scientific information regarding the potential adverse effects of the LMO (Article 12). The Protocol stresses that lack of scientific certainty due to insufficient information available about the potential negative effects of LMOs on biodiversity, including taking into account risks to human health, will *not* prevent the importing/receiving state from taking decisions in respect of LMOs in order to avoid or minimise potential adverse effects (Article 10(6)). However, such decisions must be taken in accordance with the risk assessment procedure stipulated in Article 15 and Annex III of the Protocol; and, whilst states are expressly permitted to take action more protective of biodiversity than provided for in the Protocol, such action must be consistent both with the Protocol *and* with that party's other obligations under international law (eg trade obligations).[54] The socio-economic impact of LMOs on biodiversity, especially its value to indigenous and

[51] P-T Stoll, 'Controlling the Risks of Genetically Modified Organisms: The Cartagena Protocol on Biosafety and the SPS Agreement' (1999) 10 Yearbook of International Environmental Law, 91.

[52] R Pavoni, 'Assessing and Managing Biotechnology Risk under the Cartagena Protocol on Biosafety' (2000) X Italian Yearbook of International Law, 115–6. It should be noted that Art 14 expressly provides for bilateral, regional and multilateral agreements and arrangements regarding intentional movement of LMOs so long as such arrangements do not provide a lower level of protection than that provided for by the Protocol—either equal protection or in fact a form of bilateral and/or multilateral upward derogation, and certainly precluding 'contracting out' of the Protocol's level of protection. Art 24 also envisages such agreements being concluded between contracting parties and non-parties to the Protocol.

[53] With regard to the information submitted with the notification, confidentiality may be preserved in accordance with Art 21. This includes a list of what is not considered confidential, including '[a] summary of the risk assessment of the effects on the conservation and sustainable use of biological diversity, taking into account risks to human health' (para 6) and information relating to '[a]ny methods and plans for emergency response' (para 7).

[54] See also Art 14 ('multilateralised upward derogation,) discussed in n 52 above.

local communities, may also be taken into account by contracting parties, but again at least to the extent consistent with their other international obligations.[55] Thus in both instances—a more stringent approach to LMO regulation, and taking into account in risk assessment non-scientific factors such as the socio-economic impact of LMOs on bio-diversity—individual response is conditioned by compliance with wider international obligations, including trade obligations.[56]

During the negotiation of the Protocol there was some divergence between developed and developing States regarding the purpose of risk assessment. One of the most contentious issues was whether to include in the decision making process the precautionary principle and socio-economic considerations just mentioned. For developed states, in particular those members of the 'Miami Group' keen to facilitate LMO trade,[57] the key point was to ensure that assessments were based on the most up-to-date scientific data (what we might call the 'sound science' approach). The inclusion of 'extraneous' matters such as socio-economic impact was viewed as encouraging disguised restrictions on trade.[58] Developing states considered scientific data alone to be insufficient to assess the full range of possible impacts on conservation and sustainable

[55] Art 26. This concern with non-scientific factors is reflected in the ecosystem approach of the parent Biodiversity Convention, which 'establishes the importance of including the socio-economic dimensions of nature management when implementing the CBD. Human life, activities and well-being must be included as basic factors in the wider geographical application of the ecosystem approach. Biodiversity has to be integrated into the economy of the relevant communities, and the various values of biodiversity should be captured and realised at the local level to give the right incentives to those that are nearest to guard it. This socio-economic dimension is also a reflection of the obligation of the Parties to CBD to integrate biodiversity concerns into the activities and responsibilities of the economic sectors, also mandated by the Convention.' See 'The Convention on Biological Diversity and the World Summit on Sustainable Development' at *http://www.biodiv.org/events/wssd.asp*.

[56] This may be compared with, for example, the 2003 GM Food and Feed Regulation in the EU (Regulation 1829/2003, OJ [2003] L268/1). There the legitimate objectives that may be pursued by a system of prior approval embrace not only internal market objectives and concerns for the protection of human life and health and of the environment, but also animal health and welfare and consumer interests in relation to genetically modified foodstuffs in particular. On the other hand, the 2001 Deliberate Release Directive (Directive 2001/18/EC, OJ [2001] L106/1) is addressed only to protection of human health and the environment. See further J Scott, 'European Regulation of GMOs: Thinking About Judicial Review in the WTO' in this volume.

[57] Comprising Argentina, Australia, Canada, Chile, Uruguay and the US, ie the major actual or likely exporters of LMOs. Three of the Miami Group—Argentina, Canada and the US—have launched proceedings under the WTO's dispute settlement procedure challenging the EU's biosafety regime: WT/DS292, WT/DS292 and WT/DS293, *EC—Measures Affecting the Approval and Marketing of Biotech Products*, Panel Report expected August 2005. See further 'Trade and Biosafety' below.   [58] Burgiel, n 45 above, 55.

use of biological diversity, socio-economic factors and risks to agriculture and to human health. This broader approach necessitates a multidisciplinary approach to risk assessment,[59] the implementation of which requires a case-by-case approach. Arguably the flexibility to maintain a multidisciplinary case-by-case approach is provided by the Biosafety Protocol, whilst also ensuring that possible impacts on human health and on the conservation and sustainable use of biological diversity are an integral part of the risk assessment process, the 'backbone of the decision-making process' under the Protocol.[60] Precaution is an integral part of the AIA decision-making procedure, and socio-economic concerns are catered for to an extent in the provisions permitting taking account of the concerns of indigenous and local communities. But it is clear that decision making regarding LMOs must be grounded in 'sound science' and that non-scientific factors alone—for example, a generalised consumer concern regarding genetically modified foodstuffs—will not provide unchallengeable grounds for refusal to import LMOs under the Protocol.

As for broader developing State concerns regarding implementation of the Protocol, the clearing house mechanism (CHM) established under the Protocol,[61] combined with its capacity-building provisions,[62] are designed to facilitate developing states' participation. As Kameri-Mbote observes, scientific capacity-building at the national or regional level will 'go a long way in shaping the potential of the GMO revolution used to address local needs and the requirements for sustainable development'.[63] As yet, however, the biosafety CHM does not contain any data regarding decisions taken under AIA and only seven entries regarding risk assessments (all pertaining to Dutch field trials of transgenic potatoes, carnations, chicory and apples); this may be contrasted with 348 entries under Article 11, which is the streamlined decision-making procedure in respect of LMOs for food feed and processing (showing where the real movement is for the moment).

---

[59] CBD/UNEP, n 45 above, 51.   [60] Kameri-Mbote, n 44 above, 63.

[61] See *http://bch.biodiv.org*. This builds on the clearing house mechanism already established under the CBD, as well as establishing a gateway to other biosafety information exchange sites such as UNIDO's Biosafety Information Network and Advisory Service (BINAS) at *http://binas.unido.org/binas/* and UNEP's Information Resource for the Release of Organisms (IRRO) at *http://www.chem.unep.ch/biodiv/int102.html*, as provided for in Art 20(2) of the Protocol.

[62] Which in turn are closely linked with Arts 16 (access to and transfer of technology) and 18 (technical and scientific cooperation) of the CBD. Under the Protocol, capacity building is viewed as of particular importance for developing countries without domestic biosafety systems, and is closely linked with Art 28 of the Protocol (financial mechanism and resources).   [63] Kameri-Mbote, n 44 above, 73.

Public Participation in Biosafety Decision-Making

The AIA approach of the Biosafety Protocol is dependent on the ability of receiving states to conduct some form of risk assessment; for non-contained LMOs this may be part of a broader environmental impact assessment (EIA) exercise in which public participation is central. In the biosafety field, consultation will likely embrace a wide range of stake-holders—civil society, research institutes, and the biotechnology industry, for example. The Protocol requires states to ensure that the public is actively consulted on GMOs and biosafety to promote transparency and informed decisionmaking—but only 'in accordance with their respective laws and regulations' (Article 23). Significant differences in institutional and technical capacity exist between states, differences that are only partly addressed through the Protocol's provisions on capacity building and information sharing through, *inter alia*, the clearing house mechanism already briefly touched upon. A question arises whether international rules on public participation specifically tailored to biosafety decision making are necessary.

This question has been faced squarely in the discussion of the role of civil society in biosafety decision making under the 1998 Economic Commission for Europe's Aarhus Convention on access to information, public participation in decision making, and access to justice in environmental matters.[64] The Parties to the Aarhus Convention established a Task Force (2000) and then GMO Working Groups (2001, 2002) to consider this issue, as well as adopting non-binding Guidelines on GMO decision making in 2002.[65] Having committed the GMO Working Group to the articulation of binding principles to apply to GMOs, this Group was divided on the question whether countries not yet able to implement the existing EIA obligations contained in Article 6 of the Convention should be distinguished from those states already successfully doing so. Moreover, the utility of agreeing more rigorous guidelines for GMOs in the absence of compliance with existing EIA obligations was questioned. When Article 6 was originally concluded, decisions on GMOs were expressly excluded from its binding

[64] Concluded 25 June 1998 and in force 30 October 2001, available at (1999) 38 *International Legal Materials*, 517. The Convention presently has 36 Parties.

[65] Implementation of these Guidelines was (favourably) reviewed at the second meeting of the parties in May 2005 in the light of a report by the Secretariat: see *The Report on the implementation of the Guidelines on access to information, public participation and access to justice with respect to genetically modified organisms*, ECE/MP.PP/2005/5, available at *http://www.unece.org/env/pp/mop2/mop2.docII.htm*.

requirements on public participation, with the parties required to apply its terms to decisions on whether to permit the deliberate release of GMOs into the environment only 'to the extent feasible and appropriate'. This weak provision resulted from a lack of agreement on the issue between the Parties during the negotiation of the Convention, and was clearly going to be revisited once the Convention entered into force.

This it has been, but this lack of agreement persisted in the Working Group, with clear divisions apparent between the countries of Eastern Europe, Caucasus and Central Asia and environmental NGOs on one hand, and the EU and the representatives of science and industry on the other. East European and other countries and environmental NGOs supported options that would make public participation in decisions regarding GMOs binding and which set out precise requirements on the nature of the public's participation. The EU, though to an extent internally divided on the issue, appeared to favour a non-binding, broad option that would allow countries considerable domestic flexibility in choosing how public participation should be provided for. This would provide necessary differentiation between those states with already well-developed national and regional procedures, and those still struggling with Article 6 implementation even outside the GMO context. Certainly non-EU countries have used the 2002 non-binding Guidelines on GMO decision making, referred to above, in the process of drafting their own national biosafety legislation, but gaps still persist.

The Working Group reported before the second meeting of the Conference of the Parties to the Aarhus Convention in May 2005 where, after thee days of 'intensive negotiations' in the run-up to the meeting, agreement was reached on an amendment to the Convention.[66] Once it enters into force, this amendment will require parties to inform and consult the public in decision making regarding the deliberate release and placing on the market of GMOs. The public would have the right to submit comments and public authorities would be expected to take these into account in the decision making process. Once made, the decision taken should be publicly available together with the reasons and considerations upon which it is based. Information associated with GMO decisions would be made available to the public, subject to the usual protection for commercially confidential information. However, confidentiality may not be extended to information on the intended uses of the release or regarding assessment of environmental risk. This is

[66] UNECE Press Release, 'Governments reach agreement on public participation in decision-making on genetically modified organisms', Geneva, 26 May 2005, available at *http://www.unece.org/press/pr2005/05env_p06e.htm.*

clearly to prevent abuse of the confidentiality exception, and to ensure full transparency in respect of the use and environmental impact of GMOs.[67] Upward derogation—that is, the flexibility for parties to adopt more expansive measures for public participation and access to information in GMO decision making[68]—is also provided for. Overall, this compromise embeds national and regional flexibility whilst establishing international minimum standards for public participation in GMO decision making, and seeks further to fill the biosafety regulatory gap which persists in some Central, East European and newly independent states. For states party to both the Aarhus Convention and the Biosafety Protocol (and that have also accepted the amendment and where it has entered into force), these provisions on the public right to participate in GMO decision making will serve as a modest strengthening of the public awareness and participation provisions of Article 23 of the Protocol.

Sound Science in Decision Making under the Protocol

The Biosafety Protocol provides that risk assessments 'shall be carried out in a scientifically sound manner' taking account not only of the provisions of the Protocol but also of 'recognised risk assessment techniques'—ie those recognised at the national, regional and international levels.[69] There is no definition of 'scientifically sound manner' in the Protocol though similar language may be found in other agreements.[70] 'Sound science' should entail independence, transparency, scepticism, peer review and account-ability.[71] While in general terms these are not matters prescribed at the

[67] For an analogous proviso contained in Art 21(6) of the Cartagena Protocol, see n 53 above.

[68] Access to justice, the third pillar of the Aarhus Convention, is not addressed in the amendment regarding GMOs, though clearly could be embraced in the exercise of such upward derogation.

[69] Mackenzie *et al*, n 45 above, 110. On the international level these might include UNEP's *International Technical Guidelines on for Safety in Biotechnology*, which a number of delegations in the Protocol negotiations viewed as a valuable source of guidance. See UNEP/CBD/BSWG/1/4/ paras 57–63, and CBD/UNEP, n 45 above, 50.

[70] See also the SPS Agreement—'scientific principles' (Art 2(2)); 'scientific justification' (Art3 (3)); and 'scientific evidence' (Art 2(2) and 5(2)). The provisions on the application of the precautionary approach in the 1995 Straddling Stocks Agreement refer to the 'best scientific information available' (Art 6): see Agreement for the Implementation of the Provisions of the United Nations Convention on the Law of the Sea of 10 December 1982 Relating to the Conservation and Management of Straddling Fish Stocks and Highly Migratory Fish Stocks, in force 11 December 2001, available at (1995) 34 *International Legal Materials*, 1542.

[71] A Stirling, *On Science and Precaution in the Management of Technological Risk*, vol 1, EC Institute for Prospective Technological Studies, EUR 19056 EN Spain (1998), cited in R Macrory, 'Regulating in a Risky Environment' (2001) 54 *Current Legal Problems*, 640.

international level but left for domestic or regional implementation,[72] Annex III of the Biosafety Protocol does set forth certain general principles of risk assessment which include the requirement that it 'should be carried out in a scientifically sound and transparent manner' (Article 3). As Mackenzie *et al* observe, this absence of an agreed definition of 'scientifically sound manner' may give rise to disagreements between states both as to the meaning of the phrase and as to the validity of inevitably diverging scientific views 'about the manner in which an inserted gene is likely to modify characteristics of the organism other than the intended changes, about the interpretation of data, and about the ecological and environmental effects of LMOs.'[73] Part of the difficulty in establishing international minimum harmonised standards for risk assessment, as observed by Australia in the negotiation of the Protocol,[74] is the diverse range of national regulatory measures already in place for undertaking risk assessment. As we saw above, this problem has also beset efforts to draft binding international rules on public participation in GMO decision making.

There are clearly both benefits and drawbacks to the Biosafety Protocol's approach to maintaining the diversity of national and regional approaches to living modified organisms. The benefit lies in preserving divergence, albeit consistent with other international obligations, with the principal focus the impact of LMOs on biological diversity which necessarily varies from state to state. Yet the tether for diversity is the application of the precautionary principle, which requires a degree of objectivity in the application of the principle. Subjective concerns about the impact of LMOs are left outwith this process, save to the extent that socio-economic impact may be taken into account where impacting on indigenous and local peoples. International regulation of LMOs thus reflects a rationalist faith in the objective application of scientific principles; the separation of human beings and nature, or what Holder has referred to as a 'technocratic approach to environmental problems'.[75] This is well-illustrated by the role of science in the application of the precautionary concept under the Biosafety Protocol.[76]

---

[72] For example, the Regulation establishing the European Food Safety Authority (Regulation 178/2002), which is to operate in accordance with the 'foundational values' of 'independence, scientific excellence, transparency and diligence'. Scott notes that '[t]he expert dimension has been given a glossy new exterior with the establishment of EFSA': n 56 above, 211.   [73] Mackenzie *et al*, n 45 above, 108.

[74] See CBD/UNEP, n 45 above.

[75] J Holder, 'New Age: Rediscovering Natural Law' (2000) 53 *Current Legal Problems*, 152.

[76] For an EU perspective, see T Hervey, 'Regulation of Genetically Modified Products in a Multi-Level System of Governance: Science or Citizens?' (2001) 10:3 Review of European Community and International Environmental Law, 321.

There is a risk that should an unduly narrow, positivist scientific approach emerge under the Protocol, it will sit at odds with developments in environmental science in which at least two recent trends have emerged:[77] 'post normal science' and 'sustainability science'. The former is interdisciplinary, drawing together different scientific disciplines, and relies on extended peer communities. It transcends conventional problem solving techniques (labelled 'normal science' by Kuhn[78]) considered inadequate to address fully contemporary environmental problems, and taps into systems theory. Funtowicz and Ravetz proposed the concept of post-normal science 'to deal with problems outside the realm of normal science—a realm where objectivity is not possible, prediction and control are limited, and where society and politics must play a key role'.[79] As they observe: 'The insight leading to Post-Normal Science is that in the sorts of issue-driven science relating to environmental debates, typically facts are uncertain, values in dispute, stakes high, and decisions urgent.'[80]

Sustainability science is multidisciplinary, combining scientific, economic, legal, and other disciplinary understandings and knowledge. It recognises the limitations of traditional scientific inquiry in dealing with the complex reality of social institutions interacting with natural phenomena. It is also a recent phenomenon—since 2001 or so[81]—and seeks a *rapprochement* between science and sustainable development. It has been described as a response to the perception that, '[d]uring the late '80s and early '90s ... much of the science and technology community became increasingly estranged from the preponderantly societal and political processes that were shaping the sustainable development

[77] An earlier version of this paper was delivered in the University of Edinburgh. I am grateful to the audience for their comments, in particular by Elizabeth Kirk on this section.

[78] T S Kuhn, *The Structure of Scientific Revolutions* (Chicago: University of Chicago Press, 3rd edition, 1996).

[79] As quoted in J Kay, 'About Postnormal Science', available at *www.ecologistics. com/nesh/pns.html* (visited September 2004): see S Funtowicz and J Ravetz, 'Science for the post-normal age' (1993) 25:7 *Futures*, 739–55 and ibid, 'Three Types of Risk Assessment and the Emergence of Post-Normal Science' in S Krimsky and D Golding (eds), *Social Theories of Risk* (New York: Praeger, 1992), 251–73.   [80] 'Futures', ibid.

[81] The influence of the US National Research Council's identification of sustainability science in 1999 had a catalytic effect on the development of the approach, or at any rate the rebranding of the harnessing of science and technology towards sustainability. See National Research Council, *Our Common Journey* (Washington: National Academic Press, 1999). Clark and Dickson observe that the term 'sustainability science' is controversial, suggesting 'a mature discipline with shared conceptual and theoretical components' which in fact does not exist. Some use the phrase 'science of sustainability'; whichever term is used, they note that the meaning intended, including by the US National Research Council, is 'the notion of multiple sciences addressing a common theme'. W C Clark and N M Dickson, 'Sustainability Science: The emerging research program' (2003) 100:14 *Proceedings of the National Academy of Sciences of the United States of America*, 8061.

agenda.'[82] This multidisciplinary approach is reflected in the IUCN's 2004 report cited in the introduction above, which it will be recalled identifies the single most important factor in resolving conflict over GMO regulation as the development of 'reliable information and analysis' in a multidisciplinary range of fields—biology, ecology, law, economics, ecosystem management, and social policy.[83] This is also recognised in the 2004 Addis Ababa Principles, principle 6 of which stresses the importance of interdisciplinary research for the successful implementation of the CBD.[84] However, it remains to be seen whether, in implementing the Protocol, these more dynamic scientific approaches emerge, or whether the Protocol's approach to 'sound science' risks being yet another example of the law entrenching established (and perhaps old-fashioned) ways of understanding and doing.[85]

Trade and Biosafety

Science is fundamental to the implementation of the Biosafety Protocol because the precautionary approach is such a key feature of it.[86] The Protocol permits importing countries to ban imports because of lack of scientific certainty. Unlike under the WTO Agreement on the Application of Sanitary and Phytosanitary Measures (SPS Agreement),[87] there is no obligation to seek further information to enable a more objective, informed assessment of the risk and to review the SPS measure within a reasonable time. Thus, in theory, a trade restrictive measure under the Biosafety Protocol may be of unlimited duration, or at least until the importing country decides that scientific certainty exists regarding the effects of products on biodiversity and

---

[82] R W Kates *et al*, 'Sustainability Science' (2001) 292:5517 *Science*, 641–2.

[83] IUCN Report, n 4 above, 5.

[84] The Addis Ababa Principles and Guidelines for the Sustainable Use of Biodiversity were adopted at the 7th Conference of the Parties to the CBD in 2004. For the text see *http://www.biodiv.org*.

[85] I am indebted to Elizabeth Kirk, University of Edinburgh, for these observations.

[86] In addition to the preamble and the provisions and Art 1 cited above, see Arts 10(6) and 11(8).

[87] Art 5.7 of the SPS Agreement provides that 'in cases where relevant scientific evidence is insufficient, a Member may provisionally adopt sanitary and phytosanitary measures on the basis of available pertinent information, including that from relevant international organisations as well as from sanitary and phytosanitary measures applied by other Members. In such circumstances, *Members shall seek to obtain the additional information necessary for a more objective assessment of risk and review the sanitary and phytosanitary measure accordingly within a reasonable period of time*' (emphasis added).

human health.[88] This does not, however, serve to immunise such measures from challenge elsewhere in consequence of other international legal obligations, including trade obligations under the WTO. Furthermore, as was noted above, the exercise of the AIA procedure is conditioned by the obligation of the parties under the Protocol to act consistently with their other obligations under international law.[89]

In respect of trade obligations, the Protocol does address its relationship with trade agreements—a contentious issue during negotiations—but only in the preamble,[90] which repeats nearly verbatim the rather unsatisfactory preambular language of the 1998 Rotterdam Convention on Prior Informed Consent in the pesticides context.[91] The Preamble to the Biosafety Protocol recognises that trade and environmental agreements should be mutually supportive[92] with a view to achieving sustainable development. It then emphasises that 'this Protocol shall not be interpreted as implying a change in rights and obligations of a Party under any existing international agreements' whilst immediately asserting that this recital 'is not intended to subordinate this Protocol to other international agreement'. This 'mutually-supportive, no subordination and no change in existing obligations' formula reflects the various negotiating positions taken by states on this contentious issue.[93] Given that the Protocol does not provide for any compulsory dispute settlement (in this regard it piggybacks on Article 27 CBD) then in the event of any conflict with trade rules

[88] S Zarilli, 'International Trade in GMOs and Multilateral Negotiations: A New Dilemma for Developing Countries' in F Francioni (ed), *Environment, Human Rights & International Trade* (Oxford: Hart Publishing, 2001), 57–64. See also Hagan and Weiner, n 45 above, and G L Gaston and R S Abate, 'The Biosafety Protocol and the World Trade Organisation: Can the Two Co-Exist?' (2000) 12 Pace International Law Review, 107; and Appendix 'The Cartagena Protocol and the World Trade Organization' in Mackenzie *et al*, n 45 above.   [89] See Art 26 for example.

[90] For thorough analysis see Stoll, n 51 above, and Gaston and Abate, n 88 above.

[91] As Kummer observes, '[c]ontroversy on this point appears to be inherent in multilateral environmental negtiations addressing transboundary transfer of potentially hazardous substances, since they deal with the interface of trade and environment considerations'. K Kummer, 'Prior Informed Consent for Chemicals in International Trade: The 1998 Rotterdam Convention' (1999) 8:3 Review of European Community and International Environmental Law, 323.

[92] Mutual supportiveness of trade and environment is also addressed by Principle 12 of the 1992 Rio Declaration and in paragraph 92 of the Plan of Implementation produced at the 2002 World Summit on Sustainable Development (available at *www. johannesburgsummit.org*) and in paragraph 31 of the Doha Ministerial Declaration (*available at www.wto.org*).

[93] In this sense the Biosafety Protocol's relationship with the pertinent WTO covered agreements may be located within a wider debate regarding the relationship between the WTO and multilateral environmental agreements employing trade related mechanisms, a debate which dates back a decade and more. For introductory analysis of the many complex issues, see Birnie and Boyle, n 21 above, ch 14 or Sands, n 30 above, ch 19.

the dispute is likely to arise under the WTO, which does provide for compulsory dispute settlement. Clearly the Panels and Appellate Body are limited in their jurisdiction to hearing claims based on the covered agreements.[94] However, as the US, Canada and Argentina[95] dispute with the EU over GMO regulation currently before the WTO illustrates, a moratorium on the approval of biotechnology products, as well as national marketing and import bans on such products, is susceptible to legal challenge under WTO law, in particular under the Agreement on the Application of Sanitary and Phytosanitary Measures, the Agreement on Agriculture, the Agreement on Technical Barriers to Trade, and the General Agreement on Tariffs and Trade. As this enumeration makes clear, there is no WTO side agreement on GMOs as such; thus much will turn on judicial review[96] by the Panels and Appellate Body of national decision making within the context of national biosafety frameworks, whether developed directly under the Biosafety Protocol or through regional regulation and implementation. How far the Biosafety Protocol, and its precautionary approach, will influence the interpretation of the covered agreements (SPS, TBT, GATT), if at all, may well be revealed in the Panel Report expected in August 2005.

One of the arguments by the EU is that the interpretation of the relevant WTO agreements should be consistent with the requirements of the Biosafety Protocol, including its provisions on risk assessment and the right to take precautionary measures. This raises wider questions of the scope of judicial review under the WTO and the extent to which the external treaty obligations of members—eg the Biosafety Protocol—can be taken into account in the interpretation of the WTO covered agreements.[97] We have already seen the Appellate Body in the Shrimp-Turtle dispute willing to rely on 'sustainable development' in the WTO agreement preamble in its interpretation of one of the covered agreements (GATT);[98] but how far will it step *outside* the WTO framework in its

---

[94] See the Understanding on Rules and Procedures Governing the Settlement of Disputes, Appendix I, 'Agreements Covered by the Understanding', in Annex 2 to the 1994 Agreement Establishing the World Trade Organisation, available at *www.wto.org*.

[95] Canada and Argentina are parties to the CBD and signatories to the Protocol; the US has only signed the CBD.   [96] J Scott, n 56 above.

[97] In *US–Import Prohibition of Certain Shrimp and Shrimp Products*, WTO Appellate Body (1998), WT/DS58/R, at paras 171 and 174, the Appellate Body noted that the United States, though a party to the 1973 Convention in International Trade in Endangered Species, had not sought to raise the plight of sea turtles under that Convention (nor were the unilateral measures in question legally required of it under that Convention); the United States was not party to other potentially relevant instruments such as the 1982 Law of the Sea Convention and the 1992 CBD.

[98] 'We note once more that this language demonstrates a recognition by WTO negotiators that optimal use of the world's resources should be made in accordance with the objective of sustainable development. As this preambular language reflects the intentions

interpretation of the covered agreements? A narrow but widely-held view[99] is that the Dispute Settlement Body (DSB—see below) may only apply the rules set out in the WTO covered agreements as interpreted in accordance with customary international rules on treaty interpretation.[100] This view is based on a reading of the WTO's Dispute Settlement Understanding, which expressly authorises the DSB to have recourse to customary international legal rules of treaty interpretation in the interpretation of the WTO covered agreements, whilst restraining that body from altering the obligations of the members. In the present GMO dispute, it has been argued that the interpretation of the relevant WTO agreements should be consistent with the provisions of the Biosafety Protocol, including its provisions on risk assessment and the right to take precautionary measures—as well as taking into account the recognition of the potential risks of GMOs for human health and the environment in the standard-setting body, *Codex Alimentarius*. Reliance is placed on Article 8(g) of the Biodiversity Convention, with the argument that GM products require their own distinctive authorisation procedure and are objectively different (ie not 'like') non-GM products. Inspiration may be drawn from the Appellate Body's own words in the 1998 Shrimp-Turtle case, referring to the need to take into account the 'contemporary concerns of the community of nations about the protection and conservation of the environment'.

A further question, as yet unposed directly in WTO case law, is the possibility of direct conflict between WTO agreements and external obligations of the parties, under the Biosafety Protocol, for example. We have seen that the language of the Protocol is that of mutual support and accommodation with trade rules, but without subordinating the Protocol to these

of negotiators of the WTO Agreement, we believe it must add colour, texture and shading to our interpretation of the agreements annexed to the WTO Agreement, in this case, the GATT 1994. We have already observed that Art. XX(g) of the GATT 1994 is appropriately read with the perspective embodied in the above preamble. We also note that since this preambular language was negotiated, certain other developments have occurred which help to elucidate the objectives of WTO Members with respect to the relationship between trade and environment. The most significant, in our view, was the Decision of Ministers at Marrakesh to establish a permanent Committee on Trade and Environment.' *US–Import Prohibition of Certain Shrimp and Shrimp Products*, WTO Appellate Body (1998), WT/DS58/R, paras. 153–4.

[99] See, for example, J Trachman, 'The Domain of WTO Dispute Resolution' (1999) 40 Harvard International Law Journal, 342 and M Masushita, 'Governance of International Trade under World Trade Organisation Agreements and Other Agreements', (2004) 38 *Journal of World Trade*, 185.

[100] Based on the wording of Art 3(2) of the Dispute Settlement Understanding (DSU) which refers to the 'customary rules of interpretation of public international law' which 'call for an examination of the ordinary meaning of the words of a treaty, read in their context, and in the light of the object and purpose of the treaty involved'. This is essentially

rules, reflecting the approach of other multilateral environmental agreements with trade-related environmental mechanisms and the 'mutual supportive' language of the Rio Declaration (Principle 12). Given the latitude for national implementation found in the Biosafety Protocol, it is highly unlikely that a direct conflict between obligations will arise—ie that compliance with the Biosafety Protocol necessarily implies non-compliance with WTO obligations. What is far more likely is that differences in approach to the application of the precautionary principle and the exercise of national decision making under the Protocol as compared with the covered agreements will be the subject of dispute, illustrated in part by the current GMO case before the WTO. These matters are likely to continue to be played out pursuant to the compulsory dispute settlement procedures of the WTO in the absence of such procedures in multilateral environmental agreements like the Biosafety Protocol employing trade-related mechanisms.

Conclusion

It is thus clear that the international legal regulation of biosafety and biodiversity is in a dynamic state, with very significant developments in the near and immediate term expected. The WTO Panel will report soon on the GMO case currently before the WTO, with further light shed on the role of precaution in biosafety decision making and also perhaps on the relationship between WTO and the other obligations of the parties; liability and redress provisions are being developed under the Biosafety Protocol to address environmental damage arising from transboundary movement of GMOs; and the parties to the Aarhus Convention have recently determined specific legal principles governing public participation in GMO decision making. A linking thread throughout is the need for more information on the scientific analysis and assessment of risks involved in the transboundary movement of GMOs, and divergent national approaches to risk assessment and risk management. What renders this topic so particularly challenging for international law is the stark contrast in the perceived consequences of biotechnology. On the one hand, it is hailed as a vehicle for the alleviation of world hunger and poverty;[101] on the other, there is the concern that lack of caution will lead

the text embedded in Art 31(1) of the 1969 Vienna Convention on the Law of Treaties and which is widely regarded as reflecting customary international law.

   [101] Thirteen years after the conclusion of the CBD, the ambitious prognosis in Agenda 21 of the benefits for sustainable development of biotechnology have yet fully to materialise. In 2001 the CSD Secretary-General observed that, while the biotechnology industry

to major mistakes irrevocably altering the natural world. As a recent Biodiversity Convention report on Biosafety and the Environment observes: 'For these reasons, future generations are likely to look back to our time and either thank us or curse us for what we do—or don't do—about GMOs and biosafety.' Seeking to balance the benefits of biotechnology against the risks, especially to biodiversity, is the principal contribution of the Biosafety Protocol where transboundary movement of LMOs is contemplated.

had developed and become increasingly economically important in developed states, the benefits foreseen for sustainable development had not yet materialised. *Report, Genetically Modified Organisms*, 2 para. 27.